Contemporary Theatre, Film and Television

ISSN 0749-064X

Contemporary Theatre, Film and Television

A Biographical Guide Featuring Performers, Directors, Writers, Producers, Designers, Managers, Choreographers, Technicians, Composers, Executives, Dancers, and Critics in the United States, Canada, Great Britain and the World

Thomas Riggs, Editor

Volume 70

THOMSON

GALE

Detroit • New York • San Francisco • San Diego • New Haven, Conn. • Waterville, Maine • London • Munich

Contemporary Theatre, Film & Television, Vol. 70

Editor
Thomas Riggs

CTFT Staff
Mariko Fujinaka, Janice Jorgensen, Candice Mancini, Annette Petrusso, Susan Risland, Lisa Sherwin, Arlene True, Pam Zuber

Project Editor
Allison M. Marion

Editorial Support Services
Ryan Cartmill

Composition and Electronic Capture
Gary Oudersluys, Carolyn A. Roney

Manufacturing
Drew Kalasky

LIBRARY OF CONGRESS CATALOG CARD NUMBER 84-649371

ISBN 0-7876-9043-0
ISSN 0749-064X

This title is also available as an e-book.
ISBN 1-4144-1031-X
Contact your Thomson Gale sales representative for ordering information.

Printed in the United States of America
10 9 8 7 6 5 4 3 2 1

Contents

Preface

Provides Broad, Single-Source Coverage in the Entertainment Field

Contemporary Theatre, Film and Television (*CTFT*) is a biographical reference series designed to provide students, educators, researchers, librarians, and general readers with information on a wide range of entertainment figures. Unlike single-volume reference works that focus on a limited number of artists or on a specific segment of the entertainment field, *CTFT* is an ongoing publication that includes entries on individuals active in the theatre, film, and television industries. Before the publication of *CTFT*, information-seekers had no choice but to consult several different sources in order to locate the in-depth biographical and credit data that makes *CTFT*'s one-stop coverage the most comprehensive available about the lives and work of performing arts professionals.

Scope

CTFT covers not only performers, directors, writers, and producers, but also behind-the-scenes specialists such as designers, managers, choreographers, technicians, composers, executives, dancers, and critics from the United States, Canada, Great Britain, and the world. With 240 entries in *CTFT 70*, the series now provides biographies on approximately 20,484 people involved in all aspects of theatre, film, and television.

CTFT gives primary emphasis to people who are currently active. New entries are prepared on major stars as well as those who are just beginning to win acclaim for their work. *CTFT* also includes entries on personalities who have died but whose work commands lasting interest.

Compilation Methods

CTFT editors identify candidates for inclusion in the series by consulting biographical dictionaries, industry directories, entertainment annuals, trade and general interest periodicals, newspapers, and online databases. Additionally, the editors of *CTFT* maintain regular contact with industry advisors and professionals who routinely suggest new candidates for inclusion in the series. Entries are compiled from published biographical sources which are believed to be reliable, but have not been verified for this edition by the listee or their agents.

Revised Entries

To ensure *CTFT*'s timeliness and comprehensiveness, entries from previous volumes, as well as from Gale's *Who's Who in the Theatre*, are updated for individuals who have been active enough to require revision of their earlier biographies. Such individuals will merit revised entries as often as there is substantial new information to provide. Obituary notices for deceased entertainment personalities already listed in *CTFT* are also published.

Accessible Format Makes Data Easy to Locate

CTFT entries, modeled after those in Gale's highly regarded *Contemporary Authors* series, are written in a clear, readable style designed to help users focus quickly on specific facts. The following is a summary of the information found in *CTFT* sketches:

- *ENTRY HEADING:* the form of the name by which the listee is best known.

- *PERSONAL:* full or original name; dates and places of birth and death; family data; colleges attended, degrees earned, and professional training; political and religious affiliations when known; avocational interests.

- *ADDRESSES:* home, office, agent, publicist and/or manager addresses.

- *CAREER:* tagline indicating principal areas of entertainment work; resume of career positions and other vocational achievements; military service.

- *MEMBER:* memberships and offices held in professional, union, civic, and social organizations.

- *AWARDS, HONORS:* theatre, film, and television awards and nominations; literary and civic awards; honorary degrees.

- *CREDITS:* comprehensive title-by-title listings of theatre, film, and television appearance and work credits, including roles and production data as well as debut and genre information.

- *RECORDINGS:* album, single song, video, and taped reading releases; recording labels and dates when available.

- *WRITINGS:* title-by-title listing of plays, screenplays, scripts, and musical compositions along with production information; books, including autobiographies, and other publications.

- *ADAPTATIONS:* a list of films, plays, and other media which have been adapted from the listee's work.

- *SIDELIGHTS:* favorite roles; portions of agent- prepared biographies or personal statements from the listee when available.

- *OTHER SOURCES:* books, periodicals, and internet sites where interviews or feature stories can be found.

Access Thousands of Entries Using *CTFT*'s Cumulative Index

Each volume of *CTFT* contains a cumulative index to the entire series. As an added feature, this index also includes references to all seventeen editions of *Who's Who in the Theatre* and to the four-volume compilation *Who Was Who in the Theatre.*

Available in Electronic Format

Online. Recent volumes of *CTFT* are available online as part of the Gale Biographies (GALBIO) database accessible through LEXIS-NEXIS. For more information, contact LEXIS-NEXIS, P.O. Box 933, Dayton, OH 45401-0933; phone (937) 865-6800, toll-free: 800-543-6862.

Suggestions Are Welcome

Contemporary Theatre, Film and Television is intended to serve as a useful reference tool for a wide audience, so comments about any aspect of this work are encouraged. Suggestions of entertainment professionals to include in future volumes are also welcome. Send comments and suggestions to: The Editor, *Contemporary Theatre, Film and Television,* Thomson Gale, 27500 Drake Rd., Farmington Hills, MI 48331-3535; or feel free to call toll-free at 1-800-877-GALE.

Contemporary Theatre, Film
and Television

1

AIELLO, Danny 1933(?)–

PERSONAL

Full name, Daniel Louis Aiello, Jr.; born June 20, 1933 (some sources say 1936), in New York, NY; son of Daniel Louis (a laborer) and Frances (a seamstress; maiden name, Pietrocova) Aiello; married Sandy Cohen, January 8, 1955; children: Rick (an actor), Danny III (a stunt coordinator), Jamie, Stacey.

Addresses: *Agent*—International Creative Management, 8942 Wilshire Blvd., Beverly Hills, CA 90211. *Manager*—Untitled Entertainment, 331 North Maple Dr., 3rd Floor, Beverly Hills, CA 90210. *Office*—Manhattan Pictures International, 369 Lexington Ave., New York, NY 10017

Career: Actor, producer, and writer. Manhattan Pictures International, New York, NY, partner. Previously worked in a grocery store, in a bowling alley, as a shoe shiner, as a truck loader, and selling newspapers, 1940s and 1950s; worked as a baggage clerk, then a dispatcher, with the Greyhound bus company, New York City, 1957–67; was a bouncer at the Improvisation (comedy club), New York City; also worked as a pool hustler. Served as president of Local 1202 of the Amalgamated Transit Union; was formerly a union shop steward. Involved with Broadway Cares/Equity Fights AIDS, the Hole in the Wall Gang, and the Frances Aiello Day Treatment Center. *Military service:* U.S. Army, 1951–54; served in Germany.

Awards, Honors: *Theatre World* Award, 1975, for *Lamppost Reunion;* Obie Award, distinguished performance, *Village Voice*, 1978, for *Gemini;* Emmy Award, best performer in a children's program, and *Variety* Award, 1980, both for "Family of Strangers"; Los Angeles Drama Critics Circle Award, c. 1985, for *Hurlyburly;* Gemini Award nomination, best guest performance in a series by an actor or actress, Academy of Canadian Cinema and Television, 1988, for *Night Heat;* Boston Society of Film Critics Award, best supporting actor, Los Angeles Film Critics Association Achievement Award, best supporting actor, Chicago Film Critics Association Award, best supporting actor, 1989, Academy Award nomination, best supporting actor, Golden Globe Award nomination, best performance by an actor in a supporting role in a motion picture, 1990, all for *Do the Right Thing;* Career Achievement Award, Motion Picture Bookers Club, 1989; National Board of Review Award (with others), best acting by an ensemble, 1994, for *Pret-a-Porter;* Faberage Award and two Joseph Jefferson nominations for *That Championship Season.*

CREDITS

Film Appearances:
(Unreleased) *The Godmother*, 1973.
Horse, *Bang the Drum Slowly*, Paramount, 1973.
Tony Rosato, *The Godfather II* (also known as *Mario Puzo's "The Godfather II"*), Paramount, 1976.
Danny La Gattuta, *The Front*, Columbia, 1976.
(Scenes deleted) *Annie Hall*, 1977.
Hooch, 1977.
Butch, *Fingers*, Brut, 1978.
Artie, *Blood Brothers* (also known as *A Father's Love*), Warner Bros., 1979.
Sal Carvello, *Hide in Plain Sight*, United Artists, 1980.
Carmine, *Defiance*, American International Pictures, 1980.
Morgan, *Fort Apache, the Bronx*, Twentieth Century–Fox, 1981.
Johnson, *Chu Chu and the Philly Flash*, Twentieth Century–Fox, 1981.
Amityville II: The Possession, Orion, 1982.
Police Chief Aiello, *Once Upon a Time in America* (also known as *C'era una volta in America*), Warner Bros., 1984.
Mr. Brucker, *Old Enough*, Orion, 1984.

(Uncredited) *Broadway Danny Rose,* 1984.

Captain Mike Grasso, *Deathmask* (also known as *Unknown*), 1984.

Monk, *The Purple Rose of Cairo,* Orion, 1985.

Carabello, *Key Exchange,* Twentieth Century–Fox, 1985.

Vickers, *The Stuff,* New World, 1985.

Danny Garoni, *The Protector* (also known as *Wei Long Meng Tan*), Warner Bros., 1985.

Captain Mike Gress, *Death Mask* (also known as *Unknown*), Art Theatre Guild, 1986.

Conti, *Man on Fire* (also known as *Absinthe* and *Un uomo sotto tiro*), TriStar, 1987.

Rocco, *Radio Days,* Orion, 1987.

Phil, *The Pick–Up Artist,* Twentieth Century–Fox, 1987.

Johnny Cammareri, *Moonstruck,* United Artists, 1987.

Charlie Buick, *Crack in the Mirror* (also known as *White Hot*), Jubran–Rebo, 1988.

George Sherman, *Russicum I Giorni del Diavolo* (also known as *Russicum* and *The Third Solution*), Columbia, 1988.

Sal, *Do the Right Thing,* Universal, 1989.

Phil Cantone, *Harlem Nights,* Paramount, 1989.

Captain Vincent Alcoa, *The January Man* (also known as *January Man*), United Artists, 1989.

Louis, *Jacob's Ladder* (also known as *The Inferno* and *Dante's Inferno*), TriStar, 1990.

He Ain't Heavy, 1990.

John Cunningham, *Shocktroop* (also known as *Comrades in Arms* and *Shock Troop*), Republic Pictures Home Video, 1991.

Frank Pesce, Sr., *29th Street,* Twentieth Century–Fox, 1991.

Joe Bella, *Once Around,* Universal, 1991.

Chester Grant, *The Closer,* ION Pictures, 1991.

Tommy Five–Tone, *Hudson Hawk,* TriStar, 1991.

Carmine Rasso, *Mistress* (also known as *Hollywood Mistress*), Tribeca Productions, 1992.

Jack Ruby, *Ruby,* Triumph Releasing, 1992.

Harry Stone, *The Pickle,* Columbia, 1993.

Ben Katz, *The Cemetery Club* (also known as *Looking for a Live One*), Buena Vista, 1993.

Harry, *Me and the Kid,* Orion, 1993.

Major Hamilton, *Pret–a–Porter* (also known as *Ready to Wear* and *Pret–a–Porter: Ready to Wear*), Miramax, 1994.

Tony, *Leon* (also known as *The Cleaner, The Professional,* and *Le professionnel*), Columbia/TriStar, 1994.

Ronnie, *Save the Rabbits,* 1994.

Joseph Scassi, *Power of Attorney,* Prism Pictures, 1995.

Joe Lieberman, *Lieberman in Love* (short), Chanticleer Films, 1995.

Al, *Mojave Moon,* New Moon Productions, 1996.

Councilman Frank Anselmo, *City Hall,* Columbia/TriStar, 1996.

Gene Paletto, *Two Much* (also known as *Loco de amor*), Buena Vista, 1996.

Dosmo Pizzo, *2 Days in the Valley,* Metro–Goldwyn–Mayer, 1996.

Narrator, *Unforgotten: Twenty–Five Years after Willowbrook* (documentary), Castle Hill Productions, 1996.

Danny Parente, *A Brooklyn State of Mind,* Brooklyn Pictures, 1997.

Mr. Rathbone, *Bring Me the Head of Mavis Davis,* Goldcrest Films International/BBC Films, 1998.

Phil Devereaux, *Wilbur Falls* (also known as *Dead Silence*), 1998.

Noah, *Prince of Central Park,* 1999.

Vincent Dianni, *Eighteen Shades of Dust* (also known as *Dust, Hitman's Journal, The Sicilian Code,* and *18 Shades of Dust*), MTI Home Video, 1999.

Joey, *Mambo Cafe,* Unapix Entertainment, 2000.

Louis Cropa, *Dinner Rush,* Access Motion Picture Group, 2000.

Noah Cairn, *Prince of Central Park,* Keystone Entertainment, 2000.

Fabrizio Bernini, *Off Key* (also known as *Desafinado*), 2001.

Himself, *Cannes: Through the Eyes of the Hunter* (documentary short), 2001.

Tony Santini, *Mail Order Bride,* Small Planet Pictures, 2003.

Nathan, *Zeyda and the Hitman,* 2004.

Voice of the Dummy, *The Fool* (short), 2005.

Frank Giorgio, *Brooklyn Lobster,* Meadowbrook Pictures, 2005.

Narrator, *Harry: A Communication Breakdown* (documentary), 2006.

Film Work:

Coproducer, *Leon* (also known as *The Cleaner, The Professional,* and *Le professionnel*), Columbia/TriStar, 1994.

Executive producer, *Shorty* (documentary), 2003.

Executive producer, *UnConventional* (documentary), 2004.

Television Appearances; Series:

Lieutenant Terrence McNichols, *Lady Blue,* ABC, 1985–86.

Anthony Dellaventura, *Dellaventura,* CBS, 1997–98.

Television Appearances; Miniseries:

Randy Powers, *Blood Feud,* syndicated, 1983.

Jack Ruby, *A Woman Named Jackie,* NBC, 1991.

Domenico Clericuzio, *Mario Puzo's "The Last Don"* (also known as *The Last Don*), CBS, 1997.

Don Domenico Clericuzio, *Mario Puzo's "The Last Don II"* (also known as *The Last Don II*), CBS, 1998.

Television Appearances; Movies:

Carl, *The Last Tenant,* ABC, 1978.

Bernie Serino, *Lovey: A Circle of Children, Part II,* CBS, 1978.

Martelli, *A Question of Honor,* CBS, 1982.

Coach Jacobs, *Daddy,* ABC, 1987.
Chief, *Alone in the Neon Jungle* (also known as *Command in Hell*), CBS, 1988.
Master of Ceremonies, *The Hustler of Money,* 1988.
Detective Mike Sheehan, *The Preppie Murder* (also known as *The Preppy Murder*), ABC, 1989.
Duke, *Brothers' Destiny* (also known as *Long Road Home* and *The Road Home*), 1995.

Television Appearances; Specials:
Dominic Ginetti, "Family of Strangers," *ABC Afterschool Specials,* ABC, 1980.
Frank Caruso, *The Unforgivable Secret,* ABC, 1982.
Himself, *Making "Do the Right Thing"* (documentary), 1989.
Night of 100 Stars III, NBC, 1990.
Comic Relief IV, HBO, 1990.
Richard Lewis: "I'm Doomed" (documentary), 1990.
Narrator, "Pinocchio" (animated), *We All Have Tales,* Showtime, 1994.
Sinatra: 80 Years My Way, ABC, 1995.
The NFL at 75: An All-Star Celebration (also known as *The NFL 75th Anniversary Celebration*), ABC, 1995.
The Italian Americans II: A Beautiful Song (documentary), PBS, 1998.
Comedy Central Presents the New York Friars Club Roast of Jerry Stiller, Comedy Central, 1999.
Narrator, *The Rat Pack* (documentary), HBO 1999.
Comedy Central Presents: The New York Friars Club Roast of Rob Reiner, Comedy Central, 2000.
Himself, *Last Laugh,* 2003.

Television Appearances; Awards Presentations:
The 39th Annual Tony Awards, CBS, 1985.
The 22nd Annual NAACP Image Awards, NBC, 1990.
The 62nd Annual Academy Awards, ABC, 1990.
The 63rd Annual Academy Awards, ABC, 1991.

Television Appearances; Pilots:
Frank Ravelli, *Car Wash,* NBC, 1979.
Lieutenant Terrence McNichols, *Lady Blue,* ABC, 1985.

Also appeared in *Last Laugh at Pips,* CBS.

Television Appearances; Episodic:
Matty, "Black Thorn," *Kojak,* CBS, 1976.
The Andros Targets, CBS, 1977.
Nurse, CBS, 1982.
Florist, "Babies: Growth and Development," *3-2-1 Contact,* 1983.
Tommy Vale, "The Odds," *Tales from the Darkside,* 1984.
Night Heat, CBS, 1988.
Later with Bob Costas (also known as *Later*), NBC, 1989.
Late Night with David Letterman, NBC, 1991.

Host, *Saturday Night Live* (also known as *SNL*), NBC, 1996.
The Rosie O'Donnell Show, syndicated, 1997.
Late Night with Conan O'Brien, NBC, 1997.
Himself, "The Two Hilton Lucases," *Cosby,* CBS, 1997.
Last Call with Carson Daly, NBC, 2004.
Dinner for Five, Independent Film Channel, 2004.
Good Day Live, syndicated, 2004.

Also appeared as himself, "The Films of Spike Lee," *The Directors,* Encore.

Stage Appearances:
(Broadway debut) Biggie, *Lampost Reunion,* Little Theatre (now Helen Hayes Theatre), New York City, 1975.
That Championship Season, Chicago, IL, 1975.
Chester Grant, *Wheelbarrow Closers,* Bijou Theatre, New York City, 1976.
Fran Geminiani, *Gemini,* Circle Repertory Theatre, New York City, 1977.
Damie Ruffino, *Knockout,* Helen Hayes Theatre, 1979.
Easy Money, 1980.
Max Pollack, *The Floating Light Bulb,* Vivian Beaumont Theatre, Lincoln Center, New York City, 1981.
Floyd, *A Destiny with Half Moon Street,* Coconut Grove Playhouse, Miami, FL, 1982.
Phil, *Hurlyburly,* Ethel Barrymore Theatre, New York City, 1985.
Billy Einhorn, *The House of Blue Leaves,* Vivian Beaumont Theatre, 1986.
Night of 100 Stars III, Radio City Music Hall, New York City, 1990.
Mike Francisco, *Breaking Legs,* Pacific Theatre, Cerritos, CA, 1993.
Guy Akens, *Adult Entertainment,* Truglia Theater, Rich Forum, Stamford Center for the Arts, Stamford, CT, 2002, then Variety Arts Theatre, New York City, 2002-2003.

Also appeared as Phil, *Hurlyburly,* Westwood Playhouse, Los Angeles, CA.

RECORDINGS

Albums:
I Just Wanted to Hear the Words, 2004.

Music Videos:
Appeared as the father in Madonna's "Papa Don't Preach," video, 1986.

WRITINGS

Screenplays:
Save the Rabbits, 1994.

OTHER SOURCES

Books:
International Dictionary of Films and Filmmakers, Volume 3: Actors and Actresses, 4th ed., St. James Press, 2000.

Periodicals:
Film Comment, July–August, 1991, p. 50.
New York Times, January 21, 1990; February 10, 1991, pp. 13, 19.
New York Times Magazine, January 21, 1990, p. 24.
People, February 19, 1990.

ALDER, Eugene
   See HACKMAN, Gene

ALTMAN, Bruce 1955–

PERSONAL

Born July 3, 1955, in The Bronx, NY; married Darcy McGraw (an attorney and professor of law); children: Anna. *Education:* State University of New York at Albany, B.A., English; Yale University, M.F.A., drama, 1990; studied acting at the William Esper Studio, with William Hickey in New York City, the HB Studio, New York City, and with Geraldine Page, Herbert Berghof, and Lloyd Williamson.

Addresses: *Agent*—Don Buchwald & Associates, 6500 Wilshire Blvd., Suite 2200, Los Angeles, CA 90048.

Career: Actor. Worked as a teacher at an alternative high school.

CREDITS

Film Appearances:
Bruce, *Regarding Henry,* Paramount, 1991.
Mr. Spaniel, *Glengarry Glen Ross,* New Line Cinema, 1992.
Irwin Bloom, *My New Gun,* IRS Releasing, 1992.
Title role, *Mr. Wonderful,* Samuel Goldwyn, 1993.
Jack Bradfield, *Rookie of the Year,* Twentieth Century–Fox, 1993.
David, *Mr. Jones,* TriStar, 1993.
A Dog Race in Alaska, 1993.
Gene, *Quiz Show,* Buena Vista, 1994.
Carl, *The Paper,* Universal, 1994.

Barry, *Vibrations* (also known as *Cyberstorm*), Tanglewood Films, 1995.
Ralph, *Rescuing Desire,* 1996.
Paul Wheeler, *To Gillian on Her 37th Birthday,* Sony Pictures Entertainment, 1996.
Griffin, *Dear Diary* (short), Dream Works Television, 1996.
Counselor Burt Handel, *Cop Land,* Buena Vista, 1997.
Dr. Goldstein, *The Object of My Affection,* Twentieth Century–Fox, 1998.
Professor Gilcrest, *Girl, Interrupted* (also known as *Durchgeknallt* and *Durchgeknallt—Girl, interrupted*), Columbia, 1999.
Larry, *Rituals and Resolutions,* 1999.
Marty Blizter, *L.I.E.,* Lot 47 Films, 2001.
Barry, *Get Well Soon,* Lions Gate Films,2001.
Terry Kaufman, *Changing Lanes,* Paramount, 2002.
Stan Dawes, *Marci X,* Paramount, 2003.
Dr. Klein, *Matchstick Men,* Warner Bros., 2003.
Four Simple Rules (short), 2003.
Tyler, *American Exquisite* (short), 2004.
Coach Gilmore, *Twelve and Holding,* IFC Films, 2005.
Dez, *Running Scared,* New Line Cinema, 2006.

Television Appearances; Series:
Sidney Walters, *Nothing Sacred* (also known as *Priesthood*), ABC, 1997.

Television Appearances; Movies:
Robert Mott, "Guy Hanks I," *The Cosby Mysteries,* NBC, 1994.
David Koenig, *The White Mile,* HBO, 1994.
Leonard Goldberg, *Behind the Camera: The Unauthorized Story of "Charlie's Angels,"* NBC, 2004.

Television Appearances; Pilots:
Jackson High, Fox, 1995.
Advances in Chemistry, NBC, 1998.

Television Appearances; Episodic:
Harvey "Harv" Beigel, "The Torrents of Greed: Parts 1 & 2," *Law & Order,* NBC, 1990.
Tom Morrison, "The Pursuit of Happiness," *Law & Order,* NBC, 1993.
Tommy, *The Great Defender,* Fox, 1995.
Henry, "Interview with an Angel," *Touched by an Angel,* CBS, 1995.
Henry, "The Driver," *Touched by an Angel,* CBS, 1995.
Chet Hallahan, *The Wright Verdicts,* CBS, 1995.
Feds (also known as *Feds: The War against Crime*), CBS, 1997.
Neighbor, "I've Grown Accustomed to His Face," *Now and Again,* CBS, 1999.
Brad Feldman, "Return," *Law & Order,* NBC, 2000.
Brad Feldman, "Formerly Famous," *Law & Order,* NBC, 2001.

Mark Stanford, "Stolen," *Law & Order: Special Victims Unit* (also known as *Law & Order: SVU* and *Special Victims Unit*), NBC, 2001.

Jack Crawley, "Tuxedo Hill," *Law & Order: Criminal Intent* (also known as *Law & Order: CI*), NBC, 2002.

Alan Sapinsly, "Whitecaps," *The Sopranos,* HBO, 2002.

Dr. Soper, *Ed,* NBC, 2003.

Dr. Shinsky, "Butterfly," *Rescue Me,* FX Channel, 2004.

Dr. Alvin Lawrence, "Cut," *Law & Order,* NBC, 2004.

Also appeared as Lou Jacobs, *One Life to Live,* ABC.

Stage Appearances:

From the Memoirs of Pontius Pilate, American Jewish Repertory Theatre, New York City, 1980–81.

The Restaurant; or, Your Goose Is Cooked, Theatre for the New City, New York City, 1981–82.

Gregory, *Romeo and Juliet,* Boat Basin Rotunda Theatre, New York City, 1984.

True West, Long Island Stage, Rockville Centre, NY, 1986–87.

Sarcophagus, Yale Repertory Theatre, New Haven, CT, 1987–88.

Also appeared in *Liverpool Fantasy,* New York City; *Orpheus in America,* New York City; *The Sea Gull,* New York City; as Malvolio, *Twelfth Night,* Elm Shakespeare Company.

ANDERSON, Kevin 1960–
(Kevin C. Anderson)

PERSONAL

Born January 13, 1960, in Gurnee, IL; son of Joseph Anderson. *Education:* Goodman School of Drama, De-Paul University, certificate in acting, 1981. *Avocational Interests:* Singing, playing acoustic guitar.

Addresses: *Agent*—The Gersh Agency, 232 North Canon Dr., Beverly Hills, CA 90210. *Manager*—McKeon–Valeo–Myones Management, 9150 Wilshire Blvd., Suite 102, Beverly Hills, CA 90212.

Career: Actor and stunts. Steppenwolf Theatre, Chicago, IL, member of company, beginning in 1983. Also worked as a short–order cook.

Awards, Honors: Joseph Jefferson Awards, best actor and best ensemble (with others), and *Theatre World* Award, outstanding new talent, off–Broadway, 1985, all for *Orphans;* Q Award nomination, best actor in a quality drama series, Viewers for Quality Television, and Golden Globe Award nomination, best performance by an actor in a television drama series, both 1998, for *Nothing Sacred;* Drama Desk Award, outstanding featured actor in a play, Outer Critics Circle Award, outstanding featured actor in a play, and Antoinette Perry Award, best featured actor in a play, 1999, all for *Death of a Salesman.*

CREDITS

Film Appearances:

(As Kevin C. Anderson) Chuck, *Risky Business,* Warner Bros., 1983.

Danny, *Pink Nights,* Marschall, 1985.

Phillip, *Orphans,* Lorimar, 1987.

Everett Jones, *A Walk on the Moon,* Midwest, 1987.

Terry Roberts, *Miles from Home* (also known as *Farm of the Year*), Cinecom, 1988.

Lonnie, *In Country,* Warner Bros., 1989.

Nick Kaminsky, *Liebestraum,* Metro–Goldwyn–Mayer/Pathe, 1991.

Ben Woodward, *Sleeping With the Enemy,* Twentieth Century–Fox, 1991.

Robert Kennedy, *Hoffa,* Twentieth Century–Fox, 1992.

Brian McVeigh, *The Night We Never Met,* Miramax, 1993.

Bob Richmond, *Rising Sun,* Twentieth Century–Fox, 1993.

Peter Lewis, *A Thousand Acres,* Buena Vista, 1997.

John Taylor, *Firelight* (also known as *Firelight—Le lien secret*), Miramax, 1997.

Jack Stillings, *Eye of God* (also known as *Beyond Obsessions*), Castle Hill, 1997.

Hank Kirk, *The Doe Boy,* Curb Entertainment, 2001.

Bryce, *When Strangers Appear* (also known as *The Shearer's Breakfast*), Screen Gems, 2001.

Fern's father, *Charlotte's Web,* Paramount, 2006.

Film Stunts:

Daybreak (also known as *Rapid Transit*), Off Track Productions, 2000.

Television Appearances; Series:

Father Francis Xavier "Ray" Rayneaux, *Nothing Sacred* (also known as *Priesthood*), ABC, 1997.

Tom Roam, *Skin,* Fox, 2003.

Television Appearances; Miniseries:

Ira Einhorn, *The Hunt for the Unicorn Killer,* 1999.

Television Appearances; Movies:

Val Xavier, *Tennessee Williams's "Orpheus Descending"* (also known as *Orpheus Descending*), TNT, 1990.

Nathan Hale, *Hale the Hero,* 1992.

Alex Walker, *The Wrong Man,* Showtime, 1993.
Jon, *Gregory's Two Girls,* 1999.
Billy Dupre, *Ruby's Bucket of Blood,* Showtime, 2001.
Frank Gifford, *Monday Night Mayhem,* TNT, 2002.
John F. Kennedy, *Power and Beauty* (also known as *Beauty and Power: The Judith Exner Story*), Showtime, Showtime, 2002.
Charlie, *Carry Me Home,* Showtime, 2004.

Television Appearances; Specials:
Don Alvar, *L'Africaine,* PBS, 1989.
Henrik Egerman, *A Little Night Music* (also known as *Live from Lincoln Center*), PBS, 1990.
TV's Most Censored Moments, Trio and USA Network, 2002.

Television Appearances; Episodic:
"Prodigal Son," *Miami Vice,* 1985.
Don Alvar, "L'Africaine," *Great Performances,* PBS, 1989.
Nathan Hale, "Hale the Hero," *General Motors Playwrights Theatre,* Arts and Entertainment, 1992.
"Sondheim: A Celebration at Carnegie Hall," *Great Performances,* PBS, 1993.

Stage Appearances:
Richard II, ATA Outdoor Theatre, New York City, 1983.
George, *Our Town,* Steppenwolf Theatre, Chicago, 1983.
John F. Kennedy, *One Shining Moment,* Chicago, 1983.
Fabrice, *Nude with Violin,* Church of the Heavenly Rest Theatre, New York City, 1983.
Hey, Stay a While, Goodman Theatre, Chicago, 1983–84.
Phillip, *Orphans,* Steppenwolf Theatre, then Westside Arts Theatre, then Cheryl Crawford Theatre, both New York City, 1985, later London.
Bob, *Moonchildren,* Second Stage Theatre, New York City, 1987.
Joey Evans, *Pal Joey,* Goodman Theatre, 1988.
Henry Harry, *Brilliant Traces,* Cherry Lane Theatre, New York City, 1989.
Val Xavier, *Orpheus Descending,* Neil Simon Theatre, New York City, 1989.
Jake, *Earthly Possessions,* Steppenwolf Theatre, 1991.
Joe Gillis, *Sunset Boulevard,* Adelphi Theatre, London, 1993.
Countess Maritza (opera), Santa Fe, NM, 1995.
E. G. Triplett, *The Red Address,* Second Stage Theatre, New York City, 1997.
Biff Loman, *Death of a Salesman,* Goodman Theatre, 1998, then Eugene O'Neill Theatre, New York City, 1999.
Speaking in Tongues, New York City, 2001–2002.
Taylor Collins/A City Weed, *Brooklyn,* Plymouth Theatre (also known as Schoenfeld Theatre), New York City, 2004–2005.

Also appeared in *Twelfth Night, The Three Sisters,* and *I Never Sang for My Father,* all Steppenwolf Theatre Company, Chicago, IL.

RECORDINGS

Albums:
(With others) *Sunset Boulevard,* Polydor/Really Useful Records, 1993.

OTHER SOURCES

Periodicals:
Advocate, February 17, 1998, p. 23.
Entertainment Weekly, September 26, 1997, p. 49.

APTED, Michael 1941–

PERSONAL

Full name, Michael David Apted; born February 10, 1941, in Aylesbury, Buckinghamshire, England; son of Ronald William and Frances Amelia (maiden name, Thomas) Apted; married Joan, July 9, 1966 (divorced); married Dana; children: Paul, James. *Education:* Downing College, Cambridge University, B.A., history, 1963; also attended the City of London School.

Addresses: *Agent*—Creative Artists Agency, 9830 Wilshire Blvd., Beverly Hills, CA 90212; Peters Fraser & Dunlop, Drury House, 34–43 Russell St., London WC2B 5HA England.

Career: Director, producer, screenwriter, and actor. Granada Television, London, England, researcher, director, and producer during the 1960s; American Film Institute, Center for Advanced Film and Television Studies, Hollywood, CA, cochairperson of directing discipline, 1997; Michael Apted Film Co., founder; director of television commercials. Academy of Motion Picture Arts and Sciences (Documentary Branch), member of the board of governors, 2002—.

Member: Directors Guild of America (president, 2003—).

Awards, Honors: Television Critics Award, best play, 1972, for *Another Sunday and Sweet F.A.;* Golden Prize nomination, Moscow International Film Festival, 1973, for *The Triple Echo;* Television Critics Award, best play, and Television Award, best director, British Academy of

Film and Television Arts, 1974, both for "Kisses at Fifty," *Play for Today;* International Emmy Award, 1976, for *The Collection;* International Emmy Award nomination, 1976, for *21;* Directors Guild of America Award nomination, 1980, for *Coal Miner's Daughter;* Television Award nomination, best single drama, British Academy of Film and Television Arts, 1983, for *P'tang Yang Kipperbang;* International Documentary Association Award, 1985, for *28 Up;* Grammy Award (with Sting), best music video—long form, 1987, for *Bring on the Night;* Golden St. George Award nomination, Moscow International Film Festival, 1991, for *Class Action;* Flaherty Documentary Award, British Academy of Film and Television Arts, 1992, for *35 Up;* Critics Award nomination, Deauville Film Festival, 1992, for *Incident at Oglala;* Crystal Globe Award nomination, Karlovy Vary International Film Festival, 1994, for *Blink;* Vancouver International Film Festival Award, best documentary feature, 1994, Prize of the Ecumenical Jury, Forum of New Cinema, Berlin International Film Festival, 1995, both for *Moving the Mountain;* International Documentary Association Award nomination, feature documentaries, 1998, Flaherty Documentary Award nomination (with Claire Lewis), British Academy of Film and Television Arts, 1999, all for *42 Up;* Career Award, DoubleTake Documentary Film Festival, 1998; Career Achievement Award, International Documentary Association, 1999; Silver Spire, television drama—television feature, San Francisco International Film Festival, 1999, for *Always Outnumbered;* Special Jury Award, Florida Film Festival, 2000, for *Me & Isaac Newton;* British Academy of Film and Television Arts Award, for *The Lovers;* British Academy of Film and Television Arts Award, for *Folly Foot;* Feature Film Prize in Science and Technology, Hamptons International Film Festival, British Independent Film Award nomination, best director 2001, both for *Enigma;* Directors Guild of America Award (with others), outstanding directorial achievement in dramatic series—night, 2006, for *Rome.*

CREDITS

Film Director:

Triple Echo (also known as *Soldier in Skirts*), Hemdale Releasing, 1973.
Stardust, Goodtimes/Anglo, 1974.
The Squeeze, Warner Bros., 1976.
Agatha, Casablanca/First Artists, 1978.
Coal Miner's Daughter, Universal, 1980.
Continental Divide, Universal, 1981.
Kipperbang (also known as *P'Tang Yang, Kipperbang*), Metro–Goldwyn–Mayer/United Artists, 1983.
Gorky Park, Orion, 1983.
28 Up (documentary), First Run Features, 1984.
First Born (also known as *Firstborn* and *Moving In*), Paramount, 1984.
Executive producer, *The River Rat,* Paramount, 1984.

Bring on the Night (also known as *Sting: Bring on the Night*), Samuel Goldwyn/A&M, 1985.
Critical Condition, Paramount, 1986.
Gorillas in the Mist (also known as *Gorillas in the Mist: The Story of Dian Fossey* and *The Adventures of Dian Fossey*), Universal, 1988.
Class Action, Twentieth Century–Fox, 1991.
35 Up (documentary), Samuel Goldwyn, 1991.
Thunderheart, TriStar, 1992.
Incident at Oglala, Miramax, 1992.
Blink, New Line Cinema, 1994.
Moving the Mountain (documentary), October Films, 1994.
Nell, Twentieth Century–Fox, 1994.
Extreme Measures, Warner Bros., 1996.
Inspirations (documentary), Clear Blue Sky Productions, 1997.
Fortune's Fools, Fox 2000, 1998.
The World Is Not Enough (also known as *Pressure Point* and *T.W.I.N.E.*), Metro–Goldwyn–Mayer/United Artists, 1999.
Me & Isaac Newton, 1999.
42 Up (also known as *42: Forty Two Up*), First Run Features, 1999.
Enigma (also known as *Enigma—Das Geheimnis*), Miramax, 2001.
Enough, Columbia, 2002.
Lipstick (short), 2002.
Amazing Grace, 2006.
Black Autumn, Fox 2000, 2006.

Film Producer:

28 Up (documentary), First Run Features, 1984.
35 Up (documentary), Samuel Goldwyn, 1991.
Inspirations (documentary), Clear Blue Sky Productions, 1997.
42 Up (also known as *42: Forty Two Up*), First Run Features, 1999.

Film Executive Producer:

The River Rat, Paramount, 1984.
(With others) *Bram Stoker's "Dracula"* (also known as *Dracula*), Columbia, 1992.
It's a Shame About Ray (short), 2000.

Film Appearances:

Ace Tomato agent, *Spies Like Us,* Warner Bros., 1985.
Narrator and interviewer, *42 Up* (documentary; also known as *42: Forty Two Up*), First Run Features, 1999.
Himself, *The Making of "The World Is Not Enough"* (documentary), 1999.
Himself, *More Than Enough* (documentary short), Columbia TriStar Home Video, 2003.

Television Work; Series:

Director, *Parkin's Patch,* Yorkshire TV, 1969–70.

Executive producer, *Crossroads* (also known as *C. C. Riders*), ABC, 1992.

Also worked as director and investigative reporter, *World in Action,* ITV.

Television Work; Miniseries:
Director, *Big Breadwinner Hog,* Granada TV, 1968–69.
Executive producer, *Intruders: They Are Among Us* (also known as *Intruders*), CBS, 1992.
Executive producer, *Murder Without Motive: The Edmund Perry Story* (also known as *Best Intentions: The Education and Killing of Edmund Perry* and *Best Intentions*), NBC, 1992.
Director and consulting producer, *Rome,* HBO and BBC2, 2005.

Television Director; Movies:
Seven Up (documentary), 1964.
Number 10, Granada TV, 1968.
Your Name's Not God, It's Edgar, Granada TV, 1968.
In a Cottage Hospital, Granada TV, 1969.
Don't Touch Him, He Might Resent It, Granada TV, 1970.
Slattery's Mounted Foot, London Weekend TV/Kestrel Films, 1970.
The Day They Buried Cleaver, Granada TV, 1970.
Seven Plus Seven (documentary; also known as *7 Plus Seven*), 1970.
Big Soft Nellie, Granada TV, 1971.
The Mosedale Horseshoe, Granada TV, 1971.
One Thousand Pounds for Rosebud, Granada TV, 1971.
Another Sunday and Sweet F.A. (also known as *ITV Sunday–Night Theatre: Another Sunday and Sweet F.A.*), Granada TV, 1972.
Joy, BBC, 1972.
Said the Preacher, BBC, 1972.
The Style of the Countess, Granada TV, 1972.
High Kampf (also known as *Black and Blue: High Kampf*), BBC, 1973.
Jack Point, BBC, 1973.
Poor Girl, Granada TV, 1974.
"A Great Day for Bonzo," *Childhood,* Granada TV, 1974, PBS, 1977.
Wednesday Love, BBC, 1975.
21 (documentary; also known as *21 Up*), Granada TV, 1976.
The Collection (also known as *Laurence Olivier Presents: The Collection*), Granada TV, 1976.
P'tang Yang Kipperbang (also known as *Kipperbang*), Channel 4, 1984.
The Long Way Home, Yerosha Productions/Granada TV/CBS Music Video, 1989.
Always Outnumbered (also known as *Socrates* and *Always Outnumbered, Always Outgunned*), HBO, 1998.

49 Up (documentary), ITV, 2005.

Also directed *Highway Robbery* and *Age 7 in the USSR* (documentary).

Television Work; Movies:
(Uncredited) Researcher, *Seven Up* (documentary), 1964.
Producer, *Seven Plus Seven* (documentary; also known as *7 Plus Seven*), 1970.
Executive producer, *Criminal Justice,* HBO, 1990.
Producer, *Age 7 in America* (documentary; also known as *7 Up in America*), CBS, 1992.
Executive producer, *Strapped,* HBO, 1993.
Producer, *49 Up* (documentary), ITV, 2005.

Television Director; Pilots:
The Dustbinmen, ITV, 1969.
My Life and Times, ABC, 1991.
Crossroads (also known as *C. C. Riders*), ABC, 1992.
New York News, CBS, 1995.
Marriage, HBO, 2004.

Television Work; Specials:
Director, *Murder: A Professional Job,* Granada, 1968.
Director, *There's a Hole in Your Dustbin Delilah,* Granada, 1968.
Director, *Buggins' Ermine,* Granada TV, 1972.
Director, *Haunted: Poor Girl,* 1986.
Executive producer, *14 Up in America,* Showtime, 1998.
Consulting executive, *Born in the USSR: 14 Up,* PBS, 1999.
Director, *Nathan Dixon,* CBS, 1999.
Advisor, *Being Mick* (documentary), ABC, 2001.
Director and producer, *Married in America* (documentary), Arts and Entertainment, 2002.

Television Director; Episodic:
"The Shooting War," *City '68,* Granada TV, 1967.
"There's a Hole in Your Dustbin, Delilah," *Playhouse,* Granada TV, 1968.
The Lovers, Granada TV, 1970.
"The Reporters," *Play for Today,* BBC, 1972.
"Kisses at Fifty," *Play for Today,* BBC, 1973.
"Stronger Than the Sun," *Play for Today,* BBC, 1977.
Blind Justice, ABC, 2004.

Also directed *Coronation Street* (also known as *Corrie*), ITV and CBC; *Thirty–Minute Theatre,* BBC; *Haunted; Big Breadwinner Hog,* ITV; *Folly Foot,* ITV; *Black and Blue,* BBC; *My Life and Times,* ABC; *Crossroads,* Arts and Entertainment; *New York News,* CBS.

Television Appearances; Specials:

Himself, *The Making of "Gorky Park"* (documentary), 1983.

(Uncredited) Voice of interviewer, *28 Up* (documentary), Granada TV, 1984.

(Uncredited) Voice of interviewer, *35 Up* (documentary), Granada TV, 1991.

A Personal History of British Cinema by Stephen Frears (documentary; also known as *Typically British!*), 1997.

Himself, *The James Bond Story* (also known as *007: The James Bond Story;* documentary), 1999.

Himself, *Best Ever Bond* (documentary), ITV1, 2002.

Himself, *James Bond: A BAFTA Tribute,* BBC, 2002.

Himself, *ITV 50 Greatest Shows,* ITV, 2005.

Narrator/interviewer, *49 Up* (documentary), ITV, 2005.

Himself, *The 50 Greatest Documentaries* (documentary), 2005.

Bleep! Censoring Hollywood (documentary), AMC, 2005.

Television Appearances; Episodic:

Mad TV, Fox, 1999.

This Morning (also known as *This Morning with Richard and Judy*), ITV, 2005.

Stage Work:

Director, *Strawberry Fields,* National Theatre, London, 1978.

WRITINGS

Screenplays:

Bring on the Night (also known as *Sting: Bring on the Night*), 1985.

35 Up (documentary), Samuel Goldwyn, 1991.

Moving the Mountain (documentary), October Films, 1994.

OTHER SOURCES

Books:

International Dictionary of Films and Filmmakers, Volume 2: Directors, 4th ed., St. James Press, 2000.

Periodicals:

American Film, September, 1990, p. 42.

Interview, September, 1991.

PR Newswire, June 14, 1999.

Shoot, October 24, 1997, p. 1.

Sunday Times Review (London), June 16, 1991.

ARROYO, Danny

PERSONAL

Full name, Daniel Luis Arroyo; born January 29, in the Bronx, New York, NY. *Education:* Studied acting and voice. *Avocational Interests:* Fitness workouts, boxing, gymnastics, meditation, comic books, video games.

Addresses: *Agent*—Marilyn Szatmary, SMS Talent, Inc., 8730 West Sunset Blvd., Suite 440, West Hollywood, CA 90069; (commercials) Morgan Agency, 7080 Hollywood Blvd., Suite 1009, Hollywood, CA 90028. *Manager*—Central Artists, 3310 West Burbank Blvd., Burbank, CA 91505.

Career: Actor. Appeared in television and radio commercials and print advertisements. California Predators (semiprofessional football team), football player; also worked as a bartender, boxing coach, fitness trainer, and security guard.

Member: American Federation of Television and Radio Artists, Screen Actors Guild.

Awards, Honors: Slate Award, best actor, Northern California Independent Film and Video Festival, 2000, for *Chimera House.*

CREDITS

Film Appearances:

(Scenes deleted) Brad, *Bordello of Blood* (also known as *Dead Easy* and *Tales from the Crypt Presents: "Bordello of Blood"*), Universal, 1996.

First thug on street, *The Velocity of Gary,* Next Millennium Films, 1998.

Gomez, *Lethal Weapon 4* (also known as *Lethal 4*), Warner Bros., 1998.

Lucky, *Chimera House,* Dogstar Productions, 1999.

Carlos Devon, *White Rush,* Canon Films, 2003.

Lord Grey, *Richard III,* Basilisk Films, 2006.

Detention, FilmJack Productions, c. 2006.

Appeared in the independent film *The Courier* and the short film *NYPD Jew.*

Television Appearances; Movies:

Hip hop dancer, *Let It Be Me* (also known as *Love Dance*), Starz!, 1995.

Pepe, *Hard Time,* TNT, 1998.

(Uncredited; in archive footage) Pepe, *Hard Time: The Premonition* (also known as *The Premonition*), TNT, 1999.

Television Appearances; Episodic:
House of Buggin', Fox, 1995.
Chino Espinoza, "Sweet Sorrow," *Moloney*, CBS, 1996.
Cesar, "Tomas Alcantar," *America's Most Wanted* (also known as *America's Most Wanted: America Fights Back* and *A.M.W.*), Fox, 1997.
First student, "Girls Just Wanna Have Fun," *Step by Step*, CBS, 1997.
Carlos (El Killer Bee–O), "Leo Is a Pain in My Ass," *Shasta McNasty* (also known as *Shasta*), UPN, 2000.
Dr. Reid Mooney, "Start All Over Again," *ER* (also known as *Emergency Room*), NBC, 2001.
Paco, "Val under Covers," *V.I.P.* (also known as *V.I.P.—Die Bodyguards*), syndicated, 2001.
Ralphie, "Secretos, Mentiras, y Expectativas," *Resurrection Blvd.*, Showtime, 2001.
Smuggler, *Spyder Games* (also known as *Spyder Web*), MTV, 2001.
Guillermo "Memo" Ruiz, "Bait," *Without a Trace* (also known as *Vanished*), CBS, 2004.
Bad Boy Dan, "Day 4: 11:00 a.m.–12:00 p.m.," *24* (also known as *24 Hours*), Fox, 2005.

Some sources cite additional appearances in *Spyder Games* (also known as *Spyder Web*), MTV.

Television Appearances; Pilots:
Appeared in the pilot *Times Square*, Fox.

Television Appearances; Other:
Appeared as the host of *The Funk Dance Show* and *Muscle Mania*, both ESPN 2.

RECORDINGS

Video Games:
Voices of MOS soldier, Mafia person, and other characters, *Predator: Concrete Jungle*, Vivendi Universal Games, 2005.

WRITINGS

Screenplays:
Author of the screenplay *Gamers*.

OTHER SOURCES

Electronic:
Danny Arroyo Official Site, http://www.dannyarroyo.com, January 14, 2006.

ASSANTE, Armand 1949–
(Armand Assanti)

PERSONAL

Born October 4, 1949, in New York, NY; son of a painter and a music teacher; married Karen McArn (an actress), 1982 (separated, 1994); children: Alesandra, Anya. *Education:* Attended American Academy of Dramatic Arts, New York City; studied acting with Mira Rostova. *Avocational Interests:* Playing the guitar, writing ballads.

Addresses: *Agent*—Special Artists Agency, 9465 Wilshire Blvd., Suite 890, Beverly Hills, CA 90212. *Manager*—Untitled Entertainment, 331 North Maple Dr., 3rd Floor, Los Angeles, CA. *Publicist*—Patricola/Lust Public Relations, 8383 Wilshire Blvd., Suite 530, Beverly Hills, CA 90211.

Career: Actor. Also worked in a factory.

Awards, Honors: Jehlinger Award, American Academy of Dramatic Arts, 1969; Emmy Award nomination, outstanding supporting actor in a miniseries or special, 1988, Golden Globe Award nomination, best performance by an actor in a supporting role in a series, miniseries, or motion picture made for television, 1989, both for *Jack the Ripper;* Golden Globe Award nomination, best performance by an actor in a supporting role in a motion picture, 1991, for *Q & A;* Emmy Award, outstanding lead actor in a miniseries or special, Golden Globe Award nomination, best performance by an actor in a miniseries or motion picture made for television, and Screen Actors Guild Award nomination, outstanding performance by a male actor in a television movie or miniseries, all 1997, for *Gotti;* Golden Globe Award nomination, best performance by an actor in a miniseries or motion picture for television, Golden Satellite Award nomination, best performance by an actor in a miniseries or motion picture made for television, International Press Academy, 1998, both for *The Odyssey;* Annie Award nomination, outstanding individual achievement for voice acting by a male performer in an animated feature production, ASIFA–Hollywood, 2000, for *The Road to El Dorado.*

CREDITS

Film Appearances:
(As Armand Assanti) Wedding guest, *The Lords of Flatbush* (also known as *The Lord's of Flatbush*), Columbia, 1974.

Lenny Carboni, *Paradise Alley,* Universal, 1978.

John Hawks, *Prophecy* (also known as *Prophecy: The Monster Movie*), Paramount, 1979.

Lorenzo Prado, *Love and Money,* Paramount, 1980.

Gary Callahan, *Little Darlings,* Paramount, 1980.

Henri Tremont, *Private Benjamin,* Warner Bros., 1980.

Mike Hammer, *I, the Jury,* Twentieth Century–Fox, 1982.

Maxmillian Stein, *Unfaithfully Yours,* Twentieth Century–Fox, 1983.

Belizaire Breaux (title role), *Belizaire the Cajun,* Skouras/Norstar, 1986.

Juan Mateo, *The Penitent* (also known as *Los Penitentes*), Cineworld, 1988.

Bobby Texador, *Q & A,* TriStar, 1990.

Mark Mathias, *Animal Behavior,* Cinestar, 1990.

Sean/Roni, *Eternity,* Academy Entertainment, 1990.

Bugsy Siegel, *The Marrying Man* (also known as *Too Hot to Handle*), Buena Vista, 1991.

Cesar Castillo, *The Mambo Kings* (also known as *The Mambo Kings Play Songs of Love*), Warner Bros., 1992.

Sanchez, *1492: Conquest of Paradise* (also known as *1492: La conquete du paradis,* *1492: La conquista del paraiso,* and *1492: Christophe Colomb*), Paramount, 1992.

Carol D'Allesandro, *Hoffa,* Twentieth Century–Fox, 1992.

Ned Ravine, *Fatal Instinct,* Metro–Goldwyn–Mayer, 1993.

Rusty Pirone, *Trial by Jury,* Warner Bros., 1994.

Rico, *Judge Dredd,* Buena Vista, 1995.

Lieutenant Al Garcia, *Striptease,* Columbia, 1996.

Voice, *Rashi: A Light after the Dark Ages* (documentary), 1999.

Hunt for the Devil, Fries Film Group, 1999.

Voice of Tzekel–Kan, *The Road to El Dorado* (animated), DreamWorks, 2000.

Vince "Vinnie" Pirelli, *Looking for an Echo,* Echo Productions, 2000.

Frank Banner, *Last Run,* DEJ Productions, 2001.

Holly, *One Eyed King,* Lions Gate Films, 2001.

Frank Carbone/Howard Akers, *Federal Protection,* Promark Entertainment, 2002.

Jack Cunningham, *Partners in Action,* DEJ Productions, 2002.

Ike, *Tough Luck,* Curb Entertainment, 2003.

Sam Patterson, *Citizen Verdict,* Bauer Martinez Studios, 2003.

Sam Tyler, Max Tyler, and Sam Burns, *Consequence,* Warner Bros., 2003.

Ennemis publics, 2005.

Kumal, *Children of Wax,* 2005.

Charlie Daines, *Dot.Kill,* DEJ Productions, 2005.

Benefactor, *The Third Wish,* Skyway Productions, 2005.

York, *Zerklanie voyni: Otrazhenie pervoye* (also known as *Mirror Wars: Reflection One*), 2005.

Novian, *Two for the Money,* Universal, 2005.

Argento, *Confessions of a Pit Fighter,* 2005.

Genero, *Funny Money,* 2005.

Tony Thick, *Dead Lenny,* 2006.

Harley, *Soul's Midnight,* Image Entertainment, 2006.

Film Work:

Executive producer, *Dot.Kill,* DEJ Productions, 2005.

Television Appearances; Series:

Johnny McGee, *How to Survive a Marriage,* NBC, 1974–75.

Dr. Mike Powers, *The Doctors,* NBC, 1975–77.

Mr. Smooth, *Push, Nevada,* ABC, 2002.

Television Appearances; Miniseries:

Joseph Friedman, *Evergreen,* NBC, 1985.

Napoleon Bonaparte, *Napoleon and Josephine: A Love Story,* ABC, 1987.

Richard Mansfield, *Jack the Ripper,* CBS, 1988.

Alfred DeMarigny, *Passion and Paradise,* ABC, 1989.

Alan Breck Stewart, *Kidnapped,* The Family Channel, 1995.

Odysseus, *The Odyssey* (also known as *Homer's "The Odyssey," Die abenteuer des Odysseus,* and *Odissea*), NBC, 1997.

Captain Dwight Towers, *On the Beach,* Showtime, 2000.

Television Appearances; Movies:

Johnny Turner, *Human Feelings* (also known as *Miles the Angel*), NBC, 1978.

Hamid, *Harold Robbins' "The Pirate"* (also known as *The Pirate*), CBS, 1978.

Ernest de Paulo, *Lady of the House,* NBC, 1978.

Riccardo Scicolone, *Sophia Loren: Her Own Story,* NBC, 1980.

Michael Moretti, *Rage of Angels* (also known as *Sidney Sheldon's "Rage of Angels"*), NBC, 1983.

Dr. James Stallings, *Why Me?,* ABC, 1984.

Charles Macaluso, *A Deadly Business,* CBS, 1986.

Joe Hearn, *Hands of a Stranger* (also known as *Double Standard*), NBC, 1987.

Hal Slater, *Stranger in My Bed,* NBC, 1987.

Ray Wellman, *Fever,* HBO, 1991.

Canaan, *Blind Justice* (also known as *Canaan's Way*), HBO, 1994.

John Gotti, *Gotti* (also known as *John Gotti: The Rise and Fall* and *King of the Volcano*), HBO, 1996.

Lieutenant George Dixon, *The Hunley,* TNT, 1999.

Jean–Pierre, *After the Storm,* USA Network, 2001.

Television Appearances; Specials:

Narrator, *The Life and Times of Jesus: The First Christmas* (documentary), The Learning Channel, 1993.

Intimate Portrait: Jacqueline Bisset (documentary), Lifetime, 1997.

Presenter, *The 25th International Emmy Awards,* Thirteen/WNET, 1998.

Tito Puente: The King of Latin Music (documentary), PBS, 2001.

Television Appearances; Episodic:

Tom Ryan, "Caper on a Quiet Street," *Kojak,* 1977.

Freddie Faust, "A Chilling Surprise," *Mrs. Columbo* (also known as *Kate Columbo, Kate Loves a Mystery,* and *Kate the Detective*), 1979.

Narrator (Rudolph Valentino/Archbishop Cicognani, and Cardinal Spellman), *Sex and the Silver Screen,* Showtime, 1996.

"Hoffa," *History Vs. Hollywood,* History Channel, 2001.

Himself, *Tussen de sterren,* 2003.

Stage Appearances:

(Off–Broadway debut) Christo, *Lake of the Woods,* 1971.

Leonine and Knight of Tharsus, *Perciles, Prince of Tyre,* Delacorte Theatre, New York City, 1974.

Bunce, Rob Roy Fruitwell, Vernon Equinox, Wagnerian, Fish Market Boy, and Joe Gourielli, *The Beauty Part,* American Place Theatre, New York City, 1974.

Masetto and Ferondo, *Boccaccio,* Edison Theatre, New York City, 1975.

Teddy/Ged Murray, *Comedians,* Music Box Theatre, New York City, 1976.

Tybalt, *Romeo and Juliet,* Circle in the Square Theatre, New York City, 1977.

Emperor Napoleon I, *Kingdoms,* Cort Theatre, New York City, 1981–82.

Also appeared in off–Broadway productions of *Yankees 3, Detroit 0, Rubbers,* and *Why I Went Crazy.*

OTHER SOURCES

Periodicals:

American Film, January–February, 1992, p. 22.

People, February 28, 1983, p. 95.

AVITAL, Mili 1972–

PERSONAL

Born April 3, 1972, in Jerusalem, Israel; immigrated to the United States, 1992; daughter of Iko (a graphic designer) and Noni (a graphic designer) Avital; married

Charles Randolph (a screenwriter), July 4, 2004. *Education:* Attended the Circle in the Square Professional Theater School.

Addresses: *Agent*—Innovative Artists, 1505 10th St., Santa Monica, CA 90401.

Career: Actress. Appeared in advertisements, including a television commercial for Meudenet White Cheese; previously worked as a waitress in New York City.

Awards, Honors: Israeli Film Academy Award, best supporting actress, 1991, for *Me'ever Layam;* Israeli Film Academy Award nomination, best actress, 1994, for *Groupie;* Universe Reader's Choice Award, best supporting actress in a genre motion picture, *Sci–Fi Universe Magazine,* 1995, for *Stargate;* Israeli Film Academy Award nomination, best actress, 1997, for *Minotaur.*

CREDITS

Film Appearances:

Miri, *Me'ever Layam* (also known as *Over the Ocean* and *Beyond the Seas*), Transfax Film Productions, 1992.

Groupie, 1993.

Sha'uri, *Stargate* (also known as *Stargate, la porte des etoiles*), Metro–Goldwyn–Mayer, 1994.

Thel Russell, *Dead Man* (also known as *Jim Jarmuch's "Dead Man"*), Miramax, 1995.

The End of Violence (also known as *Am ende der gewalt*), Metro–Goldwyn–Mayer/United Artists, 1997.

Thea, *Minotaur* (also known as *Mossad*), Cinema Pardes, 1997.

Fatima, *Animals* (also known as *Animals and the Tollkeeper*), Magnolia Mae, 1997.

Samantha Andrews, *Kissing a Fool,* Universal, 1998.

Sofie Pzoniak, *Polish Wedding,* Fox Searchlight, 1998.

Erin, *The Young Girl and the Monsoon,* 1999.

Emily Tylk, *Preston Tylk* (also known as *Bad Seed*), New City Releasing, 2000.

Young Iris, *The Human Stain* (also known as *La couleur du mensonge* and *Der menschliche makel*), Miramax, 2003.

Tali Shalev, *Ahava Columbianit,* 2004.

Vanessa, *When Do We Eat?,* ThinkFilm, 2005.

Film Work:

Director, producer, and editor, *I Think Myself I Am All the Time Younger* (documentary), 2004.

Television Appearances; Miniseries:

Scheherazade, *Arabian Nights,* ABC, 2000.

Devorah Baron, *Uprising,* NBC, 2001.

Television Appearances; Movies:
Theresa Barnes, *Invasion of Privacy* (also known as *Head Games*), HBO, 1996.
Conquina, *After the Storm,* USA Network, 2001.

Television Appearances; Specials:
Host (with Michael Douglas and Kevin Costner), *To Life! America Celebrates Israel's 50th,* CBS, 1998.

Television Appearances; Episodic:
Marta Stevens, "Payback," *Law & Order: Special Victims Unit* (also known as *Law & Order: SVU* and *Special Victims Unit*), NBC, 1999.
Ava Parulis/Irina Parulis, "Parasites," *Law Order: Special Victims Unit* (also known as *Law & Order: SVU* and *Special Victims Unit*), NBC, 2001.

Also appeared as Eryn Towne, "Nexus," *Haunted,* UPN.

Stage Appearances:
Cecille, *Dangerous Liaisons,* Cameri Theatre, Tel Aviv, Israel, 1987.

OTHER SOURCES

Periodicals:
Bikini, May, 1998, pp. 15–16.
People Weekly, May 8, 2000, p. 219.
Shiva Yamim, June 19, 1998, pp. 22–27.

B

BAIN, Barbara 1931–

PERSONAL

Original name, Millicent Fogel; born September 13, 1931, in Chicago, IL; married Martin Landau (an actor), 1957 (divorced, 1993); children: Susan Meredith (a writer, producer, and director), Juliet Rose (an actress). *Education:* University of Illinois, B.A., sociology; studied acting at the Actors Studio and the Neighborhood Playhouse; studied dance with Martha Graham. *Religion:* Jewish.

Addresses: *Agent*—The Artists Agency, 10000 Santa Monica Blvd., Suite 305, Los Angeles, CA 90067.

Career: Actress. Previously worked as a fashion model and dancer in New York City. Volunteer reader, Santa Monica, CA, c. 1992; Book PALS (Performing Artists for Literacy in Schools), founder, c. 1996.

Member: Actors' Equity Association, American Federation of Television and Radio Artists, Screen Actors Guild.

Awards, Honors: Emmy Awards, outstanding continued performance by an actress in a leading role in a dramatic series, 1967, 1968, 1969, Golden Globe Award nomination, best television star—female, 1968, all for *Mission: Impossible;* DramaLogue Award, *L.A. Weekly* Award, and Los Angeles Drama Critics Circle Award nomination, 1985, for *Wings;* DramaLogue Award, 1998, for *The Chairs.*

CREDITS

Film Appearances:

Cinnamon Carter, *Mission Impossible Versus the Mob* (also known as *Mission Impossible vs. the Mob*), Paramount, 1968.

Mary Casal, *Trust Me,* Cinecom, 1989.
Martha, *Skinheads* (also known as *Skinheads—The Second Coming of Hate* and *Teste Rasate*), Greydon Clark, 1990.
Hipster, *The Spirit of '76,* SVS/Triumph Home Video, 1990.
Animals, Magnolia Mae, 1997.
Madame Harwin, *Platform Six,* 1997.
Madame Richaud, *Dry Martini,* 1998.
Airtime, 1998.
The mother, *Animals and the Tollkeeper,* 1998.
Deidre, *Panic,* Artisan Entertainment, 2000.
Agnes, *Bel Air,* Load Media, Inc., 2000.
Anne Tillman, *American Gun,* 2002.
Dr. Helena Russell, *Space: 1899* (short), Fanderson, 2004.

Television Appearances; Series:

Karen Wells, *Richard Diamond, Private Detective* (also known as *Call Mr. D*), CBS, 1959.
Cinnamon Carter, *Mission: Impossible,* CBS, 1966–69.
Dr. Helena Russell, *Space: 1999* (also known as *Spazio: 1999*), syndicated, 1975–77.

Television Appearances; Movies:

Lisa Manning, *Murder Once Removed* (also known as *The Obsessive Doctor*), CBS, 1971.
Susan Lakely, *Goodnight, My Love,* ABC, 1972.
Gail Abbot, *Savage* (also known as *Watch Dog* and *The Savage File*), NBC, 1973.
Ellen Hailey, *A Summer Without Boys,* ABC, 1973.
Dr. Helena Russell, *Journey through the Black Sun,* syndicated, 1976.
Dr. Helena Russell, *Destination Moonbase Alpha* (also known as *Space: 2100*), syndicated, 1976.
Dr. Helena Russell, *Cosmic Princess,* syndicated, 1976.
Dr. Helena Russell, *Alien Attack,* syndicated, 1976.
Dr. Olga Schmetner, *The Harlem Globetrotters on Gilligan's Island,* NBC, 1981.
The Obsessive Doctor, 1992.

Audrey, *Icebergs: The Secret Life of a Refrigerator,* Lifetime, 1998.

Sarah, *Gideon,* Starz!, 1999.

Television Appearances; Specials:

Guest star, *The Mama Cass Television Program,* 1969.

Herself, *The "Space: 1999" Documentary* (documentary), 1969.

Judy Utermeyer, *Tracey Ullman in the Trailer Tales,* HBO, 2003.

Presenter, *The 12th Annual Screen Actors Guild Awards,* TNT, 2006.

Television Appearances; Pilots:

Young in Heart, CBS, 1965.

Julia Barrington, "Barrington," *CBS Summer Playhouse,* CBS, 1987.

Television Appearances; Episodic:

"The Captain's Gun," *Harbourmaster* (also known as *Adventure at Scott Island*), CBS, 1958.

"Fiddle Dee Dead," *State Trooper,* 1959.

"Small Bouquet," *Alcoa Theater,* CBS, 1959.

Prudence, "The Money Game," *Mr. Lucky,* 1959.

Judy Coyne, "Small Bouquet," *Alcoa Theatre,* 1959.

"Cold Kill," *Tightrope,* 1959.

Madelyn Terry, "The Case of the Wary Wildcatter," *Perry Mason,* CBS, 1960.

"Prisoner in Paradise," *Adventures in Paradise,* ABC, 1960.

D. J., "Christmas is a Legal Holiday," *The Law and Mr. Jones,* ABC, 1960.

"Nightmare in the Sun," *Adventures in Paradise,* ABC, 1961.

"The Craziest Race in Town," *Straightaway,* ABC, 1962.

Dorothy, "Will You Two Be My Wife?," *Dick Van Dyke Show* (also known as *Head of the Family* and *The Dick Van Dyke Daytime Show*), CBS, 1963.

Anne Munroe, "Two Million Too Much," *Hawaiian Eye,* ABC, 1963.

"I Was a Spy for the F.O.B.," *Dobie Gillis* (also known as *The Many Loves of Dobie Gillis*), CBS, 1963.

June Bates, "Hidden Asset," *Empire* (also known as *Big G*), 1963.

Cissie Van Osten, "A Touching of Hands," *Lieutenant,* NBC, 1963.

Rachel Dent, "By His Own Verdict," *77 Sunset Strip,* ABC, 1963.

Lucy Garrison, "The Fenton Canaby Story," *Wagon Train* (also known as *Major Adams, Trail Master*), ABC, 1963.

"How Does Your Garden Grow?," *Mr. Novak,* NBC, 1964.

Betty, "The Night the Monkey Died," *The Greatest Show on Earth,* ABC, 1964.

Elayna Scott, "The Case of the Nautical Knot," *Perry Mason,* CBS, 1964.

Tutor, "A Woods Full of Question Marks," *Ben Casey,* 1964.

"The Old School Tie," *Valentine's Day,* ABC, 1964.

Inge, "I'm Through Being a Nice Guy," *My Mother the Car,* NBC, 1965.

Alma Sutton, "KAOS in Control," *Get Smart,* NBC, 1965.

Gerry Hart, "Young at Heart," *Vacation Playhouse,* 1965.

Frankie, "Desperate Minutes," *My Mother the Car,* NBC, 1966.

Herself, *Dateline: Hollywood,* CBS, 1967.

Dream Girl of '67, ABC, 1967.

Everybody's Talking, ABC, 1967.

Rowan & Martin's Laugh-In, NBC, 1968.

The Andy Williams Show, NBC, 1970.

The Smothers Brothers Show, NBC, 1975.

Julia Huntley, "A Death in the Family," *Mike Hammer* (also known as *Mickey Spillane's "Mike Hammer"* and *The New Mike Hammer*), CBS, 1984.

Emily Greydon, "My Fair David," *Moonlighting,* ABC, 1985.

Christina Golitsyn, "The Khrushchev List," *Scarecrow and Mrs. King,* CBS, 1987.

Nora Morgan, "Coal Miner's Slaughter," *Murder, She Wrote,* CBS, 1988.

Ellen Lombard, "Unauthorized Obituary," *Murder, She Wrote,* CBS, 1991.

Storytime, PBS, 1994.

Vivian Wood, "Other People's Mothers," *My So-Called Life,* ABC, 1994.

The elderly Constance MacArthur, "Reunion," *The Visitor,* Fox, 1997.

Cinnamon Carter, "Discards," *Diagnosis Murder,* CBS, 1997.

Older Lilly Unser, "Matryoshka," *Millennium,* Fox, 1998.

Mother Superior, "Saving Grace," *Walker, Texas Ranger,* CBS, 1998.

Strong Medicine, Lifetime, 2002.

Also appeared in *Ben Casey,* ABC; *The Kraft Music Hall,* NBC.

Stage Appearances:

Mary Tyrone, *Long Day's Journey into Night,* Seattle, WA, 1984.

Emily Stilson, *Wings,* Odyssey Theatre, Los Angeles, 1985.

Winnie, *Happy Days,* Los Angeles Theatre Center, Los Angeles, 1986–87.

Also appeared as Kate Jerome, *Broadway Bound,* 1990; Lillian Cage, *Mrs. Cage,* 1994; in *The Price,* 1995; *All Over the Map,* 1995; Devorah, *The Yiddish Trojan Women,* 1996; Old Woman, *The Chairs,* 1997; Melissa Gardner, *Love Letters,* 1999.

RECORDINGS

Taped Readings:

(With others) *Lost in Yonkers,* L.A. Theatre Works, 2002.

(With Emily Bergl and Harriet Harris) *Agnes of God,* L.A. Theatre Works, 2002.

OTHER SOURCES

Periodicals:

Good Housekeeping, July, 1996, p. 18.

BALDWIN, Alec 1958–

PERSONAL

Full name, Alexander Rae Baldwin III; born April 3, 1958, in Massapequa (some sources say Amityville), NY; son of Alexander Rae, Jr. (a high school social studies teacher and football coach) and Carol Newcomb (maiden name, Martineau) Baldwin; brother of William, Stephen, and Daniel Baldwin (all actors); cousin of Joseph Baldwin (an actor); married Kim Basinger (an actress), August 19, 1993 (divorced, February, 2002); children: Ireland Eliesse (known as Addie). *Education:* New York University, B.A., 1993; attended George Washington University, 1976–79, and New York University, 1979–80; trained for the stage at Lee Strasberg Theatre Institute with Marcia Haufrecht and Geoffrey Horne; also studied with Mira Rostova. *Politics:* Democrat. *Religion:* Roman Catholic. *Avocational Interests:* Cuban cigars.

Addresses: *Agent*—Creative Artists Agency, 9830 Wilshire Blvd., Beverly Hills, CA 90212. *Office*—El Dorado Pictures, 725 Arizona Ave., Suite 100, Santa Monica, CA 90401.

Career: Actor, director, producer, and writer. El Dorado Pictures, Santa Monica, CA, principal; provided voices for television and radio commercials, including Chevrolet cars and trucks, 1995, Northwest Airlines, 1997, Disney World, 2003, Subaru, 2004, MTV, 2004, Iridium, General Electric, Sony, and AIG Auto Insurance; previously worked as a waiter and doorman at Studio 54, New York City, and as a lifeguard, gas station attendant, shirt salesman, driver, and landscaper. Creative Coalition, president; political fund–raiser.

Member: Actors' Equity Association, Screen Actors Guild, American Federation of Television and Radio Artists.

Awards, Honors: Acting scholarship for Tisch School of the Arts, New York University, 1980; *Soap Opera Digest* Award, outstanding new actor in a prime time serial, 1985, *Soap Opera Digest* Award nominations, best actor in a leading role on a prime time serial and outstanding villain on a prime time serial, 1986, all for *Knots Landing;* *Theatre World* Award, best performance, 1986, for *Loot;* Obie Award, best performance, *Village Voice,* and Drama Desk Award nomination, best actor in a play, 1990, both for *Prelude to a Kiss;* Antoinette Perry Award nomination, best performance by a leading actor in a play, 1992, for *A Streetcar Named Desire;* Valladolid International Film Festival Award, best actor, 1992, for *Glengarry Glenn Ross;* Emmy Award nomination, outstanding lead actor in a miniseries or a special, Golden Globe Award nomination, best performance by an actor in a miniseries or motion picture made for television, Screen Actors Guild Award nomination, outstanding performance by a male actor in a television movie or miniseries, all 1996, for "A Streetcar Named Desire," *CBS Playhouse 90s;* American Comedy Award nomination, funniest male guest appearance in a television series, 1999, for *Saturday Night Live;* Sierra Award nomination, best supporting actor, Las Vegas Film Critics Society, 2000, for *Outside Providence;* Maverick Tribute Award, Cinequest San Jose Film Festival, 2000; Emmy Award nomination (with others), outstanding miniseries, Screen Actors Guild Award nomination, outstanding performance by a male actor in a television movie or miniseries, Golden Globe Award nomination, best performance by an actor in a miniseries or motion picture made for television, Gemini Award nomination, best performance by an actor in a leading role in a dramatic program or miniseries, Academy of Canadian Cinema and Television, Gemini Award (with others), best dramatic miniseries, 2001, all for *Nuremberg;* National Board of Review Award (with others), best acting by an ensemble, 2000, Online Film Critics Society Award (with others), best ensemble cast performance, Florida Film Critics Circle Award (with others), best ensemble cast, 2001, all for *State and Main;* Emmy Award nomination, outstanding supporting actor in a miniseries or a movie, 2002, Golden Globe Award nomination, best performance by an actor in a supporting role in a series, miniseries, or motion picture made for television, 2003, both for *Path to War;* National Board of Review Award, best supporting actor, 2003, Academy Award nomination, best actor in a supporting role, Vancouver Film Critics Circle Award, best supporting actor, Screen Actors Guild Award nomination, outstanding performance by a male actor in a supporting role, Golden Satellite Award nomination, best performance by an actor in a supporting role—drama, International Press Academy, Online Film Critics Society Award nomination, best supporting actor, Golden Globe Award nomination, best performance by an actor in a supporting role in a motion picture, Dallas–Fort Worth Film Critics Association Award, best supporting actor, Broadcast Film Critics Association Award nomination, best supporting actor, 2004, all for *The Cooler;* Montclair State University, honorary doctorate of letters, 2004; Emmy Award nomination, outstanding guest actor in a comedy series, 2005, for *Will & Grace;* Screen Actors Guild Award nomination (with others), outstanding performance by a cast in a motion picture, 2005, for *The Aviator;* Golden Starfish Award, Hamptons International Film Festival, 2005, for career achievement.

CREDITS

Film Appearances:
Buck, *Forever, Lulu* (also known as *Crazy Streets*), TriStar, 1987.

Adam Maitland, *Beetlejuice,* Warner Bros., 1988.

Mick Dugan, *Working Girl,* Twentieth Century–Fox, 1988.

Davis McDonald, *She's Having a Baby,* Paramount, 1988.

Frank "The Cucumber" DeMarco, *Married to the Mob,* Orion, 1988.

Dan, *Talk Radio,* Universal, 1988.

Jimmy Lee Swaggart, *Great Balls of Fire,* Orion, 1989.

(English version) Narrator, *Tong Tana—En resa till Borneos inre* (documentary; also known as *Tong Tana* and *Tong Tana—Das verlorene paradies*), First Run Features, 1989.

Frederick J. "Junior" Frenger, *Miami Blues,* Orion, 1990.

Jack Ryan, *The Hunt for Red October,* Paramount, 1990.

Ed, *Alice,* Orion, 1990.

Charley Pearl, *The Marrying Man* (also known as *Too Hot to Handle*), Buena Vista, 1991.

Blake, *Glengarry Glen Ross,* New Line, 1992.

Peter Hoskins, *Prelude to a Kiss,* Twentieth Century–Fox, 1992.

Dr. Jed Hill, *Malice,* Columbia, 1993.

Lamont Cranston, *The Shadow,* Universal, 1994.

Carter "Doc" McCoy, *The Getaway,* Universal, 1994.

Narrator, *Wild Bill: A Hollywood Maverick; The Life and Times of William A. Wellman* (also known as *Wild Bill: Hollywood Maverick*), Turner Pictures, 1995.

(Uncredited) Narrator, *Two Bits* (also known as *A Day to Remember*), Miramax, 1995.

Teacher, *The Juror,* Columbia, 1996.

Dave Robicheaux, *Heaven's Prisoners,* New Line Cinema, 1996.

Himself/Duke of Clarence, *Looking for Richard,* Twentieth Century–Fox, 1996.

Bobby de Laughter, *Ghosts of Mississippi* (also known as *Ghosts from the Past*), Sony Pictures Entertainment, 1996.

Himself, *Sean Connery Close Up* (documentary), Blue Dolphin Film Distribution, 1996.

Robert Green, *The Edge* (also known as *Bookworm* and *The Wild*), Twentieth Century–Fox, 1997.

Robert Green, *The Edge,* 1997.

Mackin, "The Thief," *Thick as Thieves,* 1998.

Lieutenant Colonel Nicholas Kudrow, *Mercury Rising,* Universal, 1998.

Jeff King, *Notting Hill,* Universal, 1999.

Roy Bleakie, *The Confession,* 1999.

Todd Fitter, *Scout's Honor,* 1999.

Old Man Dunphy, *Outside Providence,* Miramax, 1999.

Himself, *Watch the Mercury Rising* (documentary short), Universal Studios Home Video, 1999.

Mr. Conductor, *Thomas and the Magic Railroad,* Destination Films, 2000.

Bob Barrenger, *State and Main* (also known as *Sequences et consequences*), Fine Line Features, 2000.

Himself, *The Acting Class,* 2000.

Voice of Captain Gray Edwards, Deep Eyes Sequences, *Aki's Dream* (animated short), Columbia TriStar Home Video, 2001.

Jabez Stone, *The Devil and Daniel Webster,* Family Room Entertainment, 2001.

Lieutenant Colonel James Doolittle, *Pearl Harbor* (also known as *Pearl Harbour*), Buena Vista, 2001.

Voice of Butch, *Cats & Dogs,* Warner Bros., 2001.

Voice of Captain Gray Edwards, *Final Fantasy: The Spirits Within* (animated; also known as *Fainaru fantaji*), Columbia, 2001.

Narrator, *The Royal Tennenbaums,* Buena Vista, 2001.

Himself, *Breaking the Silence: The Making of "Hannibal"* (documentary), Metro–Goldwyn–Mayer Home Entertainment, 2001.

(Uncredited) M.Z.M., *The Adventures of Pluto Nash* (also known as *Pluto Nash*), Warner Bros., 2002.

Shelly Kaplow, *The Cooler,* Lions Gate Films, 2003.

Himself, *Broadway: The Golden Age, by the Legends Who Were There* (documentary; also known as *Broadway, Broadway: The Golden Age,* and *Broadway: The Movie*), Dada Films, 2003.

Himself, *Brighter Days* (short), 2003.

Quinn, *The Cat in the Hat* (also known as *Dr. Seuss' "The Cat in the Hat"*), Universal, 2003.

(Uncredited) Himself, *Double Dare* (documentary), Balcony Releasing, 2004.

Narrator, *Thomas & Friends: Best of Gordon,* Anchor Bay Entertainment, 2004.

Joe Devine, *The Last Shot,* Buena Vista, 2004.

Stan Indursky, *Along Came Polly,* Universal, 2004.

Voice of Dennis, *The SpongeBob SquarePants Movie* (animated), Paramount, 2004.

Juan Trippe, *The Aviator,* Miramax, 2004.

Martin, *Mini's First Time,* 2005.

Brooklyn Rules, Hannover House, 2005.

Phil DeVoss, *Elizabethtown,* Paramount, 2005.

Jack McCallister, *Fun with Dick and Jane,* Sony, 2005.

Norman Burroughs, *Running with Scissors,* 2006.

The Good Shepherd, Universal, 2006.

Ellerby, *The Departed,* Warner Bros., 2006.

Also appeared in *The Chase.*

Film Work:
Executive producer, *Heaven's Prisoners*, New Line Cinema, 1996.
Producer, *The Confession*, 1999.
Executive producer, *State and Main* (also known as *Sequences et consequences*), Fine Line Features, 2000.
Producer and (uncredited) director, *The Devil and Daniel Webster*, Family Room Entertainment, 2001.

Television Appearances; Series:
Billy Allison Aldrich, *The Doctors*, NBC, 1980–82.
Dr. Hal Wexler, *Cutter to Houston*, CBS, 1983.
Joshua Rush, *Knots Landing*, CBS, 1984–85.
Host, *Raw Footage*, Independent Film Channel, 1996.
(U.S. version) Narrator and other voices, *Thomas the Tank Engine & Friends* (also known as *Thomas & Friends*, *Thomas the Tank Engine*, and *Tomas a'l Ffrindiau*), PBS and ITV, 1998–2003.
Malcolm, *Will & Grace*, NBC, 2005.

Television Appearances; Miniseries:
Rysam "Ry" Slaight, *Dress Gray*, NBC, 1986.
Justice Robert H. Jackson, *Nuremberg*, TNT, 2000.
Himself, *The Hamptons*, ABC, 2002.
Himself, *I Love the '70s*, VH1, 2003.
Himself, *TV Land Moguls*, TV Land, 2004.

Television Appearances; Movies:
Major Alex Breen, *Sweet Revenge* (also known as *Bittersweet Revenge*, *Code of Honor*, and *Her Revenge*), CBS, 1984.
Sean Carpenter, *Love on the Run*, NBC, 1985.
Colonel William Barrett Travis, *The Alamo: Thirteen Days to Glory*, NBC, 1987.
Stanley Kowalski, "A Streetcar Named Desire" (also known as "Tennessee Williams's 'A Streetcar Named Desire'"), *CBS Playhouse 90s*, CBS, 1995.
Roy Bleakie, *The Confession*, Cinemax, 1999.
Free Money, Starz!, 1999.
Macklin, *Thick as Thieves*, HBO, 2000.
Secretary of Defense Robert McNamara, *Path to War*, HBO, 2002.
Paul Kane, *Second Nature*, TNT, 2003.
Voice of Adult Timmy Turner, *Nickelodeon Presents the Fairly OddParents in: Channel Chasers* (animated), Nickelodeon, 2004.

Television Appearances; Pilots:
Sheriff Ed Cassaday, *The Sheriff and the Astronaut* (movie), CBS, 1984.
Himself, *Naked*, Bravo, 2005.

Television Appearances; Specials:
Earth '90: Children and the Environment, syndicated, 1990.
Living in America, VH1, 1991.

The 2nd Annual Saturday Night Live Mother's Day Special, NBC, 1993.
Voice, *Earth and the American Dream*, HBO, 1993.
Narrator, *A Time of AIDS*, The Discovery Channel, 1993.
Masters of Illusion: The Wizards of Special Effects, NBC, 1994.
The Universal Story, Encore Starz, 1995.
Narrator, *Blacklist: Hollywood on Trial*, AMC, 1996.
Host and narrator, "Black Market Birds: On Location with Alec Baldwin and Kim Basinger" (also known as "Vanishing Birds of the Amazon"), *Wild! Life Adventures* (also known as *TOPX*), TBS, 1996.
Indecision '96: The Republican National Convention, 1996.
Happy Birthday Elizabeth—A Celebration of Life, ABC, 1997.
Intimate Portrait: Jessica Lange, Lifetime, 1998.
The Kennedy Center Honors: A Celebration of the Performing Arts, CBS, 1998.
(Uncredited) Mr. Cherrywood, *Saturday Night Live: The Best of Phil Hartman*, NBC, 1998.
Saturday Night Live: The Best of Chris Farley, NBC, 1998.
The AFI's 100 Years ... 100 Stars, CBS, 1999.
Little Jimmy Scott, Bravo, 1999.
(Uncredited) Various characters, *Saturday Night Live: The Best of Adam Sandler*, NBC, 1999.
Host, *Paul McCartney & Friends Live: PETA's Millennium Concert*, VH1, 1999.
Saturday Night Live: 25th Anniversary Primetime Special, NBC, 1999.
Narrator, *The Democratic Promise: Saul Alinsky & His Legacy* (documentary), PBS, 1999.
Narrator, *Intimate Portrait: Judy Collins*, Lifetime, 2000.
The Man, *The Kennedy Center Presents: Speak Truth to Power*, PBS, 2000.
Voiceover, *Mailer of Mailer* (documentary), PBS, 2000.
Hollywood Salutes Bruce Willis: An American Cinematheque Tribute, TNT, 2000.
Beyond the Movie: Pearl Harbor (documentary), 2001.
The Big Show (also known as *The Big Show: Toronto International Film Festival*), CBC, 2001.
Journey to the Screen: The Making of "Pearl Harbor" (documentary), BET, 2001.
Narrator, *Into the Shadows: The CIA in Hollywood* (documentary), AMC, 2001.
Joan Rivers: The E! True Hollywood Story, E! Entertainment Television, 2001.
History vs. Hollywood: Pearl Harbor, History Channel, 2001.
Saturday Night Live: The Best of Will Ferrell, NBC, 2002.
Intimate Portrait: Joan Van Ark, Lifetime, 2002.
Host, *Dreams & Giants*, Showtime, 2003.
Making the Movie: Dr. Seuss' "The Cat in the Hat" (documentary), MTV, 2003.
(U.S. version) Narrator, *Walking with Cavemen* (documentary), BBC and The Discovery Channel, 2003.

101 Most Unforgettable SNL Moments, E! Entertainment Television, 2004.

The Rise of the Celebrity Class (documentary), BBC, 2004.

A Life Without Limits: The Making of "The Aviator" (documentary), FX Channel, 2004.

Himself and various characters, *Saturday Night Live: The Best of Alec Baldwin,* NBC, 2005.

Steve McQueen: The Essence of Cool (documentary), TNT and TCM, 2005.

Narrator, *Knots Landing Reunion: Together Again* (documentary), CBS, 2005.

Narrator, *I'm King Kong!: The Exploits of Merian C. Cooper* (documentary), TCM, 2005.

Presenter, *The 28th Annual Kennedy Center Honors: A Celebration of the Performing Arts,* CBS, 2005.

Television Appearances; Awards Presentations:

Presenter, *The 63rd Annual Academy Awards,* ABC, 1991.

The 46th Annual Tony Awards, CBS, 1992.

Presenter, *The 66th Annual Academy Awards Presentation,* 1994.

Presenter, *The 49th Annual Tony Awards,* 1995.

(Uncredited) *The 67th Annual Academy Awards,* ABC, 1995.

Presenter, *The 51st Annual Tony Awards,* CBS, 1997.

Presenter, *The 70th Annual Academy Awards,* ABC, 1998.

Presenter, *The 55th Annual Golden Globe Awards,* 1998.

Presenter, *The 52nd Annual Tony Awards,* 1998.

Presenter, *The 14th Independent Spirit Awards,* IFC and Bravo, 1999.

Presenter, *The 53rd Annual Tony Awards,* CBS, 1999.

The 5th Annual Screen Actors Guild Awards, TNT, 1999.

Presenter, *The 57th Annual Golden Globe Awards,* NBC, 2000.

The 54th Annual Tony Awards, CBS and PBS, 2000.

Host, *The 2001 ABC World Stunt Awards* (also known as *World Stunt Awards*), ABC, 2001.

The 54th Annual Primetime Emmy Awards, NBC, 2002.

Presenter, *IFP Gotham Awards 2003,* Bravo, 2003.

The 10th Annual Screen Actors Guild Awards, TNT, 2004.

The 76th Annual Academy Awards, ABC, 2004.

Television Appearances; Episodic:

Late Night with David Letterman, NBC, 1982.

Dennis Medford, "Distortions," *Hotel* (also known as *Arthur Hailey's "Hotel"*), 1985.

Guest host, *Saturday Night Live* (also known as *SNL*), NBC, 1990, 1991, 1994, 1996, 1997, 2001, 2002, 2003, 2005, 2006.

The Larry Sanders Show, HBO, 1992.

Himself, "The List," *The Larry Sanders Show,* HBO, 1993.

Inside the Actors Studio, Bravo, 1994.

Howard Stern, E! Entertainment Television, 1994, 2003.

The Charlie Rose Show, PBS, 1995.

Late Show with David Letterman (also known as *The Late Show*), CBS, 1997, 2004, 2005.

The Rosie O'Donnell Show, syndicated, 1997, 1998, 1999, 2000, 2001, 2002.

Voice of himself, "When You Dish Upon a Star," *The Simpsons* (animated), Fox, 1998.

Narrator, *Thomas the Tank Engine & Friends,* PBS, 1998.

Late Night with Conan O'Brien, NBC, 1998.

Himself, *Saturday Night Live* (also known as *SNL*), NBC, 1998, 2004, 2006.

Voice of Leonardo Leonardo, "Episode Two," *Clerks* (animated; also known as *Clerks: The Animated Series, Clerks: The Cartoon,* and *Clerks: Uncensored*), ABC, 2000.

Guest, *Who Wants to Be a Millionaire,* ABC, 2000.

Himself, "Andy Richter/Alec Baldwin," *Primetime Glick,* Comedy Central, 2002.

Himself, "Truth in the Media," *Dennis Miller Live,* HBO, 2002.

Voice of himself, "Gump Roast," *The Simpsons* (animated), Fox, 2002.

Parker, "The One With the Tea Leaves," *Friends,* NBC, 2002.

Parker, "The One in Massapequa," *Friends,* NBC, 2002.

Mad TV, Fox, 2003.

Himself, "Tenacious D a la Mode," *Player$,* G4, 2003.

The Daily Show (also known as *The Daily Show with Jon Stewart* and *The Daily Show with Jon Stewart Global Edition*), Comedy Central, 2003, 2004.

The Sharon Osbourne Show (also known as *Sharon*), syndicated, 2003, 2004.

Real Time with Bill Maher, HBO, 2003, 2005.

Jack Keller, "Hellraisers & Heartbreakers," *Las Vegas,* NBC, 2004.

Jack Keller, "Degas Away with It," *Las Vegas,* NBC, 2004.

Tinseltown TV (also known as *Tinseltown.TV*), International Channel, 2004.

"Melanie Griffith," *A&E Biography,* Arts and Entertainment, 2004.

Juan Trippe, "The Aviator," *History vs. Hollywood* (also known as *History Through the Lens* 0, History Channel, 2004.

Dr. Barrett Moore, "Joan Rivers," *Nip/Tuck,* FX Channel, 2004.

The Tony Danza Show, syndicated, 2004.

The View, ABC, 2004.

This Hour Has 22 Minutes, CBC, 2004.

Dinner for Five, Independent Film Channel, 2004.

The O'Reilly Factor, Fox News, 2004.

Hollywood Squares (also known as *H2* and *H2: Hollywood Squares*), syndicated, 2004.

HARDtalk, BBC, 2004.

Film School, Independent Film Channel, 2004.

Entertainment Tonight, syndicated, 2005.

The Oprah Winfrey Show (also known as *Oprah*), syndicated, 2005.
Corazon de ... , 2005.
Ellen: The Ellen DeGeneres Show, syndicated, 2005.
Too Late with Adam Carolla, Comedy Central, 2005.
Larry King Live, CNN, 2005.
Today (also known as *The Today Show*), NBC, 2005.
Voice of Caleb Thron, "Bonfire of the Manatees," *The Simpsons* (animated), Fox, 2005.
"The Baldwin Brothers," *The E! True Hollywood Story,* E! Entertainment Television, 2006.

Also appeared in *Hotel;* and "The Films of Michael Bay," *The Directors,* Encore.

Television Work; Series:
Creator, producer, and executive producer, *Raw Footage,* Independent Film Channel, 1996.

Television Work; Miniseries:
Executive producer, *Nuremberg,* TNT, 2000.

Television Work: Movies:
Producer, *The Confession,* Cinemax, 1999.
Executive producer, *Second Nature,* 2003.

Stage Appearances:
Lysander, *A Midsummer Night's Dream,* Lee Strasberg Theatre Institute, New York City, 1980.
Soldier, *Summertree,* Vandam Theatre, New York City, 1981.
Dennis, *Loot,* Music Box Theatre, New York City, 1986.
Grimes and Billy Corman, *Serious Money,* Royale Theatre, New York City, 1988.
Peter, *Prelude to a Kiss,* Circle Repertory Theatre, New York City, 1990.
Stanley Kowalski, *A Streetcar Named Desire,* Ethel Barrymore Theatre, New York City, 1992.
Title role, *Macbeth,* Joseph Papp Public Theatre, New York City, 1998.
Peter, "Extra," *Short Talks on the Universe,* Eugene O'Neill Theatre, New York City, 2002.
Oscar Jaffe, *Twentieth Century,* American Airlines Theater, New York City, 2004.
Entertaining Mr. Sloane, Laura Pels Theatre, New York City, 2006.

Also appeared in *A Life in the Theatre,* the Hartman Theatre, Plattsburgh, NY; *Study in Scarlet,* Williamstown, MA; and *The Wager,* New York City.

RECORDINGS

Videos:
(Uncredited) Various characters, *Saturday Night Live: The Best of Mike Myers,* 1998.

Pete Schweaty, *Saturday Night Live Christmas,* Trimark Video, 1999.
(Uncredited) Various characters, *Saturday Night Live: The Best of Molly Shannon,* 2001.

WRITINGS

Television Episodes:
"Tabloid," *Law and Order,* NBC, 1998.

OTHER SOURCES

Books:
Newsmakers, Issue 2, Gale Group, 2002.

Periodicals:
Entertainment Weekly, February 6, 2004, p. 62.
Esquire, February, 1994, p. 70; November, 1996, p. 104.
Good Housekeeping, May, 1996, p. 98.
Interview, October, 1989.
New Republic, December 8, 1997, p. 25.
People Weekly, January 29, 2001, p. 82; August 26, 2002, p. 20; November 14, 2005, p. 68; December 5, 2005, p. 116.
Redbook, February, 1994, p. 88.
Time, November 10, 1997, p. 4; December 1, 2003, p. 92.

BARGER, Greg
    See BERGER, Gregg

BARKER, Bob 1923–

PERSONAL

Full name, Robert William Barker; born December 12, 1923, in Darrington, WA; son of Byron John (a power line foreman) and Matilda Kent (maiden name, Tarleton) Barker; married Dorothy Jo Gideon, January 12, 1945 (died, October 19, 1981). *Education:* Drury College, B.A., economics, 1947 (summa cum laude). *Religion:* Protestant. *Avocational Interests:* Animal rights activism, karate, traveling, reading, sunbathing, golf, sports, Civil War buff.

Addresses: *Office*—c/o *The Price Is Right,* Price Productions, 5757 Wilshire Blvd., Suite 206, Los Angeles, CA 90036.

Career: Television host, actor, and producer. Worked as news writer, announcer, and disc jockey for KTTS–FM until 1949; news editor and staff announcer at WWPG; Bob Barker Productions, Inc., president, 1966—. *Military service:* U.S. Navy, fighter pilot, active duty, 1943–45, reserves, 1945–60; reached rank of lieutenant junior grade; American Campaign Medal, World War II Victory Medal.

Member: American Guild of Variety Artists, American Federation of Television and Radio Artists, Screen Actors Guild, Actors and Others for Animals (member of board of directors), Society Against Vivisection, Fund for Animals (national chair), Sigma Nu.

Awards, Honors: Emmy Awards, outstanding host—game show, 1982, 1984, 1987, 1988, 1990, 1991, 2000, 2002, 2004, Emmy Award (with Phillip W. Rossi and Roger Dobkowitz), outstanding audience participation show/game show, 2005, Emmy Lifetime Achievement Award, 1999, Emmy Award nominations, outstanding host—game show, 1979, 1985, 1986, 2001, 2003, 2005, Emmy Award nominations (with Rossi and Dobkowitz), outstanding audience participation show/game show, 1999, 2000, 2001, 2002, 2003, 2004, all for *The Price Is Right;* Emmy Award nomination (with others), 1985, for *CBS Tournament of Roses Parade;* MTV Movie Award (with Adam Sandler), best fight, 1996, for *Happy Gilmore;* Academy of Television Arts and Sciences Hall of Fame, inductee, 2004; Carbon Mike Award, *Pioneer Broadcaster;* named most generous host in television history and twice named most durable performer, *The Guinness Book of World Records;* named one of ten best dressed men in the United States, Custom Tailors Guild of America; received star on the Hollywood Walk of Fame.

CREDITS

Television Appearances; Series:
Host, *Truth or Consequences* (also known as *The All New Truth and Consequences* and *The New Truth and Consequences*), NBC, 1956–65, syndicated, 1966–75.
Host, *The End of the Rainbow,* NBC, 1958.
Host, *The Family Game,* ABC, 1967.
Sub–Host, *Dream Girl of '67,* 1967.
Host, *The Price Is Right* (also known as *The New Price Is Right*), CBS, 1972— syndicated version, 1977–80.
Guest panelist, *Match Game PM* (also known as *Match Game 75, Match Game 76, Match Game 77, Match Game 78, Match Game 79*), CBS, 1973, 1975–82.
Panelist, *Match Game PM,* syndicated, 1975.
Substitute host, *Tattletales,* CBS, 1975–76.
Host, *That's My Line,* 1980–81.

Television Appearances; Specials:
Host, *The Miss USA Pageant,* CBS, annually, 1966–87.
Host, *The Miss Universe Pageant,* CBS, annually, 1966–87.
Host, *The Indianapolis 500 Parade,* 1967.
Host, *Pillsbury Bake–Off,* CBS, 1969.
Host, *CBS Tournament of Roses Parade,* CBS, 1969, 1984, 1985, 1986, 1987, 1988.
Circus of the Stars #4, CBS, 1979.
TV's Funniest Gameshow Moments, ABC, 1984.
Host, *The Price Is Right Special,* CBS, 1986.
Host, *The 18th Annual Daytime Emmy Awards,* CBS, 1991.
Presenter, *The 9th Annual Television Academy Hall of Fame,* The Disney Channel, 1993.
Host, *The Price Is Right 25th Anniversary,* CBS, 1996.
Presenter, *The 23rd Annual Daytime Emmy Awards,* CBS, 1996.
The Making of Adam Sandler's Video, Comedy Central, 1996.
Segment host, "The Price is Right," *CBS: 50 Years of Funny Flubs and Screw Ups,* CBS, 1998.
The Great American History Quiz, History Channel, 1999.
Mark Goodson: Will the Real Mark Goodson Please Stand Up? (documentary), Arts and Entertainment, 2000.
Presenter, *The 28th Annual Daytime Emmy Awards,* NBC, 2001.
The Great American History Quiz: 50 States, History Channel, 2001.
Host, *The Price is Right 30th Anniversary Special* (also known as *The Price Is Right: The Showdown in Vegas*), CBS, 2002.
CBS: 50 Years from Television City, CBS, 2002.
Host, *The 29th Annual Daytime Emmy Awards,* CBS, 2002.
Host, *The Price Is Right Salutes the U.S. Marine Corps,* CBS, 2002.
Host, *The Price Is Right Million Dollar Spectacular,* CBS, 2003.
Host, *The Price Is Right Salutes the U.S. Navy,* CBS, 2003.
Host, *The Price Is Right Salutes the U.S. Air Force,* CBS, 2003.
Himself, *I Love the '70s,* VH1, 2003.
Presenter, *CBS at 75* (also known as *CBS at 75: A Primetime Celebration*), CBS, 2003.
Presenter, *The 32nd Annual Daytime Emmy Awards,* CBS, 2005.

Also hosted the *Pillsbury Bake–Off* and the *CBS Tournament of Roses Parade,* both CBS, in other years.

Television Appearances; Episodic:
Mort, "Denver McKee," *Bonanza* (also known as *Ponderosa*), 1960.
Here's Hollywood, NBC, 1961.
Substitute host, *The Tonight Show Starring Johnny Carson* (also known as *The Best of Carson*), NBC, 1966.

Dinah! (also known as *Dinah! & Friends*), 1976, 1977.
The John Davidson Show, syndicated, 1981.
Himself, "The Price is Right vs. the Young and the Restless," *Family Feud* (also known as *Family Feud Challenge* and *The New Family Feud*), CBS, 1993.
Himself, "When You Pish Upon a Star," *The Nanny,* CBS, 1994.
Ben, Carly's dad, "Something about Thanksgiving," *Something So Right,* NBC, 1996.
Himself, "Talk Ain't Cheap," *Baily Kipper's P.O.V.* (also known as *Bailey Kippper's Point of View*), CBS, 1996.
Ben, Carly's dad, "Something about a Silver Anniversary," *Something So Right,* NBC, 1997.
Himself, "Shanghai Express," *Martial Law,* CBS, 1998.
The Rosie O'Donnell Show, syndicated, 1998, 1999, 2001, 2002.
"Bob Barker: Master of Ceremonies," *Biography,* Arts and Entertainment, 1999.
Voice of himself, "Lesser of Two Evils," *Futurama* (animated), Fox, 2000.
Himself, "The Ticket," *Yes, Dear,* CBS, 2001.
Voice of himself, "Screwed the Pooch," *Family Guy* (animated; also known as *Padre de familia*), Fox, 2001.
Himself, "Price is Right," *The E! True Hollywood Story,* E! Entertainment Television, 2002.
Himself, *The Bold and the Beautiful* (also known as *Belleza y poder*), CBS, 2002.
The Wayne Brady Show, syndicated, 2003.

Also appeared as a guest, *The Gordon Elliot Show,* syndicated.

Television Work; Series:
Producer, *Lucky Pair,* syndicated, 1969.
Executive producer, *The Price Is Right* (also known as *The New Price Is Right*), CBS, 1972—.

Television Work; Specials:
Producer, *Pillsbury Bake–Off,* CBS, 1969.
Executive producer, *The Price Is Right 25th Anniversary Special,* CBS, 1996.
Executive producer, *The Price Is Right 30th Anniversary Special* (also known as *The Price Is Right: The Showdown in Vegas*), CBS, 2002.
Executive producer, *The Price Is Right Primetime Specials,* CBS, 2002.
Executive producer, *The Price Is Right Salutes the U.S. Marine Corps,* CBS, 2002.
Executive producer, *The Price Is Right Million Dollar Spectacular,* CBS, 2003.
Executive producer, *The Price Is Right Salutes the U.S. Navy,* CBS, 2003.
Executive producer, *The Price Is Right Salutes the U.S. Air Force,* CBS, 2003.

Also produced other *Pillsbury Bake–Off* competitions, CBS.

Film Appearances:
Himself, *Happy Gilmore,* Universal, 1996.

Major Tours:
Toured in *Bob Barker Fun and Games Show,* U.S. and Canadian cities.

Radio Appearances; Series:
Appeared in *The Bob Barker Show.*

BARRYMORE, Drew 1975–

PERSONAL

Full name, Drew Blythe Barrymore; born February 22, 1975, in Los Angeles, CA (some sources say Culver City, CA); daughter of John Drew, Jr. (an actor) and Ildiko Jaid (an actress) Barrymore; granddaughter of John Drew Barrymore (an actor); great–granddaughter of Maurice Costello (an actor in silent films); married Jeremy Thomas (a bar owner), March 20, 1994 (divorced, February, 1995); married Tom Green (a comedian and television personality), March, 2001 (divorced, October 15, 2002); engaged to Fabrizio Moretti (a musician), 2004. *Avocational Interests:* Photography.

Addresses: *Agent*—Creative Artists Agency, 9830 Wilshire Blvd., Beverly Hills, CA 90212. *Office*—Flower Films, 4000 Warner Blvd., Bungalow Three, Burbank, CA 91522.

Career: Actress, director, and producer. Made her television debut in a commercial at the age of eleven months; appeared in television commercials for Puppy Choice dog food, 1975, Pillsbury chocolate chip cookies, 1979, and Rice Krispies cereal, 1981; appeared in print ads for Guess? jeans, 1992–94, and Missoni, 2006; former spokesperson for Lancome; Flower Films (production company), Burbank, CA, cofounder with Nancy Juvonen.

Awards, Honors: Youth in Film Award, most promising newcomer, Film Award nomination, most outstanding newcomer, British Academy of Film and Television Arts, 1981, Young Artist Award, best young supporting actress in a motion picture, 1983, all for *E. T., the Extra–Terrestrial;* Golden Globe Award nomination, best performance by an actress in a supporting role in a motion picture, Young Artist Award nomination, best young actress in a motion picture—musical, comedy, adventure or drama, 1985, both for *Irreconcilable Differences;* Emmy Award nomination, best performance in children's programming, 1985, for "The Adventures of Con Sawyer and Hucklemary Finn," *ABC Weekend Specials;* Saturn Award nomination, best performance by a younger actor, Academy of Science Fiction, Fantasy and Horror Films, 1985, for *Firestarter;* Young Artist Award nomination, best starring performance by a young actress—motion picture, 1986, for *Cat's Eye;* Young Artist Award nomination, best young female superstar in television, 1988, for *Babes in Toyland;* Golden Globe Award, best actress in a miniseries or motion picture made for television, Best Actress Award, Mystfest, 1993, both for *Guncrazy;* Saturn Award nomination, best supporting actress, Academy of Science Fiction, Fantasy and Horror Films, 1997, for *Scream;* MTV Movie Award nomination (with Adam Sandler), best on–screen duo, MTV Movie Award (with Sandler), best kiss, 1998, Blockbuster Entertainment Award nomination, favorite actress—comedy, American Comedy Award nomination, funniest actress in a motion picture—leading role, Chlotrudis Award nomination, best actress, Chlotrudis Society for Independent Film, Nickelodeon Kids' Choice Award, favorite movie actress, 1999, all for *The Wedding Singer;* Teen Choice Award nomination, film—choice actress, 1999, Blockbuster Entertainment Award, favorite actress—comedy/romance, 2000, both for *Never Been Kissed;* Saturn Award, best actress, Academy of Science Fiction, Horror and Fantasy Films, Blockbuster Entertainment Award, favorite actress—drama/romance, Chlotrudis Award nomination, best actress, Chlotrudis Society for Independent Film, Nickelodeon Kids' Choice Award, favorite movie actress, 1999, all for *Ever After;* Actress of the Year, Hollywood Film Festival, 1999; Former Child Star Lifetime Achievement Award, Young Artist Awards, 1999; Crystal Award, Women in Film Crystal Awards, 1999; Blockbuster Entertainment Award, favorite actress—comedy/romance, American Comedy Award nomination, funniest actress in a motion picture—leading role, MTV Movie Award nominations, best female performance and best kiss (with Michael Vartan), Nickelodeon Kids' Choice Award, favorite movie actress, 2000, all for *Never Been Kissed;* Emmy Award nomination (with others), outstanding animated program—programming more than one hour, 2000, for *Olive, the Other Reindeer;* Comedy Star of the Year, ShoWest Convention, 2000; Teen Choice Award nomination, film—choice actress, 2001; Barrymore Award, Hollywood Makeup Artist and Hair Stylist Guild Awards, 2001; Woman of the Year, Hasty Pudding Theatricals, Harvard University, 2001; Golden Apple, female star of the year, 2001; Video Premiere Award nomination, best supporting actress, DVD Exclusive Awards, 2001, for *Skipped Parts;* MTV Movie Award (with others), best on–screen team, MTV Movie Award nomination, best fight, Nickelodeon Kids' Choice Award, favorite movie actress, Blockbuster Entertainment Award (with others), favorite action team, 2001, all for *Charlie's Angels;* Teen Choice Award nomina-

tion, film—choice actress, drama/action adventure, 2002, for *Riding in Cars with Boys;* MTV Movie Award (with Adam Sandler), best on–screen team, MTV Movie Award nomination, best female performance, Teen Choice Award nominations, choice movie actress—comedy, choice movie chemistry (with Sandler), and choice movie liplock (with Sandler), 2004, People's Choice Award (with Sandler), favorite on–screen chemistry, Nickelodeon Kids' Choice Award nomination, favorite movie actress, 2005, all for *50 First Dates;* Star on Hollywood Walk of Fame, 2004; Special Award, distinguished decade of achievement in film, ShoWest Convention, 2004; MTV Movie Award nomination (with others), best dance sequence, 2004, for *Charlie's Angels: Full Throttle;* named "Friend of the United Nations" by Artists for the United Nations, 2004; Audience Award nomination, best international actress, Independent Film and Television Alliance Awards, Teen Choice Award nominations, choice movie actress—comedy, choice movie chemistry (with Jimmy Fallon), choice movie liplock (with Fallon), and choice movie love scene (with Fallon), 2005, all for *Fever Pitch.*

CREDITS

Film Appearances:

(Film debut) Margaret Jessup, *Altered States,* Warner Bros., 1980.

Gertie, *E. T., the Extra–Terrestrial* (also known as *A Boy's Life, E. T. and Me, E. T.,* and *Night Skies*), Universal, 1982.

Charlie McGee, *Firestarter,* Universal, 1984.

Casey Brodsky, *Irreconcilable Differences,* Warner Bros., 1984.

Amanda, *Stephen King's "Cat's Eye"* (also known as *Cat's Eye*), Metro–Goldwyn–Mayer/United Artists, 1985.

Joleen Cox, *Far from Home,* Vestron, 1989.

Cathy Goodwin, *See You in the Morning,* Warner Bros., 1989.

Fantasy girl, *Motorama,* Columbia/TriStar Home Video, 1991.

Ivy, *Poison Ivy,* New Line Cinema, 1992.

Vampire victim, *Waxwork II: Lost in Time* (also known as *Lost in Time* and *Space Shift: Waxwork II*), Live Entertainment, 1992.

Tinsel Hanley, *No Place to Hide* (also known as *Tipperary*), Cannon, 1993.

Bjergen Kjergen, *Wayne's World 2,* Paramount, 1993.

Lilly Laronette, *Bad Girls,* Twentieth Century–Fox, 1994.

Daisy, *Inside the Goldmine,* 1994.

Holly, *Boys on the Side* (also known as *Avec ou sans hommes*), Warner Bros., 1995.

Casey Roberts, *Mad Love,* Buena Vista, 1995.

Sugar, *Batman Forever* (also known as *Forever*), Warner Bros., 1995.

Like a Lady, 1996.

Herself, *The Making of "E.T. The Extra–Terrestrial"* (documentary; also known as *E.T.: The Extra–Terrestrial—A Look Back*), 1996.

Skylar Dandridge, *Everyone Says I Love You,* Miramax, 1996.

Casey Becker, *Scream* (also known as *Scary Movie*), Dimension Films/Miramax, 1996.

Lena, the cashier, *Wishful Thinking,* Miramax, 1997.

Teena Brandon, *All She Wanted,* 1997.

Hope, *Best Men* (also known as *Independence*), Orion Pictures Entertainment, 1997.

Josie Geller, *Never Been Kissed,* Twentieth Century–Fox, 1998.

Sally Jackson, *Home Fries,* Warner Bros., 1998.

Julia Sullivan, *The Wedding Singer,* New Line Cinema, 1998.

Danielle de Barbarac, *Ever After* (also known as *Cinderella*), Twentieth Century–Fox, 1998.

Drew, *Models,* 1998.

Voice of Akima, *Titan A.E.* (animated; also known as *Titan: After Earth*), Twentieth Century–Fox, 2000.

Dream girl, *Skipped Parts* (also known as *The Wonder of Sex*), Trimark Pictures, 2000.

So Love Returns, 2000.

Dylan, *Charlie's Angels* (also known as *3 Engel fur Charlie*), Sony Pictures Entertainment, 2000.

Herself, *The Master and the Angels* (documentary short), Columbia TriStar Home Entertainment, 2000.

Herself, *Getting G'd Up* (documentary short), Columbia TriStar Home Entertainment, 2000.

Herself, *Angelic Attire: Dressing Cameron, Drew & Lucy* (documentary short), Columbia TriStar Home Entertainment, 2000.

Herself, *Behind the "Scream"* (documentary), Dimension Home Video, 2000.

Karen Pomeroy, *Donnie Darko* (also known as *"Donnie Darko" The Director's Cut*), Newmarket Films, 2001.

Mr. Davidson's receptionist, *Freddy Got Fingered,* Twentieth Century–Fox, 2001.

Beverly Donofrio, *Riding in Cars with Boys,* Columbia, 2001.

Penny, *Confessions of a Dangerous Mind* (also known as *Confessions d'un homme dangereux*), Miramax, 2002.

Herself, *The E.T. Reunion* (documentary short), 2002.

Live at the Shrine! John Williams and the World Premiere of "E.T.: The Extra Terrestrial": The 20th Anniversary, 2002.

Herself, *E.T. the Extra–Terrestrial: 20th Anniversary Celebration* (documentary), Universal Studios Home Video, 2002.

Dylan Sanders, *Charlie's Angels: Full Throttle,* Columbia, 2003.

Nancy Kendricks, *Duplex* (also known as *Der appartement–schreck* and *Our House*), Miramax, 2003.

Lucy Whitmore, *50 First Dates,* Columbia, 2004.

Herself, *My Date with Drew* (documentary), Imagination Worldwide, 2004.

Herself, *The Dating Scene* (documentary short), Columbia TriStar Home Entertainment, 2004.

Herself, *Ramones Raw* (documentary), Image Entertainment, 2004.

Herself, *"Donnie Darko": Production Diary* (documentary), Metrodome Distribution, 2004.

Lindsey Meeks, *Fever Pitch,* Twentieth Century–Fox, 2005.

Voice of Drew Barrymore, *Family Guy Presents: Stewie Griffin—The Untold Story* (animated), 2005.

Voice of Maggie, *Curious George* (animated), Universal, 2006.

Billie Offer, *Lucky You,* Warner Bros., 2006.

Film Work:

Executive Producer, *Never Been Kissed,* Twentieth Century–Fox, 1998.

Producer, *So Love Returns,* 2000.

Producer, *Charlie's Angels* (also known as *3 Engel fur Charlie*), Sony Pictures Entertainment, 2000.

Executive producer, *Charlie's Angels: Full Throttle,* 2003.

Producer, *Duplex* (also known as *Der appartement–Schrek* and *Our House*), 2003.

Producer, *Fever Pitch,* 2005.

Television Appearances; Series:

Voice of Hillary, *Star Faires,* 1986.

Lindsay Rule, *2000 Malibu Road,* CBS, 1992.

Television Appearances; Miniseries:

I Love the '70s, VH1, 2003.

I Love the '90s: Part Deux, VH1, 2005.

Television Appearances; Movies:

Bobby Graham, *Suddenly Love,* 1978.

Leslie Bogart, *Bogie,* CBS, 1980.

Lisa Piper, *Babes in Toyland,* NBC, 1986.

Jody Wykowski, *Conspiracy of Love,* CBS, 1987.

Daisy Drew, *The Sketch Artist* (also known as *Drawing Fire*), Showtime, 1992.

Anita Minteer, *Guncrazy,* Showtime, 1992.

Holly Gooding, *Doppelganger* (also known as *Doppelganger: The Evil Within*), syndicated, 1993.

Amy Fisher, *The Amy Fisher Story* (also known as *Beyond Control: The Amy Fisher Story*), ABC, 1993.

Television Appearances; Specials:

EPCOT Center: The Opening Celebration, CBS, 1983.

The Screen Actors Guild 50th Anniversary Celebration, CBS, 1984.

The Night of 100 Stars II, ABC, 1985.

Disneyland's 30th Anniversary Celebration, NBC, 1985.

Con Sawyer, "The Adventures of Con Sawyer and Huck-lemary Finn," *ABC Weekend Specials*, ABC, 1985.

Host, "Hansel and Gretel," *Great Performances*, PBS, 1986.

Happy Birthday, Hollywood! (also known as *Happy 100th Birthday Hollywood*), ABC, 1987.

The Ring, Arts and Entertainment, 1989.

Voice of letters to Margaret Sanger, *The Roots of Roe,* 1993.

100 Years of the Hollywood Western, NBC, 1994.

Hollywood's Most Powerful Women, E! Entertainment Television, 1995.

CityKids All Star Celebration, ABC, 1996.

Happy Birthday Elizabeth—A Celebration of Life, ABC, 1997.

Woody Allen: A to Z, Turner Classic Movies, 1997.

Barbara Walters Presents: Six to Watch, ABC, 1997.

Hollywood Glamour Girls (also known as *Glamour Girls*), E! Entertainment Television, 1998.

Canned Ham: The Wedding Singer, Comedy Central, 1998.

Ladies Home Journal's Most Fascinating Women of '98, CBS, 1998.

Seventeen: The Faces for Fall, The WB, 1998.

Steven Spielberg: An Empire of Dreams (documentary), Arts and Entertainment, 1998.

Take a Moment, The Disney Channel, 1998.

The AFI's 100 Years ... 100 Stars, CBS, 1999.

Assignment E! With Leeza Gibbons: Hollywood's Youth Obsession, E! Entertainment Television, 1999.

Saturday Night Live: 25th Anniversary, NBC, 1999.

Voice of Olive, *Olive, the Other Reindeer* (animated), Fox, 1999.

Host, *AFI's 100 Years ... 100 Laughs* (also known as *AFI's 100 Years, 100 Laughs: America's Funniest Movies*), CBS, 2000.

The 25 Hottest Stars Under 25, MTV, 2001.

The Tom Green Cancer Special, MTV, 2001.

(Uncredited) Herself, *Who Is Alan Smithee?* (documentary), AMC, 2002.

Herself and various characters, *Saturday Night Live: The Best of Will Ferrell,* NBC, 2002.

"E.T. the Extra-Terrestrial": 20th Anniversary Celebration, NBC, 2002.

101 Most Shocking Moments in Entertainment, E! Entertainment Television, 2003.

Herself, *The Making of "Charlie's Angels: Full Throttle"* (documentary), HBO, 2003.

Charlie's Angels Uncensored, MTV, 2003.

The Stars' First Time ... On Entertainment Tonight with Mary Hart, CBS, 2003.

Real Access: Hot 24 in 2004, The N, 2003.

101 Most Unforgettable SNL Moments, E! Entertainment Television, 2004.

Reel Comedy: 50 First Dates, Comedy Central, 2004.

Choose or Lose Presents: The Best Place to Start, MTV, 2004.

Comedy Central's Bar Mitzvah Bash!, Comedy Central, 2004.

Scream Queens: The E! True Hollywood Story, E! Entertainment Television, 2004.

Tsunami Aid: A Concert of Hope, NBC, 2005.

Television Appearances; Awards Presentations:

The 61st Annual Academy Awards, ABC, 1989.

Presenter, *The 50th Annual Golden Globe Awards,* TBS, 1993.

Presenter, *The 70th Annual Academy Awards,* ABC, 1998.

Presenter, *The 11th Annual Kids' Choice Awards,* Nickelodeon, 1998.

The 1998 Billboard Music Awards, Fox, 1998.

The 5th Annual Blockbuster Entertainment Awards, Fox, 1999.

Presenter, *Nickelodeon's 12th Annual Kids' Choice Awards,* Nickelodeon, 1999.

The 71st Annual Academy Awards, ABC, 1999.

Presenter, *The 6th Annual Blockbuster Entertainment Awards,* Fox, 2000.

Presenter, *The 72nd Annual Academy Awards Presentation,* ABC, 2000.

Presenter, *The 7th Annual Blockbuster Entertainment Awards,* Fox, 2001.

Presenter, *Nickelodeon's 14th Annual Kids' Choice Awards,* Nickelodeon, 2001.

The 8th Annual Screen Actors Guild Awards, TNT, 2002.

Nickelodeon Kids' Choice Awards '03 (also known as *Nickelodeon's 16th Annual Kids' Choice Awards*), Nickelodeon, 2003.

The 2003 MTV Movie Awards, MTV, 2003.

MTV Video Music Awards 2003, MTV, 2003.

The 2004 MTV Movie Awards, MTV, 2004.

The 31st Annual People's Choice Awards, CBS, 2005.

Presenter, *The 77th Annual Academy Awards,* ABC, 2005.

Presenter, *The 63rd Annual Golden Globe Awards,* NBC, 2005.

Television Appearances; Episodic:

Guest host, *Saturday Night Live* (also known as *SNL*), NBC, 1982, 1999, 2001, 2004, 2005.

"EPCOT Center," *The World of Disney,* CBS, 1982.

The Tonight Show Starring Johnny Carson (also known as *The Best of Carson*), NBC, 1984.

"Italo Marchiony," *An American Portrait,* CBS, 1984.

Passenger, "Ghost Train," *Amazing Stories* (also known as *Steven Spielberg's "Amazing Stories"*), NBC, 1985.

Heather Leary, "The Screaming Woman," *Ray Bradbury Theatre* (also known as *Le monde fantasique de Ray Bradbury, Mystery Theatre, Ray Bradbury presente, The Bradbury Trilogy,* and *The Ray Bradbury Theatre*), HBO, 1986.

Susan, "Fifteen and Getting Straight" (also known as "Getting Straight"), *CBS Schoolbreak Specials,* CBS, 1989.

Good Morning America, ABC, 1989.

"Former Child Stars," *Entertainment Tonight,* syndicated, 1989.

Late Night with Conan O'Brien, NBC, 1993, 2003, 2004, 2005.

Herself, "Life Cycles," *Bill Nye the Science Guy,* PBS, 1996.

Late Show with David Letterman (also known as *The Late Show*), CBS, 1996, 2004, 2005.

The Rosie O'Donnell Show, syndicated, 1996, 1998, 1999, 2000.

Herself, "Putting the 'Gay' Back in Litigation," *The Larry Sanders Show,* HBO, 1998.

The Entertainment Business, Bravo, 1998.

Ruby Wax Meets, 1998.

Herself, "Privacy," *Dennis Miller Live,* HBO, 1998.

"The Barrymores: Hollywood's Royal Family," *Famous Families,* 1998.

"Drew Barrymore," *A&E Biography* (documentary), Arts and Entertainment, 1999.

The Martin Short Show, 1999.

Diary, MTV, 2000.

Herself, *Nulle part ailleurs* (also known as *N.P.A.*), 2000.

Voice of Sophie, "Insane Clown Poppy," *The Simpsons* (animated), Fox, 2000.

Saturday Night Live (also known as *SNL*), NBC, 2000, 2006.

Mad TV, Fox, 2000, 2001.

The Tonight Show with Jay Leno, NBC, 2001, 2003, 2005.

"The 25 Most Powerful People in Entertainment," *Rank,* E! Entertainment Television, 2002.

Herself, "Charlie's Angels," *Player$,* G4, 2003.

Inside the Actors Studio, Bravo, 2003.

"Bernie Mac," *A&E Biography* (documentary), Arts and Entertainment, 2003.

Matthew's Best Hit TV, 2003.

Herself, *Bo' Selecta!* (also known as *Ho ho ho Selecta!*), Channel 4, 2003.

Herself, *Otro rollo con: Adal Ramones* (also known as *Otro rollo*), 2003.

Herself, "Charlie's Angels: Full Throttle," *HBO First Look,* HBO, 2003.

Celebrities Uncensored, E! Entertainment Television, 2003, 2004.

Herself, "50 First Dates," *HBO First Look,* HBO, 2004.

Tinseltown TV (also known as *Tinseltown.TV*), International Channel, 2004.

Total Request Live (also known as *TRL* and *Total Request with Carson Daly*), MTV, 2004.

Rove Live, Ten Network, 2004.

On–Air with Ryan Seacrest, syndicated, 2004.

Herself, "Yksinoikeudella Lordi," *4Pop,* 2004.

Real Time with Bill Maher, HBO, 2004.

The Oprah Winfrey Show (also known as *Oprah*), syndicated, 2004.

Live with Regis and Kelly, syndicated, 2004, 2005.

The Daily Show (also known as *The Daily Show with Jon Stewart* and *The Daily Show with Jon Stewart Global Edition*), Comedy Central, 2004, 2005.

Gertie, 80s, TV3, 2005.

"Sports Obsessions," *Dr. Phil,* syndicated, 2005.

Today (also known as *The Today Show*), NBC, 2005.

The View, ABC, 2005.

Herself, "Caleta Condor, Chile," *Trippin',* MTV, 2005.

Herself, *Corazon de ... ,* 2005.

Voice of Lana Lockhart, "Fast Times at Buddy Cianci Jr. High," *Family Guy* (animated; also known as *Padre de familia*), Fox, 2005.

Ahora, 2005.

Also appeared as herself, "Drew Barrymore," *Love Chain* and "Extreme Close–Up With ... Drew Barrymore," *Extreme Close Up with ... ,* both E! Entertainment Television.

Television Work; Specials:

Executive producer, *Olive, the Other Reindeer* (animated), Fox, 1999.

Director, *Chose or Lose Presents: The Best Place to Start,* MTV, 2004.

Stage Appearances:

The Night of 100 Stars II, Radio City Music Hall, New York City, 1985.

RECORDINGS

Videos:

Host, *Saturday Morning Cartoons' Greatest Hits,* MCA Music Video, 1995.

Music Videos:

Appeared in Bonnie Raitt's "You Got It," 1995; and Swirl 360's "Candy in the Sun."

WRITINGS

Autobiography:

(With Todd Gold) *Little Girl Lost,* Pocket Books (New York City), 1989.

OTHER SOURCES

Books:

Aronson, Virginia, *Drew Barrymore,* Chelsea House, 2000.

Contemporary Authors, Vol. 139, Gale (Detroit, MI), 1993.

Furman, Leah, and Elina Furman, *Happily Ever After: The Drew Barrymore Story,* Ballantine, 2000.

International Dictionary of Films and Filmmakers, Volume 3: Actors and Actresses, 4th ed., St. James Press, 2000.

Periodicals:

Entertainment Weekly, January 24, 1997, p. 58.

Esquire, February, 1994, p. 68.

Harper's Bazaar, December, 1996, p. 178; April, 2004, p. 193.

Interview, July, 1991, p. 88; October, 1994, p. 140; May, 1995, pp. 76, 94.

Movieline, April, 1994, p. 33.

People Weekly, January 16, 1990, p. 70; April 11, 1994, p. 74; May 12, 1997, p. 164; December 25, 2000, p. 98; July 23, 2001, p. 63; February 23, 2004, p. 86; April 25, 2005, p. 92.

Teen People, May 1, 2005, p. 58.

BEACH, Michael 1963–

(Mike Beach)

PERSONAL

Born October 30, 1963, in Roxbury, MA (some sources say Boston, MA); married Tracey (a homemaker); children: Ivy-Belle, Ella-Bleu, Tariah-Skye, Travon. *Education:* Graduated from the Juilliard School, 1986.

Addresses: *Agent*—Paradigm, 360 North Crescent Dr., North Bldg., Beverly Hills, CA 90210.

Career: Actor and producer.

Awards, Honors: First place, National Association for the Advancement of Colored People (NAACP) National Drama Competition, 1982; Drama Award, outstanding achievement, Juilliard School, 1984; Best Armed Combat Award, New York Shakespeare Festival, 1986; Volpi Cup (with others), best ensemble cast, Venice Film Festival, 1993, Special Golden Globe Award (with others), best ensemble cast, 1994, both for *Short Cuts;* NAACP Image Award nomination, outstanding supporting actor in a drama series, 1998, for *ER;* Black Film Award nomination, best actor, Acapulco Black Film Festival, 1998, for *Soul Food;* NAACP Image Award nomination, outstanding actor in a drama series, 2000, NAACP Image Award, outstanding actor in a drama series, 2003, both for *Third Watch;* Black Reel Award nomination, best independent actor, 2003, for *Crazy as Hell.*

CREDITS

Film Appearances:

(As Mike Beach) Sonny, *Streets of Gold,* Twentieth Century–Fox, 1986.

Parking lot attendant, *Suspect,* TriStar/ML Delphi Premier, 1987.

Alvin, *End of the Line,* Orion, 1987.

Quintas Pearch, *In a Shallow Grave,* Atlantic Releasing, 1988.

Mr. Darnell, *Lean on Me,* Warner Bros., 1989.

Barnes, *The Abyss,* Twentieth Century–Fox, 1989.

Webb, *Cadence* (also known as *Count a Lonely Cadence* and *Stockade*), New Line Cinema/Republic, 1990.

Dorian Fletcher, *Internal Affairs,* Paramount, 1990.

Dr. David Arrington, *Late for Dinner,* Columbia, 1991.

Wade "Pluto" Franklin, *One False Move,* IRS Releasing, 1992.

Hamilton, *Guilty as Charged,* IRS Releasing, 1992.

Wurlitzer, *True Romance* (also known as *Breakaway*), Warner Bros., 1993.

Jim Stone, *Short Cuts,* Fine Line Features, 1993.

Tod Stapp, *Bad Company,* Buena Vista, 1995.

Policeman outside bar, *White Man's Burden* (also known as *White Man*), Twentieth Century–Fox, 1995.

John, Sr., *Waiting to Exhale,* Twentieth Century–Fox, 1995.

Virgil, *A Family Thing,* Metro–Goldwyn–Mayer/United Artists, 1996.

Clark Cooper, *Casualties,* Trimark Pictures, 1997.

Miles, *Soul Food,* Twentieth Century–Fox, 1997.

Michael Hubbs, *Asunder,* 1998.

Terry Fitzgerald, *Spawn 3: Ultimate Battle,* 1999.

Dr. Ty Adams, *Crazy as Hell,* 2002.

Jerome Jenkins, Sr., *Like Mike 2: Street Ball,* Twentieth Century–Fox, 2006.

Paddy, *Lenexa, 1 Mile,* DEJ Productions, 2006.

Television Appearances; Series:

Shepherd Scott, *The Street,* syndicated, 1988.

Detective Desmond Beck, *Under Suspicion,* CBS, 1994–95.

Al Boulet, *ER,* NBC, 1995–97.

Voice of Terry Fitzgerald, *Spawn* (also known as *Todd McFarlane's "Spawn"*), 1997.

Monty "Doc" Parker, *Third Watch,* NBC, 1999–2004.

Television Appearances; Movies:

Rudolph Tyner, *Vengeance: The Story of Tony Cimo* (also known as *Vengeance*), CBS, 1986.

Wiley, *Weekend War,* ABC, 1988.

Calvin Jefferson, *Open Admissions,* CBS, 1988.

Steve, *Dangerous Passion,* ABC, 1990.

Perez, *Fire! Trapped on the 37th Floor,* ABC, 1991.

Tyrell, *Another Round,* 1992.

Detective Akin, *The Hit List,* Showtime, 1993.

Detective Thomas, *Final Appeal* (also known as *Lying in Wait*), NBC, 1993.

Will McQueen, "Knight Rider 2010," *Action Pack,* syndicated, 1994.

Pemberton, "Midnight Run for Your Life," *Action Pack,* syndicated, 1994.

Detective George Rydell, *Sketch Artist II: Hands That See* (also known as *A Feel for Murder* and *Sketch Artist 2*), Showtime, 1995.

Legrand, *Rebound: The Legend of Earl "The Goat" Manigault* (also known as *Angel of Harlem* and *Rebound*), HBO, 1996.

Reverend Luke, *Ms. Scrooge,* USA Network, 1997.

Mike, *Johnny Skidmarks,* HBO, 1998.

Abon Bridges, "Ruby Bridges," *The Wonderful World of Disney,* ABC, 1998.

Miles, *Made Men,* HBO, 1999.

Agent Winston, *Critical Assembly* (also known as *Ground Zero*), 2003.

Television Appearances; Specials:

Jake, "Taking a Stand" (also known as "On Our Own"), *ABC Afterschool Specials,* ABC, 1989.

Rick, *Evening Class,* Showtime, 1993.

Hobbs, *Dr. Hugo,* Lifetime, 1994.

Dee Evans, *A Room Without Doors,* Showtime, 1998.

The 31st Annual NAACP Image Awards, 2000.

Christmas in Rockefeller Center, NBC, 2001.

NBC's Funniest Outtakes, NBC, 2002.

Television Appearances; Episodic:

"Deadly Minds," *Veronica Clare,* 1991.

Michael Austin, "Birds Gotta Fly," *Gabriel's Fire,* 1991.

Nathaniel Simpson, "Justice—May 11, 1965," *Quantum Leap,* 1991.

Randy Warren, "Night of the Gladiator," *Walker, Texas Ranger,* CBS, 1993.

Officer Frank Quint, "Trials and Tribulations," *NYPD Blue,* ABC, 1994.

Officer Frank Quint, "From Whom the Skell Rolls," *NYPD Blue,* ABC, 1994.

Jonas Paige and Benjamin Paige, *Sweet Justice,* NBC, 1994.

Isaiah, *South Central,* Fox, 1994.

Attorney Brian Elliott, "Purple Heart," *Law & Order,* NBC, 1995.

Sam, "Reunion," *Touched by an Angel,* CBS, 1995.

The Rosie O'Donnell Show, syndicated, 1998, 2000.

Andy Abbott, "Lowdown," *Law & Order: Special Victims Unit* (also known as *Law & Order: SVU* and *Special Victims Unit*), NBC, 2004.

Voice of Commander, "Dark Heart," *Justice League* (animated; also known as *JL* and *Justice League*), Cartoon Network, 2004.

Voice of Devil Ray and Mr. Terrific, "To Another Shore," *Justice League* (animated; also known as *JL* and *Justice League*), Cartoon Network, 2005.

Also appeared as voice of Mr. Terrific, "Patriot Act," *Justice League* (animated; also known as *JL* and *Justice League*), Cartoon Network.

Television Work; Specials:

A Room Without Doors, Showtime, 1998.

Stage Appearances:

Nat Turner, *Ascension Day,* Hudson Guild Theatre, New York City, 1992.

RECORDINGS

Music Videos:

Appeared in "How Come, How Long," by Babyface and Stevie Wonder.

OTHER SOURCES

Books:

Contemporary Black Biography, Vol. 26, Gale Group, 2000.

Periodicals:

Entertainment Weekly, October 17, 1997, p. 43.

People, December 29, 1997, p. 138.

TV Guide, November 8, 1997, p. 5.

BECKER, Gerry 1950–

PERSONAL

Born August 6, 1950, in Buffalo, NY.

Addresses: *Agent*—Paradigm, 360 North Crescent Dr., North Bldg., Beverly Hills, CA 90210.

Career: Actor. Remains Theatre Ensemble, member of company.

Awards, Honors: National Board of Review Award of Motion Pictures (with others), best acting by an ensemble, 1998, for *Happiness.*

CREDITS

Film Appearances:

Dr. Cooperman, *The Cell,* 1983.

First officer, *Home Alone,* Miramax, 1990.

Uncle Hugh, *Men Don't Leave,* 1990.

Minister, *Hard Promises,* Goldwyn, 1992.

Business negotiator, *Hoffa,* Twentieth Century–Fox, 1992.

Conklin, *The Public Eye,* 1992.

Father Ted, *Rudy,* TriStar, 1993.

Larry Griffith, *Die Hard With a Vengeance* (also known as *Die Hard 3*), Twentieth Century–Fox, 1995.

Dr. Minceberg, *Roommates,* Herts–Lion, 1995.

Mattachine speaker, *Stonewall,* 1995.

Morehart, *Eraser,* IRS Releasing, 1996.

Dr. Gene Spitelli, *Extreme Measures,* Warner Bros., 1996.

Forensics expert, *Sleepers,* PolyGram, 1996.

Dean Blanford, *Donnie Brasco,* Sony Pictures, 1997.

New member Ted, *The Game,* Paramount, 1997.

Roger Brill, *A Perfect Murder,* Warner Bros., 1998.

Psychiatrist, *Happiness,* RKO, 1998.

Jay Tepper, *Celebrity,* 1998.

Fred Wilson, *Game Day,* 1999.

Stanley Kaufman, *Man on the Moon* (also known as *Der mondmann*), Metro–Goldwyn–Mayer, 1999.

Agent Connell, *Mickey Blue Eyes,* Warner Bros., 1999.

Banyon, *Mystery Men,* Universal, 1999.

Player's union lawyer, *Mystery, Alaska,* Buena Vista, 1999.

Mr. Fontaine, *The Story of a Bad Boy,* 1999.

Dr. Barry Cooperman, *The Cell,* New Line Cinema, 2000.

Maximillian Fargas, *Spider–Man,* Columbia, 2002.

Mr. Toliver, *Blood Work,* Warner Bros., 2002.

Dr. Stein, *Trapped* (also known as *24 Stunden Angst*), Columbia, 2002.

Doctor, *The Hire: Hostage* (short), 2002.

Dr. Skellar, *Marci X,* Paramount, 2003.

Television Appearances; Series:

Dr. West, *Central Park West* (also known as *C.P.W.*), 1996.

Myron Stone, *Ally McBeal,* Fox, 1998–2000.

Television Appearances; Miniseries:

Asteroid, NBC, 1997.

Television Appearances; Movies:

Meyer, *The Killing Floor,* PBS, 1984.

Larry, *The Imposter,* ABC, 1984.

Man at hotel, *First Steps,* The Disney Channel, 1985.

Ed Boyer, *Howard Beach: Making a Case for Murder* (also known as *In the Line of Duty: Howard Beach: Making a Case for Murder* and *Skin*), NBC, 1989.

Detective, *Without Warning: The James Brady Story,* HBO, 1991.

Judge O'Neill, *In the Shadow of a Killer,* NBC, 1992.

Samuel Adler, *Legacy of Lies,* USA Network, 1992.

Captain Pickering, *The Hunley,* TNT, 1999.

Ted Tinling, *When Billie Beat Bobby* (also known as *Billie contre Bobby: La bataille des sexes*), ABC, 2001.

Walt Rostow, *Path to War,* HBO, 2002.

Television Appearances; Pilots:

Judge Stanton, *The Guardian* (movie), CBS, 2001.

Television Appearances; Specials:

My Summer As a Girl, CBS, 1994.

Flashback, HBO, 1997.

Television Appearances; Episodic:

John Sherman, "Snatched," *Law & Order,* NBC, 1994.

"Our Lady of Cement," *The Cosby Mysteries,* NBC, 1994.

Mr. Goldman, "Simone Says," *NYPD Blue,* ABC, 1994.

Max Petrov, "The Skin Trade," *The Untouchables,* 1994.

Dr. Neal Latham, "Switch," *Law & Order,* NBC, 1995.

Davidoff, "Fun City," *New York News,* CBS, 1995.

Arnold Cassell, "Moby Greg," *NYPD Blue,* ABC, 1996.

Rupert, *Cosby,* CBS, 1996.

Hub news attorney, "Sex, Lies, and Monkeys," *The Practice,* ABC, 1997.

Thomas Robbins, "Nullification," *Law & Order,* NBC, 1997.

Attorney Stone, "Fools Night Out," *Ally McBeal,* Fox, 1998.

Dr. Cosimi, "Three Men and a Little Lady," *Spin City,* ABC, 1998.

Attorney for school, "The Pursuit of Dignity," *The Practice,* ABC, 1998.

Leo Latimer, *New York Undercover,* Fox, 1998.

Mr. Bickel, "The Music Man," *The Hughleys,* ABC, 2000.

Mr. Bickel, "The Thin Black Line," *The Hughleys,* ABC, 2000.

"Unnecessary Roughness," *Judging Amy,* CBS, 2000.

Dr. Michaels, "Faith," *Walker, Texas Ranger,* CBS, 2000.

Nathan Reed, "Blood Money," *Angel* (also known as *Angel: The Series*), The WB, 2001.

Nathan Reed, "Reprise," *Angel* (also known as *Angel: The Series*), The WB, 2001.

Nathan Reed, "Dead End," *Angel* (also known as *Angel: The Series*), The WB, 2001.

David Leary, "Blown Away," *Philly,* ABC, 2001.

Judge Stanton, "Lolita?," *The Guardian,* CBS, 2001.

Judge Stanton, "Mothers of the Disappeared," *The Guardian,* CBS, 2002.

Chester Glass, "The Greenhouse Effect," *The District,* CBS, 2002.

Network news president number one, "The Black Vera Wang," *The West Wing,* NBC, 2002.

Ramus, "Magic Wears a Mask," *Charmed,* The WB, 2002.

Robert, "Cliff Mantegna," *Nip/Tuck,* FX Channel, 2003.

"Yankee White," *Navy NCIS: Naval Criminal Investigative Service* (also known as *NCIS* and *NCIS: Naval Criminal Investigative Service*), CBS, 2003.

"Three Boys and a Gun," *The Jury,* Fox, 2004.

Gerard Wills, "Can I Get a Witness?," *Law & Order,* NBC, 2004.

Gerard Wills, "Obsession," *Law & Order,* NBC, 2005.

Also appeared as Myron Stone, "Those Lips, That Hand," *Ally,* Fox.

Stage Appearances:

Marty Frankel, *The Song of Jacob Zulu,* Plymouth Theatre, New York City, 1993.

The attendant, Ken, and Howard, *Death Defying Acts,* Variety Arts Theatre, New York City, 1995–96.

Also appeared in *Someone Who'll Watch Over Me,* Cleveland Play House, Cleveland, OH; *Common Pursuit, Inspecting Carol, Born Yesterday,* and *Ring Round the Moon,* all Steppenwolf Theatre, Chicago; *Once in Doubt, Our Country's Good,* and *Laughter in the Dark,* Remains Theatre, Chicago.

BELTRAMI, Marco 1966–

PERSONAL

Born October 7, 1966, in Fornero, Italy; immigrated to the United States. *Education:* Graduated from Brown University and the Yale School of Music; attended the University of Southern California; studied composing with Luigi Nono.

Addresses: *Manager*—Greenspan Artist Management, 8747 Holloway Dr., 2nd Floor, West Hollywood, CA 90069.

Career: Composer, orchestrator, orchestra conductor, and producer. Completed orchestral commissions to American Academy of Arts and Letters, Chicago Civic Orchestra, Sao Paulo State Orchestra, Oakland Symphony, and the Oakland East Bay Symphony; previously played in rock bands as a teenager.

Member: American Society of Composers, Authors and Publishers.

Awards, Honors: American Society of Composers, Authors and Publishers Award, top box office films, 1998, for *Scream* and *Scream 2;* American Society of Composers, Authors and Publishers Awards (with Jon Hassell), top television series, 2001, 2002, 2003, all for *The Practice;* American Society of Composers, Authors and Publishers Award, top box office films, 2003, for *Blade II;* American Society of Composers, Authors and

Publishers Award, top box office films, 2004, for *Terminator 3: Rise of the Machines;* American Society of Composers, Authors and Publishers Award, top box office films, 2005, for *I, Robot;* Emmy Award nomination, outstanding music composition for a miniseries or a movie—dramatic underscore, 1999, for *David and Lisa.*

CREDITS

Film Work:

Orchestra conductor, *Scream* (also known as *Scary Movie*), Miramax, 1996.

Music orchestrator and conductor, *Scream 2* (also known as *Scream Again, Scream Louder,* and *Scream: The Sequel*), Miramax, 1997.

Conductor and orchestrator, *The Faculty,* 1998.

Piano player, *The Minus Man,* TSG Pictures, 1999.

Score producer, orchestra conductor, and orchestrations, *Scream 3,* Miramax, 2000.

Music supervisor, score producer, orchestrations, and orchestra conductor, *Dracula 2000* (also known as *Dracula 2001* and *Wes Craven Presents "Dracula 2000"*), Miramax, 2000.

Song producer ("Driven to This"), conductor, and orchestrations, *The Watcher,* Universal, 2000.

Score coordinator, *Scary Movie 2* (also known as *Scarier Movie*), Miramax, 2001.

Score conductor, *Joy Ride* (also known as *Roadkill*), Twentieth Century–Fox, 2001.

Music conductor, *Angel Eyes,* 2001.

Conductor, *The First $20 Million is Always the Hardest,* Twentieth Century–Fox, 2002.

Music conductor and orchestrations, *Terminator 3: Rise of the Machines* (also known as *T3* and *Terminator 3–rebellion der maschinen*), Warner Bros., 2003.

Conductor, *I, Robot,* Twentieth Century–Fox, 2004.

Conductor, *Flight of the Phoenix,* Twentieth Century–Fox, 2004.

Music producer, *xXx: State of the Union* (also known as *XXX 2: The Next Level, xXx 2: The Next Level,* and *Cold Circle & Intersection*), Sony Pictures Entertainment, 2005.

Film Appearances:

Himself, *Scoring Resident Evil* (documentary), 2002.

Himself, *The Blood Pact: The Making of "Blade II"* (documentary), New Line Cinema, 2002.

Himself, *Day Out of Days: The "I, Robot" Production Diaries* (documentary), Twentieth Century–Fox, 2004.

Television Work; Movies:

Assistant to Mr. Licht, *Zooman,* Showtime, 1995.

RECORDINGS

Albums:

(With others) *Axelrod: Songs (Love Songs for the Romantic at Heart),* 1996.

Also released *I, Robot; HellBoy; Blade II; Angel Eyes; The Dangerous Lives of Altar Boys; Joy Ride; Mimic; The Minus Man; Scream; Marco CD; The Crow 3.*

WRITINGS

Film Scores:
Death Match, Horseplay Productions, 1994.
The Bicyclist, Past Due Productions, 1994.
The Whispering, A–pix Entertainment, 1996.
The Incorporated, 1996.
Scream (also known as *Scary Movie*), Miramax, 1996.
Mimic, Miramax, 1997.
Scream 2 (also known as *Scream Again, Scream Louder,* and *Scream: The Sequel*), Miramax, 1997.
54 (also known as *Fifty–Four* and *Studio 54*), Miramax, 1998.
The Faculty (also known as *Feelers*), Miramax, 1998.
The Florentine, Bcb Productions, Inc., 1999.
The Minus Man, TSG Pictures, 1999.
Scream 3, Miramax, 2000.
The Crow: Salvation, Dimension, 2000.
Texas Rangers, Dimension Films, 2000.
Walking Across Egypt, Keystone Entertainment, 2000.
Squelch, Twentieth Century–Fox, 2000.
Goodbye, Casanova, 2000.
The Crow: Salvation (also known as *The Crow III—todliche erlosung*), 2000.
The Watcher, MCA/Universal, 2000.
Highway 395, Creative Light Worldwide, 2000.
Dracula 2000 (also known as *Dracula 2001* and *Wes Craven Presents "Dracula 2000"*), Miramax, 2000.
Angel Eyes, Warner Bros., 2001.
(Uncredited) *Scary Movie 2* (also known as *Scarier Movie*), Miramax, 2001.
Joy Ride (also known as *Roadkill*), Twentieth Century–Fox, 2001.
Playing Dead: "Resident Evil" from Game to Screen (documentary short), Columbia TriStar Home Video, 2002.
Scoring Resident Evil (documentary short), Columbia TriStar Home Video, 2002.
The Dangerous Lives of Altar Boys, ThinkFilm, 2002.
I Am Dina (also known as *Jeg er Dina, Dina, Dina—Meine Geschichte, Ich bin Dina,* and *Jag ar Dina*), 2002.
Resident Evil, Screen Gems, 2002.
Blade II, New Line Cinema, 2002.
The First $20 Million Is Always the Hardest, Twentieth Century–Fox, 2002.
Dracula II: Ascension (also known as *Wes Craven Presents "Dracula II: Ascension"*), Buena Vista Home Entertainment, 2003.
Terminator 3: Rise of the Machines (also known as *T3* and *Terminator 3—Rebellion der Maschinen*), Warner Bros., 2003.
Hellboy (also known as *Super Sapiens*), Columbia, 2004.

I, Robot, Twentieth Century–Fox, 2004.
"Hellboy": The Seeds of Creation (documentary), Columbia TriStar Home Entertainment, 2004.
Flight of the Phoenix, Twentieth Century–Fox, 2004.
Cursed, Dimension, 2005.
Creature Editing 101 (documentary short), Dimension Home Video, 2005.
The Cursed Effects (documentary short), Dimension Home Video, 2005.
Behind the Fangs: The Making of "Cursed" (documentary short), Dimension Home Video, 2005.
xXx: State of the Union (also known as *XXX 2: The Next Level, xXx 2: The Next Level,* and *Cold Circle & Intersection*), Sony Pictures Entertainment, 2005.
The Three Burials of Melquiades Estrada (also known as *Les trois enterrements de Melchiades Estrada*), Sony Pictures Classics, 2005.
Red Eye, DreamWorks, 2005.
Underworld: Evolution, Screen Gems, 2006.
Captivity, 2006.
The Invisible, Buena Vista, 2006.
The Omen, Twentieth Century–Fox, 2006.
Vikaren, Sandrew Metronome, 2006.

Film Additional Music:
Nightwatch, Dimension Films, 1998.
Halloween H2O: Twenty Years Later (also known *Halloween: H20, Halloween: The Revenge of Laurie Strode, Halloween 7,* and *Halloween 7: The Revenge of Laurie Strode*), Miramax, 1998.
Halloween: Resurrection, 2002.

Television Music; Series:
Theme and score, *Land's End,* syndicated, 1995.
Score, *Dellaventura,* CBS, 1997–98.
Score, *The Practice,* ABC, 1997.
Score, *Glory Days,* The WB, 2002.

Television Scores; Movies:
"Inhumanoid" (also known as *"Circuit Breaker"*), *Roger Corman Presents,* Showtime, 1996.
Stranger in My Home (also known as *Brother's Keeper*), CBS, 1997.
David and Lisa (also known as *Oprah Winfrey Presents: "David and Lisa"*), ABC, 1998.
Dybt vand (also known as *Deep Water*), 1999.
Tuesdays with Morrie (also known as *Oprah Winfrey Presents: "Tuesdays with Morrie"*), 1999.
"There's a Nightmare in My Closet," Goodnight Moon and Other Sleepytime Tales, HBO and HBO Family, 1999.
Walking Across Egypt, Hallmark Channel, 2001.

Television Music; Specials:
Theme, *A Day With,* Fox, 1995.
Score, *Why Planes Go Down,* Fox, 1996.

Television Scores; Episodic:
"Brownstone," *Love Street,* 1994.
"See Me," *Love Street,* 1994.

BENDER, Lawrence 1958(?)–

PERSONAL

Born 1958 (some sources say 1957), in The Bronx, NY. *Education:* Earned degree in civil engineering at the University of Maine; studied acting with Sandra Seacat; studied dance with the Louis Falco Company.

Addresses: *Agent*—William Morris Agency, One William Morris Place, Beverly Hills, CA, 90212. *Office*—Lawrence Bender Productions/A Band Apart Productions, 8530 Wilshire Blvd., Suite 500, Beverly Hills, CA 90211.

Career: Producer, actor, director, writer, and grip. A Band Apart (a production company), Beverly Hills, CA, founder (with Quentin Tarantino), 1992; Lawrence Bender Productions (a production company), 1994; A Band Apart Records (record company), founder (with Quentin Tarantino), 1997; former member of Ralph Robertson Ballet Company; also worked as a flamenco dancer. Also worked as a caterer and waiter.

Awards, Honors: Independent Spirit Award nomination (with Ronna B. Wallace), best first feature, Independent Features Project, 1993, for *Reservoir Dogs;* Academy Award nomination, best picture, National Society of Film Critics Award, best picture, Society of Texas Film Critics Award, best picture, Boston Society of Film Critics Award, best picture, National Board of Review Award, best picture, Los Angeles Film Critics Association Award, best film, Palme d'Or, Cannes Film Festival, 1994, Independent Spirit Award, best feature, Film Award nomination, (with Quentin Tarantino), best film, British Academy of Film and Television Arts, MTV Movie Award, best movie, 1995, all for *Pulp Fiction;* Academy Award nomination, best picture, PGA Golden Laurel Award nomination, motion picture producer of the year, Golden Satellite Award nomination, best motion picture—drama, International Press Academy, 1998, all for *Good Will Hunting;* Cannes Prix Chopard de Producteur, 2001.

CREDITS

Film Work:
Production assistant, *Maximum Potential* (also known as *Dolph Lungren: Maximum Potential*), 1987.
Grip, *The Allnighter,* Universal, 1987.

Producer, *Intruder* (also known as *Night Crew: The Final Checkout*), Phantom Productions, 1988.
Dolly grip, *Cameron's Closet,* Sony Pictures Entertainment, 1988.
Producer, *Tale of Two Sisters,* Vista Street Entertainment, 1989.
Producer, *Reservoir Dogs,* Miramax, 1992.
Second assistant director, *Ulterior Motives,* Imperial Entertainment, 1993.
Producer, *Fresh,* Miramax, 1994.
Executive producer, *Killing Zoe,* LIVE Entertainment, 1994.
Producer, *Pulp Fiction,* Miramax, 1994.
Producer, *Four Rooms,* Miramax, 1995.
Producer, *White Man's Burden* (also known as *White Man*), Twentieth Century–Fox, 1995.
Executive producer, *From Dusk Till Dawn,* Miramax, 1996.
Executive producer, *Snakeland,* 1996.
Producer, *Good Will Hunting,* Miramax, 1997.
Producer and (uncredited) executive album producer, *Jackie Brown,* Miramax, 1997.
Producer, *A Price Above Rubies,* Miramax, 1998.
Producer, *Anna and the King,* Twentieth Century–Fox, 1999.
Executive producer, *Texas Blood Money* (also known as *From Dusk Till Dawn 2: Texas Blood Money*), Miramax, 1999.
Executive producer, *The Hangman's Daughter* (also known as *From Dusk Till Dawn 3: The Hangman's Daughter*), Miramax, 2000.
Producer, *Knockaround Guys,* New Line Cinema, 2001.
Producer, *The Mexican* (also known as *La Mexicana*), DreamWorks, 2001.
Executive producer, *Stark Raving Mad,* Newmarket Capital Films, 2002.
Producer and executive soundtrack producer, *Kill Bill: Vol. 1* (also known as *Kill Bill, Kill Bill1,* and *Quentin Tarantino's "Kill Bill: Volume One"*), Miramax, 2003.
Producer, *Dirty Dancing: Havana Nights* (also known as *Dirty Dancing 2*), Lions Gate Films, 2004.
Producer, *Kill Bill: Vol. 2* (also known as *Kill Bill, Kill Bill 2,* and *Vol. 2*), Miramax, 2004.
Producer, *Voces inocentes* (also known as *Innocent Voices*), Slowhand Cinema Releasing, 2004.
Producer, *The Chumscrubber,* Newmarket Films, 2005.
Producer, *The Great Raid,* Miramax, 2005.
Executive producer, *Goal!* (also known as *Goal! The Dream Begins*), Buena Vista, 2005.
Producer, *An Inconvenient Truth* (documentary), Paramount Classics, 2006.
Executive producer, *88 Minutes,* 2006.
Producer, *Inglorious Bastards,* Miramax, 2006.
Producer, *Manhunt,* 2007.

Film Appearances:
Officer Adams, *Intruder* (also known as *Night Crew: The Final Checkout*), Phantom Productions, 1988.

Garbage fight heckler, *Lionheart* (also known as *A.W.O.L.—Absent without Leave, A.W.O.L.,* and *Wrong Bet*), Imperial Entertainment, 1990.

Young cop and voice for background radio play, *Reservoir Dogs,* Miramax, 1992.

Third guard, *Ulterior Motives,* Imperial Entertainment, 1993.

Yuppie, *Fresh,* Miramax, 1994.

"Long haired yuppie scum," *Pulp Fiction,* Miramax, 1994.

"Long haired yuppie scum," *Four Rooms,* Miramax, 1995.

Bar patron number one, *White Man's Burden* (also known as *White Man*), Twentieth Century–Fox, 1995.

(Uncredited) Man in diner, *From Dusk Til Dawn,* 1996.

Himself, *Full Tilt Boogie* (documentary), Miramax, 1997.

Vegas onlooker, *The Mexican* (also known as *La Mexicana*), DreamWorks, 2001.

Bar patron, *Knockaround Guys,* New Line Cinema, 2001.

Himself, *Jackie Brown: How It Went Down* (documentary short), Miramax Home Entertainment, 2002.

Himself, *Pulp Fiction: The Facts* (documentary short), Miramax Home Entertainment, 2002.

(Uncredited) Hotel clerk, *Kill Bill: Vol. 2* (also known as *Kill Bill, Kill Bill 2,* and *Vol. 2*), Miramax, 2004.

Television Work; Series:

Executive producer, *Lost In Oz,* The WB, 2002.
Executive producer, *Dr. Vegas,* CBS, 2004.
Executive producer, *Build or Bust,* 2005.

Television Work; Miniseries:

Executive producer, *Legend of Earthsea,* Sci–Fi Channel, 2004.

Television Work; Movies:

Executive producer, *Anatomy of a Hate Crime,* PBS, 2001.
Executive producer, *Nancy Drew,* ABC, 2002.
Executive producer, *The Survivors Club,* CBS, 2004.

Television Work; Episodic:

Worked as a grip, *Tales from the Darkside,* syndicated.

Television Appearances; Specials:

Quentin Tarantino: Hollywood's Boy Wonder (documentary), BBC, 1994.
Himself, *Hollywood Goes to Hell* (documentary), 2000.
Himself, *The Making of "Kill Bill: Volume 2,"* 2004.
Himself, *"Pulp Fiction" on a Dime: A 10th Anniversary Retrospect* (documentary), Independent Film Channel, 2004.

Television Appearances; Episodic:

American Cinema, PBS, 1995.
Himself, "Anna and the King," *HBO First Look,* HBO, 1999.
Himself, *The Making of "Kill Bill"* (documentary), Bravo, 2003.
Himself, "Tarantino Special," *Tracks,* 2004.

WRITINGS

Film Stories:

Intruder (also known as *Night Crew: The Final Checkout*), Phantom Productions, 1988.

OTHER SOURCES

Periodicals:

Billboard, August 16, 1997, p. 6.
Interview, September, 1994, p. 130.
SHOOT, July 21, 1995, p. 1; April 19, 1996, p. 52.
Variety, May 7, 2001, p. C8; May 16, 2005, p. S24.

BENEDICT, Paul 1938–

PERSONAL

Born September 17, 1938, in Silver City, NM; son of Mitchell M. (a doctor) and Alma Marie (a journalist; maiden name, Loring) Benedict. *Education:* Suffolk University, A.B., 1960.

Addresses: *Agent*—The Gage Group, 14724 Ventura Blvd., Suite 505, Los Angeles, CA 91403.

Career: Actor and director. The Place (a theater company), cofounder; Trinity Square Repertory Company, Rhode Island, guest artist, 1986–87; Playmakers Repertory Company, Chapel Hill, NC, guest artist, 1994–95; acted in productions with Theatre Company of Boston and the American Repertory Theatre, Cambridge, MA and at Arena Stage, Washington, DC, Playhouse in the Park, Cincinnati, OH, and Center Stage, Baltimore, MD. Worked as a janitor at the Charles Playhouse, Boston, MA, 1960. *Military service:* U.S. Marine Corps Reserves, 1956–62.

Member: Actors Equity Association, American Federation of Television and Radio Artists, Screen Actors Guild, Greater Los Angeles Zoological Association.

CREDITS

Stage Appearances:

(Stage debut) Chaplain, *The Lady's Not for Burning,* Image Theatre, Boston, MA, 1962.

Sailor Shawnee, *Live Like Pigs,* Actor's Playhouse, New York City, 1965.

Mother, *The Infantry,* Eight–first Street Theatre, New York City, 1966.

Reverend Dupas, *Little Murders,* Circle in the Square Theatre, New York City, 1969.

Interviewer, news seller, man, Wills, and a man, *The Local Stigmatic,* Actor's Playhouse, 1969.

Stiles, *The White House Murder Case,* Circle in the Square Theatre, 1970.

Dr. Jason Pepper, "Ravenswood" and Hugh Gumbs, "Dunelawn," *Bad Habits,* Astor Place Theatre, New York City, 1974.

Lieutenant Drew, *The Unvarnished Truth,* Ahmanson Theatre, Los Angeles, 1985.

Ira Drew, *It's Only a Play,* Manhattan Theatre Club, New York City, 1986.

Ira Drew, *It's Only a Play,* James A. Doolittle Theatre, UCLA, 1992.

Scrooge, *A Christmas Carol,* Huntington Theatre Company, Boston, MA, 1992–93.

Arsenic and Old Lace, Long Wharf Theatre, New Haven, CT, 1994–95.

Johann Dwornitschek, *The Play's the Thing,* Criterion Center Stage Right, New York City, 1995.

Desk clerk, *Hughie,* Circle in the Square Theatre, 1996.

Mayor Shinn, *The Music Man,* Neil Simon Theatre, New York City, 2000–2001.

The Unexpected Man, Wellfleet Harbor Actors Theater, Wellfleet, MA, 2003.

Also appeared as Freddy, *Picasso at the Lapin Agile,* American Repertory Theatre, Cambridge, MA; in *Ah, Wilderness!,* Huntington, Boston, MA; *Light Up the Sky,* Hartford Stage, Hartford, CT; *Hughie,* Mark Taper Forum, Los Angeles.

Stage Director:

Frankie and Johnny in the Clair de Lune, Manhattan Theatre Club Stage I, New York City, 1987, then Westside Theatre/Upstairs, New York City.

Frankie and Johnny in the Clair de Lune, Center Theatre Group, Mark Taper Forum, Los Angeles, 1988–89.

Prelude and Liebestod, One–Act Play Festival, Nat Horne Theatre, New York City, 1989.

The Kathy & Mo Show: Parallel Lives, Westside Arts Theatre/Downstairs, New York City, 1989.

Bad Habits, Manhattan Theatre Club Stage 1, New York City, 1990.

The Old Boy, 1991–92.

Any Given Day, Longacre Theatre, New York City, 1993.

Strictly Academic, Primary Stages, New York City, 2003.

Also directed *Beyond Therapy* and *Geniuses,* both Los Angeles Public Theatre; *It's Only a Play,* Artists and Directors Theatre; *Crimes of the Heart,* Trinity Square

Playhouse, Rhode Island; *Any Given Day,* Longacre Theatre, New York City.

Film Appearances:

Wells Fargo Ferguson, *The Double–Barreled Detective Story,* Saloon, 1965.

Rutherford Melon, *The Virgin President,* New Line, 1968.

Zen Buddhist, *Cold Turkey,* Tandem Productions, 1969.

Ben Lockston, *Taking Off,* Universal, 1970.

Chestnut man, *They Might Be Giants,* Universal, 1971.

Shots O'Toole, *The Gang That Couldn't Shoot Straight* (also known as *The Gang That Couldn't Shoot*), Metro–Goldwyn–Mayer, 1971.

Dr. Beineke, *Up the Sandbox,* National General, 1972.

Reverend Lindquist, *Jeremiah Johnson,* Warner Bros., 1972.

Tramp, *Deadhead Miles,* 1972.

Plunkett, *The Front Page,* Universal, 1974.

Brownlee, *Mandingo,* Paramount, 1975.

Orren Brooks, *Smile,* United Artists, 1975.

Mark Morgenweiss, *The Goodbye Girl* (also known as *Neil Simon's "The Goodbye Girl"*), Warner Bros., 1977.

Billy's father, *Billy in the Lowlands,* FIF, 1979.

Cosmo, *Desperate Moves* (also known as *A Desperate Case, Rollerboy, Save the Last Dance for Me, Steigler and Steigler, Stiegler: A Desperate Case,* and *Stiegler: A Serious Case*), 1981.

Butler, *The Man with Two Brains,* Warner Bros., 1983.

Tucker "Smitty" Brown, *This Is Spinal Tap,* Embassy, 1984.

(Uncredited) Voice of Dr. Zook, *The Lonely Guy,* 1984.

Warden Eddie Dwyer, *The Chair* (also known as *Hot Seat*), Imperial Entertainment, 1988.

Finance teacher, *Cocktail,* Buena Vista, 1988.

Fairchild, *Arthur 2: On the Rocks,* Warner Bros., 1988.

Dr. Plotner, *Sibling Rivalry,* Columbia, 1990.

Arthur Fleeber, *The Freshman,* TriStar, 1990.

Judge Womack, *The Addams Family,* Paramount, 1991.

Mickey, *Guns and Lipstick,* 1995.

Not Guffman (Mr. Roy Loomis), *Waiting for Guffman,* Sony Pictures Classics, 1996.

(Uncredited) Walter Krasna, *The Devil's Advocate* (also known as *Devil's Advocate* and *Im auftrag des teufels*), 1997.

Who Was That Man, 1998.

Milo, *A Fish in a Bathtub,* 1998.

Professor Brainiac, *Isn't She Great* (also known as *Ist sie nicht groBartig?*), Universal, 2000.

Martin Berg, *A Mighty Wind,* Warner Bros., 2003.

Night shift guard, *After the Sunset,* New Line Cinema, 2004.

Chief Rod Rocks, *A Second Wind,* 2006.

Television Appearances; Series:

(Television debut) The mad painter, *Sesame Street* (also known as *Les Amis de Sesame, Canadian Sesame*

Street, Open Sesame, Sesame Park, and *The New Sesame Street*), PBS, 1969–74.
Harry Bentley, *The Jeffersons,* CBS, 1974–81, 1983–85.
Mr. Pratt, *The Guiding Light* (also known as *Guiding Light*), CBS, 1999.

Television Appearances; Miniseries:
Arbuthnot, *The Blue and the Gray,* CBS, 1982.

Television Appearances; Movies:
Lester Traube, *Hustling,* ABC, 1975.
Guido Fantoccini, *The Electric Grandmother,* 1981.
Mr. Magleby, *Babycakes,* CBS, 1989.
Dr. Loeb, *Attack of the 50 Ft. Woman,* HBO, 1993.

Television Appearances; Specials:
Himself, *The Making of "The Goodbye Girl"* (documentary), 1977.
Malcolm Maltved, *Sex, Shock and Censorship in the '90s,* Showtime, 1993.
Himself, *Intimate Portrait: Stockard Channing* (documentary), Lifetime, 2004.

Television Appearances; Episodic:
Donald Kauldor, "Slay Ride," *Kojak,* 1974.
Harry Bentley, "The Jeffersons Move On Up," *All in the Family* (also known as *Those Were the Days*), 1975.
Minister, "All Psyched Out," *Maude,* 1975.
Calvin Klinger, *Mama Malone,* CBS, 1984.
Frederich Hoffman, "Sticks and Stones," *Murder, She Wrote,* CBS, 1985.
Okie, "Song of the Younger World," *The Twilight Zone,* CBS, 1985.
"Top Billing," *Tales from the Crypt* (also known as *HBO's "Tales from the Crypt"*), HBO, 1991.
Mr. Ludlow, "Risk Around the Dollar," *A Different World,* NBC, 1991.
Mr. Nicolides, "The Vase Shop," *Morton & Hayes,* 1991.
Milt, "Tess Makes the Man," *Pig Sty,* UPN, 1995.
Lester, *One Life to Live,* ABC, 1996.
Mr. Elinoff, the cartoon editor at *New Yorker,* "The Cartoon," *Seinfeld,* NBC, 1998.
Jeremy, "Drew and the Life–Size Jim Thome Cut–Out," *The Drew Carey Show,* ABC, 2002.

Also appeared in *Harry–O.*

Television Work:
Director, "The Truth Hurts," *The Jeffersons,* CBS, 1985.

BENSON, Jodi 1961–

PERSONAL

Original name, Jodi Marzorati; born October 10, 1961, in Rockford, IL; married Ray Benson (an actor and singer), May 19, 1984; children: McKinley, Delaney. *Education:* Milliken University, B.F.A., musical theater. *Avocational Interests:* Skiing, hiking, going to the movies, bowling, reading, and traveling.

Addresses: *Agent*—Innovative Artists, 1505 10th St., Santa Monica, CA 90401.

Career: Actress, singer, and voice performer for animated characters. Sings soprano with orchestras, including the Indianapolis Symphony, Washington Symphony, Colorado Symphony Orchestra, and Seattle Symphony; also appeared as a guest soloist for the Kennedy Center Honors; performed at Disney's movie premieres for *Pocahontas,* Central Park, New York City, for *The Hunchback of Notre Dame,* Superdome, New Orleans, LA, and Colorado Music Fest, 1999.

Awards, Honors: Antoinette Perry Award nomination, best actress in a musical, and Helen Hayes Award nomination, Washington Theatre Awards Society, 1992, both for *Crazy for You;* Annie Award nomination, outstanding individual achievement for voice acting by a female performer in an animated feature production, International Animated Film Society (ASIFA) Hollywood, 2001, for *Lady and the Tramp II: Scamp's Adventure;* DramaLogue Award, best actress, for *Chess.*

CREDITS

Film Appearances:
(English version) Voice of Lastrelle's mother (2004), *Kaze no tani no Naushika* (animated; also known as *Kaze no tani no Nausicaa, Nausicaa, Nausicaa of the Valley of the Winds,* and *Warriors of the Wind*), 1984.
Voice of Ariel, *The Little Mermaid* (animated), Buena Vista, 1989.
Voice of Thumbelina, *Hans Christian Andersen's "Thumbelina"* (animated; also known as *Thumbelina*), Warner Bros., 1994.
Voice of Ariel, *Disney Sing–Along–Songs: Circle of Life* (animated short), Walt Disney, 1994.
Voice of Ariel, *Disney Sing–Along–Songs: Friends Like Me* (animated short), Walt Disney, 1996.
Voice of Weebo, *Flubber* (also known as *Disney's "Flubber": The Absent Minded Professor* and *The Absent Minded Professor*), Buena Vista, 1997.
Voice of Belle, *A Christmas Carol,* 1997.
Voice, *The Mighty Kong,* Legacy Releasing Corp., 1998.
Herself, *Under the Sea: The Making of Disney's Masterpiece "The Little Mermaid"* (documentary short), Walt Disney Home Video, 1998.
Voice of Barbie, *Toy Story 2* (animated), Buena Vista, 1999.
Voice of Ariel, *Wish Upon a Starfish* (also known as *Disney's "Princess Collection": Wish Upon a Starfish*), 1999.

Voice of Helen of Troy, *Hercules: Zero to Hero* (animated), 1999.

Voice of Ariel, *Giggles* (animated; also known as *Disney's "Princess Collection": Giggles*), 1999.

Voice of Ariel, *The Little Mermaid II: Return to the Sea* (animated), Buena Vista Home Video, 2000.

Voice of Asenath, *Joseph: King of Dreams* (animated), 2000.

Host of 1980s, *Disney Through the Decades* (documentary short), Walt Disney Home Video, 2001.

Voice of Lady, "Pidge," *Lady and the Tramp II: Scamp's Adventure* (animated), Walt Disney Home Video, 2001.

Voice of Ariel, *Mickey's Magical Christmas: Snowed in at the House of Mouse* (animated), Walt Disney Home Video, 2001.

Host, Sleeping Beauty, *"Beauty and the Beast": The Story Behind the Story* (documentary short), Walt Disney Home Video, 2002.

Voice of Jenna, *Balto II: Wolf Quest* (animated), 2002.

Voice of Anita, *101 Dalmatians II: Patch's London Adventure* (documentary), Walt Disney Home Video, 2003.

(Uncredited) Voice of Ariel, *Mickey's PhilharMagic* (animated), 2003.

Voice of Jenna, *Balto III: Wings of Change* (animated), Universal Studios, 2004.

Voice of Ariel, *Disney Princess Party: Volume Two* (documentary), Walt Disney Home Video, 2005.

Television Appearances; Series:
Voice of Tula, *The Pirates of Dark Water* (animated; also known as *Dark Water*), Fox, 1991–92.

Voice of Ariel, *Disney's "The Little Mermaid"* (animated; also known as *The Little Mermaid*), CBS, 1992–95.

Voice of Ariel and Belle, *House of Mouse* (animated), ABC, 2001.

Voice of Ms. Doe, Patsy Smiles, and Almondine, *Camp Lazlo* (animated), Cartoon Network, 2005.

Also appeared as voice performer for numerous cartoon series, including *P. J. Sparkles*.

Television Appearances; Specials:
Performer, *A Precious Moments Christmas*, NBC, 1991.

Presenter, *The 22nd Annual Dove Awards*, The Nashville Network, 1991.

Performer, *The Kennedy Center Honors: A Celebration of the Performing Arts*, CBS, 1992.

The Walt Disney World Very Merry Christmas Parade, ABC, 1992.

Voice of Ariel, *A Whale of a Tale*, CBS, 1992.

Performer, *The Walt Disney World Very Merry Christmas Parade*, ABC, 1995.

Performer, *The Hunchback of Notre Dame Festival of Fun Musical Spectacular*, 1996.

Performer, *A Magical Walt Disney World Christmas*, ABC, 1997.

Voice of Luella Day, *Gold Fever* (documentary), PBS, 1997.

Joshua, *The Christmas Lamb* (also known as *The Crippled Lamb*), PAX, 2000.

Voice of Lenee, *Rapsittie Street Kids: Believe in Santa* (animated), 2002.

Voice of Jenna, *Balto II: Wolf Quest* (animated), 2002.

Television Appearances; Episodic:
Police officer, "Cries of Silence," *Hunter*, NBC, 1991.

Mother, "Caroline and the Egg," *Caroline in the City*, NBC, 1997.

Voice of Helen of Troy, "Hercules & the Trojan War," *Disney's "Hercules"* (animated; also known as *Hercules*), ABC and syndicated, 1998.

Voice of Mother Cheetah, "Cheetahs Never Prosper," *The Wild Thornberrys* (animated), Nickelodeon, 2000.

Voice of Aquagirl, "The Call: Parts 1 & 2," *Batman Beyond* (animated; also known as *Batman of the Future*), The WB, 2000.

Choir soloist, "Sleeping Lions," *The Brotherhood of Poland, New Hampshire*, CBS, 2003.

Voice of Captain Torelli, "Enemy Yours/Duck Departure," *Duck Dodgers* (animated), Cartoon Network, 2003.

Voice of Princess Incense, "Pig Planet," *Duck Dodgers* (animated), Cartoon Network, 2004.

Voice of rich mom, kid number two, and Floriculture lady, "Dumb Luck/Nobody Loves Grim," *Grim & Evil* (animated; also known as *The Grim Adventures of Billy & Mandy*), Cartoon Network, 2004.

Voice of blue fairy, "Billy Ocean/Hill Billy," *Grim & Evil* (animated; also known as *The Grim Adventures of Billy & Mandy*), Cartoon Network, 2005.

Voice of wife alligator and lady admirer, "He's Not Dead, He's My Mascot/Hog Wild," *Grim & Evil* (animated; also known as *The Grim Adventures of Billy & Mandy*), Cartoon Network, 2005.

Stage Appearances:
(Broadway debut) Virginia, *Marilyn: An American Fable*, 1983.

Doria Hudson, *Smile*, Lunt–Fontanne Theatre, New York City, 1986–87.

Betty Bursteter, *Welcome to the Club*, Music Box Theatre, New York City, 1989.

Hurray! Hurray! Hollywood, Harold Clurman Theatre and John Houseman Theatre, New York City, both 1991.

Polly Baker, *Crazy for You*, Shubert Theatre, New York City, 1992–93.

Broadway Canteen 7th Annual Easter Bonnet Competition, Broadway Theatre, New York City, 1993.

Narrator, *Joseph and the Amazing Technicolor Dream Coat*, Theatre Under the Stars, 1998.

Ensign Nellie Forbush, *South Pacific*, Music Hall, Dallas, TX, 1999.

Also appeared as Flora, *Flora the Red Menace,* Pasadena Playhouse, Pasadena, CA; Florence Vassey, *Chess,* Long Beach Civic Light Opera, Long Beach, CA; Ado Annie, *Oklahoma!,* Dorothy Chandler Pavilion, Los Angeles; and Eliza Doolittle, *My Fair Lady,* Alex Theatre, Glendale, CA; Anita, *West Side Story,* Venice, Italy; Tania, *Dangerous Music,* Jupiter Theater, Jupiter, FL; Miss Edythe Herbert, *My One and Only,* European premiere; and *Broadway Follies,* Broadway production.

Major Tours:

Appeared in touring productions of *My Fair Lady; Sophisticated Ladies,* U.S. cities; and *Once Upon a Mattress,* world cities.

RECORDINGS

Albums:

Jodi Benson Sings Songs from The Beginner's Bible I and II, EMI/Sparrow, 1992.
Varese Sarabande's "Unsung Musicals I," 1994.
The Songs of Guideposts Junction, EMI/Sparrow, 1995.
Varese Sarabande's "A Hollywood Christmas," 1996.

Albums (performing voice of Ariel):

Little Mermaid (original sound track), Disney, 1989, re–released, 1997.
Sebastian, Disney, 1990.
Songs from the Sea, Disney, 1992.
Unsung Musicals, Varese Sarabande, 1994.
Thumbelina, SBK/ERG, 1994.
Classic Disney, Volume 2, Disney, 1994.
The Princess Collection, Disney, 1995.
Disney Classics Collection, Disney, 1997.

Also contributed to *Disney's "Little Mermaid": Splash Hits.*

Albums (performing voice of Thumbelina):

Thumbelina Soundtrack, Warner Bros., 1994.

Albums (performing voice of Polly Baker):

Recorded *Crazy for You* (cast album), EMI/Angel.

Songs:

"I Got Rhythm," *I Got Rhythm: The Music of George Gershwin,* 1996.

Videos:

Recorded a Christian series, *Guideposts Junction,* for Sparrow.

Video Games:

Voice of Atta, *A Bug's Life,* 1999.

Voice of Millenia and Reena, *Grandia,* Ubi Soft Entertainment, 2000.
Voice of Ariel, *Kingdom Hearts* (also known as *Kingudamu hatsu*), Square Electronic Arts, 2002.
Voice of mother, *Onimusha 3* (also known as *Onimusha 3: Demon Siege*), Capcom Entertainment, 2004.
Voice of Ariel, *Kingdom Hearts: Chain of Memories,* 2004.

BERGER, Gregg 1925–
(Greg Barger, Greg Berger)

PERSONAL

Born in 1925; raised in Akron and Cleveland, OH. *Education:* Trained for the stage at the Harvey Lembeck Comedy Workshop.

Addresses: *Agent*—Cunningham, Escott, Slevin & Doherty, 10635 Santa Monica Blvd., Suite 130, Los Angeles, CA 90025.

Career: Actor and comedian, best known for voice characterizations. The Groundlings, performing member; as a comedian, appeared at the Comedy Store, the Improv, the Laff Stop, the Masquers Club, and Disneyland, all Los Angeles; provided network promos for Kids' WB, Fox Family Channel, EPSN, and PBS, film trailers for *Being John Malkovich* and *Blair Witch 2,* internet animated series including *Julius and Friends,* and radio commercials, including BMW, Static Guard, Delta Dental, California Department of Health, and Geico Direct Insurance. Famous Fone Friends, Los Angeles, CA, volunteer.

Member: Screen Actors Guild, American Federation of Television and Radio Artists.

Awards, Honors: Annie Award nomination, best achievement for voice acting, International Animated Film Society (ASIFA) Hollywood, 1994, for *Duckman.*

CREDITS

Film Appearances:

(Uncredited) *The Stunt Man,* Twentieth Century–Fox, 1980.
Sergeant, *Attack of the Killer Tomatoes!,* NAI Entertainment, 1980.
Voice, *Revenge of the Nerds,* Twentieth Century–Fox, 1984.

Taxi driver, *Love Streams,* 1984.

Voice of William Little, *Here Come the Littles,* 1985.

Voice of Grimlock, *Transformers: The Movie* (animated; also known as *The Transformers, Matrix Forever, Transformers the Movie: Mokushiroku Matrix yo eien ni,* and *Transformers: Matrix yo eien ni*), De Laurentiis Entertainment Group, 1986.

Voice of Grimlock and Long Haul, *Transformers: Five Faces of Darkness* (animated), 1986.

Voice of Moonviper, *G.I. Joe: The Movie* (animated; also known as *Action Force: The Movie*), Marvel Entertainment, 1987.

(English version; as Greg Barger) Voice of Equestrian Master, *Little Nemo: Adventures in Slumberland* (animated), 1988.

Steve W. Klembecker, *Spaced Invaders* (also known as *Martians!!!*), Buena Vista, 1990.

Lieutenant Talinsky, *Police Academy 7: Mission to Moscow* (also known as *Police Academy: Mission to Moscow*), Warner Home Video, 1994.

Voice, *Toy Story,* Buena Vista, 1995.

Voice of circus television announcer, *The Rugrats Movie* (animated), Paramount, 1998.

Voice, *Winnie the Pooh: Seasons of Giving* (animated; also known as *Disney's "Winnie the Pooh: Seasons of Giving"*), 1999.

"Doofus and Do–Right" narrator, *Men in Black Alien Attack* (short; also known as *Men in Black: The Ride*), 2000.

Mr. Toller, *The Brainiacs.com,* PorchLight Entertainment, 2000.

Jecht, *Fainru fantaji X* (also known as *Final Fantasy X*), 2001.

Voice of tech number one, *Recess: School's Out* (animated), Buena Vista, 2001.

Voice, *Clifford's Big Red Movie* (animated), Warner Bros., 2004.

Professor Bugdonovich, *Al Roach: Private Inspector* (short), 2004.

Additional voices, *Mickey's "Twice Upon a Christmas"* (animated), Buena Vista Home Video, 2004.

Television Appearances; Series:

Additional voices, *The Smurfs* (animated; also known as *Smurfs' Adventures*), 1981.

Voice of William Little, *The Littles* (animated), 1983.

Voices of Fozzie and Scooter, *Jim Henson's "Muppet Babies,"* CBS, 1984–92.

Voices of Grimlock, Skyfire, Long Haul, Torq III, and Outback II, *The Transformers* (animated; also known as *Transformers: 2010, Super Good Robot Force, Tatakae! Cho robot seimeitai Transformer, Transformers: Generation 1,* and *Transformers*), syndicated, 1984.

Voice of Bowlhead, *The Pink Panther and Sons* (animated), 1984.

Voice of Colonel Brekhov, Cutter, Ripcord, Spirit, Firefly, Mr. Queeg, and Sparks, *G.I. Joe* (animated), 1985.

Dr. Van Werner, *St. Elsewhere,* 1987.

Voices of Odie, Orson Pig, Floyd Mouse, Weasel, and Herman the Mailman, *Garfield and Friends* (animated), CBS, 1988.

Voice, *This Is America, Charlie Brown!* (animated; also known as *Charlie Brown and Snoopy's "History of America," Charlie Brown's History of the U.S.,* and *You're On Nickelodeon Charlie Brown*), CBS, 1988–89.

Voice of A. B., *Fantastic Max* (animated), syndicated, 1988.

Voice, *The Adventures of Don Coyote and Sancho Panda* (animated), syndicated, 1990.

Voice, *Where's Waldo?* (animated; also known as *Where's Wally* and *Where's Wally?*), CBS, 1991.

Additional voices, *Toxic Crusaders* (animated), syndicated, 1991.

Voice of Mr. Skunk, Mr. Corkscrew, and Pelican, *Bonkers* (animated; also known as *Disney's "Bonkers"*), 1993.

Voices of the judge and Buck Burton, *Edith Ann: Homeless Go Home* (animated), ABC, 1994.

Voice of Cornfed, *Duckman* (animated; also known as *Duckman: Private Dick/Family Man*), USA Network, 1994–95.

Voice of The Gromble and The Viewfinder, *Aaahh!!! Real Monsters* (animated), Nickelodeon, 1994—.

Voice of Mysterio/Quentin Beck and Kraven the Hunter/Sergei Kravinoff, *Spider–Man* (animated), 1995–97.

Voice, *Channel Umptee–3* (animated), The WB, 1997.

Voice, *The Wild Thornberrys* (animated), Nickelodeon, 1998.

Additional voices, *The Powerpuff Girls* (animated; also known as *PPG* and *Youlide–Chui nu*), Cartoon Network, 1998.

Voice of Kay, *Men in Black: The Series* (animated), 1998—.

Voice talent, *Invasion of the Hidden Cameras,* Fox, 2002.

(English version) Additional voices, *Astro Boy tetsuwan atomu* (animated; also known as *Astro Boy*), 2003.

Also appeared as additional voices, *The Jetsons* (animated); (English version) voice of Devleen and Tommy David, *Majinga Zetto* (animated; also known as *TranZor Z*).

Television Appearances; Movies:

Tabloid reporter, *Running Mates* (also known as *Dirty Tricks*), HBO, 1992.

Television trainer, *Majority Rule,* Lifetime, 1992.

Voice of Golem Controller, *Batman Beyond: The Movie* (animated), The WB, 1999.

Television Appearances; Pilot Movies:

Neal, *The Hitman,* ABC, 1991.

Television Appearances; Specials:

Voice of Odie and salesman, *Here Comes Garfield* (animated), 1982.

Voice of Odie and Ali Cat, *Garfield on the Town* (animated), 1983.

Voice of Cutter, Firefly, Ripcord, Sparks, and Spirit, *G.I. Joe: The Revenge of Cobra* (animated), 1984.

Voice of Odie and ranger number one, *Garfield in the Rough* (animated), 1984.

Voice of Odie and TV announcer, *Garfield in Disguise* (animated; also known as *Garfield's Halloween Adventure*), 1985.

Voice of Odie and pigeon, *Garfield in Paradise* (animated), CBS, 1986.

Voice of Colonel Brekhov, *G.I. Joe: Arise, Serpentor, Arise!* (animated; also known as *Action Force: Arise, Serpentor, Arise!*), 1986.

Voice, *Liberty and the Littles*, 1986.

Voice of Odie, *A Garfield Christmas Special* (animated; also known as *A Garfield Christmas*), CBS, 1987.

Voices of Odie, the announcer, Bob, and Grandma Fogerty, *Garfield Goes Hollywood* (animated), CBS, 1987.

Voice of Mr. Pinkley, *Cathy* (animated), CBS, 1987.

Voice of Mr. Pinkley, *Cathy's Last Resort* (animated), CBS, 1988.

Voice, *Happy Birthday, Garfield!* (animated), CBS, 1988.

Voice, *Garfield: His Nine Lives* (animated; also known as *Garfield's Nine Lives*), CBS, 1988.

Voices of Odie and Fleebish, *Garfield's Babes and Bullets* (animated), CBS, 1989.

Voice of Mr. Pinkley, *Cathy's Valentine* (animated), CBS, 1989.

Voice, *Garfield's Thanksgiving* (animated), CBS, 1989.

Voices of Odie and Slobber Job, *Garfield's Feline Fantasies* (animated), CBS, 1990.

Voices of Odie, Stinky, and the announcer, *Garfield Gets a Life* (animated), CBS, 1991.

Additional voices, *The Story of Santa Claus* (animated; also known as *Santa Claus*), CBS, 1996.

Television Appearances; Episodic:

Bellhop, "The Last Weekend," *Too Close for Comfort* (also known as *The Ted Knight Show*), 1982.

The comedian, "But Seriously Folks," *Fame*, syndicated, 1982.

Policeman, "Alice Doesn't Work Here Anymore: Part 2," *Alice*, 1984.

Clerk, "The Lottery," *Perfect Strangers*, ABC, 1988.

Mitchell Noyes, "Sperminator," *Perfect Strangers*, ABC, 1988.

Felix, "Dancing in the Dark," *The Golden Girls*, CBS, 1989.

Parker, "What Price Gloria?—October 16, 1961," *Quantum Leap*, NBC, 1989.

Voice of Wild Bill Hiccup, "They Shoot Dogs, Don't They?," *Chip 'n Dale Rescue Rangers* (animated), 1989.

Voice of Rory, "Bart vs. Thanksgiving," *The Simpsons* (animated), Fox, 1990.

(Uncredited) "Still Another Day in the Life," *Night Court*, NBC, 1990.

Voice, *Tom and Jerry Kids Show* (animated), Fox, 1990.

Voice, *The Adventures of Don Coyote and Sancho Panda* (animated), syndicated, 1990.

Dirk, "Eclipse," *She–Wolf of London* (also known as *Love & Curses*), 1991.

Voice, *Spacecats* (animated), NBC, 1991.

Taggart, *Bob*, CBS, 1992.

Randy, *The Boys Are Back*, CBS, 1994.

Voice of Mole Man, "Mole Man," *The Fantastic Four* (animated; also known as *Marvel Action Hour: The Fantastic Four*), 1994.

Clerk, "Fools Russian," *Wings*, NBC, 1995.

(As Greg Berger) Rosie, "A Bullet for Bullock," *Batman: The Animated Series* (animated; also known as *Batman: The Animated Series* and *The Adventures of Batman & Robin*), 1995.

Mr. Douglas, "When a Man Loves a Donut," *Wings*, NBC, 1995.

Voice of Leo, "M.I.A.," *Gargoyles* (animated), 1995.

Voice of Gordon, "The Friend," *Frasier*, NBC, 1996.

Master of ceremonies, "Drew vs. the Pig," *The Drew Carey Show*, ABC, 1997.

"Daphne Hates Sherry," *Frasier*, NBC, 1997.

Voice of Captain Rossanov and guard, "General Winter," *The Real Adventures of Jonny Quest* (animated; also known as *Jonny Quest: The Real Adventures*), 1997.

Voice, "Casting the Runes," *Extreme Ghostbusters* (animated), 1997.

Voice of agent number two, *The New Batman/ Superman Adventures* (animated), The WB, 1998.

Voice of Lucky and amusement park worker, "Sid's Revenge/Roller Coaster," *Hey Arnold!* (animated), Nickelodeon, 1998.

Voice of Willie's father and policeman, "Career Day/ Hey Harold!," *Hey Arnold!* (animated), 1998.

Voice of Golem controller, "Golem," *Batman Beyond* (animated; also known as *Batman of the Future*), The WB, 1999.

Voice of anchorman, "Red, White and Drew," *The Drew Carey Show*, ABC, 1999.

Voice of pilot, "Eyewitness," *Batman Beyond* (animated; also known as *Batman of the Future*), The WB, 2000.

Voice of dispatch agent, "Zeta," *Batman Beyond* (animated; also known as *Batman of the Future*), The WB, 2000.

Clerk, "One Angry Man," *Becker*, CBS, 2000.

Voice of Bailiff and FBI Agent, "Hoss Delgado: Spectral Exterminator/Evil on Trial/To Eris Human," *Grim & Evil* (animated; also known as *The Grim Adventures of Billy & Mandy*), Cartoon Network, 2002.

Hotline voice, *Codename: Kids Next Door* (animated), Cartoon Network, 2002.

Voice of Bookworm, "The Crawling Niceness/Smarten Up!/The Grim Show," *Grim & Evil* (animated; also known as *The Grim Adventures of Billy & Mandy*), Cartoon Network, 2003.

Voice of Lawyer, "Bully Boogie/There Here Be Dwarves," *Grim & Evil* (animated; also known as *The Grim Adventures of Billy & Mandy*), Cartoon Network, 2004.

Also appeared as Billy, *Knots Landing,* CBS; voice, *Quack Pack;* voice, *Dallas,* CBS; voice, *The A–Team,* NBC; voice, *Magnum P.I.,* CBS; voice, *Solid Gold,* syndicated; in *Days of Our Lives,* NBC; and *On the Air with Roger and Roger.*

Stage Appearances:

Appeared as Mr. Shears, *Finigan's Rainbow,* Akron, OH; in *Butterscotch,* Hollywood, CA; *Loose Lips,* New York City; *Loose Lips,* Los Angeles; *Figaro Gets a Divorce,* La Jolla Playhouse, La Jolla, CA; *The Third Day Comes; One Flew Over the Cuckoo's Nest,* Deaf West Theatre Company, North Hollywood, CA; and in comedy sketches at NOTE Theatre, Los Angeles.

Radio Appearances:

Made regular appearances on *Rick Dee's Weekly Top 40,* Los Angeles.

RECORDINGS

Video Games:

Voice of Dmitri Ivanov/Burgonmeister, *Quest for Glory IV: Shadows of Darkness,* 1994.

Voice, *Blazing Dragons,* 1996.

Voice of Cornfed Pig, *Duckman,* 1997.

Voice of Cutthroat Bill, *The Curse of Monkey Island* (also known as *Monkey Island 3*), Lucas Arts, 1997.

Voice–over, *Gabriel Knight: Blood of the Sacred, Blood of the Damned,* Sierra On–Line, 1998.

Voice of Daveorn, Entar, Rieltar, and Sonner, *Baldur's Gate,* Interplay Productions, 1998.

Voice of Archer, *Small Soldiers,* 1998.

Voices of Battle Droid, Coruscant Guard, Darth Maul, Mat Rags, and Race Fan, *Star Wars: Episode I—The Phantom Menace,* 1999.

Voice of Wan Sandage, Cy Yunga, and Jinn Reeso, *Star Wars: Episode I—Racer,* 1999.

Voice of Hunter, Ripto, Foreman Bob, Master Chef, Crush, Gulp, and Yeti, *Spyro 2: Ripto's Rage!* (also known as *Spyro 2: Gateway to Glimmer* and *Spyro the Dragon 2: Ripto's Rage!*), 1999.

Voice of Kerchck, *Tarzan,* 1999.

Jedi Master Plo Koon, Darth Maul, and Khameir Sarin, *Star Wars: Episode I—Jedi Power Battles,* 2000.

Invictus (also known as *Invictus: In the Shadow of Olympus*), 2000.

Voice of Hunter the Cheetah and additional voices, *Spyro: Year of the Dragon* (also known as *Spyro the Dragon 3: Year of the Dragon*), 2000.

Voice of Everard and additional voices, *Forgotten Realms: Icewind Dale,* 2000.

Voice of Simyaz, Isea Roenal, and Oisig, *Forgotten Realms: Baldur's Gate II—Shadows of Amn,* 2000.

Voice of narrator, *Wacky Races,* Infogames Entertainment, 2000.

Voice of Paladin Magnus and Squad and Dropship voices number two, *Ground Control,* Sierra Entertainment, 2000.

(As Greg Berger) Voice, *Sacrifice,* Interplay Productions, 2000.

Voice of Battle Droid member, Plo Koon, and male citizen two, *Star Wars: Obi–Wan,* LucasArts Entertainment Company, 2001.

Voice of Confederacy trooper, *Star Wars: Galactic Battlegrounds,* LucasArts Entertainment Company, 2001.

Voice, *Fallout Tactics: Brotherhood of Steel,* Interplay Productions, 2001.

(English version) Voice of Jecht, *Fainru fantaji X* (also known as *FFX, Final Fantasy 10, Final Fantasy X,* and *Final Fantasy X International*), Square Electronic Arts, 2001.

Voice of Installer, allied boat, and intruder, *Command & Conquer: Red Alert 2* (also known as *Command & Conquer: Red Alert 2—Yuri's Revenge*), Electronic Arts, 2001.

Voice, *Command & Conquer: Yuri's Revenge* (also known as *Red Alert 2 Expansion Pack: Yuri's Revenge*), 2001.

Voice of Jessup and additional voices, *The Scorpion King: Rise of the Akkadian* (also known as *The Scorpion King*), Universal Interactive Studios, 2002.

Voice of Mantavor crew, Densadron crew, and Aquasong captain, *Treasure Planet: Battle at Procyn,* Disney Interactive, 2002.

Voice of Hunter, Ripto, Crush, and Gulp, *Spyro: Enter the Dragonfly,* 2002.

Voice of Executrix Council, *Emperor: Battle for Dune,* EA Games, 2002.

Voice of Tzidik Wrantojo and Wan Sandage, *Star Wars: Racer Revenge,* 2002.

Voice of Salty, *Pirates: The Legend of Black Kat,* EA Games, 2002.

Voice of Mendoza, *Command & Conquer: Renegade,* Electronic Arts, 2002.

Voice of Bespin guard number one, Shadow Trooper number one, and Stormtrooper number two, *Star Wars: Jedi Knight II—Jedi Outcast,* LucasArts Entertainment Company, 2002.

Voice of Cobra and additional voices, *Bruce Lee: Quest of the Dragon,* Universal Interactive Studios, 2002.

Voice of Starbase traffic controller, *Earth and Beyond,* Electronic Arts, 2002.

Voice of Small Interbot and Guard Technician, *Superman: Shadow of Apokolips,* Warner Bros., 2002.

Voice of Armitage Rook, *James Bond 007: Nightfire,* EA Games, 2002.

(As Greg Berger) Voice of Alien thug number one, Senator Trell, and wounded man, *Star Wars: Bounty Hunter,* LucasArts Entertainment, 2002.

Voice of Borneo and Jurak, *Dark Chronicle* (also known as *Dark Cloud 2*), Sony Pictures Entertainment, 2002.

Voice of Turel, *Legacy of Kain: Defiance* (also known as *Legacy of Kain: Soul Reaver III*), Eidos Interactive, 2003.

Voice, *Command & Conquer: Generals,* 2003.

(English version) Voice of Jecht, *Final Fantasy X–2* (also known as *Fainaru fantajii X–2*), Square Enix, 2003.

Voice of Samson, *Arc the Lad: Seirei no kokon* (also known as *Arc the Lad: Twilight of the Spirits*), Sony Computer Entertainment America, 2003.

Voice of Captain Blue, King Blue, and narrator, *Viewtiful Joe* (also known as *Viewtiful Joe Revival* and *Viewtiful Joe: A New Hope*), Capcom Entertainment, 2003.

Additional voices, *Star Wars: Knights of the Old Republic* (also known as *Star Wars: KOTOR*), LucasArts Entertainment Company, 2003.

Voice, *Extreme Skate Adventure* (also known as *Disney's "Extreme Skate Adventure"*), 2003.

Voice of Rax Joris, Rockettrooper Officer, Stormtrooper number two, and Merchant number one, *Star Wars: Jedi Knight—Jedi Academy,* LucasArts Entertainment Company, 2003.

Voice, *Command & Conquer: Generals Zero Hour,* EA Games, 2003.

Voice, *Rise to Honor* (also known as *Jet Li: Rise to Honor*), Sony Computer Entertainment America, 2003.

Sergeant Moody and additional voices, *Call of Duty,* Activision, 2003.

Voice of Bunyip Elder, Patch, and Foreman Norman, *Ty the Tasmanian Tiger 2,* 2004.

Sergeant Moody, *Call of Duty: United Offensive,* Activision, 2004.

Numerous voices, *EverQuest II,* Sony Online Entertainment, 2004.

(English version) Voice of The Pain, *Metal Gear Solid 3: Snake Eater* (also known as *MGS3* and *Metal Gear Solid 3*), Konami Digital Entertainment America, 2004.

Voice of Captain Blue and narrator, *Viewtiful Joe 2,* Capcom Entertainment, 2004.

Voice of Barca and additional voices, *Shadow of Rome,* Capcom Entertainment, 2005.

Voice of SkyBax patrolman, *Dinotopia: Quest for the Ruby Sunstone,* Goodtimes Entertainment, 2005.

Voice, *Chicken Little,* Buena Vista, 2005.

Voice of Frederick the Great, *Age of Empires III,* 2005.

Voice of The Pain, *Metal Gear Solid 3: Subsistence,* Konami Digital Entertainment America, 2005.

BERRY, Adam

PERSONAL

Married Nina (an actress). *Education:* University of Southern California, degree in composition and film scoring; also attended community college.

Addresses: *Manager*—Greenspan Artist Management, 8748 Holloway Dr., Second Floor, West Hollywood, CA 90069.

Career: Composer and orchestrator. Composer of musical scores for film trailers. Bass player in a band with *South Park* creators Trey Parker and Matt Stone; also played other instruments. Also worked in schools.

Awards, Honors: Daytime Emmy Award nomination, outstanding achievement in music direction and composition, 2005, for *Kim Possible.*

CREDITS

Film Work; Music Orchestrator:
The Little Death, PolyGram Filmed Entertainment, 1995.

WRITINGS

Television Music; Series:
Additional music, *F/X: The Series,* CTV and syndicated, 1996–98.

Additional music, *Roar,* Fox, 1997.

South Park (animated), Comedy Central, 1997–2001.

Hercules (animated; also known as *Disney's "Hercules"*), ABC and syndicated, 1998–99.

(And main title theme) *Buzz Lightyear of Star Command* (animated; also known as *Disney/Pixar's "Buzz Lightyear of Star Command"*), UPN and syndicated, 2000–2001, ABC, 2001.

Small Shots, Spike TV, 2001–2003.

Kim Possible (animated; also known as *Disney's "Kim Possible"*), The Disney Channel, 2002—.

The Buzz on Maggie (animated), The Disney Channel, 2005—.

Television Music; Animated Movies:
Kim Possible: A Stitch in Time (also known as *Disney's "Kim Possible: A Stitch in Time"*), The Disney Channel, 2003.

Kim Possible: So The Drama (animated; also known as *Disney's "Kim Possible: So the Drama"*), The Disney Channel, 2005.

Film Music:

Friend of the Family II (also known as *Hell Hath No Fury, Innocence Betrayed,* and *Passionate Revenge*), New City Releasing, 1996.

Fugitive Rage (also known as *Caged Fear*), A–pix Entertainment/Royal Oaks Entertainment, 1996.

Star Portal, New Concorde, 1998.

American Intellectuals, Oak Island Films, 1999.

Buzz Lightyear of Star Command: The Adventure Begins (animated; also known as *The Adventures of Buzz Lightyear*), Buena Vista Home Entertainment, 2000.

Tara (also known as *Hood Rat*), Universal Studios Home Video, 2001.

Balto II: Wolf Quest (animated), Universal Studios Home Video, 2002.

Beethoven's 5th (animated; also known as *Beethoven's 5th: Big Paw*), Universal Studios Home Video, 2003.

Balto III: Wings of Change (animated), Universal Studios Home Video, 2004.

The Trouble with Dee Dee (also known as *Dee Dee Rutherford*), Hunt and the Kill, 2005.

Film Music; Songs:

"The MacGoogle Theme Song," *Max Keeble's Big Move* (also known as *7th Grade Heart Attack*), Buena Vista, 2001.

OTHER SOURCES

Electronic:

Got Next, http://www.got-next.com, December 12, 2004.

Soundtrack.Net Web Site, http://www.soundtrack.net, December 5, 1998.

BINOCHE, Juliette 1964–

PERSONAL

Born March 9, 1964, in Paris, France; daughter of Jean–Marie (a sculptor, actor, and director) and Monique Stalens (an actress and director); sister of Marion Stalens (a photographer and actress); children: (with Andre Halle, a professional scuba diver) Raphael, (with Benoit Magimel, an actor) Hannah. *Education:* Graduated from the National Conservatory of Dramatic Arts; studied acting with Vera Gregh. *Avocational Interests:* Gardening, painting.

Addresses: *Agent*—Endeavor, 9601 Wilshire Blvd., 6th Floor, Beverly Hills, CA 90212. *Manager*—Hofflund/Polone, 9465 Wilshire Blvd., Suite 820, Beverly Hills, CA 90212. *Publicist*—Bloch/Korenbrot Public Relations, 110 S. Fairfax Ave., Suite 310, Los Angeles, CA 90036.

Career: Actress and model. Appeared in commercials for Chamallo, 1983, and Ferrero Rocher, 2002; face of Lancome's Poeme perfume, 1995–2000; face of Gentryportofino, 2003; previously worked in a Paris department store as a cashier, 1983. Does charity work for Aspecta and involved with Amnesty International.

Awards, Honors: Romy–Schneider Prize, most promising actress, 1986; Cesar Award nomination, best actress, Academie des Arts et Techniques du Cinema, 1986, for *Rendez–Vous;* Cesar Award nomination, best actress, 1987, for *Mauvais sang;* Cesar Award nomination, best actress, European Film Award, best actress, 1992, both for *Les amants du pont–neuf;* Cesar Award nomination, best actress, 1993, for *Damage;* Berline Camera, Berlin International Film Festival, Volpi Cup, best actress, Venice Film Festival, 1993, Golden Globe Award nomination, best actress in a motion picture—drama, Cesar Award, best actress, 1994, all for *Trois couleurs: Bleu;* Sant Jorid Award, best foreign actress, 1994, for *Trois couleurs: Bleu, Damage,* and *Les amants du Pont–Neuf;* Cesar Award nomination, best actress, 1996, for *Le hussard sur le toit;* named one of the fifty most beautiful people in the world, *People Weekly,* 1997; National Board of Review Award, best supporting actress, 1996, Academy Award, best supporting actress, Golden Globe Award nomination, best performance by an actress in a supporting role in a motion picture, Film Award, best performance by an actress in a supporting role, British Academy of Film and Television Arts, Screen Actors Guild Award nomination, outstanding performance by a female actor in a supporting role, Screen Actors Guild Award nomination (with others), outstanding performance by a cast, European Film Award, best actress, Silver Berlin Bear Award, best actress, Berlin International Film Festival, Chlotrudis Award, best supporting actress, Chlotrudis Society for Independent Film, Best Actress Award, Cabourg Romantic Film Festival, 1997, all for *The English Patient;* Antoinette Perry Award nomination, best actress in a play, *Theatre World* Award, 2001, both for *Betrayal;* Academy Award nomination, best actress in a leading role, Golden Globe Award nomination, best performance by an actress in a motion picture—comedy/musical, Screen Actors Guild Award nominations, outstanding performance by a female actor in a leading role and outstanding performance by the cast of a theatrical motion picture (with others), Audience Award, European Film Awards, best actress, Film Award nomination, best performance by an actress in a leading role, British Academy of Film and Television Arts, 2001, for *Chocolat;* Cesar Award nomination, best actress, 2001, for *La veuve de Sainte–Pierre;* Cesar Award nomination, best actress, 2003, for *Decalage horaire;* European Film Award nomination, best actress, 2005, for *Cache.*

CREDITS

Film Appearances:

La fille du rallye, *Liberty Belle,* 1982.

Herself, *Petites notes a propos du film "Je vous salue, Marie"* (short), 1983.

Natacha, *La vie de famille* (also known as *Family Life*), Flach–TF1, 1984.

Antoinette, *Les nanas* (also known as *The Chicks* and *Girls, Girls, Girls!*), FR3 Film, 1984.

Juliette, *Hail Mary* (also known as *Je vous salue Marie* and *The Book of Mary*), Gaumont/New Yorker, 1985.

Brigitte B., *Adieu Blareau* (also known as *Farewell blaireau*), 1985.

Une amie de Veronique, *Le meilleur de la vie* (also known as *A Better Life*), 1985.

Nina Larrieu, *Rendez–vous* (also known as *Andre Techine's "Rendez–Vous"*), Spectrafilm, 1985.

Esther Bouloire, *Mon beau–frere a tue ma soeur* (also known as *They've Killed Her!*), World Marketing, 1985.

Herself ("Joan of Arc" sequence), *Thierry Mugler,* 1985.

Anna, *Mauvais Sang* (also known as *The Night Is Young* and *Bad Blood*), AAA Classic, 1986.

Tereza, *The Unbearable Lightness of Being,* Orion, 1988.

Elsa, *Un tour de manege* (also known as *Roundabout*), 1988.

Michele, *Les amants du pont–neuf* (also known as *The Lovers on the Bridge* and *The Lovers on the Ninth Bridge*), Gaumont, 1991.

Herself, *Enqueste sur un film au–dessus de tout soupcon* (documentary), Magic Films Productions, 1991.

Anna Barton, *Damage* (also known as *Fatale*), New Line Cinema, 1992.

Catherine Earnshaw/Catherine Linton, *Emily Bronte's "Wuthering Heights"* (also known as *Wuthering Heights*), Paramount, 1992.

Herself, *Doisneau des villes, doisneau des champs* (documentary), 1993.

Julie Vignon (de Courcy), *Trois couleurs: Bleu* (also known as *Film Bleu, Trzy kolory: Niebieski, Bleu, Three Colors: Blue, Three Colours: Bleu,* and *Blue*), Miramax, 1993.

Julie Vignon (de Courcy), *Trois couleurs: Rouge* (also known as *Three Colors: Red, Three Colours: Red, Trzy kolory: Czerwony,* and *Red*), Miramax, 1994.

Julie Vignon (de Courcy), *Trois couleurs: Blanc* (also known as *Three Colors: White, Trzy kolory: Bialy, Three Colours: White, Trois couleurs: Blanc,* and *White*), Miramax, 1994.

Pauline de Theus, *The Horseman on the Roof* (also known as *Le hussard sur le toit*), Miramax, 1995.

Beatrice Saulnier, *A Couch in New York* (also known as *Un divan a New York* and *Eine Couch in New York*), Northern Arts Entertainment, 1996.

Hana, *The English Patient,* Miramax, 1996.

Alice, *Alice et Martin* (also known as *Alice and Martin* and *Alice y Martin*), October Films, 1998.

George Sand, *Les enfants du siecle* (also known as *The Children of the Century*), Alexandre Films/Les Films Alain Sande, 1999.

Voice, *Eloge de l'amour,* 1999.

Anne, *Code inconnu* (also known as *Code Unknown: Incomplete Tales of Several Journeys, Code inconnu: Recit incomplet de divers voyages, Code—Unbekannt,* and *Code Unknown*), Kino International, 2000.

Madame La, *La veuve de Saint–Pierre* (also known as *The Widow of Saint–Pierre* and *The Widow of St. Pierre*), Flach Pyramide International, 2000.

Vianne Rocher, *Chocolat,* Miramax, 2000.

Rose, *Decalage horaire* (also known as *Jet Lag*), Miramax, 2002.

Anna Malan, *Country of My Skull* (also known as *In My Country*), Sony Pictures Classics, 2004.

Anne, *Cache* (also known as *Hidden, Niente de nascondere,* and *Versteckt*), Sony Pictures Classics, 2005.

Miriam Naumann, *Bee Season,* Fox Searchlight, 2005.

Marie Palesi/Mary Magdalene, *Mary,* Wild Bunch, 2005.

Herself, *Odyssey in Rome* (documentary), 2005.

Irene, *Quelques jours en septembre,* Weinstein Company, 2006.

The mother, "2nd arrondissement," *Paris, je t'aime,* Celsius Entertainment, 2006.

Amira, *Breaking and Entering,* Weinstein Company, 2006.

Marianne, *Les Disparus,* MK2 Productions, 2006.

Also appeared in *Rouge baiser.*

Film Work:

Painter of artwork and poster designer, *Les amants du pont–neuf* (also known as *The Lovers on the Bridge* and *Lovers on the Ninth Bridge*), Gaumont, 1991.

Poster designer, *Les enfants du siecle* (also known as *The Children of the Century*), Alexandre Films/Les Films Alain Sande, 1999.

Television Appearances; Movies:

Fort bloque, 1983.

Dorthee, danseuse de corde, 1983.

Mara, *Women and Men II* (also known as *Women and Men II: In Love There Are No Rules, The Art of Seduction,* and *A Domestic Dilemma*), HBO, 1991.

Television Appearances; Specials:

Herself, *Jean–Luc Goddard: mal vu, mal dit* (documentary), 1984.

Herself, *Cinema de notre temps: Andre Techine, apres la Nouvelle Vague ...* (documentary; also known as *Cinema of Our Time: Andre Techine*), 1995.

Presenter, *The 69th Annual Academy Awards,* ABC, 1997.
Host, *The Cesar Awards,* 1998.
Herself, *Absolument cinema: Juliette Binoche,* 2000.
The Orange British Academy Film Awards, 2001.
The 7th Annual Screen Actors Guild Awards, TNT, 2001.
The 73rd Annual Academy Awards, ABC, 2001.
Louis Jouvet ou L'amour du theatre (documentary), 2002.
Judi Dench: A BAFTA Tribute, BBC, 2002.
Herself, *Un jour dans la vie du cinema francais* (documentary), 2002.
The 100 Greatest Movie Stars, Channel 4, 2003.
Herself, *Premiers pas* (documentary), 2005.
Marie Palesi, *Venecia 2005: Cronica de Carlos Boyero,* 2005.
The 100 Greatest War Films, Channel 4, 2005.
Herself, *French Beauty* (documentary), 2005.
Herself, *La Reconciliation* (documentary), 2005.

Television Appearances; Episodic:
Herself, *La nuit des Cesars,* 1986, 1998, 2001, 2003.
The Charlie Rose Show, PBS, 1997, 1999, 2000, 2005.
20 heures le journal, 1998.
Herself, "Soul Zaentz: A Tribute," *The South Bank Show,* ITV, 1998.
Herself, "Des couples dans la tourmente de l'histoire," *Bouillon de culture,* 2000.
The Rosie O'Donnell Show, syndicated, 2000.
The Big Breakfast, Channel 4, 2001.
The Tonight Show with Jay Leno, NBC, 2001, 2003.
Inside the Actors Studio, Bravo, 2002.
Tout le monde en parle, 2002, 2005.
Late Show with David Letterman (also known as *The Late Show*), CBS, 2003.
The Late Late Show with Craig Kilborn (also known as *The Late Late Show*), CBS, 2003.
The View, ABC, 2003, 2005.
The Late Late Show with Craig Ferguson, CBS, 2005.
Cinema mil, 2005.
Rose, *La Mandragora,* 2005.
Herself, "John Boorman," *The South Bank Show,* ITV, 2005.
Le Grand journal de Canal+, 2005.
L'Hebdo cinema, 2005.

Stage Appearances:
Ersilia Drei, *Naked,* The Playhouse, then Almeida Theatre, London, 1998.
Emma, *Betrayal,* Roundabout Theatre, New York City, 2000–2001.

Also appeared in French productions of *L'argent de Dieu; Henri IV; Les femmes savantes; L'ours; La mouette; Le jeu de la feuillee; Le roi se meurt; Le malade imaginaire.*

WRITINGS

Books:
(Preface only) *Le grand livre de la tendresse,* 2002.

OTHER SOURCES

Books:
International Dictionary of Films and Filmmakers, Volume 3: Actors and Actresses, 4th ed., St. James Press, 2000.
Newsmakers, Issue 3, Gale Group, 2001.

Periodicals:
Entertainment Weekly, February 23, 2001, p. 37.
Harper's Bazaar, November, 1995, p. 238.
Interview, March, 2001, p. 81.
New York Times, May 15, 1996.
People Weekly, May 9, 1994, p. 90; December 16, 1996, p. 121.
Vanity Fair, May, 1992, pp. 160–161.
Variety, August 25, 1997, p. 55; January 26, 1998, p. 8; February 23, 1998, p. 186; September 11, 2000, p. 35.

BLACK, Karen 1939(?)–
   (Karen Ziegler)

PERSONAL

Original name, Karen Blanche Ziegler; born July 1, 1939 (some sources say 1942), in Park Ridge, IL; daughter of Norman A. and Elsie (a novelist; maiden name, Reif) Ziegler; married Charles Black, 1960 (divorced); married Robert Burton, April 18, 1973 (divorced, October, 1974); married L. Minor "Kit" Carson (a writer and director), July 4, 1975 (divorced); married Steven Eckelberry (a film editor), September 27, 1987; children: (third marriage) Hunter Minor Norman; (fourth marriage) Celine. *Education:* Attended Northwestern University; trained for the stage with Lee Strasberg at Actors Studio, New York City. *Religion:* Church of Scientology.

Addresses: *Agent*—Ellis Talent Group, 4705 Laurel Canyon Blvd., Valley Village, CA 91607.

Career: Actress, writer, producer, and composer. Studied ballet until the age of 17; appeared off–Broadway in satirical reviews, 1960s; Cabaret debut at Los Angeles, Cinegrill, 1988. Also worked as Karen Ziegler. Worked as a waitress and night clerk.

Awards, Honors: New York Drama Critics Award nomination, best actress, 1965, for *The Playroom;* National Board of Review Award, best supporting actress, New York Film Critics Circle Award, best supporting actress, 1970, Academy Award nomination, best supporting actress, Golden Globe Award, best supporting actress, Golden Laurel Awards, best supporting performance—female and star of tomorrow—female, Producers Guild of America, 1971, all for *Five Easy Pieces;* Golden Globe Award, best supporting actress—motion picture, 1975, for *The Great Gatsby;* Golden Globe Award nomination, best motion picture actress in a drama, 1976, for *The Day of the Locust;* Grammy Award nomination (with others), album of best original score written for a motion picture or television special, 1976, for *Nashville;* Medalla Sitges en Plata de Ley, best actress, Catalonian International Film Festival, 1977, for *Burnt Offerings;* Hermosa Beach Film Festival Award, best actress, 1998, for *Dogtown* and *Sugar: The Fall of the West;* Chicago Alt.Film Fest Acting Award, best actress, 1999, for *Fallen Arches;* Indie Supporter Award, Method Fest, 1999; Best Actress, Fantasporto Film Festival, 2005, for *Firecracker.*

CREDITS

Film Appearances:

Painted woman, *The Prime Time* (also known as *Hell Kitten*), Essanjay, 1960.
Amy Partlett, *You're a Big Boy Now,* Warner Bros., 1966.
Ellen, *Hard Contract,* Twentieth Century–Fox, 1969.
Karen, *Easy Rider,* Columbia, 1969.
Rayette Dipesto, *Five Easy Pieces,* Columbia, 1970.
Olive, *Drive, He Said,* Columbia, 1971.
Jenny Simms, *A Gunfight* (also known as *Gunfight*), Paramount, 1971.
Parm, *Born to Win* (also known as *Born to Lose* and *Addict*), United Artists, 1971.
Mary Jane Reid (The Monkey), *Portnoy's Complaint,* Warner Bros., 1972.
Sue, *Cisco Pike,* Columbia, 1972.
Elizabeth Lucy, *The Pyx* (also known as *The Hooker Cult Murders* and *La Lunule*), Cinerama, 1973.
Laura, *Little Laura and Big John,* Crown International, 1973.
Daisy, *Rhinoceros,* American Film Theatre, 1974.
Bett Jarrow, *The Outfit,* United Artists, 1974.
Myrtle Wilson, *The Great Gatsby,* Paramount, 1974.
Nancy Pryor, *Airport, 1975,* Universal, 1974.
Gloria, *Law and Disorder,* Columbia, 1974.
Faye Greener, *The Day of the Locust,* Paramount, 1975.
Connie White, *Nashville,* Paramount, 1975.
Fran, *Family Plot,* Universal, 1976.
Susan Winters, *Crime and Passion* (also known as *Ace Up My Sleeve* and *Frankensteins Spukschlob*), American International Pictures, 1976.
Marian Rolf, *Burnt Offerings,* United Artists, 1976.

Judy Drinkwater, *Capricorn One,* Warner Bros., 1978.
Clarisse, *The Rip Off* (also known as *The Squeeze, Diamond Thieves, L'ultimo colpo, The Rip–Off, Rip Off—The Diamond Connection, Gretchko, Der Diamantencoup, Controrapina,* and *The Heist*), Worldvision, 1978.
Maya, *In Praise of Older Women* (also known as *En hommage aux femmes de trente ans*), Avco–Embassy, 1979.
Kate Neville, *Killer Fish* (also known as *Deadly Treasure of the Piranha, The Naked Sun, Treasure of the Piranha, O peixe assassino,* and *Killer fish agguato sul fondo*), Associated Films, 1979.
Paula Herbert, *The Last Word* (also known as *Danny Travis*), International, 1979.
To Noumero (also known as *1922* and *The Number*), 1979.
Amy, *Miss Right* (also known as *La donna giusta*), Image Entertainment, 1980.
Emilienne D'Alencon, *Chanel Solitaire,* United Film, 1981.
Valentine Colby, *Separate Ways,* Crown, 1981.
Joanne, *Come Back to the Five and Dime, Jimmy Dean, Jimmy Dean,* Cinecom, 1982.
Mrs. Gladys Fitzpatrick, *Growing Pains* (also known as *Bad Manners*), New World, 1982.
Breathless, Orion, 1983.
Zee, *Can She Bake a Cherry Pie?,* World Wide Classics, 1983.
Mary Turner, *Killing Heat* (also known as *The Grass Is Singing* and *Graeset sjunger*), Mainline, 1984.
There's Something Wrong in Paradise, 1984.
A Stroke of Genius, 1984.
Karen, *Martin's Day,* Metro–Goldwyn–Mayer/United Artists, 1985.
Rachel Wade, *Savage Dawn,* Media, 1985.
Linda Magnusson, *Invaders from Mars,* Cannon, 1986.
Karin, *Cut and Run* (also known as *Amazonia, Amazon: Savage Adventure, Straight to Hell,* and *Inferno in Diretta*), New World, 1986.
Gloria, *Flight of the Spruce Goose* (also known as *Lot Swierkowej Gesi*), 1986.
Herself, *The Road to Freedom: L. Ron Hubbard and Friends* (short), Church of Scientology, 1986.
Laura Lawrence, *Hostage,* Noble, 1987.
Ellen Jarvis, *It's Alive III: Island of the Alive* (also known as *Island of the Alive*), Warner Bros., 1987.
Zelma Laidlaw, *Dixie Lanes* (also known as *After These Years* and *Indian Summer*), Miramax, 1988.
Mom, *The Invisible Kid,* Taurus, 1988.
Platinum Blonde, 1988.
Rita, *Night Angel* (also known as *Hellborn*), Paragon Arts, 1988.
The Legendary Life of Ernest Hemingway (also known as *Hemingway, festa e morte*), 1988.
Ruth Wilson, *Out of the Dark,* New Line Cinema, 1989.
Belle, *Homer & Eddie,* Skouras, 1989.
Tiffany Powers, *Judgement* (also known as *Hitz*), 1989.
Homeroom teacher, *Zapped Again!,* ITC Entertainment, 1990.

Sybil Lullmer, *The Children* (also known as *Meine liebe Rose*), Hemdale Home Video, 1990.

Mrs. Trowbridge, *Overexposed* (also known as *Facade*), Concorde, 1990.

Mrs. Granger, *Twisted Justice,* Seymour Borde, 1990.

Mrs. Gordon, *Mirror, Mirror,* Academy, 1990.

Fatal Encounter, 1990.

Test Positive (also known as *A Different Life*), Alltime Productions, 1991.

Dr. Julia Harcourt, *Haunting Fear,* Troma, 1991.

Ella Purdy, *Evil Spirits,* Prism Entertainment, 1991.

Sally Rich, *Club Fed,* Prism Entertainment, 1991.

Rula, *Rubin and Ed,* IRS Releasing, 1991.

Kim Martino, *Quiet Fire,* PM Home Video, 1991.

Tarot, *The Roller Blade Seven,* 1991.

Barrett, *The Killer's Edge* (also known as *Blood Money*), PM Home Video, 1991.

Auntie Lee, *Auntie Lee's Meat Pies,* Columbia/TriStar Home Video, 1991.

Karen Thompson, *Children of the Night,* Columbia/ TriStar Home Video, 1992.

Herself, *The Player,* Fine Line Features, 1992.

Tarot, *The Legend of the Rollerblade 7,* 1992.

Inspector Wilson, *Dead Girls Don't Tango,* 1992.

Blanche, *Caged Fear* (also known as *Hotel Oklahoma, Innocent Young Female,* and *Jail Force*), New Line Home Video, 1992.

Mrs. Sorrel, *Final Judgement,* Concorde, 1993.

Mrs. Elliot, *The Double O Kid,* Prism Entertainment, 1993.

Maria Vandermeer, *The Trust,* Quadrangle Films, 1993.

Carla, *Bound and Gagged: A Love Story,* Northern Arts Entertainment, 1993.

Tarot, *Return of the Roller Blade Seven,* 1993.

Michelle, *Tuesday Never Comes,* 1993.

Evelyn, *The Wacky Adventures of Dr. Boris and Nurse Shirley* (also known as *Dr. Boris and Ms. Duluth*), Rapid Film Group, 1994.

Herself, *Jonas in the Desert* (documentary), Silver Cine, 1994.

Too Bad About Jack, 1994.

Nehor, *Plan 10 from Outer Space,* Phaedra Cinema, 1995.

June Rhodes, *Children of the Corn IV: The Gathering* (also known as *Deadly Harvest*), Dimension Films, 1996.

Rose Walsh, *Cries of Silence* (also known as *Sister Island*), Showcase Entertainment, 1996.

Millicent, *Crimetime,* Trimark, 1996.

Mrs. Tender, *New York Crossing,* 1996.

Schubert, *Every Minute Is Goodbye* (also known as *Death before Sunrise* and *Devotion*), 1996.

Ro–Kell, *Dinosaur Valley Girls,* Bruder Releasing, 1996.

Bettie, *Movies Money Murder* (also known as *Breaking Up with Paul*), 1996.

Modern Rhapsody, Rainbow Films, 1997.

Mother Coer and Lady Byron, *Conceiving Ada* (also known as *Leidenschaftliche Berechnung*), Fox Lorber Associates, 1997.

Herself, *Who Is Henry Jaglom?* (documentary), First Run Features,1997.

Courtney Whitmer, *Invisible Dad,* A–pix Entertainment, 1997.

Rose Van Horn, *Dogtown* (also known as *Howling at the Moon*), 1997.

Alex, *Men,* Hillman–Williams Productions/Shonderosa Productions, 1997.

Jessica Martin, *Malaika* (also known as *Tons of Trouble*), 1997.

Light Speed, Santelmo Entertainment, 1998.

Jude, *Charades* (also known as *Felons* and *First Degree*), Fries Film Group, 1998.

Lucy Roman, *Fallen Arches,* Saraghina Film, 1998.

The mother, *Bury the Evidence,* 1998.

Downtown Darlings, 1998.

Honey Child, *I Woke Up Early the Day I Died* (also known as *Ed Wood's "I Woke Up Early the Day I Died"* and *I Awoke Early the Day I Died*), Cinequa-non Pictures, 1998.

Dental assistant, *Waiting for Dr. MacGuffin,* Vanguard Films Home Video, 1998.

Stripping for Jesus, 1998.

Mother, *The Underground Comedy Movie,* 1998.

Dr. Gabrielle Kessler, *Stir,* 1998.

Herself, *Karen Black: Actress at Work,* 1999.

Herself, *Easy Rider: Shaking the Cage* (documentary; also known as *Shaking the Cage*), Columbia TriStar Home Entertainment, 1999.

Decoupage 2000: Return of the Goddess, 1999.

Aunt Eloise, *Mascara,* Phaedra Cinema, 1999.

Sugar: The Fall of the West, 1999.

Ma, *Paradise Cove,* 1999.

Herself, *The Independent,* New City Releasing, 2000.

Mrs. Mary Harp, *Oliver Twisted,* RGH/Lions Share Pictures, 2000.

Aunt Summer, *Red Dirt,* RGH/Lion Share Pictures, 2000.

Mrs. Springle, *The Donor,* RGH/Lions Share Pictures, 2000.

Inviati speciali, 2000.

Herself, *Plotting "Family Plot"* (documentary), Universal Studios Home Video, 2001.

Bambi LeBleau, *Gypsy 83,* Small Planet Pictures, 2001.

Aunt Judy, *Hard Luck,* Film Kitchen, 2001.

Magnificent Martha, *Soulkeeper* (also known as *The Chosen Ones*), First Look Pictures Releasing, 2001.

Dirty Dick, *Teknolust,* ThinkFilm, 2002.

Mrs. Buttleman, *Buttleman,* 2002.

Mrs. Melnick, *A Light in the Darkness,* 2002.

Herself, *Fans and Freaks: The Culture of Comics and Conventions* (documentary), 2002.

Herself, *Easy Riders, Raging Bulls: How the Sex, Drugs and Rock 'N' Roll Generation Saved Hollywood* (documentary), Shout! Factory, 2003.

Mother Firefly, *House of 1000 Corpses,* Lions Gate Films, 2003.

Chantelle, *Paris,* DEJ Productions, 2003.

Dr. McDermott, *Summer Solstice,* Echelon Entertainment, 2003.

Aunt Nelly, *Curse of the Forty–Niner* (also known as *Curse of the 49er* and *Miner's Massacre*), DEJ Productions, 2003.
Marianne Brown, *America Brown*, TLA Releasing, 2004.
Sara, *Birth of Industry* (short), 2004.
Sandra/Eleanor, *Firecracker*, 7 Arts, 2004.
Herself, *Wamego: Making Movies Anywhere* (documentary short), Dikenga Films, 2004.
Molly, *Dr. Rage*, Skouras Ventura Film Partners, 2005.
Grace's mom, *My Suicidal Sweetheart*, 2005.
Hollywood Dreams, 2006.
Mrs. Leider, *Whitepaddy*, Big Six Films, 2006.
Suffering Man's Charity, 2006.

Also appeared in *Animal Behavior; A Stroke of Genius.*

Film Work; Producer:
Charades (also known as *Felons* and *First Degree*), Fries Film Group, 1998.

Television Appearances; Series:
Marcia Garroway, *The Second Hundred Years*, ABC, 1967–68.

Television Appearances; Miniseries:
Ernestine Crawford, *Mr. Horn*, CBS, 1979.
Rose Vanda, *Power*, NBC, 1980.
Herself, *Armistead Maupin's "Tales of the City"* (also known as *Tales of the City*), PBS, 1994.

Television Appearances; Movies:
Julie Aldrich/Millicent, Larrimore/Therese, and Larrimore/Amelia, *Trilogy of Terror* (also known as *Tales of Terror* and *Terrors of the Doll*), ABC, 1975.
Miriam Oliver/Sandy, *The Strange Possession of Mrs. Oliver*, NBC, 1977.
Anne, *Because He's My Friend* (also known as *Love Under Pressure*), 1978.
Officer Evelyn Carter, *Police Story: Confessions of a Lady Cop* (also known as *The Other Side of Fear*), 1979.
Helen, *Where the Ladies Go*, ABC, 1980.
Janus, *The Blue Man* (also known as *Eternal Evil*), 1985.
Mrs. Tender, *Un Angelo a New York* (also known as *New York Crossing*), 1996.
Social worker, *My Neighbor's Daughter* (also known as *Angel Blue*), Lifetime, 1998.
Jessica Martin, *Malaika*, HBO, 1999.
Magnificent Martha, *Soulkeeper*, Sci–Fi Channel, 2001.

Television Appearances; Pilots:
Jenny Honker, *Hastings Corner*, NBC, 1970.

Television Appearances; Specials:
Presenter, *The 44th Annual Academy Awards*, NBC, 1972.

Celebrity Challenge of the Sexes, CBS, 1978.
Worlds Beyond, 1986.
Performer, *The 14th Annual Circus of the Stars*, CBS, 1989.
Mrs. Trowbridge, *Overexposed*, 1990.
Miss Kuchembacker, "Ralph S. Mouse," *ABC Weekend Specials*, ABC, 1991.
The Hunger: An MTV Sneak Preview, MTV, 1997.
Alfred Hitchcock: The E! True Hollywood Story, E! Entertainment Television, 1999.
Canned Ham: Bowfinger, Comedy Central, 1999.
Saturday Night Live: 25th Anniversary Primetime Special, NBC, 1999.
The Big Show (also known as *The Big Show: Toronto International Film Festival*), CBC, 2001.
Herself, *Wanderlust* (documentary), Independent Film Channel, 2005.

Also appeared in *Full Circle Again*, Canadian television.

Television Appearances; Episodic:
Claudia Stone, "The Ransom," *The Invaders*, ABC, 1967.
Carla, "Days of Grace," *The Big Valley*, ABC, 1967.
Lorraine Chapman, "The Satellite," *The F.B.I.*, ABC, 1967.
Patricia Dunne, "The Prisoner," *The Iron Horse*, 1967.
Elaine, "License to Kill—Limit Three People," *Mannix*, 1968.
Alethea Staunton, "The Devil's Surrogate," *Judd for the Defense*, 1968.
Susan Decker, "Log 132: Producer," *Adam–12*, 1968.
Monica, "Give Till it Hurts," *The Name of the Game*, 1969.
The Tonight Show Starring Johnny Carson (also known as *The Best of Carson*), NBC, 1971, 1972, 1973, 1976.
Barbara Sanders, "Bad Connection," *Ghost Story* (also known as *Circle of Fear*), 1972.
The Dean Martin Show (also known as *The Dean Martin Comedy Hour*), NBC, 1972.
Host, *Saturday Night Live* (also known as *SNL*), NBC, 1976, 1981.
Herself, *America 2–Night*, syndicated, 1978.
Herself, *Breakaway*, BBC, 1984.
Sheila Sheinfeld, "Enter Romance," *E/R*, 1984.
Sheila Sheinfeld, "Merry Wives of Sheinfeld: Parts 1 & 2," *E/R*, 1985.
Kay Mason, "Hired Help," *The Hitchhiker*, HBO, 1985.
Dr. Sydney Dunn, "One Good Bid Deserves a Murder," *Murder, She Wrote*, CBS, 1986.
"Suffer Little Children," *Worlds Beyond*, 1986.
Sea witch, "The Little Mermaid," *Faerie Tale Theatre* (also known as *Shelley Duvall's "Faerie Tale Theatre"*), Showtime, 1987.
Carla Ray, "A Dish Best Served Cold," *In the Heat of the Night*, NBC, 1988.

Helen Jackson, "Victims of Circumstance," *Miami Vice,* 1989.

The Pat Sajak Show, CBS, 1990.

Lorraine Pitzer, "Watching the Detectives," *Moon over Miami,* ABC, 1993.

Miss Gati, "Menage a Trois," *The Hunger,* Showtime, 1997.

Doreen Jablonsky, "One Christmas, to Go," *Party of Five,* Fox, 1998.

Crystal Garcia, *Rude Awakening,* Showtime, 1998.

Evie Long, "Cycle of Violence," *Profiler,* NBC, 1998.

Crystal Garcia, "The Grateful Living," *Rude Awakening,* Showtime, 1999.

Crystal Garcia, "One Birthday at a Time," *Rude Awakening,* Showtime, 1999.

Herself, "Celine and Brandon," *Switched!,* ABC Family, 2003.

Vera Morgan, "Con–Text," *Law & Order: Criminal Intent* (also known as *Law & Order: CI*), NBC, 2003.

Patricia Sommers, "An Adventure," *Russkie v. Gororde Angelov* (also known as *A Force of One* and *Russians in the City of Angels*), 2003.

Herself, "Jack Nicholson," *Biography,* Arts and Entertainment, 2004.

Stage Appearances:

Understudy Adele McDougall, Linda Lehman, and Liz Michaelson, *Take Her, She's Mine,* Biltmore Theatre, New York City, 1961.

Zinnia, *We're Civilized,* Jan Hus Playhouse, New York City, 1962.

Olivia, *Twelfth Night,* Hecksher Theatre, New York City, 1963.

The Uncommon Denominator, Mermaid Theater, New York City, 1963.

The Playroom, Brooks Atkinson Theater, New York City, 1965–66.

Happily Never After, Eugene O'Neill Theatre, New York City, 1966.

Hilda Brady, *Keep It in the Family,* Plymouth Theatre, New York City, 1967.

Joanne, *Come Back to the Five and Dime, Jimmy Dean, Jimmy Dean,* Martin Beck Theatre, New York City, 1982.

A View of the Heart, Ars Nova Theatre, New York City, 2004.

Also appeared with the Hecscher House Company in several Shakespearean plays.

WRITINGS

Screenplays:

Movies Money Murder (also known as *Breaking Up with Paul*), 1996.

Malaika (also known as *Tons of Trouble*), 1997.

Men, Hillman–Williams Productions/Shonderosa Productions, 1997.

Going Home, 1997.

Charades (also known as *Felons* and *First Degree*), Fries Film Group, 1998.

Edna McCoy's Festival, 1999.

The Invention of Dr. Morel, 2000.

Film Scores:

Nashville, Paramount, 1975.

Can She Bake a Cherry Pie?, World Wide Classics, 1983.

Film Songs:

The Pyx (also known as *La Lunule* and *The Hooker Cult Murders*), 1973.

Television Writing; Movies:

Additional story credits, *Malaika,* HBO, 1999.

Television Episodes:

Trauma Center, 1983.

OTHER SOURCES

Periodicals:

Interview, May, 1975.

Time Out (London), January 26, 1984.

BLACKMAN, Honor 1926(?)–

PERSONAL

Born August 22, 1926 (some sources say 1927), in London, England; father, a statistician; married Bill Sankey, 1946 (divorced, 1956); married Maurice Kaufmann (an actor), 1963 (divorced, 1975); children: (second marriage) Lottie, Barnaby. *Education:* Trained for the stage at Guildhall School of Music and Drama. *Avocational Interests:* Watching soccer, reading.

Addresses: *Agent*—NSM, 85 Shorrolds Rd., London SW6 7TU United Kingdom.

Career: Actress. Appeared in television commercials for Marks & Spencer, 2001; previously worked in the British Civil Service.

Awards, Honors: Special Television Award (with others), 2000, British Academy of Film and Television Arts, for *The Avengers.*

CREDITS

Film Appearances:
(Uncredited) Emma, *Fame is the Spur,* Two Cities, 1946.
(Uncredited) *Homecoming,* Metro–Goldwyn–Mayer, 1948.
Julie Tallent, *Daughter of Darkness,* 1948.
Paula, "The Alien Corn," *Quartet,* Rank, 1949.
Joyce Pennistone, *Conspirator,* Metro–Goldwyn–Mayer, 1949.
Mary Hart, *Diamond City,* General Film Distributors, 1949.
Susie Bates, *A Boy, a Girl, and a Bike,* 1949.
Rhoda O'Donovan, *So Long at the Fair,* Gainsborough Pictures, 1950.
Meg Cuffley, *Green Grow the Rushes* (also known as *Brandy Ashore*), 1951.
Come Die My Love (also known as *Manchas de Sangre en la Luna*), Mercurio Films, 1952.
Mrs. Tyler, *The Rainbow Jacket,* Ealing, 1953.
The Yellow Robe, 1954.
Maxine Banner, *The Delavine Affair* (also known as *Murder Is News*), 1954.
Paula Grant, *Breakaway,* RKO Radio Pictures, 1955.
Jenny Pelham, *The Glass Cage* (also known as *The Glass Tomb*), Lippert Pictures, 1955.
Dead Man's Evidence, 1955.
Lynn Pearson, *Suspended Alibi* (also known as *Suspected Alibi*), 1956.
Marelle, *Diplomatic Passport,* 1956.
Sarah Hayward, *Account Rendered,* Rank, 1957.
Susie Westlake, *You Pay Your Money,* 1957
Lesley Cartland, *The Square Peg,* Rank, 1958.
Mrs. Lucas, *A Night to Remember,* Rank, 1959.
Gillian Freeman, *Danger List,* 1959.
Sister Bryan, *A Matter of Who,* Metro–Goldwyn–Mayer, 1961.
Ann Rogers, *Serena,* Butchers, 1962.
Hera, *Jason and the Argonauts* (also known as *Jason and the Golden Fleece*), Columbia, 1963.
Pussy Galore, *Goldfinger* (also known as *Ian Fleming's "Goldfinger"*), United Artists, 1964.
Norah Hauxley, *Life at the Top,* Royal International, 1965.
Lily, Baroness von Luckenberg, *The Secret of My Success,* Metro–Goldwyn–Mayer, 1965.
Quartet, Ajay Pictures, 1966.
Daphne Fields, *Moment to Moment,* Universal, 1966.
Julie Chambois, *A Twist of Sand,* United Artists, 1968.
Lady Julia Daggett, *Shalako* (also known as *Man nennt mich Shalako*), Cinerama, 1968.
Amalaswintha, *The Fight for Rome* (also known as *The Last Roman, Struggle for Rome, La guerra per Roma—prima parte, Lupta pentru Roma I,* and *Kampf um Rom I*), Studioul Cinematografic Bucuresti, 1968.
Mummy, *Lola* (also known as *Statutory Affair, London Affair,* and *Twinky*), Rank, 1969.

Mrs. Fawcett, *The Virgin and the Gypsy,* Chevron, 1970.
Katherine Whiteley, *The Last Grenade,* Cinerama, 1970.
Mrs. Morgan, *Something Big,* National General, 1971.
Helen, *Fright* (also known as *Night Legs* and *I'm Alone and I'm Scared*), British Lion, 1971.
(Uncredited) *The Three Musketeers* (also known as *Los tres mosqueteros*), Twentieth Century–Fox, 1974.
Anna Fountain, *To the Devil a Daughter* (also known as *Child of Satan* and *Die braut des Satans*), EMI, 1975.
Summer Rain, 1976.
Mrs. Boswell, *Age of Innocence* (also known as *Ragtime Summer*), 1977.
Susan Sillsby, *The Cat and the Canary,* Grenadier Films, 1978.
Ragtime, Paramount, 1981.
The Outsiders, Warner Bros., 1983.
(Archive footage) Pussy Galore in *Goldfinger, Behind the Scenes with Thunderball* (documentary), Metro–Goldwyn–Mayer/United Artists, 1995.
Herself, *Behind the Scenes with "Goldfinger"* (documentary short; also known as *The Making of "Goldfinger"*), Metro–Goldwyn–Mayer/United Artists, 1995.
Chief Inspector Shea, *Tale of the Mummy* (also known as *Russell Mulcahy's "Tale of the Mummy"* and *Talos the Mummy*), Dimension Films, 1998.
Joy Adamson, *To Walk with Lions* (also known as *Un homme parmi les lions*), 1999.
The Music of James Bond (documentary short), 2000.
Herself, *Inside "Diamonds Are Forever"* (documentary short), 2000.
Herself, *The Best of "So Graham Norton,"* 2000.
Herself, *Harry Saltzman: Showman* (documentary short), 2000.
Herself, *Avenging the Avengers* (documentary short), Kult TV, 2000.
Madeline Dubouir, *Jack Brown and the Curse of the Crown,* 2001.
Penny Husbands–Bosworth, *Bridget Jones's Diary* (also known as *Bridget Jones* and *Le journal de Bridget Jones*), Miramax, 2001.
Herself, *To the Devil ... The Death of Hammer* (documentary short), Anchor Bay Entertainment, 2002.
Madam, *Colour Me Kubrick,* 2005.

Also appeared in *Dangerous Drugs; The Recount;* and *Set a Murderer.*

Television Appearances; Series:
Iris Cope, *Probation Officer,* 1959–60.
Nicole (Dan Dailey episodes), *The Four Just Men* (also known as *Four Just Men*), ITV, 1959.
Cathy Gale, *The Avengers,* ITV, 1962–64.
Veronica Barton, *Never the Twain,* ITV, 1981.
Laura West, *The Upper Hand,* ITV, 1990.

Mother, *Revolver*, BBC, 2004.
Narrator, *Dial a Mum*, ITV, 2005.

Television Appearances; Miniseries:
Ursula Schumann, *The First Olympics: Athens 1896* (also known as *Dream One* and *The First Modern Olympics*), NBC, 1984.
Selma, *Lace*, ABC, 1984.
Doris Asterman, *Voice of the Heart*, syndicated, 1990.
Jules, Jack's secretary, *Jake and the Beanstalk: The Real Story* (also known as *Jim Henson's "Jack and the Beanstalk: The Real Story"*), CBS, 2001.

Television Appearances; Movies:
Jocelyn Cullum, *Little Red Monkey*, 1953.
Marelle, *Diplomatic Passport*, 1954.
Man of Honour, 1960.
Ghost Squad, 1961.
Top Secret, 1962.
The Explorer, 1968.
Present Laughter, 1968.
Visit from a Stranger, 1970.
Out Damned Spot, 1972.
Lilian Stanhope, *Columbo: Dagger of the Mind*, NBC, 1972.
The Winds of Change, 1977.
Rita Vandemeyer, *The Secret Adversary* (also known as *Agatha Christie's "The Secret Adversary"* and *Partners in Crime: The Secret Adversary*), BBC, 1982, PBS, 1987.
Helen Spender, *Minder on the Orient Express*, ITV, 1985.
Voice of Mrs. Medlock, *The Secret Garden*, CBS, 1994.
Margaret Smith, *The Sight*, FX Channel, 2000.

Television Appearances; Specials:
The Incredible World of James Bond, 1965.
Margaret Stevenson, *The Rebel*, 1975.
William Tell, 1986.
The World of James Bond, Fox, 1995.
Pussy Galore, *In Search of James Bond with Jonathan Ross*, 1995.
(Uncredited) Pussy Galore, *The James Bond Story* (documentary; also known as *007: The James Bond Story*), 1999.
Herself, *Blondes: Diana Dors* (documentary), BBC, 1999.
Host, *AFI's 100 Years ... 100 Passions*, CBS, 2002.
Herself, *Bond Girls Are Forever*, AMC, 2002.
Herself, *Best Bond Ever*, ITV1, 2002.
Herself, *James Bond: A BAFTA Tribute*, BBC, 2002.
Herself, *ITV 50 Greatest Shows*, ITV, 2005.

Television Appearances; Episodic:
Paula Hickson, "Set a Murderer," *The Vise* (also known as *Detective's Diary, Saber of London, The Vise: Mark Saber,* and *Uncovered*), ABC, 1954.

Helen, "Dead Man's Evidence," *The Vise* (also known as *Detective's Diary, Saber of London, The Vise: Mark Saber,* and *Uncovered*), ABC, 1955.
Kathy, "Way Home," *Douglas Fairbanks, Jr., Presents* (also known as *Rheingold Theatre*), 1956.
Elizabeth Vernon, "The Patient in Room 21," *The New Adventures of Charlie Chan* (also known as *Charlie Chan*), 1957.
Syd Lewis, "Deep in the Heart of Chelsea," *The Vise* (also known as *Detective's Diary, Saber of London, The Vise: Mark Saber,* and *Uncovered*), ABC, 1957.
Mary Allen, "The Open and Shut Case," *Boyd Q.C.*, ITV, 1957.
Sally Evans, "The Lady Doesn't Scare," *The Vise* (also known as *Detective's Diary, Saber of London, The Vise: Mark Saber,* and *Uncovered*), ABC, 1958.
Katherine Holt, "Blind Justice," *The Invisible Man* (also known as *H.G. Wells' "Invisible Man"*), CBS, 1958.
"The Sickness," *African Patrol*, syndicated, 1958.
Isobel, "A Witness to Murder," *African Patrol*, syndicated, 1959.
Maureen, "The Widow Who Wasn't," *The Third Man*, BBC, 1959.
Syd Lewis, "Deep in the Heart of Chelsea," *The Vise* (also known as *Detective's Diary, Saber of London, The Vise: Mark Saber,* and *Uncovered*), ABC, 1959.
Joan Bernard, "Colonel Rodriguez," *Danger Man*, CBS, 1960.
Sue Brooks, "The Frame," *The Pursuers*, 1961.
Sally Evans, "The Lady Doesn't Scare," *The Vise* (also known as *Detective's Diary, Saber of London, The Vise: Mark Saber,* and *Uncovered*), ABC, 1961.
Sarah Hayward, "Account Rendered," *Kraft Mystery Theater*, NBC, 1961.
Rauch, "Destination Buenos Aires," *Top Secret*, 1961.
Diana, "The Men from Yesterday," *Top Secret*, 1961.
Pauline Stone, "The Arrow of God," *The Saint*, ITV, 1962.
Laura, "The Princess," *Ghost Squad* (also known as *G.S. 5*), ITV, 1963.
Jane Marriott/Jill Marriott, "The Wide Open Door," *ABC Stage 67*, ABC, 1967.
"Honor Blackman," *This Is Your Life*, ITV, 1969.
Bethany Cromwell, "An Agent for the Plaintiff," *The Name of the Game*, NBC, 1969.
Mary Answorth, "Boney in Venom House," *Boney*, Seven Network, 1972.
Marion Nicholls, "Love & Marriage," *Robin's Nest*, ITV, 1978.
"Patrick Macnee," *This Is Your Life*, ITV, 1984.
Professor Lasky, "Terror of the Vervoids," *Doctor Who*, BBC, 1986.
Laura West, *The Upper Hand*, Central Independent TV, 1990.
"Honor Blackman," *This Is Your Life*, ITV, 1993.
The Good Sex Guide, 1994.
So Graham Norton, Channel 4, 1998.
Rachel Knott, "A Helping Hand," *Doctors*, BBC, 2000.
Transeet Van Eyre, "Lesbian Vampire Lovers of Lust," *Dr. Terrible's House of Horrible*, BBC, 2001.

Mrs. Wellington, "Agent Provocateur," *The American Embassy,* Fox, 2002.
Isobel Hewitt, "A Talent for Life," *Midsomer Murders,* ITV and Arts and Entertainment, 2003.
Mrs. Lyons, "Snakes and Ladders," *The Royal,* ITV, 2003.
Mrs. Lyons, "Wishing and Hoping," *The Royal,* ITV, 2003.
Mrs. Lyons, "One of Those Days," *The Royal,* ITV, 2003.
Friday Night with Jonathan Ross, BBC, 2003.
The Terry and Gaby Show, Channel 5, 2004.
GMTV, ITV, 2004.
Kelly, 2004.
Rula Romanoff, *Coronation Street,* ITV and CBC, 2004.
This Morning (also known as *This Morning with Richard and Judy*), IV, 2004, 2005.
The Paul O'Grady Show, ITV, 2005.
Kitty Campbell, *New Tricks,* BBC, 2005.

Also appeared in *The Witness,* CBS.

Stage Appearances:
(Stage debut) Monica Cartwright, *The Gleam,* Globe Theatre, London, 1946.
Mary Dering, *The Blind Goddess,* Apollo Theatre, London, 1947.
Lorraine McKay, *The Fifth Season,* Cambridge Theatre, London, 1954.
Susy Henderson, *Wait Until Dark,* Strand Theatre, London, 1966.
Doris and Laura Jesson, *Mr. and Mrs.,* Palace Theatre, London, 1968.
Barbara Love, *Who Killed Santa Claus?,* Theatre Royal, Windsor, England, 1969, then Piccadilly Theatre, London, 1970.
Margaret, *The Exorcism,* Comedy Theatre, London, 1975.
Mrs. Millamant, *The Way of the World,* Arnaud Theatre, Guildford, England, 1975.
Paula Cramer, *Motive,* Arnaud Theatre, 1976.
Mrs. Millamant, *The Way of the World,* Northcott Theatre, Exeter, England, 1979.
Desiree, *A Little Night Music,* Northcott Theatre, 1979.
Mademoiselle Colombe, Bridewell, London, 2000.

Major Tours:
Mrs. Markham, *Move Over Mrs. Markham,* Australian and North American cities, 1972–73.
Hester, *The Deep Blue Sea,* British cities, 1977.
Desiree, *A Little Night Music,* British cities, 1979.
Mrs. Higgins, *My Fair Lady,* British cities, 2005.

Also toured British cities in *School for Scandal* and the solo show *Dishonourable Ladies.*

RECORDINGS

Albums:
Recorded *Everything I've Got.*

Music Videos:
Appeared in Sneaker Pimps' "Loretta Young Silks," 2003.

WRITINGS

Nonfiction:
Honor Blackman's Book of Self–Defence, 1965.

BLADES, Ruben 1948–

PERSONAL

Full name, Ruben Dario Blades, Jr.; July 16, 1948, in Panama City, Panama; immigrated to the United States, 1974; son of Ruben Dario, Sr. (a bongo player, later a police detective) and Anoland Benita (an actress, singer, and piano teacher; maiden name, Bellido de Luna) Blades; married Lisa A. Lebenzon (an actress), December 13, 1986 (divorced). *Education:* Instituto Nacional, Panama, B.A., 1966; University of Panama, license in law and political science, 1973; Harvard University, LLM., 1985; studied acting with George Loros. *Religion:* Roman Catholic. *Avocational Interests:* Baseball, soccer, boxing, dominoes, reading, collecting toy soldiers, old books, and old comic books.

Addresses: *Agent*—United Talent Agency, 9560 Wilshire Blvd., Beverly Hills, CA 90212. *Manager*—MBST Entertainment, 345 N. Maple Dr., Suite 200, Beverly Hills, CA 90210.

Career: Actor, writer, singer, producer, composer, lyricist, and politician. Banco Nacional, Panama City, Panama, member of legal staff, 1973–74; Fania Records, New York City, recording artist, 1973–83; Elektra/Asylum Records, New York City, recording artist, 1984–89. With his band Seis del Solar (Six from the Tenement), has toured U.S. cities, Central America, Europe, and South America; Blades Productions, Inc., founder; songwriter and performer with Pete Rodriguez, with the Willie Colon Orchestra, and as a solo artist; composer of music for films; performs benefit concerts for various causes, including aid for the homeless. Founder of "Papa Egoro" (Mother Earth Party), political party, Panama, 1992; ran for president of Panama in 1994; named Minister of Tourism in Panama, 2004.

Member: American Society of Composers, Authors, and Publishers (ASCAP), National Academy of Recording Arts and Sciences, Screen Actors Guild, American Federation of Television and Radio Artists, Harvard Law

School Association (vice president, 1984–85), Colegio Nacional de Abogados (Panamanian law association), Amnesty International.

Awards, Honors: Gold Records, 1977–84; Grammy Award nomination, best Latin album recording, 1982, for *Canciones del Solar de los Aburridos;* Grammy Award nomination, best tropical Latin performance album, New York Award and top ten albums of the year citations, *Time,* 1984, all for *Buscando America;* named honorary citizen, City of Chicago, 1984; Grammy Award, best tropical Latin performance, and New York Award and top ten albums of the year citations, *Time,* 1985, all for *Escenas;* New York Music Awards, best ethnic/international act and best Latin act, *New York Post,* 1986; Grammy Award nomination, best tropical Latin performance album, 1987, for *Agua de Luna;* Grammy Award nomination, best tropical Latin performance album, 1990, for *Antecedente;* American Cinema Editors Award, best acting in a movie or miniseries, for *Dead Man Out;* Emmy Award nomination, outstanding supporting actor in a miniseries or special, 1991, for *The Josephine Baker Story;* Emmy Award nomination, outstanding lead actor in a miniseries or special, 1992, for *Crazy from the Heart;* Grammy Award, best Latin pop performance, 2000, for *Tiempos;* American Latino Media Arts Award (ALMA), outstanding actor in a new series, 2001, for *Gideon's Crossing;* Grammy Award, best world music album, 2002, for *Mundo.*

CREDITS

Film Appearances:
Andy "Kid" Clave, *The Last Fight,* Best, 1982.
When the Mountains Tremble, 1983.
Beat Street, Vestron, 1984.
Rudy Valez, *Crossover Dreams,* Miramax, 1985.
Himself, *The Return of Ruben Blades* (documentary), Mug–Shot Productions, 1987.
Louis, *Critical Condition,* Paramount, 1987.
Carl Jimenez, *Fatal Beauty,* Metro–Goldwyn–Mayer, 1987.
Sheriff Bernabe Montoya, *The Milagro Beanfield War,* Universal, 1988.
Carlos Barrios, *Disorganized Crime* (also known as *Disorganised Crime*), Buena Vista, 1989.
Doctor, *Homeboy,* Twentieth Century–Fox, 1989.
Petey, *Mo' Better Blues,* Universal, 1990.
The Heart of the Deal, 1990.
Mickey Nice/Michael Weisskopf, *The Two Jakes,* Paramount, 1990.
C. W., *The Lemon Sisters,* Miramax, 1990.
Danny Archuletta, *Predator 2,* Twentieth Century–Fox, 1990.
Marlon, *The Super,* Twentieth Century–Fox, 1991.
(Uncredited) Angie's father, *Life with Mikey* (also known as *Give Me a Break*), Buena Vista, 1993.

Bartender, *A Million to Juan* (also known as *A Million to One*), Turner Home Entertainment, 1994.
Lieutenant Hector Martinez, *Color of Night,* Buena Vista, 1994.
Himself, *Yo soy, del son a la salsa* (documentary; also known as *From Son to Salsa*), 1997.
Sam Zaragosa, *Scorpion Spring,* New Line Home Video, 1997.
Jim, *Chinese Box,* Trimark, 1997.
Edwin Diaz, *The Devil's Own,* Columbia, 1997.
Diego Rivera, *Cradle Will Rock,* Buena Vista, 1999.
Don Hector Rocha y Villarael, *All the Pretty Horses,* Sony Pictures Entertainment, 2000.
Miguel, *Assassination Tango,* Metro–Goldwyn–Mayer, 2002.
FBI Agent Jorge, *Once Upon a Time in Mexico,* Sony Pictures Entertainment, 2003.
Silvio Ayala, *Imagining Argentina,* Arenas Entertainment, 2003.
Ernesto Bejarano, *Spin,* Freestyle Releasing, 2003.
Sergio, Carla's father, *Secuestro express,* Miramax, 2005.
The Hunters and the Hunted: The Making of "Predator 2" (documentary short), Twentieth Century–Fox Home Entertainment, 2005.

Also appeared in *Waiting for Salazar.*

Film Producer:
Buscando guayabas, 2000.

Television Appearances; Series:
Gideon's Crossing, ABC, 2000–2001.

Television Appearances; Movies:
Ben, *Dead Man Out* (also known as *Dead Man Walking*), HBO, 1989.
Perrone, *One Man's War,* HBO, 1991.
Ernesto Ontiveros, *Crazy from the Heart,* 1991.
Pepito Abatino, *The Josephine Baker Story,* 1991.
Pastor Beruman, *Miracle on I–880* (also known as *Miracle on Interstate 880*), NBC, 1992.
Somos un solo pueblo, 1995.
Cruz, *The Maldonado Miracle,* Showtime, 2003.

Television Appearances; Specials:
Himself, *Routes of Rhythm,* 1984.
The 28th Annual Grammy Awards, CBS, 1986.
AIDS: Changing the Rules, PBS, 1987.
The 29th Annual Grammy Awards, CBS, 1987.
A Latino Session, Cinemax, 1989.
The 31st Annual Grammy Awards, CBS, 1989.
The Best of Cinemax Sessions, Cinemax, 1990.
Routes of Rhythm with Harry Belafonte, PBS, 1990.
Count Giuseppe Pepito Abatino, *The Josephine Baker Story,* HBO, 1991.
Ernesto Ontiveros, *Crazy from the Heart,* TNT, 1991.

The 4th Annual Desi Awards, syndicated, 1992.
Let the Good Times Roll, PBS, 1993.
An American Reunion: New Beginnings, Renewed Hope, HBO, 1993.
In a New Light '93, ABC, 1993.
Concert of the Americas, PBS, 1994.
The Opening Ceremonies of the 1995 Special Olympics World Games, NBC, 1995.
Presenter, *The 37th Annual Grammy Awards,* CBS, 1995.
The 1995 NCLR Bravo Awards, Fox, 1995.
Somos un solo pueblo, 1995.
Presenter, *The 42nd Annual Grammy Awards,* 2000.
Presenter, *Sports Illustrated's Sportsman of the Year 2000,* CBS, 2000.
Soul Train Christmas Starfest, syndicated, 2000.
Presenter, *Lifetime Presents Disney's American Teacher Awards,* Lifetime, 2000.
Himself, *The Palladium: Where Mambo Was King,* 2002.
Encuentro (documentary), 2002.
Himself, *En mi pais,* 2004.

Television Appearances; Pilots:
Luis Juega, *Fall Road,* NBC, 1996.

Television Appearances; Episodic:
Late Night with David Letterman, NBC, 1985.
Sesame Street, PBS, 1986.
Rockambole, 1989.
Pero esto que es, 1989, 1990.
Storytime, PBS, 1994.
Conrad Lozano, "El mundo gira," *The X–Files* (also known as *The X Files*), Fox, 1997.
Sessions at West 54th, PBS, 1997.
Himself, *Lo + plus,* 2002.
Martin, "Verguenza," *Resurrection Blvd.,* Showtime, 2002.
Himself, "Lo latino," *La tierra de las 1000 musicas,* 2005.

Stage Appearances:
2nd Annual Hollywood Salsa and Latin Jazz Festival, Hollywood Bowl, Hollywood, CA, 1995.
Salvador, *The Capeman,* Marquis Theatre, New York City, 1998.

RECORDINGS

Albums:
(With Pete Rodriguez) *De Panama a Nueva York,* c. 1969.
(With the Willie Colon Orchestra) *Metiendo mano,* Fania, 1976.
(With the Willie Colon Orchestra) *Siembra,* Fania, 1977.
Bohemio y poeta, Fania, 1979.

Maestra Vida: Primera parte, Fania, 1980.
Maestra Vida: Segunda parte, Fania, 1980.
(With the Willie Colon Combo) *Canciones del solar de los aburridos,* Fania, 1982.
Buscando America (title means "Searching for America"), Elektra, 1984.
Escenas (title means "Scenes"), Elektra/Asylum, 1985.
Agua de luna (title means "Moon Water"), Elektra/Asylum, 1987.
Nothing but the Truth, Elektra/Asylum, 1988.
Ruben Blades Live, Elektra/Asylum, 1989.
Antecedente, Elektra, 1990.
Y son del solar (also known as *Ruben Blades y son del solar ... Live!*), Elektra, 1990.
Caminando, Sony–CBS, 1991.
Amor y control, Sony–CBS, 1992.
El que la hace la paga, Fania, 1992.
Best of Ruben Blades, Sony, 1992.
Ruben Blades with Strings, Fania, 1992.
Poeta Latina, Charly Latin, 1993.
Tras la tormenta (also known as *After the Storm*), Sony Tropical, 1995.
La rosa de los vientos (title means "The Rose of the Winds"), Sony International, 1996.
Greatest Hits, WEA International, 1996.
Tiempos, Sony Discos, 1999.
From Panama, Fania, 2000.
Sembra y Otros Favoritos Salsa Para Siempre, Musica Latina, 2001.
Salsa Caliente du Nu York, Import, 2002.
Mundo, Sony, 2002.

Recorded first album with Los Salvajes del Ritmo (meaning the Rhythm Savages), 1966; also has recorded with Elvis Costello, Lou Reed, and Sting.

Taped Readings:
Joseph and His Brothers, Rabbit Ears, 1993.

WRITINGS

Screenplays:
(With Leon Ichaso and Manuel Arce) *Crossover Dreams,* Miramax, 1985.

Film Scores:
When Mountains Tremble, 1983.
(With others) *Crossover Dreams,* Miramax, 1985.
The Return of Ruben Blades (documentary), Mug Shot Productions, 1987.
Por los caminos verdes, 1987.
The Story of Fausta (also known as *Out of My Way* and *Romance de Empregada*), Barreto/Embrafilme, 1988.
Q & A, TriStar, 1990.
A Design for a Life (short), 2001.

Empire, Universal, 2002.
Vivir pedaleando (short), 2003.

Film Songs:
The Last Fight, 1982.
Pedro Navaja, 1984.
El Hijo de Pedro Navaja, 1986.
(Theme song) *Behind the Iran–Contra Affair,* 1988.
Oliver and Company, 1988.
Chances Are, TriStar, 1989.
Do the Right Thing, 1989.
True Believer, Sony, 1989.
Gladiator, Sony, 1992.
Dance with Me, Sony, 1998.
(H) Historias cotidianas (documentary), 2001.
Empire, Universal, 2002.

Television Scores; Specials:
Gryphon, PBS, 1988.

Stage Music:
The Balcony, American Repertory Theatre, Cambridge, MA, 1986.

Other:
Contributor of articles to periodicals, including *La estrella de Panama,* the *New York Times,* and the *Village Voice.*

OTHER SOURCES

Books:
Contemporary Hispanic Biography, Vol. 3, Gale Group, 2003.
Contemporary Musicians, Vol. 2, Gale, 1990.
Marton, Betty A., *Ruben Blades,* Chelsea House, 1991.

Periodicals:
Back Stage, February 27, 1998, pp. 5–7.
Billboard, June 17, 2000, p. 68.
Chicago Tribune, October 4, 1985.
Harper's Bazaar, March, 1994, pp. 326–332.
Inter Press Service, May 26, 1998.
Interview, April, 1986, pp. 210–214.
Los Angeles Magazine, September, 1995, pp. 145–147.
Los Angeles Times, October 2, 1985.
Newsweek, September 9, 1985.
New York, August 19, 1985.
New York Times, August 18, 1985; June 21, 1987; March 17, 1994.
People Weekly, May 9, 1994, pp. 181–183.
Rolling Stone, April 23, 1987, pp. 36–40, 158.
Time, July 11, 1988; January 29, 1990, pp. 70–73.
Village Voice, March 5, 1985.
Washington Post, October 11, 1985.

BLAIR, Linda 1959–

PERSONAL

Full name, Linda Denise Blair; born January 22, 1959, in St. Louis, MO; daughter of James Frederick (an executive recruiter) and Elinore (a real estate agent; maiden name, Leitch) Blair. *Avocational Interests:* Animals, training and showing horses.

Career: Actress and producer. Falcon–Wolf Productions, affiliate. Worked as a model and appeared in several commercials and public service announcements; Linda Blair's Wild West Collection (clothing line), creator; designer of stage clothes for rock and roll musicians; performer in equestrian jumping events with her horse Northern Bound as part of a touring show, c. 1990–91. Actively involved with animal rights and charitable organizations, including Variety (a children's charity), Feed the Children, the Dolphin Research Center, Last Chance for Animals, and associations for the elderly, AIDS, cancer, diabetes, and the environment.

Member: Screen Actors Guild, American Federation of Television and Radio Artists, American Horse Shows Association.

Awards, Honors: Golden Globe Award, best supporting actress—motion picture, People's Choice Award, Academy Award nomination, best supporting actress, and Golden Globe Award nomination, most promising female newcomer, all 1974, for *The Exorcist;* South American "favorite actress" award, 1977; Saturn Award nomination, best actress in a horror film, Academy of Science Fiction, Fantasy, and Horror Films, 1978, for *Exorcist II: The Heretic;* Alcoholics Anonymous Award, for *Sarah T.—Portrait of a Teenage Alcoholic;* multiple "favorite actress" awards, *Bravo* magazine; named one of the 100 greatest kid stars, VH1, 2005; Blair's character Regan Teresa MacNeil was named one of the greatest screen heroes and villains, American Film Institute.

CREDITS

Film Appearances:
Sara Aldridge, *The Way We Live Now,* United Artists, 1969.
Barby, *The Sporting Club,* Avco–Embassy, 1970.
Regan Teresa MacNeil, *The Exorcist* (also known as *William Peter Blatty's "The Exorcist"*), Warner Bros., 1973, also released as *The Exorcist: The Version You Haven't Seen Yet* and *The Exorcist: The Version You've Never Seen.*

Janice Abbott, *Airport '75,* Universal, 1974.

Regan Teresa MacNeil, *Exorcist II: The Heretic,* Warner Bros., 1977.

Hank Bradford, *Wild Horse Hank,* Film Consortium of Canada, 1979.

Terry Barkley, *Roller Boogie,* United Artists, 1979.

Marti, *Hell Night,* Compass International Pictures, 1981.

Jenny Bellows, *Ruckus* (also known as *Big Ruckus in a Small Town, The Loner,* and *Ruckus in Madoc Country*), New World Pictures, 1982.

Carol Henderson, *Chained Heat* (also known as *Das Frauenlager*), Jensen Farley, 1983.

(In archive footage) Regan Teresa MacNeil, *Terror in the Aisles,* Universal, 1984.

Brenda, *Savage Streets,* Motion Picture Marketing, 1985.

Christine Carlson, *Red Heat* (also known as *Red Heat— Unschuld hinter Gittern*), Vestron Pictures, 1985.

Daly, *Savage Island,* Empire Entertainment, 1985.

Officer Sue Perman, *Night Patrol,* New World Pictures, 1985.

Carla, *Nightforce,* Vestron Pictures, 1987.

Doris, *SFX Retaliator* (also known as *The Heroin Deal*), 1987.

Lisa, *Grotesque,* Concorde Pictures, 1988.

Sara, *Silent Assassins,* Moviestore Entertainment, 1988.

Vickie Adderly, *Up Your Alley,* Curb/Esquire Films, 1988.

Jane Brooks, *Witchery* (also known as *Ghosthouse 2, Witchcraft, La casa 4,* and *Malefiche presenze*), FilmExport Group, 1989.

Mary Hampton, *The Chilling* (also known as *Gamma 693*), Hemdale Home Video, 1989.

Aunt Millie's Will, 1989.

Annette "Nettie" Ridgeway, *Bail Out* (also known as *W. B., Blue and the Bean* and *Wings of Freedom*), Vestron Video, 1990.

Dr. Sally Tyler, *Moving Target* (also known as *Bersaglio sull'autostrada*), Laguna Productions, 1990.

Miss Mitchell, *Zapped Again!,* Nelson Entertainment, 1990.

Nancy Aglet, *Repossessed,* New Line Cinema, 1990.

Sophie Stevens, *Bedroom Eyes II,* Vidmark, 1990.

Maggie Healey, *Dead Sleep,* Village Roadshow Production, 1991.

Leonie Stevens, *Fatal Bond,* Sony Pictures Releasing, 1992.

Phone (short film), Cowboy Films, 1992.

Evie Barnes, *Bad Blood* (also known as *A Woman Obsessed* and *A Woman's Obsession*), Platinum Pictures, 1993.

Amelia Reynolds, *Sorceress* (also known as *Temptress II*), Triboro Entertainment, 1994.

Maggie, *Skins* (also known as *Gang Boys*), Sunset Films International, 1995.

Lieutenant Cody Johnson, *Prey of the Jaguar,* Jfw Productions, 1996.

(Uncredited) Obnoxious reporter, *Scream* (also known as *Scary Movie*), Miramax, 1996.

Title role, *Marina* (short film), 1997.

Herself, *Lisa Picard Is Famous* (also known as *Famous*), First Look Pictures Releasing, 2001.

Herself, *Queen of the Whole Wide World,* 2001.

(In archive footage) *A Decade under the Influence* (documentary), IFC Films, 2003.

Herself, *UnConventional* (documentary), Revolution Earth Productions, 2004.

Brenda, *Hitters Anonymous,* Killer Parrot Films/VTA Florida, 2005.

Guest star, *Diva Dog: Pit Bull on Wheels* (short documentary), 2005.

Barbara, *All Is Normal,* Flexible Frame Productions, 2006.

Some sources cite an appearance in *He's Having a Baby,* c. 2001.

Film Work; Associate Producer:

Grotesque, Concorde Pictures, 1988.

Skins (also known as *Gang Boys*), Sunset Films International, 1995.

Television Appearances; Series:

Allyn Jatte, *Hidden Faces,* NBC, 1968–69.

Walking after Midnight, beginning 1999.

Joni, *S Club 7* (also known as *L.A. 7* and *S Club 7 in L.A.*), Fox Family Channel (later known as ABC Family Channel) and BBC, c. 2000.

Host, *The Scariest Places on Earth,* Fox Family Channel (later known as ABC Family Channel), c. 2000–2002.

A Journey through Aesthetic Realms, i (Independent Television, formerly PAX TV), beginning 2005.

Television Appearances; Miniseries:

Herself, *I Love the '70s,* VH1, 2003.

(In archive footage) Regan Teresa MacNeil, *The 100 Greatest Scary Moments* (also known as *The 100 Greatest Scary Moments from Film, TV, Advertising and Pop*), Channel 4 (England), 2004.

(In archive footage) Regan Teresa MacNeil, *The 100 Scariest Movie Moments,* Bravo, 2004.

Herself, *100 Greatest Kid Stars,* VH1, 2005.

Television Appearances; Movies:

Christine "Chris" Parker, *Born Innocent,* NBC, 1974.

Doris Mae Withers, *Sweet Hostage,* ABC, 1975.

Sarah Travis, *Sarah T.—Portrait of a Teenage Alcoholic,* NBC, 1975.

Chana Vilnofsky, *Victory at Entebbe* (also known as *Terror in the Aisles*), ABC, 1976.

Rachel Bryant, *Stranger in Our House* (also known as *Summer of Fear*), NBC, 1978.

Hannah Hawkes, *Perry Mason: The Case of the Heartbroken Bride,* NBC, 1992.

Jane Mader, *Calendar Girl, Cop, Killer? The Bambi Bembenek Story* (also known as *The Heart of the Lie*), ABC, 1992.

Professor Claudia Whyle, *Double Blast,* HBO, c. 1994.

Shelly Stoker, *Monster Makers,* The Hallmark Channel, 2003.

Television Appearances; as Herself; Specials:

Celebrity Challenge of the Sexes, CBS, 1977.

Circus of the Stars #7, CBS, 1982.

Celebrity Daredevils, ABC, 1983.

Circus of the Stars #8, CBS, 1983.

The Wildest West Show of the Stars, CBS, 1986.

America Picks the All–Time Favorite Movies (also known as *America's Favorite Movies*), ABC, 1988.

Fifteenth Annual Circus of the Stars, CBS, 1990.

The Secrets of Dick Smith, 1991.

The Golden Globe's 50th Anniversary Celebration, NBC, 1994.

The Fear of God: The Making of "The Exorcist," BBC, 1998.

AFI's 100 Years, 100 Thrills: America's Most Heart–Pounding Movies, CBS, 2001.

History's Mysteries: Exorcising the Devil, History Channel, 2001.

The 70s: Bell–Bottoms and Boogie Shoes, The Learning Channel, 2001.

(Uncredited) *Hollywood Rocks the Movies: The 1970s,* 2002.

TV's Most Censored Moments, USA Network and Trio, 2002.

The Perfect Scary Movie, 2005.

Television Appearances; Awards Presentations:

Presenter, *The 46th Annual Academy Awards,* NBC, 1974.

Presenter, *The 48th Annual Academy Awards,* ABC, 1976.

The Horror Hall of Fame, syndicated, 1990.

Presenter, *The Ninth Annual Genesis Awards,* The Discovery Channel, 1995.

Presenter, *Thirteenth Annual Genesis Awards,* Animal Planet, 1999.

(In archive footage) Regan Teresa MacNeil, *The 71st Annual Academy Awards,* ABC, 1999.

Presenter, *The 14th Annual Genesis Awards,* Animal Planet, 2000.

Presenter, *The 2001 Genesis Awards,* Animal Planet, 2001.

16th Annual Genesis Awards, Animal Planet, 2002.

Television Appearances; Episodic:

The Mike Douglas Show, syndicated, 1974.

Muffy, "Cold Feet," *The Love Boat,* ABC, 1982.

Sara Jean Rawlins, "Shadow Games," *Fantasy Island,* ABC, 1982.

Jane Pascal, "Murder Takes the Bus," *Murder, She Wrote,* CBS, 1985.

Contestant, "Halloween Week," *Win, Lose or Draw,* NBC, 1988.

Lia, "La Strega," *Monsters,* syndicated, 1989.

"Former Child Stars," *This Evening,* syndicated, 1989.

The New Hollywood Squares, syndicated, 1989.

Jenny Larson, "Jenny's Chance," *MacGyver,* ABC, 1990.

Guest, *The Howard Stern Show,* 1990.

Ida Mae, "Magnificent Seven," *Married ... with Children* (also known as *Not the Cosbys*), Fox, 1992.

Robin's Hoods, syndicated, 1994.

Teddy Ray Thompson, "Self Defense," *Renegade,* USA Network and syndicated, 1996.

Voice of Selene, "Witchy Woman," *Extreme Ghostbusters* (animated), syndicated, 1997.

Guest, "Rick James," *Behind the Music* (also known as *Behind the Music: Rick James, BtM,* and *VH1's "Behind the Music"*), VH1, 1998.

Rebecca Royce, "All Hallow's Eve," *Psi Factor: Chronicles of the Paranormal* (also known as *Psi Factor*), CanWest Global Television and syndicated, 1998.

Voice of Alexandra Springer, "S.C.A.L.E.," *Godzilla: The Series* (animated), Fox, 1999.

Herself, *Linda Blair: The E! True Hollywood Story,* E! Entertainment Television, 1999.

Ms. Hooper, "Mason–Dixon Memory," *Chicken Soup for the Soul,* PAX TV, 2000.

Herself, "Rick Springfield: Behind the Image," *Biography* (also known as *A & E Biography: Rick Springfield*), Arts and Entertainment, 2001.

Herself, *Intimate Portrait: Linda Blair,* Lifetime, 2001.

Herself, *Intimate Portrait: Tippi Hedren,* Lifetime, 2001.

Panelist, *The Conspiracy Zone* (also known as *TNN's "Conspiracy Zone with Kevin Nealon"*), The National Network, 2002.

Herself, "Linda Blair," *Biography* (also known as *A & E Biography: Linda Blair*), Arts and Entertainment, 2003.

Guest, *Hollywood Squares* (also known as *H2* and *H2: Hollywood Squares*), syndicated, multiple episodes in 2003.

Guest, *ALF's Hit Talk Show,* TV Land, 2004.

Herself, *Curse of the Exorcist: The E! True Hollywood Story,* E! Entertainment Television, 2004.

Herself, *Scream Queens: The E! True Hollywood Story,* E! Entertainment Television, 2004.

Herself, "Child Stars II: Growing Up Hollywood," *Biography* (also known as *A & E Biography*), Arts and Entertainment, 2005.

Guest, *The O'Reilly Factor,* Fox News Channel, 2005.

Guest, *Street Smarts,* 2005.

Appeared as a guest, *The Test,* FX Channel; and in *The Uncle Floyd Show,* syndicated, PBS, and other networks.

Television Appearances; Pilots:

Rock Comedy, syndicated, 1982.

On Top All Over of the World, syndicated, 1985.

Host, *The Scariest Places on Earth,* Fox Family Channel (later known as ABC Family Channel), c. 2000.

Television Work; Series:
Creative consultant, *The Scariest Places on Earth,* Fox Family Channel (later known as ABC Family Channel), c. 2000–2002.

Stage Appearances:
It Had to Be You, Canadian production, 1995.
Betty Rizzo, *Grease* (musical), Eugene O'Neill Theatre, New York City, 1997.

Appeared in *Run for Your Wife,* San Francisco, CA; and *Women behind Bars,* Los Angeles.

RECORDINGS

Videos:
Hostess, *How to Get Revenge,* 1989.
Herself, *Hollywood on Horses,* 1989.
Heather, *The Blair Bitch Project Starring Linda Blair* (also known as *The Blair Bitch Project*), 1999.

WRITINGS

Nonfiction:
(With Sunny J. Harris) *Going Vegan!,* Sunny Harris and Associates, 2001.

OTHER SOURCES

Periodicals:
Draculina, February, 1998, pp. 2–6, 55.
Entertainment Weekly, March 21, 1997, p. 92.
Oui, October, 1982, pp. 21–36, 93.
People Weekly, November 29, 1993, p. 81; December 14, 1998, p. 12.
TV Guide, June 16, 2001, pp. 41–45.

BLANC, JB 1969–
(J. B. Blanc)

PERSONAL

Born February 13, 1969, in Paris, France.

Career: Actor.

CREDITS

Film Appearances:
Undergraduate (uncredited), *Shadowlands,* Warner Bros., 1993.
Police captain (uncredited), *102 Dalmations,* Buena Vista, 2000.
Luigi Vampa, *The Count of Monte Cristo* (also known as *Alexandre Dumas' "The Count of Monte Cristo"*), Buena Vista, 2002.
Paul Holtzman, *Moonlight Serenade,* Talestic, 2006.
Leon, *Tristan + Isolde,* Twentieth Century–Fox, 2006.
The Porter, *Garfield's A Tale of Two Kitties,* Twentieth Century–Fox, 2006.

Television Appearances; Series:
DeeDee, *I My Me! Strawberry Eggs,* 2001.
Father Enrico Maxwell, *Herushingu* (also known as *Hellsing*), 2002.
(As J. B. Blanc) "Mr. Joker" Joe Carpenter, *R.O.D. the TV,* G4TechTV, 2003.
(As J. B. Blanc) Rowe Rickenbacker, waiter, *Licensed by Royalty,* Pioneer, 2003.

Television Appearances; Episodic:
Fraser, "Lust for Life," *Dr. Vegas,* CBS, 2004.
Alex Stratis, "Stratis Fear," *NYPD Blue,* ABC, 2005.

Television Appearances; Miniseries:
Mizeno, *Texhnolyze,* Fuji TV, 2003.

Television Director; Series:
Licensed by Royalty, 2003.

RECORDINGS

Video Games:
Voice of Lucian, *Radiata Stories,* Square Enix, 2005.
Voice of Kerim Bey, *James Bond 007: "From Russia with Love,"* EA Games, 2005.

BLISS, Boti 1975–
(Boti Ann Bliss)

PERSONAL

Born October 23, 1975, in NY.

Addresses: *Agent*—Paradigm, 260 North Crescent Dr., North Bldg., Beverly Hills, CA 90210. *Manager*—MBST Entertainment, 345 N. Maple Dr., Suite 200, Beverly Hills, CA 90210.

Career: Actress. Appeared in television commercials, including SBC Long Distance, 2004, Cooper Tires, 2004, and Delight coffee creamer, 2005.

CREDITS

Film Appearances:
Moira, *Broken and Bleeding,* 1998.
(As Boti Ann Bliss) Robin, *Warlock III: The End of Innocence,* Trimark Pictures, 1999.
(As Boti Ann Bliss) June, *Dumped,* Global Asylum, 2000.
(As Boti Ann Bliss) Zoe, *Panic* (also known as *Air Panic*), Nu–Image, 2001.
(As Boti Ann Bliss) Cashier, *Bubble Boy,* Buena Vista, 2001.
(As Boti Ann Bliss) Lee, *Ted Bundy* (also known as *Bundy*), First Look Pictures Releasing, 2002.
Dominique the Hooker, *National Lampoon Presents "Dorm Daze"* (also known as *Dorm Daze* and *National Lampoon's "Dorm Daze"*), Metro–Goldwyn–Mayer, 2003.
Gretyl, *The Mostly Unfabulous Social Life of Ethan Green,* Regent Releasing, 2005.
Sonny, *Stage Kiss,* 2006.
Waitress, *I'm Reed Fish,* 2006.

Television Appearances; Series:
(As Boti Ann Bliss) Maxine Valera, *CSI: Miami,* CBS, 2003–2006.

Television Appearances; Movies:
Julie's friend, *Roadracers* (also known as *Rebel Highway*), Showtime, 1994.

Television Appearances; Episodic:
(As Boti Ann Bliss) Kyra, "All of Me," *Cybill,* CBS, 1997.
Tina, "'Tis a Pity She's a Whore," *Cracker* (also known as *Fitz*), ABC, 1997.
Tyleen, *Michael Hayes,* CBS, 1997.
(As Boti Ann Bliss) Lorraine Robbins, "Rampage," *Nash Bridges* (also known as *Bridges*), CBS, 1997.
(As Boti Ann Bliss) Amy Duke, "Runaway," *Pacific Blue,* USA Network, 1997.
(As Boti Ann Bliss) Nora, "Working Girls," *The Magnificent Seven,* CBS, 1998.
(As Boti Ann Bliss) Theresa, "Smooth Sailing," *The Love Boat: The Next Wave,* UPN, 1998.
(As Boti Ann Bliss) Sandi, "Parole," *The Pretender,* NBC, 1998.
Kim number one, *The Secret Lives of Men,* ABC, 1998.
(As Boti Ann Bliss) Angela Martin, "Resurrection," *Nash Bridges* (also known as *Bridges*), CBS, 1999.
(As Boti Ann Bliss) Angela Martin, "Pump Action," *Nash Bridges* (also known as *Bridges*), CBS, 1999.
(As Boti Ann Bliss) "Hostile Witness," *Pacific Blue,* USA Network, 1999.

(As Boti Ann Bliss) Waitress, "Subject: Coelacanth This!," *FreakyLinks,* Fox, 2000.
(As Boti Ann Bliss) Abbey, "Once Upon a Time," *Charmed,* The WB, 2000.
(As Boti Ann Bliss) Abbey, "Sight Unseen," *Charmed,* The WB, 2000.
Lexie, *Providence,* NBC, 2002.

RECORDINGS

Video Games:
Voice of Maxine Valera, *CSI: Miami,* Ubi Soft Entertainment, 2004.

BLUHM, Brady 1983–

PERSONAL

Born July 6, 1983, in California.

Career: Actor.

CREDITS

Film Appearances:
Billy, *Dumb & Dumber* (also known as *Dumb Happens* and *Dumb and Dumber*), New Line Cinema, 1994.
Jason Van Arsdale, *The Crazysitter* (also known as *Two Much Trouble*), 1995.
Justin Rogers, *Alone in the Woods,* 1996.
A Thin Line Between Love and Hate (also known as *A Thin Line Between Love & Hate*), New Line Cinema, 1996.
Voice of Nello, *Gekijoban Furandaasu no inu* (also known as *Flanders no inu*), Shoc, 1997.
Voice of Christopher Robin, *Pooh's Grand Adventure: The Search for Christopher Robin* (animated; video; also known as *Winnie the Pooh's Most Grand Adventure*), Buena Vista Home Video, 1997.
Voice of Christopher Robin, *Winnie the Pooh: Seasons of Giving* (animated; video; also known as *Disney's "Winnie the Pooh: Seasons of Giving"*), Buena Vista Home Video, 1999.
Elder Johansen, *Alma and King Noah's Court* (video), Lightstone, 2005.

Television Appearances; Movies;:
Eli, *Burning Bridges,* 1990.
Police chief, *Opposites Attract,* 1990.
Marco, *In Search of Dr. Seuss,* 1994.
Voice of Christopher Robin, *Winnie the Pooh: A Valentine for You* (animated), 1999.

Television Appearances; Episodic:

Bobby Iger, *Doogie Howser, M.D.,* ABC, 1989–90.

Boy, "The Emperor's New Nose," *Designing Women,* CBS, 1991.

Bobby, "Chris and Larry Switch Lives," *Get a Life,* Fox, 1991.

Boy, "Confessions," *Life Goes On,* ABC, 1992.

Matt, "R.N. on the Rebound," *Empty Nest,* NBC, 1992.

Little boy, "It's Not Easy Being Green," *Empty Nest,* NBC, 1992.

Roseanne, ABC, 1992–93.

Henry, *Raven,* CBS, 1992–93.

The Ben Stiller Show, Fox, 1993.

Archie, "Family Matters," *Walker, Texas Ranger,* CBS, 1993.

Jackson Harris, "Western Exposure," *Baywatch,* syndicated, 1994.

Timmy, "Brown in Toyland," *Murphy Brown,* CBS, 1994.

Latika, "Time and Again," *Star Trek: Voyager,* UPN, 1995.

Walter, "Prom Misses, Prom Misses," *Clueless,* UPN, 1999.

Alan, "Bully for You," *CSI: Crime Scene Investigation* (also known as *C.S.I.* and *CSI: Weekends*), CBS, 2001.

Television Appearances; Specials:

Voice of Christopher Robin, *A Winnie the Pooh Thanksgiving,* ABC, 1998.

BOLAM, James 1938–

PERSONAL

Born June 16, 1938, in Sunderland, Tyne–and–Wear, England; son of Robert Alfred and Marion Alice (maiden name, Drury) Bolam; married Susan Jameson (an actress). *Education:* Attended school in Sunderland and Derby, England. *Avocational Interests:* Horses.

Career: Actor. Appeared in television commercials for Young's Chip Shop, 2003, 2004, 2005.

Awards, Honors: Television Award nomination, best actor, British Academy of Film and Television Arts, 1977, 1978, both for *When the Boat Comes In.*

CREDITS

Film Appearances:

Michael, *The Kitchen,* 1961.

Mike, *The Loneliness of the Long Distance Runner* (also known as *Rebel with a Cause*), British Lion, 1962.

Jeff, *A Kind of Loving,* Governor, 1962.

(Uncredited) Midshipman, *Damn the Defiant!* (also known as *H.M.S. Defiant* and *HMS Defiant*), Columbia, 1962.

Bill Hanson, *Murder Most Foul* (also known as *Agatha Christie's "Murder Most Foul"*), Metro–Goldwyn–Mayer, 1964.

Mr. Jones, *Half a Sixpence,* Paramount, 1968.

Albert, *Otley,* Columbia, 1969.

Jack Davies, *Crucible of Terror* (also known as *Unholy Terror*), Glendale, 1971.

Joey, *Straight on til Morning* (also known as *Dressed for Death, The Victim,* and *Til Dawn Do Us Part*), Hammer Films, 1972.

Attenborough and doctor, *O Lucky Man!,* Warner Bros., 1973.

Colin Shaw, *In Celebration,* AFT Distributing, 1975.

Terry Collier, *The Likely Lads,* EMI Films, 1976.

Richard Lewis, *The Unorganized Manager, Part One: Damnation* (documentary short), 1977.

Richard Lewis, *The Unorganized Manager, Part Two: Salvation* (documentary short), 1977.

Richard Lewis, *The Unorganized Manager, Part Three: Lamentations* (documentary short), 1977.

Richard Lewis, *The Unorganized Manager, Part Four: Revelations* (documentary short), 1977.

Voice of the Tod, *The Plague Dogs,* Nepenthe Productions, 1982.

Al–Mas' Ala Al–Kubra (also known as *Clash of Loyalties*), 1983.

Merlin, *Seaview Knights,* Stranger Than Fiction, 1994.

Wacky, *Clockwork Mice,* Metrodome Films, 1995.

Mr. Peters, *Stella Does Tricks,* Strand Releasing, 1997.

The Barber, 1997.

Mr. Savage, *The End of the Affair,* 1999.

Fitch, *It Was an Accident,* Pathe, 2000.

Denzil Holles, *To Kill a King,* HanWay Films, 2003.

Also appeared in *The Great Question.*

Television Appearances; Series:

Terry Collier, *The Likely Lads,* BBC, 1965–69.

Inheritance, Granada, 1967.

Terry Collier, *Whatever Happened to the Likely Lads?,* BBC, 1973.

Jack Ford, *When the Boat Comes In,* BBC, 1975–77.

Roy Figgis, *Only When I Laugh,* Yorkshire Television, 1979–83.

Nesbitt Gunn, *Room at the Bottom,* Yorkshire Television, 1986.

Trevor Chaplin, *The Beiderbecke Tapes,* Yorkshire Television, 1987.

Trevor Chaplin, *The Beiderbecke Connection,* Yorkshire Television, 1988.

Title role, *Andy Capp,* Thames Television, 1988.

Bill, *Second Thoughts,* London Weekend Television, 1991–94.

Voice, *A History of Britain,* BBC and History Channel, 2000.

Graham True, *Close & True,* ITV, 2000.

Sydney Street, *Pay and Display,* ITV, 2000.

Dr. Arthur Gilder, *Born and Bred,* BBC and PBS, 2002–2004.

Jack Halford, *New Tricks,* BBC, 2004.

Television Appearances; Miniseries:

Trevor Chaplin, *The Beiderbecke Affair,* Yorkshire Television, 1984.

Nat Oliver, *Have Your Cake and Eat It,* 1997.

Clive Peacock, *The Missing Postman,* BBC, 1997.

Narrator, *Football Diaries* (documentary), BBC, 2004.

Mr. Crump, *He Knew He Was Right,* BBC and PBS, 2004.

Television Appearances; Movies:

Frank Lambert, *The Four Seasons of Rosie Carr,* BBC, 1964.

Helmut Kranze, *The Stalker's Apprentice,* 1997.

Dr. Studjinsky, *The Island on Bird Street* (also known as *Oen I fugledgaden* and *Die Insel in der Vogelstrasse*), Showtime, 1998.

Inspector Moss, *Dirty Tricks,* 2000.

Dr. Harold Shipman, *Shipman,* ITV, 2002.

Father Leonard Tibbings, *Dalziel and Pascoe: Sins of the Father,* BBC, 2002.

Detective Superintendent Jack Halford, *New Tricks,* BBC, 2003.

Television Appearances; Specials:

Roland Maule, *Present Laughter* (also known as *A Choice of Coward No. 1: Present Laughter*), Granada, 1964.

Leslie Gaze, *Footprints in the Jungle* (also known as *W. Somerset Maugham: "Footprints in the Jungle"*), BBC, 1970.

Mark Omney, *The Limbo Connection* (also known as *Armchair Thriller: The Limbo Connection*), Thames and PBS, 1978.

Touchstone, *As You Like It* (also known as *BBC Television Shakespeare: As You Like It* and *The Complete Dramatic Works of William Shakespeare: "As You Like It"*), BBC, 1978, then 1979.

Porter, *Macbeth* (also known as *BBC Television Shakespeare: Macbeth* and *The Complete Dramatic Works of William Shakespeare: Macbeth*), BBC, 1982.

Arthur Frode, *The Maze,* PBS, 1985.

Ted Whitehead, *Eleven Men Against Eleven,* Channel 4, 1995.

Victoria Wood with All the Trimmings, BBC, 2000.

Television Appearances; Episodic:

Jake Justice, "This Stuff's Thicker Than Water," *The Odd Man,* Granada, 1963.

Tom Potter, "Supper in the Morning," *Z Cars,* BBC, 1963.

Jacob Bateson, "The Daughter–in–Law," *Cluff* (also known as *Clough*), BBC, 1964.

"The Sufferings of Peter Obiznov," *Thirty–Minute Theatre,* BBC, 1967.

McHenry, "One, Two, Sky's Blue," *Boy Meets Girl,* BBC, 1969.

Alan Grove, "I Always Wanted a Swimming Pool," *Public Eye,* ITV, 1971.

Roberts, "The Case of the Dixon Torpedo," *The Rivals of Sherlock Holmes,* 1971.

Wossname, "Dreaming of Three," *Budgie,* LWT, 1972.

Wossname, "And the Lord Taketh Away," *Budgie,* LWT, 1972.

Max Toller, "See No Evil," *The Protectors,* ITV, 1972.

"Making the Play," *Play for Today,* BBC1, 1973.

"The Maze," *Shades of Darkness,* PBS, 1984.

Himself, *Aspel & Company,* ITV, 1992.

Ronald Pringle, "Death of a Stranger," *Midsomer Murders,* ITV and Arts and Entertainment, 1999.

Ronnie, *Bedtime,* BBC1, 2002.

Billy, "The Last Will and Testament of Billy Two–Sheds," *The Afternoon Play,* BBC, 2006.

Stage Appearances:

Michael, *The Kitchen,* Royal Court Theatre, London, 1959.

Lord Mayor and Smith, *The Happy Haven,* Royal Court Theatre, 1960.

Vakov, *Platonov,* Royal Court Theatre, 1960.

Michael, *The Kitchen,* Royal Court Theatre, 1961.

Starveling, *A Midsummer Night's Dream,* Royal Court Theatre, 1961.

The Wakefield Mystery Cycle, Mermaid Theatre, London, 1961.

Tom, *The Knack ... and How to Get It* (also known as *The Knack*), Royal Court Theatre, 1962.

Tom Midway, *Semi–Detached,* Saville Theatre, London, 1962.

Attendant, *Oedipus Rex* (also known as *Oedipus the King*), Mermaid Theatre, 1965.

Mercury, *Four Thousand Brass Halfpennies,* Mermaid Theatre, 1965.

Private Meek, *Too True to Be Good,* Strand Theatre, then Garrick Theatre, both London, 1965.

Evans, *Events While Guarding the Bofors Gun,* Hampstead Theatre Club, London, 1966.

Frank More, *How's the World Treating You?,* Music Box Theatre, New York City, 1966.

Frank, *White Lies,* Lyric Theatre, London, 1968.

Brindsley Miller, *Black Comedy,* Lyric Theatre, 1968.

Colin Shaw, *In Celebration,* Royal Court Theatre, 1969.

Bamforth, *The Long and the Short and the Tall,* Belgrade Theatre, Coventry, England, 1971.

Robespierre, *The Silence of Saint–Just,* Gardner Theatre, Brighton, England, 1971.

Trevor Hollingshead, *Veterans,* Royal Court Theatre, 1972.

The Vicar of Soho, Gardner Theatre, 1972.

Title role, *Macbeth,* Young Vic Theatre, London, 1975.

Dave, *Treats,* Royal Court Theatre, 1976.

John Terry, *Who Killed "Agatha" Christie?,* Ambassadors' Theatre, London, 1978.

Title role, *King Lear,* Young Vic Theatre, 1981.

Run for Your Life, Criterion Theatre, London, 1983.

Who's Afraid of Virginia Woolf?, Birmingham, England, 1989.

Victory, Chichester, England, 1989.

Jeffrey Bernard Is Unwell, Apollo Theatre, London, 1990.

Also appeared in *Arms and the Man,* Cambridge, England.

Major Tours:

Face, *The Alchemist,* Cambridge Theatre Company, British cities, 1970.

Trepliov, *The Sea Gull* (also known as *The Seagull*), Cambridge Theatre Company, British cities, 1970.

Ben Butley (title role), *Butley,* British cities, 1973.

Leonard, *Time and Time Again,* British cities, 1974.

Arms and the Man, British cities, 1980.

BON JOVI, Jon 1962–

PERSONAL

Original name, John Francis Bongiovi, Jr.; born March 2, 1962, in Perth Amboy, NJ; son of John (a hairdresser) and Carol (a florist; maiden name, Sharkey) Bongiovi; brother of Anthony M. Bongiovi (a music video director); married Dorothea Hurley, April 29, 1989; children: Stephanie Rose, Jesse James Louis, Jacob Hurley, Romeo Jon. *Education:* Studied acting with Harold Guskin. *Avocational Interests:* Watching movies, driving cars, working out, and football.

Addresses: *Agent*—Creative Artists Agency, 9830 Wilshire Blvd., Beverly Hills, CA 90212. *Publicist*—Don Klores Communications, 386 Park Ave. South, 10th Floor, New York, NY 10016.

Career: Musician, composer, and actor. Founder, 1983, and leader, 1983–88, 1992—, of Bon Jovi (rock music band); performed in Europe, U.S.S.R., South America, Australia, New Zealand, and Hong Kong with Bon Jovi, 1988–89; leader of earlier bands, including Atlantic City Expressway, the Rest, and the Wild Ones; performed with numerous artists, including Alice Cooper, Cinderella, Ratt, Cher, Aldo Nova, and Chris Ledoux; appeared in television commercials for the Red Cross, 2001, the AFL (arena football league) on NBC, 2004, and Duracell batteries, 2004. Philadelphia Soul (an arena football league team), majority owner, 2004—; previously worked at a series of odd jobs after high school. Involved with the American Red Cross and the Special Olympics; involved with environmental causes and performed in Rainforest Benefit Concert, 1995.

Awards, Honors: American Music Award (with Bon Jovi), pop/rock band, duo or group, 1987; People's Choice Award (with Bon Jovi), favorite rock group, 1988; Michael Jackson Video Vanguard Award, MTV, 1991; American Music Award, best pop/rock song, 1990, Golden Globe Award, best original song for a motion picture, 1991, Academy Award nomination, best music for a film, 1991, Grammy Award nomination, best song written specifically for a motion picture or for television, National Academy of Recording Arts and Sciences, 1991, American Society of Composers, Authors, and Publishers Award, most performed songs from motion picture, 1991, all for "Blaze of Glory," in *Young Guns II*; Grammy Award nomination (with Bon Jovi), best music video—long form, 1997, for *Bon Jovi: Live from London;* honorary Doctorate of Humanities, Monmouth University, 2001; Award of Merit, American Music Awards, 2004.

CREDITS

Film Appearances:

Himself, *The Return of Bruno,* Hudson Hawk Films, 1988.

(Uncredited) Pit inmate, *Young Guns II* (also known as *Young Guns II: Blaze of Glory*), Twentieth Century–Fox, 1990.

The painter, *Moonlight and Valentino,* Gramercy Pictures, 1995.

Robin Grange, *The Leading Man,* J&M Entertainment, 1996.

Jon, *Destination Anywhere,* Blue Goose/Mercury Records, 1997.

Kevin, *Little City,* Miramax, 1998.

Michael, *No Looking Back* (also known as *Long Time, Nothing New*), Gramercy Pictures, 1998.

Danny, *Homegrown,* Columbia/TriStar, 1998.

Lieutenant Emmett, *U–571,* Universal, 2000.

Ricky McKinney, *Pay It Forward,* Warner Bros., 2000.

Jancy Meadows, *Row Your Boat,* Gullane Pictures, 2000.

Derek Bliss, *Vampires: Los Muertos* (also known as *John Carpenter's "Vampires: Los Muertos"*), Screen Gems, 2002.

(Uncredited) Himself, *Fahrenheit 9/11,* Lions Gate Films, 2004.

Rich Walker, *Cry_Wolf,* Rogue Pictures, 2005.

Frank Hopper, *Pucked* (also known as *National Lampoon's "Pucked"* and *National Lampoon's "The Trouble with Frank"*), National Lampoon Productions, 2006.

Television Appearances; Series:
Victor Morrison, *Ally McBeal,* Fox, 2002.

Television Appearances; Miniseries:
Retrosexual: The 80's, VH1, 2004.

Television Appearances; Specials:
Himself, *Free to Be ... a Family,* ABC, 1988.
(With band, Bon Jovi) *Moscow Music Peace Festival,* 1989.
Moscow Music Peace Festival Rockumentary (documentary), MTV, 1989.
(With band, Bon Jovi) Performer, *Especial Nochevieja 1989,* 1990.
Victory and Valor: A Special Olympics All–Star Celebration, ABC, 1991.
A Very Special Christmas II, MTV, 1992.
Rolling Stone 25: The MTV Special, MTV, 1992.
American Bandstand's Teen Idols, NBC, 1994.
The Concert for the Rock and Roll Hall of Fame, HBO, 1995.
Songs and Visions (also known as *Carlsberg Concert '97*), Fox, 1997.
A Gala for the President at Ford's Theatre, ABC, 1997.
MDA Jerry Lewis Telethon, syndicated, 1997.
Gianni Versace: The E! True Hollywood Story, E! Entertainment Television, 1997.
National Lottery, British television, 1997.
Barbara Walters Presents 6 to Watch, ABC, 1998.
Pavarotti and Friends for the Children of Liberia, BBC and PBS, 1998.
A Very Special Christmas from Washington, D.C., TNT, 1998.
Hollywood Salutes Arnold Schwarzenegger: An American Cinematheque Tribute, TNT, 1998.
NetAid, VH1, 1999.
100 Greatest Songs of Rock & Roll, VH1, 2000.
Rankin File: Voyeurism (documentary), VH1, 2000.
Greatest TV Moments: Sesame Street Music A–Z, Noggin, 2000.
Greatest Rock and Roll Moments: 2000 (documentary), VH1, 2000.
All–Star Winter Celebration: The Nobel Peace Concert, Fox Family, 2000.
A Very Special Christmas from Washington, D.C., TNT, 2000.
VH1 Presents: Bon Jovi–One Last Wild Night, 2001.
Performer, *America: A Tribute to Heroes,* 2001.
Performer, *America the Beautiful,* 2001.
(With band, Bon Jovi) Performer, *The Concert for New York,* VH1, 2001.
VH1 News Special: Listening to America, VH1, 2001.
MTV20: Live and Almost Legal, MTV and MTV2, 2001.
Macy's 4th of July Fireworks Spectacular, NBC, 2001.
Jon Bon Jovi (documentary), Bravo, 2001.
Bon Jovi Crush Tour, Fox Family, 2001.
Elvis Lives, NBC, 2002.
The 2002 Olympic Winter Games, NBC, 2002.

The Stars' First Time ... On Entertainment Tonight with Mary Hart, CBS, 2003.
(Uncredited) Himself, *Saturday Night Live: The Best of Chris Kattan,* NBC, 2003.
Command the Band: Bon Jovi, VH1, 2004.
New Year's Rockin' Eve, ABC, 2005.
(With band, Bon Jovie) Performer, *Live 8: A Worldwide Concert Event Presented by Nokia,* ABC, 2005.

Television Appearances; Awards Presentations:
The American Music Awards, ABC, 1988.
The 1989 MTV Video Music Awards, MTV, 1989.
The 63rd Annual Academy Awards, 1991.
The 33rd Annual Grammy Awards, 1991.
Presenter, *The American Music Awards,* 1991.
The 1991 MTV Video Music Awards, MTV, 1991.
The American Music Awards 20th Anniversary Special, ABC, 1993.
Presenter, *The 50th Annual Golden Globe Awards,* TBS, 1993.
Performer, *The 1995 World Music Awards,* ABC, 1994.
The 1994 MTV Movie Awards, MTV, 1994.
The 1995 MTV Video Music Awards, MTV, 1995.
Host and performer, *The 1997 World Music Awards,* ABC, 1997.
The 1997 MTV Europe Music Awards, MTV, 1997.
My VH1 Music Awards, VH1, 2000.
The 1st Annual Laureus Sports Awards, TNT, 2000.
Presenter, *The 2001 MTV Video Music Awards,* MTV, 2001.
Presenter, *My VH1 Music Awards '01,* VH1, 2001.
MTV Europe Music Awards 2002 (also known as *MTV Europe Music Awards 2002 Barcelona*), MTV, 2002.
(With band, Bon Jovi) Performer, *VH1 Big in 2002 Awards,* VH1, 2002.
(With band, Bon Jovi) Post–game performer, *Super Bowl XXXVII,* ABC, 2003.
The 32nd Annual American Music Awards, ABC, 2004.
(With band, Bon Jovi) Performer, *The 2005 World Music Awards,* ABC, 2005.
(With band, Bon Jovi) *Top of the Pops* (also known as *All New Top of the Pops* and *TOTP*), BBC, 1986, 1987, 1988, 1993, 1994, 1995, 2002.

Television Appearances; Episodic:
(With band, Bon Jovi) *MTV Rewind,* MTV, 1989.
The Howard Stern Show, syndicated, 1992.
The Late Show, ABC [Australian Broadcast Corp.], 1993.
(With band, Bon Jovi) Musical guest, *Saturday Night Live* (also known as *SNL*), NBC, 1993, 1995, 2001.
Howard Stern, E! Entertainment Television, 1994, 1997.
Storytellers, VH1, 1996.
TFI Friday (also known as *Thank Four It's Friday*), Channel 4, 1997, 2000.
The Rosie O'Donnell Show, syndicated, 1997, 1998, 2000.

Late Night with Conan O'Brien, NBC, 1997, 2002.
Seth, "Games People Play," *Sex and the City,* HBO, 1998.
Himself, "Tell Me It Was Just a Dream," *Unsolved Mysteries,* CBS, 1998.
Larry King Live, CNN, 2000.
Mundo VIP, 2000.
Himself, *Lo + plus,* 2000.
Himself, *Rove Live,* Ten Network, 2001.
Rock Across America, VH1, 2001.
The Tonight Show with Jay Leno, NBC, 2002.
(With band, Bon Jovi) *Mad TV,* Fox, 2002.
(With band, Bon Jovi) *CD:UK,* 2002.
Himself, *Operacion triunfo* (also known as *O.T.*), 2002.
Himself, *Wetten, dass ... ?* (also known as *Wetten, dass ... ? aus Dusseldorf*), 2002.
NY Graham Norton, Channel 4, 2004.
Pulse, Fox, 2004.
The Oprah Winfrey Show (also known as *Oprah*), syndicated, 2005.
RTL Comedy Nacht, 2005.
AFL owner, "Centennial," *Las Vegas,* NBC, 2005.
"Welcome to Wherever You Are," *The West Wing,* NBC, 2006.

Also appeared as guest, *The Uncle Floyd Show.*

RECORDINGS

Albums (with Bon Jovi):
Bon Jovi, PolyGram, 1984.
7800 Fahrenheit, Mercury/PolyGram, 1985.
Slippery When Wet, Mercury/PolyGram, 1986.
Bon Jovi Live, Mercury/PolyGram, 1987.
New Jersey, Mercury/PolyGram, 1988.
Keep the Faith, Mercury/PolyGram, 1992.
Cross Road, Mercury/PolyGram, 1994.
These Days, Mercury/PolyGram, 1995.
Bon Jovi, 1999.
Crush, Mercury, 2000.
One Wild Night: Live 1985-2001, Island, 2001.
Bounce, Island, 2002.
Distance, 2003.
This Left Feels Right, Island, 2003.
100,000,000 Bon Jovi Fans Can't Be Wrong, 2004.
Have a Nice Day, Island, 2005.
Live from the Have a Nice Day Tour, The Island Def Jam Music Group, 2006.

Albums (as a solo artist):
Blaze of Glory, Mercury/PolyGram, 1990.
Destination Anywhere, Mercury/PolyGram, 1997.
The Power Station Years: 1980–1983, Power Station Records, 1997.
Power Station Years, Vol. 2, Dealmakers, 2000.
The Power Station Years: The Unreleased Recordings, Masq, 2001.

Other Albums:
(As John Bongiovi) Appeared on *Christmas in the Stars.*

Singles:
"Blaze of Glory," Polygram, 1990.
"Please Come Home for Christmas," *A Very Special Christmas II,* 1995.
"Hey God," Mercury, 1995.
"Midnight in Chelsea, Part 1," Alex, 1997.

Videos:
You Give Love a Bad Name, 1986.
Breakout, 1986.
Bon Jovi: Slippery When Wet, the Videos, 1987.
Livin' on a Prayer, 1988.
Bon Jovi: New Jersey, the Videos, 1989.
Bon Jovi: Access All Areas—A Rock & Roll Odyssey, Mercury, 1990.
Ozzy Osbourne: Don't Blame Me (documentary), Sony Music Entertainment, 1991.
Turn Up the Volume 1, 1991.
Bon Jovi: Keep the Faith—An Evening with Bon Jovi, PolyGram Video, 1993.
Keep the Faith Videos, Polygram Video, 1994.
Cross Road, 1994.
Bon Jovi: Live from London, Polygram Video, 1995.
It's Only Rock 'n' Roll (documentary), 2000.
Bon Jovi: The Crush Tour, Polygram Video, 2000.
Slippery When Wet, Glass, 2003.
This Left Feels Right Live, Island, 2004.
Himself, *Late Night with Conan O'Brien: The Best of Triumph the Insult Comic Dog* (also known as *The Best of Triumph the Insult Comic Dog*), Lions Gate Films Home Entertainment, 2004.
100,000,000 Bon Jovi Fans Can't Be Wrong (short), 2004.
It's My Life, Universal International, 2005.

WRITINGS

Film Songs:
"Raise Your Hands," *Spaceballs,* Metro–Goldwyn–Mayer/United Artists, 1987.
"Blaze of Glory" and "Billy Get Your Gun," *Young Guns II* (also known as *Young Guns II: Blaze of Glory*), Twentieth Century–Fox, 1990.
"Wanted Dead or Alive," *Harley Davidson and the Marlboro Man,* Metro–Goldwyn–Mayer/Pathe, 1991.
"Mister Big Time," *Armageddon,* 1998.
"Real Life," *EDtv,* 1999.

Screenplay Stories:
One Wild Night, 2004.

OTHER SOURCES

Periodicals:

Cosmopolitan, June, 1997, p. 168.
Entertainment Weekly, September 23, 2005, p. 90.
Interview, July, 1995, p. 57.
New York, April 10, 1995, pp. 65–68.
Parade, November 2, 1997, pp. 10–11.
People Weekly, May 6, 1996, p. 97; July 14, 1997, p. 20; February 16, 1998, p. 130; November 25, 2002, p. 114.
Premiere, September, 1997, pp. 20–21.
Sports Illustrated, August 18, 2003, p. 34.
Vanity Fair, October, 1995, p. 218.

BORGNINE, Ernest 1917–
   (Ermes Effron Borgnino)

PERSONAL

Original name, Ermes Effron Borgnino; born January 24, 1917, in Hamden, CT; son of Charles B. and Anna (maiden name, Bosselli) Borgnino; married Rhoda Kemins, 1948 (divorced, 1959); married Katy Jurado (an actress), 1959 (divorced, 1963); married Ethel Merman (an actress and singer), June 1964 (divorced, July, 1964); married Donna Rancourt, 1965 (divorced, 1972); married Tova Traesnaes (a cosmetics entrepreneur), 1972; children: (first marriage) Nancee, (fourth marriage) Sharon, Christofer. *Education:* Studied acting at the Randall School of Dramatic Art, Hartford, CT. *Avocational Interests:* Playing golf.

Addresses: *Manager*—Bensky Entertainment, 15030 Ventura Blvd., Suite 343, Sherman Oaks, CA 91403.

Career: Actor. Barter Theatre, Abingdon, VA, member of repertory company, 1946–50; performed as the Grand Clown for the Great Circus Parade, Milwaukee, WI, beginning 1970s; appeared in television commercials for Pantheon Internet Kiosks, 2004. *Military service:* U.S. Navy, gunner's mate first class on destroyers, 1935–45.

Member: Masons (Order of the Grand Cross; 33rd degree).

Awards, Honors: Academy Award, National Board of Review Award, New York Film Critics Circle Award, best actor, Cannes Festival Award, best actor, Film Award, best foreign actor, British Academy of Film and Television, 1955, and Golden Globe Award, best motion picture actor—drama, 1956, all for *Marty;* Prize, Locarno International Film Festival, best actor, 1959, for *The Rabbit Trap;* Emmy Award nomination, outstanding continued performance by an actor in a series—lead, 1963, for *McHale's Navy;* Emmy Award nomination, outstanding supporting actor, 1980, for *All Quiet on the Western Front;* Golden Boot Award, Motion Picture and Television Fund, 1985; Independent Spirit Award nomination, best supporting male, Independent Features Project, 1989, for *Spike of Bensonhurst;* National Cowboy and Western Heritage Museum, inductee, 1996; King Vidor Memorial Award, San Luis Obispo International Film Festival, 1997; Daytime Emmy Award nomination, outstanding performer in an animated program, 1999, for *All Dogs Go to Heaven: The Series;* named honorary U.S. Navy Chief Petty Officer, 2004; honorary mayor, Universal City Studios; star on the Hollywood Walk of Fame.

CREDITS

Stage Appearances:
Nelson, *Mrs. McThing,* American National Theatre and Academy Theatre, New York City, 1952.

Also appeared in *Harvey,* American National Theatre and Academy Theatre.

Film Appearances:
Hu Chang, *China Corsair,* Columbia, 1951.
Hammert/Joe Castro, *The Mob* (also known as *Remember That Face*), Columbia, 1951.
Bill Street, *The Whistle at Eaton Falls* (also known as *Richer Than the Earth* and *Whistle at Eaton Falls*), Columbia, 1951.
Sergeant "Fatso" Judson, *From Here to Eternity,* Columbia, 1953.
Bull Slager, *The Stranger Wore a Gun,* Columbia, 1953.
Bill Rachin, *The Bounty Hunter* (also known as *Bounty Hunter*), Warner Bros., 1954.
Strabo, *Demetrius and the Gladiators,* Twentieth Century–Fox, 1954.
Bart Lonergan, *Johnny Guitar,* Republic, 1954.
Donnegan, *Vera Cruz,* United Artists, 1954.
Coley Trimble, *Bad Day at Black Rock,* Metro–Goldwyn–Mayer, 1955.
Mike Radin, *The Last Command* (also known as *Last Command* and *San Antonio de Bexar*), Republic, 1955.
Marty Pilletti, *Marty,* United Artists, 1955.
Morgan, *Run for Cover* (also known as *Colorado*), Paramount, 1955.
Bernie Browne, *The Square Jungle* (also known as *Square Jungle*), Universal, 1955.
Stadt, Amish farmer, *Violent Saturday,* Twentieth Century–Fox, 1955.
Lew Brown, *The Best Things in Life Are Free,* Twentieth Century–Fox, 1956.

Tom Hurley, *The Catered Affair* (also known as *Catered Affair* and *Wedding Breakfast*), Metro–Goldwyn–Mayer, 1956.

Shep Horgan, *Jubal,* Columbia, 1956.

Bernie Goldsmith, *Three Brave Men,* Twentieth Century–Fox, 1957.

John McBain, *The Badlanders* (also known as *Badlanders*), Metro–Goldwyn–Mayer, 1958.

Lieutenant Archer Sloan, *Torpedo Run,* Metro–Goldwyn–Mayer, 1958.

King Ragnar, *The Vikings,* United Artists, 1958.

Eddie Colt, *The Rabbit Trap* (also known as *Rabbit Trap*), United Artists, 1959.

Boris Mitrov, *Man on a String* (also known as *Confessions of a Counterspy* and *Ten Years of a Counterspy*), Columbia, 1960.

Lieutenant Joseph Petrosino, *Pay or Die,* Allied Artists, 1960.

Pete Stratton, *Go Naked in the World,* Metro–Goldwyn–Mayer, 1961.

Peppino Navarra, *Il Re di Poggioreale* (also known as *Black City*), 1961.

Pickpocket, *The Last Judgement* (also known as *Il giudizio universale* and *Le jugement dernier*), 1961.

Sante Carbone, *I briganti italiani* (also known as *Seduction of the South, Les Guerilleros,* and *The Italian Brigades*), 1961.

Roo, *Season of Passion* (also known as *Summer of the Seventeenth Doll* and *Summer of the 17th Doll*), United Artists, 1961.

Lucius, *Barabbas* (also known as *Barabba*), Columbia, 1962.

Lieutenant Commander Quinton McHale, *McHale's Navy,* Universal, 1964.

Trucker Cobb, *Flight of the Phoenix* (also known as *The Flight of the Phoenix*), Twentieth Century–Fox, 1965.

Barney Yale, *The Oscar,* Embassy, 1966.

Sergeant Otto Hansbach, *Chuka* (also known as *Chuka: The Gunfighter*), Paramount, 1967.

General Sam Worden, *The Dirty Dozen,* Metro–Goldwyn–Mayer, 1967.

Boris Vaslov, *Ice Station Zebra,* Filmways/Metro–Goldwyn–Mayer, 1968.

Barney Sheehan, *The Legend of Lylah Clare* (also known as *Legend of Lylah Clare*), Metro–Goldwyn–Mayer, 1968.

Bert Clinger, *The Split,* Metro–Goldwyn–Mayer, 1968.

(Uncredited) Himself, *The Man Who Makes the Difference* (documentary short), Metro–Goldwyn–Mayer, 1968.

Don Pedro Sandoval, *Vengeance Is Mine* (also known as *Quei disperati che puzzano di sudore et di morte, A Bullet for Sandoval, Desperate Men, Those Desperate Men Who Smell of Dirt,* and *Los Desperados*), Atlantida, 1969.

Dutch Engstrom, *The Wild Bunch,* Warner Bros., 1969.

Fat Cat, *The Adventurers,* Paramount, 1970.

Sheriff Harve, *Suppose They Gave a War and Nobody Came?* (also known as *War Games*), Cinerama, 1970.

Bill Green, *Bunny O'Hare,* American International Pictures, 1971.

Emmett Clemens, *Hannie Caulder,* Paramount, 1971.

Dictator, *Rain for a Dusty Summer,* Do–Bar, 1971.

Captain Perkins, *Ripped Off* (also known as *The Boxer, Counter Punch, Murder in the Ring, Ripped-Off, Tough Guy,* and *L'uomo dalla pelle dura*), Cinema Shares, 1971.

Al Martin, *Willard,* Cinerama, 1971.

Himself, *Film Portrait* (documentary), Anthology Film Archives, 1972.

Mike Rogo, *The Poseidon Adventure,* Twentieth Century–Fox, 1972.

Hoop, *The Revengers* (also known as *Los Vengadores*), National General, 1972.

Himself, *The World of Sport Fishing* (documentary), Allied Artists Pictures Corp., 1972.

Shack, *Emperor of the North Pole* (also known as *Emperor of the North*), Twentieth Century–Fox, 1973.

Chief diver Don "Mack" Mackay, *The Neptune Factor* (also known as *The Neptune Disaster, Underwater Odyssey,* and *An Underwater Odyssey*), Twentieth Century–Fox, 1973.

Cy, *Law and Disorder,* Columbia, 1974.

Jonathan Corbis, *The Devil's Rain,* Bryanston, 1975.

Santoro, *Hustle,* Paramount, 1975.

Adam Smith, *Sunday in the Country* (also known as *Vengeance Is Mine* and *Blood for Blood*), American International Pictures, 1975.

Won Ton Ton, the Dog Who Saved Hollywood (also known as *Won Ton Ton*), Paramount, 1976.

Lou, *Shoot,* Avco–Embassy, 1976.

Angelo Dundee, *The Greatest,* Columbia, 1977.

Lyle Wallace, *Convoy,* United Artists, 1978.

John Canty, *Crossed Swords* (also known as *The Prince and the Pauper*), Warner Bros., 1978.

Harry Booth, *The Black Hole,* Buena Vista, 1979.

Rann, *The Ravagers* (also known as *Ravagers*), Columbia, 1979.

Firat, *The Double McGuffin,* Mulberry Square, 1979.

Tom Conti, *When Time Ran Out* (also known as *Earth's Final Fury* and *The Day the World Ended*), Warner Bros., 1980.

Isaiah Schmidt, *Deadly Blessing,* United Artists, 1981.

Cabbie, *Escape from New York* (also known as *John Carpenter's "Escape from New York"*), Avco–Embassy, 1981.

Clint, *High Risk* (also known as *Los Gringos*), American Cinema, 1981.

Sergeant Willy Dunlop, *Super Fuzz* (also known as *Supersnooper, Super-Snooper,* and *Poliziotto superpio*), Avco–Embassy, 1981.

Lieutenant Bob Carrigan, *Young Warriors* (also known as *The Graduates of Malibu High*), Cannon, 1983.

The White Stallion, 1984.

Frank Fletcher, *Codename: Wild Geese* (also known as *Codename Wildgeese, Code Name: Wild Geese,* and *Geheimecode Wildganse*), Entertainment, 1985.

Ben Robeson, *The Manhunt* (also known as *Manhunt, Caccia all'uomo, Mad Dog,* and *Cane arrabbiato*), Samuel Goldwyn, 1986.

Isola del Tesoro, 1986.

Red Riding Hood (also known as *Cannon Movie Tales: Red Riding Hood*), 1987.

Victor, *Qualcuno paghera?* (also known as *The Opponent*), 1987.

Baldo Cacetti, *Spike of Bensonhurst* (also known as *Throw Back!*), Film Dallas, 1988.

Any Man's Death, 1988.

Bischof, *Real Men Don't Eat Gummi Bears* (also known as *Gummibarchen kusst man nicht*), [Germany], 1989.

Professor Braun, *Laser Mission* (also known as *Soldier of Fortune*), Interfilm L.A./Azimuth, 1989.

Colonel Smith, *Skeleton Coast* (also known as *Coast of Skeletons*), Silvertree, 1989.

The Big Turnaround, 1989.

Victor, *The Opponent,* Dania, 1990.

Captain Morrison, *Moving Target* (also known as *Bersaglio sull'autostrada*), Laguna Productions, 1990.

Coach, *L'ultima partita* (also known as *Opponent* and *The Last Match*), 1990.

Ernie, *Mountain of Diamonds,* 1991.

Himself, *Mistress* (also known as *Hollywood Mistress*), Rainbow Releasing/Tribeca Productions, 1992.

Ernest, *La classse americaine,* Warner Bros. TV, 1993.

Doctor, *Tides of War* (also known as *Cancellate Washington*), Arrow Releasing, 1994.

Grandfather, *Spirit of the Season,* 1994.

Arty, *Captiva Island* (also known as *Captiva*), R S Entertainment, 1995.

The Outlaws: Legend of O. B. Taggert, Northern Arts Entertainment, 1995.

Voice of Carface, *All Dogs Go to Heaven 2* (animated; also known as *All Dogs Go to Heaven II*), Metro–Goldwyn–Mayer/United Artists, 1996.

The Wild Bunch: An Album Montage (documentary short), Warner Bros., 1996.

Grandfather, *Merlin's Shop of Mystical Wonders,* 1996.

Cobra, *McHale's Navy,* Universal, 1997.

Caesar, *Gattaca* (also known as *The Eighth Day*), Columbia, 1997.

Himself, *Ernest Borgnine: On the Bus* (documentary), GoodTimes Home Video, 1997.

Ted Denslow, *BASEketball,* Universal, 1998.

Voice of Kip Killagin, *Small Soldiers,* DreamWorks, 1998.

Carface, *An All Dogs Christmas Carol,* Metro–Goldwyn–Mayer Family Entertainment, 1998.

Lucky, *12 Bucks,* 1998.

Hotis Brown, *Abilene,* Independent Artists, 1999.

Grandpa, *Mel,* 1999.

Franklin Lyle, *The Last Great Ride,* 1999.

Ben Quinn, *The Lost Treasure of Sawtooth Island,* 1999.

Nate, *Castlerock,* 2000.

Godfather Mariano, *The Kiss of Debt,* Mackinac Media, 2000.

Himself, *Sir John Mills' Moving Memories* (documentary), Carlton, 2000.

J. Edgar Hoover, *Hoover,* 2000.

Judge DuPont, *Whiplash,* 2002.

(Segment USA) *11'09"01–September 11* (also known as *11 minutes 9 secondes 1 image, 11 septembre 2001, 11'09"01: Onze minutes, neuf secondes, un cadre, Eleven Minutes, Nine Seconds, One Image: September 11, Onze minutes neuf secondes, un cadre,* and *September 11*), Empire Pictures, 2002.

Michael Bolini, *Barn Red,* 2003.

Narrator, *The American Hobo* (documentary), Echelon Entertainment, 2003.

Lucas Moat, *The Long Ride Home,* Lions Gate Films, 2003.

Rolling Star, *Blueberry* (also known as *Blueberry: L'experience secrete* and *Renegade*), Columbia TriStar, 2004.

Himself, *Passion & Poetry: The Ballad of Sam Peckinpah* (documentary), 2005.

Grandpa, *3 Below,* Dream Entertainment, 2005.

Steamtrain, *Rail Kings,* Red Distribution, 2005.

La cura del gorilla, 2006.

Bill, *Oliviero Rising,* 2006.

Judge Holliday, *Chinaman's Chance,* 2006.

Strange Wilderness, Twentieth Century–Fox, 2006.

Also appeared in *Captain Hankel; Madam Capri and Her Girls; Strike Force.*

Film Executive Producer:
Hoover, 2000.

Television Appearances; Series:
Lieutenant Commander Quinton McHale, *McHale's Navy,* ABC, 1962–66.

Officer Joe Cleaver, *Future Cop,* ABC, 1977.

Dominic Santini, *Airwolf* (also known as *Air Wolf* and *Lone Wolf*), CBS, 1984–85.

Manny Cordova, *The Single Guy,* NBC, 1995–97.

Voice of Carface, *All Dogs Go to Heaven: The Series* (animated), syndicated, 1996—.

Voice of Mermaid Man, *SpongeBob SquarePants* (animated; also known as *SpongeBob*), Nickelodeon, 1999–2002.

Television Appearances; Miniseries:
Centurion, *Jesus of Nazareth* (also known as *Gesu di Nazareth*), NBC, 1977.

J. Edgar Hoover, *Blood Feud,* syndicated, 1983.

Marcus, *The Last Days of Pompeii,* ABC, 1984.

Lion, *Alice in Wonderland* (also known as *Alice through the Looking Glass*), CBS, 1985.

Billy Bones, *L'isola del tesoro* (also known as *Der schatz im all, Space Island,* and *Treasure Island in Outer Space*), RAI–2, 1987.

Pedro El Triste, *Oceano* (also known as *Ocean*), 1989.

Television Appearances; Movies:
Deputy Sam Hill, *Sam Hill: Who Killed the Mysterious Mr. Foster?* (also known as *Sam Hill: Who Killed Mr. Foster?*), NBC, 1971.

Sam Paxton, *The Trackers* (also known as *No Trumpets, No Drums*), ABC, 1971.

Vince Boselli, *Twice in a Lifetime,* NBC, 1974.

Natale in casa d'appuntamento (also known as *Christmas Time in a Brothel, Christmas at the Brothel, Holiday Hookers,* and *Love by Appointment*), 1976.

Sam Brisbane, *Fire!,* NBC, 1977.

Dom Cimoli, *The Ghost of Flight 401,* NBC, 1978.

Stanislaus Katczinsky, *All Quiet on the Western Front,* CBS, 1979.

Mickey Doyle, *Carpool,* CBS, 1983.

Jerry, *Masquerade,* 1983.

Senator Brighton, *Love Leads the Way,* The Disney Channel, 1984.

General Sam Worden, *The Dirty Dozen: The Next Mission* (also known as *The Dirty Dozen: Next Mission*), NBC, 1985.

General Sam Worden, *The Dirty Dozen: The Deadly Mission,* NBC, 1987.

General Sam Worden, *The Dirty Dozen: The Fatal Mission* (also known as *The Dirty Dozen: Fatal Mission*), NBC, 1988.

Sal "The Salami" Piccolo, *Jake Spanner, Private Eye* (also known as *Hoodwinked, Jack Spanner, Back on the Case,* and *The Old Dick*), USA Network, 1989.

Emil Danzig, *Appearances,* NBC, 1990.

Gantz, *Any Man's Death,* 1990.

Ernie, *Mountain of Diamonds* (also known as *Burning Shore, Gluhender himmel, La montagna dei diamanti,* and *La montagne de diamants*), 1991.

Dr. Gustav Gruber, *Tieraerztin Christine,* 1993.

Hans Kroger, *Der Blaue Diamant* (also known as *Hunt for the Blue Diamond*), 1993.

Dr. Gustav Gruber, *Tieraerztin Christine II: Die Versuchung,* 1995.

Grandpa, *Me!,* HBO, 1999.

The faerie king, *The Blue Light,* 2004.

Eugene Lawson, *The Trail to Hope Rose,* Hallmark Channel, 2004.

Television Appearances; Pilots:
Lieutenant Commander Quinton McHale, "Seven Against the Sea" (pilot for *McHale's Navy*), *Alcoa Premiere,* ABC, 1962.

Joe Cleaver, *Future Cop,* ABC, 1976.

Joe Cleaver, *The Cops and Robin* (also known as *Cops and Robin*), NBC, 1978.

Take One Starring Jonathan Winters, NBC, 1981.

Dominic Santini, *Airwolf,* CBS, 1984.

Television Appearances; Specials:
The 28th Annual Academy Awards, NBC, 1956.

The General Motors 50th Anniversary Show, NBC, 1957.

Presenter, *The 29th Annual Academy Awards,* NBC, 1957.

Presenter, *The 30th Annual Academy Awards,* NBC, 1958.

The Andy Williams Show, NBC, 1963.

The Bob Hope Show, NBC, 1967.

What's Up, America?, NBC, 1971.

Vince Lombardi, *Portrait in Granite: The Vince Lombardi Story* (also known as *Legend in Granite: The Vince Lombardi Story,* ABC, 1973.

The Rowan and Martin Special, NBC, 1973.

Himself, *Sandy in Disneyland,* CBS, 1974.

Presenter, *The 46th Annual Academy Awards,* NBC, 1974.

Himself/Fatso, *The Dean Martin Celebrity Roast: Frank Sinatra,* 1977.

Superstunt, NBC, 1978.

The 50th Annual Academy Awards, ABC, 1978.

Jonathan, *Little House Years,* NBC, 1979.

The American Film Institute Salute to James Stewart, CBS, 1980.

Take One Starring Jonathan Winters, NBC, 1981.

James Bond: The First 21 Years, Thames, 1983.

The Funniest Joke I Ever Heard, ABC, 1984.

The Hollywood Christmas Parade, syndicated, 1987.

This is Your Life, NBC, 1987.

The Television Academy Hall of Fame, Fox, 1990.

MGM: When the Lion Roars (documentary; also known as *The MGM Story*), TNT, 1992.

50 Years of Television: A Celebration of the Academy of Television Arts and Sciences Golden Anniversary, HBO, 1997.

Interviewee, *Big Guns Talk: The Story of the Western* (documentary), TNT, 1997.

50 Years of Television: A Celebration of the Academy of Television Arts & Sciences Golden Anniversary, HBO, 1997.

The Best of Hollywood (also known as *50 Years: The Best of Hollywood*), 1998.

Frank Sinatra: The Very Good Years, PBS, 1998.

The 70th Annual Academy Awards, 1998.

Himself, *AFI's 100 Years ... 100 Stars,* CBS, 1999.

William Holden: An Untamed Spirit (documentary), Arts and Entertainment, 1999.

Tim Conway: Just Clowning Around (documentary), Arts and Entertainment, 1999.

The 2000 MTV Movie Awards, MTV, 2000.

Himself, *AFI's 100 Years, 100 Thrills: America's Most Heart–Pounding Movies* (also known as *AFI's 100 Years ... 100 Thrills*), CBS, 2001.

The 75th Annual Academy Awards, ABC, 2003.

Time Machine: When Cowboys Were King, 2003.

Sam Peckinpah's West: Legacy of a Hollywood Renegade (documentary), Starz!, 2004.

Also appeared in *Billy the Kid.*

Television Appearances; Episodic:
"The Copper," *Goodyear Television Playhouse* (also known as *Goodyear Playhouse*), 1951.
Gus White, "Night Visitor," *Ford Theatre*, 1954.
"The Poachers," *Fireside Theatre*, NBC, 1955.
Himself, "Ernest Borgnine," *This Is Your Life*, NBC, 1956.
Toast of the Town, CBS, 1956, 1957.
Jim Morrison, "Black Creek Encounter," *Zane Grey Theatre* (also known as *Dick Powell's "Zane Grey Theater"* and *The Westerners*), CBS, 1957.
Willy Moran, "The Willie Moran Story," *Wagon Train*, NBC, 1957.
"The Reformation of Calliope," *The O. Henry Playhouse*, 1957.
Cop, "The Flashback Show," *Make Room for Daddy* (also known as *The Danny Thomas Show*), 1957.
Host, "Human Bomb," *Navy Log*, 1957.
"Two Lives Have I," *Schlitz Playhouse of Stars* (also known as *Herald Playhouse, Schlitz Playhouse,* and *The Playhouse*), 1958.
Willy Moran, "Around the Horn," *Wagon Train*, NBC, 1958.
Major Prescott, "Circle of Fire," *Laramie*, NBC, 1959.
Estaban Zamora, "The Estaban Zamora Story," *Wagon Train*, NBC, 1959.
Jim Morrison, "Black Creek Encounter," *Frontier Justice*, 1959.
Boone Caudie, "Ride the Wild Wind," *Laramie*, NBC, 1960.
Willie, "A Gun for Willie," *Zane Grey Theatre* (also known as *Dick Powell's "Zane Grey Theater"* and *The Westerners*), CBS, 1960.
Earl Packer, "The Earl Packer Story," *Wagon Train*, NBC, 1961.
Matty Moran, "The Legend That Walks Like a Man," *The General Electric Theatre* (also known as *G. E. Theater*), CBS, 1961.
"The Blue Leaders," *The Blue Angels*, 1961.
MacHale, "Seven Against the Sea," *Alcoa Premiere*, 1962.
Major David Orlovsky, "The Bar Mitzvah of Major Orlovsky," *The General Electric Theatre* (also known as *G. E. Theater*), CBS, 1962.
Himself, *The Andy Williams Story*, NBC, 1963.
Host, *The Hollywood Palace*, ABC, 1964.
Indian, "The Indian Girl Story," *Wagon Train*, NBC, 1965.
Melvin Freebie, "The Blue–Eyed Horse," *Bob Hope Presents the Chrysler Theatre* (also known as *The Chrysler Theater* and *Universal Star Time*), NBC, 1966.

Harry, "Time and a Half on Christmas Eve," *Run for Your Life*, 1966.
Himself, *The Hollywood Squares*, NBC, 1966, 1967, 1976.
TV viewer, "The Little Black Book: Part 2," *Get Smart*, 1968.
The Tonight Show Starring Johnny Carson, NBC, 1971, 1973, 1979.
The Dean Martin Show, NBC, 1971, 1972.
Rowan & Martin's Laugh–In, NBC, 1973.
Jonathan, "The Lord Is My Shepherd: Part 2," *Little House on the Prairie*, NBC, 1974.
Earl Gianelli, "Mr. White Death," *Magnum, P.I.*, 1982.
Dominic Rosselli, "Venetian Love Song/The Arrangement/Arrividerci, Gopher/The Gigolo: Parts 1 & 2," *The Love Boat*, ABC, 1982.
Buster Ryan, "Here's Another Fine Mess," *Matt Houston*, 1983.
Guido Liggo, "Another Kind of War, Another Kind of Peace," *Highway to Heaven*, 1986.
Cosmo Ponzini, "Death Takes a Dive," *Murder, She Wrote*, CBS, 1987.
Colonel Tom Cody, "My Shining Hour," *Jake and the Fatman*, 1989.
Debbie Reynolds' Movie Memories, 1991.
Eddie Phillips, "Birds of a Feather Flock to Taylor," *Home Improvement*, ABC, 1992.
Voice of himself, "Boy Scoutz N the Hood," *The Simpsons* (animated), Fox, 1993.
Frank Nardino, "Rising Sun," *The Commish*, 1993.
Frank Nardino, "A Christmas Story," *The Commish*, 1994.
Voice of Brain's father, *Pinky and the Brain* (animated), The WB, 1996.
Artemus Sullivan, "Yesterday's Heroes," *JAG*, CBS, 1998.
Antonio Birelli, "The Last Untouchable," *Early Edition*, CBS, 1999.
Lawrence Yaeger, "Legacy," *Chicken Soup for the Soul*, PAX, 2000.
Eddie Ryan, "The Avenging Angel," *Walker, Texas Ranger*, CBS, 2000.
Himself, "The Poseidon Adventure Backstory," *Backstory* (also known as *Hollywood Backstories*), AMC, 2001.
Max, "The Blue Angel," *Touched by an Angel*, CBS, 2002.
Joe, "The Known Soldier," *7th Heaven* (also known as *Seventh Heaven*), The WB, 2002.
Frank Collero, "Alienation of Affection," *Family Law*, CBS, 2002.
Mike Murphy, "Last Waltz," *The District*, CBS, 2003.
Late Show with David Letterman (also known as *The Late Show*), NBC, 2004.

Also appeared as Nargola, *Captain Video and His Video Rangers*, Dumon.

RECORDINGS:.

Video Games:
Voice of Mermaid Man, *SpongeBob SquarePants: SuperSponge,* THQ, 2001.

OTHER SOURCES

Books:
International Dictionary of Films and Filmmakers, Volume 3: Actors and Actresses, 4th ed., St. James Press, 2000.

Periodicals:
Movieline, volume 7, issue 8, 1996, p. 30.

BORSTEIN, Alex 1971–

PERSONAL

Born February 15, 1971, in Chicago, IL; married Jackson Douglas (an actor), 1999. *Education:* Attended San Francisco State University, San Francisco, CA.

Addresses: *Agent*—Endeavor, 152 W. 57th St., 25th Floor, New York, NY 10019. *Manager*—Mosaic Media Group, 9200 Sunset Blvd., 10th Floor, Los Angeles, CA 90069.

Career: Actress.

Awards, Honors: Screen Actors Guild Award nomination (with others), outstanding performance by a cast, 2006, for *Good Night, and Good Luck.*

CREDITS

Television Appearances; Series:
Mad TV, Fox, 1997–2002.
Voice of Lois Griffin, *Family Guy* (animated), Fox, 1998–2006.
Host, *Celebrity Blackjack,* Game Show Network, 2004.

Television Appearances; Episodic:
Voice of Madame Woe, "Peace, Love, and Woe," *Mighty Morphin' Power Rangers* (animated; also known as *Day of the Dumpster, Mighty Morph'n Power Rangers, Mighty Morphin Alien Rangers* and *Power Rangers Ninja*), Fox, 1993.

Voice of contest announcer, "Birds of a Feather," *Mighty Morphin' Power Rangers* (animated; also known as *Day of the Dumpster, Mighty Morph'n Power Rangers, Mighty Morphin Alien Rangers* and *Power Rangers Ninja*), Fox, 1993.
Voice of Bloom of Doom, "Bloom of Doom," *Mighty Morphin' Power Rangers* (animated; also known as *Day of the Dumpster, Mighty Morph'n Power Rangers, Mighty Morphin Alien Rangers* and *Power Rangers Ninja*), Fox, 1994.
Voice of Lipsyncher, "Two for One," *Mighty Morphin' Power Rangers* (animated; also known as *Day of the Dumpster, Mighty Morph'n Power Rangers, Mighty Morphin Alien Rangers* and *Power Rangers Ninja*), Fox, 1994.
Voice of Queen Machina, *Power Rangers Zeo* (animated; also known as *ZeoRangers*), Fox, 1996.
Voice of Cataclaws, "Yo Ho Borgs," *Big Bad Beetleborgs* (animated; also known as *Saban's Big Bad Beetleborgs*), Fox, 1996.
Ms. Swan/Karen Goddard, *Mad TV,* Fox, 1997–2002.
Drella, Miss Celine (recurring), *Gilmore Girls,* 2000–2005.
Voice of mother (uncredited), "The Stolen Cartoons," *House of Mouse* (animated), ABC, 2001.
The Test, FX Channel, 2001.
Nicky, "Bachelor Party," *Titus,* Fox, 2002.
Becky, "New Friends," *3–South,* MTV, 2002.
Never Mind the Buzzcocks, BBC, 2002.
Becky, "Midnight Del," *3 South,* MTV, 2003.
Becky, "Joe Gets Expelled," *3–South,* MTV, 2003.
Evelyn, "Farewell, Nervosa," *Frasier,* NBC, 2003.
Voice of Catwoman, "The Deep End," *Robot Chicken* (animated), Cartoon Network, 2005.
Voice of hot French woman, "Toy Meets Girl," *Robot Chicken* (animated), Cartoon Network, 2005.
"Nightmare Generator," *Robot Chicken* (animated), Cartoon Network, 2005.
Jimmy Kimmel Live, ABC, 2005.
Too Late with Adam Carolla, Comedy Central, 2005.
Drawn Together, Comedy Central, 2005–2006.
The Late Late Show with Craig Ferguson, CBS, 2006.

Television Appearances; Specials:
Host, *All Access Pass to the 14th Annual American Comedy Awards,* Comedy Central, 2000.
The 7th Annual Blockbuster Entertainment Awards, Fox, 2001.

Television Work; Series:
Producer, *Family Guy,* Fox, 2005–2006.

Film Appearances:
Bidding customer (uncredited), *Coyote Ugly,* Buena Vista, 2000.
Registrar, *Brown Eyed Girl,* 2001.
Darcy Smits, *Bad Boy* (also known as *Dawg*), Pyramid, 2002.

Casting director, *Showtime,* Warner Bros., 2002.

Miss Ungermeyer, *The Lizzie McGuire Movie,* Buena Vista, 2003.

Milwaukee Mom with photo, *Bad Santa* (also known as *Badder Santa*), Dimension, 2003.

Tracy, *Seeing Other People,* Lantern Lane, 2004.

Sally, *Catwoman,* Warner Bros., 2004.

Hilary's Roman Adventure (video), Walt Disney, 2004.

Betty Henderson, *Billy's Dad Is a Fudge–Packer,* Power Up, 2004.

Obnoxious hummer lady, *Kicking & Screaming,* Universal, 2005.

Voice of Lois Griffin, *Family Guy Presents: Stewie Griffin–The Untold Story* (animated; video), 2005.

Natalie, *Good Night, and Good Luck,* Warner Bros., 2005.

Film Work:

Co–producer, *Family Guy Presents: Stewie Griffin–The Untold Story* (video), 2005.

WRITINGS

Television Series:

Pinky and the Brain, The WB, 1995.

Casper (also known as *The Spooktacular New Adventures of Casper*), Fox, 1996.

Mad TV, Fox, 1997–2002.

Histeria!, The WB, 1998.

Monster Farm, syndicated, 1998.

Family Guy (also known as *Padre de familia*), Fox, 2001.

Screenplays:

Family Guy Presents: Stewie Griffin—The Untold Story (video), 2005.

BOSCO, Philip 1930–

PERSONAL

Full name, Philip Michael Bosco; born September 26, 1930, in Jersey City, NJ; son of Philip Lupo (a carnival worker) and Margaret Raymond (a policewoman; maiden name, Thek) Bosco; married Nancy Ann Dunkle, January 2, 1957; children: Diane, Philip, Chris, Jenny, Lisa, Celia, John. *Education:* Graduate of St. Peter's Preparatory School, 1948; Catholic University of America, B.A., 1957; studied for the stage with James Marr, Josephine Callan, and Leo Brady. *Religion:* Roman Catholic. *Avocational Interests:* Horses.

Addresses: *Agent*—Don Buchwald & Associates, 6500 Wilshire Blvd., Suite 2200, Los Angeles, CA 90048.

Career: Actor. Arena Stage, Washington, DC, resident actor, 1957–60; Lincoln Center Repertory Company, New York City, resident actor, 1966–70; appeared in television commercials, including GE light bulbs, 1998–99, and Tidy Cat Crystals Blend, 2001; previously worked as a truck driver and at carnivals. *Military service:* U.S. Army, 1951–53, served in the signal corps and special services.

Member: Actors' Equity Association, American Federation of Television and Radio Artists, Screen Actors Guild, Catholic Actors Guild.

Awards, Honors: Shakespeare Society of Washington, DC, Award, New York Drama Critics Award, and Antoinette Perry Award nomination, best dramatic actor, 1961, all for *The Rape of the Belt;* Clarence Derwent Award—Special Citation, Actors Equity Awards, 1967, for *The Alchemist;* Antoinette Perry Award nomination, best featured actor, 1984, for *Heartbreak House;* Antoinette Perry Award nomination, best actor in a play, 1987, for *You Never Can Tell;* Daytime Emmy Award, outstanding performer in children's programming, 1988, for *Read Between the Lines;* Obie Award for sustained excellence, *Village Voice,* 1988; Antoinette Perry Award, best actor in a play, Drama Desk Award, outstanding actor in a play, and Outer Critics Circle Award, best leading actor, 1989, all for *Lend Me a Tenor;* Drama Desk Award nomination, outstanding actor in a play, 1995, for *The Heiress;* Antoinette Perry Award, best actor, 1996, for *Moon over Buffalo;* National Board of Review Award (with others), best acting by an ensemble, 1996, for *The First Wives Club;* Theater Hall of Fame, inductee, 1998; Antoinette Perry Award nomination, best actor in a play, Drama Desk Award nomination, outstanding featured actor in a play, 2005, both for *Twelve Angry Men.*

CREDITS

Stage Appearances:

(Professional debut) Bohan, *You Never Can Tell,* Olney Theatre, Olney, MD, 1954.

Brian O'Bannion, *Auntie Mame,* City Center Theatre, New York City, 1958.

Angelo, *Measure for Measure,* Belvedere Lake Amphitheatre, New York City, 1960.

Heracles, *The Rape of the Belt,* Martin Beck Theatre, New York City, 1960.

Will Danaher, *Donnybrook,* Forty–Sixth Street Theatre, New York City, 1961.

Hawkshaw, *The Ticket–of–Leave Man,* Midway Theatre, New York City, 1961–62.

Henry Bolingbroke, *Richard II,* American Shakespeare Festival Theatre, Stratford, CT, 1962.

Henry IV, *Henry IV, Part I,* American Shakespeare Festival Theatre, 1962.

Rufio, *Antony and Cleopatra,* American Shakespeare Festival Theatre, 1963.

Earl of Kent, *King Lear,* American Shakespeare Festival Theatre, 1963.

Pistol, *Henry V,* American Shakespeare Festival Theatre, 1963.

Egeon, *The Comedy of Errors,* American Shakespeare Festival Theatre, 1963.

Benedick, *Much Ado About Nothing,* American Shakespeare Festival Theatre, 1964.

Claudius, *Hamlet,* American Shakespeare Festival Theatre, 1964.

Caius Marcius Coriolanus, *The Tragedy of Coriolanus,* American Shakespeare Festival Theatre, 1965.

Duke of Buckingham, *King Richard III,* New York Shakespeare Festival, Delacorte Theatre, New York City, 1966.

Lovewit, *The Alchemist,* Vivian Beaumont Theatre, New York City, 1966.

Jack, *The East Wind,* Vivian Beaumont Theatre, 1967.

Sagredo, *Galileo,* Vivian Beaumont Theatre, 1967.

Zelda and Mr. Gray, *A Great Career* and *An Evening for Merlin Finch* (double–bill), Forum Theatre, New York City, then Vivian Beaumont Theatre, 1968.

Dunois, *St. Joan,* Vivian Beaumont Theatre, 1968.

Hector, *Tiger at the Gates,* Vivian Beaumont Theatre, 1968.

Comte de Guiche, *Cyrano de Bergerac,* Vivian Beaumont Theatre, 1968.

Curtis Moffat, Jr., *In the Matter of J. Robert Oppenheimer,* Vivian Beaumont Theatre, 1968.

Anselm, *The Miser,* Vivian Beaumont Theatre, 1970.

Nick, *The Time of Your Life,* Vivian Beaumont Theatre, 1970.

Baron de Charlus, *Camino Real,* Vivian Beaumont Theatre, 1970.

Captain Bovine, *Operation Sidewinder,* Vivian Beaumont Theatre, 1970.

Jupiter, *Amphitryon,* Forum Theatre, 1970.

Peter Stockman, *An Enemy of the People,* Vivian Beaumont Theatre, 1971.

Jimmy Farrell, *Playboy of the Western World,* Vivian Beaumont Theatre, 1971.

First god, *The Good Woman of Setzuan,* Vivian Beaumont Theatre, 1971.

Creon, *Antigone,* Vivian Beaumont Theatre, 1971.

Robert Dudley, Earl of Leicester, *Mary Stuart,* Vivian Beaumont Theatre, 1972.

Prime minister, *Narrow Road to the Deep North,* Vivian Beaumont Theatre, 1972.

Reverend John Hale, *The Crucible,* Vivian Beaumont Theatre, 1972.

Antonio, *Twelfth Night,* Vivian Beaumont Theatre, 1972.

Mikhail Skrobotov, *Enemies,* Vivian Beaumont Theatre, 1973.

Corporal Stoddart, *The Plough and the Stars,* Vivian Beaumont Theatre, 1973.

Gratiano, *The Merchant of Venice,* Vivian Beaumont Theatre, 1973.

Harold Mitchell, *A Streetcar Named Desire,* Vivian Beaumont Theatre, 1973.

Sergeant Cokes, *Streamers,* Mitzi E. Newhouse Theatre, New York City, 1976.

Crofts, *Mrs. Warren's Profession,* Vivian Beaumont Theatre, 1976.

Pistol, *Henry V,* New York Shakespeare Festival, Delacorte Theatre, 1977.

Mack the Knife, *Threepenny Opera,* New York Shakespeare Festival, Delacorte Theatre, 1977.

Richard de Beauchamp, Earl of Warwick, *St. Joan,* Circle in the Square Theatre, New York City, 1977–78.

Stages, Belasco Theatre, New York City, 1978.

Colonel Pieter Goosen, *The Biko Inquest,* Theatre Four, New York City, 1978.

Mendoza, *Man and Superman,* Circle in the Square Theatre, 1978–79.

Dr. Emerson, *Whose Life Is It, Anyway?,* Trafalgar Theatre, New York City, 1979.

Dr. Shpigelsky, *A Month in the Country,* Roundabout Stage One, New York City, 1979–80.

Andrew Undershaft, *Major Barbara,* Circle in the Square Theatre, 1980.

Cadmus, *The Bacchae,* Circle in the Square Theatre, 1980.

The devil, *Don Juan in Hell,* Roundabout Stage One, 1980–81.

Hudson, *Inadmissible Evidence,* Roundabout Stage One, 1981.

Judge Brack, *Hedda Gabler,* Roundabout Stage One, 1981.

John Tarleton, *Misalliance,* Roundabout Stage One, 1981.

Holmes Bradford, *Eminent Domain,* Circle in the Square Theatre Uptown, 1982.

Chrysale, *The Learned Ladies,* Raft Theatre, New York City, 1982.

Gaetano Altobelli, *Some Men Need Help,* Forty–Seventh Street Theatre, New York City, 1982.

Lieutenant Commander Philip Francis Queeg, *The Caine Mutiny Court–Martial,* Circle in the Square Theatre, 1983.

Nat Miller, *Ah, Wilderness!,* Roundabout Theatre, 1983.

Boss Mangan, *Heartbreak House,* Circle in the Square Theatre, 1983–84.

Doc, *Come Back, Little Sheba,* Roundabout Theatre, 1984.

Max, *The Loves of Anatol,* Circle in the Square Theatre, 1985.

Norman, *Be Happy for Me,* Douglas Fairbanks Theatre, New York City, 1985–86.

Zhdanov, *Master Class,* Roundabout Theatre, 1986.

Sir Thomas More, *A Man for All Seasons,* Roundabout Theatre, 1986–87.

Boon the waiter, *You Never Can Tell,* Circle in the Square Theatre, 1986–87.

General Burgoyne, *The Devil's Disciple,* Circle in the Square Theatre, 1988–89.

Love Letters, Promenade Theatre, New York City, 1989.

Babes in Arms, Lincoln Center, Avery Fisher Hall, New York City, 1989.

Saunders, *Lend Me a Tenor,* Morris Mechanic Theatre, Baltimore, MD, 1989, then Royale Theatre, New York City, 1989–90.

Harpagon, *The Miser,* Circle in the Square Theatre, New York City, 1990.

Mike Fransisco, *Breaking Legs,* Promenade Theatre, New York City, 1991.

Ben Marino, *Fiorello!,* City Center Theatre, 1994.

Arthur Birling, *An Inspector Calls,* Royale Theatre, 1994–95.

Dr. Austin Sloper, *The Heiress,* Cort Theatre, New York City, 1995.

George Hay, *Moon over Buffalo,* Martin Beck Theatre, New York City, 1996.

Malvolio, *Twelfth Night, Or What You Will,* Lincoln Center, New York City, 1998.

Horace J. Fletcher, *Strike Up the Band,* City Center Theatre, 1998.

Neils Bohr, *Copenhagen,* Royale Theatre, 2000–2001.

Leonardo, *Beatrice and Benedict* (concert), New York Philharmonic, New York City, 2003.

Juror number three, *Twelve Angry Men,* Roundabout Theatre Company, New York City, 2004–2005.

Tasting Memories, Neighborhood Playhouse, New York City, 2004.

Grandpa Potts, *Chitty Chitty Bang Bang,* Hilton Theatre, New York City, 2005.

Major Tours:

Brian O'Bannion, *Auntie Mame,* U.S. cities, 1958–59.

Film Appearances:

Requiem for a Heavyweight, Columbia, 1962.

Fuller, *A Lovely Way to Die* (also known as *A Lovely Way to Go*), Universal, 1968.

Doctor, *Trading Places,* Paramount, 1983.

Paulie's father, *The Pope of Greenwich Village* (also known as *Village Dreams*), Metro–Goldwyn–Mayer/United Artists, 1984.

James Flanagan, *Walls of Glass* (also known as *Flanagan*), United Film, 1985.

Brother Paul, *Heaven Help Us* (also known as *Catholic Boys*), TriStar, 1985.

Dr. Curtis Franklin, *Children of a Lesser God,* Paramount, 1986.

Curly, *The Money Pit,* Universal, 1986.

(Uncredited) *The Mission,* New Line Cinema, 1986.

Detective Melkowitz, *Three Men and a Baby,* Buena Vista, 1987.

Paul Gray, *Suspect,* TriStar, 1987.

Oren Trask, *Working Girl,* Twentieth Century–Fox, 1988.

Sam, *Another Woman,* Orion, 1988.

Sam Posner, *The Luckiest Man in the World,* Second Effort, 1989.

O'Malley, *The Dream Team,* Universal, 1989.

Frank Turner, *Blue Steel,* Metro–Goldwyn–Mayer/United Artists, 1990.

Bus driver, *Quick Change,* Warner Bros., 1990.

Senator Steubens, *True Colors,* Paramount, 1991.

Ray Silak, *FX2–The Deadly Art of Illusion* (also known as *F/X2* and *FX2*) Orion, 1991.

Mr. Paulsen, *Shadows and Fog,* Orion, 1991.

Gene Perlman, *Straight Talk,* Buena Vista, 1992.

Bertram Wolfe, *Diego Rivera: I Paint What I See* (documentary), New Deal Films, 1992.

Mort, *Safe Passage,* New Line Cinema, 1994.

Judge Flatt, *Nobody's Fool,* Paramount, 1994.

Jerry the Pope, *Milk Money,* Paramount, 1994.

Frank Scacciapensieri, *Angie,* Buena Vista, 1994.

Vincenzo, *It Takes Two* (also known as *Me and My Shadow*), Warner Bros., 1995.

Uncle Carmine Morelli, *The First Wives Club,* Paramount, 1996.

Cabby, *Surprise!* (also known as *Apologies to Bunuel*), 1996.

Walter Wallace, *My Best Friend's Wedding,* Columbia, 1997.

Dr. Hofstader, *Critical Care,* Live Entertainment, 1997.

Himself, *Moon over Broadway* (documentary), Artistic License, 1997.

Professor Clark, *Deconstructing Harry,* Fine Line Features, 1997.

Walter Wade, Sr., *Shaft* (also known as *Shaft—Noch fragen?*), Paramount, 2000.

Emily's father, *Wonder Boys* (also known as *Die Wonder Boys* and *Wonderboys—Lauter wunderknaben*), Paramount, 2000.

Uncle Chicky, *Brooklyn Sonnet* (also known as *Borough of the Kings*), Lions Gate Films, 2000.

Otis, *Kate & Leopold,* Miramax, 2001.

Professor Jergensen, *Abandon,* Paramount, 2002.

Mr. O'Brian, *Hitch,* Columbia, 2005.

Priest, *Freedomland,* Sony Pictures Releasing, 2006.

Television Appearances; Series:

Clarence Bailey, *The Guiding Light* (also known as *Guiding Light*), CBS, 1979.

Harry Yeshosky, *Tribeca,* Fox, 1993.

Eliot Markham, *As the World Turns,* CBS, 1994.

Lyle Wedgewood, *All My Children,* ABC, 2000.

Narrator—opening monologue, *Crown and Country,* PBS, 2000.

Television Appearances; Miniseries:

Thomas Colfax, *Rage of Angels: The Story Continues,* 1986.

Judge Garb, *Echoes in the Dark,* 1987.

John Wyckoff, *Internal Affairs,* 1988.

Voice of Horace Greeley, *The Civil War* (documentary; also known as *The American Civil War*), PBS, 1990.

Voice of Frederick Seward, *Lincoln* (documentary), ABC, 1992.

Voice, *Baseball* (documentary; also known as *The History of Baseball*), PBS, 1994.

Voice, *The West* (documentary), PBS, 1996.

Dr. Benjamin Franklin, *LIBERTY! The American Revolution* (documentary), PBS, 1997.

Steve Magaddino, Sr., *Bonanno: A Godfather's Story*, Showtime, 1999.

Voice, *New York: A Documentary Film* (documentary; also known as *American Experience: New York—A Documentary Film*), PBS, 1999.

Television Appearances; Movies:

Boss William Tweed, *Liberty*, 1986.

Captain John Wycoff, *Murder in Black and White*, 1990.

Art Malto, *The Return of Eliot Ness*, 1991.

Attica: Line of Fire, 1993.

Chief Wycoff, *A Silent Betrayal* (also known as *Janek: The Silent Betrayal*), CBS, 1994.

Corrections commissioner Russell Oswald, *Against the Wall*, HBO, 1994.

Chief Wycoff, *The Forget–Me–Not Murders* (also known as *Janek: The Forget–Me–Not Murders*), CBS, 1994.

Patsy, *Young at Heart* (also known as *Hoboken*), CBS, 1995.

Colonel Bailey, *Carriers* (also known as *Virus X—Die todliche Falle*), CBS, 1998.

Dominic DeAngelo, *Cupid & Cate*, CBS, 2000.

Dr. Ed Walden, *After Amy* (also known as *No Ordinary Baby*), Lifetime, 2001.

Also appeared in *Second Effort*.

Television Appearances; Specials:

Father Coyne, *Hogan's Ghost*, PBS, 1972.

Gaetano Altobelli, "Some Men Need Help," *American Playhouse*, PBS, 1985.

Gramps, "Read Between the Lines," *ABC Afterschool Specials*, ABC, 1987.

Narrator, *The Emperor's Eye: Art and Power in Imperial China* (documentary), PBS, 1989.

Narrator, *The Crash of 1929* (documentary), PBS, 1990.

Narrator, "Coney Island" (documentary), *The American Experience*, PBS, 1991.

Voice, "The Way West" (documentary), *The American Experience*, PBS, 1995.

Narrator, *Music for the Movies: Bernard Herrmann* (documentary), Bravo, 1995.

Voice, "Buckminster Fuller: Thinking Out Loud" (documentary), *American Masters*, PBS, 1996.

Voice of John Adams, *Thomas Jefferson* (documentary), PBS, 1997.

Voice, *Frank Lloyd Wright* (documentary), PBS, 1998.

Voice, *Margaret Sanger* (documentary), PBS, 1998.

Malvolio, *William Shakespeare's "Twelfth Night"* (also known as *Twelfth Night, Or What You Will*), PBS, 1998.

Narrator, *Extraordinary Cats* (documentary), PBS, 1999.

Narrator, *Iceland: Fire and Ice* (documentary), PBS, 1999.

Narrator, *The Birth of Ohio Stadium* (documentary), 1999.

Narrator, *Hollywood, D.C.* (documentary), Bravo, 2001.

Voice, *The Impressionists* (documentary), Arts and Entertainment, 2001.

Voice of Herman Melville, *Revenge of the Whale* (documentary), NBC, 2001.

Voice, *Jazz* (documentary), PBS, 2001.

Voice, *Echoes from the White House* (documentary), PBS, 2001.

Voices, *Mark Twain* (documentary), PBS, 2001.

Voices, *Horatio's Drive: America's First Road Trip* (documentary), PBS, 2003.

Voices, *Unforgivable Blackness: The Rise and Fall of Jack Johnson* (documentary), PBS, 2004.

Also appeared in *Grandpa and the Globetrotters*, PBS.

Television Appearances; Awards Presentations:

The 43rd Annual Tony Awards, CBS, 1989.

The 44th Annual Tony Awards, CBS, 1990.

The 50th Annual Tony Awards, 1996.

The 59th Annual Tony Awards, CBS, 2005.

Television Appearances; Episodic:

Duke Michael, "The Prisoner of Zenda," *The Du Pont Show of the Month*, CBS, 1961.

"Medicine Man," *Armstrong Circle Theater* (also known as *Circle Theater*), CBS, 1961.

Parnell Sullivan, "Many a Sullivan," *The Nurses* (also known as *The Doctors and Nurses*), CBS, 1963.

Hap Spencer, "The Rainbow Ride," *The Nurses* (also known as *The Doctors and Nurses*), CBS, 1964.

Ralph Maley, "A Dangerous Silence," *The Nurses* (also known as *The Doctors and Nurses*), CBS, 1965.

Dr. Manfredi, "Whipping Boy," *The Defenders*, CBS, 1965.

Willard, "The Killing of One Human Being," *For the People*, CBS, 1965.

Theo, "Charlie Has All the Luck," *Trials of O'Brien*, NBC, 1965.

Peter Stockmann, "An Enemy of the People" (also known as "Arthur Miller's Adaptation of An Enemy of the People"), *Play of the Month*, PBS, 1966.

"What's a Nice Girl Like You ... ," *N.Y.P.D.*, 1968.

"Pretenders," *The Equalizer*, CBS, 1986.

Dawson, "All This and a Gold Card, Too," *Leg Work*, 1987.

David McVane, "Substantial Justice," *Spenser: For Hire*, ABC, 1988.

Voice of himself, "Desert Giant: The World of the Saguaro's Cactus," *Reading Rainbow,* PBS, 1989.

Oscar, "Heart of Justice," *The Equalizer,* CBS, 1989.

Gordon Schell, "Happily Ever After," *Law & Order,* NBC, 1990.

Gordon Schell, "Manhood," *Law & Order,* NBC, 1993.

Gordon Schell, "Kids," *Law & Order,* NBC, 1994.

Bat Masterson/Mike Killabrew, "Bat Masterson," *Early Edition,* CBS, 1997.

Palermo Racine, "A Star in Stripes Forever," *Remember WENN,* 1997.

Dobbs, "Faccia a Faccia," *Law & Order,* NBC, 1998.

Randall Winston, Sr., "Gobble the Wonder Turkey Saves the Day," *Spin City,* ABC, 1998.

"Enter Lucas," *Cosby,* 1998.

Randall Winston, Sr., "That's Entertainment," *Spin City,* ABC, 1999.

Attorney Dobbs, "Shield," *Law & Order,* NBC, 1999.

Alan Stevens, "Losing Streak," *Ed* (also known as *Stuckeyville*), NBC, 2001.

Voice of Zeus, "Zeus on the Loose," *Cyberchase,* PBS, 2002.

Professor Winthrop, "Anti–Thesis," *Law & Order: Criminal Intent* (also known as *Law & Order: CI*), NBC, 2002.

Davis Langley, "Waste," *Law & Order: Special Victims Unit* (also known as *Law & Order: SVU* and *Special Victims Unit*), NBC, 2002.

Judge Joseph P. Terhune, "Sick," *Law & Order: Special Victims Unit* (also known as *Law & Order: SVU* and *Special Victims Unit*), NBC, 2002.

Judge Joseph P. Terhune, "Bound," *Law & Order: Special Victims Unit* (also known as *Law & Order: SVU* and *Special Victims Unit*), NBC, 2002.

Judge Joseph P. Terhune, "Obscene," *Law & Order: Special Victims Unit* (also known as *Law & Order: SVU* and *Special Victims Unit*), NBC, 2002.

Judge Joseph P. Terhune, "Outcry," *Law & Order: Special Victims Unit* (also known as *Law & Order: SVU* and *Special Victims Unit*), NBC, 2002.

Also appeared in "A Nice Place to Visit," *Play of the Month,* PBS; *Art in Our Times,* PBS; *Directions 66,* ABC; *Esso Repertory Theater,* syndicated; *Hawk,* NBC.

RECORDINGS

Taped Readings:

Trevayne, 1990.

The Day Before Midnight, 1990.

An Occasion of Sin, 1997.

Underboss: Sammy the Bull Gravano's Story of Life in the Mafia, 1997.

At All Costs, Time Warner Audio, 1998.

Swimming Across, Time Warner, 2001.

(With others) *Horatio's First Drive: America's First Road Trip,* Random House Audio, 2003.

OTHER SOURCES

Periodicals:

New York Times, August 2, 1981; January 4, 1987.

BOTTOMS, Timothy 1951(?)–
    (Tim Bottoms)

PERSONAL

Full name, Timothy James Bottoms; born August 30, 1951 (some sources say 1950), in Santa Barbara, CA; son of James "Bud" (a sculptor) and Betty Bottoms; brother of Joseph, Benjamin and Sam Bottoms (all actors); married Alicia Cory (a folksinger), 1975 (divorced, 1978); married Marcia Morehart, 1984; children: (first marriage) Bartholmew, (second marriage) Benton James, William Bodieltyle, Bridget Benita.

Addresses: *Office*—532 Hot Springs Rd., Santa Barbara, CA 93108–2014.

Career: Actor and producer. Toured Europe as a member of the Santa Barbara Madrigal Society, 1967. Also worked as a surveyor's assistant.

Member: Screen Actors Guild, American Federation of Television and Radio Artists.

Awards, Honors: Golden Globe Award nomination, most promising newcomer—male, 1972, for *The Last Picture Show;* CableACE Award, best actor, National Cable Television Association, 1987, for *The Hitchhiker;* Grand Jury Prize, best supporting actor, New York International Independent Film and Video Festival, 2000, for *Mixed Blessings.*

CREDITS

Film Appearances:

(Film debut) Joe Bonham, *Johnny Got His Gun,* Cinemation, 1971.

Sonny Crawford, *The Last Picture Show,* Columbia, 1971.

Walter Eberson, *Love and Pain (and the Whole Damn Thing),* Columbia, 1973.

Hart, *The Paper Chase,* Twentieth Century–Fox, 1973.

Daggett, *White Dawn,* Paramount, 1974.

Vrooder, *The Crazy World of Julius Vrooder* (also known as *Vrooder's Hooch*), Twentieth Century–Fox, 1974.

Jan Kubis, *Operation Daybreak* (also known as *The Price of Freedom* and *Seven Men at Daybreak*), Warner Bros., 1974.

Poke Jackson, *A Small Town in Texas,* American International Pictures, 1976.

Young man, *Rollercoaster,* Universal, 1977.

John Boothe, *The Other Side of the Mountain, Part II,* Universal, 1978.

Jack Stanford, *Hurricane* (also known as *Forbidden Paradise*), Paramount, 1979.

Jim, *The High Country* (also known as *The First Hello*), Crown International Pictures, 1981.

Casey, *Tin Man,* Thomas/Biston and Westcom, 1983.

Michael Radcliffe, *Hambone and Hillie,* New World, 1984.

Pete, *The Census Taker* (also known as *Husbands, Wives, Money & "Murder"*), Seymour Borde, 1984.

Jack Ringtree, *In the Shadow of Kilimanjaro,* Scotti Bros., 1984.

Captain Pedro Barrios, *The Sea Serpent* (also known as *Serpiente de mar, Hydra,* and *Hydra–Monster of the Deep*), 1984.

Major Elbert Stevens, *What Waits Below* (also known as *Secrets of the Phantom Caverns*), Blossom, 1984.

George Gardner, *Invaders from Mars,* Cannon, 1986.

Danny Sullivan, *The Fantasist,* ITC Entertainment Group, 1986.

The king, *Mio min Mio* (also known as *The Land of Faraway, Mio moy Mio,* and *Mio in the Land of Faraway*), Svenska Filminstitutet, 1987.

Sergeant Joseph "Hard" Case, *A Case of Honor,* Eastern Film Management Corporation, 1988.

Arthur, *The Drifter,* Concorde, 1988.

Seaman Miller, *Return to the River Kwai,* TriStar, 1989.

Sonny Crawford, *Texasville,* Columbia, 1990.

Frank Collins, *Istanbul: Keep Your Eyes Open* (also known as *Istanbul*), Cori Films–Magnum, 1990.

Hermia's father, *Ill Met by Moonlight,* Gotham Entertainment Group, 1994.

Sam, *Digger,* Paramount Home Video, 1994.

(Uncredited) Owens Ranch cowboy, *Blue Sky,* 1994.

Slayton, *Ava's Magical Adventure,* 1994.

Jurgen Brauner, *Hourglass* (also known as *The Hitcher '95*), 1995.

Ben Choice, *Horses and Champions,* Cinequanon Pictures International, 1995.

Nelson Houseman, *Top Dog,* Metro–Goldwyn–Mayer/ United Artists, 1995.

Charles Walkan, *Ripper Man,* Warner Bros., 1996.

Himself, *Ben Johnson: Third Cowboy on the Right* (documentary), FBN, 1996.

Mr. Donald Crandell, *Uncle Sam,* Solomon International Pictures, 1996.

Frank, *Fox Hunt,* 1996.

Clay, *Ringer,* 1996.

John, *The Prince,* 1996.

Mortal Challenge, New Horizons Home Video, 1997.

American Hero (also known as *Jack Armstrong*), 1997.

Lieutenant John Drake, *Absolute Force* (also known as *Total Force*), Cinequanon Pictures International, 1997.

Carl Weaver, *Mixed Blessings,* 1998.

Fouquet, *The Man in the Iron Mask,* Invisible Studio/ The Fastest Cheapest Best Film Corporation, 1998.

Illusion Infinity, 1998.

Fouquet, *The Three Musketeers Meet the Man in the Iron Mask,* 1998.

Salvatore Tandino, *The Waterfront* (also known as *Maximum Justice*), AMCO Entertainment Group, 1998.

No Rest for the Wicked, 1998.

Diamondbacks, 1998.

Marcus, *Lone Tiger* (also known as *Tiger Mask*), 1999.

(Uncredited) Johnny Canty, *The Prince and the Surfer,* A–pix Entertainment, Inc., 1999.

John Carver, *The Boy with the X–Ray Eyes* (also known as *X–Ray Boy* and *X–treme Teens*), 1999.

Jack, *A Smaller Place* (also known as *The Hiding Place*), American Multi–Cinema, 2000.

Fred Donavan, *Held for Ransom,* Cutting Edge Entertainment, 2000.

Michael McCaffery, Trevor's dad, *The Haven,* Dreadnought Films, 2000.

(Uncredited) President George Walker Bush, *The Crocodile Hunter: Collision Course,* Metro–Goldwyn–Mayer, 2002.

Francis Hiller, Douglas, Henry, Alan at 40 years, and Patricia's father, *Paradise,* 2003.

Mr. McFarland, *Elephant,* Fine Line Features, 2003.

Rotunno, *The Entrepreneurs* (also known as *Just One Look* and *The $cheme*), Cargo Films, 2003.

Mr. Kidman, *The Girl Next Door,* Twentieth Century–Fox, 2004.

Mack Cameron, *Paradise, Texas,* 2005.

Thomas, *Chinamen's Chance,* 2006.

The American Standard, 2006.

Television Appearances; Series:

Tom Porter, *Land of the Lost,* ABC, 1991–93.

President George Walker Bush, *That's My Bush!* (also known as *That's My Dick*), Comedy Central, 2001.

Television Appearances; Miniseries:

Miles Eastin, *Arthur Hailey's "The Moneychangers"* (also known as *The Moneychangers*), NBC, 1976.

Young David, *The Story of David,* ABC, 1976.

Adam Trask, *East of Eden* (also known as *John Steinbeck's "East of Eden"*), ABC, 1980.

Voice of Silver Parrish, *The Great War and the Shaping of the 20th Century* (also known as *The Great War*), PBS, 1996.

Television Appearances; Movies:

George Willard, *Winesburg, Ohio,* 1973.

Rudi Miller, *The Gift of Love,* ABC, 1978.

Steward, *Return Engagement,* 1978.

John Baker, *A Shining Season,* CBS, 1979.

Dwight Worker, *Escape,* CBS, 1980.

Morris Frank, "Love Leads the Way," *Disney Sunday Movie,* ABC, 1986.

Father Thomas O'Neil, *Perry Mason: The Case of the Notorious Nun* (also known as *The Case of the Notorious Nun*), NBC, 1986.

Tim Faraday, *Island Sons,* ABC, 1987.

Ward Derderian, *Yakuza Connection* (also known as *California Roll*), 1995.

Zach Blackwell, *Personal Vendetta,* 1995.

Jack, *Death Game* (also known as *Mortal Challenge*), Showtime, 1996.

Dean, *Black Sea 213,* TMC, 1999.

Phillip Frodden, *Mr. Atlas,* Showtime, 1999.

Detective Stepnoski, *Murder Seen* (also known as *Murder Scene*), 2000.

President George W. Bush, *DC 9/11: Time of Crisis,* Showtime, 2003.

Walter Bedell "Beetle" Smith, *Ike: Countdown to D–Day,* Arts and Entertainment, 2004.

Clarence, *Jane Doe: Now You See It, Now You Don't,* Hallmark Channel, 2005.

Hank Poelker, *Vampire Bats,* CBS, 2005.

Television Appearances; Specials:

Presenter, *The 44th Annual Academy Awards,* NBC, 1972.

Interviewee, *Picture This: The Times of Peter Bogdanovich in Archer City, Texas* (documentary), Showtime, 1991.

Voice, *500 Nations* (documentary), CBS, 1995.

Voice of Silver Parrish, *The Great War and the Shaping of the 20th Century* (documentary; also known as *1914–18*), PBS, 1996.

Narrator, *John Glenn, American Hero,* E! Entertainment Television, 1998.

Television Appearances; Episodic:

Eugene Gant, "Look Homeward, Angel," *CBS Playhouse,* CBS, 1972.

"Nose Job," *Half Nelson,* NBC, 1985.

"Joker," *The Hitchhiker* (also known as *Le Voyageur*), HBO, 1987.

Miley Judson, "The Hellgramite Method," *The Twilight Zone,* syndicated, 1988.

Mr. Franklin, "Missing Persons," *Freddy's Nightmares* (also known as *Freddy's Nightmares: A Nightmare on Elm Street: The Series*), 1989.

Forrester, "Here There Be Tygers," *The Ray Bradbury Theatre* (also known as *Le monde fantastique de Ray Bradbury, Mystery Theatre, Ray Bradbury presente, The Bradbury Trilogy,* and *The Ray Bradbury Theatre*), HBO, 1990.

Reverend Chuck, "Father Knows Best," *Gideon's Crossing,* ABC, 2000.

Reverend Chuck, "Is There a Wise Man in the House?," *Gideon's Crossing,* ABC, 2000.

Vice Principal Cole, "Tornado Prom," *That '70s Show,* Fox, 2002.

The View, ABC, 2003.

Ritt Everett, "Vanished," *Navy NCIS: Naval Criminal Investigative Service* (also known as *NCIS* and *NCIS: Naval Criminal Investigative Service*), CBS, 2004.

Mind of Mencia, Comedy Central, 2004.

Carl Murphy, "Owner of a Lonely Heart," *Grey's Anatomy,* ABC, 2005.

Television Work; Specials:

Producer, *Picture This: The Times of Peter Bogdanovich in Archer City, Texas,* Showtime, 1991.

Stage Appearances:

Kenneth Talley, Jr., *Fifth of July,* New Apollo Theatre, New York City, 1980–82.

Appeared in *West Side Story,* Santa Barbara, CA.

Major Tours:

Appeared with the Santa Barbara Madrigal Society, European cities, 1967.

RECORDINGS

Video Games:

Frank, *Fox Hunt,* Redwood Communications, 1996.

OTHER SOURCES

Periodicals:

People Weekly, May 28, 2001, p. 81.

BRADDOCK, Mickey
    See DOLENZ, Micky

BRIDGES, Todd 1965–

PERSONAL

Born May 27, 1965, in San Francisco, CA; son of James, Sr. (an agent) and Betty A. (an actress, director, and manager) Bridges; brother of Jimmy Bridges (an actor);

uncle of Penny Bae Bridges and Brook Marie Bridges (both actresses); married second wife, Dori Smith, May 25, 1998; children: Spencer Todd.

Addresses: *Agent*—Nancy Chaidez Agency, 1555 Vine St., Suite 223, Hollywood, CA 90028.

Career: Actor, producer, director, cinematographer, and writer. Little Bridge Productions, founder (with brother, James Bridges, Jr.); appeared in television commercials, including Jell–O. Todd Bridges Youth Foundation, founder, 1992; lectures teens around the United States about drugs, alcohol, and safe sex.

Awards, Honors: Young Artist Award nomination, best young actor in a comedy series, 1983, 1984, both for *Diff'rent Strokes.*

CREDITS

Film Appearances:
Himself/cyclist, *Bicycle Safety* (documentary), 1975.
Petie, *Twice Dead,* Nelson, 1988.
Water man, *She's Out of Control,* Columbia, 1989.
The Sounds of Silence, 1992.
Johnny Davis, *Homeboys,* American International Pictures Home Video, 1992.
Tyrone, *Prisoners of Love,* 1996.
Billy, *Busted,* PM Entertainment Group, 1996.
Tyrone, *Gangstaz* (also known as *Last Chance*), 1996.
Hoover Park, 1997.
The Waterfront, Ares Motion Picture Company, 1997.
Dr. Glick, *The Girl Gets Moe* (also known as *Love to Kill*), Girl Gets Moe Pictures, 1997.
Thomas, *A Devil Disguised,* 1997.
Richard, *A Day in the Life of Mia,* 1997.
Burn, *The Thief and the Stripper* (also known as *Strip 'n Run*), Bruder Releasing, 1998.
The Waterfront (also known as *Maximum Justice*), AMCO Entertainment Group, 1998.
Dr. Acosta, *Flat Out,* 1998.
Himself, *Building Bridges,* 1999.
Himself, *Labor Day,* 2000.
Night watchman, *Hollywood,* 2000.
Terry, *Flossin,* Urban Domain, 2000.
Lincoln, *Dumb Luck,* 2001.
Inhumanity, York Entertainment, 2001.
Himself, *Wrong Way to Sundance,* 2001.
Ted, *Baby of the Family,* 2002.
Harrison Dodge, *Pacino Is Missing,* 2002.
Easy T, *Welcome to America,* 2002.
Lamar, *Scream at the Sound of the Beep,* 2002.
Todd, *The Beach House,* 2002.
Eddie, *The Climb,* WorldWide Pictures, 2002.
Tupac: Resurrection (documentary), Paramount, 2003.

Himself, *Pauly Shore Is Dead,* CKrush Entertainment, 2003.
Himself, *Dickie Roberts: Former Child Star* (also known as *Dickie Roberts: (Former) Child Star*), Paramount, 2003.
Billy, *Black Ball* (also known as *Full Circle*), Cargo Films, 2003.
May Day, 2003.
Alex, *Land of the Free?,* 2004.
Herardo, *Curse of the Maya* (also known as *Evil Grave: Curse of the Maya*), David Heavener Entertainment, 2004.
Carson, *Issue,* 2005.
Henry Nails, *Treasure 'n tha Hood,* Lightyear, 2005.
Jimmy, *I Got Five On It,* Image Entertainment, 2005.
William, *Last Call,* 2006.
Dennis, *The Damned,* 2006.

Also appeared in *Fire Sale.*

Film Work:
Cinematographer, *A Devil Disguised,* 1997.
Producer and director, *Building Bridges,* 1999.
Producer and director, *Flossin,* 2000.
Producer and director, *Black Ball* (also known as *Full Circle*), Cargo Films, 2003.

Television Appearances; Series:
Loomis, *Fish,* ABC, 1977–78.
Willis Jackson Drummond, *Diff'rent Strokes,* NBC, 1978–85, then ABC, 1985–86.
Juice number two, *The Young and the Restless* (also known as *Y&R*), CBS, 2002.
Skating with Celebrities, Fox, 2006.

Television Appearances; Miniseries:
Bud, *Roots,* ABC, 1977.
I Love the '70s, VH1, 2003.
100 Greatest Kids Stars, VH1, 2005.

Television Appearances; Movies:
Robert, *Katherine* (also known as *The Radical*), ABC, 1975.
Todd York, *A Killing Affair* (also known as *Behind the Badge*), CBS, 1977.
Jason Hayes, *The Return of the Mod Squad,* ABC, 1979.
Otto Lipton, *High School U.S.A.* (also known as *High School USA*), NBC, 1983.
Circle of Pain, 1996.
Baron, *The Darkling,* 2000.
Himself, *Dancing in September,* HBO, 2000.
Power plant guard, *Ghost Dog: A Detective Tail,* PAX, 2003.
The man, *Jane Doe: Now You See It, Now You Don't,* Hallmark Channel, 2005.
Peter, *Alien Express,* Sci–Fi Channel, 2005.

Television Appearances; Specials:

NBC team member, *Battle of the Network Stars VI*, ABC, 1979.

Himself, *Good Evening, Captain,* CBS, 1981.

Circus of the Stars #6, CBS, 1981.

Roller Disco Championship, 1981.

NBC Star Salute to 1981, NBC, 1981.

Performer, *Circus of the Stars #7,* CBS, 1982.

Red team member, *Battle of the Video Games,* syndicated, 1983.

Hang Tight, Willy–Bill, syndicated, 1983.

The Lost Youth of Hollywood, NBC, 1991.

Robin Leach's Private Files: The Price of Fame, syndicated, 1993.

The Beth Littleford Interview Special, Comedy Central, 1998.

Diff'rent Strokes: The E! True Hollywood Story, E! Entertainment Television, 1998.

Crack dealer, *After Diff'rent Strokes: When the Laughter Stopped,* Fox, 2000.

TV Guide's Truth behind the Sitcoms 2, Fox, 2000.

Child Stars: Their Story (documentary), Arts and Entertainment, 2000.

Entertainment Tonight Presents: TV's Greatest Scandals, syndicated, 2000.

Celebrity Boxing, Fox, 2002.

TV Land Awards: A Celebration of Classic TV (also known as *1st Annual TV Land Awards*), TV Land, 2003.

BET Comedy Awards, Black Entertainment Television, 2004.

100 Greatest Kid Stars, VH1, 2005.

Television Appearances; Pilots:

Leonard Brown, *The Orphan and the Dude,* ABC, 1975.

Himself, *Komedy Tonite,* NBC, 1978.

Television Appearances; Episodic:

Truman Jackson, "The Hero," *Barney Miller* (also known as *The Life and Times of Captain Barney Miller*), ABC, 1975.

Solomon Henry, "The Wisdom of Solomon," *Little House on the Prairie,* NBC, 1977.

Josh, "The Stray," *The Waltons,* CBS, 1977.

Michael Jr., "The Kissing Bandit/Mike and Ike/Witness," *The Love Boat,* ABC, 1978.

Josh, "The Illusion," *The Waltons,* CBS, 1978.

Willis Jackson, "The Drummonds' Visit," *The Facts of Life,* NBC, 1979.

Himself, "CHiPs Goes Roller Disco," *CHiPs,* NBC, 1979.

Dinah! syndicated, 1979.

20/20, ABC, 1979.

Here's Boomer, NBC, 1980.

Himself, "The Great 5K Star Race and Boulder Wrap Party, Part 2," *CHiPs,* NBC, 1980.

The Mike Douglas Show, syndicated, 1980.

The Hollywood Squares, syndicated, 1980.

The John Davidson Show, syndicated, 1980.

"Boomer's Eastside Story," *Here's Boomer,* NBC, 1981.

Willis Jackson, "Bought and Sold," *The Facts of Life,* 1981.

Kids Are People, Too, ABC, 1981.

Hour Magazine, syndicated, 1981.

Dance Fever, syndicated, 1983.

All–Star Blitz, ABC, 1985.

The New Lassie, 1990.

The Howard Stern Show, syndicated, 1991.

Himself, "On Melrose Avenue," *The Ben Stiller Show,* Fox, 1992.

Himself, "Episode with Bobcat Goldthwait," *The Ben Stiller Show,* Fox, 1992.

Trevor, "Cop Star," *L.A. Heat,* TNT, 1999.

"I Love 1980," *I Love 1980's,* BBC 2, 2001.

Himself, "Newsmakers Edition," *Weakest Link* (also known as *The Weakest Link USA*), NBC, 2001.

Himself, *Oh Drama!,* Black Entertainment Television, 2001.

"It's a Nude, Nude, Nude, Nude World," *Sons of the Beach,* FX Channel, 2001.

Mad TV, Fox, 2001.

T. J. Davis, "Saved by the Bell: Jessie's Song/The Jeffersons: Florence in Love," *The Rerun Show,* NBC, 2002.

Contestant, *Cram,* Game Show Network, 2003.

Himself, *Banzai,* Fox, 2003.

Hollywood Squares (also known as *H2* and *H2: Hollywood Squares*), syndicated, 2003.

Himself, "Mel's Dinner," *The Surreal Life,* 2004.

"Gary Coleman," *A&E Biography,* Arts and Entertainment, 2005.

Himself, *Punk'd,* MTV, 2005.

Himself, "Changing Times and Trends," *TV Land Confidential,* TV Land, 2005.

Also appeared as young jockey, "The Jockey," *Here's Boomer,* and Turk, "Rocker Boomer," *Here's Boomer.*

Television Work; Specials:

Consultant, *After Diff'rent Strokes: When the Laughter Stopped,* Fox, 2000.

RECORDINGS

Music Videos:

Appeared in Moby's "We Are All Made out of Stars," 2002.

WRITINGS

Film Scripts:
Building Bridges, 1999.

OTHER SOURCES

Books:
Contemporary Black Biography, Vol. 37, Gale Group, 2003.

Periodicals:
Entertainment Weekly, January 31, 1997, p. 11; February 4, 2000, p. 84.
Jet, January 18, 1993, p. 58; February 1, 1993, p. 64; March 29, 1993, p. 34; April 5, 1993, p. 37; August 16, 1993, p. 56; December 27, 1993, p. 29; February 10, 1997, p. 48; October 18, 1999, p. 36; April 30, 2001, p. 64.
Newsweek, January 16, 1995, p. 60.
People, July 22, 2002, p. 16.

BROOKS, Joel 1949–

PERSONAL

Born December 17, 1949, in New York, NY. *Education:* Attended Hunter College and University of Minnesota.

Addresses: *Agent*—The Gage Group, 14724 Ventura Blvd., Suite 505, Los Angeles, CA 91403.

Career: Actor.

CREDITS

Film Appearances:
Len Garber, *Stir Crazy,* Columbia, 1980.
Xerox boss, *Smithereens,* New Line Cinema, 1982.
Honky Tonk Man, Warner Bros., 1982.
Best Defense, Paramount, 1984.
Ben, *Protocol,* Warner Bros., 1984.
Jake, *Skin Deep,* Twentieth Century–Fox, 1989.
Realtor, *Indecent Proposal,* Paramount, 1993.
Morgan, *Blue Flame,* Columbia/TriStar Home Video, 1995.
Pietro, *Swallows,* 1999.
Irv Katz, *Role of a Lifetime,* PorchLight Entertainment, 2001.

Vance Johnson, *The Gatekeeper,* Screen Media Films, 2002.
Frienda Victim, *Now You Know,* Miramax, 2002.
Bound by Lies (also known as *The Long Dark Kiss*), 2005.
Hat Sister, *The Mostly Unfabulous Social Life of Ethan Green,* Regent Releasing, 2005.

Television Appearances; Series:
Lieutenant Billy Dean, *Private Benjamin,* CBS, 1982.
Spud Le Boone, *Teachers Only,* NBC, 1983.
Randy, *Hail to the Chief,* ABC, 1985.
J. D. Lucas, *My Sister Sam,* CBS, 1986.
Warren Pepper, *Good Grief,* Fox, 1990–91.
Harold Krowten, *Dudley,* CBS, 1993.
Robbie, *Six Feet Under,* HBO, 2001–2002.

Television Appearances; Movies:
Paul Wagner, *The Mating Season,* CBS, 1980.
Phil Garrett, *Stranded,* NBC, 1986.
Lee, *Help Wanted: Kids,* ABC, 1986.
Rod Armitage, *Going to the Chapel* (also known as *Wedding Day* and *Wedding Day Blues*), NBC, 1988.
Max Kane, *Dinner at Eight,* TNT, 1989.
Gary Nussbaum, *Are You Lonesome Tonight?,* USA Network, 1992.
Larry Walker, *Here Come the Munsters,* Fox, 1995.
Meir, *The Man Who Captured Eichmann,* TNT, 1996.
Mr. Norris, "Toothless," *Wonderful World of Disney,* ABC, 1997.
Ferguson, *Mr. Headmistress,* ABC, 1998.
Jacob Mayhew, *Babylon 5: The River of Souls* (also known as *The River of Souls* and *River of Souls: A Babylon 5 Adventure*), TNT, 1998.
Irv Katz, *Role of a Lifetime,* NBC, 2000.
Judge, *Spring Break Lawyer,* MTV, 2001.
Raymond Garrett, *The Facts of Life Reunion,* ABC, 2001.
Alan, *Door to Door,* TNT, 2002.

Television Appearances; Pilots:
Cal Sloan, *After George,* CBS, 1983.
Mitchell, *Just Married,* ABC, 1985.
Psychiatrist, *Rowdies,* ABC, 1986.
Rigaletti, *We'll Take Manhattan,* NBC, 1990.

Television Appearances; Specials:
Grumio, *Kiss Me, Petruchio* (documentary), PBS, 1981.
Franklyn, "Gwendolyn," *NBC Presents the AFI Comedy Special,* NBC, 1987.
Paul Stengal, *Morning Glory,* 1989.

Television Appearances; Episodic:
Dr. Prescott, "Jack the Ripper," *Three's Company,* CBS, 1979.

Harwell, "Bugging the Governor," *Benson,* 1980.

Dr. Prescott, "The Root of All Evil," *Three's Company,* CBS, 1980.

Ignazio, "Cementing Relationships," *M*A*S*H,* CBS, 1980.

Bennett, "Starting Over," *Eight Is Enough,* 1981.

Nick, "Tony's Lady," *Taxi,* 1982.

Mr. Tout, "Horsing Around," *It's a Living* (also known as *Making a Living*), 1982.

Vinnie, Jr., "The Over–the–Hill Girls," *Alice,* 1983.

Raymond Garrett, "Brave New World," *The Facts of Life,* NBC, 1983.

Director, "Mr. T and mr. t," *Diff'rent Strokes,* 1983.

Blair, "Billie and the Cat," *Night Court,* NBC, 1984.

The director, "The Dukes in Hollywood," *The Dukes of Hazzard,* CBS, 1984.

Raymond Garrett, "Joint Custody," *The Facts of Life,* 1984.

Laddie Johnson, "Phantom of the Galleria," *Shadow Chasers,* ABC, 1985.

Super Password, NBC, 1985.

Jack Holland, "Cold Reading," *The Twilight Zone,* CBS, 1986.

Jerome Sedgewick, "Smiles We Left Behind: Parts 1 & 2," *Riptide,* 1986.

Kiefer Mitchell, "Dummy Dearest," *L.A. Law,* 1988.

Chad Jorgenson, "Investment in Death," *Hunter,* 1989.

Warren Pepper, *Good Grief,* 1990.

Santoro the Great, *Jack's Place,* 1992.

Don Butcher, "Silence of the Lambskins," *L.A. Law,* 1992.

Falow, "Move Along Home (aka Sore Losers)," *Star Trek: Deep Space Nine* (also known as *DS9, Deep Space Nine,* and *Star Trek: DS9*), syndicated, 1993.

Dr. Zudikoff, "A Face Worse Than Death," *Dream On,* HBO, 1994.

Judd McCoy, "Money Trouble," *Dr. Quinn, Medicine Woman,* CBS, 1994.

Harrison Powell, "Playing for Keeps," *Diagnosis Murder,* CBS, 1994.

Bernard Dubois, *The Mommies,* NBC, 1994.

Jacob Mayhew, *Babylon 5,* 1994.

Gallery owner, "Donny's Exhibit," *New York Daze* (also known as *Too Something*), 1995.

Ted Duffy, "Unwilling Witness," *Murder, She Wrote,* CBS, 1995.

Donald Rafferty/Anonymous, "Chip Off the Old Clark," *Lois and Clark: The New Adventures of Superman* (also known as *Lois and Clark* and *The New Adventures of Superman*), ABC, 1995.

Major Domo, *Homeboys in Outer Space,* UPN, 1996.

George, "A Comedy of Eros," *Murphy Brown,* CBS, 1996.

Del Stuart, "The Engagement: Part 2," *Living Single* (also known as *My Girls*), Fox, 1996.

Voice, "A Room with a Bellevue," *Duckman: Private Dick/Family Man* (animated), 1996.

Aaron Geller, "Why Can't Even a Couple of Us Get Along?" *Brooklyn South,* CBS, 1997.

Jerry Lindemann, "Do Not Go Squealing into That Good Night," *Style and Substance,* 1998.

Mr. Curtis, *For Your Love,* The WB, 1998.

Emperor Larry, "And the Sabrina Goes to ... ," *Sabrina, the Teenage Witch* (also known as *Sabrina* and *Sabrina Goes to College*), ABC, 1998.

Archibald Frost, "Recipe for Success," *The Wayans Bros.,* The WB, 1998.

Mr. Worthington, *The Parent 'Hood,* The WB, 1999.

Dr. Hubbell, "Love Unlimited," *Ally McBeal,* Fox, 1999.

Arthur, "Dharma Drags Edward out of Retirement," *Dharma and Greg,* ABC, 1999.

Dr. Van Fertle, "I Wanna Reach Right Out and Grab Ya," *Beverly Hills, 90210,* Fox, 1999.

Clark, "Arthur 2: On the Rocks," *It's Like, You Know ... ,* ABC, 1999.

Clark, "Hollywood Shuffle," *It's Like, You Know ... ,* ABC, 1999.

Dr. Hogan, "Child Care," *Strong Medicine,* Lifetime, 2001.

Rachel's attorney, "Property of Sylver Screen," *The Lot,* AMC, 2001.

Roger's doctor, "No Good Deed," *Diagnosis Murder,* CBS, 2001.

Crossing Jordan, NBC, 2002.

Patrick, "Rush to Judgment," *The Division* (also known as *Heart of the City*), Lifetime, 2003.

Mr. Hodell, "The Shower," *Everybody Loves Raymond* (also known as *Raymond*), CBS, 2003.

Mr. Franklin, "'Twas the Night Before Homecoming," *Run of the House,* The WB, 2003.

Bernard, "Chris Gets a Job," *Run of the House,* The WB, 2003.

Dr. Bruckner, "The Big Double Date with My Mate Episode," *Half & Half,* UPN, 2004.

Dr. Bruckner, "The Big Labor of Love Episode," *Half & Half,* UPN, 2004.

Fred Cohen, "Trials," *Without a Trace,* CBS, 2004.

Bridges, "Batter Up," *The Closer,* TNT, 2005.

Joel Messerschmidt, "The Giggle," *Phil of the Future,* The Disney Channel, 2005.

Joel Messerschmidt, "Phil Without a Future," *Phil of the Future,* The Disney Channel, 2005.

Joel Messerschmidt and Battina Messerschmidt, "Maybe–Sitting," *Phil of the Future,* The Disney Channel, 2005.

Felix Parker, "Zoo York," *CSI: NY,* CBS, 2005.

Joel, "Three's Company," *The War at Home,* Fox, 2006.

Dr. Mark, "Looney Tunes," *The War at Home,* Fox, 2006.

Also appeared in *It Takes Two,* ABC; as Bernard, "The Unnatural," *Run of the House,* The WB.

Stage Appearances:
The Spelling Bee, Playwrights Horizons, New York City, 1976.

Cracks, Playwrights Horizons, 1977.

Will Willard and Steve Williams, *Museum,* Delacorte Theatre, New York City, 1978.

Interpreter, lord, and soldier, *All's Well That Ends Well,* Delacorte Theatre, New York Shakespeare Festival, New York City, 1978.

Grumio, *The Taming of the Shrew,* Delacorte Theatre, New York Shakespeare Festival, 1978.

Breaking and Entering, Playwrights Horizons, 1979.

Maurice Pulvermacher and Eddie, *I Can Get It for You Wholesale,* American Jewish Theatre, New York City, 1991.

Also appeared in *Flux* and *New Jerusalem,* both New York Shakespeare Festival, New York City; *Aaron Weiss; Auto-Destruct; Fog and Mismanagement; Oedipus Rex; The Prague Spring; The Rivals; Sweet Apple Cider.*

BROWN, David 1916–

PERSONAL

Born July 28, 1916, in New York, NY; son of Edward Fisher and Lillian (maiden name, Baren) Brown; married Liberty LeGacy, April 15, 1940 (divorced, 1951); married Wayne Clark, May 25, 1951 (divorced, 1957); married Helen Gurley (an author and editor), September 25, 1959; children: (first marriage) Bruce LeGacy. *Education:* Stanford University, A.B., 1936; Columbia University, M.S., 1937.

Addresses: *Agent*—International Creative Management, 8942 Wilshire Blvd., Beverly Hills, CA 90211. *Office*—Manhattan Project, 1775 Broadway, Suite 410, New York, NY 10019.

Career: Film producer, writer, and journalist. Partner with Richard D. Zanuck. *San Francisco News,* apprentice; *Wall Street Journal,* apprentice, 1936; Fairchild Publications, night editor and assistant drama critic,1937–39; Milk Research Council, editorial director, 1939–40; Street & Smith Publications, associate editor, 1940–43; *Liberty Magazine,* associate editor, executive editor, and editor–in–chief, 1943–49; American Medical Association, editorial director, national campaign, 1949; *Cosmopolitan,* magazine, associate editor and managing editor, 1949–52; managing editor, Twentieth Century–Fox Film Corporation, story editor, and head of scenario department, 1952–56; Twentieth

Century–Fox, studio executive committee, producer, executive story editor, and head of scenario department, 1956–60; New American Library of World Literature, Inc., editorial vice–president, 1963–64; Twentieth Century–Fox, vice–president and director of story operation, 1964–69, and executive vice–president of creative operations, 1969–70; Warner Bros., executive vice–president, 1970–72; Zanuck/Brown Company, Universal Pictures, partner and director, 1972–80; Twentieth Century–Fox, producer, 1980–83; Warner Bros., producer, 1983—; Manhattan Project Ltd., president, 1987—; Island World, president, 1990–92. *Benjamin Franklin Magazine,* final judge for best short story, 1955–58. *Military service:* U.S. Army, 1943–45, Quartermaster Corps and Military Intelligence; became first lieutenant.

Member: American Film Institute (trustee, member of executive committee, 1972–80), Commission on Film, Museum of Modern Art (trustee on film, New York City), Academy of Motion Picture Arts and Sciences, Producer's Guild of America, The Century Club, Players Club, Overseas Press Club, Dutch Treat, National Press Club, New York Friar's Club.

Awards, Honors: National Association of Theatre Owners of America, Producer of the Year, 1974 and 1985; Academy Award, best picture, 1974, for *The Sting;* Academy Award nomination (with Richard D. Zanuck), best picture, 1975, for *Jaws;* Academy Award nomination (with Richard D. Zanuck), best picture, 1982, for *The Verdict;* Academy Award (with Lili Fini Zanuck and Richard D. Zanuck), best picture, Wise Owl Award second place (with Lili Fini Zanuck and Richard D. Zanuck), television and theatrical film fiction, Retirement Research Foundation, 1990, both for *Driving Miss Daisy;* Irving G. Thalberg Memorial Award (also known as Academy Award of Merit), Academy of Motion Picture Arts and Sciences, 1991; Academy Award nomination (with Rob Reiner and Andrew Scheinman), best picture, 1993, for *A Few Good Men;* Film Award nomination (with Michael Tolkin, Nick Wechsler, and Robert Altman), best film, British Academy of Film and Television Arts, Independent Spirit Award (with Tolkin and Wechsler), best feature film, 1993, both for *The Player;* David O. Selznick Lifetime Achievement Award in Theatrical Motion Pictures, Producers Guild of America, 1993; Gotham Producer Award, Independent Features Project, 1993; Wise Owl Award (with Sophie Hurst, David Manson, and Bonnie Pale), television and theatrical film fiction, Retirement Research Foundation, 1995, for *The Cemetery Club;* Hollywood Discovery Award, outstanding achievement in producing, Hollywood Film Festival, 1998; Evelyn F. Burkey Award, Writers Guild of America East, 1999; ShoWest Award (with Richard D. Zanuck), producer of the year, ShoWest Convention, 2001; Academy Award nomination (with Kit Golden and Leslie Holleran), best picture, 2001, for *Chocolat.*

CREDITS

Film Work:

Producer, *The Sting,* Universal, 1973.

Executive producer, *SSSSSSS* (also known as *SSSSnake*), Universal, 1973.

Producer, *The Sugarland Express,* Universal, 1974.

Executive producer, *The Black Windmill,* Universal, 1974.

Producer, *Willie Dynamite,* Universal, 1974.

Producer, *The Girl from Petrovka,* Universal, 1974.

Producer, *Jaws,* Universal, 1975.

Executive producer, *The Eiger Sanction,* Universal, 1975.

Producer, *MacArthur,* Universal, 1977.

Producer, *Jaws 2,* Universal, 1978.

Producer, *The Island,* Universal, 1980.

Producer, *The Verdict,* Warner Bros., 1982.

Assistant director, *The Killing Fields,* Warner Bros., 1984.

Producer, *Neighbors,* Warner Bros., 1985.

Production manager, *Defence of the Realm,* Warner Bros., 1985.

Producer, *Cocoon,* Twentieth Century–Fox, 1985.

Producer, *Target,* Warner Bros., 1985.

Producer, *Cocoon: The Return,* Twentieth Century–Fox, 1988.

Executive producer, *Driving Miss Daisy,* Warner Bros., 1989.

Associate producer, *Hear My Song,* Miramax, 1991.

Producer, *The Player,* Fine Line, 1992.

Producer, *A Few Good Men,* Columbia, 1992.

Coproducer, *Rich in Love,* Metro–Goldwyn–Mayer, 1992.

Executive producer, *Watch It,* Skouras, 1993.

Producer, *The Cemetery Club* (also known as *Looking for a Live One*), Buena Vista, 1993.

Producer, *Canadian Bacon,* Gramercy Pictures, 1994.

Producer, *Kiss the Girls,* Paramount, 1997.

Producer, *The Saint,* Paramount, 1997.

Producer, *Deep Impact,* Paramount, 1998.

Producer, *Angela's Ashes,* Paramount, 1999.

Producer, *Chocolat,* Miramax, 2000.

Producer, *Along Came a Spider* (also known as *Im netz der spinne* and *Le masque de l'araignee*), Paramount, 2000.

Producer, *The Ninth Man,* DreamWorks, 2005.

The Last Mogul: Life and Times of Lew Wasserman (documentary; also known as *The Last Mogul*), ThinkFilm, 2005.

Producer, *Peace Like a River,* Warner Bros., 2006.

Film Appearances:

Himself, *The Making of Steve Spielberg's "Jaws"* (documentary), Universal Home Video, 1995.

Himself, *Off the Menu: The Last Days of Chasen's* (documentary), Northern Arts Entertainment, 1997.

(Uncredited) Man in photo, *Chocolat,* Miramax, 2000.

Himself, *The Making of "Jaws 2"* (documentary), Universal Studios Home Video, 2001.

(Uncredited) Himself, *John Williams: The Music of "Jaws 2"* (documentary short), Universal Studios Home Video, 2001.

Himself, *The Making of "Along Came a Spider"* (documentary short), Paramount, 2001.

Final Cut: The Making of "Heaven's Gate" and the Unmaking of a Studio, Trio, 2004.

Himself, *The Last Mogul: Life and Times of Lew Wasserman* (documentary; also known as *The Last Mogul*), ThinkFilm, 2005.

Himself, *The Shark Is Still Working* (documentary), 2006.

Television Executive Producer; Miniseries:

A Season in Purgatory, CBS, 1996.

Television Producer; Movies:

Women and Men (also known as *Women and Men: Stories of Seduction, The Art of Seduction,* and *Women & Men 2*), HBO, 1990.

Women and Men II (also known as *Women and Men II: In Love There Are No Rules*), HBO, 1991.

Television Executive Producer; Movies:

Framed, 2002.

Television Executive Producer; Pilots:

Barrington, CBS, 1987.

Television Work; Pilots:

Stage producer, *Tru,* PBS, 1992.

Television Appearances; Specials:

The 63rd Annual Academy Awards Presentation, ABC, 1991.

20th Century–Fox: The First 50 Years, AMC, 1997.

Hidden Hollywood: Treasures from the 20th Century Fox Film Vaults, AMC, 1997.

20th Century Fox: The Blockbuster Years, AMC, 2000.

What is a Producer?, E! Entertainment Television, 2001.

Intimate Portrait: Raquel Welch, Lifetime, 2001.

(Uncredited) Himself, *Cleopatra: The Film That Changed Hollywood* (documentary), AMC, 2001.

Himself, *Marilyn Monroe: The Final Days* (documentary), AMC, 2001.

Making the Connection: Untold Stories of The French Connection (documentary), Fox Movie Channel, 2001.

"M*A*S*H," *History Vs. Hollywood* (documentary), History Channel, 2001.

Hello, He Lied & Other Truths from the Hollywood Trenches (documentary; also known as *Hello, He Lied*), AMC, 2002.

Guilty Pleasures: The Dominick Dunne Story, 2002.

Television Appearances; Episodic:
American Cinema, PBS, 1995.
Himself, "Darryl F. Zanuck: 20th Century Filmmaker," *A&E Biography,* Arts and Entertainment, 1995.
"Gentleman's Agreement," *Backstory,* AMC, 1999.
At Home With ... , HGTV, 1999.
Himself, "Jaws," *The E! True Hollywood Story,* E! Entertainment Television, 2002.

Stage Producer:
Tru, Booth Theatre, New York City, 1989–90.
A Few Good Men, Music Box Theatre, New York City, 1989–91.
The Cemetery Club, Brooks Atkinson Theatre, New York City, 1990.
Sweet Smell of Success, Chicago, IL, 2001, then Martin Beck Theatre, New York City, 2002.
Dirty Rotten Scoundrels, Imperial Theatre, New York City, 2005.

Also produced *Vanilla,* London.

WRITINGS

Nonfiction:
(Editor) *I Can Tell It Now,* Dutton, 1964.
(Editor with W. Richard Bruner) *How I Got That Story,* Dutton, 1967.
Brown's Guide to Growing Gray, Delacorte, 1987, revised and published as *The Rest of Your Life is the Best of Your Life: David Brown's Guide to Growing Gray Disgracefully,* Barricade Books, 1991.
Let Me Entertain You, Morrow, 1990.

Contributor to books, including *Journalists in Action,* Channel Press, 1963, and periodicals, including *American Magazine, Collier's, Harper's, Readers Digest, American Mercury, The Saturday Evening Post, Saturday Review of Literature, The New Yorker,* and *Cosmopolitan.*

OTHER SOURCES

Books:
Contemporary Authors, Volumes 13–16, first revision, Gale (Detroit, MI), 1975.

Periodicals:
Publishers Weekly, October 16, 1995, p. 17.

BURMESTER, Leo 1944–
(Leo Burmeister)

PERSONAL

Born February 1, 1944, in Louisville, KY; married Lauren Cookson, 1981; children: Colette, Daniel. *Education:* Western Kentucky University, B.A., drama; University of Denver, M.F.A., drama.

Career: Actor. Actors Theatre of Louisville, Louisville, KY, member of company, 1975–76, 1977–79, 1982–83, and 1984–85; taught acting at Kentucky Wesleyan College for one year.

CREDITS

Film Appearances:
Water Sport, *Cruising* (also known as *William Friedkin's "Cruising"*), United Artists, 1980.
Mortuary director, *Honky Tonk Freeway,* Universal, 1981.
FIB Agent number one, *Daniel,* Paramount, 1983.
Dr. Gath, *The House of God,* United Artists, 1984.
Wylie D. Daiken, *Odd Jobs* (also known as *Summer Jobs* and *This End Up*), TriStar, 1984.
Hank, *Sweet Liberty,* Universal, 1986.
Jane's dad, *Broadcast News,* Twentieth Century–Fox, 1987.
Bum, *Big Business,* Buena Vista, 1988.
The apostle Nathaniel, *The Last Temptation of Christ,* Universal, 1988.
Catfish De Vries, *The Abyss,* Twentieth Century–Fox, 1989.
Shooter Polaski, *Article 99,* Orion, 1991.
Reeves, *Passion Fish,* Miramax, 1992.
Dave Flinton, *Innocent Blood* (also known as *A French Vampire in America*), Warner Bros., 1992.
Tom Adler, *A Perfect World,* Warner Bros., 1993.
Under Pressure: Making "The Abyss" (documentary), Twentieth Century Fox Home Entertainment, 1993.
Ricky Tick, *Fly by Night,* Arrow Releasing, 1994.
Bobbie Lee Taylor, *The Neon Bible,* Channel Four Films, 1995.
Cody, *Lone Star,* Columbia TriStar, 1996.
Florida prosecutor, *The Devil's Advocate* (also known as *Devil's Advocate* and *Im auftrag des teufels*), Warner Bros., 1997.
Judge Harold Perkins, *River Red,* Frontier Films, 1997.

Shorty, *SwitchBack* (also known as *Going West* and *Going West in America*), Paramount, 1997.

Jack, *Dumbarton Bridge,* 1998.

Dallas Miller, *The Farmhouse* (also known as *Eye of the Storm*), 1998.

(As Leo Burmeister) Voice, *The Secret of Mulan* (animated), 1998.

Dad, *Saturn,* 1999.

Harmon King, *Limbo,* Screen Gems, 1999.

Himself, *Leo Burmeister and the Literature of Junk* (documentary short), 2001.

Boxing trainer, *The End of the Bar,* 2002.

Lieutenant Katt, *City by the Sea* (also known as *The Suspect*), Warner Bros., 2002.

Kit's dad, *Out of These Rooms,* 2002.

(As Leo Burmeister) Voice of telegraph operator number one, *Gangs of New York,* Miramax, 2002.

Emmet Rounds, *Red Betsy,* Lang Films, 2003.

The Suit, *Glengarry, Bob Ross* (short), 2003.

Bo Williams, *America Brown,* TLA Releasing, 2004.

Mr. Carter Moynahan, *Patch* (short), 2005.

Colonel Beauregard, *The Legend of Zorro,* Columbia, 2005.

Television Appearances; Series:

Randy Stumphill, *Flo,* CBS, 1980–81.

Officer Bill Ruskin, *Arresting Behavior* (also known as *True Blue*), ABC, 1992.

Bo Metcalf, *You're the One* (also known as *Us and Them, Us vs. Them,* and *Them!*), The WB, 1998.

Television Appearances; Miniseries:

Jim, *Rage of Angels* (also known as *Sidney Sheldon's "Rage of Angels"*), NBC, 1983.

Emmett Spence, *Chiefs,* CBS, 1983.

Eban Krutch, *George Washington,* CBS, 1984.

Eban Krutch, *George Washington II: The Forging of a Nation* (also known as *The Forging of a Nation*), CBS, 1986.

Henderson, *Queen* (also known as *Alex Haley's "Queen"*), CBS, 1993.

General Nathanael Greene, *Liberty! The American Revolution,* PBS, 1997.

Corby Judd, *Shake, Rattle, and Roll: An American Love Story,* NBC, 1999.

Television Appearances; Movies:

The doctor/prisoner, *Rattlesnake in a Cooler,* 1980.

Two By South (also known as *Precious Blood*), 1982.

Precious Blood, 1982.

Officer Red Tollin, *True Blue* (also known as *Truck One*), NBC, 1989.

Frank Vassar, *Truman,* HBO, 1995.

Harlo Ethridge, *"The Great Elephant Escape," The ABC Family Movie,* ABC, 1995.

Commissioner Russell Crane, *Mistrial,* HBO, 1996.

Bob Purdue, *... First Do No Harm,* ABC, 1997.

Dallas Miller, *The Farmhouse,* Sundance Channel, 1998.

Lamar Pike, Sr., *Getting to Know You* (also known as *Getting to Know All about You*), Sundance Channel, 1999.

Carl Lindemann, *Monday Night Mayhem,* TNT, 2002.

Grizzle, *Carry Me Home,* Showtime, 2004.

Television Appearances; Specials:

Osric, "Hamlet," *Great Performances,* PBS, 1990.

Provost Marshall Cunningham, "Hale the Hero," *General Motors Playwrights Theater,* Arts and Entertainment, 1992.

Plump convict, "Old Man" (also known as "William Faulkner's "Old Man""), *Hallmark Hall of Fame,* CBS, 1997.

Denis Leary: Behind the Anger, Comedy Central, 2003.

Television Appearances; Pilots:

Mike Selway and performer of theme song, *A Fine Romance,* CBS, 1983.

Television Appearances; Episodic:

Red Tollin, *True Blue* (also known as *Truck One*), NBC, 1989.

"The Initiation," *The Young Riders,* ABC, 1991.

Woodrow Wilton, "An Innocent Man," *Walker, Texas Ranger,* CBS, 1993.

Lester Hastings, "Snatched," *Law & Order,* NBC, 1994.

Dalton Robertson, *Chicago Hope,* CBS, 1994.

Louis Bagley, "Growth Pains," *Chicago Hope,* CBS, 1995.

Le Clair, "Charm City: Part 1," *Law & Order,* NBC, 1996.

Father Peter, "In Loco Parentis," *Trinity,* NBC, 1998.

Father Peter, "No Secrets," *Trinity,* NBC, 1998.

Father Peter, "Patron Saint of Impossible Causes," *Trinity,* NBC, 1998.

Father Peter, "Breaking In, Breaking Out, Breaking Up, Breaking Down," *Trinity,* NBC, 1999.

Max Jackson, "Soul Survivor," *Baywatch* (also known as *Baywatch Hawaii*), syndicated, 2000.

Max Jackson, "Dangerous Games," *Baywatch* (also known as *Baywatch Hawaii*), syndicated, 2000.

Lorne Cutler, "The Third Horseman," *Law & Order: Criminal Intent* (also known as *Law & Order: CI*), NBC, 2002.

"Fathers," *100 Centre Street,* Arts and Entertainment, 2002.

Lester Hastings, "Patriot," *Law & Order,* NBC, 2002.

Stage Appearances:

The Brixton Recovery, PAF Playhouse, Huntington Station, NY, 1976–77.

Carl, *Getting Out,* Paramount Manhattan Theatre, Phoenix Theatre, New York City, 1978, then Theatre De Lys, New York City, 1979.

Ray, *Lone Star* and Understudy Silvio and Woodruff Gately, *Pvt. Wars,* Century Theatre, New York City, 1979.

"Rattlesnake in a Cooler," *Two by South,* Theatre at St. Clement's Church, New York City, 1981, then Los Angeles Actors' Theatre, Los Angeles, 1982.

Eddie Ray, *Criminal Minds,* Theatre Guinevere, New York City, 1984.

Tobacco Road, Long Wharf Theatre, New Haven, CT, 1984–85.

Pap Finn, *Big River: The Adventures of Huckleberry Finn,* Eugene O'Neill Theatre, New York City, 1985.

General D., *Raggedy Ann,* Nederlander Theatre, New York City, 1986.

The nardier and chain gang leader, *Les Miserables,* Broadway Theatre, New York City, 1987.

Osric and Lord, *Hamlet,* Joseph Papp Public Theatre, New York City, 1990.

Ivanov, Yale Repertory Theatre, New Haven, CT, 1990–91.

Ray–Bud, *Dearly Departed,* Long Wharf Theatre, 1990–91.

Bud Turpin and Ray–Bud, *Dearly Departed,* Second Stage Theatre, New York City, 1991–92.

Moon, *Middle–Aged White Guys,* 1994–95.

Don, *Trudy Blue,* 1994–95.

Bradley, *Buried Child,* Brooks Atkinson Theatre, New York City, 1996.

Sid Davis, *Ah, Wilderness!* Lincoln Center, Vivian Beaumont Theatre, New York City, 1998.

Autolycus, *The Civil War,* St. James Theatre, New York City, 1999.

Officer Michaud, *Thou Shalt Not,* Plymouth Theatre, New York City, 2001–2002.

Uncle Bob, *Urban Cowboy,* Broadhurst Theatre, New York City, 2003.

RECORDINGS

Taped Readings:

Melinda Haynes' *Chalktown,* Simon & Schuster, 2001.

OTHER SOURCES

Periodicals:

Time, May 20, 1996, pp. 77–78.

C

CALABRO, Thomas 1959–

PERSONAL

Born February 3, 1959, in Brooklyn, NY; married Elizabeth Pryor, April 10, 1993; children: Conner (daughter), Augustus, and Luca. *Education:* Graduated from Fordham University; studied acting at the Actors Studio, New York City.

Addresses: *Agent*—Metropolitan Talent Agency, 4500 Wilshire Blvd., 2nd Floor, Los Angeles, CA 90010. *Manager*—Anthem Entertainment, 6100 Wilshire Blvd., Suite 1170, Los Angeles, CA 90069.

Career: Actor and director. Appeared in television commercials for Zest soap, Pound Puppies, Geo Storm cars, McDonald's, and Labatt's beer.

Member: New York Actors' Studio, Circle Repertory Lab, Screen Actors Guild.

CREDITS

Television Appearances; Series:
Joey Coltrera, *Dream Street,* NBC, 1989.
Dr. Michael Mancini, *Melrose Place,* Fox, 1992–99.

Television Appearances; Miniseries:
Nearco, *Vendetta: Secrets of a Mafia Bride* (also known as *Donna D'Onore, A Family Matter, A Woman of Honor,* and *Bride of Violence*), syndicated, 1991.
Himself, *I Love the '90s,* VH1, 2004.

Television Appearances; Movies:
Zigo's nephew, *Out of the Darkness,* 1985.
Cavanaugh, *Ladykillers,* ABC, 1988.
Andy Parma, "No Time to Die," *Columbo,* ABC, 1992.
Detective Martinson, *Sleep, Baby, Sleep,* ABC, 1995.
Richard Brown, *Stolen Innocence,* CBS, 1995.
David Abrams, *L.A. Johns* (also known as *Johns* and *Confessions*), Fox, 1997.
Narrator/Ted Gavin, *Best Actress,* E! Entertainment Television, 2000.
Ray, *Ice Angel* (also known as *L'ange de la glace*), Fox Family Channel, 2000.
Dr. Ben Cahill, *They Nest* (also known as *Creepy Crawlers*), USA Network, 2000.
Andrew West, *Single Santa Seeks Mrs. Claus,* Hallmark Channel, 2004.
Matt Thompson, *The Perfect Husband* (also known as *Her Perfect Spouse* and *Le mari ideal*), USA Network, 2004.
Disaster Zone: Volcano in New York, Sci–Fi Channel, 2006.

Television Appearances; Pilots:
Steve Hardman, *Hard Knox,* syndicated, 2001.

Television Appearances; Specials:
A Day in the Lives of Melrose Place, Fox, 1994.
The Road to Fame on "Melrose Place" and "90210," Fox, 1995.
An All Star Party for Aaron Spelling, ABC, 1998.
The 51st Annual Primetime Emmy Awards, Fox, 1999.
Intimate Portrait: Tracey Gold (documentary), Lifetime, 2003.
Intimate Portrait: Alyssa Milano (documentary), Lifetime, 2003.
Intimate Portrait: Josie Bissett (documentary), Lifetime, 2003.
Melrose Place: The E! True Hollywood Story, E! Entertainment Television, 2003.

Television Appearances; Episodic:
Ned Loomis, "Kiss the Girls and Make Them Die," *Law & Order,* NBC, 1990.

Sean McAllister, "The Royal Mystery," *Father Dowling Mysteries* (also known as *Father Dowling Investigates*), 1990.

Nick Blackwood, "Who Killed the Gadget Man?," *Burke's Law*, 1995.

Don Morelli, "New Year's Eve," *Ned and Stacey*, Fox, 1996.

The Rosie O'Donnell Show, syndicated, 1996.

Host, *Mad TV*, Fox, 1997.

Ben Mason, "The Sign of the Dove," *Touched by an Angel*, CBS, 2001.

Dr. Abrams, "Ben White," *Nip/Tuck*, FX Channel, 2005.

Television Director; Episodic:

Melrose Place, Fox, 1995–96.

Stage Appearances:

Open Admissions, Long Wharf Theatre, New Haven, CT, 1982–83.

Nickey, "Uncle Chick," *Wild Blue*, Perry Street Theatre, New York City, 1987.

The Wildman, Theatre of the Cathedral of St. John the Divine, New York City, 1987.

Vinnie, "Women and Football," Program B, *Festival of One Act Plays*, Judith Anderson Theatre, New York City, 1988.

Also appeared in *Sweet Basil*, Cincinnati Playhouse in the Park, Cincinnati, OH; as Oberon, *A Midsummer's Night Dream*, New York City; *Gravity Shoes*, Hudson Theater, New York City.

Stage Work; Director:

Stealing Souls (Bring Your Camera), Victory Theatre, New York City, 1991.

Also director of *Orphans*, New York City; *Thespians and Troglodytes*, Hudson Theatre, New York City.

Film Appearances:

Larry, *Exterminator 2*, Cannon, 1984.

Nicky "Shoes" Piazza, *Made Men*, 1997.

Philly, *Face to Face* (also known as *Italian Ties*), Bayshore Media Group, 2001.

Bernard, *Cake*, 2006.

Film Work:

Executive producer, *Falling Rue*, 2000.

OTHER SOURCES

Periodicals:

Entertainment Weekly, June 20, 1997, p. 54.

CAPLAN, Lizzy 1982–

PERSONAL

Born June 30, 1982, in Los Angeles, CA. *Education:* Graduated from Hamilton Academy of Music, Los Angeles, CA.

Addresses: *Agent*—The Gersh Agency, 232 N. Canon Dr., Beverly Hills, CA 90210. *Manager*—Blueprint Artist Management, 5670 Wilshire Blvd., Suite 2525, Los Angeles, CA 90036. *Publicist*—Bragman/Nyman/Cafarelli, 8687 Melrose Ave., Pacific Design Center, Eighth Floor, Los Angeles, CA 90069.

Career: Actress.

CREDITS

Film Appearances:

Lizzy Lyons, *Hardcore Action News*, AFI, 2002.

Party girl, *Orange County*, Paramount, 2002.

Janis Ian, *Mean Girls*, United International, 2004.

Sara Weller, *Love Is the Drug*, Alpine, 2006.

Jacqueline, *Crashing*, Pendragon, 2006.

Television Appearances; Series:

Faith Pitt, *The Pitts*, Fox, 2003.

Television Appearances; Episodic:

Sara (recurring), *Freaks and Geeks*, NBC, 1999–2000.

Sarah, "Tough Love," *Once and Again*, ABC, 2001.

Tina Greer, "X–Ray," *Smallville* (also known as *Smallville Beginnings* and *Smallville: Superman the Early Years*), Fox, 2001.

Tina Greer, "Visage," *Smallville* (also known as *Smallville Beginnings* and *Smallville: Superman the Early Years*), Fox, 2003.

The Sharon Osbourne Show, syndicated, 2004.

Avery Bishop (recurring), *Tru Calling*, Fox, 2005.

Marjee Sorelli, "Driving Miss Crazy," *Related*, The WB, 2005.

Television Appearances; Pilots:

Beautiful girl, *Undeclared*, 2001.

Television Appearances; Movies:

Lily, *From Where I Sit*, 2000.

Angela, *Everybody's Doing It*, 2002.

RECORDINGS

Videos:

"Mean Girls": Only the Strong Survive, Paramount Home Video, 2004.

CARRADINE, Robert 1954–
    (Bob Carradine, Robert Carridine)

PERSONAL

Full name, Robert Reed Carradine; born March 24, 1954, in San Mateo, CA (some sources say Los Angeles, CA); son of John (an actor) and Sonia (maiden name, Sorel) Carradine; brother of Keith Carradine (an actor) and half–brother of David Carradine (an actor); married Edie Mani, 1990; children: (with Susan Snyder) Ever (daughter); (with Mani) one daughter.

Addresses: *Agent*—Peter Strain & Associates, 5455 Wilshire Blvd., Suite 1812, Los Angeles, CA 90036.

Career: Actor and producer. A guitarist and bass player appearing in bands that played clubs in Southern California such as the Troubadour, the Palomino, the Roxy, and At My Place. Also worked as a race car driver of corvettes for Mobil Oil and BF Goodrich; won the United States Endurance Cup (with others), in a corvette, 1985.

Awards, Honors: Genie Award nomination, best performance by a foreign actor, Academy of Canadian Cinema and Television, 1982, for *Heartaches;* CableACE Award nomination, actor in a theatrical or dramatic special, National Cable Television Association, 1987, for *As Is;* Golden Boot Award, Motion Picture and Television Fund, 1998.

CREDITS

Film Appearances:

Slim Honeycutt, *The Cowboys,* Warner Bros., 1972.

Drunk's killer, *Mean Streets,* Warner Bros., 1973.

Moxey, *Aloha, Bobby and Rose,* Columbia, 1975.

(As Bob Carradine) *You and Me* (also known as *Around*), 1975.

Johnnie Chrystal, *The Pom–Pom Girls* (also known as *Palisades High*), Crown, 1976.

Spoony, *Massacre at Central High* (also known as *Blackboard Massacre*), New Line Cinema, 1976.

Bobby Ray, *Jackson County Jail* (also known as *The Innocent Victim*), New World, 1976.

Jim Crandell, *Cannonball* (also known as *Carquake*), New World, 1976.

(Uncredited) Extra in cafeteria, *Revenge of the Cheerleaders* (also known as *H.O.T.S. III*), 1976.

John, *Joyride,* Allied Artists, 1977.

Ken, *Orca* (also known as *The Killer Whale* and *Orca, the Killer Whale*), Paramount, 1977.

Christie, *Blackout* (also known as *New York Blackout, New York Escapees, Black–Out a New York, Et la terreur commence,* and *New York ne repond plus*), Cinepix, 1978.

Bill Munson, *Coming Home* (also known as *Hemkomsten*), United Artists, 1978.

Himself, *Sam Fuller and the Big Red One* (documentary), Warner Home Video, 1979.

Himself, *The Carradines Together* (documentary), Filmmakers International, 1979.

Bob Younger, *The Long Riders,* United Artists, 1980.

Private Zab and narrator, *The Big Red One* (also known as *Samuel Fuller and the Big Red One*), United Artists, 1980.

Stanley Howard, *Heartaches,* 1981.

Alex Marsh, *Tag: The Assassination Game* (also known as *Everybody Gets It In the End* and *Kiss Me, Kill Me*), 1982.

Bobby Sinclair, *Wavelength,* New World, 1983.

Sam Carpenter, *Just the Way You Are,* Metro–Goldwyn–Mayer/United Artists, 1984.

Lewis Skolnick, *Revenge of the Nerds,* Twentieth Century–Fox, 1984.

Barzak, *Number One with a Bullet,* Cannon, 1986.

Lewis Skolnick, *Revenge of the Nerds II: Nerds in Paradise,* Twentieth Century–Fox, 1987.

Herbie Altman, *Buy and Cell,* Empire Pictures, 1988.

Sammy, *Rude Awakening,* Orion, 1989.

Mark, *All's Fair* (also known as *Skirmish*), Moviestore Entertainment, 1989.

Himself, *The Player,* Fine Line Features, 1992.

Eric Parker, *Bird of Prey,* Astra Cinema, 1995.

Ben Wallace, *The Killers Within,* 1995.

Tarmac, *Firestorm* (also known as *Markus 4*), 1995.

Skinhead, *Escape from L.A.* (also known as *John Carpenter's "Escape from L.A."*), Paramount, 1996.

Bill Parker, *Lycanthrope* (also known as *Bloody Moon*), Spectrum Films, 1998.

John Burnside, *Stray Bullet,* Radiotelevisione Italiana, 1998.

John Burnside, *Stray Bullet II,* New Horizons Home Video, 1998.

"The Kid," *Gunfighter* (also known as *Ballad of a Gunfighter*), Sterling Home Entertainment, 1998.

Zack Hadley, *Breakout* (also known as *Breakout: Batteries Included* and *3 ninjas et l'invention du siecle*), 1998.

Roody, *The Effects of Magic,* 1998.

Matt Chance, *The Vegas Connection,* 1999.

Bruce Palmer, *Palmer's Pick Up,* Winchester Films, 1999.

Chuck, *The Kid With X–ray Eyes,* New Horizons Home Video, 1999.

Bill Parker, *Lycanthrope* (also known as *Bloody Moon*), 1999.

(As Robert Carridine) John Burnside, *Dangerous Curves* (also known as *Stray Bullet II*), New Horizons Home Video, 2000.

Rodale, *Ghosts of Mars* (also known as *John Carpenter's "Ghosts of Mars"*), Screen Gems, 2001.

Don Keeble, *Max Keeble's Big Move,* Buena Vista, 2001.

Bus driver, *3 Days of Rain,* Rogue Arts, 2002.

(As Robert Carradine) Sam McGuire, *The Lizzie McGuire Movie,* Buena Vista, 2003.

Big Jim, *Timecop: The Berlin Decision,* Universal, 2003.

Himself, *Hilary's Roman Adventure* (documentary short), 2004.

Himself, *The Real Glory: Reconstructing "The Big Red One"* (documentary; also known as *The Big Red One: The Reconstruction*), Warner Home Video, 2005.

Clay Sparks, *Supercross* (also known as *Supercross: The Movie*), Twentieth Century–Fox, 2005.

Thad, *Hoboken Hollow,* 2005.

Private Tomlison, *Comanche Stallion,* 2006.

George Ackerman, *Trick or Treat* (also known as *National Lampoon's "Trick or Treat"*), 2006.

Film Work:

Second assistant camera, *Americana,* 1983.

Producer, *Lycanthrope* (also known as *Bloody Moon*), Spectrum Films, 1998.

Producer, *The 1 Second Film* (animated documentary), 2006.

Television Appearances; Series:

Slim, *The Cowboys,* ABC, 1974.

Sam McGuire, *Lizzie McGuire,* The Disney Channel, 2001–2004.

Television Appearances; Miniseries:

Percy Cuthfert III, *Tales of the Klondike* (also known as *Jack London's "Klondike Tales"* and *Jack London's "Tales of the Klondike"*), 1981.

Robert Cohn, *The Sun Also Rises* (also known as *Ernest Hemingway's "The Sun Also Rises"*), NBC, 1984.

Bobby Morgan, *Monte Carlo,* CBS, 1986.

Bryant Brown, *Stephen King's "The Tommyknockers"* (also known as *The Tommyknockers*), ABC, 1993.

Himself, *Retrosexual: The 80's,* VH1, 2004.

Television Appearances; Movies:

Rolling Man, ABC, 1972.

Gas station attendant, *Footsteps* (also known as *Footsteps: Nice Guys Finish Last* and *Nice Guys Finish Last*), 1972.

Bill, *Go Ask Alice,* ABC, 1973.

Bob Hatfield, *The Hatfields and the McCoys,* ABC, 1975.

Donny Davis, *The Survival of Dana* (also known as *On the Edge: The Survival of Dana*), CBS, 1979.

John Fairchild, *The Liberators,* ABC, 1987.

Rennie Davis, *Conspiracy: The Trial of the Chicago Eight,* HBO, 1987.

Adrian Lancer, *I Saw What You Did* (also known as *I Saw What You Did ... and I Know Who You Are!*), 1988.

Gerry Franklin (some sources cite Jerry Brown), *Somebody Has to Shoot the Picture,* HBO, 1990.

Domsczek, *The Incident* (also known as *Incident at Lincoln Bluff*), 1990.

Clarence Oddbody, the title role, *Clarence,* Family Channel, 1990.

Dave Booker, *Doublecrossed,* 1991.

Lewis Skolnick, *Revenge of the Nerds III: The Next Generation,* 1992.

Greg Sanderson, *Illusions,* 1992.

Mike Kroft, *The Disappearance of Christina,* USA Network, 1993.

Bill, "The Gas Station," *Body Bags* (also known as *John Carpenter Presents "Body Bags," John Carpenter Presents "Mind Game,"* and *Mind Games*), Showtime, 1993.

Lewis Skolnick, *Revenge of the Nerds IV: Nerds in Love,* 1994.

Ted, *A Part of the Family,* Lifetime, 1994.

Wade Parker, *Humanoids from the Deep* (also known as *Roger Corman Presents "Humanoids from the Deep"*), Showtime, 1996.

Carter, *Scorpio One,* Sci–Fi Channel, 1997.

Tarmac, *Firestorm,* 1997.

Eddie, *Young Hearts Unlimited,* Fox Family, 1998.

Martian Law, 1998.

Malachi Van Helsing, *Mom's Got a Date with a Vampire,* The Disney Channel, 2000.

Sunfish Perkins, *Monte Walsh,* TNT, 2003.

Grant, *Attack of the Sabretooth* (also known as *Attack of the Sabertooth*), Sci–Fi Channel, 2005.

Television Appearances; Specials:

Rich Farrell, *As Is,* Showtime, 1986.

Maxwell Dweeb, *Disney's "Totally Minnie"* (also known as *Totally Minnie*), NBC, 1988.

Himself, *David Carradine: The E! True Hollywood Story* (documentary), E! Entertainment Television, 2000.

Himself, *The 100 Greatest War Films,* Channel 4, 2005.

Television Appearances; Pilots:

Jack Bergin, *K–9,* ABC, 1991.

Dreamweavers, syndicated, 2000.

Television Appearances; Episodic:

Phinney McLean, "A Home for Jamie," *Bonanza,* NBC, 1971.

Sonny Jim, "Dark Angel," *Kung Fu,* ABC, 1972.

"Odyssey of Death," *Police Story,* NBC, 1976.

Gardener, "October the 31st," *The Fall Guy,* ABC, 1984.

Aladdin, "Aladdin and His Wonderful Lamp," *Faerie Tale Theatre* (also known as *Shelley Duvall's "Faerie Tale Theatre"*), Showtime, 1984.

Jerry, "Night Fever," *Alfred Hitchcock Presents,* NBC, 1985.

Dan Arnold, "Still Life," *Twilight Zone,* CBS, 1986.

Frank, "Garter Belt," *The Hitchhiker* (also known as *Le Voyageur*), HBO, 1987.

John Koch, "Sleepless in Chicago," *ER,* NBC, 1994.

Joey Bermuda/The Handyman, "Home Is Where the Hurt Is," *Lois and Clark—The New Adventures of Superman* (also known as *Lois and Clark* and *The New Adventures of Superman*), ABC, 1995.

Marty Manger, "Angel Falling," *Sirens,* syndicated, 1995.

Paulson, "Quake!," *Kung Fu: The Legend Continues,* syndicated, 1995.

Taige, "Phoenix," *Kung Fu: The Legend Continues,* syndicated, 1996.

Lonnie Zamora, "Hostile Convergence," *Dark Skies,* NBC, 1996.

Gerard Salter, "What a Dump!" *NYPD Blue,* ABC, 1996.

Dr. Bruce Hartman, "Knockout," *Nash Bridges,* CBS, 1996.

Sheriff Dwight Kunkle, "Mirage," *The Pretender,* NBC, 1997.

Dr. Manheim, "Dog Bite," *The Practice,* ABC, 1997.

Darin Carter, "Friends," *Vengeance Unlimited,* ABC, 1999.

Dr. Bruce Hartman, "Skin Trade," *Nash Bridges,* CBS, 2000.

David Blake/Roger Withers, "Gone," *Law & Order: Criminal Intent* (also known as *Law & Order: CI*), NBC, 2005.

Television Producer; Movies:

(With others) *Revenge of the Nerds III: The Next Generation,* 1992.

(With others) *Revenge of the Nerds IV: Nerds in Love,* 1994.

Television Director; Episodic:

"Lizzie's Eleven," *Lizzie McGuire,* The Disney Channel, 2003.

Stage Appearances:

(Stage debut) Understudy then replacement, *Tobacco Road,* FL, 1970.

As Is, Los Angeles, 1977.

The Exonerated, 45 Bleecker, New York City, 2002–2004.

RECORDINGS

Music Videos:

Appeared in The Motels' video of "Suddenly Last Summer," 1983.

CARTER, Lynda 1951–
(Linda Carter)

PERSONAL

Original name, Lynda Jean Cordoba Carter; born July 24, 1951, in Phoenix, AZ; daughter of Colby (in business) and Jean (a factory worker) Carter; married Ron Samuels (a talent manager), 1977 (divorced, 1982); married Robert A. Altman (a lawyer), January 29, 1984; children: (second marriage) Jamie Clifford, Jessica Carter. *Education:* Attended Arizona State University; trained for the stage with Stella Adler and Charles Conrad.

Addresses: *Agent*—The Blake Agency, 1327 Ocean Ave., Suite J, Santa Monica, CA 90401. *Manager*—Melissa Prophet Management, 1640 S. Sepulveda Dr., Suite 216, Los Angeles, CA 90025.

Career: Actress, producer, singer, and dancer. Appeared in performances at the Palladium Theatre, London, England; Sporting Club, Monte Carlo, Monaco; Desert Inn Hotel, Las Vegas, NV; and Hotel de la Reforma, Mexico City, Mexico; also performed in Atlantic City, NJ, and Reno, NV. Member of the rock 'n' roll group Garfin Gathering; spokesmodel for Maybelline Cosmetics; appeared in print advertisements, including Novartis Pharmacuetical Corp.; appeared in television commercials, including Lens Express contact lenses, 1997; does professional motivational speaking engagements. Involved with nonprofit organizations, including the American Red Cross and the breast cancer research and education organizations Washington Race for the Cure and the Susan G. Komen Foundation.

Member: American Ballet Theatre, National Committee on Arts for the Handicapped, American Cancer Society (national crusade chairperson, 1985–86), Exceptional Children's Foundation (honorary chairperson, 1987–88), United Service Organization (member of the board of governors), Feed the Hungry, Committee for Creative Nonviolence.

Awards, Honors: Miss Arizona, then Miss U.S.A., 1973; Hispanic Woman of the Year Award, 1983; Emmy Award nomination, 1985, for *Lynda Carter: Body and*

Soul; Golden Eagle Award, 1986, for consistent performance in television and film; American Latino Media Arts Award (ALMA) nomination, outstanding individual performance in a made–for–television movie or miniseries in a crossover role, 1999, for *Someone to Love Me: A Moment of Truth Movie;* Ariel Award (Mexico), international entertainer of the year; Jill Ireland Award for Volunteerism; Unihealth's Pinnacle Award, for charitable work.

CREDITS

Film Appearances:
Bobbie Jo James, *Bobbie Jo and the Outlaw,* American International Pictures, 1976.
(As Linda Carter) Nikki's soldier, *The Shape of Things to Come,* Film Ventures, 1979.
Herself, *Encore!,* 1980.
Herself, *Street Life,* 1982.
(As Linda Carter) Helena, *Mercy,* 1999.
Governor Jessman, *Super Troopers* (also known as *Broken Lizard's "Super Troopers"*), Twentieth Century–Fox, 2001.
Wonder Woman, *De Superman a Spider–Man: L'aventure des super–heroes* (documentary), Gaumont/Columbia TriStar Home Video, 2002.
Herself, *Double Dare* (documentary), Balcony Releasing, 2004.
Herself, *Beauty, Brawn and Bulletproof Bracelets: A Wonder Woman Retrospective* (documentary short), Warner Home Video, 2004.
Lynette, *The Creature of the Sunny Side Up Trailer Park* (also known as *Bloodhead*), 2004.
Pauline, *The Dukes of Hazzard,* Warner Bros., 2005.
Principal Powers, *Sky High,* Buena Vista, 2005.
Herself, *Revolutionizing a Classic: From Comic Books to Television—The Evolution of Wonder Woman from Page to Screen* (documentary short), Warner Home Video, 2005.

Television Appearances; Series:
Diana Prince/Princess Diana/Wonder Woman, *Wonder Woman,* ABC, 1976–77.
Diana Prince/Princess Diana/Wonder Woman, *The New Adventures of Wonder Woman* (also known as *The New Original Wonder Woman*) CBS, 1977–79.
Carole Stanwyck, *Partners in Crime* (also known as *50/50*), NBC, 1984.
Elizabeth Shields, *Hawkeye,* syndicated, 1994–95.

Television Appearances; Movies:
Zelda, *A Matter of Wife ... and Death,* NBC, 1975.
Diana Prince/Wonder Woman, *Wonder Woman Meets Baroness Von Gunther,* ABC, 1976.
Brooke Newman and song performer, *The Last Song,* CBS, 1980.

Kate Carlin and song performer, *Born to Be Sold,* NBC, 1981.
Brianne O'Neil, *Hotline,* CBS, 1982.
Rita Hayworth, *Rita Hayworth: The Love Goddess,* CBS, 1983.
(As Linda Carter) Receptionist number two, *He's Fired, She's Hired,* 1984.
Patricia Traymore, *Stillwatch,* CBS, 1987.
Helen Durant, *Mike Hammer: Murder Takes All* (also known as *Mickey Spillane's "Mike Hammer": "Murder Takes All"* and *Murder Takes All*), CBS, 1989.
Charlotte Sampson, *Daddy* (also known as *Danielle Steel's "Daddy"*), NBC, 1991.
Meredith Lanahan, *Posing: Inspired by Three Real Stories* (also known as *I Posed for Playboy*), CBS, 1991.
Charlotte Furber and performer of song "Somehow I'll Go On," *Lightning in a Bottle,* Lifetime, 1994.
Kathryn Archer, *A Secret between Friends: A Moment of Truth Movie* (also known as *When Friendship Kills*), NBC, 1996.
(As Linda Carter) Ms. Potasher, *Shadow Zone: The Undead Express,* Showtime, 1996.
(As Linda Carter) Roxanne, *Jack Reed: Death and Vengeance,* 1996.
Susan Saroyan, *She Woke Up Pregnant* (also known as *Crimes of Silence*), ABC, 1996.
Emily Hayworth, *A Prayer in the Dark,* USA Network, 1997.
Diana Young, *Someone to Love Me: A Moment of Truth Movie* (also known as *Someone to Love Me* and *Girl in the Backseat*), NBC, 1998.
(As Linda Carter) Ella Hutch, *Execution of Justice,* 1999.
Lee Reston, *Family Blessings* (also known as *LaVyrle Spencer's "Family Blessings"*), CBS, 1999.
Dr. Janet Fraser, *Terror Peak,* PAX, 2003.
Colonel Weaver, *Slayer,* Sci–Fi Channel, 2006.

Television Appearances; Pilots:
Yeoman Diana Prince/Princess Diana/Wonder Woman, *Wonder Woman* (also known as *The New Original Wonder Woman*), ABC, 1975.

Television Appearances; Specials:
A Special Olivia Newton–John, ABC, 1976.
ABC team member, *Battle of the Network Stars,* ABC, 1976.
Performer, *Circus of the Stars,* CBS, 1977.
Presenter, *The 29th Annual Primetime Emmy Awards,* 1977.
Performer, *Circus of the Stars #2,* CBS, 1977.
The 35th Annual Golden Globe Awards, 1978.
The 30th Annual Primetime Emmy Awards, 1978.
Host, *Lynda Carter: Encore,* CBS, 1980.
Host, *Lynda Carter's Special,* CBS, 1980.
Men Who Rate a 10, 1980.

Presenter, *The American Music Awards* (also known as *The 8th American Music Awards*), 1981.

The 38th Annual Golden Globe Awards, 1981.

Host, *Lynda Carter's Celebration* (also known as *Celebration*), CBS, 1981.

Women Who Rate a 10, 1981.

Host, *Lynda Carter: Street Lights*, CBS, 1982.

Happy Birthday, Bob!, NBC, 1983.

Host, *Lynda Carter: Body and Soul*, CBS, 1984.

Night of 100 Stars II (also known as *Night of One Hundred Stars*), ABC, 1985.

Bob Hope Buys NBC?, NBC, 1985.

Happy Birthday, Hollywood, ABC, 1987.

Song performer, *Bob Hope with His Easter Bunnies and Other Friends*, NBC, 1987.

CBS: The First 50 Years, CBS, 1998.

A Very Special Christmas from Washington, D.C., TNT, 1998.

Presenter, *The 1999 ALMA Awards*, 1999.

Intimate Portrait: Loni Anderson, Lifetime, 1999.

Intimate Portrait: Lynda Carter, Lifetime, 2000.

The Mexican–Americans, 2000.

The '70s: The Decade That Changed Television, ABC, 2000.

Heart–Throbs of the 70s (documentary), Sky One, 2001.

Presenter, *The 2001 ALMA Awards*, ABC, 2001.

Lynda Carter: The E! True Hollywood Story, E! Entertainment Television, 2002.

I Love the '70s, VH1, 2003.

CBS at 75, CBS, 2003.

The Second Annual TV Land Awards: A Celebration of Classic TV, TV Land and Nickelodeon, 2004.

Ultimate Super Heroes, Ultimate Super Villains, Ultimate Super Vixens, Bravo, 2004.

Wonder Woman, *Inside TV Land: Tickeled Pink*, TV Land, 2005.

Television Appearances; Episodic:

Helen Chase, "Roots of Anger," *Nakia*, ABC, 1974.

Bobbi Dee, "Panic," *Matt Helm*, ABC, 1975.

The Tonight Show Starring Johnny Carson (also known as *The Best of Carson*), NBC, 1975, 1976, 1978, 1979, 1982, 1985.

Vicky, "The Las Vegas Strangler," *Starsky and Hutch*, ABC, 1976.

Herself, *Break the Bank*, 1976.

Cos, 1976.

Dinah! (also known as *Dinah! & Friends*), 1976, 1980.

The Mike Douglas Show, 1977.

Herself, *The Muppet Show*, syndicated, 1980.

The Midnight Special, 1981.

Television: Inside and Out, 1981.

The Merv Griffin Show, 1981, 1982.

The John Davidson Show, 1982.

Lifestyles of the Rich and Famous (also known as *Lifestyles with Robin Leach and Shari Belafonte*), ABC and syndicated, 1986.

Hour Magazine, syndicated, 1986.

Good Morning America, ABC, 1986.

Larry King Live, CNN, 1986, 1991, 1993, 1996, 2002, 2003.

The Late Show (also known as *The Late Show Starring Joan Rivers*), Fox, 1987.

Showbiz Today, CNN, 1987.

CBS This Morning, CBS, 1988.

Win, Lose or Draw, The Disney Channel, 1989.

Live with Regis & Kathie Lee, syndicated, 1991, 1994, 1997.

The Suzanne Somers Show, syndicated, 1994.

George & Alana, syndicated, 1996.

Leeza, NBC, 1996.

The Oprah Winfrey Show (also known as *Oprah*), syndicated, 1997.

The RuPaul Show, VH1, 1998.

Herself, "The Best Policy," *Work With Me*, CBS, 1999.

So Graham Norton, Channel 4, 2000.

Host, "I Love 1978" and "I Love 1979," *I Love the 1970's*, BBC, 2000.

Record executive, "Groovin'," *The Zack Files*, ITV and Fox Family, 2001.

Entertainment Tonight (also known as *E.T., ET Weekend, Entertainment This Week*, and *This Week In Entertainment*), syndicated, 2001, 2004, 2005.

The Caroline Rhea Show, syndicated, 2003.

Guest co–host, *The View*, ABC, 2003.

Summer Kirkland, "Phone Home for the Holidays," *Hope & Faith*, ABC, 2003.

Extra (also known as *Extra: The Entertainment Magazine*), syndicated, 2005.

KTLA Morning News, 2005.

20/20 (also known as *ABC News 20/20*), ABC, 2005.

This Week, BBC, 2005.

The Paul O'Grady Show, ITV, 2005.

Lorraine Dillon, "Design," *Law & Order: Special Victims Unit* (also known as *Law & Order: SVU* and *Special Victims Unit*), NBC, 2005.

Lorraine Dillon, "Flaw," *Law & Order*, NBC, 2005.

Also appeared as herself, *The Jacksons*.

Television Work; Movies:

Executive producer, *Stillwatch*, CBS, 1987.

Television Work; Specials:

Executive producer, *Lynda Carter: Body and Soul* (also known as *Body and Soul*), CBS, 1984.

Stage Appearances:

Night of 100 Stars II (also known as *Night of One Hundred Stars*), Radio City Music Hall, New York City, 1985.

Mama Morton, *Chicago*, Adelphi Theatre, London, 2005.

Also appeared in *The Vagina Monologues*, AZ.

Radio Appearances:
Steve Wright in the Afternoon, BBC Radio 2, 2005.

RECORDINGS

Albums:
Portrait, Epic, 1978.

Video Games:
Voice of Female Nord, *The Elder Scrolls III: Morrowind,* 2002.
Voice of Female Nord, *Elder Scrolls III: Bloodmoon,* Ubi Soft Entertainment, 2003.
Various characters, *The Elder Scrolls IV: Oblivion,* 2006.

Taped Readings:
Read Sandra Brown's *Where There's Smoke.*

WRITINGS

Television Songs; Movies:
Born to Be Sold, NBC, 1981.

OTHER SOURCES

Books:
Dictionary of Hispanic Biography, Vol. 4, Gale, 2003.

Periodicals:
Entertainment Weekly, September 16, 1994.
People Weekly, September 12, 1994, p. 118; July 17, 1995, p. 51.

CARTWRIGHT, Nancy 1959–

PERSONAL

Full name, Nancy Campbell Cartwright; born October 25, 1959, in Kettering, OH; daughter of Frank and Miriam Cartwright; married Warren "Murph" Murphy (a writer and producer), December 24, 1988 (divorced, 2005); children: Lucy Mae, Jackson Louis. *Education:* University of California at Los Angeles, B.A., theater arts, 1981; studied interpersonal communication at Ohio University, 1976–78; studied voice acting with Daws Butler (voice of Yogi Bear and Huckleberry Hound) and acting with Milton Katselas. *Religion:* Scientologist.

Addresses: *Agent*—Innovative Artists, 1505 Tenth St., Santa Monica, CA 90401. *Office*—Cartwright Entertainment, 9420 Reseda Blvd., Suite 572, Northridge, CA 91324.

Career: Actress and director. Co–founder (with spouse) of Happy House Productions, Inc., 1994—; conducts workshops on voice–acting; founder of SportsBlast (a production company) and Cartwright Entertainment (a production company). Spokesperson for Make America Safe; involved in numerous fundraisers for charity.

Member: Screen Actors Guild, American Federation of Television and Radio Artists.

Awards, Honors: Emmy Award, outstanding voice–over performance, 1992, Annie Award, voice acting in the field of animation, International Animated Film Society (ASIFA) Hollywood, 1995, both for *The Simpsons;* Drama–Logue Award, 1995, for *In Search of Fellini;* Daytime Emmy Award nomination, outstanding performer in an animated program, 2004, for *Kim Possible;* Faith Hubley Web of Life Award, High Falls Film Festival, 2002; Honorary Mayor of Northridge, CA, 2005.

CREDITS

Film Appearances:
Ethel, "It's a Good Life," *Twilight Zone—The Movie,* Warner Bros., 1983.
Stephanie, *Going Undercover* (also known as *Yellow Pages*), Miramax, 1984.
Voice, *Joy of Sex* (also known as *National Lampoon's "The Joy of Sex"*), Paramount, 1984.
Kathleen, *Flesh and Blood* (also known as *The Rose and the Sword* and *Los senores del acero*), Riverside, 1985.
(Uncredited) Girl at Dance, *Heaven Help Us* (also known as *Catholic Boys*), 1985.
Voice of Gusty and the fourth bushwoolie, *My Little Pony* (animated; also known as *My Little Pony: the Movie*), DeLaurentiis Entertainment Group, 1986.
Voice of Arabian Prince, *The Chipmunk Adventure* (animated), Samuel Goldwyn, 1987.
Voice of Brighteyes, *Pound Puppies and the Legend of Big Paw* (animated), TriStar, 1988.
(Uncredited) Voice of Dipped Shoe, *Who Framed Roger Rabbit,* 1988.
Stephanie, *Yellow Pages* (also known as *Going Undercover*), 1988.
Voice, *The Little Mermaid* (animated), Buena Vista, 1989.
Voice of Page, *Little Nemo: Adventures in Slumberland* (animated), Hemdale Releasing, 1990.
Voice of Fawn Deer, *Petal to the Metal* (animated short), 1992.

Caiman's secretary, *Godzilla,* TriStar/Sony Pictures Entertainment, 1998.

Voice of Dana, *The Land Before Time VI: The Secret of Saurus Rock* (animated), Universal Pictures Home Video, 1998.

Voice of Skunk, Macaws, and others, *Jungle Book: Mowgli's Story* (animated), Buena Vista Home Video, 1998.

Voice of Bart Simpson, *Bart Wars: The Simpsons Strike Back* (animated), 1999.

Voice of Mindy, *Wakko's Wish* (animated; also known as *Steven Spielberg Presents "Animaniacs: Wakko's Wish"*), 1999.

Voice of Bart Simpson, *CyberWorld* (animated short), IMAX, 2000.

Voice of Earl Squirrel, *Timber Wolf* (animated; also known as *Chuck Jones' "Timber Wolf"*), Warner Bros., 2001.

Voice of Chuckie Finster, *Rugrats Go Wild!* (animated), Paramount, 2003.

Voice of Rufus, *Kim Possible: The Secret Files* (animated), Walt Disney Home Entertainment, 2003.

Voice of Bart Simpson, *The Simpsons* (animated), Twentieth Century–Fox, forthcoming.

Film Work:

Voice coach, *Brother Bear,* Buena Vista, 2003.

Television Appearances; Series:

Voice of Gloria Paterson, *The Richie Rich/Scooby Doo Hour* (animated), ABC, 1980.

Voice of Gloria, *Rihie Rih* (animated), 1981.

Voice, *Monchhichis* (animated), ABC, 1983.

Additional voices, *Alvin & the Chipmunks* (animated; also known as *The Chipmunks* and *The Chipmunks Go to the Movies*), 1983.

Voice of Kip Kangaroo, *The Shirt Tales* (animated), 1983–85.

Voice of Daffney, *The Snorks* (animated), NBC, 1984.

Voice of Kimberly, "Space Ace," *Saturday Supercade* (animated), 1984–85.

Voice of Gilda Gossip and "Flat Freddy" Fender, *Galaxy High School* (animated; also known as *Galaxy High*), CBS, 1986.

Voice of Gusty, *My Little Pony 'n' Friends* (animated), syndicated, 1986.

Voice of Brighteyes, *Pound Puppies* (animated), ABC, 1986.

Voice of Woody, *Popeye and Son* (animated), CBS, 1987.

Voice of Arabian Prince, *The Chipmunk Adventure* (animated), 1987.

Voice, *The New Adventures of the Snorks* (animated), syndicated, 1987.

Voice of Bart Simpson, "The Simpsons" (animated short), *The Tracey Ullman Show,* Fox, 1987–89.

Voice of FX, *Fantastic Max* (animated), syndicated, 1988.

Additional voices, *Dink, the Little Dinosaur* (animated), 1989.

Voice of Bartholomew Jo–Jo "Bart" Simpson, Nelson Muntz, Todd Flanders, Ralph Wiggum, Database, Jimmy, Kearney, and others, *The Simpsons* (animated), Fox, 1989—.

Voice, *Tom and Jerry Kids Show* (animated), 1990.

Voice of Pistol Pete, *Disney's "Goof Troop"* (also known as *Goof Troop*), ABC, 1992.

Voice of Fawn Deer, Mother Grumbles, woman, and others, *Raw Toonage* (animated), 1992.

Voice of Fawn Deer, *Bonkers* (animated; also known as *Disney's "Bonkers"*), syndicated, 1993.

Voice of Mindy Sadlier and others, *Animaniacs* (animated; also known as *Steven Spielberg Presents "Animaniacs"*), Fox, 1993.

Voice of Betsy and Ross, *Problem Child* (animated), 1993.

Additional voices, *The Pink Panther* (animated), 1993.

Voice of Little Red Riding Hood, *2 Stupid Dogs* (animated), 1993.

Voices of the Sprites, *Disney's "Aladdin"* (animated; also known as *Aladdin*), CBS, 1994.

Voice of Margo Sherman and additional voices, *The Critic* (animated), ABC, 1994–95.

Ruby Jillette, *The Fresh Prince of Bel–Air,* NBC, 1994.

Additional voices, *Timon and Pumbaa* (animated; also known as *The Lion King's "Timon and Pumbaa"*), CBS, 1995.

Additional voices, *The Twisted Adventures of Felix the Cat* (animated; also known as *The Twisted Tales of Felix the Cat*), 1995.

Voice of Melissa Screech, *Steven Spielberg Presents "Toonsylvania"* (animated; also known as *Toonsylvania*), Fox, 1998.

Voice of Rudy Mookich, *Pinky, Elmyra & the Brain* (animated), The WB, 1998.

Additional voices, *Big Guy and Rusty the Boy Robot* (animated), 1999—.

Voice of Lu, *Mike, Lu & Og* (animated), Cartoon Network, 1999.

Voice of Megan Allman, *God, the Devil and Bob* (animated), NBC, 2000.

Voice of Charles "Chuckie" Finster, Jr., *Rugrats* (animated), Nickelodeon, 2001–2005.

Rufus, *Kim Possible* (animated; also known as *Disney's "Kim Possible"*), Disney, 2002.

Voice of Chuckie Finster, *All Grown Up* (also known as *Rugrats All Grown Up*), Nickelodeon, 2003.

Voice of Billy and Kenji, *Betsy's Kindergarten Adventure* (animated), 2006.

Also appeared in *On Hollywood Blvd.; Fame.*

Television Appearances; Miniseries:

Jill Murray, *The Rules of Marriage,* CBS, 1982.

Television Appearances; Movies:

(Uncredited) *Skokie* (also known as *Once They Marched Through a Thousand Times*), 1981.

Title role, *Marian Rose White,* CBS, 1982.

Libby Dean, *Deadly Lessons,* ABC, 1983.

Jean, *Not My Kid,* CBS, 1985.

Ruth Potter, *Precious Victims,* CBS, 1993.

Terry Michaels, *A Tangled Web* (also known as *Deadly Seduction*), CBS, 1996.

Dell, *Suddenly* (also known as *An Urban Legend* and *When Somebody Loves You*), ABC, 1996.

Terry Michaels, *Vows of Deception* (also known as *Deadly Seduction* and *Tangled Web*), CBS, 1996.

Voice of Rufus, *Kim Possible: So the Drama* (animated), The Disney Channel, 2005.

Television Appearances; Specials:

Voice of Karen and second baby, "The Amazing Bunjee Adventure" (animated), *ABC Weekend Specials,* ABC, 1984.

Voice of Bart Simpson, *The Simpsons: Family Portrait* (animated), Fox, 1988.

Voice, "P. J. Funnybunny" (animated), *ABC Weekend Specials,* ABC, 1989.

Voice of Bart Simpson, *The Simpsons: Family Therapy* (animated), Fox, 1989.

Voice of Bart Simpson, Todd Flanders, and others, *Simpsons Roasting on an Open Fire* (animated; also known as *The Simpsons Christmas Special*), Fox, 1989.

Voice of Bart Simpson, *The Ice Capades 50th Anniversary Special,* ABC, 1990.

Voice of Bart Simpson, *Dangerous,* Fox, 1991.

The American Music Awards, ABC, 1991.

Voice of Bart Simpson, *Comic Relief IV,* 1991.

Voice of Wally Funnybunny, Heidi Funnybunny, and Potts Pig, "P. J.'s Unfunnybunny Christmas" (animated), *ABC Weekend Specials,* ABC, 1993.

Secretary, *The Great O'Grady,* Showtime, 1993.

Voice of Pistol Pete, *A Goof Troop Christmas* (animated), 1993.

Secrets Revealed, ABC, 1994.

Voice, *P. J. Funnybunny: A Very Cool Easter* (animated), ABC, 1996.

(Uncredited) Voice of herself, *The 51st Annual Primetime Emmy Awards,* Fox, 1999.

The 5th Annual Screen Actors Guild Awards, TNT, 1999.

Herself, *"The Simpsons": America's First Family* (documentary), BBC, 2000.

Voice of Todd, *Rapsittie Street Kids: Believe in Santa* (animated), 2002.

Voice of Rufus, *Kim Possible: A Sitch in Time* (animated; also known as *Disney's "Kim Possible: A Sitch in Time"*), 2003.

VH1 Goes Inside South Park, VH1, 2003.

50 Cutest Child Stars: All Grown Up, E! Entertainment Television, 2005.

Voice of Chuckle, *All Grown Up: Dude, Where's My Horse?* (animated), Nickelodeon, 2005.

Television Appearances; Pilots:

Annie Monacan, *In Trouble,* ABC, 1981.

Marge, *Chain Letter,* ABC, 1989.

Television Appearances; Episodic:

Holly, "Terminal Case," *Tucker's Witch,* CBS, 1982.

Muffin, "Some Kind of Harmony," *Fame,* 1983.

Muffin, "Secrets," *Fame,* 1984.

Cynthia, "Diane's Nightmare," *Cheers,* NBC, 1985.

"Growing Up, Growing Old," *Our House,* 1987.

Gwen, "The Initiation," *Mr. Belvedere,* 1987.

Belinda, the waitress, "On the Road," *TV 101,* 1989.

Ann, "Tears of a Clown," *Empty Nest,* 1989.

Voice of the junk food kid, "Showdown at Teeter–Totter Gulch," *Rugrats* (animated), Nickelodeon, 1992.

Voice of Bart Simpson, "Dial 'M' for Mother," *The Critic* (animated), 1994.

Frances O'Reilly, "976 Ways to Say I Love You," *Baywatch Nights,* 1995.

Ruby Jillette, "Save the Last Trance for Me," *The Fresh Prince of Bel–Air,* NBC, 1995.

Herself, *The Brains Trust,* BBC, 1996.

Voice of Bart Simpson, *Sesame Street* (also known as *Les amis de Sesame, Canadian Sesame Street, Open Sesame, Sesame Park,* and *The New Sesame Street*), PBS, 1996.

Herself, *Blue Peter,* 1999.

Herself, *Happy Hour,* USA Network, 1999.

Herself, *TFI Friday* (also known as *Thank Four It's Friday*), Channel 4, 1999.

Fully Booked, BBC, 1999.

(Uncredited) Voice of Bart Simpson doll, "A Big Piece of Garbage," *Futurama* (animated), 1999.

Herself, *Pyramid,* syndicated, 2002, 2004.

Inside the Actors Studio, Bravo, 2003.

Voice of Phantasmo: Experiment 375, "Phantasmo: Experiment 375," *Lilo & Stitch: The Series* (animated), The Disney Channel, 2003.

Herself, *GMTV,* ITV, 2004.

Rove Live, Ten Network, 2005.

Herself, *Dokument: Humor,* 2005.

Voice of Daffney, "Brian the Bachelor," *Family Guy* (animated; also known as *Padre de familia*), Fox, 2005.

Voice of Rufus, "Rufus: Experiment #607," *Lilo & Stitch: The Series* (animated), The Disney Channel, 2005.

Also appeared as voice of Babysitter, "Adventures in Bobby Sitting," *Bobby's World;* in *Generation; Bridges to Cross.*

Television Director; Episodic:

Uncredited, directed episodes of *The Simpsons* (animated).

Stage Appearances:

Karen, *The Transgressor,* Dynarski Theatre, Los Angeles, 1980.

Adelaide, *Guys and Dolls,* Showboat Dinner Theatre, Stockton, CA, 1984.

Coming Attractions, Skylight Theatre, Los Angeles, 1985.

In Search of Fellini (one–woman show), Theatre Geo, Hollywood, CA, 1995.

Louella Parsons, *The Cat's Meow,* Coast Playhouse, and Matrix Theatre, Los Angeles, 1997–98.

Also appeared in *Potpourrie and Porcupines; Comedy Cabaret.*

RECORDINGS

Video Games:

Voice of Bart Simpson, *The Simpsons: Bart vs. the Space Mutants,* 1991.

Voice of Bart Simpson, *The Simpsons,* 1991.

Voice of Bart Simpson, *The Simpsons: Bart's Nightmare,* 1993.

Voice of Bart Simpson, Bartman, Nelson Muntz, and Ralph Wiggum, *The Simpsons: Cartoon Studio,* 1996.

Voice of Nelson Muntz, Ralph Wiggum, Rod Flanders, and Todd Flanders, *The Simpsons: Virtual Springfield* (also known as *Virtual Springfield*), 1997.

Voice of Bart Simpson, *The Simpsons: Wrestling,* Activision, 2001.

Voice of Bart Simpson and others, *The Simpsons: Road Rage,* 2001.

Voice of Bart Simpson and Nelson Muntz, *The Simpsons: Skateboarding,* 2002.

Voice of Bart Simpson, Ralph Wiggum, Nelson Muntz, and others, *The Simpson: Hit & Run,* Vivendi Universal Games, 2003.

Albums:

The Simpsons Sing the Blues, Geffen, 1990.

Songs in the Key of Springfield, 1997.

The Simpsons Yellow Album, 1998.

Go Simpsonic with the Simpsons, 1999.

Music Videos:

Voice of Bart Simpson, "Black or White," *Dangerous: The Short Films* (also known as *Michael Jackson— Dangerous: The Short Films*), 1993.

WRITINGS

Stage Plays:

In Search of Fellini (one–woman stage play), produced at Theatre Geo, Hollywood, CA, 1995.

Autobiography:

My Life as a Ten–Year–Old Boy, Hyperion, 2000.

OTHER SOURCES

Periodicals:

Los Angeles Times TV Times, March 22, 1992.

People Weekly, December 14, 1998, p. 25.

CASS, David S., Sr.
    (Dave Cass; Dave Cass, Sr.; David Cass; David S. Cass; David Cass, Sr.)

PERSONAL

Father of David Cass, Jr. (an assistant director).

Addresses: *Contact*—Larry Levinson Productions, 500 South Sepulveda Blvd., Suite 610, Los Angeles, CA 90049.

Career: Stunt coordinator, stunt performer, actor, director, producer, and writer. Also worked as an extra and double in films. Also known as David S. Cass.

CREDITS

Film Producer:

One Block Away (short film), 1975.

(With others) *Texas Rangers,* Miramax/Dimension Films, 2001.

Film Second Unit Director:

(As David Cass) *Savannah Smiles,* Gold Coast Productions, 1982.

(As David Cass) *Smokey and the Bandit Part 3,* Universal, 1983.

(As Dave Cass) *Uphill All the Way,* New World Pictures, c. 1984.

(As Dave Cass) *Tequila Sunrise,* Warner Bros., 1988.

(As Dave Cass) *DeepStar Six* (also known as *Deep Star Six*), TriStar, 1989.

(As Dave Cass) *The Horror Show* (also known as *Horror House, House 3,* and *House III: The Horror Show*), Metro–Goldwyn–Mayer/United Artists, 1989.

(As Dave Cass) *Suburban Commando,* New Line Cinema, 1991.

(As Dave Cass) *The Family Man,* MCA/Universal, 2000.

Film Stunt Coordinator:

All Night Long, Universal, 1981.

Savannah Smiles, Gold Coast Productions, 1982.

(As David Cass) *Get Crazy* (also known as *Flip Out*), Rosebud, 1983.

(As David Cass) *Smokey and the Bandit Part 3,* Universal, 1983.

(As Dave Cass) *Uphill All the Way,* New World Pictures, c. 1984.

(As Dave Cass) *Tequila Sunrise,* Warner Bros., 1988.

(As Dave Cass) *Suburban Commando,* New Line Cinema, 1991.

Film Stunt Performer:

(Uncredited) *McLintock!,* United Artists, 1963.

(Uncredited) *Shenandoah,* Universal, 1965.

(Uncredited) *The Good Guys and the Bad Guys,* Warner Bros./Seven Arts, 1969.

(Uncredited) *Heaven with a Gun,* Metro–Goldwyn–Mayer, 1969.

(Uncredited) *Young Billy Young,* United Artists, 1969.

(Uncredited) *Earthquake,* Universal, 1974.

(Uncredited) *Farewell, My Lovely,* Avco–Embassy, 1975.

(Uncredited) *Blue Sunshine,* Cinema Shares International, 1976.

(Uncredited) *Trackdown,* United Artists, 1976.

(Uncredited) *Two–Minute Warning,* Universal, 1976.

(Uncredited) *The Jerk,* MCA/Universal, 1979.

(As Dave Cass) *The Lady in Red* (also known as *Guns, Sin and Bathtub Gin*), New World Pictures, 1979.

(Uncredited) *More American Graffiti* (also known as *Purple Haze*), MCA/Universal, 1979.

(As Dave Cass) *The Island,* MCA/Universal, 1980.

(As David Cass) *Six Pack,* Twentieth Century–Fox, 1982.

The Sword and the Sorcerer, Group 1 International, 1982.

(As Dave Cass) *Heart Like a Wheel,* Twentieth Century–Fox, 1983.

(As Dave Cass) *Smokey and the Bandit Part 3,* Universal, 1983.

(As Dave Cass) *My Demon Lover,* New Line Cinema, 1987.

(As Dave Cass) *Revenge,* Columbia, 1990.

(As David Cass) *Suburban Commando,* New Line Cinema, 1991.

Overnight Delivery, New Line Cinema, 1998.

Film Work; Other:

Stunt driver, *Roadhouse 66,* Atlantic Releasing, 1984.

Production assistant, *No Man's Land,* Orion, 1987.

Action coordinator, *My Boyfriend's Back* (also known as *Johnny Zombie*), Buena Vista, 1993.

Film Appearances:

(As David Cass) Ray, *Shenandoah,* Universal, 1965.

Deputy Dave, *Suppose They Gave a War and Nobody Came?* (also known as *War Games*), Cinerama Releasing, 1970.

(As David Cass) Trooper, *Dirty Dingus Magee,* Metro–Goldwyn–Mayer, 1970.

Jason Brooks, *Enter the Devil* (also known as *Disciples of Death*), Sunset International Releasing, 1972.

Deputy, *The Boy Who Cried Werewolf,* Universal, 1973.

(Uncredited) Sheriff Merle, *Earthquake,* Universal, 1974.

Big Jake, *One Block Away* (short film), 1975.

McDonald, *The Master Gunfighter,* Taylor–Laughlin Productions, 1975.

Green's henchman, *Two–Minute Warning,* Universal, 1976.

(As Dave Cass) Spangler's gang member, *Treasure of Matecumbe,* Buena Vista, 1976.

(As David Cass) Bearman, *The Island of Dr. Moreau,* American International Pictures, 1977.

(As Dave Cass) Boss kidnapper, *Mr. Billion* (also known as *The Windfall*), Twentieth Century–Fox, 1977.

(As Dave Cass) Strip club drunk, *The Goodbye Girl* (also known as *Neil Simon's "The Goodbye Girl"*), Metro–Goldwyn–Mayer/Warner Bros., 1977.

(As Dave Cass) Jack, *Hot Lead and Cold Feet* (also known as *Hot Lead & Cold Feet*), Buena Vista, 1978.

Second henchman, *The Apple Dumpling Gang Rides Again* (also known as *Trail's End*), Buena Vista, 1979.

(As David Cass) Mercenary with a moustache, *Heaven's Gate* (also known as *Johnson County Wars*), United Artists, 1980.

Hotwire, Comworld Pictures, 1980.

(As Dave Cass) Factory guard, *Tron,* Buena Vista, 1982.

Wes, *Endangered Species,* Metro–Goldwyn–Mayer, 1982.

(As Dave Cass) Local tough man, *Smokey and the Bandit Part 3,* Universal, 1983.

Grady's partner, *My Demon Lover,* New Line Cinema, 1987.

Lou, *Flicks* (animated; also known as *Hollyweird* and *Loose Joints*), Media Home Entertainment, 1987.

Police officer in depository, *Best Seller,* Orion, 1987.

Smokey, *Geddon,* 2000.

Television Second Assistant Director; Series:

dr. vegas, CBS, 2004.

Television Stunt Performer; Series:

Dundee and the Culhane, CBS, 1967.

Here Come the Brides, ABC, 1968–70.

The Streets of San Francisco, ABC, 1972–77.

(Uncredited) *The Six Million Dollar Man,* ABC, 1973–78.

(Uncredited) *The Rockford Files* (also known as *Jim Rockford, Private Investigator*), NBC, 1974–80.

Starsky and Hutch, ABC, 1975–79.

Walker, Texas Ranger, CBS, beginning c. 1993.

Television Director; Miniseries:

Johnson County War, The Hallmark Channel, 2002.

Television Second Unit Director; Miniseries:
(As Dave Cass) *Kenny Rogers as The Gambler: The Adventure Continues,* CBS, 1983.
(As Dave Cass) *Kenny Rogers as The Gambler, Part III: The Legend Continues* (also known as *The Gambler III: The Legend Continues*), CBS, 1987.
Nothing Lasts Forever (also known as *Sidney Sheldon's "Nothing Lasts Forever"*), CBS, 1995.
Streets of Laredo (also known as *Larry McMurtry's "Streets of Laredo"*), CBS, 1995.
Dead Man's Walk (also known as *Larry McMurtry's "Dead Man's Walk"*), ABC, 1996.
True Women, CBS, 1997.
(As Dave Cass) *Attila* (also known as *Attila the Hun*), USA Network, 2001.
Helen of Troy, USA Network, 2003.

Television Stunt Coordinator; Miniseries:
(As Dave Cass) *Kenny Rogers as The Gambler: The Adventure Continues,* CBS, 1983.
(As Dave Cass) *Dream West,* CBS, 1986.
Kenny Rogers as The Gambler, Part III: The Legend Continues (also known as *The Gambler III: The Legend Continues*), CBS, 1987.
The Gambler Returns: The Luck of the Draw (also known as *The Luck of the Draw: The Gambler Returns*), NBC, 1991.
(As David Cass) *Queen* (also known as *Alex Haley's "Queen"*), CBS, 1993.
(As Dave Cass) *The Gambler V: Playing for Keeps,* CBS, 1994.
(As David Cass) *Heaven & Hell: North & South, Book III* (also known as *John Jakes' "Heaven & Hell: North & South, Book III"* and *North and South III*), ABC, 1994.
Scarlett, CBS, 1994.
Buffalo Girls, CBS, 1995.
Nothing Lasts Forever (also known as *Sidney Sheldon's "Nothing Lasts Forever"*), CBS, 1995.
Streets of Laredo (also known as *Larry McMurtry's "Streets of Laredo"*), CBS, 1995.
True Women, CBS, 1997.
(As Dave Cass, Sr.) *Only Love,* CBS, 1998.

Television Stunt Performer; Uncredited; Miniseries:
Centennial, NBC, 1978.
Kenny Rogers as The Gambler: The Adventure Continues, CBS, 1983.

Television Director; Movies:
Hard Time: The Premonition (also known as *The Premonition*), TNT, 1999.
Gentle Ben (also known as *Terror on the Mountain*), Animal Planet, 2002.
Night of the Wolf, Animal Planet, 2002.
Gentle Ben 2: Danger on the Mountain (also known as *Black Gold*), Animal Planet, 2003.
Monster Makers, The Hallmark Channel, 2003.

Straight from the Heart, The Hallmark Channel, 2003.
The Hollywood Mom's Mystery (also known as *The Dead Hollywood Moms Society*), The Hallmark Channel, 2004.
Life on Liberty Street, The Hallmark Channel, 2004.
The Trail to Hope Rose, The Hallmark Channel, 2004.
Back to You and Me, The Hallmark Channel, 2005.
Desolation Canyon, The Hallmark Channel, 2005.
Detective (also known as *Arthur Hailey's "Detective"*), 2005.
The Family Plan, The Hallmark Channel, 2005.
Mystery Woman: Game Time, The Hallmark Channel, 2005.
Thicker Than Water, The Hallmark Channel, 2005.
Mystery Woman: Redemption, The Hallmark Channel, 2006.
Mystery Woman: Wild West Mystery, The Hallmark Channel, 2006.

Television Second Unit Director; Movies:
Wet Gold, ABC, 1984.
(As David Cass) *The Alamo: Thirteen Days to Glory,* NBC, 1987.
Rio Diablo, CBS, 1993.
Everything That Rises, TNT, 1998.
(As Dave Cass) *"The Ransom of Red Chief," The Wonderful World of Disney,* ABC, 1998.
Hard Time: Hostage Hotel (also known as *Hostage Hotel*), TNT, 1999.

Television Producer; Movies:
Hard Time, TNT, 1998.
Hard Time: Hostage Hotel (also known as *Hostage Hotel*), TNT, 1999.

Television Stunt Coordinator; Movies:
Kenny Rogers as The Gambler (also known as *The Gambler*), CBS, 1980.
Angel Dusted (also known as *Angel Dust*), NBC, 1981, also broadcast on *ABC Afterschool Specials,* ABC.
(As Dave Cass) *Coward of the County,* CBS, 1981.
Rascals and Robbers: The Secret Adventures of Tom Sawyer and Huck Finn, CBS, 1982.
The Toughest Man in the World, CBS, 1984.
Wet Gold, ABC, 1984.
(As Dave Cass) *Wild Horses,* CBS, 1985.
Assassin, CBS, 1986.
Louis L'Amour's "Down the Long Hills" (also known as *Down the Long Hills*), ABC and The Disney Channel, 1986.
(As Dave Cass) *The Alamo: Thirteen Days to Glory,* NBC, 1987.
Case Closed (also known as *Death by Diamonds*), CBS, 1988.
(As David Cass) *In the Line of Duty: The FBI Murders,* NBC, 1988.
Longarm (also known as *Showdown in Silver City*), ABC, 1988.

(As Dave Cass) *Desperado: Badlands Justice,* NBC, 1989.

(As Dave Cass) *Desperado: The Outlaw Wars,* NBC, 1989.

Rio Diablo, CBS, 1993.

River of Rage: The Taking of Maggie Keene (also known as *Murder on the Rio Grande*), CBS, 1993.

(As Dave Cass) *Breathing Lessons,* CBS, 1994.

(As Dave Cass) *MacShayne: Final Roll of the Dice,* NBC, 1994.

Tidal Wave: No Escape, ABC, 1997.

Everything That Rises, TNT, 1998.

(As Dave Cass) "The Ransom of Red Chief," *The Wonderful World of Disney,* ABC, 1998.

(As Dave Cass) *It Came from the Sky* (also known as *Les visiteurs impromtus*), Romance Classics, 1999.

Television Stunt Performer; Movies:

Kenny Rogers as The Gambler (also known as *The Gambler*), CBS, 1980.

(As Dave Cass) *Desperado,* NBC, 1987.

(Uncredited) *Longarm* (also known as *Showdown in Silver City*), ABC, 1988.

Howard Beach: Making a Case for Murder (also known as *In the Line of Duty: Howard Beach, Making a Case for Murder* and *Skin*), NBC, 1989.

Knight Rider 2000, NBC, 1991.

Hard Time, TNT, 1998.

Television Stunt Coordinator; Pilots:

(As Dave Cass) *The Georgia Peaches,* CBS, 1980.

(As Dave Cass) *Brotherhood of the Gun* (also known as *Hollister*), CBS, 1991.

Television Stunt Performer; Pilots:

(As Dave Cass) *The Georgia Peaches,* CBS, 1980.

(As Dave Cass) *Brotherhood of the Gun* (also known as *Hollister*), CBS, 1991.

(As Dave Cass) *The Keys,* NBC, 1992.

Television Appearances; Miniseries:

Frank Pettis, *Centennial,* NBC, 1978.

(Uncredited) Crazy director, *Family Album* (also known as *Danielle Steel's "Family Album"*), NBC, 1994.

Sheriff Boone, *The Gambler V: Playing for Keeps,* CBS, 1994.

Sheriff Doniphan, *Streets of Laredo* (also known as *Larry McMurtry's "Streets of Laredo"*), CBS, 1995.

Looter, *True Women,* CBS, 1997.

(As David Cass) Third companion, *Attila* (also known as *Attila the Hun*), USA Network, 2001.

Television Appearances; Movies:

Man, *Black Noon,* CBS, 1971.

(As Dave Cass) Dump truck driver, *Ohms,* CBS, 1980.

(As Dave Cass) Juanita's brother, *More Wild Wild West,* CBS, 1980.

(As Dave Cass) Seaman Dodge, *Donovan's Kid,* The Disney Channel, 1980.

Winters, *Kenny Rogers as The Gambler* (also known as *The Gambler*), CBS, 1980.

Overseer, *Rascals and Robbers: The Secret Adventures of Tom Sawyer and Huck Finn,* CBS, 1982.

Expatriate, *Wet Gold,* ABC, 1984.

(As Dave Cass) Keough, *Pigs vs. Freaks* (also known as *Off Sides*), ABC, 1984.

Louis L'Amour's "Down the Long Hills" (also known as *Down the Long Hills*), ABC and The Disney Channel, 1986.

(As Dave Cass) *Desperado,* NBC, 1987.

Man, *Miracle Landing,* CBS, 1990.

Cabe Winslow, *Rio Diablo,* CBS, 1993.

Gunfighter, *Everything That Rises,* TNT, 1998.

(As David Cass, Sr.) Pike, *Hard Ground,* The Hallmark Channel, 2003.

(As Dave Cass) Cab driver, *The Family Plan,* The Hallmark Channel, 2005.

Television Appearances; Specials:

(As Dave Cass) Himself, *Attila: The Making of an Epic Mini-Series,* USA Network, 2001.

Television Appearances; Episodic:

(As Dave Cass) Minister, "The Other Half," *Gunsmoke* (also known as *Gun Law* and *Marshal Dillon*), CBS, 1964.

(As Dave Cass) Harper, "Hondo and the Death Drive," *Hondo,* ABC, 1967.

(As Dave Cass) Corporal, "Sangre," *The High Chaparral,* NBC, 1971.

(As Dave Cass) Pinari, "Cat's Paw," *Mission: Impossible,* CBS, 1971.

(As Dave Cass) Deputy Coghlan, "One Ace Too Many," *Bonanza* (also known as *Ponderosa*), NBC, 1972.

(As Dave Cass) Deputy sheriff, "Frenzy," *Bonanza* (also known as *Ponderosa*), NBC, 1972.

Hugo, "Speed," *Mission: Impossible,* CBS, 1973.

The deputy, "The Breakdown," *The Waltons,* CBS, 1975.

(Uncredited) Sid, "Chicken Little Is a Little Chicken," *The Rockford Files* (also known as *Jim Rockford, Private Investigator*), NBC, 1975.

(As Dave Cass) Mort, "The Trees, the Bees, and T. T. Flowers: Parts 1 & 2," *The Rockford Files* (also known as *Jim Rockford, Private Investigator*), NBC, 1977.

(As Dave Cass) Janos, "Rancho Outcast," *The Bionic Woman,* NBC, 1978.

(As Dave Cass) Casey, "A Different Drummer," *The Rockford Files* (also known as *Jim Rockford, Private Investigator*), NBC, 1979.

"Clancy," *Young Maverick,* CBS, 1979.

(As Dave Cass) Ashley, "Details at Eleven," *Simon & Simon,* CBS, 1981.

(As Dave Cass) Major Jason Samos, "The Satyr," *Buck Rogers in the 25th Century,* NBC, 1981.

"Snow Job," *Enos,* CBS, 1981.

(As Dave Cass) Alex Webster, "Not a Drop to Drink," *Knight Rider,* NBC, 1982.

Andrew, "Created Equal," *Voyagers!,* NBC, 1982.

Goodwin, "Who's Woo in America," *The Greatest American Hero,* ABC, 1982.

Luke, "The Angel's Triangle/Natchez Bound," *Fantasy Island,* ABC, 1982.

(As Dave Cass) Second bodyguard, "Bail Out," *Simon & Simon,* CBS, 1983.

Chuck, "I Shall Be Re–Released," *Legmen,* NBC, 1984.

(As Dave Cass) Louis, "Knight by a Nose," *Knight Rider,* NBC, 1985.

Morris, "New Orleans Nightmare," *Matt Houston,* ABC, 1985.

(As Dave Cass) Benny, "A Little Bit of Luck ... a Little Bit of Grief," *Magnum, P.I.,* CBS, 1986.

Connie, "The Avenging Angel," *Misfits of Science,* NBC, 1986.

Third man on ranch, "Fighting for Your Life," *Highway to Heaven,* NBC, 1987.

(As Dave Cass) Gus, "Winner Takes All," *B. L. Stryker* (also known as *ABC Monday Mystery Movie* and *The ABC Saturday Mystery Movie*), ABC, 1990.

As David Cass, appeared in *The Yellow Rose,* NBC.

Television Appearances; Pilots:

(As Dave Cass) Dent, *Royce,* CBS, 1976.

First hand, *Law of the Land* (also known as *The Deputies*), NBC, 1976.

Biker, *The Golden Gate Murders* (also known as *Specter on the Bridge*), CBS, 1979.

(As Dave Cass) *The Georgia Peaches,* CBS, 1980.

(As David Cass) Second dock worker, *Command 5,* ABC, 1985.

WRITINGS

Screenplays:

Enter the Devil (also known as *Disciples of Death*), Sunset International Releasing, 1972.

Teleplays; Miniseries:

(Story) *The Gambler V: Playing for Keeps,* CBS, 1994.

Teleplays; Movies:

(As David Cass) *Rio Diablo,* CBS, 1993.

Hard Time, TNT, 1998.

Hard Ground, The Hallmark Channel, 2003.

CHANNING, Carol 1921–

PERSONAL

Full name, Carol Elaine Channing; born January 31, 1921, in Seattle, WA; raised in San Francisco, CA; daughter of George (a newspaper editor and a Christian Scientist lecturer) and Adelaide (maiden name, Glaser) Channing; married Theodore Naidish (a writer; divorced); married Al Carson (a professional football player; divorced, September, 1956); married Charles F. Lowe (a television producer and manager), September 5, 1956 (filed for divorce May 19, 1998; died, September 2, 1999); married Harry Kullijian, May 10, 2003; children: (second marriage) Channing George Lowe (a political cartoonist). *Education:* Attended Bennington College. *Religion:* Christian Scientist. Politics: Democrat.

Addresses: *Agent*—William Morris Agency, One William Morris Pl., Beverly Hills, CA 90212; Vox, Inc., 5670 Wilshire Blvd., Suite 820, Los Angeles, CA 90036.

Career: Actress and singer. Cabaret performer at various venues, including the Tropicana Hotel, Las Vegas, NV, 1957, the Nugget Hotel, Reno, NV, 1972, and the Palmer House, Chicago, IL, 1972. Performer at the Inaugural Gala for President Lyndon B. Johnson, Washington, DC, 1965; appeared in television commercials, including General Foods; also a performer at the Apollo Theatre, Harlem, and at resorts in the Pocono Mountains; sold her "Broadway Collection" jewelry on home shopping networks. Previously worked as a model and as an usher in the Alvin Theater, New York City.

Member: Actors' Equity Association.

Awards, Honors: New York Drama Critics Circle Award, 1948, for *Lend an Ear; Theatre World Award,* 1949; Antoinette Perry Award nomination, best actress in a musical, 1956, for *The Vamp;* Antoinette Perry Award nomination, best actress in a musical, 1961, for *Show Girl;* Antoinette Perry Award and New York Drama Critics Award, 1964, both for *Hello Dolly!;* Golden Apple Award, female star of the year, 1967; Golden Globe Award, best supporting actress, Academy Award nomination, best supporting actress, Golden Laurel Award, female supporting performance, Producers Guild of American, 1968, all for *Thoroughly Modern Millie;* Antoinette Perry Special Award, 1968; London Critics Award, 1970, for *Carol Channing and Her Ten Stout–Hearted Men;* Woman of the Year Award, Hasty Pudding Theatricals, Harvard University, 1971; Antoinette Perry Award nomination, best actress in a musical, 1974, for *Lorelei, or Gentlemen Still Prefer Blondes;* Antoinette Perry Award, for lifetime achievement in the theater, 1995; Distinguished Lifetime Service Award, League of American Theatres and Producers, 1998; Los Angeles Drama Critics Lifetime Achievement Award, 1996; Julie Harris Award, Actors' Fund, 2002; Star on the Broadway Walk of Stars, 2002; Woman of the Year, Nevada Ballet Theatre, 2003; Star on the Hollywood Walk of Fame—Television.

CREDITS

Stage Appearances:

Singer, *No for an Answer,* Center Theatre, New York City, 1941.

Understudy Maggie Watson, *Let's Face It,* Imperial Theatre, New York City, 1941.

Steve, *Proof Through the Night,* Morosco Theatre, New York City, 1942.

(Broadway debut) Various roles, *Lend an Ear,* National Theatre, 1948.

Lorelei Lee, *Gentlemen Prefer Blondes,* Ziegfeld Theatre, New York City, 1949, later Palace Theatre, Chicago, 1951.

Ruth Sherwood, *Wonderful Town,* Winter Garden Theatre, New York City, 1953.

Flora Weems, *The Vamp,* Winter Garden Theatre, 1955.

Show Business, Curran Theatre, San Francisco, CA, 1959.

Various roles, *Show Girl,* Eugene O'Neill Theatre, New York City, 1961.

Dolly Gallagher Levi, *Hello, Dolly!,* St. James Theatre, New York City, 1964–65, then Shubert Theatre, New York City, 1966, later Lunt–Fontanne Theatre, New York City, 1978, and 1995–96, also Shaftesbury Theatre, London, 1980.

Mrs. Dunkelmayer, "House of Dunkelmayer," Betty, "Betty," Irene, "Toreador," and Mrs. Wexel, "The Swingers," *Four on a Garden,* Broadhurst Theatre, New York City, 1971.

Carol Channing and Her Ten Stout Hearted Men, Drury Lane Theatre, London, 1971.

Carol Channing and Her Gentlemen Prefer Blondes, Princess Theatre, Melbourne, Australia, and Regent Theatre, Sydney, Australia, both 1972.

Lorelei Lee, *Lorelei, or Gentlemen Still Prefer Blondes* (also known as *Lorelei*), Palace Theatre, New York City, 1974.

Lorelei Lee, *Parade of Stars Playing the Palace,* Palace Theatre, 1983.

The Night of 100 Stars II (also known as *Night of One Hundred Stars*), Radio City Music Hall, New York City, 1985.

Legends, Los Angeles, 1985–86.

Happy Birthday, Mr. Abbott! Or Night of 100 Years, Palace Theatre, 1987.

Herself and performer of song "Little Girl from Little Rock," *Night of 100 Stars III* (also known as *Night of One Hundred Stars*), Radio City Music Hall, 1990.

Give My Regards to Broadway, Carnegie Hall, New York City, 1991.

Razzle Dazzle!, Los Angeles, 2004.

Carol Channing: The First Eighty Years Are the Hardest, Feinstein's at the Regency, New York City, 2005.

Also appeared in *So Proudly We Hail.*

Major Tours:

Lorelei Lee, *Gentlemen Prefer Blondes,* U.S. cities, 1951–52.

Eliza Doolittle, *Pygmalion,* U.S. cities, 1953.

Ruth, *Wonderful Town,* U.S. cities, 1954.

Show Business, U.S. cities, 1959.

Show Girl Revue, U.S. cities, 1961.

George Burns–Carol Channing Musical Revue, U.S. cities, 1962.

Dolly Gallagher Levi, *Hello, Dolly!,* U.S. cities, 1965–66, 1967, 1977–80, 1983, and 1994–96.

The Carol Channing Show, U.S. cities, 1971.

Lorelei Lee, *Lorelei, or Gentlemen Still Prefer Blondes* (also known as *Lorelei*), U.S. cities, 1975.

Alma, *The Bed before Yesterday,* Florida cities, 1976.

Jerry's Girls, Florida cities, 1984.

Sylvia Glenn, *Legends,* U.S. cities, 1985–86.

Film Appearances:

Mrs. Peters, *Paid in Full,* 1950.

Molly Wade, *The First Traveling Saleslady,* Universal, 1956.

Herself, *Carol Channing's Los Angeles,* 1966.

Muzzy, *Thoroughly Modern Millie,* Universal, 1967.

Narrator, *All About People,* 1967.

Flo Banks, *Skidoo,* Paramount, 1968.

Voice of Mehitabel, *Shinbone Alley,* 1971.

Voice, *Free to Be ... You & Me,* 1974.

Heartland guest, *Sgt. Pepper's Lonely Hearts Club Band,* 1978.

Herself, *George Burns—His Wit and Wisdom,* 1989.

Voice of Muddy, *Happily Ever After* (animated), First National Film Corporation, 1990.

Herself, *Wisecracks,* Alliance Releasing, 1991.

Voice of Miss Fieldmouse, *Hans Christian Andersen's "Thumbelina"* (animated; also known as *Thumbelina*), Warner Bros., 1994.

Herself, *Line King: The Al Hirschfeld Story* (also known as *The Line King*), Castle Hill Productions, 1996.

Edie & Pen (also known as *Desert Gamble*), 1996.

(Uncredited) Herself, *Homo Heights* (also known as *Happy Heights*), 1998.

(Uncredited) Herself, *The Kid Stays in the Picture* (documentary), Focus Features, 2002.

Herself, *Broadway: The Golden Age, by the Legends Who Were There* (documentary; also known as *Broadway, Broadway: The Golden Age,* and *Broadway: The Movie*), Dada Films, 2003.

Television Appearances; Series:
Voice, *Where's Waldo?* (animated; also known as *Where's Wally*), CBS, 1991.
Voice of Granny, *The Addams Family* (animated), 1992.
Herself, *The Bold and the Beautiful* (also known as *Glamour* and *Top Models*), 1993.
Herself, *Hollywood Squares,* 1998.

Television Appearances; Movies:
White Queen, *Alice in Wonderland* (also known as *Alice Through the Looking Glass*), CBS, 1985.
Voice of Ceiling Fan, *The Brave Little Toaster Goes to Mars* (animated), The Disney Channel, 1998.

Television Appearances; Pilots:
The Carol Channing Show, CBS, 1967.

Television Appearances; Specials:
Svengali and the Blonde, NBC, 1955.
Crescendo, CBS, 1957.
The Best on Record, NBC, 1965.
The Wonderful World of Burlesque, NBC, 1966.
Carol Channing's Los Angeles, 1966.
Carol Channing and 101 Men, ABC, 1967.
Host, *Carol Channing and Pearl Bailey: On Broadway,* ABC, 1969.
Carol Channing Proudly Presents the Seven Deadly Sins, ABC, 1969.
Guest, *Danny Thomas Looks at Yesterday, Today and Tomorrow,* CBS, 1970.
Host, *I'm a Fan,* CBS, 1972.
Performer, *One More Time,* CBS, 1974.
Bob Hope Comedy Special, NBC, 1974.
Voice of herself, *Free to Be ... You & Me,* 1974.
The Royal Variety Performance 1979, 1979.
Night of 100 Stars, 1982.
Parade of Stars, ABC, 1983.
George Burns Celebrates 80 Years in Show Business, NBC, 1983.
The Night of 100 Stars II (also known as *Night of One Hundred Stars*), ABC, 1985.
George Burns 90th Birthday Party (also known as *Kraft Salutes the George Burns 90th Birthday Special*), CBS, 1986.
Herself and performer of song "Little Girl from Little Rock," "Broadway Sings: The Music of Jule Styne" (also known as "The Music of Jule Styne"), *Great Performances,* PBS, 1987.
The 12th Annual Circus of the Stars (also known as *Circus of the Stars*), CBS, 1987.
Herself, *11–22–63: The Day the Nation Cried* (also known as *JFK: The Day the Nation Cried*), 1989.

Herself and performer of song "Little Girl from Little Rock," *Night of 100 Stars III* (also known as *Night of One Hundred Stars*), NBC, 1990.
Macy's Thanksgiving Day Parade, NBC, 1992.
The Carol Burnett Show: A Reunion, 1993.
Herself, *Jerry Herman's "Broadway at the Bowl"* (also known as *Broadway at the Hollywood Bowl*), PBS, 1994.
The Golden Globe's 50th Anniversary Celebration, NBC, 1994.
The First 100 Years: A Celebration of American Movies, HBO, 1995.
Gail Sheehy's "New Passages," ABC, 1996.
Annie, ABC, 1999.
Halston: The E! True Hollywood Story, E! Entertainment Television, 1999.
Broadway's Lost Treasures, PBS, 2003.
The Desilu Story: The Rags to Riches Success of the Desilu Empire, Bravo, 2003.
Broadway: The American Musical (documentary), PBS, 2004.

Television Appearances; Awards Presentations:
Presenter, *The 19th Annual Tony Awards,* WWOR (New York City), 1965.
The 40th Annual Academy Awards, ABC, 1968.
The 32nd Annual Tony Awards, 1978.
Presenter, *The 34th Annual Tony Awards,* CBS, 1980.
The 24th Annual Grammy Awards, CBS, 1982.
The 38th Annual Tony Awards, CBS, 1984.
The 1st Annual Comedy Awards, 1987.
The 43rd Annual Tony Awards, 1989.
The 45th Annual Tony Awards, 1991.
Presenter, *The 46th Annual Tony Awards,* CBS, 1992.
The 49th Annual Golden Globe Awards, TBS, 1992.
Presenter, *The 46th Annual Tony Awards,* 1992.
The Golden Globe's 50th Anniversary Celebration, NBC, 1994.
The 49th Annual Tony Awards, 1995.
The 50th Annual Tony Awards, CBS, 1996.
Presenter, *The 58th Annual Tony Awards* (also known as *The 2004 Tony Awards*), CBS, 2004.

Television Appearances; Episodic:
Herself, *The Milton Berle Show* (also known as *Texaco Star Theater* and *The Buick–Berle Show*), 1953.
"This Little Kitty Stayed Cool," *Omnibus,* CBS, 1953.
Person to Person, CBS, 1956.
Mabel, "Three Men on a Horse," *Playhouse 90,* CBS, 1957.
Toast of the Town (also known as *The Ed Sullivan Show*), 1957, 1958, 1959, 1961, 1964, 1967, 1971.
The Spike Jones Show, 1957.
Daisy June, "Clem in New York," *The Red Skelton Show* (also known as *The Red Skelton Hour*), 1957.
Herself, "Comedy Time," *Shower of Stars* (also known as *Chrysler Shower of Stars*), 1957.

Herself, *The Big Record,* 1958.
Promenade member, "The Christmas Tree," *Hallmark Hall of Fame* (also known as *Hallmark Television Playhouse*), NBC, 1958.
"George Signs Carol Channing," *The George Burns Show,* NBC, 1959.
"At Carol Channing's," *The Big Party for Revlon,* CBS, 1959.
Here's Hollywood, 1962.
What's My Line?, 1962–66.
I've Got a Secret, 1963.
The Andy Williams Show, 1963.
Password (also known as *Password All–Stars*), 1963, 1964, 1965.
Guest panelist, *To Tell the Truth,* 1964.
Daisy June, "Clem Strikes Oil," *The Red Skelton Show* (also known as *The Red Skelton Hour*), 1964.
The Carol Burnett Show (also known as *Carol Burnett and Friends*), 1968, 1971, 1972.
Playboy After Dark, 1969.
Rowan & Martin's Laugh–In (also known as *Laugh–In*), 1969, 1970, 1972.
The Tonight Show with Johnny Carson, NBC, 1970, 1971.
The Flip Wilson Show, 1971, 1972.
"David Hartman," *This Is Your Life,* 1972.
The Dean Martin Show (also known as *The Dean Martin Comedy Hour*), 1972, 1974.
The Mike Douglas Show, 1974.
Herself, *The Muppet Show,* syndicated, 1980.
Aunt Sylvia, "Aunt Sylvia," *The Love Boat,* ABC, 1981.
Aunt Sylvia, "My Aunt, The Warrior," *The Love Boat,* ABC, 1982.
Aunt Sylvia, "My Friend the Executrix," *The Love Boat,* ABC, 1982.
Herself, "Distant Relative," *Magnum, P.I.,* CBS, 1983.
Aunt Sylvia, "Authoress! Authoress!," *The Love Boat,* ABC, 1984.
"Soap Star," *The Love Boat,* ABC, 1985.
"Who Killed Maxwell Thorn?," *The Love Boat,* ABC, 1987.
The New Hollywood Squares, syndicated, 1988.
Super Password, NBC, 1988.
Lifestyles of the Rich and Famous, syndicated, 1989.
Sweethearts, syndicated, 1989.
"Carol Channing's Broadway," *Evening at Pops,* PBS, 1989.
Voice of Canina LaFur, "A Chorus Crime," *Chip 'n Dale Rescue Rangers* (animated), 1990.
Voice of Canina LaFur, "They Shoot Dogs, Don't They?," *Chip 'n Dale Rescue Rangers* (animated), 1990.
Voice of Granny Frump, *The Addams Family* (animated), ABC, 1992.
Herself, "Smoke Gets in Your Lies," *The Nanny,* CBS, 1993.
Voice of Dr. Contralto, *The Magic School Bus* (animated), PBS, 1994.
"Who Killed the Fashion King?," *Burke's Law,* 1994.
Herself, "Girlie Show," *Space Ghost Coast to Coast,* Cartoon Network, 1995.

The Dana Carvey Show, ABC, 1996.
The Rosie O'Donnell Show, syndicated, 1996.
Herself, "New York and Queens," *The Drew Carey Show,* ABC, 1997.
Herself, "The Comeback," *Touched by an Angel,* CBS, 1997.
Herself, "Chelsea's First Date," *Style and Substance,* CBS, 1998.
"Angela Lansbury: A Balancing Act," *Biography,* Arts and Entertainment, 1998.
CBS News Sunday Morning (also known as *Sunday Morning*), CBS, 2005.
Martha, syndicated, 2005.
Voice, *American Dad* (animated), Fox, 2005.
Voice of herself, "Patriot Games," *Family Guy* (animated; also known as *Padre de familia*), Fox, 2006.

Also appeared in *Captain Kangaroo,* CBS; *The Lucy Show,* CBS:

WRITINGS

Autobiography:
Just Lucky, I Guess: A Memoir of Sorts, Simon & Schuster, 2002.

OTHER SOURCES

Periodicals:
Entertainment Weekly, June 2, 1995, p. 29.
Interview, October, 1995, p. 84.
Newsweek, June 1, 1998, p. 76.
People Weekly, December 16, 1985, p. 194; June 8, 1998, p. 132.
Vanity Fair, October, 1995, pp. 262–66, 268, 292–93.

CHARENDOFF–STRONG, Tara
See STRONG, Tara

CHILL
See MITCHELL, Daryl

COLEMAN, Beth Toussaint
See TOUSSAINT, Beth

COOPER, Chuck 1954–

PERSONAL

Born November 8, 1954, in Cleveland, OH; son of an actor; children: Eddie, Alex, Lilli. *Education:* Graduated from Ohio University.

Addresses: *Agent*—SMS Talent, 8730 Sunset Blvd., Suite 440, Los Angeles, CA 90069; Don Buchwald and Associates, 10 East 44th St., New York, NY 10017.

Career: Actor.

Awards, Honors: Antoinette Perry Award, best featured actor in a musical, 1997, for *The Life;* Vivian Robinson/AUDELCO Recognition Award for excellence, outstanding performance in a musical—male, 2004, for *Caroline, or Change.*

CREDITS

Stage Appearances:
Isaac, Blind John, Abner, and Bert, *Colored People's Time,* Negro Ensemble Company, Cherry Lane Theatre, New York City, 1982.
Brother Boxer, *Amen Corner,* Nederland Theatre, New York City, 1983.
Caliban, *The Tempest,* Alliance Theatre Company, Atlanta, GA, 1984–85.
Memphis, *The Life,* Westbeth Theatre Center, New York City, 1990.
Man number one, "break" man, "Agnes," man in dirty dungarees, "Eulogy for Mister Hamm," and cabbie, "Lucky Nurse," *Four Short Operas,* Playwrights Horizons Theatre, New York City, 1991.
Adam, *Someone Who'll Watch over Me,* Booth Theatre, New York City, 1992–93.
Title role, *Othello,* New Jersey Shakespeare Festival, Drew University, Madison, NJ, 1993–94.
Roscoe, *Avenue X,* Playwrights Horizons Theatre, 1994.
Understudy Fosca's father, Lieutenant Barri, Lieutenant Torasso, Major Rizzoli, and Private Augenti, *Passion,* Plymouth Theatre, New York City, 1994–95.
Captain Jabali Abdul LaRouche, *Police Boys,* Playwrights Horizons Theatre, 1995.
Standby Dan Gerard, *Getting Away with Murder,* Broadhurst Theatre, New York City, 1996.
Memphis, *The Life,* Ethel Barrymore Theatre, New York City, 1997.
Frank Schaeffer, *Marco Polo Sings a Solo,* Signature Theatre, New York City, 1998.
King Mostansir, *Nicolette and Aucassin,* Westport County Playhouse, Westport, CT, 2000.
Billy Flynn, *Chicago,* Ethel Barrymore Theatre, New York City, 2001.
Jaguar Senior and Dregster Dupree, *Thunder Knocking on the Door,* Minetta Lane Theater, New York City, 2002.
Title role, *Robseon,* Mill Hill Playhouse, Trenton, NJ, 2002.
W. E. B. Dubois, *The World Beyond the Hill: The Life and Times of W. E. B. Dubois,* Berkshire Festival, 2003.

Shoulda Woulda Coulda (cabaret), Don't Tell Mama, New York City, 2003.
The dryer and the bus, *Caroline, or Change,* Eugene O'Neill Theatre, New York City, 2003–2004.
Hair, New Amsterdam Theatre, New York City, 2004.
Lennon, Orpheum Theater, San Francisco, CA, then Colonial Theatre, Boston, MA, then Broadhurst Theatre, New York City, 2005.

Also appeared as Brutus, *Julius Caesar,* Philadelphia Drama Guild, Philadelphia, PA; Tullus Aufidius, *Coriolanus,* and *The Doctor Is Out,* both Old Globe Theatre, San Diego, CA; title role, *Othello,* New Jersey Shakespeare Festival; Caliban, *The Tempest,* Alliance Theatre, Atlanta, GA; in *Getting Away with Murder, The Tap Dance Kid, Passion,* and *Rumors,* all Broadway productions; *Primary English Class, Riff Raff Revue,* and *Jawbone,* all Off–Broadway productions; Badfoot, *St. Louis Woman,* City Center Encores!, New York City; and *King's Island Christmas.*

Major Tours:
William, *The Tap Dance Kid,* 1986–87.

Also toured in *Eubie!* and *Whistle Down the Wind.*

Film Appearances:
Himself, *The Hollywood Knights,* Columbia, 1980.
Drag race passenger, *Collision Course,* De Laurentiis Entertainment Group, 1989.
Customer, *Malcolm X* (also known as *X*), Warner Bros., 1992.
Umpire, *North,* Columbia, 1994.
Mark the cop, *Sweet Nothing,* Warner Bros., 1995.
Stockbroker, *The Juror,* Columbia, 1996.
New York City cop, *The Peacemaker,* DreamWorks Pictures, 1997.
Male guard, *Gloria,* Columbia, 1999.
Earl Martin, *The Hurricane,* Buena Vista, 1999.
Armon, *The Opportunists,* First Look Pictures Releasing, 1999.
Benjamin, *Our Song,* IFC Films, 2000.
Jim, *3 Days of Rain,* Rogue Arts, 2002.
Sergeant Williams, *Downtown: A Street Tale,* 2004.
Find Me Guilty, 2006.

Film Work:
Stunts, *The Adventures of Buckaroo Banzai Across the 8th Dimension* (also known as *The Adventures of Buckaro Banzai*), 1984.

Television Appearances; Series:
Charlie the Bridgeman, *100 Centre Street,* Arts and Entertainment, 2001–2002.

Television Appearances; Movies:
Cop, *Action Family,* 1987.
Judge Whitney, *Criminal Justice,* HBO, 1990.

Television Appearances; Specials:
Gym teacher, "That Funny Fat Kid," *Young People's Specials,* syndicated, 1986.
The 51st Annual Tony Awards, CBS, 1997.
Cop Shop, PBS, 2004.

Television Appearances; Episodic:
Drew MacDaniel, "Sonata for Solo Organ," *Law & Order,* NBC, 1990.
Art Samuels, "Blue Bamboo," *Law & Order,* NBC, 1994.
Prosecutor, "Expert Witness," *Cosby Mysteries,* NBC, 1994.
"One Day at a Time," *Cosby Mysteries,* NBC, 1994.
Sawyer, "Man's Best Friend," *New York Undercover* (also known as *Uptown Undercover*), Fox, 1995.
Walters' attorney, "Custody," *Law & Order,* NBC, 1996.
Bus driver, "Moby Greg," *NYPD Blue,* ABC, 1996.
Referee, *Strangers with Candy,* Comedy Central, 1999.
Lowell Griffin, "The Naked Are the Dead," *NYPD Blue,* ABC, 2000.
James Vesey, "The Perfect Valentine," *Cosby,* CBS, 2000.
Rolando August, "Burn, Baby, Burn," *Law & Order,* NBC, 2000.
Lieutenant Kyle, "Man Enough," *Third Watch,* NBC, 2001.
Barry's ex–boss, "Fallout: Part 1," *Without a Trace,* CBS, 2003.
Mr. Tassler, "Perfect," *Law & Order: Special Victims Unit* (also known as *Law & Order: SVU* and *Special Victims Unit*), NBC, 2003.
Hayden, "See No Evil," *Hack,* CBS, 2003.

Also appeared in *I'll Fly Away,* NBC; *The Bold and the Beautiful,* CBS; "Past Imperfect," *New York News.*

RECORDINGS

Albums (Cast Recordings):
Appeared on *The Life; King Island Christmas; Caroline, or Change; Avenue X; St. Louis Woman; The Confidence Man.*

COVER, Franklin Edward 1928–2006

PERSONAL

Full name, Franklin Edward Cover; born November 20, 1928, in Cleveland, OH; died of pneumonia, February 5, 2006, in Englewood, NJ. Actor. Though Cover worked extensively in theatre, he was best recognized as Tom Willis, the white neighbor of George and Louise Jefferson in the popular television series *The Jeffersons,* which ran from 1975 to 1985. Cover enjoyed a long acting career that began in 1945 with his stage debut at the Cain Park Theatre in Cleveland Heights, OH. He appeared with the Cleveland Playhouse from 1954 to 1958 before heading to New York City, where he performed in such Broadway productions as *Any Wednesday* at the Music Box Theatre and *Born Yesterday* at the 46th Street Theatre. Cover also appeared in a number of feature films, including *The Great Gatsby, The Stepford Wives,* and *Wall Street,* but he was better known for his television work. Cover made numerous episodic appearances in such popular series as *All in the Family, The Love Boat, Will & Grace,* and the soap opera *All My Children.*

PERIODICALS

Variety, February 20, 2006.

D

DAMON, Matt 1970–

PERSONAL

Full name, Matthew Paige Damon; born October 8, 1970, in Cambridge, MA; son of Kent Damon (a tax preparer and stockbroker) and Nancy Carlsson–Paige (a professor of childhood education); married Luciana Barroso, December 9, 2005; children: Alexia (stepdaughter). *Education:* Studied English at Harvard University, 1988–91.

Addresses: *Agent*—Endeavor, 9601 Wilshire Blvd., 6th Floor, Beverly Hills, CA 90212. *Publicist*—PMK/HBH Public Relations, 700 San Vicente Blvd., Suite G910, West Hollywood, CA 90069.

Career: Actor, producer, and writer. Appeared in a radio commercial for Samuel Adams beer, 2001, and National Mentoring Month, 2005.

Awards, Honors: National Board of Review Award (with Affleck), special achievement in filmmaking, 1997, Academy Award (with Ben Affleck), best writing—screenplay written directly for the screen, Academy Award nomination, best actor in a leading role, Golden Globe Award (with Affleck), best screenplay—motion picture, Golden Globe Award nomination, best performance by an actor in a motion picture—drama, Silver Berlin Bear, outstanding single achievement, Berlin International Film Festival, Writers Guild of America Screen Award nomination (with Affleck), best screenplay written directly for the screen, Humanitas Prize (with Affleck), feature film category, Human Family Educational and Cultural Institute, Broadcast Film Critics Association Awards, best screenplay–original (with Affleck) and breakthrough artist, MTV Movie Award nominations, best kiss (with Minnie Driver), best on–screen duo (with Affleck), and best male performance, Florida Film Critics Circle Award (with Affleck), newcomer of the year, Online Film Critics Society Award nomination (with Affleck), best screenplay, Screen Actors Guild Award nominations, outstanding performance by a cast (with others), and outstanding performance by a male actor in a leading role, Golden Satellite Award (with Affleck), best motion picture screenplay—original, International Press Academy, Golden Satellite Award nomination, best performance by an actor in a motion picture—drama, Chicago Film Critics Award, most promising actor, Sierra Award, most promising actor, Las Vegas Film Critics Society Award, all 1998, London Critics Circle Award nominations, screenwriter of the year (with Affleck) and actor of the year, Blockbuster Entertainment Award, favorite actor in a video, 1999, all for *Good Will Hunting;* Blockbuster Entertainment Award nomination, favorite actor—drama, 1998, for *John Grisham's "The Rainmaker";* ShoWest Award, male star of tomorrow, National Association of Theatre Owners, 1998; chosen as one of the fifty most beautiful people in the world, *People Weekly,* 1998; Screen Actors Guild Award nomination (with others), outstanding performance by a cast, Online Film Critics Society Award (with others), best ensemble cast performance, 1999, both for *Saving Private Ryan;* Golden Globe Award nomination, best actor in a motion picture drama, Blockbuster Entertainment Award nomination, favorite actor—suspense, Sierra Award nomination, best actor, Las Vegas Film Critics Society, and MTV Movie Award nominations, best musical performance (with others) and best villain, Teen Choice Award nominations, film—choice actor and film—choice liar, all 2000, for *The Talented Mr. Ripley;* Sierra Award nomination, Las Vegas Film Critics Society, best actor, 2000, Blockbuster Entertainment Award nomination, favorite actor—drama/romance, 2001, both for *All the Pretty Horses;* Phoenix Film Critics Society Award nomination (with others), best acting ensemble, MTV Movie Award nomination (with others), best on–screen team, 2002, DVD Premiere Award nomination (with Brad Pitt and Andy Garcia), best audio commentary—new release, DVD Exclusive

Awards, 2003, all for *Ocean's Eleven;* Bronze Wrangler (with others), theatrical motion picture, Western Heritage Awards, Blimp Award nomination, favorite voice from an animated movie, Kids' Choice Awards, 2003, for *Spirit: Stallion of the Cimarron;* Emmy Award nomination (with others), outstanding non-fiction program—reality, 2002, Television Producer of the Year Award nomination (with others), reality/game/informational series, PGA Golden Laurel Awards, 2003, both for *Project Greenlight;* Emmy Award nomination (with others), outstanding reality program, Television Producer of the Year Award nomination (with others), reality/game/informational series, PGA Golden Laurel Awards, 2004, both for *Project Greenlight 2;* Teen Choice Award nomination, choice movie actor—action/adventure/thriller, MTV Movie Award nomination, best male performance, Empire Award, best actor, *Empire* magazine, Saturn Award nomination, best actor, Academy of Science Fiction, Fantasy and Horror Films, 2005, all for *The Bourne Supremacy;* Emmy Award nomination (with others), outstanding reality program, 2005, for *Project Greenlight 3;* Broadcast Film Critics Association Award nomination (with others), best acting ensemble, 2005, for *Ocean's Twelve;* ShoWest Award, male star of the year, National Association of Theatre Owners, 2005.

CREDITS

Film Appearances:

Extra, *The Good Mother* (also known as *The Price of Passion*), Buena Vista, 1988.

Steamer, *Mystic Pizza,* Samuel Goldwyn, 1988.

Charlie Dillon, *School Ties,* Paramount, 1992.

Second Lieutenant Britton Davis, *Geronimo: An American Legend,* Columbia, 1993.

Edgar Pudwhacker, *Glory Daze* (also known as *Last Call*), Columbia TriStar, 1995.

Specialist Ilario, *Courage Under Fire,* Twentieth Century–Fox, 1996.

Executive number two, *Chasing Amy* (also known as *Comic Strip*), Miramax, 1997.

Rudy Baylor, *John Grisham's "The Rainmaker"* (also known as *The Rainmaker*), Paramount, 1997.

Will Hunting, *Good Will Hunting,* Miramax, 1997.

Mike McDermott, *Rounders,* Miramax, 1998.

Private James Francis Ryan, *Saving Private Ryan,* DreamWorks Distribution, 1998.

Himself, *Return to Normandy* (documentary; also known as *The Making of "Saving Private Ryan"*), 1998.

Himself, *Into the Beach: "Saving Private Ryan"* (documentary short), 1998.

Loki/Larry, *Dogma,* Lions Gate Films, 1999.

Tom Ripley, *The Talented Mr. Ripley* (also known as *The Mysterious Yearning Secretive Sad Lonely Trouble Confused Loving Musical Gifted Intelligent Beautiful Tender Sensitive Haunted Passionate Talented Mr. Ripley*), Miramax, 1999.

Himself, *"The Talented Mr. Ripley": Making the Soundtrack* (documentary short), Paramount 1999.

Himself, *Inside "The Talented Mr. Ripley"* (documentary short), Paramount, 1999.

Voice of Cal, *Planet Ice* (animated), Twentieth Century–Fox, 1999.

Himself, *Reflections on "The Talented Mr. Ripley"* (documentary), 2000.

Voice of Cale, *Titan A.E.* (animated; also known as *Titan: After Earth*), Twentieth Century–Fox, 2000.

Rannulph Junuh, *The Legend of Bagger Vance,* DreamWorks, 2000.

John Grady Cole, *All the Pretty Horses,* Sony Pictures Entertainment, 2000.

Steven Sanderson, *Finding Forrester,* Columbia, 2000.

Linus Caldwell, *Ocean's Eleven* (also known as *11* and *O11*), Warner Bros., 2001.

Voice of Luke Trimble, *The Majestic,* Warner Bros., 2001.

Himself, *Judge Not: In Defense of Dogma* (documentary short), Lions Gate Films Home Entertainment, 2001.

Himself and Will Hunting, *Jay and Silent Bob Strike Back,* Dimension, 2001.

Voice of Spirit, *Spirit: Stallion of the Cimarron* (animated; also known as *Spirit*), DreamWorks, 2002.

Jason Bourne, *The Bourne Identity* (also known as *Die Bourne Identitat*), Universal, 2002.

Title role, *Gerry,* ThinkFilm, 2002.

Kevin, *The Third Wheel,* Miramax, 2002.

Matt, bachelor number two, *Confessions of a Dangerous Mind* (also known as *Confessions d'un homme dangereux*), Miramax, 2002.

Himself, *Saltlake Van Sant* (documentary short), Miramax, 2003.

Bob, *Stuck on You,* Twentieth Century–Fox, 2003.

Donny, *EuroTrip,* DreamWorks, 2004.

Public relations executive number two, *Jersey Girl,* Miramax, 2004.

Jason Bourne, *The Bourne Supremacy* (also known as *Die Bourne Verschworung*), Universal, 2004.

Linus Caldwell, *Ocean's Twelve,* Warner Bros., 2004.

Himself, *"Saving Private Ryan": Boot Camp* (documentary short), DreamWorks Home Entertainment, 2004.

Himself, *Making "Saving Private Ryan"* (documentary), 2004.

Himself, *"Saving Private Ryan" Miller and His Platoon* (documentary short), DreamWorks Home Entertainment, 2004.

Narrator, *Howard Zinn: You Can't Be Neutral on a Moving Train* (documentary short), DreamWorks Home Entertainment, 2004.

Himself, *Sur les traces de Gerry* (documentary short; also known as *From Gerry to Elephant*), 2004.

Voice, *Magnificent Desolation: Walking on the Moon 3D* (animated documentary short), IMAX, 2005.

Wilhelm Grimm, *The Brothers Grimm,* Miramax, 2005.

Bryan Woodman, *Syriana,* Warner Bros., 2005.

Mr. Aaron, *Margaret,* Fox Searchlight, 2006.

Edward Wilson, *The Good Shepherd*, Universal, 2006.
Colin Sullivan, *The Departed*, Warner Bros., 2006.
Jason Bourne, *The Bourne Ultimatum*, Universal, 2007.

Film Work:
Producer, *Stolen Summer*, Miramax, 2002.
Executive producer, *Speakeasy*, Miramax, 2002.
Executive producer, *The Third Wheel*, Miramax, 2002.
Editor, *Gerry*, ThinkFilm, 2002.
Executive producer, *The Battle of Shaker Heights*, Miramax, 2003.
Executive producer, *Turning It Over*, 2004.
Executive producer, *Feast*, 2005.

Television Appearances; Series:
Himself, *Project Greenlight*, HBO, 2001.
Himself, *Project Greenlight 2*, HBO, 2003.
Himself, *Project Greenlight 3*, HBO, 2005.

Television Appearances; Miniseries:
Narrator, *Journey to Planet Earth*, 2003.

Television Appearances; Movies:
Charlie Robinson, *Rising Son*, TNT, 1990.
Cotton Calloway, *The Good Old Boys*, TNT, 1995.

Television Appearances; Specials:
Seventeen: The Faces for Fall, The WB, 1998.
The Untitled Jay Lacopo Project, Sundance, 1999.
AFI's 100 Years, 100 Thrills: America's Most Heart–Pounding Movies, CBS, 2001.
(Uncredited) Himself, *Shirtless: Hollywood's Sexiest Men* (documentary), AMC, 2002.
Ben Affleck & Matt Damon: The E! True Hollywood Story, E! Entertainment Television, 2003.
Reel Comedy: Stuck on You, Comedy Central, 2003.
Tsunami Aid: A Concert of Hope, 2005.
Red Carpet Confidential, CBS, 2005.

Television Appearances; Awards Presentations:
Presenter, *The 70th Annual Academy Awards*, ABC, 1998.
Presenter, *The 56th Annual Golden Globe Awards*, 1999.
Presenter, *The 71st Annual Academy Awards*, ABC, 1999.
The 2000 Blockbuster Entertainment Awards, Fox, 2000.
Presenter, *The 2002 MTV Movie Awards*, MTV, 2002.

Television Appearances; Episodic:
The Rosie O'Donnell Show, syndicated, 1997, 1998, 2000, 2002.
The Oprah Winfrey Show (also known as *Oprah*), syndicated, 1998, 2002.

Howard Stern, E! Entertainment Television, 1998.
Mundo VIP, 1998.
Himself, "Saving Private Ryan," *HBO First Look*, HBO, 1998.
The Howard Stern Radio Show, syndicated, 1999.
Late Night with Conan O'Brien, NBC, 1999, 2002, 2003.
Himself, "The Legend of Bagger Vance," *HBO First Look*, HBO, 2000.
Himself, "Billy Bob Thorton," *Bravo Profiles*, Bravo, 2000.
(Uncredited) Himself, *Inside the Actors Studio*, Bravo, 2001.
(Uncredited) Himself, *Saturday Night Live* (also known as *SNL*), NBC, 2001.
Himself, "Matt Damon," *Revealed with Jules Asner*, E! Entertainment Television, 2001.
The Tonight Show with Jay Leno, NBC, 2001, 2002, 2005.
Host, *Saturday Night Live* (also known as *SNL*), NBC, 2002.
(Uncredited) Himself, *Extra* (also known as *Extra: The Entertainment Magazine*), syndicated, 2002.
Himself, "Keep It on the Short Grass," *The Bernie Mac Show*, Fox, 2002.
Owen, "A Chorus Lie," *Will & Grace*, NBC, 2002.
Celebrities Uncensored, E! Entertainment Television, 2003.
Bob Tenor, "Stuck on You," *HBO First Look*, HBO, 2003.
Tinseltown TV (also known as *Tinseltown.TV*), International Channel, 2003, 2004.
Late Show with David Letterman (also known as *Late Show Backstage* and *The Late Show*), CBS, 2004.
MovieReal, Arts and Entertainment, 2004.
Himself, "Ocean's Twelve," *HBO First Look*, HBO, 2004.
Live with Regis and Kelly, syndicated, 2004.
Enough Rope with Andrew Denton, ABC [Australian Broadcast Corp.], 2004.
Rove Live, Ten Network, 2004.
The Panel, Ten Network, 2004.
Mondo Thingo, ABC [Australian Broadcast Corp.], 2004.
60 Minutes, CBS, 2004.
Tout le monde en parle, 2004.
GMTV, ITV, 2004, 2005.
Himself, "Syriana," *HBO First Look*, HBO, 2005.
Cinema mil, Televisio de Catalunya, 2005.
Corazon de ... , 2005.
"Bruce Willis," *Biography*, Arts and Entertainment, 2005.
(Uncredited) Voice of himself, "The Unblinking Eye," *Law & Order: Criminal Intent* (also known as *Law & Order: CI*), 2005.
The Film Programme, BBC, 2005.

Television Executive Producer; Series:
Project Greenlight, HBO, 2001.
Push, Nevada, ABC, 2002.

Project Greenlight 2, HBO, 2003.
Project Greenlight 3, HBO, 2005.

Television Executive Producer; Pilots:
General Manager, 2003.
Los Angeles, ABC, 2003.
All Grown Up, CBS, 2003.

Stage Appearances:
(London stage debut) *This Is Our Youth,* London, 2002.

WRITINGS

Screenplays:
(With Ben Affleck) *Good Will Hunting,* Miramax, 1997.
Gerry, ThinkFilm, 2002.

OTHER SOURCES

Books:
Diamond, Maxine and Harriet Hemmings, *Matt Damon: A Biography,* Pocket Books (New York City), 1998.
International Dictionary of Films and Filmmakers, Volume 3: Actors and Actresses, 4th ed., St. James Press, 2000.

Periodicals:
Entertainment Weekly, July 23, 2004, p. 22.
Interview, December, 1997, p. 118.
Los Angeles Times, November 30, 1997, pp. 3, 78–79.
Parade, November 30, 2003, pp. 6–7.
People Weekly, February 23, 1998, p. 87; August 2, 2004, p. 67.
Teen People, August 1, 2004, p. 106.
Time, December 1, 1997, p. 78.

DAVIES, Geraint Wyn 1957–
(Gary Davies, Geraint Davies)

PERSONAL

Born April 20, 1957, in Swansea, Wales; immigrated to Canada, 1964; father, a pastor; mother, a teacher; married Alana Davies (an artist), 1985; children: Galen, Pyper. *Education:* Graduated from Upper Canada College; attended University of Western Ontario.

Addresses: *Agent*—Paradigm, 360 North Crescent Dr., North Bldg., Beverly Hills, CA 90210.

Career: Actor, director, and producer. Stratford Shakespeare Festival, Stratford, Ontario, Canada, member of company, 1988–89; Shaw Festival, Niagara–on–the–Lake, Ontario, Canada, member of company; Theatre Clwyd (the Welsh National Performing Arts Company), actor and associate director, for two seasons; Roundtable Films (a production company), founder.

Member: Screen Actors Guild.

Awards, Honors: Regional Theatre Best Actor Award, 1992, for *Hamlet;* Gemini Award nominations, best performance by an actor in a continuing leading dramatic role, Academy of Canadian Cinema and Television, 1993, 1996, both for *Forever Knight;* Gemini Award nomination, best performance by an actor in a continuing leading dramatic role, 1998, for *Black Harbour;* Garland Awards (with others), best ensemble cast, Backstage West, 1998; Helen Hayes Award, outstanding lead actor—resident play, Washington Theatre Awards Society, 2005, for *Cyrano.*

CREDITS

Film Appearances:
(As Gary Davies) Michael Franklin, *Deadly Harvest,* 1977.
Michael Wilson, *One of the Hollywood Ten* (also known as *Punto de mira*), Alibi Films International, 2000.
Eric Daniels, *American Psycho II: All American Girl* (also known as *American Psycho 2*), Lions Gate Films, 2002.
Simon Grady, *Cube 2: Hypercube* (also known as *Hypercube*), 2002.
Colin, *The Wild Dogs,* Mongrel Media, 2002.
Zin, *Alien Tracker,* Lions Gate Films Home Entertainment, 2003.
(Archive footage) Simon Grady, *Re–Entering the Nightmare* (documentary short), Savage Dog Film & Digitals, 2005.

Film Work:
Executive producer, *Cocktailed Confusion,* 1999.
Coproducer and director, *The Quantum Heist,* Power Point Films, 2006.

Television Appearances; Series:
So the Story Goes, 1977.
Glen, *High Hopes,* CBC, 1978.
Thomas, *The Canadian,* 1978.
Jimmy Hogan, *To Serve and Protect,* 1985.
Allan Pearson, *The Judge,* CBC, 1986.
Major Mike Rivers, *Airwolf* (also known as *Lonewolf* and *Airwolf II*), USA Network, 1987.

Nicholas de Brabant/Detective Nicholas "Nick" Knight, *Forever Knight,* CBS, 1992–94, syndicated, 1994–96.
Nick Haskell, *Black Harbour,* CBC, 1996—.
Zin, *Tracker,* syndicated, 2001.
James Nathanson, *24,* Fox, 2006.

Television Appearances; Miniseries:
David Kaydick, *RoboCop: Prime Directives,* Sci–Fi Channel, 2000.
Premier William G. Davis, *Trudeau,* CBC, 2002.

Television Appearances; Movies:
Drake, *Hangin' in Plasma Suite,* syndicated and CBC, 1977.
Jon, *D.O.A.,* 1978.
Rick Jarrell, *A Paid Vacation,* 1979.
Antipholus of Syracuse, *The Boys from Syracuse,* 1986.
Young pilot, *Learning to Fly,* 1986.
Angus, *Ikwe* (also known as *Daughters of the Country: "Ikwe"*), 1987.
Hortensio, *The Taming of the Shrew,* 1988.
Allan Devlin, *Bionic Showdown: The Six Million Dollar Man and the Bionic Woman* (also known as *Return of the Six Million Dollar Man and the Bionic Woman II*), NBC, 1989.
Anton ("Tony"), *Terror Stalks the Class Reunion* (also known as *For Better and for Worse* and *Mary Higgins Clark: Pour le meilleur et pour le pire*), syndicated, 1992.
Dr. Martin Nolan, *Hush Little Baby* (also known as *Mother of Pearl*), USA Network, 1993.
Matt Stewart, *Other Women's Children,* Lifetime, 1993.
Martin Mallory, *Ghost Mom* (also known as *Bury Me in Niagara* and *Bury Me in St. Louis, Louis*), Fox, 1993.
Dr. Lambert, *Dancing in the Dark,* Lifetime, 1995.
Ben, "The Graveyard Rats," *Trilogy of Terror II,* USA Network, 1996.
Straker, *The Conspiracy of Fear* (also known as *Bridge of Spies* and *The Losers*), HBO, 1996.

Also appeared as in *Cope.*

Television Appearances; Episodic:
(As Gary Davies) Joey, "Cementhead," *For the Record,* 1977.
Thomas, "Ambush at Iroquois Point," *The Canadians,* 1978.
Robert Sutcliffe, "Death on Delivery," *The Great Detective,* CBC, 1979.
David Barrington, "Once Upon a Tyme," *The Littlest Hobo,* CTV and syndicated, 1982.
Dez Ranger, "The Case of the Missing Guitar," *Edison Twins II,* CBC and The Disney Channel, 1983.
Adam Coulter, "Scavenger Hunt: Parts 1 & 2," *The Littlest Hobo,* CTV and syndicated, 1983.

Anthony Davis, "The Wedding," *Street Legal,* CBC, 1986.
"Leap of Faith," *Diamonds,* USA Network, 1988.
Dan Bright, "The Reluctant Candidate," *The Campbells,* The Family Channel, 1988.
Paul Stebbins, "The Reunion," *Alfred Hitchcock Presents,* USA Network, 1989.
Klaus Helsing, "The Vampire Solution," *Dracula: The Series,* syndicated, 1990.
Klaus Helsing, "Black Sheep," *Dracula: The Series,* syndicated, 1990.
Boswell, "Count Your Blessings," *Katts and Dog* (also known as *Rin Tin Tin: K–9 Cop*), CTV and The Family Channel, 1990.
Anthony Davis, "Wedding," *Street Legal,* CBC, 1990.
Frank Hallstead, "For a Song," *Sweating Bullets* (also known as *Tropical Heat*), 1991.
Victor, "Dangerous Dreams," *The Hidden Room,* Lifetime, 1991.
Hartley Jeffco, "Three Men and a Skull," *My Secret Identity,* syndicated, 1991.
Captain Tom Reeves, "Collateral Damage," *Matrix,* syndicated, 1993.
Michael Moore/Quentin Barnes, "Turnabout," *Highlander* (also known as *Highlander: The Series*), syndicated, 1993.
Martin, "Provision 22," *Robocop* (also known as *RoboCop: The Series*), syndicated, 1994.
Lawrence, "The Possessed," *Kung Fu: The Legend Continues,* syndicated, 1994.
Sheriff Grady Markham, "Paradise," *The Outer Limits,* Showtime and syndicated, 1996.
David, "Worlds Within," *The Outer Limits,* Showtime and syndicated, 2001.
Dr. Sims, "Victoria," *1–800–MISSING* (also known as *Missing*), Lifetime, 2003.
Lawyer, "Buttons on a Hot Tin Roof," *Puppets Who Kill,* Comedy Central, 2005.

Also appeared (as Gary Davies) as Gary, "Once a Hero," *Side Street,* CBC; Nick, "The Loyalists," *In Their Shoes;* Morgan, "The Hand That Feeds," *Not My Department.*

Television Executive Producer; Movies:
The Fifteen Streets, 1989.

Television Director; Episodic:
Forever Knight, CBS, 1995–97.
"The Smell of Violets," *North of 60,* CBC, 1997.
"The Mask," *Power Play,* CBC, 1997.
"Manipulation," *Power Play,* CBC, 1999.

Also directed episodes of *Black Harbour,* CBC; *Pit Pony,* CBC.

Stage Appearances:
(Professional debut) *The Fantasticks,* Quebec City, 1976.

Red Emma, Quebec City, 1976.

A Midsummer's Night Dream, Quebec City, 1976.

Petruchio, *The Taming of the Shrew,* 1996.

Gross Indecency: The Three Trials of Oscar Wilde, Mark Taper Forum, Los Angeles, 1998.

An Evening with Dylan Thomas, Atlantic Theatre Festival, Nova Scotia, Canada, 1999.

Dylan Thomas and Shakespeare: In the Envy of Some Greatness, Atlantic Theatre Festival, 2000.

Stranger in Paradise, Atlantic Theatre Festival, 2001.

Henry Higgins, *My Fair Lady,* Stratford Festival, Stratford, Ontario, Canada, 2002.

Hughie, Atlantic Theatre Festival, 2003.

Dylan Thomas, *Do Not Go Gentle,* Chicago Shakespeare Theatre, Chicago, 2003.

(New York debut) Edmund, *King Lear,* Vivian Beaumont Theatre, New York City, 2004.

Dylan Thomas, *Do Not Go Gentle,* ArcLight Theater, New York City, 2005.

Cyrano, Shakespeare Theatre, c. 2005.

Days Without End, ArcLight Theatre, 2005.

Also appeared as Antipholus, *The Boys from Syracuse;* Marchbanks, *Candida;* Christian, *Cyrano de Bergerac;* d'Artagnan, *The Three Musketeers;* title role, *Henry V;* title role, *Pericles;* Stockman, *Enemy of the People;* in *The Last Englishman,* British Actors Theatre Company; *Henry VIII,* Chichester Festival, Chichester, England; *The Music Cure; The Vortex; Goodnight Disgrace; My Fat Friend,* Los Angeles; *Sleuth,* Toronto, Ontario, Canada; *Hereward the Wake; Buckingham.*

Major Tours:

Title role, *Hamlet,* Theatre Clwyd, British cities, 1992.

Also toured in *An Enemy of the People,* Theatre Clwyd, British cities.

Stage Director:

Joy of the Desolate, Highland Park, IL, 2000.

RECORDINGS

Albums:

Bar Talk, 2000.

OTHER SOURCES

Periodicals:

Cinescape, July, 1995, p. 73.

Sci-Fi Universe, March, 1996.

Starlog, March, 1995.

Venue, Summer, 1996.

DERN, Bruce 1936–

PERSONAL

Full name, Bruce MacLeish Dern; born June 4, 1936, in Chicago (some sources say Winnetka), IL; son of John and Jean (MacLeish) Dern; grandson of George Dern (a former governor of Utah and Federal Secretary of War); nephew of Archibald Macleish (a poet); married Marie Dean (divorced); married Diane Ladd (an actress), 1960 (divorced, 1969); married Andrea Beckett, October 20, 1969; children: (second marriage) Laura Elizabeth (an actress), Diane E. (deceased). *Education:* Attended the University of Pennsylvania, 1954–57; studied for the theatre with Gordon Phillips and at the American Foundation of Dramatic Art; studied acting at the Actors Studio.

Addresses: *Agent*—Creative Artists Agency, 9830 Wilshire Blvd., Beverly Hills, CA 90212.

Career: Actor. Actors Studio, member, 1959—.

Member: Actors' Equity Association, Screen Actors Guild, Santa Monica Track Club.

Awards, Honors: National Society of Film Critics Award, best supporting actor, 1972, for *Drive, He Said;* Pacific Archives Award, Berkeley, CA, actor of the year, 1972; Bronze Wrangler (with others), theatrical motion picture, Western Heritage Awards, 1972, for *The Cowboys;* Golden Globe Award nomination, best supporting actor, 1974, for *The Great Gatsby;* Academy Award nomination, best supporting actor, Golden Globe Award nomination, best supporting actor, 1979, both for *Coming Home;* Genie Award nomination, best performance by a foreign actor, Academy of Canadian Cinema and Television, 1980, for *Middle Age Crazy;* Silver Bear Award, best actor, Berlin International Film Festival, 1983, for *That Championship Season;* Genie Award nomination, best performance by a foreign actor, 1983, for *Middle Age Crazy;* Golden Boot Award, Motion Picture and Television Fund, 2002.

CREDITS

Film Appearances:

Jack Roper, *Wild River,* Twentieth Century–Fox, 1960.

Joe Krajac, *The Crimebusters,* Metro–Goldwyn–Mayer, 1961.

Bedtime Story, Universal, 1963.

John Mayhew, *Hush ... Hush, Sweet Charlotte* (also known as *Cross of Iron* and *What Ever Happened to Cousin Charlotte?*), Twentieth Century–Fox, 1964.

Sailor, *Marnie,* Universal, 1964.

Joey Kerns and a loser, *The Wild Angels,* American International Pictures, 1966.

John, *The Trip,* American International Pictures, 1967.

Hammond, *The War Wagon,* Universal, 1967.

Deputy Samuel P. Tippen, *Waterhole No. 3* (also known as *Waterhole #3* and *Waterhole 3*), Paramount, 1967.

John May, *The St. Valentine's Day Massacre,* Twentieth Century–Fox, 1967.

Steve Davis, *Psych–Out* (also known as *Love Children*), American International Pictures, 1968.

Miller, Cooper Hanging Party, *Hang 'em High,* United Artists, 1968.

Rafe Quint, *Will Penny,* Paramount, 1968.

Richie Fowler, *Number One,* United Artists, 1969.

Joe Danby, *Support Your Local Sheriff,* United Artists, 1969.

Billy Bix, *Castle Keep,* Columbia, 1969.

Keeg, *The Cycle Savages,* American International Pictures, 1969.

(Uncredited) Himself (actor), *The Moviemakers* (documentary short), Anchor Bay Entertainment, 1969.

Kevin Dirkman, *Bloody Mama,* American International Pictures, 1970.

James, *They Shoot Horses, Don't They?,* Cinerama, 1970.

J. J. Weston, *Rebel Rousers* (also known as *Limbo*), Four Star, 1970.

Coach Bullian, *Drive, He Said,* Columbia, 1971.

Dr. Roger Girard, *The Incredible Two–Headed Transplant* (also known as *The Incredible Transplant*), American International Pictures, 1971.

Asa "Long Hair" Watts, "Long Hair," *The Cowboys,* Warner Bros., 1972.

Lowell Freeman, *Silent Running* (also known as *Running Silent*), Universal, 1972.

Himself, *The Making of Silent Running* (documentary), Universal, 1972.

Jason Staebler, *The King of Marvin Gardens,* Columbia, 1972.

Smitty, *Thumb Tripping,* Avco–Embassy, 1972.

Leo Larsen, *The Laughing Policeman* (also known as *An Investigation of Murder*), Twentieth Century–Fox, 1973.

Tom Buchanan, *The Great Gatsby,* Paramount, 1974.

"Big Bob" Freelander, *Smile,* United Artists, 1975.

Jack Strawhorn, *Posse,* Paramount, 1975.

George Lumley, *Family Plot,* Universal, 1976.

Grayson Potchuck, *Won Ton Ton, the Dog Who Saved Hollywood* (also known as *Won Ton Ton*), Paramount, 1976.

William Brandels, *Folies bourgeoises* (also known as *The Twist, Pazzi borghesi, Die verruckten reichen*), UGC/Parafrance, 1976.

Michael Lander, *Black Sunday,* Paramount, 1977.

Captain Bob Hyde, *Coming Home* (also known as *Hemkomsten*), United Artists, 1978.

Detective, *The Driver,* Twentieth Century–Fox, 1978.

Bobby Lee, *Middle Age Crazy* (also known as *Heartfarm*), Twentieth Century–Fox, 1980.

Karl Kinsky, *Tattoo,* Twentieth Century–Fox, 1981.

George Sitkowski, *That Championship Season,* Cannon, 1982.

Harry Tracy, *Harry Tracy—Desperado* (also known as *Harry Tracy* and *Harry Tracy: Dead or Alive*), Quartet, 1982.

Wes Holman, *On the Edge,* New Front Films, 1986.

Mr. Edwards, *The Big Town* (also known as *The Arm*), Columbia, 1987.

Retour, 1987.

Ethan, *World Gone Wild,* Lorimar, 1988.

Cliff, *1969,* Atlantic, 1988.

Mark Rumsfield, *The 'Burbs,* Universal, 1989.

Garrett "Uncle Bud" Stoker, *After Dark, My Sweet,* Avenue Entertainment, 1990.

John Gillon, *Diggstown* (also known as *Midnight Sting*), Metro–Goldwyn–Mayer, 1992.

Will Plummer, *Wild Bill* (also known as *Deadwood* and *Wild Bill Hickok*), Metro–Goldwyn–Mayer/United Artists, 1995.

Patrick Leary, *Mrs. Munck,* 1995.

Rear Admiral Yancy Graham, *Down Periscope,* Twentieth Century–Fox, 1996.

Sheriff Ed Galt, *Last Man Standing* (also known as *The Bodyguard, Gundown,* and *Welcome to Jericho, Gangster!*), New Line Cinema, 1996.

(Uncredited) The chief, *Mulholland Falls,* Metro–Goldwyn–Mayer/United Artists, 1996.

Voice of Link Static, *Small Soldiers,* DreamWorks, 1998.

Mr. Dudley, *The Haunting* (also known as *La Maldicion*), DreamWorks, 1999.

Harry Volpi, *Madison,* Metro–Goldwyn–Mayer, 2000.

Judge, *All the Pretty Horses,* Sony Pictures Entertainment, 2000.

Begleiter, *The Glass House,* Columbia, 2001.

Himself, *Plotting "Family Plot"* (documentary), Universal Studios Home Video, 2001.

Editor, *Masked and Anonymous,* Sony Pictures Classics, 2003.

Sean McNally, *Milwaukee, Minnesota,* Tartan USA, 2003.

Thomas, *Monster,* Newmarket Films, 2003.

Himself, *Tune In Trip Out* (documentary short), Metro–Goldwyn–Mayer/United Artists Home Entertainment, 2003.

Himself, *A Decade Under the Influence* (documentary), IFC Films, 2003.

Himself, *Love & Haight* (documentary short), Metro–Goldwyn–Mayer Home Entertainment, 2003.

Gene, *The Hard Easy,* Lightening Entertainment, 2005.

Walker, 2005.

Charlie, *Down in the Valley,* ThinkFilm, 2005.

Ellis Brawley, *Believe In Me,* 2005.

The Astronaut Farmer, Warner Bros., 2006.

Television Appearances; Series:

E. J. Stocker, *Stoney Burke,* ABC, 1962–63.

Host, *Lost Drive–In,* Speedvision, 1996.

Franklin, *Big Love,* HBO, 2006.

Television Appearances; Miniseries:

Stanley Mott, *Space* (also known as *James Michener's "Space"*), CBS, 1985.

Television Appearances; Movies:

Deputy Doyle Pickett, *Sam Hill: Who Killed the Mysterious Mr. Foster?* (also known as *Sam Hill: Who Killed Mr. Foster?*), ABC, 1971.

Rob Charles, *Toughlove* (also known as *Tough Love*), ABC, 1985.

Augustine St. Clare, *Uncle Tom's Cabin*, Showtime, 1987.

Douglas Osborne, *Roses Are for the Rich*, CBS, 1987.

John Hollander, *Trenchcoat in Paradise*, CBS, 1989.

Scout Ed Higgins, *The Court–Martial of Jackie Robinson*, TNT, 1990.

T. L. Barston, *Into the Badlands*, USA Network, 1991.

Junior Stoker, *Carolina Skeletons*, NBC, 1991.

Billy Archer, *It's Nothing Personal*, NBC, 1993.

Payton McCay, *Dead Man's Revenge* (also known as *You Only Die Once*), USA Network, 1994.

George Putnam, *Amelia Earhart: The Final Flight*, TNT, 1994.

John Walker, *A Mother's Prayer*, USA Network, 1995.

Patrick Leary, *Mrs. Munck*, Showtime, 1996.

Captain Swaggert, *Perfect Prey* (also known as *When the Bough Breaks II*), Showtime, 1998.

McGurdy, *If ... Dog ... Rabbit ...* (also known as *One Last Score*), Cinemax, 1999.

Ray Earl Winston, *Hard Time: The Premonition* (also known as *The Premonition*), TNT, 1999.

Nate Hutchinson, *Hard Ground*, Hallmark Channel, 2003.

Television Appearances; Specials:

Himself, *Big Guns Talk: The Story of the Western* (documentary), TNT, 1997.

Voice of Mojave Max, *Mojave Adventure* (animated), TBS and syndicated, 1997.

(Uncredited) *Warner Bros. 75th Anniversary: No Guts, No Glory*, 1998.

Mia Farrow: The E! True Hollywood Story, E! Entertainment Television, 1998.

Intimate Portrait: Laura Dern, 1999.

Jane Fonda: The E! True Hollywood Story, E! Entertainment Television, 2000.

Rona Barrett: The E! True Hollywood Story, E! Entertainment Television, 2000.

It Conquered Hollywood! The Story of American International Pictures (documentary), AMC, 2001.

Television Appearances; Pilots:

Comfort, Texas (also known as *The Untitled Brian Benben Project*), 1997.

Frank Henderson, *Big Love*, HBO, 2006.

Television Appearances; Episodic:

"The Man on the Monkey Board," *Route 66*, CBS, 1960.

"Crime at Sea," *Sea Hunt*, syndicated, 1961.

"Bullets Cost Too Much," *Naked City*, ABC, 1961.

"The Fault in Our Stars," *Naked City*, ABC, 1961.

Johnny Page, "Daphne, Girl Detective," *Surfside 6*, ABC, 1961.

Billy Harris, "A Dark Night for Bill Harris," *Ben Casey*, ABC, 1961.

Johnny Norton, "The Remarkable Mrs. Hawk," *Thriller* (also known as *Boris Karloff's "Thriller"*), NBC, 1961.

"Crime and Punishment: Part 1," *Cain's Hundred*, 1961.

Jud Treadwell, "Act of God," *The Detectives* (also known as *Robert Taylor's "Detectives," The Detectives Starring Robert Taylor*, and *The Detectives, Starring Robert Taylor*), ABC, 1961.

"Poor Eddie's Dad," *The Law and Mr. Jones*, ABC, 1962.

"Old Man and the City," *The Dick Powell Show* (also known as *The Dick Powell Theatre*), NBC, 1962.

Martin, "The Other Side of the Mountain," *The Fugitive*, ABC, 1963.

Seth Bancroft, "The Eli Bancroft Story," *Wagon Train*, ABC, 1963.

Maynard, "The Hunt," *Kraft Suspense Theatre*, NBC, 1963.

Ben Garth, "The Zanti Misfits," *The Outer Limits*, ABC, 1963.

Deering, "Squadron," *The Dick Powell Show* (also known as *The Dick Powell Theatre*), NBC, 1963.

Ralph Wheeler, "Lover's Lane," *77 Sunset Strip*, ABC, 1964.

Charley, "Come Watch Me Die," *The Fugitive*, ABC, 1964.

"Beyond the Sea of Death," *Alfred Hitchcock Hour*, CBS, 1964.

Pell, "First to Thine Own Self," *The Virginian* (also known as *Major Adams, Trail Master*), NBC, 1964.

Vernon, "The Last of the Strongmen," *The Greatest Show on Earth*, ABC, 1964.

Jud Fisher, "Those Who Stay Behind," *Wagon Train*, ABC, 1964.

Jesse, "Lonely Place," *Alfred Hitchcock Hour*, NBC, 1964.

Lee Darrow, "The Payment," *The Virginian* (also known as *Major Adams, Trail Master*), NBC, 1964.

Lieutenant Michaels, "The Mission," *Twelve O'Clock High*, ABC, 1964.

Lieutenant Danton, "The Lorelei," *Twelve O'Clock High*, ABC, 1965.

Cody, "Corner of Hell," *The Fugitive*, ABC, 1965.

Lieutenant Michaels, "The Mission," *Twelve O'Clock High*, ABC, 1965.

Wilkins, "The Indian Girl Story," *Wagon Train*, ABC, 1965.

Ed Rankin, "Walk into Terror," *Rawhide*, CBS, 1965.

Durkee, "Rendezvous at Amarillo," *Laredo*, CBS, 1965.

Doyle Phleger, "Ten Little Indians," *Gunsmoke* (also known as *Gun Law* and *Marshall Dillon*), CBS, 1965.

Bobby Ballantin, "The Verdict," *A Man Called Shenandoah*, ABC, 1965.

Judd Print, "South Wind," *Gunsmoke* (also known as *Gun Law* and *Marshall Dillon*), CBS, 1965.

Sergeant Jones, "The Jones Boys," *Twelve O'Clock High,* ABC, 1965.

Hank, "The Good Guys and the Bad Guys," *The Fugitive,* ABC, 1965.

Private First Class Byron Landy, "Pound of Flesh," *The F.B.I.,* ABC, 1965.

Gallagher, 1965.

Bert Kramer, "A Little Learning," *The Virginian* (also known as *Major Adams, Trail Master*), NBC, 1965.

Les, "The Wolfers," *Branded,* NBC, 1966.

Jack, "Under a Dark Star," *The Big Valley,* ABC, 1966.

Merrick, "To Hang a Dead Man," *The Loner,* CBS, 1966.

Dixon, "By Force of Violence," *The Big Valley,* ABC, 1966.

Collis, "The Lost Treasure," *The Big Valley,* ABC, 1966.

Lou Stone, "The Jailer," *Gunsmoke* (also known as *Gun Law* and *Marshall Dillon*), CBS, 1966.

Turk, "Gallagher Goes West," *The World of Disney* (also known as *Walt Disney Presents, Walt Disney's "Wonderful World of Color," Walt Disney, The Wonderful World of Disney, The Magical World of Disney, The Disney Sunday Movie,* and *Disney's "Wonderful World"*), NBC, 1966.

Alex Ryder, "The Treasure Seekers," *Run for Your Life,* NBC, 1966.

Hutch, "The Devil's Disciples," *The Fugitive,* ABC, 1966.

Turk, gunslinger, "The Crusading Reporter," *Gallagher Goes West,* 1966.

Alex Ryder, "Trip to the Far Side," *Run for Your Life,* NBC, 1967.

Alex Ryder, "At the End of the Rainbow There's Another Rainbow," *Run for Your Life,* NBC, 1967.

Gabe Skeels, "Four Days to Furnace Hill," *The Big Valley,* ABC, 1967.

Cully Maco, "The Trackers," *Bonanza* (also known as *Ponderosa*), NBC, 1968.

Thorg, "Wild Journey," *Land of the Giants,* ABC, 1968.

Lucas, "Julie," *Lancer,* CBS, 1968.

Virgil Roy Phipps, "The Nightmare," *The F.B.I.,* ABC, 1968.

John Weaver, "The Prize," *The Big Valley,* ABC, 1968.

Guerin, "The Long Night," *Gunsmoke* (also known as *Gun Law* and *Marshall Dillon*), CBS, 1969.

Bucky O'Neill, "Amid Splinters of the Thunderbolt," *Then Came Bronson,* NBC, 1969.

Tom Nevill, "A Person Unknown," *Lancer,* CBS, 1969.

Thorg, "Wild Journey," *Land of the Giants,* ABC, 1970.

"The Gold Mine," *Bonanza* (also known as *Ponderosa*), NBC, 1970.

Wade, "Only the Bad Come to Sonora," *High Chaparral,* NBC, 1970.

Luther Seacombe, "To the Gods Alone," *The Immortal,* ABC, 1970.

The Tonight Show Starring Johnny Carson, NBC, 1972, 1973.

Guest host, *Saturday Night Live* (also known as *NBC's "Saturday Night," Saturday Night,* and *SNL*), NBC, 1982, 1983.

Voice of Randy Strickland, "Boxing Luanne," *King of the Hill* (animated), Fox, 2003.

Also appeared in *Fallen Angels,* Showtime; as himself, "The Films of Roger Corman," *The Directors,* Encore.

Stage Appearances:

Maguire, *The Shadow of a Gunman,* New York City, 1958–59.

Stuff, *Sweet Bird of Youth,* Martin Beck Theatre, New York City, 1959–60.

Sinclair "Hal" Lewis, *Strangers,* John Golden Theatre, New York City, 1979.

Chicken, Lillian Theater, Hollywood, CA, 2005.

Also appeared in *Orpheus Descending.*

OTHER SOURCES

Books:

International Dictionary of Films and Filmmakers, Volume 3: Actors and Actresses, 4th ed., St. James Press, 2000.

Periodicals:

Films in Review, October, 1980.
People Weekly, March, 1994, p. 210.
Take One (Montreal, Quebec, Canada), July, 1973.

DOLENZ, Micky 1945–
   (Mickey Braddock, Micky Braddock, Michael Dolenz, Mickey Dolenz)

PERSONAL

Full name, George Michael Dolenz, Jr.; born March 8, 1945, in Los Angeles, CA; son of George (an actor) and Janelle Dolenz; married Samantha Just (a model), 1967 (divorced, 1975); married Trina Dow, 1977 (divorced, 1991); married Donna Quinter, September 20, 2002; children: (first marriage) Ami (an actress); (second marriage) three daughters. *Education:* Studied architectural design at Valley College and the Los Angeles Technical Institute; studied physics at Open University. *Avocational Interests:* Painting, crafts, and building things.

Addresses: *Agent*—Agency for the Performing Arts, 9200 Sunset Blvd., Suite 900, Los Angeles, CA 90069.

Career: Actor, director, producer, musician, and screenwriter. Actor and musician in bands such as Mickey and the One Nighters and the Missing Links, 1958–66; member of The Monkees, 1966–70, 1985—; cartoon voiceover actor, actor, and musician, 1970–77; television producer and director in England, 1977–85; WCBS–FM, New York City, morning DJ, 2005; Independent Entertainment, Los Angles, CA, principal; appeared in commercials for Sugar Pops cereal, Oscar Mayer, Safeway grocery stores, and Pizza Hut.

Member: Screen Actors Guild.

Awards, Honors: Star on the Hollywood Walk of Fame (with The Monkees).

CREDITS

Film Appearances:

(Uncredited) Jungle Gino, *Good Times* (also known as *Sonny & Cher in Good Times*), 1967.

Micky, *Head,* Columbia, 1968.

(Uncredited) Audience member, *Monterey Pop,* 1968.

Keep Off My Grass!, 1971.

Vance, *Night of the Strangler* (also known as *Dirty Dan* and *Vengeance Is Mine*), Howco Productions, 1975.

Keep Off! Keep Off!, 1975.

Lieutenant Fenwick, *Linda Lovelace for President* (also known as *Hot Neon*), 1976.

Heart and Soul (also known as *The Monkees: Heart and Soul*), Rhino, 1986.

Bart, *Deadfall,* Trimark, 1993.

Himself, *The Making of "A Hard Day's Night"* (documentary; also known as *You Can't Do That! The Making of "A Hard Day's Night"*), MPI Home Video, 1995.

Contest judge, *The Brady Bunch Movie,* Paramount, 1995.

Mom, Can I Keep Her?, New Horizons Home Video, 1998.

Bernard, *Invisible Mom II,* New Horizons Home Video, 1999.

Himself, *The Monkees: Live Summer Tour,* Pioneer, 2002.

Himself, *Easy Riders, Raging Bulls: How the Sex, Drugs, and Rock 'N' Roll Generation Saved Hollywood* (documentary), Shout! Factory, 2003.

Himself, *Mayor of Sunset Strip* (documentary), First Look Pictures Releasing, 2003.

Film Work:

Director, *Malpractice,* 2001.

Also directed *The Box.*

Television Appearances; Series:

(As Mickey Braddock) Corky, *Circus Boy,* NBC, 1956–57, then ABC, 1957–58.

Micky, *The Monkees,* NBC, 1966–68.

Voice, *Scooby–Doo* (animated), 1969.

Voice of Skip, *The Funky Phantom* (animated), ABC, 1971–72.

Voice of Harvey, *Butch Cassidy and the Sundance Kids* (animated), NBC, 1973.

Voice of Tod Devlin, *Devlin* (animated), ABC, 1974.

(As Mickey Dolenz) Voice of Wheelie Sheeler, *The Skatebirds* (animated; also known as *The Robonic Stooges, Wonder Wheels, Woofer and Whimper,* and *Mystery Island*), CBS, 1977–78.

Voice of Arthur, *The Tick* (animated), Fox, 1994–95.

Mayor Micky Dolenz, *Pacific Blue,* USA Network, 1996.

Voice of Ralph and Scribble, *The Secret Files of the Spy Dogs,* 1998.

Television Appearances; Movies:

Donny Shotz, "The Love Bug," *The Wonderful World of Disney,* ABC, 1997.

(Uncredited) Himself, *Hendrix,* Showtime, 2000.

Television Appearances; Specials:

The 18th Annual Primetime Emmy Awards, 1967.

Himself, *33 1/3 Revolutions per Monkee,* NBC, 1969.

Dick Clark Television Special, 1974.

NBC 60th Anniversary Celebration, NBC, 1986.

MTV Video Music Awards, MTV, 1986.

Walt Disney World's 15th Birthday Celebration, 1986.

The 14th Annual American Music Awards, ABC, 1987.

Voices That Care, Fox, 1991.

(As Micky Braddock) Melvin, *Rod Serling: Submitted for Your Approval* (documentary), PBS, 1995.

Miss Teen USA Pageant, CBS, 1996.

Micky, *Hey, Hey It's the Monkees,* ABC, 1997.

The Monkees: The E! True Hollywood Story, E! Entertainment Television, 1999.

(Uncredited) Himself, *Hollywood Rocks the Movies: The Early Years (1955–1970),* 2000.

100 Greatest Number One Singles, 2001.

Rock Gardens, HGTV, 2003.

Television Appearances; Episodic:

Today (also known as *NBC News Today* and *The Today Show*), 1956, 1966, 1982, 1986, 1993, 1996, 1997.

(As Mickey Braddock) Ted Matson, "The Vaunted," *Zane Grey Theater* (also known as *Dick Powell's "Zane Grey Theater"* and *The Westerners*), CBS, 1958.

Playhouse 90, CBS, 1958.

(As Micky Braddock) Melvin, "The Velvet Alley," *Playhouse 90,* 1959.

Peyton Place, ABC, 1962.

The New Steve Allen Show, 1962.

Mr. Novak, NBC, 1964.

Peyton Place, ABC, 1965.

American Bandstand (also known as *AB*), 1966, 1976.

Top of the Pops, BBC, 1967, 1968.

The Hollywood Squares, 1968.

The Glen Campbell Goodtime Hour, 1969.

It's Happening (also known as *Happening '69*), 1969.

The Joey Bishop Show, 1969.

The Tonight Show Starring Johnny Carson (also known as *The Best of Carson*), NBC, 1969.

The Johnny Cash Show, 1969.

Rowan & Martin's Laugh–In (also known as *Laugh–In*), 1969.

Dinah! (also known as *Dinah! & Friends*), syndicated, 1971, 1976.

"Barbara Lost," *My Three Sons,* CBS, 1972.

Oiler, "Dirt Duel," *Adam-12,* NBC, 1972.

Cappy, "Bitter Legion," *Cannon,* CBS, 1972.

"The Camerons Are a Special Clan," *Owen Marshall, Counselor at Law,* ABC, 1973.

Voice, *Partridge Family: 2200 A.D.* (animated), CBS, 1974.

Contestant, *Break the Bank,* ABC, 1976.

Rock Concert (also known as *Don Kirshner's "Rock Concert"*), 1976.

The Mike Douglas Show, 1976.

The Tomorrow Show (also known as *Tomorrow* and *Tomorrow Coast to Coast*), 1977.

CBS News Nightwatch, CBS, 1986.

Entertainment Tonight (also known as *ET, ET Weekend, Entertainment This Week,* and *This Week in Entertainment*), syndicated, 1986, 1995, 2000, 2001, 2002.

Solid Gold (also known as *Solid Gold in Concert*), syndicated, 1986.

Showbiz Today, CNN, 1986, 1993, 1996.

Good Morning America, ABC, 1986, 1987, 1996.

"Deadly Collection," *Mickey Spillane's "Mike Hammer"* (also known as *Mike Hammer* and *The New Mike Hammer*), CBS, 1987.

Nightlife, 1987.

The Morning Program, 1987.

Sally Jessy Raphael (also known as *Sally*), 1987.

Saturday Morning Live, 1988.

The Factory, 1988.

Midday, 1988, 1996.

Aspel & Company, 1989.

Good Morning Britain (also known as *TV–am*), 1989.

The Pat Sajak Show, 1989.

Midday, 1989.

A.M. Los Angeles, 1989, 1990, 1991.

Nashville Now, 1989.

Inside Edition, syndicated, 1990.

Pick of the Pilots (also known as *Denis Norden's "Pick of the Pilots"*), 1990.

Totally Hidden Video, 1991.

Crook & Chase, The Nashville Network, 1991.

Country Kitchen (also known as *Florence Henderson's "Country Kitchen"*), 1991.

Mr. Josh Goldsilver, "Episode with Rob Morrow," *The Ben Stiller Show* (also known as *The Best Man*), Fox, 1992.

Breakfast Television, 1992.

Voice of Min and Max, "Two–Face: Parts 1 & 2," *Batman* (animated; also known as *Batman: The Animated Series* and *The Adventures of Batman & Robin*), 1992.

Vicki!, 1993.

CBS News Up to the Minute, CBS, 1993.

Late Night with Conan O'Brien, NBC, 1993.

Larry King Live, CNN, 1993.

Norm, "Band on the Run," *Boy Meets World,* ABC, 1994.

Marilu, 1994.

The Tonight Show with Jay Leno, NBC, 1994, 1996, 1997.

(As Mickey Dolenz) Voice of Min and Max, "Second Chance," *Batman* (animated; also known as *Batman: The Animated Series* and *The Adventures of Batman & Robin*), 1994.

Gordy, "Rave On," *Boy Meets World,* ABC, 1995.

Muppets Tonight (also known as *The New Muppet Show* and *Muppets Live!*), ABC, 1996.

George & Alana, syndicated, 1996.

Good Day L.A., Fox, 1996.

Politically Incorrect with Bill Maher, ABC, 1996, 1997, 1998.

Arthel & Fred, 1997.

Breakfast News, 1997.

The National Lottery (also known as *The National Lottery Live*), 1997.

Noel's House Party, 1997.

Debt, Lifetime, 1997.

Access Hollywood, syndicated, 1997, 2000.

This Morning (also known as *This Morning with Richard and Judy*), ITV, 1997, 2002.

Pictionary, syndicated, 1998.

The Roseanne Show, syndicated, 2000.

Extra (also known as *Extra: The Entertainment Magazine*), syndicated, 2000.

Himself, "The Monkees," *Behind the Music* (also known as *VH1's "Behind the Music"*), VH1, 2000.

Himself, "Anniversary Special," *Behind the Music* (also known as *VH1's "Behind the Music"*), VH1, 2000.

Men Are From Mars, Women Are From Venus, 2000.

(As Mickey Dolenz) Voice of Lefty, "Fallen Arches/The Man Event," *The Powerpuff Girls* (animated; also known as *PPG* and *Youlide–Chui nu*), Cartoon Network, 2000.

(As Mickey Dolenz) Voice of Lefty, "Getting' Twiggy with It/Cop Out," *The Powerpuff Girls* (animated; also known as *PPG* and *Youlide–Chui nu*), Cartoon Network, 2000.

Mr. Metcalf, "Drew and the King," *The Drew Carey Show,* ABC, 2001.

Himself, "I Love 1980," *I Love the 1980's,* BBC2, 2001.

Himself, "Pure Pop," *Walk On By: The Story of Popular Song* (documentary; also known as *The Story of Pop*), BBC and ABC, 2001.

Live with Regis & Kelly, syndicated, 2001.
The Early Show (also known as *The Saturday Early Show*), CBS, 2001.
Breakfast, BBC, 2002.
The Vicar, *As the World Turns,* CBS, 2002.
Himself, "Bill Oddie," *This Is Your Life,* BBC, 2002.
Open House (also known as *Open House with Gloria Hunniford*), Channel 5, 2002.
(Uncredited) Himself, "Trump–ed to Triumph," *Queer Eye for the Straight Guy,* 2005.

Also appeared as Eli Campbell, "My Dad Could Beat Up Your Dad," *Monty.*

Television Work; Series:
(As Michael Dolenz) Producer and creator, *Metal Mickey,* London Weekend Television, 1980–83.
Producer, *No Problem,* London Weekend Television, 1983–85.
Creator and producer, *Luna,* 1983.

Television Work; Movies:
Director, *Aladdin,* 1990.

Television Work; Specials:
Executive producer, *Hey, Hey It's the Monkees,* ABC, 1997.

Television Director; Episodic:
"Mijacogeo," *The Monkees,* NBC, 1968.
(As Michael Dolenz) *Metal Mickey,* London Weekend Television, 1980–83.
No Problem, London Weekend Television, 1983–85.
(As Michael Dolenz) *Luna,* 1983.
Murphy's Mob, 1986.
Pacific Blue, 1996.
Boy Meets World, ABC, 1999.
Malpractice, Lifetime, 2002.

Also directed episodes of *Fernwood 2–Night.*

Stage Appearances:
Huckleberry Finn, *Tom Sawyer,* Sacramento, CA, 1976.
Vince Fontaine, *Grease,* Eugene O'Neill Theatre, New York City, 1994.

Also appeared as The Count's Kid, *The Point,* London; Pseudolus, *A Funny Thing Happened on the Way to the Forum.*

Major Tours:
Vince Fontaine, *Grease,* U.S. cities, 1994–95.
Aida, 2003–2004.

Stage Director:
Directed *Bugsy Malone,* London.

RECORDINGS

Albums (with The Monkees):
The Monkees, Rhino, 1966.
More of the Monkees, Rhino, 1967.
Headquarters, Rhino, 1967.
Pisces, Aquarius, Capricorn and Jones, Ltd., Rhino, 1967.
The Birds, the Bees and The Monkees, Rhino, 1968.
Head (film soundtrack), Rhino, 1968.
Instant Replay, Rhino, 1969.
The Monkees Present, Rhino, 1969.
The Monkees Greatest Hits, Arista, 1969.
Changes, Rhino, 1970.
A Barrel Full of Monkees, Colgems, 1971.
Refocus, Bell, 1972.
The Monkees Golden Hits, RCA Victor, 1972.
40 Timeless Hits, EMI, 1980.
Best of the Monkees, MFP, 1981.
More Greatest Hits, Arista, 1982.
20 Golden Greats, Rhino, 1982.
Monkee Flips, Rhino, 1984.
Pool It!, Rhino, 1986.
Then and Now, the Best of the Monkees, Arista, 1986.
20th Anniversary Tour (live recording), Rhino, 1986.
Live 1967, Rhino, 1987.
Missing Links, Rhino, 1987.
Missing Links, Volume II, Rhino, 1990.
Listen to the Band, Rhino, 1991.
Greatest Hits, Rhino, 1995.
Missing Links, Volume III, Rhino, 1996.
Justus, Rhino, 1996.
I'm a Believer and Other Hits, Rhino Flashback, 1997.
The Monkees: Anthology, Rhino, 1998.
Daydream Believer, Rhino Flashback, 1998.

Also recorded *MonkeeMania.*

Albums (as a Solo Artist):
(As Mickey Dolenz) *Mickey Dolenz Puts You to Sleep,* Rhino, 1991.
(As Mickey Dolenz) *Broadway Mickey,* Rhino, 1994.

Albums; Other:
Dolenz, Jones, Boyce and Hart, 1976.
Concert in Japan, 1996.

Singles:
Appeared on "Voices That Care."

Music Videos:
Appeared in "Voices That Care."

Video Games:
Himself, *Hey, Hey We're the Monkees*, 1996.

WRITINGS

Screenplays:
(Uncredited) *Head,* Columbia, 1968.

Television Episodes:
"Mijacogeo," *The Monkees,* NBC, 1968.

Television Theme Songs:
The Yesterday Show with Johnny Kerwin, Trio, 2004.

Stage Musicals (Book):
Wrote *Bugsy Malone,* London.

Autobiography:
(With Mark Bego) *I'm a Believer: My Life of Monkees Music and Madness,* Hyperion, 1993.

OTHER SOURCES

Books:
Contemporary Authors, Vol. 152, Gale, 1997.

DOTCHIN, Angela Marie 1974–
  (Angela Dotchin, Angela Marie Dotchins)

PERSONAL

Born March 31, 1974, in Auckland, New Zealand. *Avocational Interests:* Art, graphic design, music, writing, travel, and kickboxing.

Career: Actress. Also worked as a model.

Awards, Honors: New Zealand Television Award, best actress, 1999, for *Lawless.*

CREDITS

Television Appearances; Series:
Kirsty Knight, *Shortland Street,* TVNZ, 1992–98.
Kora, *Young Hercules,* syndicated, 1998.
Jodie Keane, *Lawless,* 1999.
(As Angela Dotchin) Mrs. Emilia Smythe Rothschild, *Jack of All Trades,* Fox, 2000.

Chrissy, *Serial Killers,* 2004.

Television Appearances; Movies:
(As Angela Dotchin) Jodie Keane, *Lawless: Dead Evidence* (also known as *Dead Evidence*), TV2, 2000.
(As Angela Dotchin) Jodie Keane, *Lawless: Beyond Justice* (also known as *Lawless 2*), TV2, 2001.
Renee Price, *Maiden Voyage,* 2004.

Television Appearances; Specials:
(As Angela Marie Dotchins) Kirsty Knight, *Happy Birthday 2 You,* TV2, 2000.

Television Appearances; Pilots:
Jodie Keane, *Lawless,* Fox, 1999.

Television Appearances; Episodic:
Soraya, "Tsunami," *Xena: Warrior Princess,* syndicated, 1998.
Nautica, "Love on the Rocks," *Hercules: The Legendary Journeys,* syndicated, 1999.
Nautica, "My Best Girl's Wedding," *Hercules: Legendary Journeys,* syndicated, 1999.

OTHER SOURCES

Periodicals:
Pavement, December/January, 2000.
TV Guide (New Zealand), September 2, 2000, pp. 8–9.
Woman's Day (New Zealand), November 8, 1999, pp. 6–7; January 10, 2000, p. 6.

DOUGLAS, Illeana 1965–

PERSONAL

Original name, Illeana Hesselberg; born July 25, 1965, in Quincy, MA; daughter of Gregory and Joan Douglas; granddaughter of Melvyn Douglas (an actor); stepgranddaughter of Helen Gahagan Douglas (an actress, singer, and politician); married Jonathan Axelrod (a television producer), May 16, 1998 (divorced, March 13, 2001). *Education:* Attended American Academy of Dramatic Arts and Neighborhood Playhouse School of the Theatre.

Addresses: *Agent*—Innovative Artists, 1505 10th St., Santa Monica, CA 90401.

Career: Actress, director, producer, and writer. Worked as a stand-up comedian while in her teens; owned a production company; played rock band Aerosmith's manager in the preshow at Walt Disney World's Rock 'n' Roll Coaster, 1999. Worked for Peggy Siegal (a publicist) in New York City, 1988.

Awards, Honors: Best Short Film Prize, Aspen Film Festival, 1993, for *The Perfect Woman;* Prize, Aspen Film Festival, 1995, for *Boy Crazy, Girl Crazier;* Chlotrudis Award nomination, best supporting actress, Chlotrudis Society for Independent Film, Saturn Award nomination, best supporting actress, Academy of Science Fiction, Fantasy, and Horror Films, 1996, both for *To Die For;* Blockbuster Entertainment Award nomination, favorite supporting actress in a drama or romance, 2000, for *Message in a Bottle;* Golden Satellite Award, best performance by an actress in a comedy or musical series, International Press Academy, 2000, for *Action;* Emmy Award nomination, outstanding guest actress in a drama series, 2002, for *Six Feet Under.*

CREDITS

Film Appearances:
Mother in park, *Hello Again,* Buena Vista, 1987.
Voice in crowd, *The Last Temptation of Christ,* Universal, 1988.
Paulette's friend, "Life Lessons," *New York Stories,* Buena Vista, 1989.
Rosie, *Goodfellas* (also known as *GoodFellas*), Warner Bros., 1990.
Nan, *Guilty by Suspicion* (also known as *La liste noire*), Warner Bros., 1991.
Lori Davis, *Cape Fear,* Universal, 1991.
(Scenes deleted) Angie's neighbor, *Jungle Fever,* 1991.
Lilliana Methol, *Alive* (also known as *Alive: The Miracle of the Andes*), Buena Vista, 1993.
Leslie, *Grief,* Strand Releasing, 1993.
Evelyn Santangelo, *Household Saints,* Fine Line Features, 1993.
The Perfect Woman (short), 1993.
Elizabeth, woman at book party, *Quiz Show,* Buena Vista, 1994.
Celena, *Boy Crazy, Girl Crazier* (short), 1995.
Marie Davenport, *Search and Destroy* (also known as *The Four Rules*), October Films, 1995.
Janice Maretto, *To Die For,* Columbia, 1995.
Laurel, *Judgement,* 1995.
Jasmine, *Wedding Bell Blues,* Curb Entertainment, 1996.
Edna Buxton/Denise Waverly, *Grace of My Heart,* Gramercy Pictures, 1996.
Darcy O'Neil, *Picture Perfect,* Twentieth Century–Fox, 1997.
Georgia Feckler, *Hacks* (also known as *The Big Twist* and *Sink or Swim*), Shoreline Entertainment, 1997.
Laura, *Flypaper,* Trimark, 1997.
Herself, *Pitch* (documentary), The Asylum, 1997.
Julia Bullock, *The Thin Pink Line,* 1998.
Lina Paul, *Message in a Bottle,* Warner Bros., 1999.

Anita Dick, *Can't Stop Dancing,* 1999.
Lisa Weil, *Stir of Echoes,* Artisan Entertainment, 1999.
Ms. Schaefer, *Happy, Texas,* Miramax, 1999.
Elizabeth Ryder, *The Next Best Thing,* Paramount, 2000.
Roberta Allsworth, *Ghost World,* Metro–Goldwyn–Mayer, 2001.
Heidi, *Dummy,* Artisan Entertainment, 2002.
Kiki Pierce, *The New Guy,* Columbia, 2002.
Dr. Mona Zimmer, *The Adventures of Pluto Nash* (also known as *Pluto Nash*), Warner Bros., 2002.
Herself, *Making of "Ghost World"* (documentary short), Metro–Goldwyn–Mayer, 2002.
Joyce Rothman, *The Kiss,* 2003.
Julie Conroy, *Missing Brendan,* 2003.
Cameo, *Surviving Eden,* 2004.
Herself, *Supermarket* (short), Illeanarama, 2004.
Donna, *I'm Perfect,* 2005.
Olive Ransom, *The Californians,* Fabrication Films, 2005.
Elaine Edwards, *Bondage,* Eccentric Cattle Entertainment, 2006.
Jill, *Walk the Talk,* 2006.
Expired, 2006.

Film Work:
Director, *The Perfect Woman* (short), 1993.
Director, *Everybody Just Stay Calm,* 1994.
Director, *Boy Crazy, Girl Crazier* (short), 1995.
Executive producer, *Life Without Dick,* TriStar, 2001.
Producer and director, *Devil Talk* (short), 2003.
Producer and director, *Supermarket* (short), Illeanarama, 2004.
Director, *Sorority Rule,* 2005.

Television Appearances; Series:
Wendy Ward, *Action,* Fox, 1999.
Herself, *Illeanarama,* Oxygen, 2005.

Television Appearances; Miniseries:
Teresa Luciano, *Bella Mafia,* CBS, 1997.
Edith Roosevelt, *Rough Riders* (also known as *Teddy Roosevelt and the Rough Riders*), TNT, 1997.

Television Appearances; Movies:
Rita Pascoe, *Weapons of Mass Distraction,* HBO, 1997.
Anna Lansky, *Lansky,* HBO, 1999.
Kate, *Point of Origin* (also known as *In the Heat of the Fire*), 2002.
K. J., *Alchemy,* ABC Family, 2005.

Television Appearances; Specials:
Host, *Everybody Just Stay Calm—Stories in Independent Filmmaking,* Independent Film Channel, 1994.
Presenter, *The 14th Independent Spirit Awards* (also known as *The 2001 IFP/West Independent Spirit Awards*), Independent Film Channel, 1998.

Politically Incorrect After Party Presented by Pepsi, ABC, 1999.

Host and narrator, *It's Only Rock & Roll!* ABC, 2000.

Presenter, *The 16th Annual IFP/West Independent Spirit Awards,* Independent Film Channel, 2001.

Narrator and host, *Flops 101: Lessons from the Biz,* 2004.

Television Appearances; Pilots:

Celia Thompson, *The Coven,* Lifetime, 2004.

Herself, *Illeanarama,* Oxygen, 2005.

Television Appearances; Episodic:

Gina Doolen, "Autofocus," *Homicide: Life on the Street* (also known as *Homicide*), NBC, 1995.

Martha, "Sister," *The Single Guy,* NBC, 1995.

Late Show with David Letterman (also known as *The Late Show*), CBS, 1996.

Loretta, "The Strongbox," *Seinfeld,* NBC, 1997.

Herself, "Just the Perfect Blendship," *The Larry Sanders Show,* HBO, 1998.

Herself, "Putting the 'Gay' Back in Litigation," *The Larry Sanders Show,* HBO, 1998.

Ginny, "Dating the Teacher," *Brother's Keeper,* ABC, 1999.

Late Night with Conan O'Brien, NBC, 1999.

The Martin Short Show, syndicated, 1999.

Mad TV, Fox, 1999.

Host, *The List,* VH1, 1999.

The Late Late Show with Craig Kilborn (also known as *The Late Late Show*), CBS, 2001.

Kenny's wife, "Hungry Heart," *Frasier,* NBC, 2001.

Rachel Murray, "Drew and the Activist: Parts 1 & 2," *The Drew Carey Show,* ABC, 2001.

Dr. Helen Mead, "A Change Will Do You Good," *Strange Frequency,* VH1, 2001.

Angela, "The New Person," *Six Feet Under,* HBO, 2001.

Hollywood Unleashed, Animal Planet, 2001.

Herself, "The Perfect Pitch," *Brilliant But Cancelled,* Trio, 2002.

Gina Bernardo, "Juvenile," *Law & Order: Special Victims Unit* (also known as *Law & Order: SVU* and *Special Victims Unit*), NBC, 2002.

Gina Bernardo, "Resilience," *Law & Order: Special Victims Unit* (also known as *Law & Order: SVU* and *Special Victims Unit*), NBC, 2002.

Dinner for Five, Independent Film Channel, 2002, 2003.

Gina Bernardo, "Tortured," *Law & Order: Special Victims Unit* (also known as *Law & Order: SVU* and *Special Victims Unit*), NBC, 2003.

(Uncredited) Angela, "Time Flies," *Six Feet Under,* HBO, 2005.

The Late Late Show with Craig Ferguson, CBS, 2005.

Angela, "Hold My Hand," *Six Feet Under,* HBO, 2005.

Television Work; Series:

Executive producer, *Illeanarama,* Oxygen, 2005.

Television Work; Specials:

Executive producer and director, *Everybody Just Stay Calm—Stories in Independent Filmmaking,* Independent Film Channel, 1994.

Television Work; Pilots:

Executive producer, *Illeanarama,* Oxygen, 2005.

Stage Appearances:

Lynn, "Dream House," *New Works 1987,* Cubiculo Theatre, New York City, 1987.

Alice, *The Moment When,* Playwrights Horizons, New York City, 2000.

Kate Griswald, *Surviving Grace,* Union Square Theatre, New York City, 2002.

Mrs. Shinn, *Music Man,* Pittsburgh Civic Light Opera, Pittsburgh, PA, 2004.

Also appeared in *As Sure As You Live, Black Eagles,* and *Takes on Women.*

WRITINGS

Screenplays:

The Perfect Woman (short), 1993.

Boy Crazy, Girl Crazier (short), 1995.

Supermarket (short), Illeanarama, 2004.

Television Specials:

Everybody Just Stay Calm—Stories in Independent Filmmaking, Independent Film Channel, 1994.

Television Pilots:

Illeanarama, Oxygen, 2005.

Television Episodes:

Illeanarama, Oxygen, 2005.

OTHER SOURCES

Periodicals:

Premiere, Volume 8, 1994, pp. 37–38.

DRESCHER, Fran 1957–

PERSONAL

Full name, Francine Joy Drescher; born September 30, 1957, in Flushing, NY; daughter of Mort (a naval systems analyst) and Sylvia (a bridal consultant)

Drescher; married Peter Marc Jacobson (a producer), November 4, 1978 (divorced, 1999). *Education:* Attended Queens College of the City University of New York and Ultissima Beauty Institute.

Addresses: *Agent*—International Creative Management, 8942 Wilshire Blvd., Beverly Hills, CA 90211.

Career: Actress, comedian, producer, director, and writer. Miss New York Teenager, runner–up, 1973; High School Sweethearts (production company), founder and partner with Peter Marc Jacobson; appeared in television commercials, including Hanes' Smooth Illusions, 1994, Three Musketeers, 1997–98, Old Navy, 2003, and Pizza Hut. Loaf and Kisses Gourmet Croutons, cofounder, 1988. M.D. Anderson Cancer Centre, Houston, TX, patient advocate on the external advisory board.

Awards, Honors: "Five–Minute Oscar" Award, *Esquire* magazine, for *American Hot Wax;* American Comedy Award nomination, funniest female performer in a television series leading role—network, cable, or syndication, 1996, Emmy Award nominations, outstanding lead actress in a comedy, 1996, 1997, Golden Globe Award nominations, best television comedy or musical actress, 1996, 1997, Golden Satellite Award nomination, best performance by an actress in a television series—musical or comedy, International Press Academy, 1997, and *TV Guide* Award nomination, favorite actress in a comedy, 1999, all for *The Nanny;* chosen as one of the fifty most beautiful people in the world, *People Weekly,* 1996; Public Service Award, Gynecologic Cancer Foundation, 2002.

CREDITS

Film Appearances:
Connie, *Saturday Night Fever,* Paramount, 1977.
Sheryl, *American Hot Wax,* Paramount, 1978.
Evie, *G.O.R.P.* (also known as *Gorp*), Filmways, 1980.
Sally, *The Hollywood Knights,* Columbia, 1980.
Mameh, *Ragtime,* Paramount, 1981.
Karen Blittstein, *Doctor Detroit,* Universal, 1982.
Bobbi Flekman, *This Is Spinal Tap* (also known as *Spinal Tap*), Embassy, 1984.
Young Lust, 1984.
Linda, *The Rosebud Beach Hotel* (also known as *Big Lobby;* re–released in 1994 as *The No–Tell Hotel*), Almi, 1985.
Polo Habel, *The Big Picture,* Columbia, 1989.
Pamela Finklestein, *UHF* (also known as *The Vidiot from UHF*), Orion, 1989.
It Had to Be You, 1989.
Joy Munchak, *Cadillac Man,* Orion, 1990.
Veronica, *Wedding Band,* IRS Releasing, 1990.

Valerie, *We're Talkin' Serious Money,* Columbia TriStar Home Video, 1992.
Velma Velour, *Car 54, Where Are You?* Orion, 1994.
Dolores "D. D." Durante, *Jack,* Buena Vista, 1996.
Joy Miller, *The Beautician and the Beast,* Paramount, 1997.
Herself, *The Stars of Star Wars: Interviews from the Cast* (documentary), IMC Vision, 1999.
Kerry, *Kid Quick* (short; also known as *The Adventures of Kid Quick*), 2000.
Virginia Mason, *Santa's Slay,* Lions Gate Films, 2005.

Film Work:
Executive producer, *The Beautician and the Beast,* Paramount, 1997.

Television Appearances; Series:
Melissa Kirschner, *Princesses,* CBS, 1991.
Fran Fine Sheffield, *The Nanny,* CBS, 1993–99.
Fran Reeves, *Living with Fran,* The WB, 2005—.

Also appeared in *WIOU.*

Television Appearances; Miniseries:
Herself, *Heroes of Jewish Comedy,* Comedy Central, 2003.

Television Appearances; Movies:
Carolyn, *Stranger in Our House* (also known as *Summer of Fear*), 1978.
Jody Levin, "Rock 'n' Roll Mom," *Disney Sunday Movie,* ABC, 1988.
Germaine, *Love and Betrayal* (also known as *Throw Away Wives*), CBS, 1989.
Rosemarie Russo, *Without Warning: Terror in the Towers,* NBC, 1993.
Sister Frida, *Picking Up the Pieces,* Cinemax, 2000.
Amanda Wasserman, *Beautiful Girl,* ABC Family, 2003.

Television Appearances; Specials:
Today at Night, NBC, 1994.
Comic Relief VII, HBO, 1995.
Interviewee, *Hollywood's Most Powerful Women,* E! Entertainment Television, 1995.
Voice of Nanny Fran Fine, *Oy to the World* (animated; also known as *The Nanny Christmas Special: Oy to the World*), CBS, 1995.
Up for the Golden Globes, NBC, 1996.
Interviewee, *Very Personal with Naomi Judd,* Family Channel, 1997.
Canned Ham: Deconstructing Harry, Comedy Central, 1997.
Guest host, *CBS: The First 50 Years,* CBS, 1998.
Interviewee, *Intimate Portrait: Judith Light,* Lifetime, 1998.
To Life! America Celebrates Israel's 50th, CBS, 1998.

True or False: Teenagers Mean Trouble, CBS, 1998.
Influences: From Yesterday to Today, CBS, 1999.
Herself, *Intimate Portrait: Fran Drescher* (documentary), Lifetime, 1999.
Herself, *Finding Lucy* (documentary; also known as *American Masters: Finding Lucy*), PBS, 2000.
Lifestory: Rosie O'Donnell, Nickelodeon, 2001.
Marshalls' Women in Comedy, PAX, 2002.
Intimate Portrait: Lucille Ball, Lifetime, 2002.
The 3rd Annual Women Rock! Girls and Guitars, Lifetime, 2002.
CBS at 75, CBS, 2003.
TV's Greatest Sidekicks, Lifetime, 2004.
Presenter, *Women Rock!,* Lifetime, 2004.
The Nanny Reunion: A Nosh to Remember, Lifetime, 2004.

Television Appearances; Awards Presentations:
The 9th Annual American Comedy Awards, 1995.
Host, *The 4th Annual VH1 Honors,* VH1, 1997.
Presenter, *The 54th Annual Golden Globe Awards,* NBC, 1997.
Presenter, *The 25th International Emmy Awards,* Thirteen (New York)/WNET, 1998.
Blockbuster Entertainment Awards, UPN, 1998.

Television Appearances; Pilots:
Carolyn Baker, *Stranger in Our House* (also known as *Summer of Fear*), NBC, 1978.
Leslie Harper Weinstein, *I'd Rather Be Calm,* CBS, 1982.
Maggie Newton, *P.O.P.,* NBC, 1984.
Gail Hoffstetter, *What's Alan Watching?,* CBS, 1989.
Jo Finc, *WIOU,* 1990.
Rene Gianelli, *Hurricane Sam* (also known as *Mother's Day*), CBS, 1990.
Fran Fine, *The Simple Life,* CBS, 1998.

Television Appearances; Episodic:
Rhonda, "Metamorphosis," *Fame,* NBC, 1982.
Mrs. Baker, "The Refrigerator," *227,* NBC, 1985.
Carol Patrice, "The Heiress," *Who's the Boss?,* ABC, 1985.
Miriam Brody, "Author, Author," *Night Court,* NBC, 1986.
Joyce Columbus, "Charmed Lives," *Who's the Boss?,* ABC, 1986.
"Manos Arriba Mrs. Greely," *Once a Hero,* 1987.
Sales assistant, "By Stuff Possessed," *The Tracy Ullman Show,* Fox, 1989.
"The Second Greatest Story Ever Told," *Dream On,* HBO, 1990.
Roxanne, "Future's So Bright, I Gotta Wear Shades," *ALF,* 1990.
The Tonight Show Starring Johnny Carson (also known as *The Best of Carson*), NBC, 1990, 1991.
Kathleen, "The Second Greatest Story Ever Told," *Dream On,* HBO, 1991.

The Dennis Miller Show, syndicated, 1992.
"A Bus Named Desire," *Civil Wars,* ABC, 1992.
Today at Night, NBC, 1994.
Late Show with David Letterman (also known as *The Late Show*), CBS, 1994, 1995, 1996, 1997, 1998.
Interviewee, "Girlie Show," *Space Ghost Coast to Coast* (animated; also known as *SGC2C*), Cartoon Network, 1994.
Howard Stern, E! Entertainment Television, 1994, 1995, 1996, 1997, 1998, 2005.
Late Night with Conan O'Brien, NBC, 1994, 1997, 1998, 2005.
The Rosie O'Donnell Show, syndicated, 1996, 1997, 1998, 2001, 2002.
The Ruby Wax Show (also known as *Ruby Wax Meets*), Fox, 1997.
The Tonight Show with Jay Leno, NBC, 1997, 2002, 2005.
Celebrity square, *Hollywood Squares,* syndicated, 1998.
Host and Bobbi Flekman, *The List,* VH1, 1999.
Herself, *Mad TV,* Fox, 1999.
The Late Late Show with Craig Kilborn (also known as *The Late Late Show*), CBS, 2003.
Herself, *The Restaurant,* NBC, 2003.
Dinner for Five, Independent Film Channel, 2003.
Roberta Diaz, "Fear and Loathing in Miami," *Good Morning, Miami,* NBC, 2003.
Roberta Diaz, "About a Ploy," *Good Morning, Miami,* NBC, 2003.
Roberta Diaz, "Three Weeks Notice," *Good Morning, Miami,* NBC, 2003.
Access Hollywood, syndicated, 2004.
Irene Slater, "Cinderella in Scrubs," *Strong Medicine,* Lifetime, 2004.
Ellen: The Ellen DeGeneres Show, syndicated, 2004, 2005.
Live with Regis and Kelly, syndicated, 2005.
Herself, "Malibu Charity Bash," *I Married a Princess,* Lifetime, 2005.
Kathy Griffin: My Life on the D–List, Bravo, 2005.
Jimmy Kimmel Live, ABC, 2005.
The View, ABC, 2005.
Herself, "Casting and Character Creation," *TV Land Confidential,* TV Land, 2005.
The Late Late Show with Craig Ferguson, CBS, 2005.
Fran Reeves, "Girls Gone Wild," *What I Like About You,* The WB, 2005.
Herself, "Every Dog Had His Day," *The Apprentice: Martha Stewart,* NBC, 2005.
The Tony Danza Show, syndicated, 2005, 2006.

Also appeared in *Nine to Five,* syndicated.

Television Work; Series:
Creator and producer, *The Nanny,* CBS, 1993–97.
Executive producer, *The Nanny,* CBS, 1996–99.
Executive producer, *Living with Fran,* The WB, 2005—.

Television Work; Specials:
Executive producer, *Oy to the World* (animated), CBS, 1995.
Executive producer, *The Nanny Reunion: A Nosh to Remember,* Lifetime, 2004.

Television Work; Pilots:
Executive producer and director, *Daytrippers,* MTV, 1998.

Television Director; Episodic:
"Call Me Fran," *The Nanny,* CBS, 1998.
"Maggie's Wedding," *The Nanny,* CBS, 1999.
"Like Cures Like," *Strong Medicine,* Lifetime, 2004.

Stage Appearances:
The Exonerated, 45 Bleecker, New York City, c. 2002–2004.

RECORDINGS

Videos:
Pamela Finklestein, "UHF," *Alapalooza: The Videos,* BMG Music, 1994.
Pamela Finklestein, "UHF," *"Weird Al" Yankovic: The Videos,* 1996.
Pamela Finkelstein, "UHF," *"Weird Al" Yankovic: The Ultimate Video Collection,* Volcano Entertainment Group, 2003.

WRITINGS

Television Specials:
Oy to the World (animated; also known as *The Nanny Christmas Special: Oy to the World*), CBS, 1995.

Television Pilots:
Daytrippers, MTV, 1998.

Television Stories; Pilots:
The Nanny, CBS, 1993.

Television Episodes:
(With Peter Marc Jacobson) "Christmas Episode," *The Nanny,* CBS, 1993.
(With Peter Marc Jacobson) "Personal Business," *The Nanny,* CBS, 1993.
(With Peter Marc Jacobson) "Schlepped Away," *The Nanny,* CBS, 1994.
(With Peter Marc Jacobson) "The Will," *The Nanny,* CBS, 1995.
(With Peter Marc Jacobson) "Oy to the World," *The Nanny,* CBS, 1995.

(With Peter Marc Jacobson, Robert Sternin, and Prudence Fraser) "The Chatterbox," *The Nanny,* CBS, 1995.

Television Stories; Episodic:
(With Robert Sternin) "Immaculate Conception," *The Nanny,* CBS, 1998.
"Healing with Fran," *Living with Fran,* The WB, 2006.

Autobiographies:
Enter Whining, Regan Books (New York City), 1996.
Cancer Schmancer, Warner Books (New York City), 2002.

OTHER SOURCES

Periodicals:
People Weekly, September 2, 1996, p. 39; March 10, 1997, p. 39.

DUNN, Kevin 1956–

PERSONAL

Born August 24, 1956, in Chicago, IL; brother of Nora Dunn (an actress); married Katina Alexander; children: one son.

Addresses: *Agent*—The Gersh Agency, 232 North Canon Dr., Beverly Hills, CA 90210.

Career: Actor.

CREDITS

Film Appearances:
Agent Bird, *Mississippi Burning,* Orion, 1988.
Venkman's talk show guest, *Ghostbusters II,* Columbia, 1989.
Tom Killian, *The Bonfire of the Vanities,* Warner Bros., 1990.
Roselli, *Marked for Death* (also known as *Screwface*), Twentieth Century–Fox, 1990.
Assistant Chief Stanley Hoyt, *Blue Steel,* Metro–Goldwyn–Mayer/United Artists, 1990.
Patrick, *Only the Lonely,* Twentieth Century–Fox, 1991.
Lieutenant Commander Block, *Hot Shots!,* Twentieth Century–Fox, 1991.
J. Edgar Hoover, *Chaplin* (also known as *Charlot*), TriStar, 1992.

Captain Mendez, *1492: The Conquest of Paradise* (also known as *1492: Christophe Colomb, 1492: La Conquete du paradis,* and *1492: La Conquista del paraiso*), Paramount, 1992.

Alan Reed, *Dave,* Warner Bros., 1993.

(Uncredited) Brillo, *Beethoven's 2nd,* 1993.

Arthur Goslin, *Little Big League,* Columbia, 1994.

Clifford Leland, *Mad Love,* Buena Vista, 1995.

Charles "Chuck" Colson, *Nixon,* Buena Vista, 1995.

FBI Agent Doyle, *Chain Reaction* (also known as *Dead Drop*), Twentieth Century–Fox, 1996.

Mr. Mercer, *Picture Perfect,* Twentieth Century–Fox, 1997.

Mikulski, *The Sixth Man* (also known as *The 6th Man*), Buena Vista, 1997.

Hidalgo, *Almost Heroes* (also known as *Edwards and Hunt* and *Edwards and Hunt: The First American Road Trip*), Warner Bros., 1998.

Colonel Hicks, *Godzilla,* TriStar, 1998.

Stuart Abernathy, *Small Soldiers,* DreamWorks Distribution, 1998.

Lou Logan, *Snake Eyes,* Paramount, 1998.

Frank McCarthy, *Stir of Echoes,* Artisan Entertainment, 1999.

Marty, *I Heart Huckabees* (also known as *I Love Huckabees*), Fox Searchlight, 2004.

Monson, *Live Free or Die,* 2006.

All the King's Men, Sony, 2006.

Dexter, *Gridiron Gang,* Columbia, 2006.

Cleo Short, *The Black Dahlia,* Universal, 2006.

Television Appearances; Series:

Anthony Kubecek, *Jack and Mike,* ABC, 1986–87.

Al O'Brien, *Arsenio,* ABC, 1997.

Voice of Tony Hicks, *Godzilla: The Series,* syndicated, 1998.

Roy, *Bette!* 2000–2001.

Television Appearances; Miniseries:

Lieutenant Gladstone, *Blind Faith* (also known as *The Toms River Case*), NBC, 1990.

Murray Wilson, *The Beach Boys: An American Family,* ABC, 2000.

Television Appearances; Movies:

Policeman, *Night of Courage* (also known as *In This Fallen City*), ABC, 1987.

Jeff Lombardi, *Taken Away,* CBS, 1989.

Jacob Waldner, "Kennonite" (also known as "Gideon Oliver"), *The ABC Mystery Movie,* ABC, 1989.

Webber, *Double Edge* (also known as *Hit Woman: The Double Edge, Hit Women,* and *Two Women*), CBS, 1992.

Mark Evola, *Shadow of a Doubt,* NBC, 1995.

Charles Millard/Charles the Mysterious, *The Four Diamonds,* The Disney Channel, 1995.

Phil Brenner, *Jack Reed: A Killer Among Us* (also known as *Jack Reed: One of Our Own* and *Jack Reed: The Ridges Case*), NBC, 1996.

Milton Stella, *Unforgivable,* CBS, 1996.

Eric Silver, *Shattered Mind* (also known as *The Terror Inside*), 1996.

Jimmy Cannon, *The Second Civil War,* HBO, 1997.

Dr. Nigel Shore, *On the Edge of Innocence* (also known as *Blue Heaven* and *On the Edge*), NBC, 1997.

Title role, *The First Gentleman,* 1999.

Lieutenant Bob Coughlan, *L.A. Sheriff's Homicide* (also known as *LA County 187*), UPN, 2000.

Gleason's manager Jack Philbin, *Gleason* (also known as *Gleason: The Jackie Gleason Story*), 2002.

The Stranger Beside Me (also known as *Ann Rule Presents: The Stranger Beside Me*), 2003.

Cyrus, *NTSB: The Crash of Flight 323,* 2004.

Television Appearances; Pilots:

Anthony Kubecek, *Jack and Mike,* ABC, 1986.

Francis Xavier Hennessey, *The First Gentleman,* CBS, 1994.

Admiral Al Brovo, the Judge Advocate General, *JAG,* NBC, 1995.

Banning, *NYPD 2069,* Fox, 2003.

George Sr., *Carol Potter Gets a Life,* ABC, 2005.

Television Appearances; Episodic:

Dr. Sasha Dorn, "Bad Cats and Sudden Death," *Cannon,* 1972.

Jim McNulty, "The Last Angry Mailman," *Cheers,* NBC, 1987.

Lawyer Barry Braunstein, "Beauty and Obese," *L.A. Law,* NBC, 1988.

Bob, "The Boys Next Door," *Family Ties,* 1988.

Glen, "All in the Neighborhood: Part 1," *Family Ties,* 1989.

"Blu Flu," *21 Jump Street,* Fox, 1989.

Lawyer Barry Braunstein, "Izzy Ackerman or Is He Not," *L.A. Law,* NBC, 1989.

Burt, "House of Grown–Ups," *Roseanne,* ABC, 1989.

Joel, "Male Unbonding," *Seinfeld,* NBC, 1990.

Bob Morris, *Dear John,* NBC, 1990.

Himself, "Small Soldiers," *HBO First Look,* HBO, 1998.

Voice of Dr. Hodges, "Heroes," *Batman Beyond* (animated), 1999.

Voice, "There's Too Much Sex on TV," *God, the Devil and Bob* (animated), NBC, 2000.

Voice, "God's Girlfriend," *God, the Devil and Bob* (animated), NBC, 2000.

Voice, "Bob Gets Involved," *God, the Devil and Bob* (animated), NBC, 2000.

Bill Munce, "Man and Superman," *The Practice,* ABC, 2002.

Mitch Mann, "Jim's Domain," *Push, Nevada,* ABC, 2002.

Ron Berman, "The David McNorris Story," *Boomtown,* NBC, 2002.

J. J. Halsted, "Let's Make a Deal," *Dragnet* (also known as *L.A. Dragnet*), ABC, 2003.

"Chapter Seventy–Five," *Boston Public,* Fox, 2003.

Vic Tilden, "Out of Control," *LAX,* NBC, 2004.

Berkowitz, "Control," *Huff,* Showtime, 2004.

Coach Terry Hardwick, "Major League," *7th Heaven* (also known as *7th Heaven: Beginnings* and *Seventh Heaven*), The WB, 2004.

Coach Terry Hardwick, "Lost and Found," *7th Heaven* (also known as *7th Heaven: Beginnings* and *Seventh Heaven*), The WB, 2004.

Coach Terry Hardwick, "Waynes World," *7th Heaven* (also known as *7th Heaven: Beginnings* and *Seventh Heaven*), The WB, 2004.

Arnie MacLaren, "Publish and Perish," *Law & Order,* NBC, 2005.

Gordy, "The Long Con," *Lost,* ABC, 2006.

Stage Appearances:

The Front Page, Goodman Theatre, Chicago, 1981–82.

The Time of Your Life, Goodman Theatre, 1983–84.

Dealing, Northlight Theatre, Evanston, IL, 1986–88.

E

ECHIKUNWOKE, Megalyn 1983–

PERSONAL

Born May 28, 1983, in Spokane, WA. *Avocational Interests:* Singing, dancing, surfing, traveling.

Addresses: *Agent*—Bresler, Kelly and Associates, 11500 West Olympic Blvd., Suite 352, Los Angeles, CA 90064. *Manager*—Ira Belgrade, Ira Belgrade Management, 5850 East West Third St., Los Angeles, CA 90036.

Career: Actress.

CREDITS

Television Appearances; Series:
Cherish Pardee, *Spyder Games* (also known as *Spyder Web*), MTV, 2001.
Nicole Palmer, a recurring role, *24* (also known as *24 Hours*), Fox, 2001–2002.
Claudia Gibson, *For the People* (also known as *Para la gente*), Lifetime, 2002–2003.
Danika Ward, *Like Family,* The WB, 2003–2004.
Angie Barnett, a recurring role, *That '70s Show,* Fox, 2004–2005.

Television Appearances; Miniseries:
Elizabeth, *Creature* (also known as *Peter Benchley's "Creature"*), ABC, 1998.

Television Appearances; Movies:
Lauren, *Funny Valentines,* Starz!, 1999.

Television Appearances; Specials:
The Sixth Annual Sears Soul Train Christmas Starfest, UPN, 2003.

Television Appearances; Episodic:
Allison Hightower, "Uncle Steve," *The Steve Harvey Show,* The WB, 1998.
Randy, "Three Dudes and a Baby," *Malibu, CA,* syndicated, 2000.
"Chapter Twenty–Four," *Boston Public,* Fox, 2001.
Janel, "Coming to Africa," *Sheena,* syndicated, 2002.
Karen, "The Parrot Trap," *What I Like about You,* The WB, 2002.
Terry Welch, "Bygones," *ER* (also known as *Emergency Room*), NBC, 2002.
Vaughne, "The Killer in Me," *Buffy the Vampire Slayer* (also known as *BtVS, Buffy,* and *Buffy the Vampire Slayer: The Series*), UPN, 2003.
Rain/Debbie, "Drinking the Kool–Aid," *Veronica Mars,* UPN, 2004.
Cassie Robinson, "Route 666," *Supernatural,* The WB, 2006.

Also appeared in an episode of *Odd Man Out,* ABC.

Television Appearances; Pilots:
Cherish Pardee, *Spyder Games* (also known as *Spyder Web*), MTV, 2001.
Claudia Gibson, *For the People* (also known as *Para la gente*), Lifetime, 2002.
Shannon Cross, *BS** (also known as *Boarding School*), Fox, 2002.
Danika Ward, *Like Family,* The WB, 2003.

Some sources cite an appearance as Christina Chase in the pilot *Hitched,* Fox.

Film Appearances:
Elena, *Great Lengths* (short film), University of Southern California, 2004.
Sista Strada Cast, *Camjackers,* Eu Topos Productions/LAFCO, 2006.

EDELMAN, Randy 1947–

PERSONAL

Born June 10, 1947, in Paterson, NJ; son of an accountant and a first–grade teacher; married Jackie DeShannon (a singer and songwriter); children: Noah. *Education:* Attended the Cincinnati Conservatory of Music and the University of Cincinnati. *Religion:* Jewish.

Addresses: *Agent*—The Gorfaine/Schwartz Agency, 13245 Riverside Dr., Suite 450, Sherman Oaks, CA 91423.

Career: Composer, orchestrator, arranger, conductor, keyboard player, and vocalist. Worked as an arranger at King Records; CBS Records, New York City, staff songwriter, 1970; composed the Soarin' (Ride) theme for Disney's California Adventure.

Awards, Honors: BMI Film Music Award, 1989, for *Twins;* BMI Film Music Award, 1990, for *Ghostbusters II;* BMI Television Music Award, 1991, for *MacGyver;* BMI Film Music Award, 1992, for *Kindergarten Cop;* Golden Globe Award nomination (with Trevor Jones), best original score for a motion picture, 1992, Film Award nomination (with Jones), best original film score, British Academy of Film and Television Arts, 1993, BMI Film Music Award, 1994, all for *The Last of the Mohicans;* BMI Film Music Award, 1995, for *The Mask;* BMI Film Music Award, 1996, for *While You Were Sleeping;* Saturn Award nomination, Academy of Science Fiction, Fantasy and Horror Films, 1997; BMI Film Music Award, 1998, for *Anaconda;* BMI Film Music Award, 1999, for *Six Days, Seven Nights;* BMI Film Music Award, 2003, for *xXx;* Richard Kirk Career Achievement Award, BMI Film and Television Awards, 2003.

CREDITS

Film Work:

Music performer, *Red, White and Busted* (also known as *Outside In*), Robbins International, 1972.

Choral arranger and orchestrator, "Kumbaya," *Troop Beverly Hills,* Columbia, 1989.

Music conductor, *The Last of the Mohicans,* Twentieth Century–Fox, 1992.

Music conductor, *The Distinguished Gentleman,* Buena Vista, 1992.

Orchestrator, *Dragon: The Bruce Lee Story,* Universal, 1993.

Orchestrator, *The Big Green,* Buena Vista, 1995.

Music conductor, *The Indian in the Cupboard,* Columbia/Paramount, 1995.

Music conductor, *Dragonheart,* Universal, 1996.

Music conductor, *Daylight,* Universal, 1996.

Music conductor and pianist, *Diabolique,* Warner Bros., 1996.

Music conductor, and producer and arranger of song "Down in the Everglades," *Gone Fishin',* Buena Vista, 1997.

Orchestra conductor, *For Richer or Poorer,* Universal, 1997.

Score conductor, *Six Days, Seven Nights* (also known as *6 Days 7 Nights*), Touchstone, 1998.

Orchestra conductor, *EDtv* (also known as *Ed TV*), 1999.

Orchestra conductor, *Shanghai Noon,* 2000.

Song conductor ("The Hong Kong Cha Cha"), *Rush Hour 2,* New Line Cinema, 2001.

Orchestra conductor, *Corky Romano* (also known as *Corky Romano: "Special" Agent*), Buena Vista, 2001.

Conductor, *xXx* (also known as *Triple X*), Sony, 2002.

Orchestra conductor, *Shanghai Knights,* Buena Vista, 2003.

Music conductor, *Surviving Christmas,* DreamWorks, 2004.

Songs producer, orchestra conductor, music conductor, and band arrangements, *Connie and Carla,* Universal, 2004.

Film Appearances:

A guest at Heartland, *Sgt. Pepper's Lonely Hearts Club Band* (also known as *Banda de los corazones*), Universal, 1978.

Himself, *The Making of "Dragonheart"* (documentary), 1997.

Television Work; Movies:

Music performer, *Dennis the Menace: Dinosaur Hunter!* (also known as *Dennis the Menace*), 1993.

Television Appearances; Episodic:

Rod and Emu's Saturday Special, 1983.

Stage Work:

Keyboardist, *The Boyfriend,* Broadway production, c. 1970.

RECORDINGS

Albums:

Randy Edelman, 1972.

Laughter and Tears, 1973.

Prime Cuts, 1975.

Fairwell Fairbanks, Vivid Sound, 1976.

If Love Is Real, 1977.

Uptown Uptempo, 1979.
You're the One, 1979.
On Time, 1982.
Randy Edelman & His Piano, 1984.
The Very Best Of ... , Rev–Ola, 20–03.

WRITINGS

Film Scores:
Executive Action, National General, 1973.
Sgt. Pepper's Lonely Hearts Club Band, Universal, 1978.
The Chipmunk Adventure, Samuel Goldwyn, 1987.
Feds, Warner Bros., 1988.
Troop Beverly Hills, Columbia, 1989.
Ghostbusters II (also known as *Ghostbusters 2*), Columbia, 1989.
(With Howard Shore) *Quick Change,* Warner Bros., 1990.
Kindergarten Cop, Universal, 1990.
Come See the Paradise, Twentieth Century–Fox, 1990.
Quick Change, 1990.
V. I. Warshawski (also known as *V. I. Warshawski, Detective in High Heels*), Buena Vista, 1991.
Shout, Universal, 1991.
Drop Dead Fred (also known as *My Special Friend*), New Line Cinema, 1991.
Eyes of an Angel (also known as *The Tender*), Trans World Entertainment, 1991.
Beethoven, Universal, 1992.
(With Trevor Jones) *The Last of the Mohicans,* Twentieth Century–Fox, 1992.
The Distinguished Gentleman, Buena Vista, 1992.
My Cousin Vinny, Twentieth Century–Fox, 1992.
Dragon: The Bruce Lee Story, Universal, 1993.
Gettysburg, New Line Cinema, 1993.
Beethoven's 2nd, Universal, 1993.
Angels in the Outfield (also known as *Angels*), Buena Vista, 1994.
Greedy, Imagine Entertainment, 1994.
Pontiac Moon, Paramount, 1994.
The Mask, Dark Horse Entertainment/New Line Cinema, 1994.
Billy Madison, Universal, 1995.
Tall Tale: The Unbelievable Adventures of Pecos Bill (also known as *Tall Tale*), Walt Disney Productions, 1995.
The Big Green, Buena Vista, 1995.
The Indian in the Cupboard, Columbia/Paramount, 1995.
While You Were Sleeping, Buena Vista, 1995.
Daylight, Universal, 1996.
Diabolique, Warner Bros., 1996.
Down Periscope, Twentieth Century–Fox, 1996.
Dragonheart, Universal, 1996.
The Quest, Universal, 1996.
Anaconda, Sony Pictures Entertainment, 1997.
For Richer or Poorer, Universal, 1997.

Gone Fishin', Buena Vista, 1997.
Leave It to Beaver, Universal, 1997.
Six Days, Seven Nights (also known as *6 Days 7 Nights*), Touchstone, 1998.
The Gelfin (also known as *Crazy Gelfins*), Universal, 1999.
EDtv (also known as *Ed TV*), Universal, 1999.
The Whole Nine Yards (also known as *Le nouveau voisin*), Warner Bros., 2000.
Passion of Mind, Paramount Classics, 2000.
Shanghai Noon, Buena Vista, 2000.
The Replacements, Warner Bros., 2000.
The Skulls (also known as *Le clan des Skulls*), Twentieth Century–Fox, 2000.
Head Over Heels, Universal, 2001.
China: The Panda Adventure, IMAX, 2001.
Osmosis Jones, Warner Bros., 2001.
Corky Romano (also known as *Corky Romano: "Special" Agent*), Buena Vista, 2001.
Black Knight, Twentieth Century–Fox, 2001.
Frank McKlusky, C.I., Buena Vista, 2002.
xXx (also known as *Triple X*), Sony, 2002.
Who Is Cletis Tout?, Paramount Classics, 2002.
National Security, Sony, 2003.
Shanghai Knights, Buena Vista, 2003.
Gods and Generals, Warner Bros., 2003.
Surviving Christmas, DreamWorks, 2004.
Connie and Carla, Universal, 2004.
Cartoon Logic (documentary short), New Line Home Video, 2005.
Return to Edge City (documentary short), New Line Home Video, 2005.
Introducing Cameron Diaz (documentary short), New Line Home Video, 2005.
Chow Bella: Hollywood's Pampered Pooches (documentary short), New Line Home Video, 2005.
What Makes Fido Run? (documentary short), New Line Home Video, 2005.
Son of the Mask, New Line Cinema, 2005.
Creating "Son of the Mask": Digital Diapers and Dog Bytes (documentary short), New Line Home Video, 2005.
Paw Prints and Baby Steps: On the Set of "Son of the Mask" (documentary short), New Line Home Video, 2005.

Film Additional Music:
Twins, Universal, 1988.
Miss Congeniality 2: Armed and Fabulous, Warner Bros., 2005.

Film Songs:
Red, White and Busted (also known as *Outside In*), Robbins International, 1972.

Television Scores; Series:
Ryan's Four, ABC, 1983.
(Theme song) *Maximum Security,* HBO, 1985.

(And theme) *MacGyver,* ABC, 1985–87.
Mr. Sunshine, ABC, 1986.
(And theme music) *The Adventures of Brisco County, Jr.* (also known as *Brisco County, Jr.*), Fox, 1993.
The Mask (animated), CBS, 1995–98.

Television Scores; Movies:
Snatched, ABC, 1973.
Blood Sport, ABC, 1973.
When Your Lover Leaves, NBC, 1983.
A Doctor's Story, NBC, 1984.
Scandal Sheet (also known as *The Devil's Bed*), ABC, 1985.
Taking Back My Life (also known as *Taking Back My Life: The Nancy Ziegenmeyer Story*), CBS, 1992.
Dennis the Menace: Dinosaur Hunter! (also known as *Dennis the Menace*), 1993.
Citizen X, HBO, 1995.
The Hunley, TNT, 1999.
A Season on the Brink, ESPN, 2002.

Television Scores; Pilots:
MacGyver, ABC, 1985.

Television Scores; Specials:
All the Kids Do It, CBS, 1984.
Happily Ever After, PBS, 1985.
A Family Again, ABC, 1988.
(Closing music) *The 1996 Summer Olympic Games,* NBC, 1996.
(Theme music) *Super Bowl XXXII,* ABC, 1998.
Surviving Christmas: Unwrapping the Comedy, 2004.

Television Songs; Specials:
"Weekend in New England," *Manilow Country,* The Nashville Network, 2000.

Television Scores; Episodic:
"Surviving Christmas," *HBO First Look,* HBO, 2004.

OTHER SOURCES

Periodicals:
People Weekly, May 5, 1980, p. 129.

EDELSON, Kenneth
(Kenneth L. Edelson)

PERSONAL

Career: Actor. Sometimes credited as Kenneth L. Edelson.

CREDITS

Film Appearances:
Dorothy's Christmas party guest, *Alice,* Orion, 1990.
Gabe's novel montage, *Husbands and Wives,* TriStar, 1992.
Ken, *Mighty Aphrodite,* 1995.
Bar Mitzvah guest, *Deconstructing Harry,* Fine Line Features, 1997.
Rabbi Kaufman, *Celebrity,* Miramax, 1998.
(Uncredited) Party guest, *Sweet and Lowdown,* 1999.
Potter party guest, *Small Time Crooks,* DreamWorks, 2000.
Voltan's participant, *The Curse of the Jade Scorpion* (also known as *Im bann des jade skorpions*), DreamWorks, 2001.
Dr. Koch, *Hollywood Ending,* DreamWorks, 2002.
Hotel desk clerk, *Anything Else* (also known as *Anything else, la vie et tout le reste* and *La vie et tout le reste*), DreamWorks, 2003.
(Uncredited) Disco guest, *Melinda and Melinda,* Fox Searchlight, 2004.

EDWARDS, Stacy 1965–

PERSONAL

Born March 4, 1965, in Glasgow, MT; daughter of Preston (an Air Force officer) and Patty Edwards; married Eddie Bowz (an actor), June 1, 1996. *Education:* Studied at Lou Conte Dance Studio and with Hubbard Street Dance Company, both Chicago, IL.

Addresses: *Manager*—Interlink Management, 19366 Rosita St., Tarzana, CA 91356.

Career: Actress and dancer.

Awards, Honors: *Soap Opera Digest* Award nomination, outstanding newcomer–daytime, 1988, for *Santa Barbara;* Independent Spirit Award nomination, best female lead, Chicago Film Critics Association Award nomination, most promising actress, 1998, both for *In the Company of Men;* Screen Actors Guild Award nomination (with others), outstanding performance by an ensemble in a drama series, 1998, for *Chicago Hope;* Video Premiere Award nomination, best actress, DVD Exclusive Awards, 2001, for *Prancer Returns.*

CREDITS

Film Appearances:
Peggy Bell, *Spontaneous Combustion,* LIVE Entertainment, 1989.

Mary Ann, *Skeeter,* Columbia/TriStar Home Video, 1993.

Toni Keely, *Relentless 3,* New Line Cinema, 1993.

Mrs. Cooper, *Private Lessons 2,* Tohokushinsha Film, 1994.

Becky, *The Fear,* A–Pix Entertainment, 1995.

The Cottonwood, 1996.

Christine, *In the Company of Men* (also known as *En compagnie des hommes*), Sony Pictures Classics, 1997.

Jennifer, *Men Seeking Women* (also known as *The Bet*), IFM Film Associates, 1997.

Jill Gates, *Tumbling After,* 1997.

Jennifer Rogers, *Primary Colors* (also known as *Perfect Couple* and *Mit aller macht*), Universal, 1998.

Park Day, 1998.

Sheila King, *Black and White,* Screen Gems, 1999.

Zoe, *The Bachelor,* New Line Cinema, 1999.

Holly, *Four Dogs Playing Poker* (also known as *4 Dogs Playing Poker*), Behaviour Entertainment, 1999.

Finn, *The Next Best Thing,* Paramount, 2000.

Mitch Cobb, *Mexico City,* Curb Entertainment, 2000.

Lucretia Clan, *Driven* (also known as *A toute vitesse*), Warner Bros., 2001.

Sophie Hickman, *Speakeasy,* Miramax, 2002.

Jessica Dobson, *Local Boys,* First Look Pictures Releasing, 2002.

Maggie, *Joshua,* Artisan Entertainment, 2002.

Television Appearances; Series:

Hayley Benson Capwell, *Santa Barbara,* NBC, 1986–88.

Lindy Hammersmith, *Sons and Daughters* (also known as *The Hammersmiths*), CBS, 1991.

Dr. Lisa Catera, *Chicago Hope,* CBS, 1997–99.

Television Appearances; Miniseries:

Barbara Richardson, *Innocent Victims,* ABC, 1996.

Television Appearances; Movies:

(Uncredited) Model in red hat, *Born Beautiful,* NBC, 1982.

Andrea Moran, *Glory Days,* CBS, 1988.

Paula Jordan, *Dinner at Eight,* TNT, 1989.

Rachel Bauer, *Matlock: The Scam,* ABC, 1995.

Innocent Victims, 1996.

Bess Houdini, *Believe: The Houdini Story* (also known as *Houdini*), TNT, 1998.

Denise Holton, *Prancer Returns* (also known as *Le retour du petit renne*), USA Network, 2001.

Biddy, *Back When We Were Grownups,* CBS, 2004.

Television Appearances; Pilots:

Barbara Bailey, *The Hat Squad,* CBS, 1992.

Elaine Weinstein, *Pacific Blue,* 1996.

Alexandra Kelly, *Wolf Lake* (movie), CBS, 2001.

Television Appearances; Specials:

Michelle Munson, "A Hard Rain," *Showtime 30–Minute Movie,* Showtime, 1994.

Television Appearances; Episodic:

Kimberley Bauer, "I'll Be Seeing You," *Jake and the Fatman,* 1988.

"Everything You've Always Wanted to Know About Teenagers (But Were Afraid to Ask)," *TV 101,* 1988.

Rebecca, "Whose Choice Is It Anyways?" *21 Jump Street,* Fox, 1988.

"The Promise," *Vietnam War Story,* HBO, 1988.

Sara, "Boy Meets Girl," *Valerie* (also known as *Valerie's Family*), 1989.

Sara, "Boy Loses Girl," *Valerie* (also known as *Valerie's Family*), 1989.

Nicole Corry, "Placenta Claus Is Coming to Town," *L.A. Law,* NBC, 1989.

Officer Frances Xavier Rawley, "O'Malley's Luck," *Murder, She Wrote,* CBS, 1990.

Elisabeth Spokane, "Animal Frat—October 19, 1967," *Quantum Leap,* NBC, 1990.

Laurie Bascom, "The Perfect Couple Mystery," *Father Dowling Mysteries,* 1990.

Sydney, "Helter Skelter," *L.A. Law,* NBC, 1992.

Elaine Brown, "Flim Flam," *Murder, She Wrote,* CBS, 1995.

Rachel Bauer, "The Scam," *Matlock,* 1995.

Elaine Weinstein, "Captive Audience," *Pacific Blue,* USA Network, 1996.

Mildred "Millie" Austin, "callme@murder.com," *Silk Stalkings,* USA Network, 1997.

Jenny Butler, "Jenny," *The Fugitive,* CBS, 2001.

Jenny Butler, "Strapped," *The Fugitive,* CBS, 2001.

Emily Muller, "He Saw, She Saw," *Without a Trace,* CBS, 2002.

Lorena, "A Feather on the Breath of God," *Touched by an Angel,* CBS, 2002.

Vickie Winston, "Feeling the Heat," *CSI: Crime Scene Investigation* (also known as *C.S.I.*), CBS, 2003.

Susan Cardiff, "Resolutions," *Cold Case,* CBS, 2004.

Meredith Rice, "Head," *Law & Order: Special Victims Unit* (also known as *Law & Order: SVU* and *Special Victims Unit*), NBC, 2004.

Commander Janice Byers, "Heart Break," *Navy NCIS: Naval Criminal Investigative Service* (also known as *NCIS* and *NCIS: Naval Criminal Investigative Service*), CBS, 2004.

Lucy Palermo, "The Socratic Method," *House, M.D.* (also known as *House*), Fox, 2004.

Debbie Montenassi, "Tanglewood," *CSI: New York* (also known as *CSI: NY*), CBS, 2005.

Gail Hoke, "Sacrifice," *Numb3rs,* CBS, 2005.

District attorney Chelios, "Ass Fat Jungle," *Boston Legal,* ABC, 2005.

Linda Caleca, "The Sea," *Night Stalker,* ABC, 2005.

Also appeared in "Doubles or Nothing," *Robin's Hoods.*

Stage Appearances:
Appeared in *Agnes of God* and *In the Boom Boom Room,* Chicago; *Rounders.*

OTHER SOURCES

Periodicals:
Entertainment Weekly (special issue), November–December, 1997, p. 55.
Parade, December 6, 1998, p. 22.
People Weekly, August 25, 1997, p. 66.

ELLIOTT, Chris 1960–

PERSONAL

Born May 31, 1960, in New York, NY; son of Bob (a comedian and writer) and Lee Elliott; married Paula Niedert (a talent coordinator), 1986; children: Abigail, Bridget.

Addresses: *Agent*—United Talent Agency, 9560 Wilshire Blvd., Suite 500, Beverly Hills, CA 90212. *Manager*—Hofflund/Polone, 9465 Wilshire Blvd., Suite 820, Beverly Hills, CA 90212; Bauer Company, 9720 Wilshire Blvd., Mezzanine, Beverly Hills, CA 90212.

Career: Actor, director, producer, series creator, and writer. Rockefeller Center, New York City, tour guide, c. 1979; *Late Night with David Letterman,* gofer and talent coordinator, then writer and performer, 1981–1993; performer in improvisational theatre and summer stock productions; Elliottland Productions, founder; appeared in television commercials, including Tostitos tortilla chips, 1994–95, and Frosted Cheerios, 1995–96.

Awards, Honors: Emmy Awards (with others), outstanding writing in a variety or music program, 1984, 1985, 1986, 1987, Emmy Award nominations (with others), outstanding writing in a variety or music program, 1984, 1985, 1988, 1989, 1990, all for *Late Night with David Letterman;* Emmy Awards (with others), outstanding writing in a variety or music program, 1986, for *Late Night with David Letterman 4th Anniversary Special;* Emmy Awards (with others), outstanding writing in a variety or music program, 1987, for *Late Night with David Letterman 5th Anniversary Special;* Emmy Award nominations (with others), outstanding writing in a variety or music program, 1988, for *Late Night with David Letterman 6th Anniversary Special;* Emmy Award nominations (with others), outstanding writing in a variety or music program, 1989, for *Late Night with*

David Letterman 7th Anniversary Special; American Comedy Award nomination, best supporting male in a motion picture, 1994, for *Groundhog Day;* American Comedy Award nomination, funniest supporting actor in a motion picture, 1999, for *There's Something About Mary.*

CREDITS

Film Appearances:
Lighting assistant, *Lianna,* United Artists, 1983.
Mr. Spooner, *My Man Adam,* 1985.
Zeller, *Manhunter* (also known as *Red Dragon: The Pursuit of Hannibal Lechter*), De Laurentiis Entertainment Group, 1986.
Bendix, *The Abyss,* Twentieth Century–Fox, 1989.
Robber, "Life Without Zoe," *New York Stories,* Touchstone, 1989.
U.F.O. scientist, *Hyperspace* (also known as *Gremloids*), Earl Owensby, 1990.
Larry, *Groundhog Day,* Columbia, 1993.
Alan Squire, *The Traveling Poet,* Worldwide Pants/Elliottland Productions, 1993.
A. White, *CB4,* Universal, 1993.
Nathaniel Mayweather, *Cabin Boy,* Touchstone, 1994.
Pool man, *Poolside Ecstasy* (also known as *Velvet Pictures Present Poolside Ecstasy*), 1994.
Chris the diva, *Housewives: The Making of the Cast Album,* Worldwide Pants/Elliottland Productions, 1994.
The gambler, *Kingpin,* Metro–Goldwyn–Mayer, 1996.
Dom, *There's Something about Mary* (also known as *There's Something More About Mary*), Twentieth Century–Fox, 1998.
Santa Claus, *The Sky Is Falling,* Showcase Entertainment, 1999.
Buffet waiter, *Nutty Professor II: The Klumps* (also known as *The Klumps*), Universal, 2000.
Roger the snowplowman, *Snow Day,* Paramount, 2000.
Hanson, *Scary Movie 2* (also known as *Scarier Movie*), Dimension Films, 2001.
Bob, *Osmosis Jones,* Warner Bros., 2001.
Eugene the Gator Guy, *First Time Caller,* 2006.
Scary Movie 4, Weinstein Company, 2006.

Film Director:
The Traveling Poet, Worldwide Pants/Elliottland Productions, 1993.
Poolside Ecstasy (also known as *Velvet Pictures Present Poolside Ecstasy*), 1994.
Housewives: The Making of the Cast Album, Worldwide Pants/Elliottland Productions, 1994.

Television Appearances; Series:
The "Man Under the Seats," the "Panicky Guy," the "Fugitive Guy," and other characters, *Late Night with David Letterman,* NBC, 1982–93.

Spin, *Nick and Hillary* (also known as *Tattinger's*), NBC, 1989.

Chris Peterson, *Get a Life,* Fox, 1990–92.

Various characters, *Saturday Night Live* (also known as *NBC's Saturday Night, Saturday Night,* and *SNL*), NBC, 1994–95.

Bradley Crosby, *The Naked Truth* (also known as *Wilde Again*), NBC, 1997.

Voice of Dogbert, *Dilbert* (animated), UPN, 1999–2000.

Larry Heckman, *Cursed* (also known as *The Weber Show*), NBC, 2000.

Peter MacDougall, *Everybody Loves Raymond,* CBS, 2003–2005.

Television Appearances; Movies:
Ratbag Hero, 1991.
Jase Wallenberg, *The Barefoot Executive,* 1995.
Himself, *The Swinger,* Showtime, 2001.

Television Appearances; Pilots:
Chris Tollman, *Out There,* ABC, 1997.
Lonny, *Better Days,* CBS, 1998.
Arlo, *The Ripples,* NBC, Fox, 2005.

Television Appearances; Specials:
Himself, "Chris Elliott: A Television Miracle," *Late Night with David Letterman 2nd Annual Holiday Film Festival,* NBC, 1986.

Chris, *Action Family,* Cinemax, 1987.

Franklin Delano Roosevelt, *Chris Elliott's FDR: A One-Man Show,* Cinemax, 1987.

Just for Laughs, Showtime, 1987.

Late Night with David Letterman 5th Anniversary Show, NBC, 1987.

Late Night with David Letterman 6th Anniversary Show, NBC, 1988.

Late Night with David Letterman 7th Anniversary Show, NBC, 1989.

Late Night with David Letterman 8th Anniversary Show, NBC, 1990.

Andy, *Medusa: Dare to Be Truthful* (also known as *Dare to Be Truthful*), Showtime, 1992.

Voice characterization, *Springfield's Most Wanted* (animated), Fox, 1995.

Himself, *Reel Comedy: Something About Mary* (also known as *Reel Comedy: There's Something About Mary*), 1998.

Himself, *Here, There and Everywhere: A Concert for Linda,* 1999.

Chris, *The Victoria's Secret Fashion Show 2002,* CBS, 2002.

Denis Leary's "Merry F#%$in Christmas," Comedy Central, 2005.

Television Appearances; Episodic:
Professor Schooner, "Coal Black Soul," *The Equalizer,* CBS, 1986.

Cryptographer, "Down for the Count: Part 2," *Miami Vice,* NBC, 1987.

Late Show with David Letterman (also known as *The Late Show*), CBS, 1993–2003.

Psychic meter reader, "Sick Day," *The Adventures of Pete and Pete,* Nickelodeon, 1995.

Himself, "Larry's Sitcom," *The Larry Sanders Show,* HBO, 1995.

Steve, "The Ten Percent Solution," *Murphy Brown,* CBS, 1995.

Steve, " ... Like a Neighbor Scorned," *Wings,* NBC, 1996.

Steve, "Underdogs," *Murphy Brown,* CBS, 1996.

Voice of Dr. Reamus Elliott, "All About Elliott," *Duckman* (animated; also known as *Duckman: Private Duck/Family Man*), USA Network, 1997.

Warren, "Mars Attracts!," *Sabrina, the Teenage Witch* (also known as *Sabrina*), ABC, 1997.

Chris Malley, "Oh, Say, Can You Ski?," *The Nanny,* CBS, 1998.

Voice of Triton, "Hercules and the Son of Poseidon," *Hercules* (animated; also known as *Disney's "Hercules"*), The Disney Channel, 1998.

Late Night with Conan O'Brien, NBC, 1998, 2005.

Gilbert Bronson, "Books," *Tracey Takes On ... ,* 1999.

Jack Parson, "Judgment Day," *The Outer Limits* (also known as *The New Outer Limits*), Showtime and syndicated, 2000.

F. Moynihan, "Lyin' Hearted," *The King of Queens,* CBS, 2001.

Chet Bellafiore, "The New World," *Ed* (also known as *Stuckeyville*), NBC, 2002.

Reverend Gaylord Pierson, "Father Disfigure," *According to Jim,* ABC, 2002.

Reverend Gaylord Pierson, "We Have a Bingo," *According to Jim,* ABC, 2003.

Voice of Rob Holguin, "After the Mold Rush," *King of the Hill* (animated), CBS, 2003.

Reverend Gaylord Pierson, "Dana Dates the Reverend," *According to Jim,* ABC, 2004.

Jeffery Barton, "The Hunter, Hunted," *Third Watch,* NBC, 2004.

Jeffrey Barton, "Greatest Detectives in the World," *Third Watch,* NBC, 2004.

"The Swinger," *Jump Cuts,* Comedy Central, 2004.

Bray, "2000 Light Years from Home," *That '70s Show,* Fox, 2005.

The Daily Show (also known as *The Daily Show with Jon Stewart* and *The Daily Show with Jon Stewart Global Edition*), Comedy Central, 2005.

Jimmy Kimmel Live, ABC, 2005.

Television Work; Series:
Creator and producer, *Get a Life,* Fox, 1990–92.

Television Work; Pilots:
Executive producer, *Out There,* ABC, 1997.

Television Work; Specials:
Executive producer, *Chris Elliott's "FDR: A One–Man Show"* (also known as *FDR: A One Man Show*), Cinemax, 1987.

WRITINGS

Film Stories:
(With Adam Resnick) *Cabin Boy,* Touchstone, 1994.

Television Specials:
(With others) *Late Night with David Letterman 2nd Annual Holiday Film Festival,* NBC, 1986.
(With others) *Late Night with David Letterman 4th Anniversary Show,* NBC, 1986.
Action Family, Cinemax, 1987.
Chris Elliott's "FDR: A One–Man Show" (also known as *FDR: A One Man Show*), Cinemax, 1987.
(With others) *Late Night with David Letterman 5th Anniversary Show,* NBC, 1987.
(With others) *Late Night with David Letterman 6th Anniversary Show,* NBC, 1988.
(With others) *Late Night with David Letterman 7th Anniversary Show,* NBC, 1989.
(With others) *Late Night with David Letterman 8th Anniversary Show,* NBC, 1990.

Television Pilots:
Get a Life, Fox, 1990.
Out There, ABC, 1997.
Better Days, CBS, 1998.

Television Episodes:
(With others) *Late Night with David Letterman,* NBC, 1982–93.
"Terror on the Hell Loop," *Get a Life,* Fox, 1990.
"The Prettiest Week of My Life," *Get a Life,* Fox, 1990.
"Pile of Death," *Get a Life,* Fox, 1990.

Books:
(With Bob Elliott) *Daddy's Boy: A Son's Shocking Account of Life with a Famous Father* (satire), Delacorte, 1989.
The Shroud of the Thwacker (novel), Miramax, 2005.

OTHER SOURCES

Books:
Contemporary Authors, Vol. 147, Gale, 1995.

Periodicals:
Entertainment Weekly, January 21, 1994, pp. 36–37; July 22, 1994, p. 59.
Gentleman's Quarterly, May, 1989, p. 246.

Interview, September, 1987, p. 46.
New York Times, June 14, 1989.
People Weekly, November 5, 1990; January 24, 1994, p. 17.
Playboy, January, 1986, p. 185.
Time, January 10, 1994, p. 63.
Us, August 21, 1989.

ELMES, Frederick 1946–
    (Fred Elmes)

PERSONAL

Born November 4, 1946, in Mountain Lakes, NJ (some sources say Orange, NJ). *Education:* American Film Institute, undergraduate degree, 1972; New York University, graduate degree, 1975; studied photography at the Rochester Institute of Technology.

Addresses: *Contact*—Mirisch Agency, 1801 Century Park East, Suite 1801, Los Angeles, CA 90067.

Career: Cinematographer. Also worked as a cinematographer on student films, educational films, and commercials; worked as cinematographer on *The Hire: Chosen* (short), BMWFilms.com, 2001.

Member: American Society of Cinematographers.

Awards, Honors: Caixa de Catalunya, outstanding cinematography for a miniseries or special, Catalonian International Film Festival, 1986, National Film Critics Award, best cinematography, Independent Spirit Award nomination, best cinematography, Boston Society of Film Critics Award, best cinematography, 1987, all for *Blue Velvet;* Independent Spirit Award, best cinematography, 1990, for *Wild at Heart;* Independent Spirit Award, best cinematography, 1991, for *Night on Earth;* Excellence in Cinematography Award, Hawaii International Film Festival, 1996; Emmy Award nomination, outstanding cinematography for a miniseries or special, 1997, for *In the Gloaming;* Gold Special Award, Worldfest Houston, Directors' Week Award, best cinematography, Fantasporto, 1997, both for *The Empty Mirror;* Chicago Film Critics Association Award nomination, best cinematography, 1998, for *The Ice Storm;* Special Award (with David Lynch), best duo—director/cinematographer, Camerimage, 2000.

CREDITS

Film Cinematographer:
(As Fred Elmes) *Street Scenes* (also known as *Street Scenes 1970*), 1970.
The Amputee, 1974.

(Uncredited) *The Killing of a Chinese Bookie,* Faces, 1976.

Number One, 1976.

Breakfast in Bed, William Haugse, 1977.

(With Herbert Cardwell) *Eraserhead,* Libra, 1977.

(Uncredited) *Opening Night,* Faces, 1977.

(With others) *Real Life,* Paramount, 1978.

Citizen: The Political Life of Allard K. Lowenstein (documentary), M J and E Productions, 1982.

Valley Girl (also known as *Bad Boyz* and *Rebel Dreams*), Atlantic, 1983.

(Second unit) *Red Dawn,* 1984.

Broken Rainbow (documentary), 1985.

(Second unit) *Real Genius,* TriStar, 1985.

Blue Velvet, De Laurentiis Entertainment Group, 1986.

"Liebestod," *Aria,* Miramax/Warner Bros., 1987.

(With Joe Kelly) *Heaven* (documentary), Columbia, 1987.

Allan Quatermain and the Lost City of Gold, Cannon, 1987.

River's Edge, Island, 1987.

(Anthology segments) *Moonwalker* (also known as *Michael Jackson: Moonwalker*), Ultimate Productions, 1988.

Permanent Record, Paramount, 1988.

Cold Dog Soup, Anchor Bay, 1990.

Wild at Heart (also known as *David Lynch's "Wild at Heart"*), Samuel Goldwyn, 1990.

Hollywood Mavericks, 1990.

Night on Earth (also known as *Une nuit sur terre*), Fine Line Features, 1991.

The Saint of Fort Washington, Warner Bros., 1993.

Coffee and Cigarettes III (also known as *Coffee and Cigarettes: Somewhere in California*), 1993.

Trial by Jury, Warner Bros., 1994.

Reckless, Samuel Goldwyn, 1995.

The Empty Mirror, 1996.

The Ice Storm, Fox Searchlight, 1997.

To Live On (also known as *Civil War*), Universal, 1998.

(Uncredited; additional) *The Object of My Affection,* 1998.

Ride with the Devil, 1999.

Chain of Fools, 2000.

Storytelling, New Line Cinema, 2001.

Ten Minutes Older: The Trumpet, 2002.

Trapped (also known as *24 Studen Angst*), Sony, 2002.

Hulk, Universal, 2003.

"Somewhere in California," *Coffee and Cigarettes,* United Artists, 2003.

Kinsey, Fox Searchlight, 2004.

Broken Flowers, Focus Features, 2005.

The Namesake, Fox Searchlight, 2006.

Film Work; Other:

Assistant camera, *Invasion of the Blood Farmers,* 1972.

(As Fred Elmes) Assistant camera, *A Woman Under the Influence,* 1974.

Special effects photography, *Eraserhead,* Libra, 1977.

Camera operator, *Opening Night,* 1977.

Additional photographer, *Real Life,* 1979.

Camera operator, *Modern Romance,* 1981.

Additional unit supervisor, additional unit photography supervisor, and second unit director, *Dune,* Universal, 1985.

Second unit director, *Allan Quatermain and the Lost City of Gold,* Cannon, 1987.

Film Appearances:

Himself, *Visions of Light: The Art of Cinematography* (documentary), American Film Institute, 1992.

Himself, *Mysteries of Love,* 2002.

Himself, *The Kinsey Report: Sex on Film,* 2005.

Television Cinematographer; Miniseries:

"The Cowboy and the Frenchman," *Les francais vus par* (also known as *The Cowboy and the Frenchman* and *The French as Seen by ...*), 1988.

The Wedding (also known as *Oprah Winfrey Presents "The Wedding"*), 1998.

Television Cinematographer; Movies:

Conspiracy: The Trial of the Chicago 8, 1987.

In the Gloaming, HBO, 1997.

Television Cinematographer; Specials:

The Louie Anderson Show, HBO, 1988.

"The Closed Set," *Tales from the Hollywood Hills* (also known as *Great Performances*), PBS, 1988.

(Concert sequences) *The Judds: Across the Heartland,* CBS, 1989.

Television Camera; Specials:

The Judds: Across the Heartland, CBS, 1989.

Television Cinematographer; Pilots:

(As Fred Elmes) "Roughhouse" (also known as "House and Home"), *CBS Summer Playhouse,* CBS, 1988.

Television Appearances; Specials:

(Uncredited) Presenter, *The 1987 IFP/West Independent Spirit Awards,* Independent Film Channel, 1987.

Jonathon Ross Presents for One Week Only: David Lynch, Channel 4, 1990.

EVANS, David M. 1962–
(David Mickey Evans)

PERSONAL

Born October 20, 1962, in Wilkes Barre, PA; married; children: four. *Education:* Loyola Marymount University, undergraduate degree and M.A., film arts and screenwriting.

Addresses: *Agent*—The Endeavor Agency, 9701 Wilshire Blvd., 10th Floor, Beverly Hills, CA 90212. *Manager*—Key Creatives, 9595 Wilshire Blvd., Suite 800, Beverly Hills, CA 90212.

Career: Director, writer, producer, and actor. Also worked as a bartender, security guard, and phone installer while attending college.

Awards, Honors: Jack Haley Award, best student film, 1983, and Sam Arkoff Award (with others), best screenplay, 1984, both given by Loyola Marymount University, both for *Route 666;* DVDX Award nomination (with Evan Spiliotopoulos), best screenplay (for a DVD Premiere Movie), DVD Exclusive Awards, 2005, for *Mickey, Donald, Goofy: The Three Musketeers.*

CREDITS

Film Director:
(Uncredited) *Radio Flyer,* Columbia, 1992.
(As David Mickey Evans) *The Sandlot* (also known as *The Sandlot Kids*), Twentieth Century–Fox, 1993.
First Kid, Buena Vista, 1996.
The Fountain of Truth, Twentieth Century–Fox, 1997.
L. C. Soul Unlimited, Twentieth Century–Fox, 1999.
(As David Mickey Evans) *Beethoven's 3rd,* Universal Studios Home Video, 2000.
Snooze, Lotus Pictures, 2000.
Way Outside, Lotus Pictures, 2000.
(As David Mickey Evans) *Beethoven's 4th,* Universal Studios Home Video, 2001.
After School Special (also known as *National Lampoon's "Barely Legal"*), Barely Legal Productions, 2003.
The Solitary Man, 2004.
(With others) *Ozzie & Dobbs Get Stoked!,* 2004.
The Sandlot 2, Twentieth Century–Fox, 2005.
The Final Season, 2006.

Film Work; Other:
Executive producer, *Radio Flyer,* Columbia, 1992.
Coproducer, *Ozzie & Dobbs Get Stoked!,* 2004.

Film Appearances:
(Uncredited) Narrator, *The Sandlot* (also known as *The Sandlot Kids*), Twentieth Century–Fox, 1993.
Hammett, *Beethoven's 4th,* Universal Studios Home Video, 2001.
Dave, *After School Special* (also known as *National Lampoon's "Barely Legal"*), Barely Legal Productions, 2003.
(As David Mickey Evans) Narrator, *The Sandlot 2,* Twentieth Century–Fox, 2005.

Television Work; Movies:
The Craig Kielburger Story, Showtime, 2000.
101 Ways to Bug Your Parents, The Disney Channel, 2000.
Wilder Days, TNT, 2003.

Television Work; Pilot Movies:
(As David Mickey Evans) Co–executive producer, *Journey to the Center of the Earth,* NBC, 1993.

WRITINGS

Screenplays:
Terminal Entry, United Film Distribution Company, 1986.
Open House, Intercontinental, 1987.
(Uncredited) *The Class of 1999,* Vestron, 1988.
Route 666, 1988.
The Black Pearl, Columbia Pictures, 1991.
Radio Flyer, Columbia, 1992.
(With David Mickey Evans) *The Sandlot* (also known as *The Sandlot Kids*), Twentieth Century–Fox, 1993.
(Uncredited; narration only) *Far Off Place,* Walt Disney Pictures, 1993.
(Uncredited) *Hocus Pocus,* Walt Disney Pictures, 1993.
Katz & Doggs, Twentieth Century–Fox, 1994.
Gravity Hill, Twentieth Century–Fox, 1994.
(Uncredited) *Far From Home: The Adventures of Yellow Dog,* Twentieth Century–Fox, 1994.
Ed, 1996.
The Fountain of Truth, Twentieth Century–Fox, 1997.
L. C. Soul Unlimited, Twentieth Century–Fox, 1999.
Way Outside, Lotus Pictures, 2000.
Snooze, Twentieth Century–Fox, 2000.
(Uncredited) *Beethoven's 4th,* Universal Studios Home Video, 2001.
Mickey, Donald, Goofy: The Three Musketeers (animated), Buena Vista, 2004.
(With others) *The Solitary Man,* 2004.
(With others) *Ozzie & Dobbs Get Stoked!,* 2004.
The Sandlot 2, Twentieth Century–Fox, 2005.

Television Movies:
The Craig Kielburger Story, Showtime, 2000.
101 Ways to Bug Your Parents, Disney Channel, 2000.

Television Pilot Movies:
Journey to the Center of the Earth, NBC, 1993.

OTHER SOURCES

Periodicals:
Drama–Logue, August 22, 1996.

F

FINCHER, David 1962–

PERSONAL

Born May 10, 1962, in Denver, CO; son of Jack Fincher (a writer and bureau chief for Life magazine); married Donya Farentino (divorced); children: Phelix Imogen (daughter). *Education:* Graduated from Ashland High School, Ashland, Oregon.

Addresses: *Agent*—Creative Artists Agency, 9830 Wilshire Blvd., Beverly Hills, CA 90212.

Career: Director and producer. Industrial Light and Magic (ILM), camera operator and crew member, c. 1981–84; Propaganda Films (a production company), cofounder, 1987. Filmed numerous television commercials for various organizations and products, including the American Cancer Society, Nike, Hondo, Pepsi, Budweiser, Levi's, AT&T, Coca–Cola, and Hewlett–Packard, beginning 1985; director of music videos, beginning 1986.

Awards, Honors: MTV Music Video Award, best director, 1989, for Madonna's "Express Yourself"; MTV Music Video Award, best director, 1990, for Madonna's "Vogue"; Saturn Award nomination, best director, Academy of Science Fiction, Fantasy, and Horror Films, 1993, for *Alien 3;* Grammy Award, best music video—short form, National Academy of Recording Arts and Sciences, 1995, for the Rolling Stones' "Love Is Strong"; Saturn Award, best director, Academy of Science Fiction, Fantasy, and Horror Films, Hochi Film Award, best foreign language film, International Fantasy Film Award, best film, Fantasporto, 1996, Blue Ribbon Award, best foreign language film, 1997, Video Premiere Award nomination, best DVD audio commentary, DVD Exclusive Awards, 2001, all for *Seven;*

Online Film Critics Society Award nomination, best director, 1999, for *Fight Club;* Directors Guild of America Award, 2004, for outstanding director achievement in commercials.

CREDITS

Film Work:

Special photographic effects artist, *Twice Upon a Time* (animated), Warner Bros., 1983.

Assistant camera operator in miniature and optical effects unit, *Return of the Jedi* (also known as *Star Wars: Episode VI—Return of the Jedi*), Twentieth Century–Fox, 1983.

Matte photography artist, *Indiana Jones and the Temple of Doom,* Paramount, 1984.

Matte photography assistant: ILM, *The NeverEnding Story* (also known as *Die Unendliche Geschchte*), 1984.

Director, *The Beat of the Live Drum,* 1985.

Director, *Alien 3,* Twentieth Century–Fox, 1992.

Director, *Seven* (also known as *Se7en*), New Line Cinema, 1995.

Director, *The Game,* Polygram Filmed Entertainment, 1997.

Director, *Fight Club,* Twentieth Century–Fox, 1999.

Second unit director, *Star Wars: Episode I* (also known as *Star Wars: The Balance of the Force, Star Wars: The Beginning,* and *Star Wars: Genesis*), Twentieth Century–Fox, 1999.

Director, *Rendezvous with Rama,* 1999.

Executive producer, *The Hire: Ambush* (short), BMW Films, 2001.

Executive producer, *The Hire: Chosen* (short), BMW Films, 2001.

Executive producer, *The Hire: The Follow* (short), BMW Films, 2001.

(Uncredited) Executive producer, *The Car Thief and the Hit Man,* 2001.

Executive producer, *The Hire: Star* (short), BMW Films, 2001.

Executive producer, *The Hire: Powder Keg* (short), BMW Films, 2001.

Executive producer, *The Hire: Ticker* (short), BMW Films, 2002.

Director, *Panic Room,* Columbia TriStar, 2002.

Executive producer, *Lords of Dogtown,* TriStar, 2005.

Executive producer, *Love and Other Disasters,* 2006.

Producer and director, *Zodiac,* Paramount, 2006.

Also worked on *The Blue Iguana,* Paramount, 1988.

Film Appearances:

Christopher Bing, *Being John Malkovich,* USA Films, 1999.

Himself, *On Location: Fight Club* (documentary short), Twentieth Century–Fox, 2000.

Film director, *Full Frontal,* 2002.

Himself, *The Making of "Alien 3"* (documentary), Twentieth Century–Fox Home Entertainment, 2003.

Himself, *Shooting "Panic Room"* (documentary), Columbia TriStar Home Entertainment, 2004.

Television Appearances; Specials:

(Uncredited) Himself, *The Making of "Alien 3"* (documentary), 1992.

Himself, *Alien Evolution* (documentary), Channel 4, 2001.

Himself, *Murder by Numbers* (documentary), IFC, 2001.

Himself, *The Making of "Panic Room"* (documentary), 2002.

Television Appearances; Pilots:

Himself, *The Henry Rollins Show,* IFC, 2004.

Television Appearances; Episodic:

Himself, *Henry's Film Corner,* IFC, 2004.

RECORDINGS

Music Videos (as Director):

Paula Abdul's "The Way That You Love Me," 1988.

Steve Winwood's "Roll with It," 1988.

Paula Abdul's "Straight Up," 1989.

Paula Abdul's "Forever Your Girl," 1989.

Paula Abdul's "Cold Hearted," 1989.

Aerosmith's "Janie's Got a Gun," 1989.

Madonna's "Express Yourself," 1989.

Madonna's "Oh Father," 1990.

Madonna's "Bad Girl," 1993.

Michael Jackson's "Who Is It?," *Dangerous: The Short Films* (also known as *Michael Jackson—Dangerous: The Short Films*),1993.

Aerosmith, "Big Ones You Can Look At," 1994.

Rolling Stones's "Love Is Strong," 1994.

Sting's "Englishman in New York," *The Best of Sting: Fields of Gold 1984–1994,* 1994.

Madonna's "Bad Girl," *The Video Collection 93:99,* 1999.

George Michael's "Freedom '90," *Ladies & Gentleman: The Best of George Michael,* 1999.

A Perfect Circle's "Judith," 2000.

Video Hits: Paula Abdul, EMI Distribution, 2005.

Nine Inch Nails' "Only," 2005.

Also directed Madonna's "Vogue"; the Wallflowers's "6th Avenue Heartbreak"; Billy Idol's "Rock the Cradle of Love"; Don Henley's "The End of Innocence"; Johnny Hates Jazz's "Shattered Dreams" and "Heart of Gold."

OTHER SOURCES

Books:

Authors and Artists for Young Adults, Vol. 36, Gale Group, 2000.

International Dictionary of Films and Filmmakers: Volume 2, Directors, 4th ed., St. James Press, 2000.

Periodicals:

Entertainment Weekly, September 19, 1997, p. 32; April 9, 2004, p. 69.

Interview, March, 2002, p. 78.

Los Angeles Times, September 9, 1997.

National Review, October 13, 1997, p. 76.

New York Times, August 31, 1997, pp. 9H, 14H.

Rolling Stone, October 17, 1996, p. 44; April 3, 1997, p. 52.

FLANERY, Sean Patrick 1965–

PERSONAL

Born October 11, 1965, in Lake Charles, LA. *Education:* Studied business and drama at University of St. Thomas, Houston, TX, 1988. *Avocational Interests:* Black belt in karate, competing in triathalons.

Addresses: *Agent*—Paradigm, 360 North Crescent Dr., North Bldg., Beverly Hills, CA 90210. *Manager*—The Firm, 9465 Wilshire Blvd., 6th Floor, Beverly Hills, CA 90212.

Career: Actor. Appeared in television commercials. Also worked as a waiter in Los Angeles, CA.

Awards, Honors: Winning driver in the Dodge Neon Challenge Race, 1994; MTV Movie Award nomination, best breakthrough performance, 1996, for *Powder;* winning driver in the 21st Annual Toyota Pro/Celebrity Race, 1997.

CREDITS

Film Appearances:
Buddy, *A Tiger's Tale,* 1987.
Kingdom Come, 1993.
Zack Murphy, *Frank & Jesse,* 1994.
Riley Henderson, *The Grass Harp,* Fine Line Features, 1995.
Jeremy "Powder" Reed, *Powder,* Buena Vista, 1995.
Chris D'Amico, *Raging Angels* (also known as *Spirit Realm* and *Spirit*), Chako Films International, 1995.
Ray, a lawyer, *Just Your Luck* (also known as *Whiskey Down*), Polygram Video, 1996.
Louis, *Pale Saints,* Norstar Entertainment, 1997.
Dave Edgerton, *Eden,* Legacy Releasing, 1997.
Billy Phillips, *Best Men,* Orion, 1997.
Christian, *The Method,* Roundtable Productions, 1997.
Max Minot, *Suicide Kings,* Artisan Entertainment, 1998.
Zack Blanton, *Zack and Reba,* 1998.
Tom Bartlett, *Simply Irresistible* (also known as *Einfach unwiderstehlich*), Twentieth Century–Fox, 1999.
Todd Sparrow, *Girl,* Kushner–Locke International, 1999.
Conner MacManus, *The Boondock Saints* (also known as *Mission des dieux*), South Boondock Productions, 1999.
Rick Hamilton, *Body Shots,* New Line Cinema, 1999.
Conner, *D–Tox* (also known as *Eye See You* and *Im auge der angst*), Universal, 2002.
John, *Lone Hero* (also known as *Heroes solitaire*), Promark Entertainment Group, 2002.
Alex Brooks, *Con Express,* 2002.
Ed Baikman, *Borderline* (also known as *Borderline—Unter mordverdacht*), Columbia TriStar Home Video, 2002.
Himself, *Overnight* (documentary), ThinkFilm, 2003.
Ben, *The Gunman,* Curb Entertainment, 2004.
John, *The Storyteller,* 2005.
Veritas, *Veritas, Prince of Truth,* 2005.
Jake Greyman, *Demon Hunter,* Anchor Bay Entertainment, 2005.
Walter Harwig, Jr., *Into the Fire,* Slowhand Cinema Releasing, 2005.
Clay Arrendal, *Crystal River,* 2005.
Harry, *The Insatiable,* 2006.

Film Work:
Executive producer, *The Method,* 1997.

Television Appearances; Series:
Indiana Jones (age sixteen), *The Young Indiana Jones Chronicles,* ABC, 1992–93.
Elvis Ford, *The Strip,* UPN, 1999.

Greg Stillson, *The Dead Zone,* USA Network, 2002–2005.

Television Appearances; Miniseries:
Johnny Lance, *Diamond Hunters,* syndicated, 2001.

Television Appearances; Movies:
"Just Perfect," *Mickey Mouse Club,* 1990.
"My Life As a Babysitter," *Mickey Mouse Club,* 1990.
The driver, *The Accident,* 1993.
Young Indiana Jones, *Young Indiana Jones and the Hollywood Follies,* The Family Channel, 1994.
Zack Murphy, *Frank and Jesse,* HBO, 1994.
King Arthur, *Guinevere* (also known as *Bound in Blood*), Lifetime, 1994.
Young Indiana Jones, *Young Indiana Jones and the Attack of the Hawkmen,* The Family Channel, 1995.
Young Indiana Jones, *Young Indiana Jones and the Treasure of the Peacock's Eye,* The Family Channel, 1995.
Young Indiana Jones, *Young Indiana Jones Travels with Father,* The Family Channel, 1996.
Tom Walker, *Run the Wild Fields,* Showtime, 2000.
Bobby, *Acceptable Risk* (also known as *Robin Cook's "Acceptable Risk"*), 2001.
Cole, *30 Days Until I'm Famous,* VH1, 2004.
Tom Terranova, *Kiss the Bride,* Lifetime, 2004.
Wayne, *K.A.W.,* 2006.

Television Appearances; Pilots:
Sheriff Ben Jones, *Then Came Jones,* Sci–Fi Channel, 2003.
Jimmy Blake, *Dead Lawyers,* ABC, 2004.

Television Appearances; Episodic:
The Dennis Miller Show, syndicated, 1992.
Himself, "Young Indy and the Sidewalk of Doom," *Sidewalks Entertainment,* 1994.
Eric, "Stasis," *The Outer Limits* (also known as *The New Outer Limits*), Showtime and syndicated, 2000.
Orlin, "Ascension," *Stargate SG–1,* Showtime, 2001.
Daniel Lee Corbitt, "Famous Last Words," *Touched by an Angel,* CBS, 2001.
Adam, "Happily Ever After," *Charmed,* The WB, 2002.
Dr. Paul Thorson, "Cold Fusion," *The Twilight Zone,* UPN, 2003.

RECORDINGS

Albums:
Johnson Was a Snowball Who Loved the Beach, 1993.

OTHER SOURCES

Periodicals:
Entertainment Weekly, November 10, 1995, p. 36.
Variety, October 30, 1995, p. 72; November 13, 1995, p. 54.

FLOCKHART, Calista 1964–

PERSONAL

Full name, Calista Kay Flockhart; born November 11, 1964, in Freeport, IL; daughter of Ronald (a business executive) and Kay (a school teacher) Flockhart; engaged to Harrison Ford (actor), 2002; children: Liam. *Education:* Graduated from Shawnee High School, Medford, NJ, 1983; Rutgers College, B.F.A., theater, 1988.

Addresses: *Agent*—International Creative Management, 8942 Wilshire Blvd., Beverly Hills, CA 90211; Special Artists Agency, 9465 Wilshire Blvd., Suite 890, Beverly Hills, CA 90212.

Career: Actress. Appeared in regional theatre productions in Cleveland, OH, Louisville, KY, Chicago, IL, and Houston, TX; Malaparte (a theater company), former member. V–Day Global Youth Initiative, cofounder (with Eve Ensler) and spokesperson.

Awards, Honors: *Theatre World* Award, best new talent, Clarence Derwent Award, most promising female performer, Actor's Equity Association, 1995, both for *The Glass Menagerie;* Emmy Award nominations, outstanding lead actress in a comedy series, 1998, 1999, 2001, Golden Globe Award, best performance by an actress in a television series—comedy/musical, 1998, Golden Globe Award nominations, best performance by an actress in a television series—comedy/musical, 1999, 2000, 2001, 2002, People's Choice Award, favorite female television performer, 2000, People's Choice Award nominations, favorite female performer in a new television series, 1998, 1999, Screen Actors Guild Award (with others), outstanding performance by an ensemble in a comedy series, 1999, Screen Actors Guild Award nominations, outstanding performance by a female actor in a comedy series, 1998, 1999, 2000, 2001, and outstanding performance by an ensemble in a comedy series (with others), 1998, 2000, 2001, Q Award, best actress in a quality comedy series, Viewers for Quality Television, 1998, Q Award nomination, Viewers for Quality Television, best actress in a quality comedy series, 2000, American Comedy Award nomination, funniest female performer in a TV series (leading role) network, cable or syndication, 1999, *TV Guide* Award nominations, favorite actress in a comedy, 1999, 2000, Golden Satellite Award nomination, best performance by an actress in a television series—comedy or musical, International Press Academy, 1999, 2000, all for *Ally McBeal;* TV Prizes, Aftonbladet TV Prize, Sweden, best foreign television personality, 1999, 2000.

CREDITS

Film Appearances:

Barnard girl, *Quiz Show,* Buena Vista, 1994.

Amanda Morel, *Getting In* (also known as *Student Body*), Trimark Pictures, 1994.

Acting student, *Naked in New York,* Columbia TriStar Home Video, 1994.

Clear Cut, 1994.

Jane, *Jane Doe* (also known as *Pictures of Jane Doe*), 1995.

Helen, *Drunks,* 1995.

Barbara Keeley, *The Birdcage* (also known as *Birds of a Feather*), Metro–Goldwyn–Mayer, 1996.

Christine, *Milk and Money,* 1997.

Diney Majeski, *Telling Lies in America,* Banner Entertainment, 1997.

Helena, *A Midsummer Night's Dream* (also known as *William Shakespeare's "A Midsummer Night's Dream"* and *Sogno di una notte di mezza estate*), Fox Searchlight, 1999.

Like a Hole in the Head, Fox Searchlight, 1999.

Christine, "Goodnight Lilly, Goodnight Christine" and "This Is Dr. Keener," *Things You Can Tell Just By Looking at Her,* United Artists, 2000.

Valerie Watson, *The Last Shot,* Buena Vista, 2004.

Amy, *Fragile,* Bauer Martinez Studios, 2005.

Television Appearances; Series:

Elise, *The Guiding Light* (also known as *Guiding Light*), 1989.

Title role, *Ally McBeal,* Fox, 1997–2002.

Television Appearances; Movies:

Helen, *Drunks,* Showtime, 1995.

Amy, *Venecia 2005: Cronica de Carlos Boyero,* 2005.

Television Appearances; Specials:

Mary Lynn, *An American Story,* CBS, 1991.

Lillian Anderson, "Darrow," *American Playhouse,* PBS, 1991.

Mary–Margaret Carter, "The Secret Life of Mary–Margaret: Portrait of a Bulimic," *Lifestories: Families in Crisis,* HBO, 1992.

Barbara Walters Presents the 10 Most Fascinating People of 1998, ABC, 1998.

Herself, *McBeal Appeal,* Channel 4, 1999.

Bash: Latter–Day Plays, Showtime, 2000.

Narrator, *Science of Love* (documentary), Discovery Health, 2001.

(Uncredited) *The 100 Greatest TV Characters,* Channel 4, 2001.

Intimate Portrait: Calista Flockhart (documentary), Lifetime, 2001.

All About Ally, E! Entertainment Television, 2001.

America: A Tribute to Heroes, 2001.

Intimate Portrait: Young Hollywood (documentary), Lifetime, 2002.

Intimate Portrait: Lisa Gay Hamilton (documentary), Lifetime, 2002.

Intimate Portrait: Melissa Joan Hart (documentary), Lifetime, 2003.

Intimate Portrait: Eve Ensler (documentary), Lifetime, 2003.

TV Revolution, Bravo, 2003.

(Uncredited) Herself, *Michael Moore, el gran agitador,* 2004.

Herself, *101 Biggest Celebrity Oops,* E! Entertainment Television, 2004.

(Uncredited) Herself, *The AFI Tribute to George Lucas,* USA Network, 2005.

Television Appearances; Awards Presentations:

The 50th Annual Primetime Emmy Awards, NBC, 1998.

The 5th Annual Screen Actors Guild Awards, TNT, 1999.

The 51st Annual Primetime Emmy Awards, Fox, 1999.

The 53rd Annual Tony Awards, Fox, 1999.

The 56th Annual Golden Globe Awards, NBC, 1999.

The 1st Annual TV Guide Awards, Fox, 1999.

The 6th Annual Screen Actors Guild Awards, TNT, 2000.

The 57th Annual Golden Glob Awards, NBC, 2000.

The 2nd Annual TV Guide Awards, Fox, 2000.

The 14th Annual American Comedy Awards, Fox, 2000.

The 7th Annual Screen Actors Guild Awards, TNT, 2001.

The 53rd Annual Primetime Emmy Awards, CBS, 2001.

Presenter, *My VH1 Music Awards '01,* VH1, 2001.

The 59th Annual Golden Globe Awards, NBC, 2002.

The 56th Annual Tony Awards, CBS, 2002.

Presenter, *The 60th Annual Golden Globe Awards,* NBC, 2003.

The 75th Annual Academy Awards, ABC, 2003.

The 2003 MTV Movie Awards, MTV, 2003.

Television Appearances; Episodic:

Ally McBeal, "Axe Murderer," *The Practice,* ABC, 1997.

The Rosie O'Donnell Show, syndicated, 1998, 2000, 2002.

Voice of Vanna Van, "Rip Van Winkle," *Happily Ever After: Fairy Tales for Every Child* (animated), HBO, 1999.

Host, *Saturday Night Live* (also known as *SNL*), NBC, 2000.

Guest, *The Tonight Show with Jay Leno,* NBC, 2001, 2002.

Celebrities Uncensored, E! Entertainment Television, 2003.

Guest, *Corazon, corazon,* 2004.

Guest, *Magacine,* 2005.

Guest, *Corazon de...,* 2005.

Stage Appearances:

Skidie, *Beside Herself,* Circle Repertory Theatre, New York City, 1989.

Lucia, Student, and Doctor, *Mad Forest,* Stage I, Manhattan Theatre Club, New York City, 1991–92.

Class 1 Acts: '91–'92, MCC Theater, New York City, 1992.

Emily, *Our Town,* Alley Theatre, Houston, TX, 1992–93.

Anita Merendino, *Wrong Turn at Lungfish,* Promenade Theatre, New York City, 1993.

Robin Smith, *Sophistry,* Playwrights Horizons, New York City, 1993.

Joanna, *Sons and Fathers,* Malaparte Theatre Company, New York City, 1994.

Irina, *Three Sisters,* Goodman Theatre, Chicago, 1994–95.

(Broadway debut) Laura, *The Glass Menagerie,* Criterion Stage Right, Roundabout Theatre, New York City, 1994–95.

Natalya Ivanova, *The Three Sisters,* Roundabout Theatre, 1997.

"Medea Redux," *Bash: Latter–Day Plays,* Douglas Fairbanks Theater, New York City, 1999.

The Vagina Monologues, Westside Theater Downstairs, New York City, 2000.

Also appeared as Juliet, *Romeo and Juliet,* Hartford Stage, Hartford, CT; Cordelia, *King Lear;* Emily, *Our Town,* Williamstown Theater Festival, Williamstown, MA; in *Bover Boys,* Primary Stages; *All for One,* Ensemble Studio Theatre, New York City; *The Loop,* Alice's 4th Floor; *Beside Herself; The Imposter,* Alice's 4th Floor; *Death Takes a Holiday,* Williamstown Theater Festival; *Jittas' Atonement,* Berkshire Theater Festival, Berkshire, MA.

RECORDINGS

Taped Readings:

Carl Best's Shrinking Violet, Weston Books, 2003.

OTHER SOURCES

Periodicals:

Backstage, February 14, 1997, p. 33.

Cosmopolitan, January, 1998, p. 128.

Entertainment Weekly, January 30, 1998, p. 20; October 16, 1998, p. 12.

People Weekly, May 11, 1998, p. 175; January 29, 2001, p. 58; May 20, 2002, p. 60; December 1, 2003, p. 57.

TV Guide, February 26, 1998, pp. 16–22; May 1, 1999, p. 22.

FOLEY, Dave 1963–
(David Foley)

PERSONAL

Full name, David Scott Foley; born January 4, 1963, in Toronto, Ontario, Canada; son of Michael (a steam–fitter) and Mary (a homemaker) Foley; married Tabatha Southey, December 31, 1991 (divorced, c. 1997); married Crissy Guerrero, August 1, 2002; children: (first marriage) Edmund "Ned" Southey, Basil Patrick Southey; (second marriage) Alina Chiara. *Education:* Attended an improvisational workshop with the Second City theatre group, c. 1981.

Addresses: *Agent*—United Talent Agency, 9560 Wilshire Blvd., Suite 500, Beverly Hills, CA 90212. *Manager*—Brillstein–Grey Entertainment, 9150 Wilshire Blvd., Suite 350, Beverly Hills, CA 90212.

Career: Actor, comedian, director, producer, editor, and writer. Began comedy career, 1981; member of the comedy troupe Kids in the Hall, including tours of Canadian and U.S. cities, 1984–94, 2002—. Also worked as a stand–up comedian and a movie theatre usher.

Member: Screen Actors Guild.

Awards, Honors: Gemini Awards (with Kids in the Hall), Academy of Canadian Cinema and Television, best writing in a comedy or variety program or series, 1989, 1990, best performance in a variety or performing arts program, 1989, and best performance in a comedy program or series (individual or ensemble), 1993, Gemini Award nominations (with Kids in the Hall), best performance in a comedy program or series (individual or ensemble), 1992, 1994, 1996, and best writing in a comedy or variety program or series, 1995, 1996, Emmy Award nominations (with others), outstanding achievement in writing for a variety or music program, 1993, 1994, 1995, all for *The Kids in the Hall;* Petcabus Award nomination (with others), best ensemble cast in a comedy or drama series, 1998, for *NewsRadio;* Film Showcase Jury Award (with others), best screenplay, U.S. Comedy Arts Festival, 1999, Canadian Comedy Award nomination, best male film performance, 2000, both for *The Wrong Guy;* Gemini Award nomination (with others), best performance or host in a variety program or series, 2003, for *The True Meaning of Christmas Specials;* Vancouver Film Critics Circle Award, best supporting actor—Canadian film, 2005, for *Childstar.*

CREDITS

Film Appearances:
(As David Foley) Bo Baker, *High Stakes,* 1986.

Grocery store clerk, *Three Men and a Baby,* Buena Vista, 1987.

Chris, *It's Pat* (also known as *It's Pat: The Movie*), Buena Vista, 1994.

Marv, psychiatrist, suicidal businessman, new guy, and Raymond Hurdicure, *Kids in the Hall: Brain Candy* (also known as *Brain Candy, Kids in the Hall: La pilule du bonheur,* and *The Drug*), Paramount, 1996.

Neal, *Hacks* (also known as *The Big Twist* and *Sink or Swim*), Rigorous Productions, 1997.

Nelson Hibbert, *The Wrong Guy,* Lions Gate Films, 1998.

Troy, *Blast from the Past,* New Line Cinema, 1998.

Voice of Flik, *A Bug's Life* (animated; also known as *Bugs*), Buena Vista, 1998.

Voice of the Baldwin Brothers, *South Park: Bigger, Longer, and Uncut,* Paramount, 1999.

Bob Haldeman, *Dick* (also known as *Dick, les coulisses de la presidence*), Sony Pictures Entertainment, 1999.

Voice of Flik, *Toy Story 2* (animated), Buena Vista, 1999.

Voice of Flik, *It's Tough to Be a Bug* (animated), 1999.

Himself, *The Making of "Dick"* (documentary short), 1999.

Herb, Stu's agent, *Monkeybone,* Twentieth Century–Fox, 2000.

Voice of Hank the Technician, *CyberWorld* (animated short), IMAX, 2000.

Higgins, *On the Line,* Miramax, 2001.

Himself/panelist, *Wild Desk Ride* (also known as *Conan O'Brien's "Wild Desk Ride"*), 2001.

Himself and various characters, *Kids in the Hall: Same Guys, New Dresses* (documentary), Eclectic DVD Distribution, 2001.

Himself, *The Frank Truth* (documentary), 2001.

Kids in the Hall: Tour of Duty, Razor & Tie Direct, 2002.

Roy, *Stark Raving Mad,* Columbia TriStar Home Entertainment, 2002.

Nat Porter, *Fancy Dancing* (also known as *Au rythme de l'amour*), Mackinac Media, 2002.

Michael Barnes, *$windle* (also known as *Swindle*), 2002.

Network executive number one, *Run Ronnie Run,* New Line Cinema, 2002.

Himself, *Love & Support,* 2003.

Tour manager, *Grind,* Warner Bros., 2003.

(Uncredited) Henderson, *My Boss's Daughter,* Dimension Films, 2003.

Eric, *Employee of the Month,* DEJ Productions, 2004.

Tom Brennemen, *Ham & Cheese* (also known as *Tom Brennemen*), Decade Distribution, 2004.

Voice of Randall the Goose, *Goose!,* Freestyle Releasing LLC, 2004.

Dr. Denton Whiteside, *Intern Academy* (also known as *Medecin en herbe*), TVA Films, 2004.

Philip Templeman, *Childstar,* Hart Sharp Video, 2004.

Mr. Boy, *Sky High,* Buena Vista, 2005.
Stu Gainor, *Out of Omaha,* 2006.

Film Work:
Executive producer, *The Wrong Guy,* Paragon Entertainment, 1997.
Director, *Kids in the Hall: Same Guys, New Dresses,* Eclectic DVD Distribution, 2001.
Editor, *Kids in the Hall: Tour of Duty,* Razor & Tie Direct, 2002.

Television Appearances; Series:
Various characters, *The Kids in the Hall,* CBC, 1989–95, HBO, 1989–92, and CBS, 1992–95.
David "Dave" Nelson, *NewsRadio* (also known as *News Radio* and *The Station*), NBC, 1995–99.
Stuart Lamarack, *Will & Grace,* NBC, 2004.
Host, *Celebrity Poker Showdown,* Bravo, 2005—.

Television Appearances; Miniseries:
Lewis Allen, *Anne of Green Gables: The Sequel* (also known as *Anne of Avonlea;* re–edited material from *Anne of Avonlea*), CBC, then *WonderWorks,* PBS, 1988.
Al Bean, *From the Earth to the Moon,* HBO, 1998.
Himself, *I Love the '70s,* VH1, 2003.

Television Appearances; Movies:
(Uncredited) *Echoes in the Darkness,* 1987.
Welsh Rabbit in Part 1, Old Ironsides/Smith in Parts 2–3, *The Lawrenceville Stories* (also known as *The Lawrenceville Stories: The Return of Hickey* and *The Prodigious Mr. William Hicks*), 1988.
Principal Warrick, *Prom Queen: The Marc Hall Story* (also known as *Prom Queen*), CTV, 2004.
Eric, *Employee of the Month,* Showtime, 2004.

Television Appearances; Specials:
Welsh Rabbit, *The Prodigious Hickey,* PBS, 1987.
George Barker Smith, "The Return of Hickey," *American Playhouse,* PBS, 1988.
George Barker Smith, "The Beginning of the Firm," *American Playhouse,* PBS, 1989.
The 2000 Canadian Comedy Awards, Comedy Network [Canada], 2000.
Comedy Central Presents the Second Annual Kennedy Center Mark Twain Prize Celebrating the Humor of Jonathan Winters, Comedy Central, 2000.
(With Kids in the Hall) *Sketch Pad,* HBO, 2001.
Himself and David Bowie, *The True Meaning of Christmas Specials,* CBC, 2002.
Host, *The 6th Annual Academy of Interactive Arts & Sciences Awards,* 2003.
Uncensored Comedy: That's Not Funny!, Trio, 2003.
Presenter, *Comedy Central Presents: The Commies,* Comedy Central, 2003.
Great Things About the Holidays, Bravo, 2005.

Television Appearances; Pilots:
John Wilkes Booth, *Toonces, the Cat Who Could Drive a Car* (also known as *Toonces and Friends*), NBC, 1992.
Augustus Friendly, *The Friendlys,* NBC, 2004.
Voice of Principal Galway, *Testing Bob,* ABC, 2005.

Also appeared as title role, *Peter Fuddy,* Fox.

Television Appearances; Episodic:
Mad TV, Fox, 1995.
"Operation Hell on Earth," *Mr. Show,* HBO, 1996.
Robin, *Howie Mandel's Sunny Skies,* 1995, later CBC, 1997.
The Pet Shop, Animal Planet, 1997.
Late Night with Conan O'Brien, NBC, 1997, 1998, 1999.
The Daily Show (also known as *The Daily Show with Jon Stewart* and *The Daily Show with Jon Stewart Global Edition*), Comedy Central, 1999.
Owen, "Hanging with Jake," *Becker,* CBS, 2001.
The Andy Dick Show, MTV, 2001.
Win Ben Stein's Money, Comedy Central, 2002.
Himself, "Mike Myers," *Revealed with Jules Asner,* E! Entertainment Television, 2002.
Francis, "Arthur, Interrupted," *The Tick,* Fox, 2002.
Jay, "Blind Ambition," *Just Shoot Me!,* NBC, 2002.
Voice of Laslow Oswald, "High–Tech House of Horrors," *What's New, Scooby–Doo?* (animated), The WB, 2002.
Various, *The Toronto Show,* 2003.
Voice of Priest, "Fibber: Experiment 032," *Lilo & Stitch: The Series* (animated), The Disney Channel, 2003.
Derek Purcell, "Baby Come Back," *Grounded for Life,* Fox, 2003.
Psychiatrist, "Jung Frankenstein," *The King of Queens,* CBS, 2003.
Last Call with Carson Daly, NBC, 2004.
Principal Harris, "Friends in Low Places," *I'm With Her,* ABC, 2004.
Dinner for Five, Independent Film Channel, 2005.
Himself, "Joey and the Poker," *Joey,* NBC, 2005.
(Uncredited) Voice of himself, *Saturday Night Live* (also known as *SNL*), NBC, 2005.
Voice of Kelsey Grammer's cat, "Stage Fright," *Father of the Pride* (animated), NBC, 2005.
Real Time with Bill Maher, 2005.
The Late Late Show with Craig Ferguson, CBS, 2005, 2006.

Also appeared as Gary Gerbil, "The Wheel Is Not Enough," *Odd Job Jack.*

Television Work; Specials:
Executive producer and director, *The True Meaning of Christmas Specials,* CBC, 2002.

Television Work; Pilots:
Executive producer, *The Hollow Men,* Comedy Central, 2005.

Television Director; Episodic:
"Padded Suit," *NewsRadio* (also known as *News Radio* and *The Station*), NBC, 1999.

Also directed episodes of *The Kids in the Hall.*

RECORDINGS

Video Games:
Voice of Flik, *A Bug's Life,* 1999.

WRITINGS

Screenplays:
(With David Anthony Higgins and Jay Kogen) *The Wrong Guy,* Paragon Entertainment, 1997.
Kids in the Hall: Tour of Duty, Razor & Tie Direct, 2002.

Television Specials:
The True Meaning of Christmas Specials, CBC, 2002.

Television Episodes:
(With others) *The Kids in the Hall,* CBC, 1989–95, HBO, 1989–92, and CBS, 1992–95.

Writings for the Stage:
With others, wrote material for the Kids in the Hall comedy troupe's tour of Canadian and U.S. cities.

OTHER SOURCES

Periodicals:
Advocate, April 30, 1996, p. 56.
Entertainment Weekly, March 24, 1995, p. 72.
Newsweek, April 22, 1996, p. 73.
People Weekly, December 4, 1995, pp. 69–70.
Variety, March 20, 1995, p. 30.

FONTANA, Tom 1951–

PERSONAL

Full name, Thomas Michael Fontana; born September 12, 1951, in Buffalo, NY; son of Charles Louis (in sales) and Marie Angelica (a hospital unit coordinator; maiden name, Internicola) Fontana; married Sagan Lewis (an actress), December 18, 1982 (marriage ended). *Education:* State University College at Buffalo, B.A., speech and theatre arts, 1973. *Religion:* Roman Catholic.

Addresses: *Agent*—United Talent Agency, 9560 Wilshire Blvd., Suite 500, Beverly Hills, CA 90212. *Office*—Levinson/Fontana Company, 185 Broome St., New York, NY 10002.

Career: Writer, producer, creative consultant, and television series creator. Writers Theatre, New York City, playwright in residence, 1975–90; Williamstown Theatre Festival, Williamstown, MA, playwright in residence, 1978–80; Levinson/Fontana Company (production company), partner.

Member: Academy of Television Arts and Sciences, Dramatists Guild, Writers Guild of America West, Authors League of America, American Writers Theatre Foundation (member of the board of directors, 1975–90.)

Awards, Honors: Peabody Award, 1983; Emmy Awards, outstanding writing for a drama series, 1984, 1986, Emmy Award nominations (with others), outstanding writing for a drama series, 1984, 1985, 1986, 1987, 1988, Emmy Award nominations (with others), outstanding drama series, 1984, 1985, 1986, 1987, 1988, Humanitas Prize (with John Masius), 60 minute category, Los Angeles Human Family Institute, 1985, Writers Guild of America Award, Golden Award, New York International Film and Television Festival, People's Choice Award (with John Tinker and John Masius), outstanding writing—drama series, 1987, all for *St. Elsewhere;* Christopher Award, National Association of Catholic Broadcasters, 1986; Maggie Award, Planned Parenthood Association, 1986; Distinguished Alumnus Award, State University at Buffalo, 1987; Hall of Fame, Canisius High School, 1991; Peabody Awards, 1993, 1996, and 1998, Emmy Award, outstanding writing for a drama series, 1993, Television Awards, (with Frank Pugliese, Bonnie Mark, and Julie Martin), episodic drama, Writers Guild of America, 1994, 1996, Founders Award, Viewers for Quality Television, 1995, Best Drama Series, Viewers for Quality Television, 1996, Television Critics Association Awards, program of the year, 1996, best drama series, 1996, 1997, all for *Homicide: Life on the Street;* CableACE Award, best drama series, 1998, Television Award nomination (with Bradford Winters), best episodic drama, Writers Guild of America Award, 2000, for *Oz;* honorary doctorate of letters, State University College at Buffalo, 1998; Emmy Award nomination (with others), outstanding writing for a miniseries or a movie, 2000, for *Homicide: The Movie;* Golden Satellite Award, best television series—drama, International Press Academy, 2000, for *An*

American Tragedy; Evelyn F. Burkey Award, Writers Guild of America (East), 2001; Emmy Award nomination (with others), outstanding writing for a variety, music or comedy program, 2002, for *America: A Tribute to Heroes;* Special Edgar Award, Edgar Allan Poe Awards, Mystery Writers of America, 2005, for *Homicide: Life on the Streets, Oz, The Jury,* and others.

CREDITS

Television Work; Series:

Producer, *St. Elsewhere,* NBC, 1982–88.
Executive producer and creator, *Tattinger's* (also known as *Nick & Hillary*), NBC, 1988–89.
Executive producer and creator, *Home Fires,* NBC, 1991–92.
Executive producer, *Homicide: Life on the Street* (also known as *H: LOTS* and *Homicide*), NBC, 1993–99.
Executive producer, *Philly Heat,* 1994.
Executive producer and creator, *Oz,* HBO, 1997–2003.
Creative consultant, *The Hoop Life,* Showtime, 1999–2000.
Executive producer and series creator, *The Beat,* UPN, 2000.
Executive producer and creator, *The Jury,* Fox, 2004–2005.
Producer and executive producer, *The Bedford Diaries,* The WB, 2006.

Television Work; Miniseries:

Executive producer, *American Tragedy,* 2000.

Television Work; Movies:

Executive producer, *The Prosecutors,* 1996.
Executive producer, *Firehouse,* 1997.
Executive producer, *Homicide: The Movie,* NBC, 2000.
Producer, *The Path to War,* 2000.
Executive producer, *Shot in the Heart,* HBO, 2001.
Executive producer, *Judas,* ABC, 2004.
Executive producer, *Strip Search,* HBO, 2004.
Executive producer, *Anytown, USA,* Film Movement, 2005.

Television Executive Producer; Specials:

Barry Levinson on the Future in the 20th Century: Yesterday's Tomorrows (also known as *The 20th Century: Yesterday's Tomorrows*), 1999.

Television Executive Producer; Pilots:

New Year, ABC, 1993.
Philly Heat, ABC, 1995.
The Prosecutors (movie), NBC, 1996.
The Family Brood, CBS, 1998.
Good Guys, Bad Guys, NBC, 2000.
Utopia, Lifetime, 2001.
Hudson's Law, CBS, 2001.

Bradford, CBS, 2001.
Baseball Wives, HBO, 2002.

Television Appearances; Specials:

Himself, *Anatomy of a "Homicide: Life on the Street"* (documentary), PBS, 1998.
The 70s: The Decade That Changed Television, ABC, 2000.
Les Miserable (documentary), The Learning Channel, 2000.
Himself, *Comedy Central Presents: The N.Y. Friars Club Roast of Hugh Hefner,* Comedy Central, 2001.
Himself, *TV's Most Censored Moments,* Trio and USA Network, 2002.
Himself, *Brilliant But Cancelled: Pilot Season,* Trio, 2003.

Television Appearances; Episodic:

The Museum of Television and Radio: Influences, Bravo, 2000.

Film Work:

Executive producer, *The Press Secretary,* 2001.

Film Appearances:

Himself, *Homicide: Life at the Start* (documentary short), A&E Home Video, 2003.

WRITINGS

Television Episodes:

St. Elsewhere, NBC, 1982–88.
Tattinger's, NBC, 1988–89.
Nick and Hillary, NBC, 1989.
Home Fires, NBC, 1991–92.
Homicide: Life on the Street (also known as *H: LOTS* and *Homicide*), NBC, 1993–99.
Philly Heat, 1994.
Under Fire, 1995–96.
Oz, HBO, 1997–2003.
"The Beat Goes On," *The Beat,* UPN, 2000.
"Bangers," *The Jury,* Fox, 2004–2005.
The Bedford Diaries, The WB, 2006.

Television Stories; Episodic:

(With John Tinker and Bruce Paltrow) "Madonna and Child Reunion," *Home Fires,* NBC, 1992.
(With John Tinker and Bruce Paltrow) "Sibling Rivalry," *Home Fires,* NBC, 1992.
(With Bradford Winters) "U.S. Male," *Oz,* HBO, 1999.
(With James Yoshimura) "Lamentation on the Reservation," *The Jury,* Fox, 2004.
(With James Yoshimura) "The Boxer," *The Jury,* Fox, 2004.

(With James Yoshimura) "Too Jung to Die," *The Jury,* Fox, 2004.

(With James Yoshimura) "Last Rites," *The Jury,* Fox, 2004.

(With James Yoshimura) "Three Boys and a Gun," *The Jury,* Fox, 2004.

(With James Yoshimura) "The Honeymoon Suite," *The Jury,* Fox, 2004.

(With James Yoshimura) "Mail Order Mystery," *The Jury,* Fox, 2004.

(With James Yoshimura) "Memories," *The Jury,* Fox, 2004.

Also wrote (with Channing Gibson) "Tour of Doody," *Tattinger's* (also known as *Nick & Hillary*), NBC; (with John Tinker) "El Sid," *Tattinger's* (also known as *Nick & Hillary*), NBC; numerous stories for *Homicide: Life on the Streets* (also known as *H: LOTS* and *Homicide*), NBC; numerous stories for *St. Elsewhere,* NBC.

Television Movies:
Firehouse, 1997.
Homicide: The Movie, NBC, 2000.
Judas, ABC, 2004.
Strip Search, HBO, 2004.

Television Specials:
The Fourth Wiseman, ABC, 1985.
America: A Tribute to Heroes, 2001.

Television Pilots:
Home Fires, NBC, 1992.
New Year, ABC, 1993.
Philly Heat, ABC, 1995.
The Prosecutors (movie), NBC, 1996.
The Family Brood, CBS, 1998.
Good Guys, Bad Guys, NBC, 2000.
Hudson's Law, CBS, 2001.
(And story, with James Yoshimura) *The Jury,* Fox, 2004.
The Bedford Diaries, The WB, 2006.

Screenplays:
First Thing Monday, 2000.

Stage Plays:
Johnny Appleseed: A Noh Play (one–act play), Studio Arena, Buffalo, NY, 1970.
This Is on Me: Dorothy Parker (two–act adaptation), American Contemporary Theatre, Buffalo, NY, 1971, then Williamstown Theatre Festival, Williamstown, MA, 1979.
An Awfully Big Adventure: An Entertainment (two–act play), Writers Theatre, New York City, 1975.
One/Potato/More, Direct Theatre, New York City, 1975.
Nonsense!, Writers Theatre, 1977.

The Underlings (two–act play), Cincinnati Playhouse in the Park, Cincinnati, OH, 1978, then Writers Theatre, 1979, later Williamstown Theatre Festival, 1980, then Eisenhower College, Elmira, NY, 1981, later Studio Arena, Buffalo, NY, 1982, then Thomas More College, Crestview Hills, KY, 1983, later Friends Theatre Company, New York City, 1984.
The Overcoat; or Clothes Make the Man (two–act adaptation from a short story by Nikolay Gogol), Williamstown Theatre Festival, 1978, then Writers Theatre, 1981.
Old Fashioned, Chelsea Theatre Center, New York City, 1979, then Linwood Summer Theatre, Linwood, NY, 1980, later Colonnades Theatre Lab, New York City, 1981.
The Spectre Bridegroom, Williamstown Theatre Festival, 1981.
Movin' Mountains (two–act play), McCarter Theatre, Princeton, NJ, 1981, then Writers Theatre, 1982.
Mime (one–act play), One Act Theatre, San Francisco, CA, 1982, then One Act Theatre, Los Angeles, 1983.
Imaginary Lovers (one–act play), American Conservatory Theatre, San Francisco, 1982, then One Act Theatre, Los Angeles, 1983, later Writers Theatre, 1984.

Graphic Novels:
Wrote a Batman graphic novel, Marvel, 2006.

OTHER SOURCES

Books:
Contemporary Authors, Vol. 130, Gale, 1990.

Periodicals:
Entertainment Weekly, July 11, 1997, p. 36.
New York, July 14, 1997, p. 38.
The Writer, March, 2003, p. 33.

FORBES, Michelle 1967–

PERSONAL

Born January 8 (some sources February 17), 1967, in Austin, TX; married Ross Kettle (an actor), 1990 (divorced).

Addresses: *Agent*—Domain, 9229 Sunset Blvd., Suite 415, Los Angeles, CA 90069. *Manager*—Framework Entertainment, 9057 Nemo St., Suite C, West Hollywood, CA 90069.

Career: Actress.

Awards, Honors: Daytime Emmy Award nomination, outstanding supporting actress, 1988, *Soap Opera Digest* Award nomination, outstanding villainess—daytime, 1990, both for *Guiding Light;* Saturn Award nomination, best actress, Academy of Science Fiction, Fantasy and Horror Films, 1994, for *Kalifornia;* Screen Actors Guild Award nomination (with others), outstanding performance by an ensemble in a drama, 2003, for *24.*

CREDITS

Film Appearances:
Maggie Rudden, *The Playboys,* 1992.
Carrie Laughlin, *Kalifornia,* Gramercy Pictures, 1993.
Nerissa, *Love Bites* (also known as *Love Bites: The Reluctant Vampire*), 1993.
Helen, *The Road Killers* (also known as *Roadflower*), Miramax, 1994.
Dawn Lockard, *Swimming with Sharks* (also known as *The Boss* and *The Buddy Factor*), Trimark, 1995.
Rinda Woolley, *Black Day Blue Night* (also known as *Black Day/Blue Night*), Republic Pictures Home Video, 1995.
Brazen, *Escape from L.A.* (also known as *John Carpenter's "Escape from L.A."*), Paramount, 1996.
Mary, *Just Looking,* 1997.
Valeria, *Dry Martini,* 1998.
Mary, *Bullfighter,* Phaedra Cinema, 2000.
Francene, *Perfume* (also known as *Dress to Kill*), Lions Gate Films, 2001.
Madge Grubb, *American Girl* (also known as *Confessions of an American Girl*), New Line Cinema, 2002.
Mrs. Voss, *Dandelion,* Ruth Pictures, 2004.
Dede Dragonfly, *Al Roach: Private Insectigator* (animated short), 2004.

Television Appearances; Series:
Solita Carrera/Dr. Sonni Wells y Carrera Lewis, *Guiding Light* (also known as *The Guiding Light*), CBS, 1987–89.
Lieutenant Ro Laren, *Star Trek: The Next Generation* (also known as *Star Trek: TNG*), syndicated, 1991–94.
Chief Medical Examiner Julianna Cox, *Homicide: Life on the Street* (also known as *Homicide* and *H: LOTS*), NBC, 1996–98.
Dr. Lyla Garrity, *Wonderland,* ABC, 2000.
Helen York, *The District,* CBS, 2000.
Lynne Kresage, *24,* Fox, 2002–2003.

Television Appearances; Miniseries:
Susan Metcalfe, *Messiah* (also known as *Messiah I: The First Killings*), BBC, 2001.
Susan Metcalfe, *Messiah 2: Vengeance Is Mine,* BBC, 2002.

Rory Hammett, *Johnson County War,* Hallmark Channel, 2002.
Susan Metcalfe, *Messiah III: The Promise,* BBC, 2004.

Television Appearances; Movies:
Dr. Julianna Cox, *Homicide: The Movie,* NBC, 2000.
Miranda Zero, *Global Frequency,* 2005.

Television Appearances; Specials:
Dr. Julianna Cox, *Anatomy of a "Homicide: Life on the Street"* (documentary), PBS, 1998.
Herself, *24: Access All Areas* (documentary), BBC, 2003.

Television Appearances; Awards Presentations:
The 15th Annual Daytime Emmy Awards, CBS, 1988.

Television Appearances; Pilots:
District Attorney Rachel Simone, *The Prosecutors* (movie), NBC, 1996.
Dr. Lyla Garrity, *Wonderland,* 2000.

Television Appearances; Episodic:
"The Inside Man," *Shannon's Deal,* NBC, 1990.
Dara, "Half a Life," *Star Trek: The Next Generation* (also known as *Star Trek: TNG*), syndicated, 1991.
Gym instructor, "The Fugitive Priest Mystery," *Father Dowling Mysteries* (also known as *Father Dowling Investigates*), NBC, 1991.
Julie, "The Big Salad," *Seinfeld,* NBC, 1994.
FBI agent Jamie Pratt, "A Stitch in Time," *The Outer Limits* (also known as *The New Outer Limits*), Showtime, 1996.
Assistant district attorney Julia Trent, "Executioner," *Brimstone,* 1998.
Assistant district attorney Jill Sorenson, "Rape Kit," *Strong Medicine,* Lifetime, 2002.
Jules Sorenson, "Recovery Times," *Strong Medicine,* Lifetime, 2002.
Lena, "Get Your Mack On," *Fastlane,* Fox, 2002.
Herself, *Pure 24,* BBC3, 2003.
Reena, *Love Is the Drug,* 2004.
Dr. Maggie Sinclair, "Another Mister Sloane," *Alias,* ABC, 2005.
Zoya Petikof, "Thief of Hearts," *The Inside,* Fox, 2005.
Female agent, "End of the Tunnel," *Prison Break,* Fox, 2005.
Admiral Helena Cain, "Pegasus," *Battlestar Galactica,* Sci–Fi Channel and Sky One, 2005.
Prison Break, Fox, 2005.
Admiral Helena Cain, "Resurrection Ship: Parts 1 & 2," *Battlestar Galactica,* Sci–Fi Channel and Sky One, 2006.

Also appeared in *Nasty Boys,* NBC.

Stage Appearances:
Follies, Golden Nugget Casino, Atlantic City, NJ, 1982.
Call It Clover, Los Angeles, 1994.

Also appeared in *Blithe Spirit; Much Ado about Nothing.*

RECORDINGS

Video Games:
Ensign Ro Laren, *Star Trek: The Next Generation Companion,* 1999.
Voice of Dr. Judith Mossman, *Half–Life 2,* Sierra Studios, 2004.

OTHER SOURCES

Periodicals:
Entertainment Weekly, May 26, 1995, p. 22; August 23, 1996, p. 134.
New York, December 2, 1996, pp. 130–31.
Variety, September 12, 1994, p. 40.

FORMAN, Milos 1932–
(Jan Tomas)

PERSONAL

First name pronounced "Mee–losh"; original name, Jan Tomas Forman; born February 18, 1932, in Caslav, Czechoslovakia; immigrated to the United States, 1968; naturalized citizen, November 30, 1977; son of Rudolf (a professor) and Anna (maiden name, Svabova) Forman (both died in German concentration camps during World War II); raised by family members; married Jana Brejchova (an actress), 1951 (divorced, 1956); married Vera Kresadlova (a singer), 1964 (divorced, 1999); married Martina Zborilova (Forman's film crew assistant), November 28, 1999; children: (second marriage) Matej and Petr (twins); (third marriage) Andrew and James (twins). *Education:* Studied screenwriting at the Film Institute at the University of Prague, 1950–55; also studied at the Academy of Music and Dramatic Art, Prague, and Laterna Magika, Prague, 1958–62.

Addresses: *Agent*—Lantz Office, 200 W. 57th St., Suite 503, New York, NY 10019. *Manager*—Nancy Seltzer & Associates, 6220 Del Valle Dr., Los Angeles, CA 90048.

Career: Director, producer, writer, and actor. Directed documentaries for Czech television, 1954–56; worked as an assistant writer and director with Laterna Magika (Magic Lantern, theater group), 1958–62; Columbia University, New York City, co–director film studies, 1975—, film professor, 1978—; Cannes Film Festival, 1972, 1985.

Member: Director's Guild of America (Guild's President Committee, 1986—).

Awards, Honors: Czechoslovak Film Critics Award, and first prize, Locarno Film Festival, 1963, both for *Peter and Pavla;* Golden Sail Award, best feature film, Locarno International Film Festival, 1964, for *Black Peter;* Grand Prix Award, 17th International Film Festival, Locarno, 1964; Academy Award nomination, best foreign film, Golden Lion Award nomination, Venice Film Festival, 1965, French Film Academy Award, best film, 1966, Bodil Award, best European film, Bodil Festival, 1967, all for *Loves of a Blonde;* Jussi Award, best foreign director, 1967, for *Black Peter* and *Loves of a Blonde;* Academy Award nomination, best foreign film, 1967, for *The Fireman's Ball;* Grand Prize of the Jury and Golden Film Award nomination, Cannes International Film Festival, 1971, Writers Guild of America Award screen nomination (with Jean–Claude Carriere, John Guare and John Klein), best comedy written directly for the screen, Film Award nominations, best screenplay (with Jean–Claude Carriere, John Guare and John Klein), best director, British Academy of Film and Television Arts, Bodil Award, best American film, Bodil Festival, 1972, all for *Taking Off;* Academy Award, best director, Directors Guild of America Award (with others), outstanding directorial achievement in motion pictures, 1975, Golden Globe Award, best director—motion picture, Silver Ribbon Award, best director—foreign film, Italian National Syndicate of Film Journalists, Bodil Award, best American film, David di Donatello Award, best director—foreign film, 1976, Film Award, best direction, British Academy of Film and Television Arts, Reader's Choice Award, best foreign language film director, Kinema Junpo, Kansas City Film Critics Circle Award, best director, Cesar Award nomination, best foreign film, 1977, all for *One Flew Over the Cuckoo's Nest;* David di Donatello Award, best director—foreign film, 1979, Cesar Award nomination, best foreign film, 1980, both for *Hair;* Golden Globe Award nomination, best director—motion picture, 1982, for *Ragtime;* Academy Award, best director, Directors Guild of America Award (with Michael Hausman), outstanding directorial achievement in motion pictures, Los Angeles Film Critics Association Award, best director, 1984, Golden Globe Award, best director—motion picture, Cesar Award, best foreign film, Silver Ribbon Award, best director—foreign film, Italian National Syndicate of Film Journalists, Robert Award, best foreign film, Jussi Award, best foreign filmmaker, Joseph Plateau Award, best director, David di Donatello Award, best director—foreign film, Amanda Award, best foreign feature film, 1985, Film Award nomination (with Saul Zaentz), best film, British

Academy of Film and Television Arts, Kinema Junpo Award, best foreign language film, Guild Film Award—Gold, foreign film, 1986, DVD Premiere Award nomination (with Peter Shaffer), best audio commentary, library release, 2003, all for *Amadeus;* Cesar Award nomination, best director, 1990, for *Valmont;* Freedom of Expression Award (with Oliver Stone), National Board of Review, 1996, Academy Award nomination, best director, Golden Globe Award, best director—motion picture, Golden Bear award, Berlin Film Festival, European Film Award, outstanding European Achievement in World Cinema, 1997, Czech Lion Award nomination, Czech Film and Television Academy, best foreign language film, 1998, all for *The People vs. Larry Flynt;* John Huston Award, Artists Rights Foundation, 1997; Special Prize for Outstanding Contribution to World Cinema, Karlovy Vary International Film Festival, 1997; Artistic Achievement Award, Czech Film and Television Academy, 1998; Lifetime Achievement Award, Palm Springs International Film Festival, 2000; CineMerit Award, Munich Film Festival, 2000; Silver Berlin Bear, best director, and Golden Berlin Bear Award nomination, Berlin International Film Festival, 2000, Czech Lion Award nomination, best foreign language film, 2001, all for *Man on the Moon;* Film Society Award for Lifetime Achievement in Directing, San Francisco International Film Festival, 2004; Billy Wilder Award, National Board of Review, 2004.

CREDITS

Film Director:

Il laterna magika (also known as *Magic Lantern II*), 1960.

Kdyby Ty Muziky Nebyly (also known as *The Glory of the Brass Bands, If It Weren't for Music, If There Were No Music,* and *Why Do We Need All the Brass Bands?*), 1963.

Audition (also known as *Konkurs;* composed of two short films, *If Only They Ain't Had Them Bands* and *Talent Competition*), 1963.

Black Peter (also known as *Cerny Petr* and *Peter and Pavla*), 1963.

Loves of a Blonde (also known as *Lasky jedne plavovlasky* and *A Blonde in Love*), Prominent, 1966.

The Firemen's Ball (also known as *Hori, ma panenko, Al fuoco pompieri!,Fuoco, ragazza mia, The Fireman's Ball* and *Lottery,* and *Like a House on Fire*), Cinema V, 1967.

Taking Off, Universal, 1971.

I Miss Sonia Henie (also known as *Nedostaje mi Sonja Henie*), 1971.

"The Decathlon," *Visions of Eight* (documentary; also known as *Munchen 1972—8 beruhmte Regisseure sehen die Spiele der XX. Olympiade, Olympiade Munchen 1972,* and *Olympic Visions*), Cinema V, 1973.

One Flew Over the Cuckoo's Nest, United Artists, 1975.

Hair, United Artists, 1979.

Ragtime, Paramount, 1981.

Amadeus (also known as *Peter Shaffer's "Amadeus"*), Orion, 1984.

Valmont, Orion, 1989.

The People vs. Larry Flynt (also known as *Larry Flynt*), Columbia, 1996.

The Little Black Book, Universal, 1998.

Man on the Moon (also known as *Andy Kaufman* and *Der Mondmann*), Universal, 1999.

Goya's Ghosts, 2006.

Film Work; Other:

First assistant director, *Stenata,* 1957.

Second assistant director, *Dedecek automobil,* 1957.

Assistance, *Voices from the Attic,* Siren Pictures, 1988.

Producer, *Dreams of Love,* 1990.

Executive producer, *Way Past Cool,* Redeemable Features/Act III Communications/Price1, 2000.

Executive producer, *Nomad,* 2004.

Film Appearances:

Stribrny vitr (also known as *Strieborny vietor* and *The Silver Wind*), 1954.

Dedecek automobil, 1957.

Himself, *Meeting Milos Forman,* Macmillan Films, 1971.

Himself, *Chytilova Versus Forman* (documentary), 1981.

Before the Nickelodeon: The Cinema of Edwin S. Porter (documentary), First Run Features, 1982.

Himself, *Chytilova Versus Forman,* 1984.

Himself, *50 Years of Action!,* 1986.

Dmitri, *Heartburn,* Paramount, 1986.

Lazlo–the landlord, *New Year's Day,* International Rainbow, 1989.

Narrator, *Why Havel?* (documentary), 1991.

Behind the Scenes: A Portrait of Pierre Guffroy (documentary; also known as *L'Envers du decors: Portrait de Pierre Guffroy*), Ariane Distribution, 1992.

Himself, *Who Is Henry Jaglom?* (documentary), First Run Features, 1997.

Himself, *Completely Cuckoo* (documentary; also known as *The Making of "One Flew Over the Cuckoo's Nest"*), Warner Home Video, 1997.

Father Havel, *Keeping the Faith,* Buena Vista, 2000.

Himself, *In the Shadow of Hollywood* (documentary; also known as *A l'ombre d'Hollywood*), National Film Board of Canada, 2000.

Himself, *Man on the Moon: Behind the Moonlight* (documentary short; also known as *Spotlight on Location: Man on the Moon*), Universal Studios Home Video, 2000.

Himself, *The Making of "Amadeus"* (documentary), Warner Home Video, 2002.

Himself, *A Decade Under the Influence* (documentary), IFC Films, 2003.

Himself, *Charlie: The Life and Art of Charles Chaplin* (documentary), 2003.

Himself, *Tell Them Who You Are* (documentary), Think-Film, 2004.

Himself, *Francois Truffaut, an Autobiography,* 2004.

Himself, *Cineastes contra magnats* (documentary), Canonigo Films, 2005.

Television Appearances; Miniseries:
Interviewee, *Cold War,* CNN, 1998.

Television Director; Movies:
Dobre placena prochazka, 1966.

Television Appearances; Specials:
The 48th Annual Academy Awards, ABC, 1976.
James Cagney: That Yankee Doodle Dandy (documentary), 1981.
The 57th Annual Academy Awards, ABC, 1985.
The Statue of Liberty (documentary), PBS, 1985.
The Way We Wear (documentary), PBS, 1988.
Milos Forman: Portrait (documentary), PBS, 1989.
American Tribute to Vaclav Havel and a Celebration of Democracy in Czechoslovakia, PBS, 1990.
Havel's Audience with History, PBS, 1990.
The Republic Pictures Story (documentary), AMC, 1991.
Drawn from Memory, PBS, 1995.
Cannes ... Les 400 Coups, 1997.
The 69th Annual Academy Awards, ABC, 1997.
Inside the Academy Awards, TNT, 1997.
Charlie Chaplin: A Tramp's Life (documentary), Arts and Entertainment, 1998.
One Flew over the Cuckoo's Nest (documentary), The Learning Channel, 1998.
Himself, *V centru filmu–v teple domova* (also known as *In the Center of Film—In the Warmth of Home*), 1998.
Himself, *Eigentlich ist nichts geschehen–Der Film des Prager Fruhlings,* 1998.
Himself, *Milos Forman: Kino ist Wahrheit,* 2000.
The Beatles Revolution (documentary), 2000.
(Uncredited) Himself, *Hollywood Rocks the Movies: The 1970s,* 2002.
AFI's 100 Years ... 100 Heroes & Villains (also known as *AFI's 100 Years, 100 Heroes & Villains: America's Greatest Screen Characters*), CBS, 2003.
Voice of himself, *A Room Nearby,* PBS, 2003.
Francois Truffaut, une autobiographie, 2004.
San Sebastian 2005: Cronica de Carlos Boyero, 2005.

Television Appearances; Episodic:
Late Night with David Letterman, NBC, 1986.
Mundo VIP, 1997.
Himself, *Paskvil,* 1997.
Himself, "Saul Zaentz: A Tribute," *The South Bank Show,* ITV, 1998.

Conversations in World Cinema, Sundance, 2000.
Himself, *Cinema mil,* 2005.

Also appeared as himself, "The Films of Milos Forman," *The Directors,* Encore.

Stage Director:
The Little Black Book, Helen Hayes Theatre, New York City, 1972.

WRITINGS

Screenplays:
Nechte to na mne (also known as *Leave It to Me*), 1955.
Stenata, 1957.
Laterna magika II (also known as *Magic Lantern II*), 1960.
Kdyby ty muziky nebyly (also known as *If It Weren't for Music, If There Were No Music, The Glory of the Brass Bands,* and *Who Do We Need All the Brass Bands?*), 1963.
Audition (also known as *Konkurs* and *Competition*), 1963.
Black Peter (also known as *Cerny Petr* and *Peter and Pavla*), 1963.
Loves of a Blonde (also known as *Lasky jedne plavovlasky* and *A Blonde in Love*), 1965.
Dedecek automobil, 1965.
The Firemen's Ball (also known as *Hori, ma panenko, Al fuoco pompieri!, Fuoco, ragazza mia, The Firemen's Ball and Lottery,* and *Like a House on Fire*), 1967.
The Nail Clippers (also known as *La pince a ongles*), 1969.
Taking Off, Universal, 1971.
Valmont, Orion, 1989.
Goya's Ghosts, 2006.

Autobiography:
(With Jan Novak) *Turnaround: A Memoir,* Villard Books, 1994.

OTHER SOURCES

Books:
Authors and Artists for Young Adults, Vol. 63, Thompson Gale, 2005.
Dizdarevic, Jasmin, *Konkurs na rezisera Milose Formana,* AG Kult (Prague), 1990.
Foll, January, *Milos Forman,* Cs. Filmovy ustav (Prague), 1989.
International Dictionary of Films and Filmmakers, Volume 2: Directors, 4th ed., St. James Press, 2000.
Slater, Thomas J., *Milos Forman: A Bio–Bibliography,* Greenwood Press, 1987.

FOX, Emilia 1974–

PERSONAL

Full name, Emilia Rose Elizabeth Fox; born July 31, 1974, in London, England; daughter of Edward Fox (an actor) and Joanna David (an actress); married Jared Harris (an actor), July 16, 2005. *Education:* Attended Oxford University.

Addresses: *Agent*—Kathryn Fleming, Peters, Fraser & Dunlop, Drury House, 34–43 Russell St., London WC2B 5HA, England.

Career: Actress. Graduate Fashion awards, judge, 2002; British Fashion awards, host, 2005; Whitbread Book awards, panelist. Voice–over artist and appeared in commercials. Performer at benefits.

Awards, Honors: Tric Award, new television talent of the year, Television and Radio Industries Club, 1998; Cult TV Festival, breakthrough performance, 2000, for *Randall & Hopkirk (Deceased)*; Benjamin Franklin Award for adult fiction, c. 2002, for *I Capture the Castle*; Eagle Award nomination, best actress, Polish Film awards, 2003, for *The Pianist*; Spoken Word Award, female reader of the year, 2004; Audie Award, solo narration—female, Audio Publishers Association, 2005, for *Destination Unknown.*

CREDITS

Television Appearances; Series:
Georgiana Darcy, *Pride and Prejudice,* BBC and Arts and Entertainment, 1995.
Dale Carver, *Other People's Children,* BBC, 2000.
Jeannie Hurst, *Randall & Hopkirk (Deceased)* (also known as *Randall & Hopkirk (Deceased)—Series I*), BBC, 2000–2001.
Dr. Nikki Alexander, *Silent Witness,* BBC, beginning 2004, also broadcast on Arts and Entertainment.

Television Appearances; Miniseries:
Mrs. de Winter, *Rebecca,* Carlton Television, 1997, broadcast on *Masterpiece Theatre* (also known as *ExxonMobil Masterpiece Theatre* and *Mobil Masterpiece Theatre*), PBS, 1997.
Vanessa Ratcliffe, *The Round Tower* (also known as *Catherine Cookson's "The Round Tower"*), Tyne Tees Television, 1998.
Jackie Shipton, *Bad Blood,* Carlton Television, 1999.
Minette Roland, *The Scarlet Pimpernel,* BBC and Arts and Entertainment, 1999.

Spig, *Shooting the Past,* BBC, 1999, broadcast on *Masterpiece Theatre* (also known as *ExxonMobil Masterpiece Theatre* and *Mobil Masterpiece Theatre*), PBS, 1999.
Cassandra (princess of Troy), *Helen of Troy,* USA Network, 2003.
Jane Seymour, *Henry VIII,* Independent Television, 2003, broadcast on *Masterpiece Theatre* (also known as *ExxonMobil Masterpiece Theatre* and *Mobil Masterpiece Theatre*), PBS, 2004.
Lady Margaret, *Gunpowder, Treason & Plot,* BBC–2, 2004.
Amy Dudley, *The Virgin Queen,* broadcast on *Masterpiece Theatre* (also known as *ExxonMobil Masterpiece Theatre* and *Mobil Masterpiece Theatre*), PBS, 2005, then broadcast on BBC–4, 2006.

Television Appearances; Movies:
Ann Devenish, *Bright Hair* (also known as *Der Moerder von Jenners Wood*), BBC, 1997.
Clara Copperfield, *David Copperfield,* BBC, 1999, broadcast on *Masterpiece Theatre* (also known as *ExxonMobil Masterpiece Theatre* and *Mobil Masterpiece Theatre*), PBS, 2000.
The Life and Death of Peter Sellers, HBO, 2003.

Television Appearances; Specials:
Karoline von Esterhazy, *The Temptation of Franz Schubert* (also known as *The Double Life of Franz Schubert* and *The Temptation of Schubert*), Channel 4 (England), 1997.
Niki, *Blink* (short), Channel 4, 1998.
Narrator, *The Private Lives of Pompeii* (documentary), Channel 4, 2002.
Voice of the nightingale, "The Nightingale and the Rose," *Wilde Stories* (animated), Channel 4, 2003.

Television Appearances; Awards Presentations:
Herself, *The Evening Standard Theatre Awards,* Independent Television, 2003.
Presenter, *Classical Brits 2004* (also known as *Classical Brit Awards*), Independent Television, 2004.
Herself, *The Evening Standard British Film Awards,* Independent Television 3, 2005.

Television Appearances; Episodic:
Princess Alice, "Queen Victoria's Holiday Home," *Treasure Houses,* BBC, c. 1987.
Charlie Moyes, "The Doctor's Opinion," *Verdict,* Yorkshire Television, 1998.
GMTV, Independent Television, 2001, 2003, multiple episodes in 2004, 2006.
Voice of Kate Bartram, "The Empire of Good Intentions," *A History of Britain* (also known as *Simon Schama, A History of Britain*), BBC and History Channel, 2002.

Voice of the young Queen Victoria, "Victoria and Her Sisters," *A History of Britain* (also known as *Simon Schama, A History of Britain*), BBC and History Channel, 2002.

Wilma Lettings, "Faithless," *Coupling,* BBC, 2002.

Wilma Lettings, "Unconditional Sex," *Coupling,* BBC, 2002.

RI:SE, Channel 4 (England), 2002.

Bo' Selecta! (also known as *Bo' Selecta! Vol. 3* and *Ho Ho Ho Selecta!*), Channel 4, 2003.

Today with Des and Mel, Independent Television, 2003.

Richard & Judy, Channel 4, 2005.

Joanna Burton, "The Moving Finger," *Marple* (also known as *Agatha Christie's "Marple,"* *Agatha Christie's "Miss Marple,"* *Marple: The Moving Finger,* and *Miss Marple*), Independent Television, 2006, also broadcast on Arts and Entertainment and CBC.

Narrator, "Stephen Poliakoff—A Brief History of Now," *Time Shift,* BBC–4, 2006.

Film Appearances:

Pippa, *The Rat Trap* (short film), AtomFilms, 1999.

Gina, *The Magic of Vincent* (short film), Vera Films, 2000.

Dorota, *The Pianist* (also known as *Der Pianist, Pianista,* and *Le pianiste*), Focus Features, 2002.

Reader, *Cover Stories: Pride and Prejudice* (documentary), 2002.

Sabina Spielrein, *Prendimi l'anima* (also known as *The Soul Keeper* and *L'ame en jeu*), Medusa Distribuzione, 2002.

Swinging girl, *Hideous Man* (short film), Harry Nash Films, 2002.

Claire Bligh, *Three Blind Mice* (also known as *Une souris verte*), First Look Home Entertainment, 2003.

Fay, *The Republic of Love,* Seville Pictures, 2003.

Sharon, *Cashback* (short film), British Film Institute, 2004.

Kate, *Things to Do before You're 30* (also known as *You Don't Have to Say You Love Me*), Warner Bros., 2005.

Nancy Browning, *La tigre e la neve* (also known as *The Tiger and the Snow*), Focus Features, 2005.

Rosie Jones, *Keeping Mum,* Independent Films, 2005.

Sharon Pintey, *Cashback* (full–length film), Left Turn Films/Ugly Duckling Films, 2006.

Voice of Bettina (an animal activist), *Free Jimmy* (animated), Storm Studio, 2006.

Some sources cite appearances in *Cabbages and Queens,* c. 2003; *Save Angel Hope,* IAC Film, 2005; and *Spirit Trap,* Archangel Filmworks, 2005.

Stage Appearances:

Anya Ranyevskaya, *The Cherry Orchard,* Royal Shakespeare Company, Albery Theatre, London, 1997.

An Evening of Words and Music (benefit), Imperial War Museum, London, 1997.

Title role, *Katherine Howard,* Chichester Festival Theatre, Chichester, England, 1998.

Anne, *Good,* Donmar Warehouse Theatre, London, 1999.

Isabel, *Richard II,* and Virgilia, *Coriolanus* (double–bill), Almeida Theatre, London, 2000, then Brooklyn Academy of Music, Harvey Theatre, Brooklyn, New York City, 2000.

Alison, *Look Back in Anger,* Old Fire Station Theatre, Oxford, England, 2002.

Madame de Tourvel, *Les Liaisons Dangereuses,* Playhouse Theatre, London, 2003.

Appeared as Ellie, *Heartbreak House,* Oxford Playhouse, Oxford, England.

Radio Appearances; Series:

Harriet, *Georgiana, Duchess of Devonshire,* BBC Radio 4, 1999.

Narrator, *The Montana Stories* (consists of "A Cup of Tea," "The Doll's House," "Honeymoon," and "Marriage a la Mode"), BBC Radio 4, 2001.

Reader, *Girl from the South,* BBC Radio 4, 2002.

Reader, *Madame Bovary,* 2002.

Voice of Joan, *Love Lessons,* BBC Radio 4, 2003.

Where Angels Fear to Tread, BBC Radio 4, 2003.

Radio Appearances; Miniseries:

Title role, *Effi Briest,* BBC Radio 4, 1998.

Sydney Bidulph, *The Memoirs of Sydney Bidulph,* BBC Radio 4, 2000.

Amy Reardon, *New Grub Street,* BBC Radio 4, 2002.

Clelia Conti, *The Charterhouse of Parma,* BBC Radio 4, 2002.

Radio Appearances; Specials:

Marie–Jo Simenon, "Murder in Paris," *Saturday Playhouse,* BBC Radio 4, 1998.

Eva, *Don't Be a Stranger,* BBC Radio 4, 1999.

"Killing Me Softly," *Thriller Playhouse,* BBC Radio 4, c. 2000.

Molly Bloxham, *Barnes and Molly,* BBC Radio 4, 2000.

Celia Cumber, *Queen Gertrude PLC,* BBC Radio 4, 2001.

Hero, *Much Ado about Nothing,* BBC Radio 3, 2001.

Theodora Darrell, *Agatha Christie's "Magnolia Blossom,"* BBC Radio 4, 2002.

Reader, *Carlyle's House and Other Sketches,* BBC Radio 4, 2003.

Voice of Nella, *Missing Pieces,* BBC Radio 4, 2003.

Also appeared in *Barnes Wallace Letters,* BBC Radio.

Radio Appearances; Episodic:

Lady Isabel, "The Day Trip," *Devonia,* BBC Radio 4, 1999.

"Black Earth City," *Book of the Week,* BBC Radio 4, 2002.

Reader, *Poetry Please,* BBC Radio 4, multiple episodes in 2002.

"The Explorer's Daughter," *Book of the Week,* BBC Radio 4, 2004.

RECORDINGS

Videos:

Spig, *Shooting the Past: Spig's Story,* 1999.

Audiobooks:

Daphne du Maurier, *The Daphne du Maurier Collection: "Rebecca/Frenchman's Creek/Jamaica Inn,"* Hodder & Stoughton, 1997.

Daphne du Maurier, *Rebecca,* 1997, Acorn Media, 2000, abridged version released by Hodder Headline, 2003.

Anne Bronte, *Agnes Grey,* Chivers Audio Books, 1998.

Tim Bowler, *River Boy,* Chivers Children's Audio Books, 1999.

Ben Elton, *Inconceivable,* HarperCollins, 1999.

Jane Green, *Mr. Maybe,* Penguin Audiobooks, 1999.

Josie Lloyd and Emlyn Rees, *Come Again,* Random House Audiobooks, 1999.

Jared Diamond, *Why Is Sex Fun?: The Evolution of Human Sexuality,* Orion Audio, 2000.

Honey Moon, Hodder & Stoughton, 2000.

Val McDermid, *Killing the Shadows,* HarperCollins, 2001.

Barbara Vine, *Grasshopper,* Chivers Audio Books, 2001.

Dodie Smith, *I Capture the Castle,* CSA Telltapes/Chivers Audio Books/Audio Partners, c. 2001.

Celia Rees, *Witch Child,* Bloomsbury Audio Books, 2002.

William Shakespeare, *King Lear,* Naxos Audiobooks, 2002.

Anita Shreve, *Sea Glass,* Orion Audio, 2002.

Linda Chapman, *Bright Lights,* Penguin Children's Audiobooks, 2003.

Ann Halam, *Dr. Franklin's Island,* Chivers Audio Books, 2003.

Joanne Harris, *Holy Fools,* Random House Audiobooks, 2003.

Diana Wynne Jones, *The Merlin Conspiracy,* 2003.

Carole Matthews, *For Better, For Worse,* HarperAudio, 2003.

Celia Rees, *Sorceress,* Bloomsbury Audio Books, 2003.

Peter Robinson, *Caedmon's Song,* Macmillan Audio Books, 2003.

Meg Cabot, *Nicola and the Viscount,* BBC Audiobooks, 2004.

Agatha Christie, *Death Comes as the End,* HarperCollins, 2004.

Agatha Christie, *Destination Unknown,* HarperCollins, 2004.

Agatha Christie, *The Man in the Brown Suit,* HarperCollins, 2004.

Agatha Christie, *Why Didn't They Ask Evens?,* HarperCollins, 2004.

Paulo Coelho, *Eleven Minutes,* Thorsons, 2004.

Gustave Flaubert, *Madame Bovary,* Hodder & Stoughton, 2004.

Sally Gardner, *The Smallest Girl Ever,* Orion Audio, 2004.

D. H. Lawrence, *Lady Chatterley's Lover,* CSA Word, 2004.

William Shakespeare, *The Tempest,* Naxos Audiobooks, 2004.

Georgie Adams, *The Three Little Witches Storybook,* Orion Audio, 2005.

Agatha Christie, *They Came to Baghdad,* HarperCollins, 2005.

Philippa Gregory, *The Constant Princess,* edited by Kati Nicholl, HarperCollins, 2005.

Kate Mosse, *The Labyrinth,* Orion Audio, 2005.

Asne Seierstad, *The Bookseller of Kabul,* Time Warner AudioBooks, 2005.

Agatha Christie, *The Seven Dials Mystery,* HarperCollins, 2006.

Philippa Gregory, *The Last Boleyn,* edited by Kati Nicholl, HarperCollins, 2006.

Sophie Kinsella, *The Secret Dreamworld of a Shopaholic,* Corgi Audio, 2006.

Sophie Kinsella, *Shopaholic Abroad,* Corgi Audio, 2006.

FRANCKS, Don 1932–

PERSONAL

Born February 28, 1932, in Vancouver, British Columbia, Canada; children: Cree, Rainbow.

Career: Actor.

CREDITS

Film Appearances:

Andy, *Ivy League Killers* (also known as *The Fast Ones*), Astral, 1959.

Narrator, *The Price of Fire* (also known as *La rancon du feu*), National Film Board of Canada, 1961.

Russel, *Drylanders* (also known as *Un autre pays*), Columbia, 1963.

Alexander MacKenzie, *Alexander Mackenzie: The Lord of the North,* National Film Board of Canada, 1964.

Narrator, *High Steel* (also known as *Charpentier du ciel*), National Film Board of Canada, 1965.

The Circle, National Film Board of Canada, 1967.

Woody Mahoney, *Finigan's Rainbow,* Pioneer, 1968.
Buffalo, *McCabe & Mrs. Miller,* Warner Bros., 1971.
Drylanders Episode 1, National Film Board of Canada, 1977.
Flashpoint, National Film Board of Canada, 1977.
Peter Brennan, *Drying Up the Streets,* Vestron Video, 1978.
Elder, *Fast Company,* Danton, 1979.
Deut Boggs, *Fish Hawk,* AVCO Embassy, 1979.
Albert, *Summer's Children,* 1979.
Chief Jake Newby, *My Bloody Valentine,* Paramount, 1981.
Voice of Grimaldi, *Heavy Metal,* Columbia, 1981.
Voice of Mok, *Rock & Rule* (also known as *Ring of Power* and *Rock 'n' Rule*), Metro–Goldwyn–Mayer/United Artists, 1983.
Chauncy Rand, *Terminal Choice* (also known as *Critical List, Death Bed, Death List* and *Trauma*), Almi, 1985.
Voice of Wolf Breath, *Madballs: Escape from Orb!,* Hi–Tops Video, 1986.
Carl Hooker, *The Big Town,* Columbia, 1987.
Voice of Len Roos, *Those Roos Boys and Friends,* 1987.
George Taip, *Oklahoma Smugglers,* Sharp, 1988.
Sol Chamberlain, *Married to It,* Orion, 1991.
Maitland Burns, *Paint Cans,* National Film Board of Canada, 1994.
Hooky, *Johnny Mnemonic* (also known as *Johnny Mnemoniue*), TriStar, 1995.
Lou Matlin, *First Degree* (video), Norstar, 1996.
Harrison Withers, *Harriet the Spy,* Paramount, 1996.
Dr. Surprise, *Bogus,* Warner Bros., 1996.
Michael Baer, *The Minion* (also known as *Fallen Knight* and *Guerrier des tenebres*), Buena Vista, 1998.
Bayliss Hatcher, *Summer of the Monkeys* (also known as *L' Ete des singes*), Buena Vista Home Video, 1998.
Gus, *Dinner at Fred's,* Imperial, 1999.
King, *Inspector Gadget: Gadget's Greatest Gadgets* (video), Buena Vista, 1999.
Chinawsky, *My Name Is Tanino,* Medusa, 2002.
Lie with Me, Eurocine, 2005.

Television Appearances; Series:
Burns Chuckwagon from the Stampede Corral, CBC, 1954.
Riding High, 1955.
Long Shot, CBC, 1959.
Host, *Other Voices,* CBC, 1964.
Franklin Sheppard, *Jericho,* CBS, 1966.
Mr. Anybody, *Mister Rogers' Neighborhood,* PBS, 1968–70.
Host, *This Land,* 1978–82.
David Brook, *The Phoenix Team,* CBC, 1980.
Inspector Gadget (animated; also known as *Inspecteur Gadget*), syndicated, 1983–84.
Voice of Umwak, Dulok Shaman, *Ewoks* (also known as *Ewoks & Droids Adventure Hour, Star Wars: Ewoks* and *The All New Ewoks*), 1985–86.

Alf, NBC, 1987–91.
Announcer, *Top Cops,* CBS, 1990.
Dr. Arcane, *Swamp Thing,* USA Network, 1991.
Voice of Girth/Hobbs, *Cadillacs and Dinosaurs* (animated), 1993.

Television Appearances; Movies:
Ouellette, *Riel,* CBC, 1979.
Warden, *984: Prisoner of the Future* (also known as *The Tomorrow Man*), 1982.
Don Geller, *Countdown to Looking Glass,* 1984.
Don Spatulo, *Hot Paint,* 1988.
Social arranger, *The Christmas Wife,* 1988.
Labor of Love, 1990.
On Thin Ice: The Tai Babilonia Story, 1990.
Singer, *The Trial of Red Riding Hood,* CBC, 1992.
Dr. Martin, *Quiet Killer* (also known as *Black Death* and *New York, alerte a la peste*), CBS, 1992.
Royland, *The Diviners,* 1993.
Peter, *Small Gifts,* CBC, 1994.
Jerome Kirkland, *Madonna: Innocence Lost,* 1994.
Smithford, *A Vow to Kill,* 1995.
Marcel, *The Possession of Michael D.* (also known as *Legacy of Evil*), 1995.
Norman, *The Conspiracy of Fear,* 1996.
Red, *Heck's Way Home* (also known as *Un drole de cabot*), 1996.
Hector, *The Deliverance of Elaine,* 1996.
Risser, *Captive Heart: The James Mink Story,* 1996.
Marty, *Hostile Advances: The Kerry Ellison Story,* 1996.
Ken, *A Prayer in the Dark,* 1997.
Zal Adamchyk, *Mr. Music,* Showtime, 1998.
Lou Massey, *A Killing Spring* (also known as *Copie non conforme*), 2002.

Television Appearances; Episodic:
Constable Bill Mitchell, *R.C.M.P.* (also known as *Royal Canadian Mounted Police*), CBC, 1959.
Sanders, "The Game Reserve," *The Forest Rangers* (also known as *Les Cadets de la foret*), 1963.
"You Wanna Know What Really Goes on in a Hospital?," *Ben Casey,* ABC, 1965.
"Why Did the Day Go Backwards?," *Ben Casey,* ABC, 1965.
T. Wigget Jones, "The Night of the Grand Emir," *The Wild Wild West,* CBS, 1966.
Artie King, "The Round Table Affair," *The Man from U.N.C.L.E.,* NBC, 1966.
The Merv Griffin Show, syndicated, 1968.
Nicholas Groat, "A Game of Chess," *Mission: Impossible,* CBS, 1968.
Caleb and Jack Welles, "The Land Dreamer," *The Virginian* (also known as *The Men from Shiloh*), NBC, 1969.
Major Alex Denesch, "The Numbers Game," *Mission: Impossible,* CBS, 1969.
"Memory: Zero," *Mannix,* CBS, 1969.

Noah Fletcher, "Little Darling of the Sierras," *Lancer,* CBS, 1969.

Reverend Dobson, "The Good Shepherd," *The Littlest Hobo,* CTV/syndicated, 1984.

Sunshine, "I'm Looking Through You," *Seeing Things,* CBC, 1984.

Droids (animated; also known as *Droids: The Adventures of R2D2 and C3PO* and *Star Wars: Droids*), ABC, 1985.

Gary, "Blind Alley," *Seeing Things,* CBC, 1985.

The Care Bears Family (animated), ABC, 1986.

Voice of Admiral Franklin Brinkley, *Starcom: The U.S. Space Force,* 1987.

Voice of Lacchi, *Captain Power and the Soldiers of the Future,* syndicated, 1987.

Mel, "I'll Be Home for Christmas," *Street Legal,* CBC, 1987.

AlfTales (also known as *Alf*), NBC, 1988.

"Spirit Cabinet," *The Hidden Room,* Lifetime, 1991.

Gun shop owner, *Secret Service,* NBC, 1992.

Narrator, *Hollywood Babylon,* syndicated, 1992.

Dick, "Transfigured Night," *The Hidden Room,* Lifetime, 1993.

Stranger, "Enter the Tiger," *Kung Fu: The Legend Continues,* syndicated, 1994.

"The Great Chendini," *Side Effects,* CBC, 1994.

Abe Pike, "The Return of Gus Pike," *Road to Avonlea* (also known as *Avonlea* and *Tales from Avonlea*), Disney and CBC, 1995.

Dr. Simon Gorfleisch, *The Great Defender,* Fox, 1995.

Levi Cole, "Thanksgiving," *Little Men,* PAX, 1998.

Voice of Kalok, *The Silver Surfer* (animated), Fox, 1998.

Sandman, "Nightmare on Eerie Street," *Eerie, Indiana: The Other Dimension,* NBC, 1998.

Bad Dog, Fox, 1998.

Walter, "Double Date," *La Femme Nikita,* 1998.

Second sailor, "Jason and the Argonauts," *Mythic Warriors: Guardians of the Legend,* 1998.

Blue–eyed wolf, "Ulysses and Circe," *Mythic Warriors: Guardians of the Legend,* 1998.

Jake Whitney, "Flag Day," *Relic Hunter* (also known as *Relic Hunter—Die schatzjagerin* and *Sydney Fox l'aventuriere*), 1999.

Samuel Thompson, "Wendigo," *PSI Factor: Chronicles of the Paranormal,* syndicated, 2000.

Phil Phelps, "Backstage Pass," *The Famous Jett Jackson,* The Disney Channel, 2000.

Kyle Madrid, "Trapped by Time," *Earth: Final Conflict* (also known as *EFC, Gene Roddenberry's Earth: Final Conflict, Invastion planete terre* and *Mission Erde: Sie sind unter uns*), 2001.

Mr. Goldstein, "Reversal of Fortune," *Street Time,* Showtime, 2002.

Voice of skunk, *My Dad the Rock Star* (animated; also known as *Moi Willy, fils de rockstar*), Teletoon, 2003.

Stan Puck, *This Is Wonderland,* CBC, 2004.

The evil head, "The Twilight Place," *Puppets Who Kill,* Comedy Central, 2004.

Voice of Maximus Sr., *Atomic Betty* (animated), Cartoon Network, 2004–2005.

Also appeared in many episodes of *X–Men,* Fox.

Television Appearances; Miniseries:

Captain Savard, *Blauvogel* (also known as *Bluehawk*), 1994.

Johnny Moore, *Degree of Guilt,* 1995.

Reverend Doctor Garshwin, *Seasons of Love,* CBS, 1999.

President Stanz, *The Last Chapter II: The War Continues* (also known as *Le Dernier chapitre: La vengeance*), CBC, 2003.

Television Appearances; Specials:

Jimmy Rae, *Moment of Truth,* CBS, 1992.

Swamp hermit, *The Werewolf of Fever Swamp,* Fox, 1996.

Voice of Boss Mouse, *The True Meaning of Crumbfest* (animated), PAX, 1998.

Voice of Maximus Sr., *Atomic Betty: The No–L Nine* (animated), Cartoon Network, 2005.

Stage Appearances:

Don Francks, *Leonard Bernstein's Theatre Songs,* Lucille Lortel Theatre, New York City, 1965.

Hop Kelly, *Kelly,* Broadhurst Theatre, New York City, 1965.

Theo, *The Flip Side,* Booth Theatre, New York City, 1968.

Also appeared in *On a Clear Day; Man Inc.,* St. Lawrence Centre, Toronto, Canada; *Spring Thaw* and *The Connection.*

Stage Work:

Directed and produced *The Connection.*

RECORDINGS

Video Games:

Voice of Sabretooth, *Marvel vs. Capcom 2: New Age of Heroes,* Capcom, 2000.

Voice of Sabretooth/Victor Creed, *X–Men: Mutant Academy,* Activision, 2000.

X–Men: Mutant Academy 2, Activision, 2001.

WRITINGS

Stageplays:

Wrote *Spring Thaw* and *The Connection.*

G

GALEOTTI, Bethany Joy
See LENZ, Joie

GARCIA, Jorge 1973–

PERSONAL

April 28, 1973 (some sources cite 1979), in Omaha, NE. *Education:* Attended college. *Avocational Interests:* Singing.

Addresses: *Agent*—Agency for the Performing Arts, 9200 Sunset Blvd., Suite 900, Los Angeles, CA 90069; (commercials) David Ziff, Cunningham/Escott/Slevin & Doherty Talent Agency, 10635 Santa Monica Blvd., Suite 140, Los Angeles, CA 90025. *Manager*—Erik Kritzer, Fenton–Kritzer Entertainment, 8840 Wilshire Blvd., Third Floor, Beverly Hills, CA 90211.

Career: Actor. Stand–up comedian at the Comedy Store, Los Angeles, and Laugh Factory, Hollywood, CA; appeared in advertisements. Worked in music stores.

Awards, Honors: Member of the cast of *Lost* that was named entertainer of the year, *Entertainment Weekly,* 2005; Teen Choice Award nominations, choice male breakout television performance and choice television sidekick, both 2005, Golden Globe Award, best television series—drama, and Screen Actors Guild Award, outstanding performance by an ensemble in a drama series, both with others, both 2006, all for *Lost.*

CREDITS

Television Appearances; Series:
Hector Lopez, *Becker,* CBS, 2003–2004.
Hugo "Hurley" Reyes, *Lost,* ABC, 2004—.

Television Appearances; Miniseries:
Himself, *I Love the '80s 3–D,* VH1, 2005.

Television Appearances; Movies:
Julius, *Columbo: Columbo Likes the Nightlife,* ABC, 2003.

Television Appearances; Specials:
Hugo "Hurley" Reyes, *Lost: The Journey,* ABC, 2005.

Television Appearances; Awards Presentations:
The 57th Annual Primetime Emmy Awards, CBS, 2005.
12th Annual Screen Actors Guild Awards (also known as *Screen Actors Guild 12th Annual Awards*), TNT and TBS, 2006.

Television Appearances; Episodic:
Cab driver, "The Arrival," *Spin City* (also known as *Spin*), ABC, 2001.
Vizzy, "Would I Lie to You?," *Rock Me Baby,* UPN, 2003.
Drug dealer, "The Car Pool Lane," *Curb Your Enthusiasm,* HBO, 2004.

Television Guest Appearances; Episodic:
"When Real Life and Screen Life Collide," *TV Land Confidential,* TV Land, 2005.
Entertainment Tonight (also known as *Entertainment This Week, ET, E.T., ET Weekend,* and *This Week in Entertainment*), syndicated, 2005.
Live with Regis and Kelly, syndicated, 2005.
The Tonight Show with Jay Leno, NBC, 2005.
The Tony Danza Show, syndicated, 2005.
Jimmy Kimmel Live, ABC, 2005, 2006.

Television Appearances; Pilots:
Hugo "Hurley" Reyes, *Lost,* ABC, 2004.

Film Appearances:

Monty, *Raven's Ridge,* The Asylum, 1997.

Jay, *Tomorrow by Midnight* (also known as *Midnight 5*), VCL Communications, 1999.

Meatloag, *King of the Open Mics,* Soby Entertainment, 2000.

Teddy, *The Slow and the Cautious* (short film), IFILM, 2002.

Chris, *Happily Even After,* Hotbed Media, 2004.

Gardener, *Our Time Is Up* (short film), Station B, 2004.

Mount Rushmore, *The Good Humor Man,* —80 Films, c. 2005.

Pedro, *Little Athens,* Legaci Pictures, 2005.

Sergio, *Sweetzer,* Wildcat Entertainment, 2006.

Stage Appearances:

Appeared in productions of the musicals *Fiddler on the Roof* and *Guys and Dolls,* both Beverly Hills Playhouse, Beverly Hills, CA; appeared in other productions, including *Hurlyburly, The Midnight Zone, Romancing Valentino,* and *Something Borrowed, Something Blue.*

RECORDINGS

Videos:

Racoon Head, *Tales from the Crapper,* Troma Team Video, 2004.

GLOVER, Danny 1947–

PERSONAL

Full name, Danny Lebern Glover; born July 22, 1947 (some sources say 1946), in San Francisco, CA; son of James (a postal worker) and Carrie (a postal worker; maiden name, Hunley) Glover; married Asake Bomani (a jazz singer and gallery owner), 1975 (filed for divorce, May, 1999); children: Mandisa. *Education:* San Francisco State University, degree in economics; studied acting at Black Actors' Workshop, American Conservatory Theatre, beginning in 1975.

Addresses: *Office*—Carrie Productions, 2625 Alcatraz Ave., Suite 243, Berkeley, CA 94705. *Agent*—International Creative Management, 8942 Wilshire Blvd., Beverly Hills, CA 90211. *Manager*—Anonymous Content, 3532 Hayden Ave., Culver City, CA 90232. *Publicist*—Rogers & Cowan Public Relations, 8687 Melrose Ave., 7th Floor, Los Angeles, CA 90069.

Career: Actor, producer, and director. Began acting in the late 1960's with San Francisco State University's Black Students Union; Carrie Productions, president;

appeared in television commercials, including The Gap, 2002, Winsor Pilates, 2002, MCI Long Distance, 2003, and for United Nations Development Program. City of Berkeley, CA, worked as evaluator of social programs; Office of the Mayor, San Francisco, CA, researcher, 1971–75; United Nations Development Program, appointed United Nations Goodwill Ambassador, 1998; active in the Coors Foundation for Family Literacy; spokesperson for the National Association for Sickle Cell Disease.

Awards, Honors: *Theatre World* Award, 1981–82, for "*Master Harold*" ... *and the Boys;* Image Award, outstanding lead actor in a motion picture, National Association for the Advancement of Colored People, 1989, for *Lethal Weapon;* Emmy Award nomination, outstanding actor in a miniseries or special, 1988, CableACE Award, actor in a movie or miniseries, 1989, Image Award, outstanding lead actor in a drama series, miniseries, or television movie, 1990, all for *Mandela;* Emmy Award nomination, outstanding supporting actor in a miniseries or special, 1989, for *Lonesome Dove;* Independent Spirit Award, best male lead, Independent Features Project, 1991, for *To Sleep With Anger;* Black Filmmakers Hall of Fame, inductee, 1990; Phoenix Award, Black American Cinema Society, 1990; honorary D.H.L., Paine College, 1990; Image Award nomination, outstanding lead actor in a motion picture, 1993, for *Bopha!;* Piper–Heidsieck Award, San Francisco International Film Festival, 1993; MTV Movie Award (with Mel Gibson), best on–screen duo, 1993, for *Lethal Weapon 3;* Humanitarian Award, Women in Film Crystal Award, 1994; Humanitarian Award, Video Software Dealers Association, 1995; Image Award nomination, outstanding actor in a telefilm or miniseries, 1995, for *Queen;* received star on Hollywood Walk of Fame, 1996; CableACE Award nominations, dramatic or theatrical special (with others; two episodes), CableACE Awards, dramatic or theatrical special (with others) and actor in a dramatic special/series, 1996, for *America's Dream;* Emmy Award nomination, outstanding guest actor in a drama series, 1996, for *Fallen Angels;* Image Award nomination, outstanding performance in an animated/live action/dramatic youth or children's series/special, 1996, for "The Frog Prince," *Happily Ever After: Fairy Tales for Every Child;* Grammy Award nomination, spoken word, 1997, for *Long Walk to Freedom;* honorary D.F.A., San Francisco State University, 1997; appointed Goodwill Ambassador, United Nations Development Program, 1998; Image Award nomination, outstanding lead actor in a television movie, miniseries, or drama special, 1998, for *Buffalo Soldiers;* Image Award nomination, outstanding supporting actor in a motion picture, 1998, for *John Grisham's "The Rainmaker";* Blockbuster Entertainment Award nomination (with Mel Gibson), favorite duo—action/adventure, MTV Movie Award nomination (with Mel Gibson), best action sequence 1999, both for *Lethal Weapon 4;* Image Award, outstanding lead actor in a motion picture, Black Film Award nomination, Acapulco Black Film Festival, 1999, both for *Beloved;* Emmy Award nomination, outstanding supporting actor in a miniseries or a movie, 2000, Screen Actors Guild Award nomination, outstanding performance by a male actor in a television movie or miniseries, Image Award, outstanding actor in a television movie, miniseries, or dramatic special, 2001, all for *Freedom Song;* Phoenix Film Critics Society Award nomination (with others), best acting ensemble, 2002, for *The Royal Tenenbaums;* Lifetime Achievement Award, Jamerican International Film Festival, 2002; Lifetime Achievement Award, Los Angeles Pan African Film Festival, 2003; Daytime Emmy Award nomination, outstanding directing in a children's special, 2003, for *Just a Dream;* Image Award nomination, outstanding actor in a television movie, miniseries, or dramatic special, Black Reel Award nomination, television—best actor, 2004, both for *Good Fences.*

CREDITS

Film Appearances:

(Film debut) Inmate, *Escape from Alcatraz,* Paramount, 1979.

Morgan, *Chu Chu and the Philly Flash,* Twentieth Century–Fox, 1981.

Title role, *Oscar Micheaux, Film Pioneer,* 1981.

Fojol and Roland, *Out* (also known as *Deadly Drifter*), Cinegate, 1982.

Birdy, TriStar, 1984.

Loomis, *Iceman,* Universal, 1984.

Moses, *Places in the Heart,* TriStar, 1984.

James McFee, *Witness,* Paramount, 1984.

The Stand–In, 1984.

Malachi, *Silverado,* Columbia, 1985.

Albert, *The Color Purple,* Warner Bros., 1985.

Roger Murtaugh, *Lethal Weapon,* Warner Bros., 1987.

Captain Bartholomew Clark, *Bat*21,* TriStar, 1988.

Roger Murtaugh, *Lethal Weapon 2,* Warner Bros., 1989.

Himself, *Hollywood on Horses* (documentary), 1989.

(English version) Narrator, *Rabbit Ears: How the Leopard Got His Spots* (also known as *Apple Rabbit Ears*), 1989.

Harry Mention, *To Sleep with Anger,* Samuel Goldwyn, 1990.

Lieutenant Mike Harrigan, *Predator 2,* Twentieth Century–Fox, 1990.

Commander Frank "Dooke" Camparelli, *Flight of the Intruder,* Paramount, 1991.

Easy–Money, *A Rage in Harlem,* Miramax, 1991.

Raymond Campanella, *Pure Luck,* Universal, 1991.

Simon, *Grand Canyon,* Twentieth Century–Fox, 1991.

Narrator, *The Talking Eggs,* 1992.

Roger Murtaugh, *Lethal Weapon 3,* Warner Bros., 1993.

Jerry and narrator, *The Saint of Fort Washington,* Warner Bros., 1993.

Micah Mangena, *Bopha!,* Paramount, 1993.

George Knox, *Angels in the Outfield* (also known as *Angels*), Buena Vista, 1994.

(Uncredited) Bank robber, *Maverick,* 1994.

Kidnapped, 1994.

Captain Sam Cahill, *Operation Dumbo Drop* (also known as *Dumbo Drop*), Buena Vista, 1995.

Narrator, *Can't You Hear the Wind Howl?* (documentary; also known as *Can't You Hear the Wind Howl? The Life and Music of Robert Johnson*), Win-Star Home Entertainment, 1997.

Gus Green, *Gone Fishin',* Buena Vista, 1997.

(Uncredited) Judge Tyrone Kippler, *John Grisham's "The Rainmaker"* (also known as *The Rainmaker*), Paramount, 1997.

Bob Goodall, *Switchback* (also known as *Going West* and *Going West in America*), Paramount, 1997.

(Uncredited) Mountain man, *Wild America,* Warner Bros., 1997.

Voice of Barbarus, *Antz* (animated; also known as *Ants*), DreamWorks, 1997.

Roger Murtaugh, *Lethal Weapon 4,* Warner Bros., 1998.

Paul D., *Beloved,* Buena Vista, 1998.

Voice of Jethro, *The Prince of Egypt* (animated), Dream-Works Distribution, 1998.

(Scenes deleted) *How Stella Got Her Groove Back,* Twentieth Century–Fox, 1998.

Narrator, *Soldier Child* (documentary), Winghead Pictures, 1998.

Host and himself, *Pure Lethal* (short), Warner Bros., 1998.

Narrator, *The People vs. Shintech,* 1999.

Wings Against the Wind, 1999.

Henry Johnson, *The Monster,* 1999.

Himself, *The Making of "Silverado"* (documentary), Sony Pictures Entertainment,1999.

Voice of Train Conductor, *Our Friend, Martin,* 1999.

Boesman, *Boesman and Lena* (also known as *Boesman & Lena*), Kino International Corp., 2000.

Himself, *Ennis' Gift* (documentary), 2000.

Battu, 2000.

Henry Sherman, *The Royal Tenenbaums,* Buena Vista, 2001.

XXI Century (documentary), 2003.

Himself, *A Collaboration of Spirits: Casting and Acting "The Color Purple"* (documentary short), 2003.

Himself, *Cultivating a Classic: The Making of "The Color Purple"* (documentary short), 2003.

Detective David Tapp, *Saw,* Lions Gate Films, 2004.

Judge Crowley, *The Cookout,* Lions Gate Films, 2004.

Narrator, *Picture This: A Fight to Save Joe* (documentary), 2005.

Himself, *The Hunters and the Hunted: The Making of "Predator 2"* (documentary short), Twentieth Century–Fox Home Entertainment, 2005.

Himself, *Aristide and the Endless Revolution* (documentary), 2005.

Himself, *The Peace! DVD* (documentary), Cinema Libre Studio, 2005.

Wilhelm, *Manderlay,* IFC Films, 2005.

Jake, *Missing in America*, First Look Home Entertainment, 2005.

Himself and Wilhelm, *The Cannes Experience: Manderlay 2005* (documentary short), 2005.

Narrator, *In Pursuit of Happiness*, 2005.

District Attorney Ken Hollister, *The Shaggy Dog*, Buena Vista, 2006.

Brer Turtle, *The Adventures of Brer Rabbit* (animated), Universal Studios, 2006.

Nujoma: Where Others Wavered, 2006.

Voice of Miles, *Barnyard* (animated), Paramount, 2006.

Marty Madison, *Dreamgirls*, DreamWorks, 2006.

Film Work:

Executive producer, *To Sleep With Anger*, Samuel Goldwyn, 1990.

Executive producer, *The Final Act*, 1998.

Financier, *Woman Thou Art Loosed*, Magnolia Pictures, 2004.

Television Appearances; Series:

Harley, *Palmerstown, U.S.A.* (also known as *Palmerstown*), CBS, 1980.

Voice of Professor Pollo, *Captain Planet and the Planeteers* (animated; also known as *The New Adventures of Captain Planet*), 1990.

Host, *Civil War Journal*, Arts and Entertainment, 1993.

Hollywood Squares, 1998.

Host, *Courage*, Fox Family, 2000.

Himself, *Independent View*, PBS, 2002.

Television Appearances; Miniseries:

Marshall Peters, *Chiefs*, CBS, 1983.

Joshua Deets, *Lonesome Dove*, CBS, 1989.

Alec Haley, *Queen* (also known as *Alex Haley's "Queen"*), CBS, 1993.

Narrator, *The Untold West: The Black West*, TBS, 1993.

Host, *Life by the Numbers* (also known as *M: The Invisible Universe*), PBS, 1998.

Narrator, *Pandemic: Facing AIDS* (documentary), HBO, 2003.

Ogion, *Legend of Earthsea* (also known as *Earthsea*), Sci–Fi Channel, 2004.

Television Appearances; Movies:

Lester, *Keeping On*, 1981.

Gary, *The Face of Rage*, ABC, 1983.

Nelson Mandela, *Mandela*, HBO, 1987.

Alex, *Dead Man Out* (also known as *Dead Man Walking*), HBO, 1989.

Silas, "Long Black Song," *America's Dream*, HBO, 1996.

Sergeant Wyatt, *Buffalo Soldiers*, TNT, 1997.

Will Walker, *Freedom Song*, TNT, 2000.

Hershey, *3 A.M.*, Showtime, 2001.

Tom Spader, *Good Fences*, Showtime, 2003.

David, *The Exonerated*, Court TV, 2005.

Television Appearances; Specials:

Willie Monroe, *Memorial Day*, 1983.

Nelson Mandela, *Mandela* (documentary), PBS, 1986.

Ultimate Stuntman: A Tribute to Dar Robinson, ABC, 1987.

Mr. Scott, *A Place at the Table*, NBC, 1988.

The R.A.C.E., NBC, 1989.

All–Star Tribute to Kareem Abdul–Jabbar, NBC, 1989.

Walter Lee Younger, "A Raisin in the Sun," *American Playhouse*, PBS, 1989.

Premiere: Inside the Summer Blockbusters, Fox, 1989.

The 2nd Annual Valvoline National Driving Test, CBS, 1990.

A Party for Richard Pryor, CBS, 1991.

Mel Gibson's Unauthorized Video Diary, HBO, 1991.

Mel Gibson's Video Diary 2: "Lethal Weapon 3," HBO, 1991.

Lonesome Dove: The Making of an Epic (documentary), TNN, 1992.

The American Film Institute Salute to Sidney Poitier, NBC, 1992.

First Person with Maria Shriver, NBC, 1992.

Hollywood Hotshots, Fox, 1992.

Narrator, "The Black West," *The Untold West* (documentary), TBS, 1993.

Apollo Theater Hall of Fame, NBC, 1993.

Host and narrator, "How the Leopard Got His Spots," *Celebrate Storytelling with Danny Glover* (animated), PBS, 1994.

Movie News Hot Summer Sneak Preview, CBS, 1994.

The American Film Institute Salute to Steven Spielberg (also known as *The AFI Salute to Steven Spielberg*), NBC, 1995.

The First 100 Years: A Celebration of American Movies, HBO, 1995.

Voice, *Africans in America—America's Journey Through Slavery* (documentary), PBS, 1998.

The Secret World of Antz (documentary), NBC, 1998.

Celebrity Profile: Danny Glover, E! Entertainment Television, 1998.

Warner Bros. 75th Anniversary: No Guts, No Glory, TNT, 1998.

Host and narrator, *The Black Cowboys* (documentary), History Channel, 1999.

Kennedy Center Mark Twain Prize Celebrating the Humor of Richard Pryor, 1999.

Voice of Train Conductor, *Our Friend, Martin*, Starz!, 1999.

Host, *Scared Straight! 20 Years Later* (documentary), UPN, 1999.

Arista Records' 25th Anniversary Celebration, 1999.

Presenter, *25 Years of No. 1 Hits: Arista Records' Anniversary Celebration*, 2000.

Narrator, "Casey at Bat," *Cincinnati Pops Holiday: Fourth of July from the Heartland*, PBS, 2000.

Heroes for the Planet—A Tribute to National Geographic, CNBC, Fox News, and National Geographic, 2001.

Ennis' Gift: A Film About Learning Differences, HBO, 2002.

Narrator, *The Real Eve* (documentary; also known as *Where We Came From*), Discovery Channel, 2002.

Host, *What's Going On?* (documentary), Showtime, 2003.

The John Garfield Story (documentary), TCM, 2003.

Mel Gibson: The E! True Hollywood Story, E! Entertainment Weekly, 2004.

The Road to Manderlay (documentary), 2005.

La Marato 2005, 2005.

Television Appearances; Awards Presentations:

Presenter, *The 60th Annual Academy Awards Presentation,* 1988.

The 20th NAACP Image Awards, NBC, 1988.

The 16th Annual Black Filmmakers Hall of Fame, syndicated, 1989.

Presenter, *The 21st Annual NAACP Image Awards,* NBC, 1989.

The 22nd Annual NAACP Image Awards, NBC, 1990.

The 24th Annual Victor Awards, syndicated, 1990.

The 5th Stellar Gospel Music Awards, syndicated, 1990.

The 17th Annual People's Choice Awards, CBS, 1991.

Presenter, *The 63rd Annual Academy Awards Presentation,* ABC, 1991.

Host, *The 26th Annual Victor Awards,* TBS, 1992.

Host, *The 13th Annual ACE Awards,* TNT, 1992.

The 46th Annual Tony Awards, CBS, 1992.

Host, *The Essence Awards,* CBS, 1993.

Host, *One Child, One Dream: The Horatio Alger Awards,* NBC, 1993.

Jim Thorpe Pro Sports Awards, ABC, 1994.

The 36th Annual Grammy Awards, CBS, 1994.

VH1 Honors, VH1, 1994.

The Blockbuster Entertainment Awards, CBS, 1995.

The 1996 Essence Awards, Fox, 1996.

The 1999 Essence Awards, Fox, 1999.

The 2000 ESPY Awards, ESPN, 2000.

Honoree, *The 2000 Essence Awards,* Fox, 2000.

The 2001 Essence Awards, Fox, 2001.

The 8th Annual Screen Actors Guild Awards, TNT, 2002.

The 34th NAACP Image Awards, Fox, 2003.

Presenter, *The 57th Annual Tony Awards,* CBS, 2003.

The 2004 BET Awards, Black Entertainment Television, 2004.

Television Appearances; Pilots:

Henry Lee, *The Law and Henry Lee,* CBS, 2003.

Television Appearances; Episodic:

Leroy, "Slammer," *Lou Grant,* CBS, 1979.

Joyner, "Fire Man," *The Greatest American Hero,* ABC, 1981.

Jesse John Hudson, "The Second Oldest Profession," *Hill Street Blues,* NBC, 1981.

Jesse John Hudson, "The Last Man on East Ferry Avenue," *Hill Street Blues,* NBC, 1981.

Jesse John Hudson, "Hearts and Minds," *Hill Street Blues,* NBC, 1981.

Jesse John Hudson, "Blood Money," *Hill Street Blues,* NBC, 1981.

Bill, "A Man in Nell's Room," *Gimme a Break!,* NBC, 1981.

William, "And the Children Shall Lead," *WonderWorks,* PBS, 1985.

Title role, "John Henry," *Shelley Duvall's Tall Tales and Legends,* Showtime, 1985, 1987.

The Barbour Report, ABC, 1986.

Narrator, "The Talking Eggs," *Long Ago and Far Away,* PBS, 1989.

Host and narrator, "How the Leopard Got Its Spots," *Storybook Classics,* Showtime, 1989.

Host, "Thumbelina," *Storybook Classics,* Showtime, 1989.

(Uncredited) Roger Murtaugh, *Saturday Night Live* (also known as *SNL*), NBC, 1989.

Host, "The Three Little Pigs/The Three Billy Goats Gruff," *Storybook Classics,* Showtime, 1989.

Host, "The Fisherman and His Wife," *Storybook Classics,* Showtime, 1989.

Host, "Red Riding Hood/Goldilocks," *Storybook Classics,* Showtime, 1990.

Host, "Paul Bunyan," *Storybook Classics,* Showtime, 1990.

Host, "The Emperor's New Clothes," *Storybook Classics,* Showtime, 1990.

Host and narrator, "Br'er Rabbit and the Wonderful Tar Baby," *Storybook Classics,* Showtime, 1990.

The Arsenio Hall Show, syndicated, 1991, 1992.

Narrator of "Br'er Rabbit and Boss Lion," *American Heroes and Legends,* Showtime, 1992.

The Tonight Show Starring Johnny Carson (also known as *The Best of Carson*), NBC, 1992.

Howard Stern, E! Entertainment Television, 1994.

Philip Marlowe, "Red Wind," *Fallen Angels,* Showtime, 1995.

Voice, "The Frog Prince," *Happily Ever After: Fairy Tales for Every Child* (animated), HBO, 1995.

Inside the Actors Studio, Bravo, 1998.

The Rosie O'Donnell Show, syndicated, 1998, 2000, 2001, 2002.

Mundo VIP, 1998, 2000.

"St. Louis to Timbuktu," *Great Railway Journeys,* PBS, 1999.

The Oprah Winfrey Show (also known as *Oprah*), syndicated, 2001.

The Wayne Brady Show, syndicated, 2003.

Narrator, "James Baldwin: Witness," *A&E Biography* (also known as *Biography*), Arts and Entertainment, 2003.

Tavis Smiley, PBS, 2004.

Richard & Judy, Channel 4, 2004.

Ruben & Joonas, 2005.

Caiga quien caiga, 2005.

Le vrai journal, 2005.

Charlie Pratt, Sr., "The Show Must Go On," *ER,* NBC, 2005.

Charlie Pratt, Sr., "Nobody's Baby," *ER*, NBC, 2005.
Charlie Pratt, Sr., "Wake Up," *ER*, NBC, 2005.
Charlie Pratt, Sr., "Dream House," *ER*, NBC, 2005.

Also appeared in *B.J. and the Bear*, NBC; *Many Mansions*, PBS; "AIDS in the Caribbean," *What's Going On?*.

Television Work; Series:
Executive producer, *Courage*, Fox Family, 2000.
Producer, *The Henry Lee Project*, CBS, 2003.

Television Executive Producer; Movies:
America's Dream, HBO, 1996.
Deadly Voyage, HBO, 1996.
Buffalo Soldiers, TNT, 1997.
Freedom Song, TNT, 2000.
3 A.M., Showtime, 2001.

Television Producer; Movies:
Good Fences, Showtime, 2003.

Television Director; Movies:
Just a Dream, Showtime, 2002.

Television Work; Specials:
Director, "Override," *Directed By*, Showtime, 1994.

Television Work; Pilots:
Executive producer, *The Law and Henry Lee*, CBS, 2003.

Stage Appearances:
(Off–Broadway debut) Zachariah, *Blood Knot*, Roundabout Theatre, New York City, 1980.
(Broadway debut) Willie, *"Master Harold' ... and the Boys*, Lyceum Theatre, New York City, 1982.
Sam, *"Master Harold' ... and the Boys*, Royale Theatre, New York City, 2003.
Lord Justice Steyn, *Guantanamo: Honor Bound to Defend Freedom*, 45 Bleecker, New York City, 2004.

Also appeared in *The Island*, Eureka Theatre, San Francisco, CA; *Macbeth* and *Sizwe Banzi Is Dead*, Actors Theatre, Los Angeles; *Suicide in B Flat*, Magic Theatre, San Francisco, CA; *Nevis Mountain Dew*, Los Angeles; *Jukebox*, Oakland, CA.

RECORDINGS

Videos:
(Contributor) *Thomas Jefferson: A View from the Mountain* (documentary), 1996.

Music Videos:
Himself, "Liberian Girl," *Michael Jackson: HIStory on Film—Volume II*, Sony Music, 1997.

Taped Readings:
Nelson Mandela's *Long Walk to Freedom*, Time Warner Audio Books, 1996.

OTHER SOURCES

Books:
Contemporary Black Biography, Vol. 24, Gale Group, 2000.
International Dictionary of Films and Filmmakers, Volume 3: Actors and Actresses, 4th ed., St. James Press, 2000.

Periodicals:
Ebony, March, 1986, p. 82.
Essence, July, 1994, p. 52.
GQ, July, 1989.
People, February 10, 1992, pp. 91–92.
Playbill, June 30, 2003, pp. 12–13.
Premiere, February, 1992, pp. 70, 73–74.

GOLDBERG, Lee
(Ian Ludlow)

PERSONAL

Married; children: one daughter. *Education:* Attended University of California at Los Angeles.

Addresses: *Agent*—The Stein Agency, 5125 Oakdale Ave., Woodland Hills, CA 91364.

Career: Writer, producer, story editor, and creative consultant. Worked as a freelance writer for publications such as *American Film, Starlog, Newsweek, Los Angeles Times* syndicated, *Washington Post*, and *San Francisco Chronicle*.

Member: International Society of Crime Writers, Writers Guild of America, Authors Guild, Mystery Writers of America.

Awards, Honors: Edgar Allan Poe Award nomination (with William Rabkin), best television episode, Mystery Writers of America, 1993, for *Likely Suspects* and, 2002, for *A Nero Wolfe Mystery*.

CREDITS

Television Work; Series:
Story editor, *Hunter*, NBC, 1984.
Story editor, *Baywatch* (also known as *Baywatch Hawaii*), 1989–90.
Supervising producer, *She–Wolf of London* (also known as *Love & Curses*), syndicated, 1990.
Executive story editor, *Baywatch* (also known as *Baywatch Hawaii*), 1990.
Producer, *Likely Suspects,* Fox, 1992.
Supervising producer, *SeaQuest DSV* (also known as *SeaQuest 2032*), NBC, 1993.
Supervising producer, *Cobra,* syndicated, 1993.
Supervising producer, *The Cosby Mysteries,* NBC, 1994.
Supervising producer, *Stick With Me, Kid,* 1995.
Supervising producer, *Diagnosis Murder,* CBS, 1996–97.
Executive producer, *Diagnosis Murder,* CBS, 1997–99 producer, *Martial Law,* CBS, 1998.
Creative Consultant and co–executive producer, *Missing* (also known as *1–800–MISSING*), Lifetime, 2003—.

Television Work; Specials:
Executive producer, *The Best TV Shows That Never Were,* ABC, 2004.

WRITINGS

Television Episodes (With William Rabkin):
"On Air," *Hunter,* NBC, 1984.
(With Burt Pearl and Steven L. Sears) "Haunted Highway," *The Highwayman,* NBC, 1988.
Murphy's Law, 1988–89.
Baywatch (also known as *Baywatch Hawaii*), syndicated, 1989–90.
She Wolf of London (also known as *Love & Curses*), syndicated, 1990–91.
Diagnosis Murder, CBS, 1994–99.
"The Car Mechanic," *Deadly Games,* UPN, 1995.
"Chains of Command," *SeaQuest DSV* (also known as *SeaQuest 2032*), NBC, 1995.
"Resurrection," *SeaQuest DSV* (also known as *SeaQuest 2032*), NBC, 1995.
"Smoke on the Water," *SeaQuest DSV* (also known as *SeaQuest 2032*), NBC, 1995.
"The Prince of Wails," *Sliders,* Fox, 1995.
"That's a Moray!" (also known as "Skeleton Garden"), *Flipper* (also known as *The New Adventures of Flipper*), PAX, 1995.
"Sammo Blammo," *Martial Law,* CBS, 1999.
"Final Conflict: Part 2," *Martial Law,* CBS, 2000.
"Freefall," *Martial Law,* CBS, 2000.
Nero Wolfe, Arts and Entertainment, 2000–2002.
"Crossed Out," *She Spies,* syndicated, 2003.

Missing (also known as *1–800–MISSING*), Lifetime, 2003–2005.
"Mr. Monk Meets the Godfather," *Monk,* USA Network, 2004.

Also wrote episodes of *Spenser: For Hire,* ABC; *Likely Suspects,* Fox; *Cobra,* syndicated; *Stick with Me, Kid;* and *The Cobsy Mysteries,* NBC.

Television Episode Stories (With William Rabkin):
"Haunted Highway," *The Highwayman,* NBC, 1988.
(With Abbie Bernstein) "Nice Girls Don't," *She Wolf of London,* syndicated, 1990.
(With Gabe Torres) "What's Got into Them?," *She Wolf of London,* syndicated, 1991.
(With Arthur Sellers) "Beyond the Beyond," *She Wolf of London,* syndicated, 1991.
(With Gerry Conway) "Physician, Murder Thyself," *Diagnosis Murder,* CBS, 1997.
(With Dick Van Dyke) "Comedy is Murder," *Diagnosis Murder,* CBS, 1997.
"Murder, My Suite," *Diagnosis Murder,* CBS, 1999.

Television Movies:
Wrote *Dame Edna: Megastar Detective.*

Television Specials:
"Terror for Rent" and "Motel Hell," *Haunted Lives: True Ghost Stories,* CBS, 1992.
"Terror for Rent" and "Motel Hell," *Real Ghosts III,* UPN, 1996.
The Best TV Shows That Never Were, ABC, 2004.

Books; Nonfiction:
The Jewish Student's Guide to American College, Sure Sellers, 1989.
Unsold Television Pilots 1955–1988, McFarland & Co., 1990.
Unsold TV Pilots: The Almost Complete Guide to Everything You Never Saw on TV, 1955–1990, Carol Publications Group, 1991.
The New Jewish Student's Guide to American Colleges, Ulversoft, 1992.
Television Series Revivals: Sequels & Remakes of Canceled Series, McFarland & Co., 1993.
(With others) *Science Fiction Film–Making in the 1980s,* McFarland & Co., 1995.
The Dreamweavers: Fantasy Film–Makers of the 1980s, McFarland & Co., 1996.
Successful Television Writing, John Wiley, 2003.

Books; Fiction:
(As Ian Ludlow) *.357 Vigilante #1,* Pinnacle Books, 1983–85.
(As Ian Ludlow) *.357 Vigilante #2: Make Them Pay,* Pinnacle Books, 1983–85.

.357 Vigilante #3: White Wash, Pinnacle Books, 1983–85.

(As Ian Ludlow) *.357 Vigilante #4: Killstorm,* Pinnacle Books, 1983–85.

My Gun Has Bullets, St. Martins Press, 1995.

Beyond the Beyond, St. Martins Press, 1997.

The Silent Partner, New American Library, 2003.

Walk, Five Star, 2004.

Diagnosis Murder #2: The Death Merchant, Signet, 2004.

Shooting Script, Signet, 2004.

Diagnosis Murder #4: Waking Nightmare, Signet, 2005.

Diagnosis Murder #5: The Past Tense, 2005.

The Man with the Iron–On Badge, Five Star, 2005.

Mr. Monk Goes to the Firehouse, Signet, 2006.

Mr. Monk Goes to Hawaii, 2006.

Diagnosis Murder #6: The Dead Letter, 2006.

GRACE, Maggie 1983–

PERSONAL

Full name, Margaret Grace Denig; raised in Worthington, OH; born September 21, 1983, in Columbus, OH. *Avocational Interests:* Reading.

Addresses: *Agent*—Chris Hart, International Creative Management, 8942 Wilshire Blvd., Beverly Hills, CA 90211. *Manager*—Darren Goldberg, Darren Goldberg Management, 5225 Wilshire Blvd., Suite 419, Los Angeles, CA 90036.

Career: Actress.

Awards, Honors: Young Artist Award nomination, best performance in a television movie, miniseries, or special by a leading young actress, Young Artist Foundation, 2003, for *Murder in Greenwich;* member of the cast of *Lost* that was named entertainer of the year, *Entertainment Weekly,* 2005; Teen Choice Award nomination, choice female television breakout performance, 2005, Golden Globe Award, best television series—drama, and Screen Actors Guild Award, outstanding performance by an ensemble in a drama series, both with others, both 2006, all for *Lost.*

CREDITS

Television Appearances; Series:
Elke, a recurring role, *Oliver Beene,* Fox, 2004.
Shannon Rutherford, *Lost,* ABC, 2004–2005.

Television Appearances; Movies:
Martha Moxley, *Murder in Greenwich* (also known as *Dominick Dunne Presents: "Murder in Greenwich"*), USA Network, 2002.
Dulcie Landis, *Twelve Mile Road,* CBS, 2003.

Television Appearances; Specials:
(In archive footage) Shannon Rutherford, *Lost: The Journey,* ABC, 2005.

Television Appearances; Awards Presentations:
The 57th Annual Primetime Emmy Awards, CBS, 2005.
World Music Awards 2005, ABC, 2005.
The 63rd Annual Golden Globe Awards, NBC, 2006.
12th Annual Screen Actors Guild Awards (also known as *Screen Actors Guild 12th Annual Awards*), TNT and TBS, 2006.

Television Appearances; Episodic:
Amy Gorman, "Spring Break," *CSI: Miami,* CBS, 2003.
Hannah Cottrell, "Mother's Daughter," *Miracles* (also known as *The Calling*), ABC, 2003.
Jessie Dawning, "Obscene," *Law & Order: Special Victims Unit* (also known as *Law & Order: SVU* and *Special Victims Unit*), NBC, 2004.
Mary, "My Two Moms," *Like Family,* The WB, 2004.
Rene, "Volunteers," *Cold Case,* CBS, 2004.
Guest, *Entertainment Tonight* (also known as *Entertainment This Week, ET, E.T., ET Weekend,* and *This Week in Entertainment*), syndicated, 2005.
Guest, *Jimmy Kimmel Live,* ABC, 2005.
Guest, *The View,* ABC, 2005.

Appeared as Haley Dugan in "Beach House," an unaired episode of *The Lyon's Den,* NBC.

Television Appearances; Pilots:
Shannon Rutherford, *Lost,* ABC, 2004.

Appeared as Hope Wilde in the pilot *Septuplets,* Fox.

Film Appearances:
Rachel Reed, *Rachel's Room,* Sony Digital Entertainment, 2001.
Shop Club, A Few Miles North Productions/Ghetto Pictures/Kitty Films/Rated R Films, 2002.
Amanda, *Creature Unknown,* Creative Light Entertainment, 2004.
Elizabeth Williams, *The Fog,* Columbia, 2005.

Stage Appearances:
Appeared in community theatre productions.

OTHER SOURCES

Periodicals:
Interview, October, 2005, p. 64.
USA Today, October 18, 2005.

USA Weekend, (some sources cite October 14, 2005, p. 14.

GREER, Pam
See GRIER, Pam

GRIER, David Alan 1955(?)–
(David Alan Griers)

PERSONAL

Born June 30, 1955 (some sources cite 1956), in Detroit, MI; son of William Henry (a writer) and Aretas Ruth (maiden name, Dudley) Grier; married Maritza Rivera (some sources spell first name Maritsa; divorced). *Education:* University of Michigan, B.A., 1978; Yale University, M.F.A., 1981.

Addresses: *Agent*—Nick Nuciforo, Creative Artists Agency, 9830 Wilshire Blvd., Beverly Hills, CA 90212; Sean Elliott, Endeavor, 9601 Wilshire Blvd., Sixth Floor, Beverly Hills, CA 90212.

Career: Actor, producer, and writer. Stand–up comedian at various venues.

Awards, Honors: *Theatre World* Award, 1981, and Antoinette Perry Award nomination, best actor in a featured role in a musical, 1982, both for *The First;* Volpi Cup (with others), best actor, Venice International Film Festival, 1983, for *Streamers;* Image Award nomination, outstanding supporting actor in a comedy series, National Association for the Advancement of Colored People, 1999, for *Damon;* Bronze Wrangler Award (with others), outstanding television feature film, Western Heritage awards, 2003, for *King of Texas;* Image Award nomination, outstanding supporting actor in a comedy series, 2003, and Golden Satellite Award nomination, best performance by an actor in a supporting role in a series, comedy or musical, International Press Academy, 2004, both for *Life with Bonnie;* named one of the 100 greatest stand–up comedians of all time, Comedy Central, 2004.

CREDITS

Television Appearances; Series:
Oliver Royce, *All Is Forgiven,* NBC, 1986.
Various characters, *In Living Color,* Fox, 1990–93.
David Preston, *The Preston Episodes,* Fox, 1995.

Bernard, *Damon,* Fox, 1998.
Host, *Random Acts of Comedy,* Fox Family Channel, 1999.
Agent Jerome Daggett, *DAG,* NBC, 2000–2001.
Host, *Premium Blend* (also known as *Comedy Central's "Premium Blend"*), Comedy Central, 2001–2002.
David Bellows, *Life with Bonnie,* ABC, 2002–2004.
Voice of Landanlius "The Truth" Truefield, *Crank Yankers,* Comedy Central, between 2002 and 2005.

Television Appearances; Miniseries:
Fred Hampton, *The '60s,* NBC, 1999.
(In archive footage) Himself, *Comedy Central Presents: 100 Greatest Stand–Ups of All Time,* Comedy Central, 2004.

Television Appearances; Movies:
Dan Anderson, "A Saintly Switch" (also known as "In Your Shoes"), *The Wonderful World of Disney,* ABC, 1998.
Detective Augustus, *Top of the World* (also known as *Cold Cash* and *Showdown*), HBO, 1998.
Bob Bugler, "Angels in the Infield," *The Wonderful World of Disney,* ABC, 2000.
Rip, *King of Texas,* TNT, 2002.

Television Appearances; Specials:
Host, *Pure Insanity II,* Fox, 1990.
Himself and multiple characters, *The Best of Robert Townsend & His Partners in Crime,* HBO, 1991.
Spy Magazine's Hit List: The 100 Most Annoying and Alarming People and Events of 1992 (also known as *The Spy 100*), NBC, 1992.
(In archive footage) Vulcan, *Mo' Funny: Black Comedy in America,* HBO, 1993.
TV Guide: 40th Anniversary Special, Fox, 1993.
Himself, *The Making of "Blankman,"* HBO, 1994.
Host, *Fox Fall Preview Party,* Fox, 1995.
Extreme Comedy, ABC, 1996.
Host, *When New Year's Eve Attacks!* (also known as *Fox's New Year's Eve Live* and *1997 New Year's in Las Vegas*), Fox, 1997.
Himself, *Elmopalooza,* ABC, 1998.
Host, *American Comedy Awards Viewer's Choice: Class of '99* (also known as *Comedy Central Presents the American Comedy Awards Viewer's Choice*), Comedy Central, 1999.
NFL All–Star Comedy Blitz, CBS, 1999.
Saturday Night Live: 25th Anniversary (also known as *Saturday Night Live: 25th Anniversary Primetime Special*), NBC, 1999.
Cohost, *Macy's Fourth of July Fireworks Spectacular,* NBC, 2000.
Host, *My VH1 Music Awards Pre–Show,* VH1, 2000.
Voice of King Maynard, *Princess and the Pauper: An Animated Special from the "Happily Ever After: Fairy Tales for Every Child" Series* (animated), HBO, 2000.

AFI's 100 Years ... 100 Laughs (also known as *AFI's 100 Years, 100 Laughs: America's Funniest Movies*), CBS, 2000.

Himself, *Laugh Track: 20 Years of Comedy on MTV,* MTV, 2001.

Himself, *MTV Icon: Janet Jackson,* MTV, 2001.

Voice of Bonyo, *The Valiant Little Tailor: An Animated Special from the "Happily Ever After: Fairy Tales for Every Child" Series* (animated), HBO, 2001.

Himself, *The Book of David: The Cult Figure's Manifesto,* Comedy Central, 2002.

Rock Stars Do the Dumbest Things, VH1, 2003.

Voice of Landanlius "The Truth" Truefield, *Crank Yankers Christmas Special,* Comedy Central, 2004.

Uncle Henry, "The Muppets' Wizard of Oz" (musical), *The Wonderful World of Disney,* ABC, 2005.

Television Appearances; Awards Presentations:

Presenter, *Soul Train Comedy Awards,* 1993.

Met Life Presents the Apollo Theatre Hall of Fame (also known as *Apollo Theatre Hall of Fame*), NBC, 1994.

Performer, *The 67th Annual Academy Awards,* ABC, 1995.

Presenter, *The 11th Annual American Comedy Awards,* ABC, 1997.

Presenter, *The 12th Annual American Comedy Awards,* Fox, 1998.

Presenter, *The 30th Annual NAACP Image Awards,* Fox, 1999.

Presenter, *My VH1 Music Awards,* VH1, 2000.

Himself, *VH1 Big in 2002 Awards* (also known as *Big in 2002*), VH1, 2002.

Host, *Young Hollywood Awards,* American Movie Classics, 2003.

Presenter, *The Fifth Annual Family Television Awards,* The WB, 2003.

Himself, *BET Comedy Awards,* Black Entertainment Television, 2004.

Performer, *The 20th IFP Independent Spirit Awards,* Bravo and Independent Film Channel, 2005.

Television Appearances; Episodic:

Desk sergeant, "The Lock Box," *The Equalizer,* CBS, 1985.

Hometown, CBS, 1985.

Professor Byron Wallcott, "Romancing Mr. Stone," *A Different World,* NBC, 1987.

Harold, "Soldiers," *Tour of Duty,* CBS, 1988.

Secret Service man, "Child's Play," *Tanner '88* (also known as *Tanner: A Political Fable*), HBO, 1988.

Howard, *Baby Boom,* NBC, 1988.

First FBI agent, "Wanted: Dead or Alive," *ALF,* NBC, 1989.

Reverend Leon Lonnie Love, "The Break Up: Part 2," *Martin,* Fox, 1993.

Reverend Leon Lonnie Love, "Checks, Lie, and Videotape," *Martin,* Fox, 1993.

Himself, "Darker Than Me," *The South Bank Show,* Independent Television, 1994.

Reverend Leon Lonnie Love, "Wedding Bell Blues," *Martin,* Fox, 1995.

(As David Alan Griers) Voice of one of the three bears, "Goldilocks and the Three Bears," *Happily Ever After: Fairy Tales for Every Child* (animated), HBO, 1995.

Voice of Marlon, *Steven Spielberg Presents "Pinky and the Brain"* (animated; also known as *Pinky and the Brain*), The WB, 1995.

"Take Two Tablets, and Get Me to Mt. Sinai," *Dream On,* HBO, 1995, also broadcast on Fox.

Reverend Leon Lonnie Love, "I, Martin, Take Thee, Pam?," *Martin,* Fox, 1997.

Himself, "Kenan & Kel Go to Hollywood," *Kenan & Kel,* Nickelodeon, 1998.

Gil, "Chemistry," *Cosby,* CBS, 1998.

Voice, *Hercules* (animated; also known as *Disney's "Hercules"*), ABC and syndicated, 1998.

Himself, "Aww, Here It Goes to Hollywood: Part 2," *Kenan & Kel,* Nickelodeon, 1999.

Himself, *Pulp Comics: David Alan Grier* (also known as *Pulp Comedy*), Comedy Central, 1999.

(Uncredited) Audience member, "Hollywood A.D.," *The X–Files,* Fox, 2000.

Voice of Tubunch, "Stress Test," *Buzz Lightyear of Star Command* (animated; also known as *Disney/Pixar's "Buzz Lightyear of Star Command"*), UPN and syndicated, 2000.

Himself, "African Americans in Television," *Inside TV Land* (also known as *Inside TV Land: African Americans in Television*), TV Land, 2002.

Laurence Williams, "Chapter Forty–Two," *Boston Public,* Fox, 2002.

Aladdin, *Sesame Street* (also known as *Canadian Sesame Street, The New Sesame Street, Open Sesame, Sesame Park,* and *Les amis de Sesame*), PBS, 2002.

Ed Bradley, *Mad TV,* Fox, 2002.

Jimmy, "The Sweet Hairafter," *My Wife and Kids* (also known as *Wife and Kids*), ABC, 2003.

Himself, *Mad TV,* Fox, 2003.

Lunch Box Lewis, *Mad TV,* Fox, 2004.

Jimmy, "The Bahamas: Parts 1 & 2," *My Wife and Kids* (also known as *Wife and Kids*), ABC, 2005.

Appeared in *All My Children,* ABC. Some sources cite an appearance as Jazz Moe in *Life with Bonnie,* ABC.

Television Guest Appearances; Episodic:

Guest host, *Later* (also known as *Later with Bob Costas, Later with Cynthia Garrett,* and *Later with Greg Kinnear*), NBC, 1994.

Guest host, *Saturday Night Live* (also known as *NBC's "Saturday Night," Saturday Night, Saturday Night Live '80, SNL,* and *SNL 25*), NBC, 1995, 1997.

The Rodman World Tour (also known as *Dennis Rodman's World Tour '96*), MTV, 1996.

The Chris Rock Show, HBO, 1997.

The Rosie O'Donnell Show, syndicated, multiple appearances between 1997 and 2002.

Politically Incorrect with Bill Maher (also known as *Politically Incorrect*), ABC, 1998.

Host and panelist, *The List,* VH1, 1999.

The Daily Show (also known as *The Daily Show with Jon Stewart* and *The Daily Show with Jon Stewart Global Edition*), Comedy Central, 1999.

Late Night with Conan O'Brien, NBC, 1999, 2002, 2005.

Howard Stern, 2000.

Pajama Party, 2000.

The Late Late Show with Craig Kilborn (also known as *The Late Late Show*), CBS, multiple appearances between 2000 and 2004.

Contestant, *Who Wants to Be a Millionaire,* ABC, 2001.

Tough Crowd with Colin Quinn (also known as *Tough Crowd*), Comedy Central, 2002.

Jamie Foxx Presents Laffapalooza, Showtime, c. 2002.

Himself, "The Best of Chappelle's Show: Volume 2 Mixtape," *Chappelle's Show,* Comedy Central, 2003.

Cedric the Entertainer Presents, Fox, 2003.

Dinner for Five, Independent Film Channel, 2003.

E! News Daily (also known as *E! News Live* and *E! News Live Weekend*), E! Entertainment Television, 2003.

The Isaac Mizrahi Show, Oxygen Network, 2003.

Last Call with Carson Daly, NBC, 2004.

Late Show with David Letterman (also known as *The Late Show* and *Late Show Backstage*), CBS, 2004.

Live with Regis and Kelly, syndicated, 2004, 2005.

Jimmy Kimmel Live, ABC, multiple appearances in 2004 and 2005, 2006.

The Tony Danza Show, syndicated, 2005.

Too Late with Adam Carolla, Comedy Central, 2005.

Unscripted (also known as *Untitled Section Fight Comedy*), HBO, 2005.

The View, ABC, 2005.

Television Appearances; Pilots:

Dieter Philbin, "Kingpins," *CBS Summer Playhouse,* CBS, 1987.

Host, *Pure Insanity!,* Fox, 1990.

Various characters, *In Living Color,* Fox, 1990.

David Preston, *The Preston Episodes,* Fox, 1995.

Bernard, *Damon,* Fox, 1998.

The Next Big Thing, CBS, 1999.

Agent Jerome Daggett, *DAG,* NBC, 2000.

Voice of dog, *Dog Days,* NBC, 2000.

David Bellows, *Life with Bonnie,* ABC, 2002.

The Davey Gee Show, Fox, 2005.

Television Producer:

Executive producer, *The Preston Episodes* (series), Fox, 1995.

Producer, *The Book of David: The Cult Figure's Manifesto* (special), Comedy Central, 2002.

Executive producer, *The Davey Gee Show* (pilot), Fox, 2005.

Film Appearances:

Roger Hicks, *Streamers,* United Artists, 1983.

Corporal Cobb, *A Soldier's Story,* Columbia, 1984.

Elliot Morrison, *Beer* (also known as *The Selling of America*), Orion, 1986.

Don "No Soul" Simmons, *Amazon Women on the Moon* (also known as *Cheeseburger Film Sandwich*), Universal, 1987.

Steve Hadley, *From the Hip,* De Laurentiis Entertainment Group, 1987.

Newsperson, *I'm Gonna Git You Sucka,* Metro–Goldwyn–Mayer, 1988.

Peter Conklin, *Ich und Er* (also known as *Me and Him*), Columbia, 1988.

Rogers, *Off Limits* (also known as *Saigon*), Twentieth Century–Fox, 1988.

Detective Bill, *Almost an Angel,* Paramount Home Video, 1990.

Drummond, *Loose Cannons,* TriStar, 1990.

Himself, *The Player,* Fine Line Features, 1992.

Gerard Jackson, *Boomerang,* Paramount, 1992.

Fred Ostroff, *In the Army Now* (also known as *You're in the Army Now*), Buena Vista, 1994.

Kevin Walker, *Blankman,* Columbia, 1994.

Carl, *Tales from the Hood,* Savoy Pictures, 1995.

Carl Bentley, *Jumanji,* TriStar, 1995.

Detective Augustus, *Top of the World,* 1997.

Ensign Charles T. Parker, *McHale's Navy,* Universal, 1997.

The Devil, *Damned If You Do,* Mixed Media, 1999.

Mr. Butz, *Freeway 2* (also known as *Freeway II: Confessions of a Trickbaby*), Full Moon Entertainment, 1999.

Voice of Red, *Stuart Little,* Columbia, 1999.

Charlie Johnson, *Return to Me* (also known as *Distance Calls*), Metro–Goldwyn–Mayer, 2000.

Jenkins, *3 Strikes,* Metro–Goldwyn–Mayer, 2000.

Measures, *The Adventures of Rocky and Bullwinkle* (also known as *Die Abenteuer von Rocky und Bullwinkle*), Universal, 2000.

Mugger in Central Park, *15 Minutes* (also known as *15 Minuten Ruhm*), New Line Cinema, 2001.

Strip club owner, *I Shaved My Legs for This,* 2001.

Art City 3: A Ruling Passion (documentary), Twelve Films, 2002.

Jerry Robin, Jr., *Tiptoes* (also known as *Tiny Tiptoes*), Reality Check Productions, 2003.

Limousine driver, *Blue Collar Comedy Tour: The Movie,* Warner Bros., 2003.

Bob, *The Woodsman,* Newmarket Films, 2004.

Clyde Houston, *How to Get the Man's Foot outta Your Ass* (also known as *Baadasssss!, Badass,* and *Gettin' the Man's Foot outta Your Baadasssss!*), Sony Pictures Classics, 2004.

Himself, *Lexie,* York Entertainment, 2004.
Jim Fields, *Bewitched,* Columbia, 2005.
Brother James, *East of A,* Cinema Libre Studio, 2006.
Himself, *Hooked* (short film), 2006.

Stage Appearances:

Mahagonny (opera; also known as *The Rise and Fall of the City of Mahagonny*), Yale Repertory Theatre, New Haven, CT, 1978–79.
Measure for Measure, Yale Repertory Theatre, 1979–80.
Timon of Athens, Yale Repertory Theatre, 1979–80.
An Attempt at Flying, Yale Repertory Theatre, 1980–81.
The Suicide, Yale Repertory Theatre, 1980–81.
Winterset, Yale Repertory Theatre, 1980–81.
Jackie Robinson, *The First* (musical), Martin Beck Theatre, New York City, 1981.
Love's Labour's Lost, Yale Repertory Theatre, 1981–82.
Private C. J. Memphis, *A Soldier's Play,* Negro Ensemble Company, Theatre Four, New York City, 1981–82, then Goodman Theatre, Chicago, IL, 1982–83.
James Thunder Early, *Dreamgirls* (musical), Imperial Theatre, New York City, between 1981 and 1985.
Murderer and Richmond, *King Richard III,* New York Shakespeare Festival, Public Theatre, Delacorte Theatre, New York City, 1983.
Aslak, *Peer Gynt,* Williamstown Theatre Festival, Main Stage, Williamstown, MA, 1984.
Thomas, *Distant Fires,* Hartford Stage Company, Hartford, CT, 1985–86.
Master Frank Ford, *The Merry Wives of Windsor,* New York Shakespeare Festival, Public Theatre, Delacorte Theatre, 1994.
Whitelaw Savory, *One Touch of Venus,* City Center Theatre Encores!, Great American Musicals in Concert, New York City, 1996.
Pseudolus and Prologus, *A Funny Thing Happened on the Way to the Forum* (musical), St. James Theatre, New York City, c. 1997–98.
Fernando Perez, *The Mambo Kings* (musical), Golden Gate Theatre, San Francisco, CA, 2005.
The Second Annual New York Comedy Festival, New York City, 2005.

Radio Appearances; Series:

Supporting role, "Star Wars," *NPR Playhouse,* National Public Radio, 1981.
Supporting role, "The Empire Strikes Back," *NPR Playhouse,* National Public Radio, 1983.

Radio Appearances; Episodic:

The Howard Stern Radio Show, 2000.

Frequent guest, *Loveline,* KROQ (Los Angeles) and syndicated.

RECORDINGS

Videos:

Himself, *Late Night with Conan O'Brien: The Best of Triumph the Insult Comic Dog* (also known as *The Best of Triumph the Insult Comedy Dog*), Lions Gate Films Home Entertainment, 2004.
Himself, *Bewitched: Star Shots,* Sony Pictures Home Entertainment, 2005.
Himself, *Casting a Spell: Making "Bewitched,"* Sony Pictures Home Entertainment, 2005.
(Uncredited) Himself, *Kermit: A Frog's Life,* Walt Disney, 2005.
Himself, *Why I Love "Bewitched,"* Sony Pictures Home Entertainment, 2005.

WRITINGS

Teleplays; Series:

Special material, *In Living Color,* Fox, 1992–93.
Stand-up material, *Premium Blend* (also known as *Comedy Central's "Premium Blend"*), Comedy Central, 2001–2002.

Teleplays; Specials:

The Book of David: The Cult Figure's Manifesto, Comedy Central, 2002.

Teleplays; Episodic:

Pulp Comics: David Alan Grier (also known as *Pulp Comedy*), Comedy Central, 1999.

As a comedian, contributed material to episodes of various series.

Teleplays; Pilots:

The Davey Gee Show, Fox, 2005.

OTHER SOURCES

Books:

Contemporary Black Biography, Volume 28, Gale, 2001.
Who's Who among African Americans, 18th edition, Gale, 2005.

Periodicals:

Movieline, August, 1994, pp. 16–17.
People Weekly, December 2, 2002, p. 183.
Playbill, August 18, 1997.

GRIER, Pam 1949–
    (Pam Greer, Pamela Grier)

PERSONAL

Full name, Pamela Suzette Grier; born May 26, 1949, in Winston–Salem, NC; daughter of Clarence Ransom (a military aircraft mechanic) and Gwendolyn Sylvia (a registered nurse; maiden name, Samuels) Grier; cousin of Roosevelt Grier (a professional football player and actor). *Education:* Attended Metropolitan State College, Denver, CO, and the University of California, Los Angeles; studied acting. *Religion:* Methodist. *Avocational Interests:* Skiing, scuba diving, horseback riding, tennis.

Addresses: *Agent*—Steve LaManna, Innovative Artists, 1505 10th St., Santa Monica, CA 90401.

Career: Actress. Performed as a singer and participated in beauty pageants. Switchboard operator at a talent agency and for American International Pictures, c. 1969. Some sources state that Grier founded a production company, sang at various venues with the singer Snoop Dogg, worked as a cheerleader for the Denver Broncos, was a presenter at the Newark Black Film Festival, and operated a design firm. Also known as Pam Greer.

Member: Screen Actors Guild, American Federation of Television and Radio Artists, Actors' Equity Association, Academy of Motion Picture Arts and Sciences, Amnesty International.

Awards, Honors: Image Award, best actress, National Association for the Advancement of Colored People, 1986, for *Fool for Love;* Achievement awards, National Black Theatre Festival and African–American Film Society, both 1993; Tuesday, October 13, 1998, declared Pam Grier Day in Denver, CO, by Denver mayor Wellington E. Webb; Career Achievement awards, Chicago International Film Festival, 1998, and Acapulco Black Film Festival, 1999; Golden Globe Award nomination, best performance by an actress in a comedy or musical film, Screen Actors Guild Award nomination, outstanding performance by a female actor in a leading role, Image Award nomination, outstanding lead actress in a motion picture, Golden Satellite Award nomination, best performance by an actress in a motion picture—comedy or musical, International Press Academy, and Saturn Award nomination, best actress, Academy of Science Fiction, Fantasy, and Horror Films, all 1998, and Golden Slate, best female performance, Csapnivalo awards, 2000, all for *Jackie Brown;* Image Award nominations, outstanding lead actress in a comedy series, 1999 and 2000, both for *Linc's;* Daytime Emmy Award nomination, outstanding performer in an animated program, 2000, for "The Empress's Nightingale," *Happily Ever After: Fairy Tales for Every Child;* Susan B. Anthony "Failure Is Impossible" Award, High Falls Film Festival, 2001; Black Reel Award nomination, best actress in a theatrical film, Foundation for the Advancement of African Americans in Film, 2002, for *Bones;* Image Award nomination, outstanding actress in a television movie, miniseries, or dramatic special, 2002, for *3 A.M.;* Trumpet Award for

film, 2003; Image Award nominations, outstanding supporting actress in a drama series, 2003 and 2004, both for *Law & Order: Special Victims Unit;* Image Award nominations, outstanding supporting actress in a drama series, 2005 and 2006, both for *The L Word;* named one of the 100 most fascinating women of the twentieth century, *Ebony* magazine.

CREDITS

Film Appearances:

(As Pamela Grier) Partygoer, *Beyond the Valley of the Dolls* (also known as *Hollywood Vixens*), Twentieth Century–Fox, 1970.

Grear, *The Big Doll House* (also known as *Bamboo Dolls House, Women's Penitentiary,* and *Women's Penitentiary II*), New World, 1971.

Alabama, *Women in Cages* (also known as *Women's Penitentiary III*), New World, 1972.

Blossom, *The Big Bird Cage* (also known as *Women's Penitentiary II*), New World, 1972.

(As Pamela Grier) Gozelda, *Hit Man,* Metro–Goldwyn–Mayer, 1972.

Lee Daniels, *Black Mama, White Mama* (also known as *Chained Women, Chains of Hate, Hot, Hard, and Mean,* and *Women in Chains*), American International Pictures, 1972.

(As Pamela Grier) Mona, *Cool Breeze,* Metro–Goldwyn–Mayer, 1972.

Aleysa the panther woman, *Twilight People* (also known as *Beasts* and *Island of the Twilight People*), Dimension Films, 1973.

Title role, *Coffy,* American International Pictures, 1973.

Lisa, *Scream, Blacula, Scream!* (also known as *Blacula Is Beautiful, Blacula Lives Again!, Blacula II,* and *The Name Is Blacula*), American International Pictures, 1973.

Title role, *Foxy Brown,* American International Pictures, 1974.

Mamawi, *The Arena* (also known as *Naked Warriors* and *La rivolta delle gladiatrici*), New World, 1974.

Aretha, *Bucktown,* American International Pictures, 1975.

Title role, *Friday Foster,* American International Pictures, 1975.

Sheba Shayne, *Sheba, Baby,* American International Pictures, 1975.

(As Pamela Grier) Regine, *Drum,* United Artists, 1976.

Mary Jones, *Greased Lightning,* Warner Bros., 1977.

(As Pamela Grier) Sandra, *La notte dell'alta marea* (also known as *The Night of the High Tide* and *Twilight of Love*), 1977.

Charlotte, *Fort Apache, the Bronx,* Twentieth Century–Fox, 1981.

Dust witch, *Something Wicked This Way Comes,* Buena Vista, 1983.

Myra, *Tough Enough,* Twentieth Century–Fox, 1983.

Cathryn Bolan, *Stand Alone,* New World, 1985.

Cora, *On the Edge,* Skouras Pictures, 1985.

Hunter, *The Vindicator* (also known as *Frankenstein '88*), Fox Home Video, 1986.

Sergeant MacLeish, *The Allnighter,* Universal, 1987.

Delores "Jacks" Jackson, *Above the Law* (also known as *Nico* and *Nico: Above the Law*), Warner Bros., 1988.

Ruth Butler, *The Package,* Orion, 1989.

Ms. Connors, *Class of 1999,* Taurus Entertainment, 1990.

Ms. Wardroe, *Bill & Ted's Bogus Journey,* Orion, 1991.

Phoebe, *Posse,* Gramercy Pictures, 1993.

Captain Maggie Davis, *Serial Killer,* Republic, 1996.

Hershe Las Palmas, *Escape from L.A.* (also known as *John Carpenter's "Escape from L.A."*), Paramount, 1996.

Laurie Thompson, *Original Gangstas* (also known as *Hot City*), Orion, 1996.

Louise Williams, *Mars Attacks!,* Warner Bros., 1996.

Annabelle Lee, *Fakin' da Funk,* Octillion Entertainment, 1997.

Title role, *Jackie Brown,* Miramax, 1997.

Janette, *Strip Search,* A–pix Entertainment/Quadra Entertainment, 1997.

Detective Vera Cruz, *Jawbreaker,* Columbia/TriStar, 1998.

Diane, *No Tomorrow,* PM Entertainment Group, 1998.

Woo, *New Line Cinema, 1998.

Carol, *Holy Smoke!,* Miramax, 1999.

Detective Angela Wilson, *In Too Deep,* Dimension Films, 1999.

Susan Mendenhall (some sources cite Susan Teller), *Fortress 2* (also known as *Fortress 2: Re–Entry*), 1999.

Detective Della Wilder (title role), *Wilder* (also known as *Slow Burn* and *Wilder: Profession detective*), Dream Rock/Bedford Entertainment, 2000.

Tina, *Snow Day,* Paramount, 2000.

Commander Helena Braddock, *Ghosts of Mars* (also known as *John Carpenter's "Ghosts of Mars"*), Screen Gems/Columbia/TriStar, 2001.

Pearl, *Bones,* New Line Cinema, 2001.

Linda Fox, *Love the Hard Way,* Vine International Pictures, 2001, Kino International, 2003.

Flura Nash, *The Adventures of Pluto Nash* (also known as *Pluto Nash*), Warner Bros., 2002.

Mrs. Williams, *Baby of the Family,* DownSouth Filmworks, 2002.

(Uncredited; in archive footage) Herself, *Undercover Brother,* Universal, 2002.

Herself, *A Decade under the Influence* (documentary), IFC Films, 2003.

Zelda, *Untitled Ryan McKinney Project,* Dark Portal, c. 2006.

Film Work:

Performer of title song, *The Big Doll House* (also known as *Bamboo Dolls House, Women's Penitentiary,* and *Women's Penitentiary II*), New World, 1971.

Performer of songs that have appeared in other films.

Television Appearances; Series:

Suzanne Terry, *Crime Story,* NBC, c. 1986–88.

Eleanor Braithwaite Winthrop, *Linc's,* Showtime, 1998–2000.

Host, *Women & the Badge,* Oxygen Network, beginning 2002.

Kit Porter, *The L Word* (also known as *Earthlings*), Showtime, beginning 2004.

Television Appearances; Miniseries:

Francey, *Roots: The Next Generations,* ABC, 1979.

Suzette Lermontant, *Feast of All Saints* (also known as *Anne Rice's "The Feast of All Saints"*), Showtime, 2001.

Herself, *The 100 Most Memorable TV Moments,* TV Land, 2004.

Television Appearances; Movies:

Alexandra "Alie" Horn, *Badge of the Assassin,* CBS, 1985.

Linda Holman, *A Mother's Right: The Elizabeth Morgan Story* (also known as *Shattered Silence*), ABC, 1992.

Mrs. Quincy, *Family Blessings* (also known as *LaVyrle Spencer's "Family Blessings"*), CBS, 1996.

Sam, *Hayley Wagner, Star,* HBO, 1999.

George, *3 A.M.,* Showtime, 2001.

Claire Washburn, *1st to Die* (also known as *F1rst to Die* and *James Patterson's "F1rst to Die"*), NBC, 2003.

Mrs. Cooper, *Back in the Day,* Black Entertainment Television, 2005.

Television Appearances; Specials:

Herself, *The Making of "Something Wicked This Way Comes,"* 1983.

Narrator, *Paul Robeson: Speak of Me As I Am,* PBS, 1998.

(As Pamela Grier) Voice of the nightingale, "The Empress's Nightingale," *Happily Ever After: Fairy Tales for Every Child* (animated; also known as *The Empress's Nightingale: An Animated Special from "The Happily Ever After: Fairy Tales for Every Child"* Series), HBO, 1999.

Herself, *It Conquered Hollywood! The Story of American International Pictures* (documentary), American Movie Classics, 2001.

The Sandra Bernhard Experience, Arts and Entertainment, 2001.

Herself, *Totally Gayer,* VH1, 2004.

Television Appearances; Awards Presentations:

16th Annual Black Filmmakers Hall of Fame, syndicated, 1989.

Herself, *Fourth Annual Screen Actors Guild Awards* (also known as *Screen Actors Guild Fourth Annual Awards*), TNT, 1998.

Presenter, *The 25th Annual American Music Awards,* ABC, 1998.

Presenter, *The 29th NAACP Image Awards,* Fox, 1998.

Presenter, *The Source Hip–Hop Music Awards,* UPN, 2001.

Presenter, *World Stunt Awards,* ABC, 2001.

Herself, *2003 Trumpet Awards,* TBS, 2003.

Television Appearances; Episodic:

Guest, *The Tonight Show Starring Johnny Carson* (also known as *The Best of Carson*), NBC, multiple episodes in 1973.

Guest, *Soul Train,* syndicated, 1973, 1977.

Cynthia Williams, "The Kinfolk/Sis and the Slicker/Moonlight and Moonshine/Affair: Parts 1 & 2," *The Love Boat,* ABC, 1980.

Valerie Gordon, "Prodigal Son," *Miami Vice,* NBC, 1985.

Valerie Gordon, "Rites of Passage," *Miami Vice,* NBC, 1985.

Benet Collins, "Hurricane: Parts 1 & 2," *Night Court,* NBC, 1986.

Samantha, "Planning Parenthood," *The Cosby Show,* NBC, 1987.

Neema Sharone, "Frank's Place: The Movie," *Frank's Place,* CBS, 1988.

Susan Province, "Blood Red," *Midnight Caller,* NBC, 1989.

Lieutenant Guthrie, "Dead but Not Buried: Part 1," *Knots Landing,* CBS, 1990.

Lieutenant Guthrie, "What If?," *Knots Landing,* CBS, 1990.

Valerie Gordon, "Too Much, Too Late," *Miami Vice,* NBC, 1990.

"Hostile Takeover," *Monsters,* 1991.

Grace Ballard, "My Favorite Dad," *Pacific Station,* NBC, 1992.

Janice Robertson, "M Is for the Many Things She Gave Me," *The Fresh Prince of Bel–Air,* NBC, 1994.

Lynn Montgomery, "The Telethon," *The Sinbad Show,* Fox, 1994.

Major Vanetta Brown, "Rainbow Comix," *The Marshal,* ABC, 1995.

Herself, "All the Players Came," *Martin,* Fox, 1995.

Anita Grayson, "Pillow Talk," *Sparks* (also known as *Sparks, Sparks, and Sparks*), UPN, 1996.

Erica, "Goin' to the Net," *The Wayans Bros.,* The WB, 1996.

Herself, "Show n97," *Mundo VIP,* 1998.

Voice of Julie Auburn, "Inherit the Wheeze," *Steven Spielberg Presents "Pinky and the Brain"* (animated; also known as *Pinky and the Brain*), The WB, 1998.

Guest host, *Mad TV,* Fox, 1998.

Guest, *The Rosie O'Donnell Show,* syndicated, 1998.

Brenda, "The Sins of the Mother and ... the Boyfriend," *For Your Love,* The WB, 1999.

Voice of Mother Springbok, "Stick Your Neck Out," *The Wild Thornberrys* (animated), Nickelodeon, 1999.

Herself, *Intimate Portrait: Pam Grier,* Lifetime, 1999.

Bar owner, "Time Is on My Side," *Strange Frequency,* VH1, 2001.

Guest, *The Late Late Show with Craig Kilborn* (also known as *The Late Late Show*), CBS, 2001.

Herself, *Miami Vice: The E! True Hollywood Story,* E! Entertainment Television, 2001.

Hollywood Unleashed, Animal Planet, 2001.

The Test, FX Channel, 2001.

Assistant United States attorney Claudia Williams, "Disappearing Acts," *Law & Order: Special Victims Unit* (also known as *Law & Order's Sex Crimes, Law & Order: SVU,* and *Special Victims Unit*), NBC, 2002.

Dr. Lewis, "Switch," *Night Visions,* Fox, 2002.

Voice of My'ria'h, "A Knight of Shadows: Parts 1 & 2," *Justice League* (animated; also known as *JL, JLA,* and *Justice League of America*), Cartoon Network, 2002.

Assistant United States attorney Claudia Williams, "Pandora," *Law & Order: Special Victims Unit* (also known as *Law & Order's Sex Crimes, Law & Order: SVU,* and *Special Victims Unit*), NBC, 2003.

Guest, *The Wayne Brady Show,* syndicated, 2004.

Herself, *Snoop Dogg: The E! True Hollywood Story,* E! Entertainment Television, 2005.

Also appeared in an episode of *In Living Color,* Fox.

Television Appearances; Pilots:

Kit Porter, *The L Word* (also known as *Earthlings*), Showtime, 2004.

Stage Appearances:

Frankie and Johnny at the Clair de Lune, c. 1980.

May, *Fool for Love,* Los Angeles Theatre Center, Los Angeles, 1985–86.

Telltale Hearts, Crossroads Theatre Company, New Brunswick, NJ, 1993–94.

Also appeared in *The Piano Lesson.*

RECORDINGS

Videos:

Herself, *Baadasssss Cinema* (documentary), New Video Group, 2002.

Herself, *Diggin' Up "Bones"* (short), New Line Home Video, 2002.

Herself, *Jackie Brown: How It Went Down* (short documentary), Miramax Home Entertainment, 2002.

(In archive footage) Herself, *Sex at 24 Frames per Second* (documentary; also known as *Playboy Presents "Sex at 24 Frames per Second: The Ultimate Journey through Sex in Cinema"*), Playboy Entertainment Group, 2003.

Albums:
Performed as a backup singer for albums recorded by Bobby Womack, early 1970s.

Music Videos:
Snoop Dogg (as Snoop Doggy Dogg), "Doggy Dogg World," 1994.

OTHER SOURCES

Books:
Contemporary Black Biography, Volume 31, Gale, 2001.
St. James Encyclopedia of Popular Culture, five volumes, St. James Press, 2000.
Who's Who among African Americans, 18th edition, Gale, 2005.

Periodicals:
Essence, July, 1996, p. 28; September, 2001, p. 72.
Fangoria, January, 2002, pp. 50–53.
Femme Fatales, May, 2002, pp. 60–61.
Interview, January, 1998, p. 78.
Jet, March 2, 1998; April 13, 1998, p. 36; August 3, 1998, p. 62; March 1, 1999, p. 49; August 23, 1999, p. 36.
People Weekly, May 13, 1996, p. 137; January 26, 1998, p. 138.
Request, May/June, 2002, p. 41.
TV Guide, August 1, 1998, pp. 20–22; February 1, 2003, pp. 20–22.

GROH, David 1941–

PERSONAL

Full name, David Lawrence Groh; born May 21, 1939 (some sources cite 1941), in New York, NY; son of Benjamin and Mildred Groh; married Denise Arsenault, 1984 (marriage ended); married Karla Pergande (some sources spell first name Carla), 1988; children: Spencer Arthur. *Education:* Brown University, B.A., 1961; also attended London Academy of Music and Dramatic Art.

Addresses: *Agent*—Sharon Kemp Agency, 447 South Robertson Blvd., Suite 204, Beverly Hills, CA 90211; The Gersh Agency, 222 North Canon Dr., Beverly Hills, CA 90210.

Career: Actor. Appeared in commercials. *Military service:* U.S. Army, 1963–64.

Member: Actors' Equity Association, Screen Actors Guild, American Federation of Television and Radio Artists, Phi Beta Kappa.

Awards, Honors: Fulbright scholar, 1962–63.

CREDITS

Television Appearances; Series:
Hangman's assistant and one–armed man, *Dark Shadows,* ABC, beginning c. 1966.
Simon, *Love Is a Many Splendored Thing,* CBS, 1972–73.
Joe Gerard, *Rhoda,* CBS, 1974–77.
Don Gardner, *Another Day,* CBS, 1978.
D. L. Brock, *General Hospital,* ABC, 1983–85.
Lieutenant Walker, *Black Scorpion* (also known as *Roger Corman Presents "Black Scorpion"*), Sci–Fi Channel, 2001.

Television Appearances; Miniseries:
Rocco Salvatore, *The Dream Merchants,* Operation Prime Time, 1980.
Tony Guidice, *Power,* NBC, 1980.
Bert Allenberg, *Sinatra* (also known as *The Frank Sinatra Story*), CBS, 1992.

Television Appearances; Movies:
Benjamin Wise, *Victory at Entebbe,* ABC, 1976.
Dale, *Smash–Up on Interstate 5,* ABC, 1976.
Harry Benson, *Murder at the Mardi Gras,* NBC, 1978.
Jack Farnham, *The Child Stealer,* ABC, 1979.
Jim Huggins, *Tourist,* Operation Prime Time, 1980.
Jeff Bennett, *This Is Kate Bennett,* ABC, 1982.
Michael (some sources cite Mason) Drumm, *Broken Vows,* 1987.
Marty Alberts, *Menu for Murder* (also known as *Murder at the P.T.A. Luncheon*), CBS, 1990.
Bendix, *Last Exit to Earth* (also known as *Roger Corman Presents "Last Exit to Earth"*), Showtime, 1996.
Martin Crispin, *Acts of Betrayal* (also known as *True Blue*), HBO, 1997.
Adrian Friar, *The Cowboy and the Movie Star* (also known as *Love on the Edge*), Fox Family Channel, 1998.
Abe, *Take My Advice: The Ann and Abby Story,* Lifetime, 1999.
Captain Barnett, *Blowback* (also known as *Guardian*), HBO, 1999.

Television Appearances; Specials:
CBS team member, *Battle of the Network Stars,* ABC, 1977.

Television Appearances; Episodic:
Dick Elmore, "Face for a Shadow," *Police Story,* NBC, 1975.

Joe Gerard, "Mary Richards Falls in Love," *Mary Tyler Moore* (also known as *The Mary Tyler Moore Show*), CBS, 1975.

Himself, *Celebrity Sweepstakes,* NBC, 1975.

Detective Frank Benson, "The Other Side of the Fence," *Police Story,* NBC, 1976.

Bert Fredicks, "Help, Murder," *The Love Boat,* ABC, 1977.

Dan Gentry, "Hard Rock Brown," *Police Story,* NBC, 1977.

Marty Lacayo, "Prime Rib," *Police Story,* NBC, 1977.

Guest, *Dinah!* (also known as *Dinah! & Friends*), syndicated, 1977.

Major Duke Danton, "Planet of the Slave Girls," *Buck Rogers in the 25th Century,* NBC, 1979.

Himself, "The Great 5K Star Race and Boulder Wrap Party: Part 2," *CHiPs,* NBC, 1980.

Ben Daniels, "Romance Times Three," *Fantasy Island,* ABC, 1981.

Donnelly, "Creepy Time Gal," *Trapper John, M.D.,* CBS, 1982.

Jack Brenner, "The Zertigo Diamond Caper," *CBS Children's Mystery Theatre,* CBS, 1982.

Joe, "Bank Job," *Today's F.B.I.,* ABC, 1982.

Stuart Glick, "The Visitors," *Matt Houston,* ABC, 1983.

Devon Sinclair, "Watch Out!" *Whiz Kids,* CBS, 1984.

Bass, "Under Special Circumstances," *MacGruder and Loud,* ABC, 1985.

Brad Evans, "Haunted Memories," *Finder of Lost Loves,* ABC, 1985.

Dr. Stan Garfield, "Murder Digs Deep," *Murder, She Wrote,* CBS, 1985.

Howard Terrell, "Hearts and Minds," *Hotel* (also known as *Arthur Hailey's "Hotel"*), ABC, 1985.

Jonathan, "The Skull of Nostradamus," *Simon & Simon,* CBS, 1985.

Bill Malone, "The Bully," *Kate & Allie,* CBS, 1986.

Angel/Aldo, "Let the Games Begin," *Tales from the Darkside,* syndicated, 1987.

Tony Romano, "Thanksgiving," *Spenser: For Hire,* ABC, 1987.

Gordon Tully, "How to Make a Killing," *Murder, She Wrote,* CBS, 1989.

Ken Martin, "Yesterday's Child," *Hunter,* NBC, 1989.

Dr. Jacob Lowenstein, "Indifference," *Law & Order,* NBC, 1990.

Dr. Stephen Harbaugh, "Vowel Play," *L.A. Law,* NBC, 1990.

Frank Larkin, "The Trophy: Parts 1 and 2," *Baywatch* (also known as *Baywatch Hawaii*), syndicated, 1991.

Henry Waverly, "Lines of Excellence," *Murder, She Wrote,* CBS, 1991.

"Let's Call the Whole Thing Off," *Jake and the Fatman,* CBS, 1991.

Barnum, "The Highest Court," *Dark Justice,* CBS, 1992.

Lieutenant Nolandt, "Things Are Tough All Over," *Sisters,* NBC, 1993.

Bryan Chase, "Days of Rage," *M.A.N.T.I.S.,* Fox, 1994.

Judge Joel Thayer, "Censure," *Law & Order,* NBC, 1994.

Dr. McFetridge, "Child Support," *Courthouse,* CBS, 1995.

Vince Parezi, "Free Kimmy," *Melrose Place,* Fox, 1995.

William Barnes, "Ace in the Hole," *Renegade,* USA Network and syndicated, 1995.

Jacob Weiss, "Kaddish," *The X–Files,* Fox, 1996.

Tony Blanton, "Guess Who's Coming to Dinner," *Baywatch* (also known as *Baywatch Hawaii*), syndicated, 1996.

Vince Parezi, "The Bobby Trap," *Melrose Place,* Fox, 1996.

Vince Parezi, "No Lifeguard on Duty," *Melrose Place,* Fox, 1996.

Chief petty officer "Dad" Harridan, "Heroes," *JAG,* CBS, 1997.

"Countdown to Murder," *Mike Hammer, Private Eye,* syndicated, 1998.

Don Franco, "Raging Val," *V.I.P.* (also known as *V.I.P.—Die Bodyguards*), syndicated, 1999.

Vince Terman, "Safe House," *Walker, Texas Ranger,* CBS, 1999.

Don Franco, "Franco in Love," *V.I.P.* (also known as *V.I.P.—Die Bodyguards*), Fox, 2000.

Dr. Carlton, "Family Therapy," *The Huntress,* USA Network, 2001.

Michael Goldberg, "Howdy Partner," *Girlfriends* (also known as *My Girls*), UPN, 2003.

Dr. Jacob Lowenstein, "Fixed," *Law & Order,* NBC, 2004.

Television Appearances; Pilots:

Keith Hammett, *Room for Two,* ABC, 1992.

Film Appearances:

Don Carbo, *Colpo rovente,* 1969.

Change in the Wind (also known as *Irish Whiskey Rebellion*), Cinerama, 1972.

Al, *Two–Minute Warning,* Universal, 1976.

Cohen, *A Hero Ain't Nothin' but a Sandwich,* New World, 1977.

Jerry Norton, *Hotshot* (also known as *El rey del futbol*), International Film Marketing/Arista, 1987.

Inspector Wolinski, *The Return of Superfly,* Triton Pictures/Vidmark, 1990.

Warren Wajakawakawitz, *The Stoned Age* (also known as *The Stoëned Age* and *Tack's Chicks*), Trimark Pictures, 1994.

(Uncredited) Buddy Lupton (some sources cite surname as Lufkin), *Get Shorty,* Metro–Goldwyn–Mayer, 1995.

District attorney Frank Jacobi, *Illegal in Blue,* Orion, 1995.

The lieutenant, *The Confidence Man,* One World Media, 1996.

Tony, *White Cargo* (also known as *Body Angels*), Third Coast Entertainment, 1996.

Dylan Perry, *Swimsuit: The Movie,* All Channel Films, 1997.

Jack, Sr., *Every Dog Has Its Day,* Red Dog Films, 1997.
Television station manager, *Most Wanted,* New Line Cinema, 1997.
Uncle Hutchy, *Spoiler,* 1998.
Frankie, *Black Leather Soles* (short film), 2005.
Alan, *The Trouble with Ross,* Bedford Communications, 2006.
Mr. Santucci, *Crazylove,* PorchLight Entertainment, 2006.

Stage Appearances:
The Importance of Being Earnest, off–Broadway production, 1963.
The Hot L Baltimore, off–Broadway production, 1973.
George Schneider, *Chapter Two,* Imperial Theatre, New York City, beginning 1978, play also produced at the Eugene O'Neill Theatre.
Craig Blaisdell, *Dead Wrong,* Riverwest Theatre, New York City, 1986.
Phil, *Be Happy for Me,* Douglas Fairbanks Theatre, New York City, 1986.
Andy Broude, *Road Show,* Circle Repertory Theatre, New York City, 1987.
Jack, *Tea with Mommy and Jack,* Hudson Guild Theatre, New York City, 1988.
Kenneth Hayes, *Beyond a Reasonable Doubt,* Paper Mill Playhouse, Millburn, NJ, 1988–89.
Walter Gold, *The Twilight of the Golds,* Booth Theatre, New York City, 1993.
Sam Zilinsky, *Mizlansky/Zilinsky,* Geffen Playhouse, University of California, Los Angeles, 2000.

Alan George, *The Waverly Gallery,* Pasadena Playhouse, Pasadena, CA, 2002.

Also appeared in *Antony and Cleopatra* and *Elizabeth the Queen,* both Broadway productions; and in *Face to Face,* Player's Theatre.

Stage Director:
Mango Mango, Lee Strasberg Creative Center Theatre, West Hollywood, CA, 2000.

RECORDINGS

Videos:
King Lear (also known as *The Plays of William Shakespeare—King Lear*), Kultur, c. 1983.

Video Games:
Sylvio Donato, *Voyeur II,* 1996.

OTHER SOURCES

Periodicals:
Entertainment Weekly, December 16, 1994, p. 83.
New Leader, November 15, 1993, p. 22.
TV Zone, August, 1997, pp. 18–22.

H

HACKMAN, Gene 1930–
(Eugene Alder)

PERSONAL

Full name, Eugene Alden Hackman; born January 30, 1930, in San Bernardino (some sources cite Riverside), CA; raised in Danville, IL; son of Eugene Ezra (a newspaper press operator) and Lydia Hackman; married Fay Maltese (a bank secretary), January 1, 1956 (divorced, 1986); married Betsy Arakawa, December, 1991; children: (first marriage) Christopher, Elizabeth, Leslie. *Education:* Attended University of Illinois at Urbana–Champaign; attended School of Radio Technique and Art Students League of New York, both New York City; trained at Pasadena Playhouse. *Avocational Interests:* Flying, race car driving, landscape painting, drawing, film collecting.

Addresses: *Agent*—Fred Specktor, Creative Artists Agency, 9830 Wilshire Blvd., Beverly Hills, CA 90212–1804; (voice) Special Artists Agency, 9465 Wilshire Blvd., Suite 890, Beverly Hills, CA 90212. *Publicist*—Dick Guttman, Guttman Associates, 118 South Beverly Dr., Suite 201, Beverly Hills, CA 90212.

Career: Actor and writer. Sometimes credited as Eugene Alder. The Premise (improvisational comedy group), member of company, c. 1961; Chelly Ltd. (production company), founder; New Actors Workshop teacher; voice performer for television and radio commercials; worked as a radio announcer in the Midwest; some sources cite work as an assistant director for television productions and as a floor manager at television studios. Permanent Charities Committee of the Entertainment Industries, honorary chair; worked at various jobs in New York City, 1956–58, including positions as a doorman, truck driver, and shoe salesperson; worked at a soda fountain and as a furniture mover. *Military service:* U.S. Marine Corps, radio operator and broadcaster for Armed Forces Radio, c. 1946–49; served in China, Japan, and Hawaii.

Member: Actors' Equity Association, Screen Actors Guild, American Federation of Television and Radio Artists, Academy of Motion Picture Arts and Sciences.

Awards, Honors: Clarence Derwent Award, most promising new actor, Actors' Equity Association, 1963, for *Children from Their Games;* National Society of Film Critics Award, best supporting actor, and Academy Award nomination, best actor in a supporting role, both 1968, for *Bonnie and Clyde;* Golden Laurel Award nomination, best male new face, Producers Guild of America, 1968; Academy Award nomination, best actor in a supporting role, 1971, for *I Never Sang for My Father;* New York Film Critics Circle Award, best actor, and Star of the Year Award, National Association of Theatre Owners, both 1971, Academy Award, best actor in a leading role, Golden Globe Award, best motion picture actor—drama, National Board of Review Award, best actor, and Kansas City Film Critics Circle Award, best actor, all 1972, and Film Award, best actor, British Academy of Film and Television Arts, 1973, all for *The French Connection;* Film Award, best actor, British Academy of Film and Television Arts, 1973, for *The Poseidon Adventure;* Cannes International Film Festival Award, 1973, for *Scarecrow;* Star of the Year Award, National Association of Theatre Owners, 1974; National Board of Review Award, best actor, 1974, Golden Globe Award nomination, best motion picture actor—drama, 1975, Film Award nomination, best actor, British Academy of Film and Television Arts, 1975, New York Film Critics Circle Award nomination, best actor, and performance as named one of the 100 greatest performances of all time, *Premiere* magazine, 2006, all for *The Conversation;* Bronze Wrangler Award (with others), outstanding theatrical motion picture, Western

Heritage awards, 1976, for *Bite the Bullet;* Golden Globe Award nomination, best motion picture actor—drama, and Film Award nomination, best actor, British Academy of Film and Television Arts, both 1976, for *The French Connection II;* Film Award nomination, best actor, British Academy of Film and Television Arts, 1976, for *Night Moves;* Film Award nomination, best supporting actor, British Academy of Film and Television Arts, 1979, for *Superman;* Golden Globe Award nomination, best performance by an actor in a supporting role in a motion picture, 1984, for *Under Fire;* Golden Globe Award nomination, best performance by an actor in a motion picture—drama, 1986, for *Twice in a Lifetime;* National Board of Review Award and National Society of Film Critics Award, both best actor, 1988, Silver Berlin Bear, best actor, Berlin International Film Festival, Academy Award nomination, best actor in a leading role, and Golden Globe Award nomination, best performance by an actor in a motion picture—drama, all 1989, all for *Mississippi Burning;* New York Film Critics Award and Los Angeles Film Critics Association Award, both best supporting actor, 1992, Academy Award, best actor in a supporting role, Golden Globe Award, best performance by an actor in a supporting role in a motion picture, Film Award, British Academy of Film and Television Arts, best actor in a supporting role, National Society of Film Critics Award, Boston Society of Film Critics Award, and Kansas City Film Critics Circle Award, all best supporting actor, and Bronze Wrangler Award (with others), outstanding theatrical motion picture, all 1993, all for *Unforgiven;* Bronze Wrangler Award (with others), outstanding theatrical motion picture, 1994, for *Geronimo: An American Legend;* American Comedy Award nomination, funniest actor in a motion picture (leading role), 1996, for *Get Shorty;* Golden Apple Award nomination, male star of the year, Hollywood Women's Press Club, 1996; Blockbuster Entertainment Award, favorite supporting actor—comedy, Golden Satellite Award nomination, best performance by an actor in a supporting role in a motion picture—comedy or musical, International Press Academy, and Screen Actors Guild Award (with others), outstanding performance by a cast, all 1997, for *The Birdcage;* Blockbuster Award nomination, favorite supporting actor—action/adventure, 1999, for *Enemy of the State;* Golden Globe Award, best performance by an actor in a motion picture—musical or comedy, National Society of Film Critics Award, best actor, AFI (American Film Institute) Film Award, featured actor of the year—male—movies, Chicago Film Critics Association Award, best actor, National Board of Review Award, Golden Satellite Award nomination, best performance by an actor in a motion picture, comedy or musical, Phoenix Film Critics Society Award nomination, best actor in a leading role, and Phoenix Film Critics Society Award nomination (with others), best acting ensemble, all 2002, for *The Royal Tenenbaums;* Cecil B. DeMille Award, Golden Globe awards, 2003; subject of the song "Gene Hackman," by the Hoodoo Gurus.

CREDITS

Film Appearances:

(Uncredited) Police officer, *Mad Dog Coll,* Columbia, 1961.

Norman, *Lilith,* Columbia, 1964.

Harmsworth, *A Covenant with Death,* Warner Bros., 1966.

Reverend John Whipple, *Hawaii,* United Artists, 1966.

Buck Barrow, *Bonnie and Clyde* (also known as *Bonnie and Clyde ... Were Killers!*), Warner Bros./Seven Arts, 1967.

Sergeant Tweed, *First to Fight,* Warner Bros., 1967.

Tommy Del Gaddo, *Banning,* Universal, 1967.

Out by the Country Club, 1967.

Detective lieutenant Walter Brill, *The Split,* Metro–Goldwyn–Mayer, 1968.

Buzz Lloyd, *Marooned* (also known as *Space Travelers*), Columbia, 1969.

Eugene Claire, *Downhill Racer,* Paramount, 1969.

Joe Browdy, *The Gypsy Moths,* Metro–Goldwyn–Mayer, 1969.

Red Fletcher (some sources cite surname as Fraker), *Riot!,* Paramount, 1969.

Gene Garrison, *I Never Sang for My Father,* Columbia, 1970.

Brandt Ruger, *The Hunting Party,* United Artists, 1971.

Detective James "Jimmy"/"Popeye" Doyle, *The French Connection,* Twentieth Century–Fox, 1971.

Dr. Dave Randolph, *Doctors' Wives,* Columbia, 1971.

Officer Leo Holland, *Cisco Pike,* Columbia, 1971.

Mary Ann, *Prime Cut,* National General, 1972.

Reverend Frank Scott, *The Poseidon Adventure,* Twentieth Century–Fox, 1972.

Max Millan, *Scarecrow,* Warner Bros., 1973.

Harold the blind hermit, *Young Frankenstein* (also known as *Frankenstein Jr.*), Twentieth Century–Fox, 1974.

Harry Caul, *The Conversation,* Paramount, 1974.

Zandy Allan, *Zandy's Bride* (also known as *For Better, for Worse*), Warner Bros., 1974.

Harry Moseby, *Night Moves,* Warner Bros., 1975.

James "Jimmy"/"Popeye" Doyle, *The French Connection II,* Twentieth Century–Fox, 1975.

Kibby, *Lucky Lady,* Twentieth Century–Fox, 1975.

Sam Clayton, *Bite the Bullet,* Columbia, 1975.

(In archive footage) *America at the Movies,* Cinema 5 Distributing, 1976.

Himself, *A Look at Liv* (documentary), Win Kao Productions, 1977.

Major general Stanislaw Sosabowski, *A Bridge Too Far,* United Artists, 1977.

Major William Sherman Foster, *March or Die,* Columbia, 1977.

Roy Tucker, *The Domino Principle* (also known as *The Domino Killings* and *El domino principe*), Avco–Embassy, 1977.

Himself, *Formula uno, febbre della velocita* (also known as *Speed Fever*), 1978.

Lex Luthor, *Superman* (also known as *Superman: The Movie*), Warner Bros., 1978.

Lex Luthor, *Superman II,* Warner Bros., 1980.

George Dupler, *All Night Long,* Universal, 1981.

Pete Van Wherry, *Reds,* Paramount, 1981.

Alex Grazier, *Under Fire,* Orion, 1983.

Colonel Jason Rhodes, *Uncommon Valor,* Paramount, 1983.

Jack McCann, *Eureka,* United Artists, 1983.

Voice of God, *Two of a Kind,* Twentieth Century–Fox, 1983.

Ned Rawley, *Misunderstood* (also known as *L'ultimo sole d'estate*), Metro–Goldwyn–Mayer/United Artists, 1984.

Harry MacKenzie, *Twice in a Lifetime,* Yorkin Company/Pan Canadian, 1985.

Walter Lloyd/Duncan "Duke" Potter, *Target,* Warner Bros., 1985.

Coach Norman Dale, *Hoosiers* (also known as *Best Shot*), Orion, 1986.

Wilfred Buckley, *Power,* Twentieth Century–Fox, 1986.

Defense secretary David Brice, *No Way Out,* Orion, 1987.

Lex Luthor and voice of Nuclear Man, *Superman IV: The Quest for Peace,* Warner Bros., 1987.

Agent Rupert Anderson, *Mississippi Burning,* Orion, 1988.

Dan McGuinn, *Split Decisions* (also known as *Kid Gloves*), New Century–Vista, 1988.

Floyd, *Full Moon in Blue Water,* Trans World Entertainment, 1988.

Larry Lewis, *Another Woman,* Orion, 1988.

Lieutenant colonel Iceal Hambleton, *Bat*21* (also known as *Bat 21*), TriStar, 1988.

Jedediah Tucker Ward, *Class Action,* Twentieth Century–Fox, 1989.

Lowell Korshack, *Postcards from the Edge,* Columbia, 1989.

Sergeant Johnny Gallagher, *The Package,* Orion, 1989.

MacArthur Stern, *Loose Cannons* (also known as *The Von Metz Incident*), TriStar, 1990.

Robert Caulfield, *Narrow Margin,* TriStar, 1990.

Sam Boyd/John Jones, *Company Business,* Metro–Goldwyn–Mayer/Pathe, 1990.

Sheriff "Little Bill" Daggett, *Unforgiven* (also known as *The William Munny Killings*), Warner Bros., 1992.

Avery Tolar, *The Firm,* Paramount, 1993.

Brigadier general George Crook, *Geronimo: An American Legend,* Columbia, 1993.

Nicholas Earp, *Wyatt Earp,* Warner Bros., 1994.

Captain Frank Ramsey, *Crimson Tide,* Buena Vista, 1995.

Harry Zimm, *Get Shorty,* Metro–Goldwyn–Mayer, 1995.

John Herod, *The Quick and the Dead,* TriStar, 1995.

Dr. Lawrence Myrick, *Extreme Measures,* Sony Pictures Entertainment, 1996.

Sam Cayhall, *The Chamber,* Universal, 1996.

Senator Kevin Keeley, *The Birdcage* (also known as *Birds of a Feather*), Metro–Goldwyn–Mayer, 1996.

President Allen Richmond, *Absolute Power,* Sony Pictures Entertainment, 1997.

Edward "Brill" Lyle, *Enemy of the State,* Buena Vista, 1998.

Jack Ames, *Twilight* (also known as *The Magic Hour*), Paramount, 1998.

Voice of General Mandible, *Antz* (animated), Dream-Works, 1998.

Henry Hearst, *Under Suspicion* (also known as *Suspicion*), Lions Gate Films, 1999.

Jimmy McGinty, *The Replacements,* Warner Bros., 2000.

Admiral Leslie McMahon Reigart, *Behind Enemy Lines,* Twentieth Century–Fox, 2001.

Arnold Margolese, *The Mexican* (also known as *La mexicana*), DreamWorks, 2001.

Himself, *Cannes: Through the Eyes of the Hunter* (documentary short film), 2001.

Joe Moore, *Heist* (also known as *Le vol*), Warner Bros., 2001.

Royal Tenenbaum, *The Royal Tenenbaums,* Buena Vista, 2001.

William B. Tensy, *Heartbreakers,* Metro–Goldwyn–Mayer, 2001.

(In archive footage) Himself, *The Kid Stays in the Picture* (documentary), Focus Features/USA Films, 2002.

Narrator, *Colors of Courage: Sons of New Mexico, Prisoners of Japan* (documentary), Center for Regional Studies, University of New Mexico, 2002.

Rankin Fitch, *Runaway Jury,* Twentieth Century–Fox, 2003.

Monroe Cole, *Welcome to Mooseport,* Twentieth Century–Fox, 2004.

Film Work:

Executive producer, *Under Suspicion* (also known as *Suspicion*), Lions Gate Films, 1999.

Television Appearances; Movies:

Reverend Thomas Davis, *Shadow on the Land,* ABC, 1968.

Television Appearances; Specials:

Himself, *The Making of "Superman: The Movie,"* 1978.

Night of 100 Stars II (also known as *Night of One Hundred Stars*), ABC, 1985.

Charlie Bragg: One of a Kind, PBS, 1986.

The Third Annual Hollywood Insider Academy Awards Special, USA Network, 1989.

Himself, *Clint Eastwood on Westerns,* 1992.

Himself, *Eastwood & Co.: Making "Unforgiven,"* ABC, 1992.

Himself, *Clint Eastwood—The Man from Malpaso,* Cinemax, 1993.

Voice, *Earth and the American Dream,* HBO, 1993.

Host, *100 Years of the Hollywood Western,* NBC, 1994.

Star Trek: 30 Years and Beyond, UPN, 1996.

(Uncredited) Himself, *Sports on the Silver Screen,* HBO, 1997.

Himself, *The Best of Hollywood* (also known as *50 Years: The Best of Hollywood*), 1998.

Himself, *The Secret World of Antz,* 1998.

Narrator, "Hitchcock, Selznick and the End of Hollywood," *American Masters* (also known as *American Masters: Hitchcock, Selznick and the End of Hollywood*), PBS, 1999.

AFI's 100 Years ... 100 Stars, CBS, 1999.

Himself, "Clint Eastwood: Out of the Shadows," *American Masters,* PBS, 2000.

Himself, *The Poughkeepsie Shuffle: Tracing "The French Connection,"* 2000.

Himself, *History vs. Hollywood,* History Channel, 2001.

Himself, *Making the Connection: Untold Stories of "The French Connection"* (also known as *The French Connection 30th Anniversary Special*), Fox Movie Channel, 2001.

Host and narrator, *Heroes of Iwo Jima,* Arts and Entertainment, 2001.

(In archive footage) *AFI's 100 Years ... 100 Heroes and Villains,* CBS, 2003.

Narrator, *Imaginary Witness: Hollywood and the Holocaust,* American Movie Classics, 2004.

Television Appearances; Awards Presentations:

Presenter, *The 44th Annual Academy Awards,* NBC, 1972.

Presenter, *The 45th Annual Academy Awards,* NBC, 1973.

Presenter, *The 56th Annual Academy Awards,* ABC, 1984.

Presenter, *The 61st Annual Academy Awards Presentation,* ABC, 1989.

Presenter, *The 46th Annual Tony Awards,* CBS, 1992.

Presenter, *The 65th Annual Academy Awards Presentation,* ABC, 1993.

And the Winner Is, syndicated, 1993.

The 50th Annual Golden Globe Awards, TBS, 1993.

Presenter, *The 66th Annual Academy Awards Presentation,* ABC, 1994.

Himself, *The 60th Annual Golden Globe Awards,* NBC, 2003.

Television Appearances; Episodic:

Joey Carlton, "Little Tin God," *The U.S. Steel Hour* (also known as *The United States Steel Hour*), CBS, 1959.

Steve, "The Pink Burro," *The U.S. Steel Hour* (also known as *The United States Steel Hour*), CBS, 1959.

Reverend MacCreighton, "Big Doc's Girl," *The U.S. Steel Hour* (also known as *The United States Steel Hour*), CBS, 1959.

"Bride of the Fox," *The U.S. Steel Hour* (also known as *The United States Steel Hour*), CBS, 1960.

Jerry Warner, "Quality of Mercy," *The Defenders,* CBS, 1961.

"Brandenberg Gate," *The U.S. Steel Hour* (also known as *The United States Steel Hour*), CBS, 1961.

Ed, "Far from the Shade Tree," *The U.S. Steel Hour* (also known as *The United States Steel Hour*), CBS, 1962.

"Prime of Life," *Naked City,* ABC, 1963.

Guard, "Judgment Eve," *The Defenders,* CBS, 1963.

Douglas McCann, "Ride with Terror," *DuPont Show of the Week,* NBC, 1963.

Police officer, "Creeps Live Here," *East Side, West Side,* CBS, 1963.

Motorist, "Who Will Cheer My Bonnie Bride," *Route 66,* CBS, 1963.

Houston Worth, "Do Not Mutilate or Spindle," *Hawk,* ABC, 1966.

Roger Nathan, "The Only Game in Town," *Trials of O'Brien,* CBS, 1966.

Herb Kenyon, "The Courier," *The F.B.I.,* ABC, 1967.

Tom Jessup, "The Spores," *The Invaders,* ABC, 1967.

Harry Wadsworth, "Leopards Try, but Leopards Can't!," *Iron Horse,* ABC, 1967.

"My Father and My Mother," *CBS Playhouse,* CBS, 1968.

Frank Hunter, "Happy Birthday ... Everybody," *I Spy,* NBC, 1968.

Insight, syndicated, 1971.

Guest, *Rowan and Martin's Laugh–In* (also known as *Laugh–In*), NBC, multiple episodes in 1972.

Guest, *The Tonight Show Starring Johnny Carson* (also known as *The Best of Carson*), NBC, 1972, 1973, 1975.

Guest, *V.I.P.–Schaukel,* 1978.

Guest, *Revista de cine,* 1979.

"Gene Hackman," *The South Bank Show,* Independent Television, 1983.

Champlin on Film, Bravo, 1989.

Guest, *The Rosie O'Donnell Show,* syndicated, 1998.

Himself, "Gene Hackman," *Bravo Profiles* (also known as *Bravo Profiles: Gene Hackman* and *Gene Hackman*), Bravo, c. 2000.

Himself, "Bonnie and Clyde," *Backstory* (also known as *Hollywood Backstories*), American Movie Classics, 2001.

Guest, *Inside the Actors Studio,* Bravo, 2001.

(In archive footage) Himself, *Headliners & Legends: Denzel Washington,* MSNBC, 2002.

Himself, "Runaway Jury," *HBO First Look,* HBO, 2003.

Himself, "Dustin Hoffman," *The Hollywood Greats* (also known as *Hollywood Greats*), BBC, 2004.

Guest, *Larry King Live,* Cable News Network, 2004.

Appeared as Frank Collins in "The End of the Story," an episode of *Look Up and Live,* CBS; also appeared in "The Films of Richard Donner," *The Directors,* Encore.

Stage Appearances:

Chaparral, Sheridan Square Playhouse, New York City, 1958.

The Curious Miss Caraway, Pasadena Playhouse, Pasadena, CA, c. 1958.

The Saintliness of Margery Kempe, York Playhouse, 1959.

Pilgrim's Progress, off–Broadway production, early 1960s.

Who'll Save the Plowboy?, off–Broadway production, early 1960s.

Charles Widgin Rochambeau, *Children from Their Games,* Morosco Theatre, New York City, 1963.

Sidney Rice, *A Rainy Day in Newark,* Belasco Theatre, New York City, 1963.

Sydney Carroll, *Poor Richard,* Helen Hayes Theatre, New York City, 1964.

Cass Henderson, *Any Wednesday,* Music Box Theatre, New York City, c. 1964–66, George Abbott Theatre, New York City, 1966.

Baxter in "Fragments" and Zach in "Basement," *Fragments,* Cherry Lane Theatre, New York City, 1967.

The Natural Look, Longacre Theatre, New York City, 1967.

Billyboy, *Come to the Palace of Sin,* Theatre de Lys (now Lucille Lortel Theatre), New York City, 1969.

Night of 100 Stars II (also known as *Night of One Hundred Stars*), Radio City Music Hall, New York City, 1985.

Roberto Miranda, *Death and the Maiden,* Brooks Atkinson Theatre, New York City, 1992.

RECORDINGS

Videos:

Himself, *Making "Superman": Filming the Legend,* Warner Bros. Home Video, 2001.

Himself, *Taking Flight: The Development of "Superman,"* Warner Bros. Home Video, 2001.

Himself, *All on Accounta Pullin' a Trigger,* Warner Home Video, 2002.

(In archive footage) Lex Luthor, *De Superman a Spider–Man: L'aventure des super–heros* (animated), Gaumont/Columbia/TriStar Home Video, 2002.

Himself, *The Making of "Runaway Jury,"* Twentieth Century–Fox Home Entertainment, 2004.

Himself, *Hoosier History: The Truth behind the Legend,* Metro–Goldwyn–Mayer Home Entertainment, 2005.

WRITINGS

Novels:

(With Daniel Lenihan) *Wake of the Perdido Sea: A Novel of Shipwrecks, Pirates, and the Sea,* Newmarket Press, 1999.

(With Lenihan) *Justice for None,* St. Martin's Press, 2004.

OTHER SOURCES

Books:

Hunter, Allan, *Gene Hackman,* St. Martin's Press, 1987.

International Dictionary of Films and Filmmakers, Volume 3: *Actors and Actresses,* 4th edition, St. James Press, 2000.

Munn, Michael, *Gene Hackman,* Robert Hale Limited, 1987.

St. James Encyclopedia of Popular Cultures, five volumes, St. James Press, 2000.

Periodicals:

American Film, March, 1983.

Boston Herald, December 21, 2001.

Entertainment Weekly, October 17, 2003, pp. 45–47.

Film Comment, September/October, 1974; November/December, 1988, pp. 21–24, 70–74.

Films and Filming, May, 1986.

Films in Review, January, 1975.

Literature/Film Quarterly, January, 1993.

Los Angeles Times, December 16, 2001.

New York Times Magazine, March 19, 1989.

Oui, August, 1981, p. 32.

Parade, December 30, 2001, p. 20.

People Weekly, March 26, 2001.

Premiere, February, 1991, p. 68; February, 2002, p. 88.

Prevue, October, 1991, p. 36.

Publishers Weekly, March 22, 1999, p. 28.

Radio Times, March 11, 1989, p. 21; April 29, 1995.

Stars, September, 1992.

Stills, April, 1986.

Time, June 7, 2004, p. 139.

TV Guide, January 18, 2003, pp. 41–43.

USA Today, October 11, 1996.

HAGGERTY, Dan 1941–
(Dan Haggarty, Daniel Haggerty)

PERSONAL

Born November 19, 1941, in Hollywood, CA; son of Don (an actor) Haggerty; married Diane Rooker, 1959 (divorced, 1984); married Samantha, 1984; children: (first marriage) Tracey, Tammy; (second marriage) one son.

Career: Actor and animal trainer. Haggerty's Bistro (restaurant), Studio City, CA, owner, beginning 1991; also developed and sold his recipe for barbecue sauce.

Awards, Honors: People's Choice Award, best male performer in a new program, 1978, for *The Life and Times of Grizzly Adams;* received a star on the Hollywood Walk of Fame.

CREDITS

Television Appearances; Series:
James Capen "Grizzly" Adams, *The Life and Times of Grizzly Adams,* NBC, 1977–78.

Television Appearances; Movies:
Benjamin Ward, *Desperate Women,* NBC, 1978.
Nick Willis, *Terror Out of the Sky* (also known as *The Revenge of the Savage Bees*), CBS, 1978.
Sam Harrison, *Condominium,* Operation Prime Time, 1980.
California Gold Rush, 1981.
James Capen "Grizzly" Adams, *The Capture of Grizzly Adams,* NBC, 1982.
Barkley, *Cheyenne Warrior,* 1994.

Television Appearances; Specials:
(As Dan Haggarty) NBC team captain, *Battle of the Network Stars III,* ABC, 1977.
NBC team member, *Battle of the Network Stars II,* ABC, 1977.
NBC team member, *Battle of the Network Stars IV,* ABC, 1978.
NBC Salutes the 25th Anniversary of the Wonderful World of Disney, NBC, 1978.

Television Appearances; Episodic:
Thug, "Killers from Kansas," *Texas John Slaughter,* series broadcast on *Walt Disney Presents,* ABC, 1959.
"No Laughing Matter," *Richard Diamond, Private Detective,* CBS and NBC, 1959.
"Epitaph for a Gambler," *Maverick,* ABC, 1961.
Guest, *The Mike Douglas Show,* syndicated, 1977.
Himself, "CHiPs Goes Roller Disco: Part 2," *CHiPs* (also known as *CHiPs Patrol*), NBC, 1979.
Bo Thompson, "Waikiki Angels," *Charlie's Angels,* ABC, 1981.
Guest, *The American Sportsman,* ABC, 1982.
"The World's Greatest Kisser," *The Love Boat,* ABC, 1983.

Television Appearances; Pilots:
Voice of Terl, *Battlefield Earth: The Anime Series* (anime; also known as *Battlefield Earth*), syndicated, 2001.

Television Work; Series:
(Uncredited) Stunt performer, *Tarzan,* NBC, 1966–68.

Film Appearances:
Riff, *Muscle Beach Party,* American International Pictures, 1964.
(Uncredited) Charlie, *Girl Happy* (musical), Metro–Goldwyn–Mayer, 1965.
(Uncredited) Man in commune, *Easy Rider* (also known as *The Loners*), Columbia, 1969.
Angels Die Hard! (also known as *Rough Boys* and *The Violent Angels*), New World, 1970.
(Uncredited) Biker, *Chrome and Hot Leather,* American International Pictures, 1971.
Biker, *The Pink Angels,* 1971.
Cal, *The Tender Warrior,* Safari, 1971.
Ken, *Bury Me an Angel,* New World, 1972.
(Uncredited) Biker, *Superchick* (also known as *Superchic* and *Super Chick*), 1973.
Brother Billy, *Hex* (also known as *The Shrieking*), Twentieth Century–Fox, 1973.
Starbird and Sweet William (also known as *The Adventures of Starbird*), 1973.
Tsezar, *When the North Wind Blows,* 1974.
James Capen "Grizzly" Adams, *The Life and Times of Grizzly Adams,* Sunn Classics, 1976.
Frontier Fremont, *The Adventures of Frontier Fremont* (also known as *Spirit of the Wild*), Sunn Classics, 1977.
(As Dan Haggarty) Jake, *Americana,* Sherwood, 1981.
James Capen "Grizzly" Adams, *Legend of the Wild,* Taft International Pictures, 1981.
Rick, *King of the Mountain,* Universal, 1981.
Ladies Night, 1983.
Joe Evans, *Abducted* (also known as *Abduction*), Prism Entertainment, 1986.
Dr. Mike Campbell, *Night Wars,* Action, 1988.
Mike McGavin, *Elves,* American International Pictures, 1989.
Sergei, *Mind Trap* (also known as *Danger*), 1989.
Skating coach, *Ice Pawn,* 1989.
Sergeant Vince Marlow, *The Chilling* (also known as *Gamma 693* and *A Woman Obsessed*), 1989, Coyote Home Video, 1992.
Arnie, *The Channeler,* 1990.
Big Eli McDonaugh, *Spirit of the Eagle,* Shapiro Glickenhaus Home Video, 1990.
Dr. Berquist, *Inheritor,* Film World–VidAmerica, 1990.
Jake Baxter, *Repo Jake,* PM Home Video, 1990.
(As Daniel Haggerty) Ted Michaels, *Terror Night* (also known as *Bloody Movie*), Double Helix Films, 1990.
Zack, *Chance,* PM Entertainment, 1990.
Macon County War, American International Pictures, 1990.
Hollis Bodine, *Soldier's Fortune* (also known as *Soldiers of Fortune*), Republic Pictures, 1991.
Deadly Diamonds, AMI Entertainment, 1991.
Frank, *Love and Dynamite,* 1992.
Voices of King Ferdinand and swarm lord, *The Magic Voyage* (animated; also known as *Pico and Columbus* and *Die Abenteuer von Pico und Columbus*),

Atlas Film, dubbed version released by Hemdale Film Corporation, 1992.

Joe Evans, *Abducted II: The Reunion,* Astral Films, 1994.

Colonel Rose, *The Little Patriot* (also known as *Sign of the Otter*), Sultan Films, 1995.

King of Storyland, *Father Frost,* Plaza Entertainment, 1996.

Himself, *Motorcycle Cheerleading Mommas,* 1997.

Jeremiah, *Grizzly Mountain,* Legacy Releasing, 1997.

Buck McCoy, *Born Champion,* 1998.

King, *Puss in Boots,* Plaza Entertainment, 1999.

Jeremiah, *Escape to Grizzly Mountain,* Metro–Goldwyn–Mayer Home Entertainment, 2000.

Bear Madigan, *Motocross Kids,* Tag Entertainment, 2004.

Detective Jim LeBaron, *An Ordinary Killer,* 2004, Anthem Pictures International, 2006.

Hebron, *Crossing the King's Highway,* Pretty Dangerous Films, 2006.

Jake, *Wild Michigan* (short film), American World Pictures, 2006.

Film Work; Animal Trainer:

It. Robin Crusoe, USN, Buena Vista, 1966.

Monkeys, Go Home!, Buena Vista, 1967.

L'arbe de Noel (also known as *The Christmas Tree, When Wolves Cry,* and *L'albero di Natale*), Les Films Corona/Valoria Films, 1969, dubbed version released by Continental Distributing, 1970.

Film Work; Other:

(Uncredited) Motorcycle builder, *Easy Rider* (also known as *The Loners*), Columbia, 1969.

Set decorator, *Gentle Savage* (also known as *Camper John*), Cinemation Industries, 1973.

Associate producer, *Chance,* PM Entertainment, 1990.

RECORDINGS

Videos:

Himself, *Beyond Ordinary: The Making of "An Ordinary Killer,"* CDI Distribution, 2005.

OTHER SOURCES

Periodicals:

Entertainment Weekly, August 19, 1994, p. 68.

HALMI, Robert, Jr. 1957–

(Robert Halmi: Robert H. Halmi, Jr.)

PERSONAL

Born March 7, 1957, in Weston, CT; son of Robert H. Halmi (a filmmaker and studio executive); married; wife's name, Leah; children: Winter (daughter), Bela (son), Colt (son), Thomas. *Education:* Syracuse University, graduated, 1979; Harvard University, M.B.A.

Addresses: *Office*—Hallmark Entertainment Holdings, 1325 Avenue of the Americas, 21st Floor, New York, NY 10019.

Career: Producer, director, and studio executive. Robert Halmi Productions, began as an assistant to the producer, 1980, became associate producer, producer, and executive producer; RHI Entertainment, cofounder, 1984, then president and chief executive officer; Robert Halmi, Inc., president, c. 1985–88; Quintex, affiliate, 1990; Hallmark Entertainment Holdings, New York City, president, chief executive officer, and cochair, beginning 1994; Hallmark Entertainment Networks, founder, 1995; Crown Media Holdings, founder and board chair, 1995; Hallmark Cards, Inc., member of corporate executive council. Worked as a professional photographer, with work published in periodicals, including *Newsweek,* the *New York Times, Paris Match,* and *Time.*

Awards, Honors: Emmy Award nomination (with others), outstanding children's program, 1985, for *The Night They Saved Christmas;* Emmy Award nomination (with Robert Halmi, Sr.), outstanding drama or comedy special, 1987, for "Pack of Lies," *Hallmark Hall of Fame;* Emmy Award nomination, outstanding miniseries, 1989, George Foster Peabody Broadcasting Award, Henry W. Grady School of Journalism, University of Georgia, 1990, and Golden Globe Award, best miniseries or motion picture made for television, 1990, all with others, all for *Lonesome Dove;* Emmy Award (with others), outstanding drama or comedy special, 1990, for *The Incident;* Bronze Wrangler Award (with others), outstanding television feature film, Western Heritage awards, 1996, for *Streets of Laredo;* Antoinette Perry Award nomination (with others), best revival of a musical, 1998, for *1776;* Antoinette Perry Award nomination (with others), best revival of a musical, 1998, for *The Sound of Music;* Emmy Award nomination (with others), outstanding television movie, 1999, for *The Baby Dance;* Emmy Award nomination (with others), outstanding miniseries, 2000, for *Arabian Nights;* Daytime Emmy Award nomination (with others), outstanding children's special, 2000, for *A Gift of Love: The Daniel Huffman Story;* Daytime Emmy Award (with others), outstanding children's special, 2001, for *Run the Wild Fields;* Daytime Emmy Award (with others), outstanding children's special, 2001, for *A Storm in Summer;* Emmy Award nomination (with others), outstanding miniseries, 2002, for *Dinotopia;* Daytime

Emmy Award nomination (with others), outstanding children's special, 2002, for *Off Season;* Daytime Emmy Award nomination (with others), outstanding children's special, 2002, for *They Call Me Sirr;* Camie Award (with others), Character and Morality in Entertainment awards, 2003, for *Love Comes Softly;* Emmy Award nomination (with others), outstanding television movie, 2004, for *The Lion in Winter;* Camie Award (with others), 2005, for *Love's Enduring Promise;* Broadcast Film Critics Award nomination (with others), best picture made for television, 2005, for *The Five People You Meet in Heaven.*

CREDITS

Television Executive Producer; Series:
Learning the Ropes, syndicated, 1988.
Chillers (also known as *Mistress of Suspense*), beginning 1990.
Dracula—The Series, syndicated, 1990–91.
The Secret World of Alex Mack (also known as *Alex Mack*), Nickelodeon, 1994–98.
Lonesome Dove: The Outlaw Years, CTV and syndicated, c. 1995–96.
Farscape (also known as *Far Horizon* and *Space Chase*), Sci–Fi Channel, c. 1999–2004.
America!, Odyssey, beginning 2000.
Adoption, The Hallmark Channel, beginning 2002.
Dinotopia (live action and animated; also known as *Dinotopia: The Series*), ABC, 2002–2003.

Television Producer; Series:
The Earth Journal with Dr. Richard Leakey, syndicated, beginning 1991.
(As Robert H. Halmi, Jr.) Senior producer, *Space Rangers,* CBS, 1993.

Television Executive Producer; Miniseries:
Ford: The Man and the Machine, syndicated, 1987.
(With others) *Lonesome Dove,* CBS, 1989.
The Fire Next Time, CBS, 1993.
Return to Lonesome Dove, CBS, 1993.
The Old Curiosity Shop, The Disney Channel, 1995.
Streets of Laredo (also known as *Larry McMurtry's "Streets of Laredo"*), CBS, 1995.
Dead Man's Walk (also known as *Larry McMurtry's "Dead Man's Walk"*), ABC, 1996.
Creature (also known as *Peter Benchley's "Creature"*), ABC, 1998.
Aftershock: Earthquake in New York (also known as *Aftershock—Das grosse Beben* and *Erdbeben–Inferno: Wenn die Welt untergeht*), CBS, 1999.
Cleopatra, ABC, 1999.
Journey to the Center of the Earth, USA Network, 1999.
Arabian Nights, ABC, 2000.
David Copperfield, TNT, 2000.
Hamlet, Odyssey, 2000.

In the Beginning, NBC, 2000.
Jason and the Argonauts, NBC, 2000.
The 10th Kingdom (also known as *Das 10te Koenigreich* and *Das Zehnte Koenigreich*), NBC, 2000.
A Girl Thing, Showtime, 2001.
Hans Christian Andersen: My Life as a Fairy Tale, The Hallmark Channel, 2001.
The Infinite Worlds of H. G. Wells, The Hallmark Channel, 2001.
The Lost Empire (also known as *Monkey King—Ein Krieger zwischen den Welten*), NBC, 2001.
Voyage of the Unicorn, Odyssey, 2001.
Dinotopia (live action and animated), ABC, 2002.
Johnson County War, The Hallmark Channel, 2002.
Roughing It (also known as *Mark Twain's "Roughing It"*), The Hallmark Channel, 2002.
DreamKeeper, ABC, 2003.
Farscape: The Peacekeeper Wars (also known as *The Farscape Miniseries*), The Hallmark Channel, 2004.
Frankenstein, The Hallmark Channel, 2004.
King Solomon's Mines, The Hallmark Channel, 2004.
La Femme Musketeer, The Hallmark Channel, 2004.
Legend of Earthsea (also known as *Earthsea*), Sci–Fi Channel, 2004.
Hercules, NBC, 2005.
Icon (also known as *Frederick Forsyth's "Icon"*), The Hallmark Channel, 2005.
Mysterious Island, The Hallmark Channel, 2005.
Supernova, The Hallmark Channel, 2005.
Blackbeard, The Hallmark Channel, 2006.
The Curse of King Tut's Tomb, The Hallmark Channel, 2006.

Television Executive Producer; Movies:
Nairobi Affair, CBS, 1984.
The Night They Saved Christmas, ABC, 1984.
The Mysterious Death of Nina Chereau, 1988.
Margaret Bourke–White (also known as *Double Exposure*), TNT, 1989.
(As Robert Halmi) *The Incident,* CBS, 1990.
Bump in the Night, Starz!, 1991.
Eyes of a Witness, CBS, 1991.
(As Robert Halmi) *The Josephine Baker Story,* HBO, 1991.
Against Her Will: An Incident in Baltimore, CBS, 1992.
Blind Spot, CBS, 1993.
Reunion, CBS, 1994.
Seasons of the Heart, NBC, 1994.
The Yearling, CBS, 1994.
Black Fox, CBS, 1995.
Black Fox: Good Men and Bad, CBS, 1995.
Black Fox: The Price of Peace, CBS, 1995.
(With others) *September* (also known as *Rosamunde Pilcher's "September"*), Showtime, 1996.
The Baby Dance, Showtime, 1998.
Hard Time, TNT, 1998.
"*The Ransom of Red Chief,*" *The Wonderful World of Disney,* ABC, 1998.

Still Holding On: The Legend of Cadillac Jack (also known as *Cadillac Jack*), CBS, 1998.

The Tale of Sweeney Todd, Showtime, 1998.

Alice in Wonderland (also known as *Alice in Wunderland*), NBC, 1999.

A Gift of Love: The Daniel Huffman Story, Showtime, 1999.

Hard Time: Hostage Hotel (also known as *Hostage Hotel*), TNT, 1999.

Hard Time: The Premonition (also known as *The Premonition*), TNT, 1999.

In a Class of His Own, Showtime, 1999.

The Wishing Tree, Showtime, 1999.

By Dawn's Early Light, Showtime, 2000.

Finding Buck McHenry, Showtime, 2000.

The Prince and the Pauper, pay–per–view, 2000.

Run the Wild Fields, Showtime, 2000.

Seventeen Again, Showtime, 2000.

A Storm in Summer, Showtime, 2000.

Back to the Secret Garden, Showtime, 2001.

Off Season, Showtime, 2001.

Prince Charming, TNT, 2001.

"Snow White" (also known as *"Snow White: The Fairest of Them All"* and *"Blanche–Neige"*), *The Wonderful World of Disney,* ABC, 2001.

They Call Me Sirr, Showtime, 2001.

Walter and Henry, Showtime, 2001.

Gentle Ben (also known as *Terror on the Mountain*), Animal Planet, 2002.

I Was a Teenage Faust, Showtime, 2002.

Just a Dream, Showtime, 2002.

"Mr. Saint Nick," *The Wonderful World of Disney,* ABC, 2002.

Night of the Wolf, Animal Planet, 2002.

The Red Sneakers, Showtime, 2002.

Santa, Jr., The Hallmark Channel, 2002.

Snow Queen, The Hallmark Channel, 2002.

Audrey's Rain, The Hallmark Channel, 2003.

A Carol Christmas, The Hallmark Channel, 2003.

Gentle Ben 2: Danger on the Mountain (also known as *Black Gold*), Animal Planet, 2003.

Hard Ground, The Hallmark Channel, 2003.

The King and Queen of Moonlight Bay, The Hallmark Channel, 2003.

The Last Cowboy, The Hallmark Channel, 2003.

The Lion in Winter, Showtime, 2003.

Love Comes Softly, The Hallmark Channel, 2003.

Monster Makers, The Hallmark Channel, 2003.

Mystery Woman, The Hallmark Channel, 2003.

Out of the Ashes, Showtime, 2003.

Straight from the Heart, The Hallmark Channel, 2003.

A Time to Remember, The Hallmark Channel, 2003.

Angel in the Family, The Hallmark Channel, 2004.

A Boyfriend for Christmas, The Hallmark Channel, 2004.

Cavedweller, Showtime, 2004.

A Christmas Carol: The Musical, NBC, 2004.

Crown Heights, Showtime, 2004.

The Five People You Meet in Heaven, ABC, 2004.

Gone but Not Forgotten, Showtime, 2004.

The Hollywood Mom's Mystery (also known as *The Dead Hollywood Moms Society*), The Hallmark Channel, 2004.

Just Desserts, The Hallmark Channel, 2004.

Life on Liberty Street, The Hallmark Channel, 2004.

The Long Shot: Believe in Courage, The Hallmark Channel, 2004.

Love, Clyde, The Hallmark Channel, 2004.

Love's Enduring Promise, The Hallmark Channel, 2004.

Murder without Conviction, The Hallmark Channel, 2004.

A Place Called Home, The Hallmark Channel, 2004.

Single Santa Seeks Mrs. Claus, The Hallmark Channel, 2004.

The Trail to Hope Rose, The Hallmark Channel, 2004.

Wedding Daze, The Hallmark Channel, 2004.

Annie's Point, The Hallmark Channel, 2005.

Back to You and Me, The Hallmark Channel, 2005.

Detective (also known as *Arthur Hailey's "Detective"*), 2005.

A Family of Strangers, The Hallmark Channel, 2005.

The Family Plan, The Hallmark Channel, 2005.

Fielder's Choice, The Hallmark Channel, 2005.

Jane Doe: Now You See It, Now You Don't, The Hallmark Channel, 2005.

Jane Doe: Til Death Do Us Part, The Hallmark Channel, 2005.

Jane Doe: Vanishing Act, The Hallmark Channel, 2005.

Jane Doe: The Wrong Face, The Hallmark Channel, 2005.

Love's Long Journey, The Hallmark Channel, 2005.

McBride: Anybody Here Murder Marty?, The Hallmark Channel, 2005.

McBride: The Chameleon Murder, The Hallmark Channel, 2005.

McBride: The Doctor Is Out ... Really Out, The Hallmark Channel, 2005.

McBride: Fallen Idol, The Hallmark Channel, 2005.

McBride: It's Murder, Madam, The Hallmark Channel, 2005.

McBride: Murder Past Midnight, The Hallmark Channel, 2005.

McBride: Tune In for Murder, The Hallmark Channel, 2005.

Meet the Santas, The Hallmark Channel, 2005.

Mystery Woman: At First Sight, The Hallmark Channel, 2005.

Mystery Woman: Game Time, The Hallmark Channel, 2005.

Mystery Woman: Mystery Weekend, The Hallmark Channel, 2005.

Mystery Woman: Redemption, The Hallmark Channel, 2005.

Mystery Women: Sing Me a Murder, The Hallmark Channel, 2005.

Mystery Woman: Snapshot, The Hallmark Channel, 2005.

Mystery Woman: Vision of a Murder, The Hallmark Channel, 2005.

Ordinary Miracles, The Hallmark Channel, 2005.

Out of the Woods, The Hallmark Channel, 2005.
The Poseidon Adventure, NBC, 2005.
Thicker Than Water, The Hallmark Channel, 2005.
Falling in Love with the Girl Next Door, The Hallmark Channel, 2006.
Hidden Places, The Hallmark Channel, 2006.
Jane Doe: The Brigadoon Effect, The Hallmark Channel, 2006.
Jane Doe: The Harder They Fall, The Hallmark Channel, 2006.
Jane Doe: Yes, I Remember It Well, The Hallmark Channel, 2006.
Murder 101, The Hallmark Channel, 2006.
Mystery Woman: Wild West Mystery, The Hallmark Channel, 2006.
Our House, The Hallmark Channel, 2006.
The Reading Room, The Hallmark Channel, 2006.
McBride: Murder at the Mission, The Hallmark Channel, c. 2006.
Though None Go with Me, The Hallmark Channel, c. 2006.

Television Producer; Movies:
My Old Man, CBS, 1979.
Associate producer, *When the Circus Came to Town,* CBS, 1981.
China Rose, CBS, 1983.
Cook & Peary: The Race to the Pole, CBS, 1983.
The Phantom of the Opera, NBC, 1983.
Associate producer, *Svengali,* CBS, 1983.
Terrible Joe Moran, CBS, 1984.
(As Robert Halmi) *The Murders in the Rue Morgue,* CBS, 1986.
Grand Larceny, syndicated, 1987.
Pals, 1987.
Spies, Lies & Naked Thighs, CBS, 1988.
Trouble in Paradise, CBS, 1989.
Face to Face, CBS, 1990.
Lifepod, Fox, 1993.

Television Assistant to the Producer; Movies:
(Some sources cite producer) *A Private Battle,* CBS, 1980.

Television Executive Producer; Specials:
"Pack of Lies," *Hallmark Hall of Fame,* CBS, 1987.
"April Morning," *Hallmark Hall of Fame,* CBS, 1988.
(With others) *Kenny Rogers: Keep Christmas with You,* CBS, 1992.
Hal Roach: Hollywood's King of Laughter, The Disney Channel, 1994.
Crayola Kids Adventures: Tales of Gulliver's Travels, CBS, 1997.
Crayola Kids Adventures: The Trojan Horse, CBS, 1997.
Crayola Kids Adventures: 20,000 Leagues under the Sea, CBS, 1997.
Hogwatch, Sky One, 2006.

Television Production Manager; Specials:
Peking Encounter, syndicated, 1981.

Television Producer; Other:
Adventures of William Tell, 1986.
Associate producer, *Best of Friends,* 1987.

Film Executive Producer:
Lily in Love (also known as *Playing for Keeps* and *Jatszani kell*), New Line Cinema, 1984.
Leader of the Band, New Century Vista, 1987.
(As Robert Halmi) *Mr. & Mrs. Bridge,* Miramax, 1990.
The Ascent, RHI Entertainment, 1994.
Dinotopia: Quest for the Ruby Sunstone (animated), Goodtimes Entertainment, 2005.

Film Producer:
Hugo a vizilo (animated; also known as *Hugo the Hippo*), Twentieth Century–Fox, 1975.
Associate producer, *Hosszu vagta* (also known as *Brady's Escape* and *Long Ride*), Satori, 1984.
Braxton, Atlatique Productions/Robert Halmi, Inc., 1989.

Film Director:
(As Robert Halmi) *Braxton,* Atlatique Productions/Robert Halmi, Inc., 1989.

Film Unit Production Manager:
Lily in Love (also known as *Playing for Keeps* and *Jatszani kell*), New Line Cinema, 1984.

Stage Producer:
1776 (musical), Criterion Center Stage Right Theatre, New York City, 1997, then George Gershwin Theatre, New York City, 1997–98.
The Sound of Music (musical), Martin Beck Theatre, New York City, 1998–99.

OTHER SOURCES

Periodicals:
Variety, January 12, 2006.

HARGITAY, Mariska 1964–
(Marishka Hargitay)

PERSONAL

First name is pronounced Ma–rish–ka; full name, Mariska Magdolina Hargitay; born January 23, 1964, in Los Angeles, CA; daughter of Mickey Hargitay (a bodybuilder and actor and in real estate) and Jayne Mansfield (an actress); stepdaughter of Ellen Siano (a flight attendant); married Peter Hermann (an actor and teacher), August 28, 2004; children: one. *Education:* Studied theatre at the University of California, Los Angeles.

Addresses: *Agent*—Erwin More, William Morris Agency, One William Morris Place, Beverly Hills, CA 90212.

Career: Actress. Appeared in the public service campaign "The More You Know," broadcast by NBC; performed public service announcements for Safe Horizons. Joyful Heart Foundation, founder and president; Spirit of the Dolphin, founder; Mount Sinai Sexual Assault and Violence Intervention, board member; certified rape crisis counselor and volunteer for other support organizations, including Santa Monica Rape Crisis Treatment Center, Project ALS, and the James Redford Institute for Transplant Awareness. Named Miss Beverly Hills, 1982.

Awards, Honors: Golden Satellite Award nomination, best performance by an actress in a drama series, International Press Academy, 2000, Q Award nomination, best actress in a quality drama series, Viewers for Quality Television, 2000, *TV Guide* Award nomination, favorite actress in a new series, 2000, Prism Award nomination, outstanding performance in a television drama series episode, 2004, Gracie Allen Award, individual achievement for best female lead in a drama series, American Women in Radio and Television, 2004, Emmy Award nominations, outstanding lead actress in a drama series, 2004 and 2005, Screen Actors Guild Award nominations, outstanding performance by a female actor in a drama series, 2004 and 2006, and Golden Globe Award, best performance by an actress in a television series—drama, 2005, all for *Law & Order: Special Victims Unit.*

CREDITS

Television Appearances; Series:
Jesse Smith, *Downtown,* CBS, 1986–87.
Carly Fixx, *Falcon Crest,* CBS, 1987–89.
Officer Angela Garcia, *Tequila and Bonetti,* CBS, 1992.
Didi Edelstein, *Can't Hurry Love,* CBS, 1995–96.
Detective Nina Echeverria, *Prince Street,* NBC, 1997.
Cynthia Hooper, a recurring role, *ER* (also known as *Emergency Room*), NBC, 1997–98.
Detective Olivia Benson, *Law & Order: Special Victims Unit* (also known as *Law & Order's Sex Crimes, Law & Order: SVU,* and *Special Victims Unit*), NBC, 1999—.

Television Appearances; Miniseries:
Etta Place, *The Gambler V: Playing for Keeps,* CBS, 1994.

Paige Price, *Night Sins,* CBS, 1997.
Herself, *I Love the '80s,* VH1, 2002.

Television Appearances; Movies:
Lisa Karsh, *Finish Line,* TNT, 1989.
Melanie, *Blindside* (also known as *Blind Side*), HBO, 1993.
Rendi, *The Advocate's Devil,* ABC, 1997.
Ellie Harrison, *Plain Truth,* Lifetime, 2004.

Television Appearances; Specials:
Host, *The Fiesta Bowl Parade,* CBS, 1995.
Christmas in Rockefeller Center, NBC, 2003.
InStyle Celebrity Weddings, ABC, 2005.

Television Appearances; Awards Presentations:
Presenter, *The 56th Annual Writers Guild Awards,* Starz!, 2004.
Presenter, *The 10th Annual Screen Actors Guild Awards,* TNT, 2004.
Herself, *The 62nd Annual Golden Globe Awards,* NBC, 2005.
Presenter, *The 57th Annual Primetime Emmy Awards,* CBS, 2005.

Television Appearances; Episodic:
Audine, "And Then You Die," *In the Heat of the Night,* NBC, 1988.
Marsha, "Freddy's Tricks and Treats," *Freddy's Nightmares* (also known as *Freddy's Nightmares: A Nightmare on Elm Street, the Series*), syndicated, 1988.
Lisa Peters, "Second Wave," *Baywatch* (also known as *Baywatch: Hawaii*), syndicated, 1989.
Carmen, "Windows," *Gabriel's Fire,* ABC, 1990.
Courtney Dunn, "Fathers and Lovers," *thirtysomething,* ABC, 1990.
Debbie Vitale, "Romp," *Wiseguy,* CBS, 1990.
Michelle Larkin, "Black Diamond Run," *Booker* (also known as *Booker, P.I.*), Fox, 1990.
Katie, "The Katie and Adam Story," *Grapevine,* CBS, 1992.
Diane, "Getting Rid of Robby," *Hotel Room* (also known as *David Lynch's "Hotel Room"*), HBO, 1993.
Laurel, "Less Moonlight," *Key West,* Fox, 1993.
Melissa Shannon, "The Pilot," *Seinfeld,* NBC, 1993.
Jane, "Young Americans," *All–American Girl,* ABC, 1995.
Dara, "The Mugging," *Ellen* (also known as *These Friends of Mine*), ABC, 1996.
Police officer Kate Conklin, "Kept Man," *The Single Guy,* NBC, 1996.
Police officer Kate Conklin, "Pilot Redux aka Mounted Cop," *The Single Guy,* NBC, 1996.
Police officer Kate Conklin, "The Virgin," *The Single Guy,* NBC, 1996.

Guest, *The Tonight Show with Jay Leno*, NBC, 1999, 2005.

Detective Olivia Benson, "Entitled," *Law & Order*, NBC, 2000.

Detective Olivia Benson, "Fools for Love," *Law & Order*, NBC, 2000.

Guest, *The Late Show with David Letterman* (also known as *The Late Show* and *Late Show Backstage*), CBS, 2002.

Guest, *The Rosie O'Donnell Show*, syndicated, 2002.

Herself, *Intimate Portrait: Joely Fisher*, Lifetime, 2002.

Herself, *TV Land Moguls*, TV Land, c. 2003.

Guest, *The View*, ABC, 2003, 2005.

Gust, *Late Night with Conan O'Brien*, NBC, 2004.

Detective Olivia Benson, "Day," *Law & Order: Trial by Jury*, NBC, 2005.

Detective Olivia Benson, "Flaw," *Law & Order*, NBC, 2005.

(In archive footage) Herself, *Corazon de ...* , Television Espanola (Spain), 2005.

Television Appearances; Pilots:

Penny Hadfield, "True Romance: Parts 1 & 2," *Cracker* (also known as *Cracker: Mind over Murder* and *Fitz*), ABC, 1997.

Wendy, "Love and the Blind Date," *Love, American Style*, ABC, 1999.

Film Appearances:

Donna, *Ghoulies*, Empire Pictures, 1985.

Joey, *Welcome to 18* (also known as *Summer Release*), American Distribution Group, 1986.

Nicole, *Jocks* (also known as *Road Trip*), Crown International Pictures, 1986.

Mr. Universe, Cine Universe, 1988, subtitled version released by Zeitgeist Films, 1990.

Anita, *Hard Time Romance* (also known as *Vaya con Dios*), 1991.

Jennifer, *The Perfect Weapon*, Paramount, 1991.

Jill Banner, *Strawberry Road* (also known as *Sutoroberi rodo*), Toho Company, 1991.

Marisa Benoit, *Bank Robber*, IRS Releasing, 1993.

Prostitute at bar, *Leaving Las Vegas*, Metro–Goldwyn–Mayer/United Artists, 1995.

Myra Okubo, *Lake Placid* (also known as *Lac Placid*), Twentieth Century–Fox, 1999.

(As Marishka Hargitay) Darcy, *Perfume* (also known as *Dress to Kill*), Lions Gate Films, 2001.

Some sources cite an appearance in *Star 80,* Warner Bros., 1983.

Film Work:

Associate producer, *Thira*, 2006.

Stage Appearances:

The Exonerated, Forty–Five Bleecker Street Theatre, New York City, 2003.

The American National Theatre Founders' Celebration Honoring August Wilson, Dodger Stages, New York City, 2005.

RECORDINGS

Video Games:

Voice of Deena Dixon, *True Crime: New York City,* Activision, 2005.

OTHER SOURCES

Periodicals:

Allure, August, 2005.

Cosmopolitan, October, 2005.

Entertainment Weekly, March 4, 2005.

Esquire, October, 1999, p. 135.

Good Housekeeping, October, 2004, p. 162.

InStyle, June, 2000, pp. 374–79.

Parade, July 13, 1997, p. 18; November 5, 2000, pp.8–9; February 13, 2005, p. 16.

People Weekly, April 6, 1992, pp. 105–107; December 10, 2001, pp. 151–52; September 13, 2004, p. 86; May 9, 2005.

TV Guide, November 8, 1997, p. 6; August 17, 2002, pp. 38–39; July 31, 2005, pp. 16–18.

USA Today, November 13, 1997, p. 3D.

US Weekly, April 24, 2000, p. 20.

Electronic:

Mariska.com, http://www.mariska.com, February 21, 2006.

HEDER, Jon 1977–
   (John Heder, Jonathan Heder)

PERSONAL

Full name, Jonathan Joseph Heder; born October 26, 1977, in Fort Collins, CO; raised in Salem, OR; married Kirsten, 2002. *Education:* Brigham Young University, B.F.A., computer animation, 2004. *Religion:* Church of Jesus Christ of Latter–Day Saints (Mormons). *Avocational Interests:* Drawing, animation, dancing.

Addresses: *Agent*—Joel Lubin, Creative Artists Agency, 9830 Wilshire Blvd., Beverly Hills, CA 90212. *Manager*—Julie Wixon–Darmody, Mosaic Media Group, 9200 Sunset Blvd., 10th Floor, Los Angeles, CA 90069.

Career: Actor. Appeared in commercials. Greasy Entertainment (production company), cofounder. Missionary in Japan.

Awards, Honors: MTV Movie awards, best break-through male performance and best musical performance, Teen Choice awards, choice movie dance scene and choice movie hissy fit, Teen Choice Award nominations, choice male movie breakout performance, choice movie actor in a comedy, choice movie liar, choice movie chemistry (with Efren Ramirez), choice movie love scene (with Tina Majorino), choice movie rumble and choice movie blush scene (both with Jon Gries), and Online Film Critics Society Award nomination, best breakthrough performance, all 2005, for *Napoleon Dynamite*.

CREDITS

Film Appearances:
Audience member, *The Wrong Brother* (short film), Candlelight Media Group, 2000.
(As Jonathan Heder) Officer Hardy, *Funky Town*, 2000.
Seth, *Peluca* (short film), 2003.
Title role, *Napoleon Dynamite*, Paramount/Fox Searchlight Pictures, 2004.
Darryl, *Just Like Heaven* (also known as *If Only It Were True*), DreamWorks, 2005.
Orlie, *Moving McAllister*, Camera 40 Productions/Revel Entertainment, 2005.
Clark, *The Benchwarmers*, Sony Pictures Entertainment, 2006.
Roger, *School for Scoundrels*, The Weinstein Company, 2006.
Voice of Skull, *Monster House* (animated; also known as *Zemeckis/Spielberg Motion Capture Project*), Sony Pictures Entertainment, 2006.
Ice skater, *Blades of Glory*, DreamWorks, 2007.
Voice, *Surf's Up* (animated), Sony Pictures International, 2007.
Mama's Boy, Warner Independent Pictures, 2007.

Television Appearances; Specials:
Himself, *Best Summer Ever*, VH1, 2004.
MTV Movie Awards 2005 Pre Show, MTV, 2005.
Himself, *Teen Nick*, Nickelodeon, 2006.

Television Appearances; Awards Presentations:
The Teen Choice Awards 2004, Fox, 2004.
The Teen Choice Awards 2005, Fox, 2005.
The 20th IFP Independent Spirit Awards, Independent Film Channel and Bravo, 2005.
The 2005 MTV Movie Awards, MTV, 2005.

Television Appearances; Episodic:
Guest, *The View*, ABC, 2004.
(Uncredited) Napoleon Dynamite, *The Late Show with David Letterman* (also known as *The Late Show*), CBS, 2004.
Percy, *Mad TV*, Fox, 2004.
(As John Heder) Voice of Napoleon Bonamite, "The Black Cherry," *Robot Chicken* (live action and animated), Cartoon Network, 2005.
Guest, *Dinner for Five*, Independent Film Channel, 2005.
Guest, *Late Night with Conan O'Brien*, NBC, 2005.
Guest, *Mad TV*, Fox, 2005.
Guest, *The Tonight Show with Jay Leno*, NBC, 2005.
Guest host, *Saturday Night Live* (also known as *NBC's "Saturday Night," Saturday Night,* and *SNL*), NBC, 2005.
Himself, *Punk'd*, MTV, 2005.
Himself, *Jimmy Kimmel Live*, ABC, 2006.
Himself, *Rome Is Burning* (also known as *Jim Rome Is Burning*), ESPN, 2006.
Himself, *Teen Nick*, Nickelodeon, 2006.

OTHER SOURCES

Periodicals:
Interview, June, 2004, p. 44.
Parade, March 26, 2006, p. 16.

Electronic:
Cinema Confidential News, http://www.cinecom.com, June 11, 2004.

HOLLOWAY, Josh 1969–

PERSONAL

Full name, Joshua Lee Holloway; born July 20, 1969, in San Jose, CA; raised in GA; father a surveyor; mother a nurse; married Yessica Kumala (a retail director), October 1, 2004. *Education:* Attended University of Georgia. *Avocational Interests:* Fishing, sailing, camping, snowboarding, martial arts, motorcross activities, playing the guitar.

Addresses: *Agent*—Leland LaBarre, Diverse Talent Group, 1875 Century Park East, Suite 2250, Los Angeles, CA 90067. *Manager*—Jai Khanna, Brillstein–Grey Entertainment, 9150 Wilshire Blvd., Suite 350, Beverly Hills, CA 90212. *Publicist*—Patricola/Lust Public Relations, 8383 Wilshire Blvd., Suite 530, Beverly Hills, CA 90211.

Career: Actor. Appeared in commercials and worked as a model. Operated a development company in Georgia and a restaurant in Los Angeles; also worked at a farm.

Awards, Honors: Member of the cast of *Lost* that was named entertainer of the year, *Entertainment Weekly,* 2005; Teen Choice Award nomination, choice male television breakout performance, 2005, Golden Globe Award, best television series—drama, and Screen Actors Guild Award, outstanding performance by an ensemble in a drama series, both with others, both 2006, all for *Lost.*

CREDITS

Television Appearances; Series:
James "Sawyer" Ford, *Lost,* ABC, 2004—.

Television Appearances; Specials:
(In archive footage) James "Sawyer" Ford, *Lost: The Journey,* ABC, 2005.

Television Appearances; Awards Presentations:
The 57th Annual Primetime Emmy Awards, CBS, 2005.
12th Annual Screen Actors Guild Awards (also known as *Screen Actors Guild 12th Annual Awards*), TNT and TBS, 2006.

Television Appearances; Episodic:
Handsome man and vampire, "City of," *Angel* (also known as *Angel: The Series*), The WB, 1999.
Ben Wiley, "Medieval Crimes," *Walker, Texas Ranger,* CBS, 2001.
Kenny Richmond, "Assume Nothing," *CSI: Crime Scene Investigation* (also known as *CSI, CSI: Las Vegas, CSI: Weekends,* and *Les experts*), CBS, 2003.
Eric, "Addicted to Love," *Good Girls Don't...* (also known as *My Roommate Is a Big Fat Slut*), Oxygen, 2004.
"My Other Left Foot," *Navy NCIS: Naval Criminal Investigative Service* (also known as *Naval CIS, Navy CIS, Navy NCIS, NCIS,* and *NCIS: Naval Criminal Investigative Service*), CBS, 2004.
Guest, *Entertainment Tonight* (also known as *Entertainment This Week, ET, E.T., ET Weekend,* and *This Week in Entertainment*), syndicated, 2005.
Himself, *Live with Regis and Kelly,* syndicated, 2006.

Appeared as Lana's young man in "Separation Anxiety," an unaired episode of *The Lyon's Den,* NBC.

Television Appearances; Pilots:
James "Sawyer" Ford, *Lost,* ABC, 2004.

Film Appearances:
Sean, *Cold Heart,* Diary Productions/Nu–Image Films, 2001.
Loren Carol, *Moving August,* MC–One, 2002.
Trent Parks, *Sabretooth,* Lions Gate Films, 2002.

Younger pal, *Mi amigo,* Azalea Film Corporation, 2002. (Uncredited) *My Daughter's Tears* (also known as *Against All Evidence* and *Meine Tochter ist kleine Moerderin*), Beta Film, 2002.
Pheb, *Dr. Benny,* Outrider Pictures, 2003.
Jake Hunt, *Skinner Box* (also known as *Sorority Asylum*), Global Vision Entertainment, 2006.
Max Truemont, *Whisper* (also known as *Hellion*), Universal, 2006.

RECORDINGS

Music Videos:
Aerosmith, "Cryin'," 1993.

OTHER SOURCES

Periodicals:
Boston Herald, December 8, 2004.
InStyle Weddings, summer, 2005.
People Weekly, March 21, 2005, p. 118.
TV Guide, January 2, 2005, pp. 38–40; April 3, 2005, pp. 24–29; June 5, 2005, p. 34.
TV Zone, March, 2005, pp. 34–36, 38–40.
USA Today, November 29, 2005.

Electronic:
Joshholloway.com, http://www.joshholloway.com, January 16, 2006.

HORN, Michelle 1987–

PERSONAL

Born February 28, 1987, in Pasadena, CA.

Addresses: *Agent*—The Kohner Agency, 9300 Wilshire Blvd., Suite 555, Beverly Hills, CA 90212.

Career: Actress.

Awards, Honors: Film Award, best child actress performance, Burbank International Children's Film Festival, 2001, for *The Ruby Princess Runs Away.*

CREDITS

Film Appearances:
Young Jodie, *Stuart Saves His Family,* Paramount, 1995.

Voice of young Kiara, *The Lion King II: Simba's Pride* (animated; video), Buena Vista Home Video, 1998.

Margaret Craven, *Return to the Secret Garden,* Alpha, 2000.

Ruby Princess, *The Ruby Princess Runs Away,* KOAN, 2001.

Megan, *Mental Hygiene,* 2001.

Jennifer Smith, *Hostage,* Miramax, 2005.

Emily, *Little Athens,* Legaci, 2005.

Kristen, *Loving Annabelle,* 2006.

Television Appearances; Episodic:

Small Talk, The Family Channel, 1996.

Amy Webster, "Bloodlust," *Profiler,* NBC, 1998.

Amy Webster, "Cycle of Violence," *Profiler,* NBC, 1998.

Saghi, "Tears of the Prophets," *Star Trek: Deep Space Nine* (also known as *DS9, Deep Space Nine* and *Star Trek: DS9*), syndicated, 1998.

Fields, "Burden of Proof," *The Practice,* ABC, 1998.

Kayla, "Fast Friends," *The Journey of Allen Strange,* Nickelodeon, 1999.

Saghi, "Penumbra," *Star Trek: Deep Space Nine* (also known as *DS9, Deep Space Nine* and *Star Trek: DS9*), syndicated, 1999.

Little Rona, "The Art of Give and Take," *Arli$$,* HBO, 1999.

Rayna, "Hero," *Angel,* The WB, 1999.

Voice of Eliza Pinchley, "One If by Clam, Two If by Sea," *Family Guy* (animated; also known as *Padre de familia*), Fox, 2001.

Voice of Mylaar, "Lovebeam #9," *Lloyd in Space* (animated), ABC, 2001.

Voice of Eileen, "The Big Sleepover," *Lloyd in Space* (animated), ABC, 2002.

Cassie (recurring), *Family Law,* CBS, 2002.

Fields, "Privilege," *The Practice,* ABC, 2002.

Fields, "Convictions," *The Practice,* ABC, 2002.

Jesse Campbell (recurring), *Strong Medicine,* Lifetime, 2004–2005.

Tara Patterson, "4.0," *Without a Trace,* CBS, 2005.

Television Appearances; Movies:

Megan, *Chance of a Lifetime,* 1998.

RECORDINGS

Video Games:

Young Kiara, *The Lion King II: Simba's Pride Activity Center* (also known as *Disney's "The Lion King II: Simba's Pride Activity Center"*), 1998.

Amanda Sparkle, Tiara Damage, *Walt Disney World Quest Magical Racing Tour,* Eidos Interactive, 2000.

J-K

JAMES, Colton 1988–

PERSONAL

Born February 22, 1988.

Career: Actor.

CREDITS

Film Appearances:

Benjamin, *The Lost World: Jurassic Park* (also known as *Jurassic Park: The Lost World, Jurassic Park 2, The Lost World,* and *The Lost World: Jurassic Park 2*), MCA/Universal, 1997.

Friendly son, *Austin Powers: The Spy Who Shagged Me* (also known as *Austin Powers 2: The Spy Who Shagged Me*), New Line Cinema, 1999.

Edward Baines, *The Cell,* New Line Cinema, 2000.

Jason Brascoe, *Extreme Honor* (also known as *Last Line of Defence 2*), Dreamfactory, 2001.

First boy, *Thank Heaven,* Showcase Entertainment, 2002.

Ross, *Carpool Guy,* L.S. Ideas, 2005.

Television Appearances; Series:

Neil Kanelos, *Port Charles* (also known as *Port Charles: Desire, Port Charles: Fate, Port Charles: The Gift, Port Charles: Miracles Happen, Port Charles: Naked Eyes, Port Charles: Secrets, Port Charles: Superstitions, Port Charles: Surrender, Port Charles: Tainted Love, Port Charles: Tempted, Port Charles: Time in a Bottle,* and *Port Charles: Torn*), ABC, 1998–2000.

Television Appearances: Miniseries:

Denny, *House of Frankenstein 1997,* NBC, 1997.

Television Appearances; Movies:

Danny Bridges, *Emma's Wish,* CBS, 1998.

Ethan, *A Memory in My Heart,* CBS, 1999.

Marty, *The Santa Trap,* PAX TV, 2002.

Skeeze, *Monster Makers,* The Hallmark Channel, 2003.

Television Appearances; Episodic:

Bill's kid, "Kids," *NewsRadio* (also known as *News Radio* and *The Station*), NBC, 1997.

Jimmy, "The Blood," *Seinfeld,* NBC, 1997.

Kid, "Johnny Hollywood," *The Single Guy,* NBC, 1997.

Matthew, "The Alternateville Horror," *Sliders,* Sci–Fi Channel, 1998.

Young Schulte, "Victims of Victims," *Profiler,* NBC, 1998.

Tommy, "Artie Comes to Town," *The Norm Show* (also known as *Norm*), ABC, 1999.

Josh Underwood, "Invocation," *The X–Files,* Fox, 2000.

Roy, "Deprogramming Erin," *Titus,* Fox, 2001.

Alex, "Still Rocking," *Still Standing,* CBS, 2002.

Leo, "Birthday Boy," *Without a Trace* (also known as *Vanished*), CBS, 2002.

Mickey, "Damage Is Done," *ER* (also known as *Emergency Room*), NBC, 2002.

Mickey, "A Simple Twist of Fate," *ER* (also known as *Emergency Room*), NBC, 2002.

Charlie Easton, "Got Murder?," *CSI: Crime Scene Investigation* (also known as *CSI, CSI: Las Vegas, CSI: Weekends,* and *Les experts*), CBS, 2003.

Jacob Foster, "Kilt Trip," *Judging Amy,* CBS, 2003.

Tennyson Singer, "The 3–H Club," *NYPD Blue,* ABC, 2004.

Josh Feldman, "Hold My Hand," *Six Feet Under,* HBO, 2005.

Appeared as Billy in *Beyond Belief: Fact or Fiction* (also known as *Beyond Belief* and *Strange Truth: Fact or Fiction*), Fox; and as Jonathon in *Moloney,* CBS.

Television Work; Series:

Casting assistant, *Supernatural,* The WB, 2005—.

JAMES, Pell 1977–

PERSONAL

Born April 30, 1977, in VA; father a lawyer; mother a substance abuse counselor. *Education:* Attended New York University.

Addresses: *Agent*—Bonnie Bernstein, Endeavor, 9601 Wilshire Blvd., Sixth Floor, Beverly Hills, CA 90212. *Manager*—Widescreen Management, 270 Lafayette St., Suite 402, New York, NY 10012.

Career: Actress. Appeared in commercials and promotional spots.

CREDITS

Film Appearances:
(Uncredited) Pell, *Black and White,* Screen Gems, 2000.
Julie, *Uptown Girls* (also known as *Molly Gunn*), Metro–Goldwyn–Mayer, 2003.
Annie, *Satellite,* Gigantic Pictures/Satellite, 2004.
Brier Tucket, *Undiscovered,* Lions Gate Films, 2005.
Isabel, *Confess,* Centrifugal Films, 2005.
Sun Green, *Broken Flowers,* Focus Features, 2005.
Wendi, *Neighborhood Watch,* Cafe Productions, 2005.
Cecilia Shepard, *Zodiac* (also known as *Chronicles*), Paramount, 2006.
Malerie Sandow, *The King,* ThinkFilm, 2006.
The American Standard, Eleven Eleven Films/Continental Productions, 2006.

Some sources cite an appearance as the title role in *Beautiful Swimmer;* and as Lynn Collins in *Trainwreck.*

Television Appearances; Movies:
Willa Shields, *Strip Search,* HBO, 2004.

Television Appearances; Episodic:
Chloe, "Access Nation," *Law & Order,* NBC, 2002.
Alicia Morley, "Brotherhood," *Law & Order: Special Victims Unit* (also known as *Law & Order: SVU* and *Special Victims Unit*), NBC, 2004.

Television Appearances; Pilots:
Appeared as Ellie Parker in the pilot *Hudson's Way,* CBS.

OTHER SOURCES

Periodicals:
Interview, September, 2005, pp. 164–67.

Electronic:
Pell James, http://www.pelljames.com, January 16, 2006.

J–LO
See LOPEZ, Jennifer

JOSEPH, Kimberley 1973–

PERSONAL

Born August 30, 1973, in Vancouver, British Columbia, Canada; raised in Gold Coast, Queensland, Australia; daughter of Joe (an operator of fast–food restaurant franchises) and Wendy (an operator of fast–food restaurant franchises) Joseph. *Education:* Attended Bond University; also studied in Switzerland and New York City.

Addresses: *Manager*—Bauer Company, 9720 Wilshire Blvd., Mezzanine, Beverly Hills, CA 90212; Marsala/Tappan Management, 8324 Fountain Ave., Suite B, Los Angeles, CA 90069; June Cann Management Australia, 73 Jersey Rd., Woollahra, New South Wales 2025, Australia.

Career: Actress and ballet dancer.

CREDITS

Television Appearances; Series:
Cassie Barsby, *Paradise Beach,* Australian Broadcasting Corporation and syndicated, 1993.
Host, *Gladiators* (also known as *Australian Gladiators*), Seven Network (Australia), c. 1995–96.
Joanne "Jo" Brennan, *Home and Away,* Seven Network, 1996.
Clare Devon, *Tales of the South Seas,* Ten Network (Australia), beginning 1998.
Herself, *E! News* (also known as *E!*), E! Entertainment Television, 2000–2001.
Jo Ellison, *Cold Feet,* Bravo, 2001–2003.
Dr. Grace Connelly, a recurring role, *All Saints,* Seven Network, 2004.
Cindy, a recurring role, *Lost,* ABC, 2004–2005.

Television Appearances; Movies:
Sophie Duvet, *Go Big,* Ten Network (Australia), 2004.

Television Appearances; Episodic:
Nemesis, "Two Men and a Baby," *Hercules: The Legendary Journeys* (also known as *Hercules*), syndicated, 1997.

Mary Worth, "Dangerous Encounters," *Water Rats,* Nine
   Network (Australia), 1999.
Andrea Thatcher, "Scent of Evil," Nine Network, 2000.
Herself, *Greeks on the Roof,* Seven Network (Australia),
   2003.

Television Appearances; Pilots:
Cindy, *Lost,* ABC, 2004.

Film Appearances:
Tracey, *Fight Night* (short film), Rivetting Productions,
   2005.

RECORDINGS

Videos:
Host, *Gladiators Greatest Hits* (also known as *The Best
   of "Gladiators": Series One*) Castle Video, 1995.

OTHER SOURCES

Periodicals:
Age (Melbourne, Australia), May 29, 2003.

KAUFMAN, Adam (II),

PERSONAL

Addresses: *Agent*—Thruline Entertainment, 9250
Wilshire Blvd., Ground Floor, Beverly Hills, CA 90212.

Career: Actor.

CREDITS

Television Appearances; Series:
Jamie Harper, *Brookfield,* ABC, 1999.

Television Appearances; Episodic:
Douglas Burke, "Past Imperfect," *Law & Order,* 1997.
Parker Abrams (recurring), *Buffy the Vampire Slayer*
   (also known as *Buffy* and *Buffy the Vampire Slayer:
   The Series*), The WB, 1999.
"Starlight StarBright," *Chicken Soup for the Soul,* PAX,
   1999.
Ethan (recurring), *Dawson's Creek,* 2000.
Michael Goren, "Wrong Is Right," *Law & Order: Special
   Victims Unit* (also known as *Law & Order SVU*),
   2000.
Dom, "To Serve, With Love," *Dead Last,* 2001.

Ted, "Spring Break," *CSI: Miami,* 2003.
Andre, "The Girl Next Door," *Veronica Mars,* 2004.
Jared Vogel, "Delta Does Detroit," *E–Ring,* 2005.

Television Appearances; Miniseries:
Charlie Keys, *Taken* (also known as *Steven Spielberg
   Presents "Taken "*), 2002.

Film Appearances:
James Roberts, *Between,* Opus, 2005.
Michael, *Vieni via con me* (also known as *Come Away
   with Me*), Medusa, 2005.
Wyatt, *Altered,* Rogue, 2006.

KIM, Yoon–jin 1973–
   (Yunjin Kim, Kim Yoon–jin)

PERSONAL

Born November 7, 1973, in Seoul, South Korea; raised
in New York, NY. *Education:* Boston University, B.F.A.;
graduate study at Oxford University; attended the British American Drama Academy; studied drama, dance,
and martial arts.

Addresses: *Agent*—Esther Chang, William Morris
Agency, One William Morris Place, Beverly Hills, CA
90212. *Manager*—Alex Chaice, Artistry Management,
525 Westbourne Dr., Los Angeles, CA 90048.

Career: Actress. Also a dancer. Appeared in commercials; Kanebo (cosmetics company), spokesperson.

Awards, Honors: Member of the cast of *Lost* that was
named entertainer of the year, *Entertainment Weekly,*
2005; Asian Excellence Award, outstanding female
television performance, Golden Globe Award (with others), best television series—drama, and Screen Actors
Guild Award (with others), outstanding performance by
an ensemble in a drama series, all 2006, for *Lost;* some
sources cite multiple awards for the films *Shiri* and
Milae.

CREDITS

Television Appearances; Series:
Gina, *Weding Deureseu* (also known as *Wedding
   Dress*), KBS (South Korea), beginning 1998.
With Love, Fuji Television, beginning 1999.
(As Yunjin Kim) Sun Paik Kwon, *Lost,* ABC, 2004—.

Television Appearances; Miniseries:
Mi Sook, *Beautiful Vacation* (also known as *A Gorgeous Vacation* and *Splendid Holiday*), MBC (South Korea), 1996.
The Hunch, MBC, 1997.

Television Appearances; Specials:
(As Yunjin Kim; in archive footage) Sun–Hwa Kwon, *Lost: The Journey,* ABC, 2005.

Television Appearances; Awards Presentations:
The 57th Annual Primetime Emmy Awards, CBS, 2005.
The 63rd Annual Golden Globe Awards, NBC, 2006.
12th Annual Screen Actors Guild Awards (also known as *Screen Actors Guild 12th Annual Awards*), TNT and TBS, 2006.
2006 Asian Excellence Awards, AZN Television, 2006.

Television Appearances; Episodic:
Guest cohost, *The View,* ABC, 2005.
Guest, *Jimmy Kimmel Live,* ABC, 2005, 2006.

Television Appearances; Other:
Some sources cite an appearance in *Foreboding.*

Film Appearances:
Areumdawoon sheejul (also known as *Spring in My Hometown*), [South Korea], 1998.
Myung–hyun Lee (some sources cite role as Bang–hee or Hyun Lee), *Shiri* (also known as *Swiri*), 1999, subtitled version, Samuel Goldwyn Company, 2002.
Yeon, *Danjeogbiyeonsu* (also known as *Gingko Bed 2, The Legend of Gingko,* and *Muyuru Tsuki: The Legend of Gingko*), CJ Entertainment, 2000.
Seo–Yeong, *Rush!,* 2001.
Hui–su, *Yesterday,* CJ Entertainment, 2002.
Ji–ni, *Iron Palm* (also known as *Mr. Iron Palm*), Korea Pictures, 2002.
Mi–heun, *Milae* (also known as *Ardor*), 2002.
(As Kim Yoon–jin) Seo Yun–hee, *6wol–ui–ilgi* (also known as *Diary of June*), Cinewise Film, 2005.

Some sources cite an appearance in *Georgia Heat.*

Stage Appearances:
Anya, *The Cherry Orchard,* National Asian American Theatre Company (NAATCO), New York City, 1993.
Fa Mu Lan, *The Woman Warrior,* Berkeley Repertory Theatre, Berkeley, CA, 1994.
Huoy, *Survivor: A Cambodian Odyssey* (also known as *Survivor*), 18th Annual Humana Festival of New American Plays, Actors Theatre of Louisville, Louisville, KY, 1994.

Wife, *The Woman Warrior,* Ahmanson Theatre, James A. Doolittle Theatre, Los Angeles, 1995.
Diana, *Junk Bonds,* Capital Repertory Company, Albany, NY, c. 1996.
Jing–Mei "June" Woo, *The Joy Luck Club,* Long Wharf Theatre, New Haven, CT, 1997.
Yachiyo, *The Ballad of Yachiyo,* Seattle Repertory Theatre, Seattle, WA, 1997.

Appeared as a sylph, *The Forest Song,* and as a museum lecturer, *Waterfall/Reflections,* both LaMama Experimental Theatre Club, New York City; and as Ophelia, *Hamlet,* National Academy of Dramatic Arts.

RECORDINGS

Music Videos:
Appeared in the S. G. Wananbe music video "Timeless."

WRITINGS

Photography:
Author of *XOXO,* a book of photographs.

OTHER SOURCES

Periodicals:
Honolulu Star–Bulletin, September 22, 2004.

Electronic:
Yunjin Kim, http://www.yunjinkim.com, January 16, 2006.

KLUGMAN, Brian

PERSONAL

Father, a real estate broker; mother, a schoolteacher; nephew of Jack Klugman (an actor). *Education:* Attended Carnegie–Mellon University.

Addresses: *Agent*—Endeavor, 9601 Wilshire Blvd., Sixth Floor, Beverly Hills, CA 90212. *Manager*—Michael Garnett, Leverage Management, 3030 Pennsylvania Ave., Santa Monica, CA 90404.

Career: Actor and writer. Appeared in commercials. Participant at the June Filmmakers and Screenwriters Lab, Sundance Institute.

CREDITS

Film Appearances:

First Long Island teen, *Fly by Night,* Lumiere Productions, 1993.

Medical student, *Wishmaster* (also known as *Wes Craven Presents "Wishmaster"* and *Wes Craven's "Wishmaster"*), Imperial Entertainment/Live Film & Mediaworks, 1997.

Man on drugs, *Can't Hardly Wait* (also known as *The Party*), Columbia, 1998.

Suicide, the Comedy (also known as *The Intervention*), Cargo Films, 1998.

Johnathan, *Random Acts of Violence,* The Asylum, 1999.

(Uncredited) Student, *Teaching Mrs. Tingle,* Miramax/Dimension Films, 1999.

Charles, *Burning Annie,* Armak Productions, 2003.

Military guard, *The Princess Diaries 2: Royal Engagement* (also known as *The Princess Diaries 2*), Buena Vista, 2004.

Munch, *Adam and Eve,* Lightning Entertainment, 2005.

Abraham, *Dreamland,* Echo Lake Productions/Heller Highwater Productions/Hunter Films, 2006.

Griffin and Phoenix, Gold Circle Films, 2006.

Appeared in *The Great Upside Down* (short film).

Film Director:

Director of *The Great Upside Down* (short film). With Lee Sternthal, director of *The Unknown.*

Television Appearances; Series:

Guy, a recurring role, *Felicity,* The WB, 1998–99.

Kirby, a recurring role, *Frasier* (also known as *Dr. Frasier Crane*), NBC, 2001–2002.

Television Appearances; Miniseries:

Wahoo, *The '60s,* NBC, 1999.

Television Appearances; Movies:

Brent Corman, *Monster Makers,* The Hallmark Channel, 2003.

Television Appearances; Specials:

Joshua, "The Bel Air Witch Project" segment, *The Bogus Witch Project,* 2000.

Television Appearances; Episodic:

First teenager, "Nineteen," *The Single Guy,* NBC, 1996.

Big Mo, "Curfew–sion," *The Parent 'Hood,* The WB, 1997.

Gail, "Zargtha," *Baywatch Nights* (also known as *Detectives on the Beach*), syndicated, 1997.

Jason, "A Girl's Gotta Deck the Halls," *Jenny,* NBC, 1997.

Timothy, "Over the Edge," *The Pretender,* NBC, 1997.

Big Mo, "Money Shot," *The Parent 'Hood,* The WB, 1998.

Russell, "Of Past Regret and Future Fear," *ER* (also known as *Emergency Room*), NBC, 1998.

White Chocolate, "Choose Your Own Evil," *GvsE* (also known as *G vs. E*), USA Network, 1999, later known as *Good versus Evil,* Sci–Fi Channel.

Pizza delivery boy, *Shasta McNasty* (also known as *Shasta*), UPN, c. 1999.

Noodle, "Jimmy Dot Com," *Ladies Man,* CBS, 2000.

Jerry Gaviola, "Better Laid Than Never: Part 2," *NYPD Blue,* ABC, 2002.

Cashier/God, "Requiem for a Third Grade Ashtray," *Joan of Arcadia,* CBS, 2004.

Television Appearances; Pilots:

Appeared as Bean Dip in the television pilot *Misconceptions,* The WB.

RECORDINGS

Videos:

(In archive footage) Medical student from *Wishmaster, Boogeymen: The Killer Compilation,* Flixmix, 2001.

WRITINGS

Screenplays:

Warrior, Icon Productions/Solaris, 2006.

Wrote the short film *The Great Upside Down.* With Lee Sternthal, author of *The Unknown.* Some sources cite Klugman as the author of the screenplays *Mephisto* and *Tron 2.0.*

KNOTTS, Don 1924–2006

PERSONAL

Original name, Jesse Donald Knotts; born July 21, 1924, in Morgantown, WV; died of complications from lung cancer, February 24, 2006, in Beverly Hills, CA. Actor, comedian, and writer. Known for his comedic portrayals of affable yet somewhat dimwitted characters, Knotts worked in the entertainment industry for half a century. His most recognized characters included bumbling Deputy Barney Fife in *The Andy Griffith Show,* a role that garnered Knotts five Emmy Awards, and lascivious landlord Ralph Furley in *Three's*

Company. Knotts began his career as a ventriloquist and appeared in his first television series, the soap opera *Search for Tomorrow,* from 1953 to 1955. It was the only dramatic role in his career. He appeared as a regular in *The Steve Allen Show* before landing his seminal role in *The Andy Griffith Show,* which ran for five seasons, from 1960 to 1965. Knotts also hosted his own variety show and in the late 1980s appeared with former costar Andy Griffith in the series *Matlock.* Knotts' film career reflected his love of lighthearted humor. He appeared in such films as *It's a Mad, Mad, Mad, Mad World,* the animated and live action film *The Incredible Mr. Limpet, The Reluctant Astronaut,* and *The Apple Dumpling Gang.* Knotts' final film performance was as the voice of Mayor Turkey Lurkey in the animated film *Chicken Little.* Knotts was also a writer. He wrote the screenplay *The Barney Fife Guide to Life, Love, and Self-Defense* in 1993 as well as a memoir, *Barney Fife and Other Characters I Have Known,* published in 1999.

OTHER SOURCES

Periodicals:
Broadcasting & Cable, March 6, 2006.
Entertainment Weekly, March 10, 2006.
Newsweek, March 10, 2006.
People Weekly, March 10, 2006.
Variety, March 6, 2006.

KRAEMER, Joe

PERSONAL

Born in western NY; father, a bank employee; married Heidi Van Lier (an actress, writer, and director); children: one. *Education:* Attended Berklee School of Music and University of Southern California.

Career: Composer, music conductor, sound designer and editor, director, and producer. Performed as a musician; record producer for other performers; worked as an intern at a theatre.

CREDITS

Film Work:
Dialogue editor, *Dumb & Dumber* (also known as *Dumb Happens* and *Misled and Uninformed*), New Line Cinema, 1994.
Sound editor, *The Grass Harp,* Fine Line Features, 1995.

Music editor and sound editor, *Kingpin,* Metro–Goldwyn–Mayer/United Artists, 1996.
Sound designer and associate producer, *Chi Girl,* Tri-Shore Entertainment, 1999.
Assistant to main music editor, *Hanging Up* (also known as *Aufgelegt!*), Columbia, 2000.
Music conductor and song performer of song "How to Make a Margarita," *The Way of the Gun,* Artisan Entertainment, 2000.
Sound effects editor, *Frailty* (also known as *Daemonisch* and *Nessuno e al sicuro*), Lions Gate Films, 2001.
Producer, *Monday,* 2006.

Director of various films that he also wrote and scored, beginning in high school.

Film Appearances:
Voice of Randy, *Chi Girl,* TriShore Entertainment, 1999.
Monday, 2006.

Appeared in various films he wrote and directed and super 8 film projects.

Television Work; Series:
Sound editor, *Land's End,* syndicated, 1995–96.

Television Work; Movies:
Music consultant, *The Pentagon Wars,* HBO, 1998.
Music arranger and music producer, *Hard Ground,* The Hallmark Channel, 2003.

RECORDINGS

Albums:
Recorded albums, including *Phonographic Memory.*

Album Producer:
Producer of albums, including the Dylan Kussman album *Unemployed on This Asteroid.*

WRITINGS

Film Music:
(With Kevin Kliesch) Songs, *Kingpin,* Metro–Goldwyn–Mayer/United Artists, 1996.
Burn, 1998.
Final Decision, 1998, York Entertainment, 2003.
Chi Girl, TriShore Entertainment, 1999.
Additional music, *We Married Margo,* KOAN, Inc., 2000.
Temporary score, *Hanging Up* (also known as *Aufgelegt!*), Columbia, 2000.
Slammed, A la Carte Entertainment, 2000.

The Way of the Gun, Artisan Entertainment, 2000.

Additional music, *The Circle* (short film), Mercury Films/Too Fat to Fish, 2001.

Temporary score, *Osmosis Jones,* Warner Bros., 2001.

(Uncredited; scenes deleted) *A Beautiful Mind,* Universal, 2001.

Dynamite (also known as *Family under Siege*), PorchLight Entertainment, 2002.

Esmeraldero (also known as *Emerald Cowboy*), Indican Pictures 2003.

The Hitcher II: I've Been Waiting (also known as *Hitcher 2* and *Hitcher 2: The Prey*), Universal Studios Home Video, 2003.

The Last Stop Cafe (short film), Dalvey Road Entertainment, 2003.

Open House, Bugeater Films/NeoFight Film, 2004.

Somewhere, Summerland Story Company, 2004.

All Souls Day: Dia de los muertos (also known as *Dia de los muertos*), IDT Entertainment Sales, 2005.

My Big Fat Independent Movie, Aloha Pictures/Film Threat/Anchor Bay Entertainment, 2005.

Ten 'til Noon, Shut Up & Shoot Pictures, 2005.

The Darkroom, CFQ Films/Mindfire Entertainment, 2006.

Monday, 2006.

Room 6, CFQ Films/Haunted Hospital Productions, 2006.

An Unreasonable Man (also known as *Ralph Nader: An Unreasonable Man*), 2006.

Composer, director, and actor in various films, beginning in high school. Wrote music for super 8 film projects. Some sources cite Kraemer as the composer for *Grand Junction.*

Television Music; Series:

Contributing composer, *Undressed* (also known as *MTV's "Undressed"*), MTV, 1999–2002.

Television Music; Movies:

Framed, TNT, 2002.

Hard Ground, The Hallmark Channel, 2003.

Mystery Woman, The Hallmark Channel, 2003.

A Time to Remember, The Hallmark Channel, 2003.

A Place Called Home, The Hallmark Channel, 2004.

The Trail to Hope Rose, The Hallmark Channel, 2004.

House of the Dead 2: Dead Aim, Sci-Fi Channel, 2005.

McBride: Murder Past Midnight, The Hallmark Channel, 2005.

Mystery Woman: Game Time, The Hallmark Channel, 2005.

Mystery Woman: Mystery Weekend, The Hallmark Channel, 2005.

Mystery Women: Sing Me a Murder, The Hallmark Channel, 2005.

Mystery Woman: Snapshot, The Hallmark Channel, 2005.

Mystery Woman: Vision of a Murder, The Hallmark Channel, 2005.

The Poseidon Adventure, NBC, 2005.

Television Music; Episodic:

Composer of music for an animated project that appeared in *Liquid Television,* MTV.

Television Music; Pilots:

The Underworld, 1997.

Some sources cite Kraemer as the composer for the pilot *Hollywood Vice.*

Albums:

Recorded albums, including *Phonographic Memory.* Some of Kraemer's compositions have been included in soundtrack recordings.

OTHER SOURCES

Electronic:

IGN Web Site, http://filmforce.ign.com, September 19, 2000.

Joe Kraemer, http://www.joekraemer.com, January 16, 2006.

KURODA, Emily 1952–
(Emily K. Kuroda)

PERSONAL

Born October 30, 1952, in Fresno, CA; daughter of William and Kay Kuroda; married Alberto Isaac (an actor and director), July 2, 1984. *Education:* California State University, Fresno, M.A., 1978; studied drama.

Addresses: *Agent*—Stone Manners Talent and Literary, 6500 Wilshire Blvd., Suite 550, Los Angeles, CA 90048.

Career: Actress. East West Players, Los Angeles, former member of company; also affiliated with the Asian American Theatre Project at the Los Angeles Theatre Center and Nobu McCarthy's Theatre Nova. Held various jobs.

Member: Actors' Equity Association, Screen Actors Guild, American Federation of Television and Radio Artists, Asian–Pacific American Artists Association.

Awards, Honors: *DramaLogue* awards, outstanding actress, c. 1984, *Visitors from Nagasaki,* c. 1989, *Minamata,* c. 1994, *The Maids,* and c. 1996, for *Ikebana; DramaLogue* Award (with others), best ensemble acting, 1990, *The Golden Gate;* commendation from the City of Los Angeles, 1993, for *About Love;* Garland Award, outstanding performance, and nomination for L.A. Ovation Award, 2000, both for *Straight as a Line;* named one of the top ten, *Los Angeles Times,* 2001, for *Red;* Best Actress Award, *Entertainment Today,* 2004, for *A Winter People;* Playwrights' Arena Award, outstanding contribution to Los Angeles theatre, 2006; Golden Eagle Award, for *Solo.*

CREDITS

Television Appearances; Series:
(As Emily K. Kuroda) Yukiko, *Gung Ho,* ABC, 1986–87.
Ronnie Page, a recurring role, *L.A. Law,* NBC, 1988–89.
Nurse Candice Katsumoto, *The Young and the Restless* (also known as *Y & R*), CBS, 1998.
Mrs. Kim, *Gilmore Girls* (also known as *Gilmore Girls: Beginnings* and *The Gilmore Way*), The WB, 2000—.

Television Appearances; Miniseries:
Nurse Liu, *Dynasty: The Reunion* (also known as *Dynasty: The Miniseries*), ABC, 1991.

Television Appearances; Movies:
Kikusen, *American Geisha,* 1986.
Reporter, *The Preppie Murder* (also known as *The Preppy Murder*), ABC, 1989.
Intensive care unit nurse, *Donor,* CBS, 1990.
Regina, *She Said No,* NBC, 1990.
Linda, *Caution: Murder Can Be Hazardous to Your Health* (also known as *Columbo: Caution! Murder Can Be Hazardous to Your Health*), ABC, 1991.
Jack's secretary, *Ladykiller,* USA Network, 1992.
Dr. Nancy Lee, *A Perry Mason Mystery: The Case of the Lethal Lifestyle* (also known as *The Case of the Famous Fatality, The Case of the Lethal Lifestyle,* and *A Perry Mason Mystery: The Case of the Famous Fatality*), NBC, 1994.
Operating room nurse, *Never Say Never: The Deidre Hall Story* (also known as *Deidre Hall's Story: After All*), ABC, 1995.
Awake to Danger (also known as *Awake to Murder, The Other Side of Dark,* and *Out of the Dark*), NBC, 1995.
Dr. Alice Morisaki, *Heartless,* USA Network, 1997.
Min, *Stranger Inside,* HBO, 2001.

Television Appearances; Specials:
Voice of Yeh–Shen, "Yeh–Shen: A Cinderella Story from China" (animated), *CBS Storybreak,* CBS, 1985.
Jeanette Kim, *About Love,* International Channel, 1993.

Television Appearances; Episodic:
Akemi, "You're Steele the One for Me," *Remington Steele,* NBC, 1982.
(As Emily K. Kuroda) Geisha girl, "Naka Jima Kill," *Tales of the Gold Monkey,* ABC, 1983.
Trauma Center, ABC, 1983.
Karen Matsuga, "The Spoilers," *MacGyver,* ABC, 1988.
Dr. Kito, "Life after Death," *Life Goes On,* ABC, 1991.
Janet Masuda, "It's a Damm Shaman," *Doogie Howser, M.D.,* ABC, 1991.
Woman, "Play, Pause, Search: Part 2," *Knots Landing,* CBS, 1991.
Reporter, "Crash and Born," *Sisters,* NBC, 1992.
Waitress, "Ottuma 52501," *The Jackie Thomas Show,* ABC, 1992.
Waitress, "The Player," *The Jackie Thomas Show,* ABC, 1993.
Dottie, "Take These Broken Wings," *ER* (also known as *Emergency Room*), NBC, 1996.
Attending physician, *Moloney,* CBS, c. 1996.
Dr. Garson, "Bloodlust," *The Profiler,* NBC, 1998.
Nurse Wolfe, *Party of Five,* Fox, c. 1998.
Janice Heinz, "Free Dental," *The Practice,* ABC, 1999.
Melinda Harris, "The Grinch," *Snoops,* ABC, 1999.
Mrs. Kwan, "F Is for Framed," *L.A. Heat,* TNT, 1999.
Third executive storyteller, "Romeo and Julie," *Working,* NBC, 1999.
Dr. Edwina Bates, "Simon Sez," *Chicago Hope,* CBS, 2000.
Dr. Ellen Braun, "Affairs of the State," *Family Law,* CBS, 2000.
Nurse, "The Sugar Pill," *Shasta McNasty* (also known as *Shasta*), UPN, 2000.
Claire Yamada, "God's Work," *The Agency,* CBS, 2001.
Claire Yamada, "Nocturne," *The Agency,* CBS, 2001.
Lily, "Sight Gag," *The King of Queens,* CBS, 2001.
Restaurant employee, "The Shrimp Incident," *Curb Your Enthusiasm,* HBO, 2001.
Claire Yamada, "Son Set," *The Agency,* CBS, 2002.
Yuki Takami, *Presidio Med,* CBS, c. 2002.
Dr. Kim Anderson, "Under Color of Law," *The Handler,* CBS, 2003.
Brenda's professor, "Grinding the Corn," *Six Feet Under,* HBO, 2004.
"Dr. Thorton Hears a Who," *Strong Medicine,* Lifetime, 2006.

Appeared in episodes of *Arli$$,* HBO; *Count on Me; The Division* (also known as *Heart of the City*), Lifetime; *General Hospital,* ABC; multiple episodes of *Life Stories* (multiple episodes); *Married ... with Children* (also known as *Not the Cosbys*), Fox; *Matlock,* NBC and ABC; *Party Girl,* Fox; and *Port Charles* (also known as *Port Charles: Desire, Port Charles: Fate, Port Charles: The Gift, Port Charles: Miracles Happen, Port Charles: Naked Eyes, Port Charles: Secrets, Port Charles: Superstitions, Port Charles: Surrender, Port*

Charles: Tainted Love, Port Charles: Tempted, Port Charles: Time in a Bottle, and *Port Charles: Torn*), ABC. Some sources cite appearances in *Highway to Heaven,* NBC.

Television Appearances; Pilots:

(As Emily K. Kuroda) Yukiko, *Gung Ho,* ABC, 1986.

Mikoto, *Party Girl,* Fox, 1996.

Mrs. Kim, *Gilmore Girls* (also known as *Gilmore Girls: Beginnings* and *The Gilmore Way*), The WB, 2000.

Television Work; Series:

Additional voices, *Potsworth & Co.* (animated; also known as *Midnight Patrol*), beginning 1990.

Stage Appearances:

Hokusai Sketchbooks, East West Players, Los Angeles, 1980–81.

Christmas in Camp, East West Players, 1981–82.

Asaga Kimashita, East West Players, 1983–84.

Visitors from Nagasaki, East West Players, c. 1984.

Three Penny Opera (musical theatre), East West Players, c. 1985.

Standby, *The Sound of a Voice/As the Crow Flies,* Los Angeles Theatre Center, Los Angeles, 1985–86.

A Chorus Line (musical), East West Players, c. 1987.

Justine, *Jacques and His Master,* Los Angeles Theatre Center, 1987–88.

Old woman and dying man's wife, *Minamata,* East West Players, Los Angeles Theatre Center, c. 1989.

The Golden Gate, Fountain Theatre, Los Angeles, c. 1990, and Zephyr Theatre, San Francisco, CA.

Understudy, *The Wash,* Center Theatre Group, Mark Taper Forum, Los Angeles, 1990–91.

Sansho the Bailiff (musical), Brooklyn Academy of Music Theatre, Brooklyn, New York City, c. 1993.

The Maids, East West Players, Los Angeles Theatre Center, c. 1994.

The Woman Warrior, Center Theatre Group, Doolittle Theatre, Ahmanson Theatre, Los Angeles, 1994–95.

Mother's youth and a teacher, *The Woman Warrior: A Girlhood among Ghosts,* Huntington Theatre Company, Boston, MA, 1994–95, and other regional venues.

The Glass Menagerie, Singapore Repertory Theatre, Singapore, 1996.

Ikebana, East West Players, Los Angeles, 1996.

Sumiko Takamura (Okusan), *Ballad of Yachiyo,* New York Shakespeare Festival, Public Theatre, Martinson Hall, New York City, 1997, as well as South Coast Repertory Theatre, Costa Mesa, CA, and other regional venues.

Dogeaters, La Jolla Playhouse, La Jolla, CA, 1998.

Pacific Overtures (musical), East West Players, c. 1998.

Straight as a Line, Playwright's Arena Theatre, Los Angeles, 1999.

Carlotta Campion, *Follies* (musical), East West Players, David Henry Hwang Theatre at the Union Center for the Arts, Los Angeles, 2000.

Second wife, *Golden Child,* David Henry Hwang Theatre at the Union Center for the Arts, 2000.

Red, East West Players, David Henry Hwang Theatre at the Union Center for the Arts, 2001.

Sisters Matsumoto, East West Players, c. 2001.

Question 27, Question 28 (reading), Noh Space, San Francisco, CA, 2003.

Comrade Chin, Suzuki, and Shu Fang, *M Butterfly,* David Henry Hwang Theatre at the Union Center for the Arts, 2004.

Madam Xia, *A Winter People,* Theatre@Boston Court, Pasadena, CA, 2004.

Wardina, *A Distant Shore,* Center Theatre Group, Kirk Douglas Theatre, Culver City, CA, 2005.

Appeared in *Big Tiger Prophecy, Bird's Nest Soup, Hymn to Her,* and *Watcher,* all Mark Taper Forum; *Cold Tofu,* East West Players, Los Angeles Theatre Club; *Flower Drum Song,* San Francisco Musical Theatre, San Francisco; *The Grapevine,* East West Players; *Macbeth,* Los Angeles Theatre Center; *Our Town,* South Coast Repertory Theatre; *Petals and Thorns,* Company of Angels; *Pirandello in Singapore,* Cast Theatre; *Rhubarb Shoots,* Pan Andreas Theatre; *Two Gentlemen of Verona,* Los Angeles Shakespeare Festival, Los Angeles; and in the workshop production of *Avocado Kid, or Zen and the Art of Guacamole* (musical).

Stage Work:

(With others) Developer, *29 1/2 Dreams, Women Walking through Walls,* East West Players, c. 1993.

Film Appearances:

Cory Chu, *Worth Winning,* Twentieth Century–Fox, 1989.

News anchor, *Why Me?,* Triumph Releasing, 1989.

Vicki, *Dad,* Universal, 1989.

Nurse Ruth, *Late for Dinner,* Columbia, 1991.

Mrs. Lee, *Yellow,* Phaedra Cinema, 1997.

Mrs. Lee Lee, *The Suburbans,* Columbia/TriStar, 1999.

Japanese woman, *Shopgirl,* Buena Vista, 2005.

Flora Nakano, *The Sensei,* Heitmann Entertainment/Zen Mountain, c. 2006.

Some sources cite appearances in *2 Days in the Valley* (also known as *Two Days in the Valley*), Metro–Goldwyn–Mayer, 1996; and *Minority Report,* Twentieth Century–Fox, 2002; as well as appearances in *Doctors* and *Solo.*

WRITINGS

Writings for the Stage:

(With others) *29 1/2 Dreams, Women Walking through Walls,* East West Players, c. 1993.

OTHER SOURCES

Electronic:
Emily Kuroda, http://www.emilykuroda.com, February 21, 2006.

KURUP, Shishir 1961–
(Gupta Shishir Kurup)

PERSONAL

Full name, Shishir Ravindran Kurup; also known as Gupta Shishir Kurup, according to some sources; born November 2, 1961, in Bombay, India; son of Ravi and Bhavani (maiden name; Mathews) Kurup; companion of Page Leong (an actress). *Education:* University of Florida, B.F.A., 1984; University of California, San Diego, M.F.A., 1987; studied with Tadashi Suzuki, 1986.

Career: Actor, director, writer, and composer. Cornerstone Theatre Company, founding member, 1986—; Los Angeles Theatre Center, Los Angeles, director of Asian American Theatre Project, 1990–91; Raven Group, codirector, 1991—; Artists Collective, associate director, 1992—; Audrey Skirball Kenis Theatre, member of playwrights' advisory committee, 1992—; South Coast Repertory Theatre, member of the advisory committee of the Nexus Program, 1993—. Young Conservatory, faculty member, 1990–92; University of California, Irvine, member of drama faculty, 1992; University of California, Los Angeles, member of Asian studies faculty, 1993; University of Southern California, adjunct assistant professor. Los Angeles County Museum of Art, audiovisual technician, 1988–91; Museum of Contemporary Art, member of Asian access advisory committee, 1992—. L.A. Ovation awards, presenter, 2003.

Awards, Honors: Grant from the Japan–America Friendship Committee, 1986; Flintridge Foundation awards, 1991, for *Skeleton Dance,* and 1992, *On Caring for the Beast;* Princess Grace Award, 1993, for theatre apprenticeship, Cornerstone Theatre Company; L.A. Ovation Award (with others), best play, c. 1995, for *The Central Ave. Chalk Circle.*

CREDITS

Stage Appearances:
Celestial Alphabet Event, One Dream Theatre, New York City, 1991.

EXILE: Ruminations on a Reluctant Martyr (solo show), Highways Performance Space, Santa Monica, CA, 1992, and other productions, including ones at the Mark Taper Forum, Los Angeles, Whittier College, Whittier, CA, the New York Shakespeare Festival, New York City, the University of Massachusetts, Amherst, MA, the Green Room, Manchester, England, and the Institute of Contemporary Art, London.
A Slice of Rice, Frijoles, and Greens, Great Leap Theatre, 1992, Loyola University Theatre, Chicago, IL, 1998.
Assimilation (solo show), Mark Taper Forum, 1992, the Village, Hollywood, CA, 2002.
Life and Death: The Vaudeville Show, The Artists' Collective/Los Angeles Theatre Center, Santiago, Cuba, 1993.
The Central Ave. Chalk Circle, Cornerstone Theatre Company, Watts, Los Angeles, 1995.
Malliere, Cornerstone Theatre Company, Santa Monica Place Mall, Santa Monica, CA, 1996.

Major Tours:
The California Seagull, California and Massachusetts cities, c. 1995–96.

Stage Director:
Skeleton Dance, New Works Festival, Los Angeles Theatre Center, Los Angeles, 1991.
Ghurba, Cornerstone Theatre Company, Los Angeles Theatre Festival, University of California, Los Angeles, 1993.
Cleveland Raining, East West Players, 1995.
(With Bill Rauch) *Everyman at the Mall* (also known as *Everyman*), Cornerstone Theatre Company, Santa Monica Place Mall, Santa Monica, CA, c. 1995, also produced at multiple southern California malls, 1997.

Film Appearances:
Khoudri, *Coneheads,* Paramount, 1993.
Raji, *The Trigger Effect,* Gramercy Pictures, 1996.
Jimmy, *City of Angels* (also known as *Stadt der Engel*), Warner Bros., 1998.
Abu Statlin, *Dill Scallion,* The Asylum, 1999.
Voice of Hisham Badir, *Anywhere but Here,* Twentieth Century–Fox, 1999.
Turbans (short film), Different Drum Productions, 2000.
Loy, *The Want,* 2001.
Surfer clerk, *The Zeros,* Zilch Company, 2001.
Alex, *A Day without a Mexican* (also known as *Un dia sin mexicanos*), Altavista Films, 2004.
Maitre d', *In Good Company* (also known as *Synergy*), Universal, 2004.
Sharif and Attah, *Sharif Don't Like It,* 2006.

Film Work:
Director, *Sharif Don't Like It,* 2006.

Television Appearances; Series:

X–Ray the cab driver, *Murder in Small Town X* (also known as *Endgame*), Fox, 2001.

Dr. Krishna Singh, *Surface* (also known as *Fathom*), NBC and Sci–Fi Channel, beginning 2005.

Television Appearances; Movies:

Sujat, *The Prime Gig,* Independent Film Channel, 2000.

Television Appearances; Specials:

California Seagull—The Short Cut (short), KCET (PBS affiliate), 1996.

Television Appearances; Episodic:

Dr. Rajid, "The Bad Boy in the Plastic Bubble," *Nurses,* NBC, 1992.

Dr. Tarica, "Perfectly Perfect," *Beverly Hills 90210,* Fox, 1993.

Pakistani medical student, "Feb 5, '95," *ER* (also known as *Emergency Room*), NBC, 1995.

Anesthesiologist, "Sweet Surrender," *Chicago Hope,* CBS, 1996.

Anesthesiologist, "A Time to Kill," *Chicago Hope,* CBS, 1996.

Harshad Ghafoor, "Chapter Thirteen," *Murder One,* ABC, 1996.

Gurdip Sahel, "Eight Pounds of Pressure," *C–16: FBI* (also known as *C–16*), ABC, 1997.

Glenn, "Welcome to Bent Copper," *Soldier of Fortune, Inc.* (also known as *SOF, Inc., S.O.F., Inc.* and *S.O.F. Special Ops Force*), syndicated, 1999.

Obstetrician and gynecologist, "Oh What a Piece of Work Is Man," *Chicago Hope,* CBS, 1999.

Anesthesiologist, "Cold Hearts," *Chicago Hope,* CBS, 2000.

Jayanti Salimpour, *City of Angels,* CBS, c. 2000.

Nitin Sharma, "Darkness for Light," *Judging Amy,* CBS, 2001.

Restaurant owner, "The Room," *Six Feet Under,* HBO, 2001.

Zach, "Bad Moon Rising," *The West Wing,* NBC, 2001.

Zach, "The Stackhouse Filibuster," *The West Wing,* NBC, 2001.

Doctor, "Bite Me," *Charmed,* The WB, 2002.

Saeed Akhtar, "Passage: Part 1," *Alias,* ABC, 2002.

Carmole Swarma, "Mr. Monk and the Sleeping Suspect," *Monk,* USA Network, 2003.

Vedic astrologer, "Who's Sari Now?," *Miss Match,* NBC, 2003.

"Blocked Lines," *Strong Medicine,* Lifetime, 2003.

Howard, "The People vs. Sergius Kovinsky," *The D.A.,* ABC, 2004.

Adeeb Amar, "Bale to the Chief," *NYPD Blue,* ABC, 2005.

Emergency room doctor, "Flashpoint," *The Closer,* TNT, 2005.

Television Appearances; Pilots:

Mr. Shandra, *Veronica's Video,* UPN, 1997.

Dr. Krishna Singh, *Surface* (also known as *Fathom*), NBC and Sci–Fi Channel, 2005.

RECORDINGS

Audiobooks:

His Holiness Dalai Lama, Victor Chan, and Bstan–'Dzin–Rgy, *The Wisdom of Forgiveness: Intimate Journeys and Conversations,* Riverhead, 2004.

WRITINGS

Stage Plays:

Skeleton Dance, New Works Festival, Los Angeles Theatre Center, Los Angeles, 1991.

EXILE: Ruminations on a Reluctant Martyr (solo show), Highways Performance Space, Santa Monica, CA, 1992, and other productions, including ones at the Mark Taper Forum, Los Angeles, Whittier College, Whittier, CA, the New York Shakespeare Festival, New York City, the University of Massachusetts, Amherst, MA, the Green Room, Manchester, England, and the Institute of Contemporary Art, London.

On Caring for the Beast, Highways Performance Space, c. 1992, Currican Theatre, New York City, 2001, also produced elsewhere.

Assimilation (solo show), Mark Taper Forum, 1992, the Village, Hollywood, CA, 2002.

Ghurba, Cornerstone Theatre Company, Los Angeles Theatre Festival, University of California, Los Angeles, 1993.

(With others) *Life and Death: The Vaudeville Show,* The Artists' Collective/Los Angeles Theatre Center, Santiago, Cuba, 1993.

(Adaptation) *Sid Arthur* (adaptation of the Hermann Hesse work *Siddhartha*), Cornerstone Theatre Company, St. John's United Methodist Church, Watts, Los Angeles, c. 1994–95.

Merchant on Venice (based on the William Shakespeare play *The Merchant of Venice*), South Asian League of Artists in America, New York City, 2001, Lark Theatre Studio, New York City, 2004.

As Vishnu Dreams, Cornerstone Theatre Company and East West Players, David Henry Hwang Theatre at the Union Center for the Arts, Los Angeles, 2004.

Music for the Stage:

Songs, *Sid Arthur* (adaptation of the Hermann Hesse work *Siddhartha*), Cornerstone Theatre Company, St. John's United Methodist Church, Watts, Los Angeles, c. 1994–95.

Songs, *The Central Ave. Chalk Circle,* Cornerstone Theatre Company, Watts, Los Angeles, 1995.

Everyman at the Mall (also known as *Everyman*), Cornerstone Theatre Company, Santa Monica Place Mall, Santa Monica, CA, c. 1995, also produced at multiple southern California malls, 1997.

As You Like It: A California Concoction (based on the William Shakespeare play *As You Like It*), Corner-

stone Theatre Company, P.L.A.Y./Center Theatre Group, Pasadena, CA, 2006.

Screenplays:

Sharif Don't Like It, 2006.

L

LAGESON, Lincoln
(Linc Lageson)

PERSONAL

Career: Producer, director, set production worker, stunt performer, and actor.

Awards, Honors: Camie Award (with others), Character and Morality in Entertainment awards, 2005, for *Love's Enduring Promise.*

CREDITS

Television Production Assistant; Series:
(As Linc Lageson) *Zoolife with Jack Hanna,* syndicated, beginning 1992.

Television Work; Miniseries:
Key set production assistant, *Gambler V: Playing for Keeps,* CBS, 1994.
Production assistant and stunt performer, *Streets of Laredo* (also known as *Larry McMurtry's "Streets of Laredo"*), CBS, 1995.
Set production coordinator, *Dead Man's Walk* (also known as *Larry McMurtry's "Dead Man's Walk"*), ABC, 1996.

Television Producer; Movies:
Set producer, *Rough Riders* (also known as *Teddy Roosevelt & the Rough Riders*), TNT, 1997.
Associate producer, *Everything That Rises,* TNT, 1998.
Associate producer, *Hard Time,* TNT, 1998.
(With others) *Hard Time: Hostage Hotel* (also known as *Hostage Hotel*), TNT, 1999.
(With others) *Hard Time: The Premonition* (also known as *The Premonition*), TNT, 1999.

A Carol Christmas, The Hallmark Channel, 2003.
Hard Ground, The Hallmark Channel, 2003.
Mystery Woman, The Hallmark Channel, 2003.
Line producer, *The King and Queen of Moonlight Bay,* The Hallmark Channel, 2003.
The Hollywood Mom's Mystery (also known as *The Dead Hollywood Moms Society*), The Hallmark Channel, 2004.
Just Desserts, The Hallmark Channel, 2004.
Life on Liberty Street, The Hallmark Channel, 2004.
Love's Enduring Promise, The Hallmark Channel, 2004.
Detective (also known as *Arthur Hailey's "Detective"*), 2005.
Mystery Woman: Game Time, The Hallmark Channel, 2005.
Mystery Woman: Mystery Weekend, The Hallmark Channel, 2005.
(With others) *Mystery Woman: Sing Me a Murder,* The Hallmark Channel, 2005.
(With others) *Mystery Woman: Snapshot,* The Hallmark Channel, 2005.
(With others) *Mystery Woman: Vision of a Murder,* The Hallmark Channel, 2005.
Out of the Woods, The Hallmark Channel, 2005.
The Poseidon Adventure, NBC, 2005.
(With others) *Mystery Woman: At First Sight,* The Hallmark Channel, 2006.
(With others) *Mystery Woman: Redemption,* The Hallmark Channel, 2006.
Mystery Woman: Wild West Mystery, The Hallmark Channel, 2006.
Our House, The Hallmark Channel, 2006.

Television Second Assistant Director; Movies:
Blue Tiger (also known as *Irezumi*), HBO, 1994.
Mystery Woman: Game Time, The Hallmark Channel, 2005.
Mystery Woman: Mystery Weekend, The Hallmark Channel, 2005.
Mystery Woman: Sing Me a Murder, The Hallmark Channel, 2005.

Mystery Woman: Snapshot, The Hallmark Channel, 2005.

Mystery Woman: Vision of a Murder, The Hallmark Channel, 2005.

Mystery Woman: At First Sight, The Hallmark Channel, 2006.

Mystery Woman: Redemption, The Hallmark Channel, 2006.

Mystery Woman: Wild West Mystery, The Hallmark Channel, 2006.

Our House, The Hallmark Channel, 2006.

Television Work; Movies:

Production assistant, *Victim of Love,* CBS, 1991.

Key set production assistant, *MacShayne: Final Roll of the Dice,* NBC, 1994.

Key set production assistant, *MacShayne: Winner Takes All,* NBC, 1994.

Television Stunt Performer; Movies:

Everything That Rises, TNT, 1998.

Hard Time, TNT, 1998.

Hard Time: Hostage Hotel (also known as *Hostage Hotel*), TNT, 1999.

Hard Ground, The Hallmark Channel, 2003.

Utility stunt performer, *The King and Queen of Moonlight Bay,* The Hallmark Channel, 2003.

Stunt driver, *The Hollywood Mom's Mystery* (also known as *The Dead Hollywood Moms Society*), The Hallmark Channel, 2004.

Stunt driver and utility stunt performer, *Life on Liberty Street,* The Hallmark Channel, 2004.

Utility stunt performer, *Love's Enduring Promise,* The Hallmark Channel, 2004.

Mystery Women: Sing Me a Murder, The Hallmark Channel, 2005.

Utility stunt performer, *Detective* (also known as *Arthur Hailey's "Detective"*), 2005.

Mystery Woman: Redemption, The Hallmark Channel, 2006.

Television Second Assistant Director; Specials:

When You Believe: Music from "The Prince of Egypt," NBC, 1998.

Television Stunt Performer; Episodic:

"After Life," *Buffy the Vampire Slayer* (also known as *BtVS, Buffy,* and *Buffy the Vampire Slayer: The Series*), UPN, 2001.

"Flooded," *Buffy the Vampire Slayer* (also known as *BtVS, Buffy,* and *Buffy the Vampire Slayer: The Series*), UPN, 2001.

Television Stunt Performer; Pilots:

68, ABC, 1999.

Television Appearances; Miniseries:

Dock hand, *Gambler V: Playing for Keeps,* CBS, 1994.

Television Appearances; Movies:

Bellman, *MacShayne: Final Roll of the Dice,* NBC, 1994.

Porter, *Edie & Pen* (also known as *Desert Gamble*), HBO, 1996.

Hearst lackey, *Rough Riders* (also known as *Teddy Roosevelt & the Rough Riders*), TNT, 1997.

Death row guard, *Hard Time: The Premonition* (also known as *The Premonition*), TNT, 1999.

Plainclothes police officer, *Hard Time: Hostage Hotel* (also known as *Hostage Hotel*), TNT, 1999.

Paul Granger, *Mystery Woman,* The Hallmark Channel, 2003.

Tilley's first assistant director, *A Carol Christmas,* The Hallmark Channel, 2003.

First assistant director, *The Hollywood Mom's Mystery* (also known as *The Dead Hollywood Moms Society*), The Hallmark Channel, 2004.

Takedown police officer, *Detective* (also known as *Arthur Hailey's "Detective"*), 2005.

Television Appearances; Episodic:

Security guard, "Smoochas Gracias," *City of Angels,* CBS, 2000.

Ambulance driver, "Defending His Honor," *JAG,* CBS, 2002.

Film Work:

Set production assistant, *American Yakuza,* First Look Pictures Releasing, 1993.

Transportation coordinator, *Wild Cactus,* Imperial Entertainment/Lincolnwood Motion Pictures/Metropolis Motion Pictures, 1993.

First assistant director, *Timemaster,* 1995.

Second unit first assistant director, *Tales from the Hood,* Savoy Pictures, 1995.

Production supervisor, *Texas Rangers,* Miramax/Dimension Films, 2001.

Film Appearances:

One of the group of rangers and outlaws, *Texas Rangers,* Miramax/Dimension Films, 2001.

RECORDINGS

Video Second Assistant Director:

Playboy: Fabulous Forties (also known as *Playboy's Fabulous Forties*), Playboy Entertainment Group, 1994.

OTHER SOURCES

Periodicals:

American Cowboy, July/August, 2005.

LALAINE, 1987–
(Lalaine Paras)

PERSONAL

Full name, Lalaine Ann Vergara–Paras; born June 3, 1987, in Burbank, CA; daughter of Lilia Paras.

Addresses: *Manager*—Leslie Allan–Rice, Leslie Allan–Rice Management, 1007 Maybrook Dr., Beverly Hills, CA 90210.

Career: Actress and singer. Concert performer at various venues; appeared in commercials and promotions, and spokesperson for Power Play, a healthy eating campaign. Appeared in "Express Yourself," a public service campaign broadcast on The Disney Channel, 2001; volunteer for charities and at charity events.

Awards, Honors: Young Artist Award nomination (with others), best performance by a young ensemble in a feature film or television movie, 2000, for "Annie," *The Wonderful World of Disney*; Young Artist Award nominations, best performance by a supporting young actress in a television comedy series, 2002, and best ensemble in a television comedy or drama series, both with others, 2002 and 2003, and Imagen Award, best supporting actress in television, Imagen Foundation, 2003, all for *Lizzie McGuire*.

CREDITS

Television Appearances; Series:
Miranda Isabella Sanchez, *Lizzie McGuire* (live action and animated; also known as *What's Lizzie Thinking?*), The Disney Channel, 2001–2003.
Host, *Flipside,* Living Asia Channel, beginning 2004.

Television Appearances; Movies:
Kate, "Annie" (musical), *The Wonderful World of Disney,* ABC, 1999.
(As Lalaine Paras) Theresa Rodriguez, *Border Line,* NBC, 1999.
Abby, *You Wish!,* The Disney Channel, 2003.

Television Appearances; Episodic:
Chloe, "Showtime," *Buffy the Vampire Slayer* (also known as *BtVS, Buffy,* and *Buffy the Vampire Slayer: The Series*), UPN, 2003.
Chloe, "Get It Done," *Buffy the Vampire Slayer* (also known as *BtVS, Buffy,* and *Buffy the Vampire Slayer: The Series*), UPN, 2003.
Guest, *SOP Gigsters* (also known as *S.O.P.*), GMA Network (Philippines), multiple episodes in 2004.
Guest, *U–Pick Live,* Nickelodeon, 2005.

Also had an uncredited appearance in an episode of *Rank,* E! Entertainment Television.

Television Appearances; Pilots:
Some sources cite an appearance as Miranda Isabella Sanchez in *Stevie Sanchez,* The Disney Channel.

Television Work; Movies:
Song performer, "If You Wanna Rock," *Pixel Perfect,* The Disney Channel, 2004.

Some sources state that Lalaine provided voices for *Mrs. Santa Claus* (musical), 1996; and "Geppetto" (musical), *The Wonderful World of Disney,* ABC, 2000.

Film Appearances:
Norma, *Promised Land,* Adriana Chiesa Enterprises, 2004.
Tutti, *Her Best Move,* Summertime Films, 2006.
Princess, *Royal Kill* (also known as *Princess*), 2007.

Film Work:
Some sources state that Lalaine provided voices for *Babe* (also known as *Babe, the Gallant Pig*), Universal; *Lolita,* Lions Gate Films, 1997; and *Inspector Gadget* (also known as *The Real Inspector Gadget*), Buena Vista, 1999.

Stage Appearances:
Appeared as Annette in the opera *Brundibar,* Opera Pacific.

Major Tours:
Little Cosette/Eponine, *Les Miserables* (musical), U.S. cities, 1997–98.

Also toured with *Disney's "Imagineers"* and the *Radio Disney Mall Tour.*

RECORDINGS

Albums:
Inside Story (also known as *Lalaine Inside Story!*), LVP Entertainment, 2003.

Albums; with Others:
Pixel Perfect (soundtrack), Disney, 2000.
You Wish! (soundtrack), 2003.
DisneyMania, Volume 3, Disney, 2005.

DisneyRemixMania, Disney, 2005.

Singles:
"Haunted," c. 2004.
"I'm Not Your Girl," Reprise Records/Warner Bros., 2005.

Other singles include "Fly Away" and "We All Fall Down." Lalaine's songs have appeared in television productions.

Music Videos:
Tom Petty, "Walls," 1996.
"I'm Not Your Girl," 2005.

WRITINGS

Albums; with Others:
Inside Story (also known as *Lalaine Inside Story!*), LVP Entertainment, 2003.

Singles:
"Haunted," c. 2004.
"I'm Not Your Girl," Reprise Records/Warner Bros., 2005.

Other singles include "Fly Away" and "We All Fall Down." Lalaine's songs have appeared in television productions.

LAW, Phyllida 1932–

PERSONAL

Full name, Phyllida Ann Law; born May 8, 1932, in Glasgow, Scotland; daughter of William and Megsie Law; married Eric Norman Thompson (an actor and director), May, 1957 (died, December 1, 1982); children: Emma (an actress), Sophie (an actress).

Career: Actress. Arena Stage, Washington, DC, member of company, 1966–67.

CREDITS

Film Appearances:
Jean, *Otley,* Columbia, 1968.
Fraulein Manzialy, *Hitler: The Last Ten Days* (also known as *Gli ultimi 10 giorni di Hitler*), Paramount, 1973.

Julia, *Tree of Hands* (also known as *Innocent Victim*), Castle Hill Productions, 1989.
Vera, *Peter's Friends,* Samuel Goldwyn, 1992.
Ursula, *Much Ado about Nothing,* Samuel Goldwyn, 1993.
Anne's mother, *Before the Rain* (also known as *Pred dozhdot*), Gramercy Pictures, 1994.
(Uncredited) Dr. Talbot, *Junior,* Universal, 1994.
Mrs. Bates, *Emma,* Miramax, 1996.
Elspeth, *The Winter Guest,* Fine Line Features, 1997.
Vronskaya, *Anna Karenina* (also known as *Leo Tolstoy's "Anna Karenina"* and *Anne Karenine*), Warner Bros., 1997.
First woman at hairdresser's shop, *I Want You* (also known as *Beloved*), USA Films, 1998.
The grandmother, *L'amante perduto* (also known as *Lost Lover*), 1999.
Lady Drake, *Mad Cows,* Entertainment Film Distributors, 1999.
Veronica, *Milk,* Arrow Releasing, 1999.
Margaret Sutton, *Saving Grace,* Fine Line Features, 2000.
Mrs. Watchett, *The Time Machine,* Warner Bros./DreamWorks, 2002.
Mrs. Williams, *I'll Be There,* Warner Bros., 2003.
Bella Black, *Blinded,* Guerilla Films, 2004.
Faith, *Two Men Went to a War,* Indican Pictures, 2004.
Mrs. Claus, *Tooth,* Redbus Film Distribution, 2004.
Distinguished lady, *Danny the Dog* (also known as *Unleashed*), Rogue Pictures, 2005.
Mrs. Coogan, *Mee–Shee: The Water Giant* (also known as *Ogopogo* and *The Water Giant*), ContentFilm, 2005.
Esperanza di Mendoza, *Day of Wrath,* American World Pictures/Screen Media Ventures, 2006.
Headmistress, *A Little Trip to Heaven,* A–Film Distribution, 2006.
Mother Canisius, *Copying Beethoven,* Myriad Pictures, 2006.
Sarah, *Mia Sarah,* Filmax International, 2006.
Viscountess Cumbermere, *Nanny McPhee,* Universal, 2006.

Some sources cite an appearance in *Opium Royale.*

Television Appearances; Series:
Presenter, *Play School,* BBC–2, beginning c. 1964.
Mrs. Beauchamp, *A Picture of Katherine Mansfield,* BBC, 1973.
Aunt Gwen, *Come Back, Lucy,* Associated Television, 1978.
Mrs. Blandy, *A Question of Guilt,* BBC, beginning 1980.
Aunt Lizzie, *Fame Is the Spur,* BBC, 1982.
Mrs. Vesey Stanhope, *The Barchester Chronicles,* BBC, 1982, broadcast on *Masterpiece Theatre* (also known as *ExxonMobil Masterpiece Theatre* and *Mobil Masterpiece Theatre*), PBS, 1984, and on Arts and Entertainment.

Edith Makepeace, *Hell's Bells,* BBC, 1986.

Lady Broughton, *Ffizz,* Independent Television (England), 1987–89.

Multiple roles, *Thompson,* BBC, 1988, PBS, 1989.

Babs, *That's Love,* Television South, 1988–92.

Olivia Esholt, *Chelworth,* BBC, 1989.

Edith Duglass, *The House of Eliott,* BBC and Arts and Entertainment, 1991–94.

Margot, *Degrees of Error,* BBC, beginning 1995.

Eve, *Wonderful You,* Independent Television, 1999.

Marjorie Tollworth, *Stig of the Dump* (also known as *Stig*), BBC, 2002.

Television Appearances; Miniseries:

Mademoiselle Vatnaz, *Sentimental Education,* BBC, 1970.

Marjorie Phelps, "The Unpleasantness at the Bellona Club," *Lord Peter Wimsey* (also known as *Lord Peter Wimsey: Unpleasantness at the Bellona Club*), BBC and PBS, 1973.

Madame Annette de Lancel, *Till We Meet Again* (also known as *Judith Krantz's "Till We Meet Again"*), CBS, 1989.

Lady Margaret, *The Magical Legend of the Leprechauns* (also known as *Leprechauns* and *Kampf der Kobolde*), NBC, 1999.

Rose Trenchard, *The Swap,* Independent Television (England), 2002.

Television Appearances; Movies:

The Poisoned Earth, Associated Television, 1961.

Mrs. Timpson, *All or Nothing at All,* London Weekend Television, 1993.

Maria, *Brush with Fate,* CBS, 2003.

Lady Lucia Pinochet, *Pinochet in Suburbia,* BBC–2 and HBO, 2006.

Television Appearances; Specials:

The wife, "Evelyn," *Play for Today* (also known as *Play for Today: Evelyn*), BBC, 1971.

"Buffet," *Play for Today* (also known as *Play for Today: Buffet*), BBC, 1976.

Lady Faulconbridge, *The Life and Death of King John* (also known as *The BBC Television Shakespeare, The Complete Dramatic Works of William Shakespeare: The Life and Death of King John,* and *King John*), BBC–2, 1984.

Marie's mother, *The Blue Boy,* BBC, 1994, broadcast on *Masterpiece Theatre* (also known as *ExxonMobil Masterpiece Theatre* and *Mobil Masterpiece Theatre*), PBS, 1994.

How Proust Can Change Your Life, [Great Britain], 2000.

Herself, *The 100 Greatest Kids TV Shows,* Channel 4 (England), 2001.

Television Appearances; Episodic:

Rosie McCallion, "Green Wedding," *Dixon of Dock Green,* BBC, 1963.

Sergeant Ruth Beckett, "Within the Law," *Dixon of Dock Green,* BBC, 1965.

Mary Fielding, "Women and Business Never Did Mix," *The Troubleshooters* (also known as *Mogul*), BBC, 1967.

Miss Cummins, "The Princess," *The Jazz Age,* BBC, 1968.

Laura Rankin, "The Singing Sands," *Detective,* BBC, 1969.

Mrs. Tetley, "Good Morning, Yesterday!," *Menace,* BBC, 1970.

Winifred Holland, "Golden Island," *Fraud Squad,* Associated Television, 1970.

Louise Maitland–Douglas, "The Condemned," *Sutherland's Law,* BBC, 1974.

Lady Constance Weir, "The Hero's Farewell," *Upstairs, Downstairs,* London Weekend Television, 1974, broadcast on *Masterpiece Theatre* (also known as *ExxonMobil Masterpiece Theatre* and *Mobil Masterpiece Theatre*), PBS, 1976.

Ann Kingsley, "First Impressions," *Angels,* BBC, 1978.

Ann Kingsley, "Fraternity," *Angels,* BBC, 1978.

Mrs. Thripp, "Rumpole and the Married Lady," *Rumpole of the Bailey* (also.

known as *Rumpole of the Bailey, Series I*), Independent Television (England), broadcast on *Mystery!,* PBS, c. 1980.

Mrs. Lucas, "Holy Wars," *Agony,* London Weekend Television, 1981.

Maggie Patton, "A Sad Loss," *Tales of the Unexpected* (also known as *Roald Dahl's "Tales of the Unexpected"*), Anglia Television and syndicated, 1983.

Jessica Truscott, "Fingers," *C.A.T.S. Eyes,* Independent Television, 1985.

Honoria Bird, "Rumpole and the Blind Tasting," *Rumpole of the Bailey* (also known as *Rumpole of the Bailey, Series IV*), Independent Television, 1987, broadcast on *Mystery!,* PBS, c. 1988.

Lady Ann, "Gracie," *About Face,* Independent Television, 1989.

Lady Carrington, "Incredible Theft," *Poirot* (also known as *Agatha Christie's "Poirot"* and *Poirot, Series One*), Independent Television, 1989, broadcast on *Mystery!,* PBS, c. 1990, and on Arts and Entertainment.

Joan Mathieson, "Forbidden Fruit," *Taggart,* Independent Television, 1994.

Magistrate, "Bring Me the Head of Arthur Daley," *Minder,* Independent Television, 1994.

Nancy Bellow, "Witch Hunt," *Heartbeat,* Independent Television, 1994.

Vicky Jeffreys, "A Pillar of the Community," *Hamish Macbeth,* BBC, 1995.

Herself, *A Bit of Fry and Laurie,* BBC, 1995.

Mrs. Ferris, "Impasse," *Paul Merton in Galton and Simpson's ... ,* Independent Television, 1996.

Guest, *The Rosie O'Donnell Show,* syndicated, 1997.

Elaine Porter, "Angel," *Dangerfield,* BBC, 1998.

Felicity Dinsdale, "Blood Will Out," *Midsomer Murders,* Independent Television and Arts and Entertainment, 1999.

Isobel Marchmont, "Laurels Are Poison," *The Mrs. Bradley Mysteries,* BBC and BBC America, 2000.

Professor Isobel Hogg, *Monarch of the Glen,* BBC Scotland, 2000, BBC America, 2001.

Jean, "Preserves," *Table 12,* BBC, 2001.

May Beauchamp, "Orpheus in the Undergrowth," *Rosemary & Thyme,* Independent Television, 2004.

Mrs. Carstairs, "The Hardest Word," *Waking the Dead,* BBC, 2004.

(In archive footage) Herself, *This Morning* (also known as *This Morning with Richard and Judy*), Independent Television, 2004.

Irene Moser, "The 7:59 Club," *Afterlife,* Independent Television, 2005.

Stage Appearances:
Major Barbara, Bristol Old Vic Company, 1956.
Red Roses for Me, 1962.
A Voyage 'round My Father, Haymarket Theatre, London, 1971.
Habeus Corpus, Haymarket Theatre, 1973.
Dotty, *Noises Off,* Savoy Theatre, London, c. 1983.
La Cage aux Folles (musical), London Palladium, c. 1986.
Elspeth, *The Winter Guest,* 1995.
The Tuesday Group, King's College, London (University of London), Franklin–Wilkins Building, c. 2003.

Appeared in *The Merry Wives of Windsor,* London production. Appeared in other productions, including performances at the Old Vic, London.

Stage Work:
Director, *The Duchess of Malfi,* National Theatre, King's Theatre, Edinburgh, Scotland, 2003.

RECORDINGS

Audiobooks:
Virginia Woolf, *Mrs. Dalloway,* Chivers, 2001.
Virginia Woolf, *To the Lighthouse,* Chivers, 2001.

WRITINGS

Nonfiction:
(Illustrator) Kenneth Branagh, *Beginning,* Chatto & Windus, 1989, American edition, St. Martin's Press, 1991.

OTHER SOURCES

Periodicals:
Guardian, January 5, 1998.
Independent, January 9, 1998.

LEE, Mushond 1967–
(Steven Lee, Steven Mushond Lee)

PERSONAL

Born September 17, 1967, in North Trenton, NJ.

Career: Actor and location manager.

CREDITS

Film Appearances:
(As Steven Lee) Richard Armand, *Lean on Me,* Warner Bros., 1989.
Helicopter, *Helicopter* (short film), Carousel Film & Video, 1993.
Joker, *Street Knight,* Cannon, 1993.
Joe, *P.C.H.* (also known as *Kill Shot*), 1995.
Intern (Carl), *Conspiracy Theory,* Warner Bros., 1997.
Duane, *The Pinston Cafe* (short film), University of Southern California, 2000.
Pretty Nate, *Love and a Bullet,* TriStar, 2002.
With or Without You, Screen Media Ventures, 2003.
FBI agent, *Charlie's Angels: Full Throttle,* Sony Pictures Releasing, 2003.
Malcolm, *2001 Maniacs,* Lions Gate Films, 2005.

Film Work:
Location manager, *Love and a Bullet,* TriStar, 2002.

Television Appearances; Series:
Jamahl "JoJo Grimes" Muhammad, *Sunset Beach,* NBC, 1997.

Television Appearances; Miniseries:
Huey Newton, *The '60s,* NBC, 1999.

Television Appearances; Movies:
Jonesy, *Blade Squad,* Fox, 1998.
Luther, *Behind Enemy Lines,* HBO, 1998.
Blake, *Operation Sandman: Warriors in Hell,* UPN, 2000.
Billy, *James Dean,* TNT, 2001.

Television Appearances; Pilots:
All AX–S, ABC, 1993.

Television Appearances; Episodic:
(As Steven Mushond Lee) Slide, "Period of Adjustment," *The Cosby Show,* NBC, 1990.
Slide, "Just Thinking about It: Parts 1 & 2," *The Cosby Show,* NBC, 1990.

Slide, "Attack of the Killer B's," *The Cosby Show,* NBC, 1991.

Beverly High football team member, "Home and Away," *Beverly Hills, 90210,* Fox, 1992.

Wendell, *Where I Live,* ABC, 1992.

Orlando, "Blood Is Thicker Than Mud," *The Fresh Prince of Bel–Air,* NBC, 1993.

Wesley, "Three Homies and a Baby," *Martin,* Fox, 1995.

Frank Matthews, "The Medal," *Early Edition,* CBS, 1997.

Jackson, "The Thin Dead Line," *Angel* (also known as *Angel: The Series*), The WB, 2001.

LENK, Tom 1976–
(Tom Lenck, Thomas Lenk)

PERSONAL

Full name, Thomas Loren Lenk; born June 16, 1976, in Westlake Village, CA; son of Fred (a tuba player and high school music teacher [some sources cite a computer programmer]) and Pam (a teacher) Lenk. *Education:* Attended Moorpark College; University of California, Los Angeles, B.A. *Avocational Interests:* Art, bowling, kickboxing.

Addresses: *Agent*—Michael Greenwald, Don Buchwald and Associates, 6500 Wilshire Blvd., Suite 2200, Los Angeles, CA 90048; (commercials) Cunningham/Escott/Dipene, 10635 Santa Monica Blvd., Suite 140, Los Angeles, CA 90025. *Manager*—Michael Valeo, McKeon–Valeo–Myones Management, 9150 Wilshire Blvd., Suite 102, Beverly Hills, CA 90212.

Career: Actor and writer. Comedy performer at clubs in Los Angeles; appeared in commercials. Also appeared at conventions.

Awards, Honors: Winner of Carol Burnett Music Theatre Competition, University of California, Los Angeles, 1997; Golden Fang Award, best wannabe villain, 2002, named to Emmy wish list, best supporting actor in a drama, *TV Guide,* 2003, Golden Tater, breakout star, Couch Potato awards, E! Entertainment Television, and named one of the top scene stealers, *San Francisco Examiner,* all for *Buffy the Vampire Slayer.*

CREDITS

Television Appearances; Series:
Andrew Wells, *Buffy the Vampire Slayer* (also known as *BtVS, Buffy,* and *Buffy the Vampire Slayer: The Series*), UPN, 2001–2003.

Television Appearances; Episodic:
(As Thomas Lenk) Alan Higgins, "The God Thing," *Judging Amy,* CBS, 2000.

Cyrus, "Real Me," *Buffy the Vampire Slayer* (also known as *BtVS, Buffy,* and *Buffy the Vampire Slayer: The Series*), The WB, 2000.

Young man, "The Brain Game," *Popular,* The WB, 2001.

Andrew Wells, "Damage," *Angel* (also known as *Angel: The Series*), The WB, 2004.

Andrew Wells, "The Girl in Question," *Angel* (also known as *Angel: The Series*), The WB, 2004.

Thomas Wheeler, "Joey and the Big Audition," *Joey,* NBC, 2004.

Young poet, "In Case of Rapture," *Six Feet Under,* HBO, 2004.

Allen, "Spin," *House* (also known as *House, M.D.*), Fox, 2005.

Appeared in *Cousin Skeeter,* Nickelodeon; some sources cite an appearance in *The Tonight Show with Jay Leno,* NBC.

Television Appearances; Pilots:
Some sources cite appearances in the pilots *Mystery Girl,* UPN; and in *The Ruling Class.*

Film Appearances:
(As Thomas Lenk) Uncle Floyd's second kid, *Boogie Nights,* New Line Cinema, 1997.

(As Tom Lenck) Chris, *Boy Next Door* (short film), 1999.

Drunk boy at party, *And Then Came Summer,* 10% Productions, 2000.

Sean, *Window Theory,* Wingman Productions/American World Pictures, 2004.

Teddy, *Straight–Jacket,* Regent Releasing/here! Films, 2004.

Himself, *Bandwagon,* 2004.

Billy, *Loretta* (short film), Wallace House Productions, 2005.

Frodo Baggins, *Date Movie* (also known as *Untitled Aaron Seltzer/Jason Friedberg Project*), Twentieth Century–Fox, 2006.

Kronos, *The Thirst,* CFQ Films/Mindfire Entertainment, 2006.

Stage Appearances:
Save Me from My Sister, Hudson Theatre, Los Angeles, c. 2001.

There's Someone Living in the House That Jack Built, 2nd Stage Theatre, Hollywood, CA, 2003.

Charity Takes Nationals by Storm, c. 2003.

Various characters, *Strangely Attractive* (sketch comedy show), Lillian Theatre, Los Angeles, c. 2005.

Will You Be My Special Friend?, Acme Comedy Theatre, Los Angeles, c. 2005.

Duncan Trask, *The Book of Liz,* Blank Theatre Company, 2nd Stage Theatre, 2005–2006.

Franz Klinemann, *Rock of Ages* (musical), Vanguard Hollywood, Hollywood, CA, 2006.

Appeared as Hugo, *Bye, Bye Birdie* (musical), in *Hello, Dolly* (musical), and in *Peter Pan,* all Cabrillo Music Theatre, Thousand Oaks, CA; appeared as a balladeer, *Assassins* (musical); as Jack, *Into the Woods* (musical); as Peter, *Jesus Christ Superstar* (rock opera); as George, *Our Town;* as the title role, *Scooby Doo;* in *Steps in Time, Shreek!* (also known as *Disney's "Steps in Time"* and *Disney's "Steps in Time, Shreek!"*); and in the solo show *The Tom Lenk Show.* Appeared in community theatre productions.

Major Tours:
Toured as Doody in the musical *Grease,* European cities.

Stage Work:
Production stage manager, *The Grave White Way* (musical revue), Hudson Backstage Theatre, Hollywood, CA, 2001.

Some sources cite Lenk as the director of *Annie* (musical), Camarillo Youth Center, c. 1993.

RECORDINGS

Videos:
Himself, *"Buffy": Season 7 Overview,* Fox Box, 2004.

Music Videos:
The Offspring, "The Kids Aren't Alright," 1999.
3rd Faze, "Shy," 2001.

WRITINGS

Writings for the Stage:
Save Me from My Sister, Hudson Theatre, Los Angeles, c. 2001.
Charity Takes Nationals by Storm, c. 2003.
(With others) *Strangely Attractive* (sketch comedy show), Lillian Theatre, Los Angeles, c. 2005.
Will You Be My Special Friend?, Acme Comedy Theatre, Los Angeles, c. 2005.

Author of *It's Too Chilly for a Salad* and *The Orphan Project;* and of the solo show *The Tom Lenk Show.*

OTHER SOURCES

Periodicals:
Buffy (Great Britain), July, 2002.

Buffy the Vampire Slayer, June, 2002, p. 48; June, 2003, pp. 38–42; April, 2004, pp. 12–13.
TV Zone Special, July, 2003, pp. 78–83.

LENZ, Joie 1981–
(Bethany Galeotti, Bethany Joy Galeotti, Bethany Joy Lenz)

PERSONAL

Original name, Bethany Joy Lenz; born April 2, 1981, in Hollywood, FL; married Michael Galeotti (a musician), January 1, 2006. *Education:* Studied voice with Eric Vetro and Richard Barrett. *Avocational Interests:* Photography, painting, writing, horseback riding, knitting, and making stationary.

Addresses: *Agent*—Paradigm, 360 North Crescent Dr., North Bldg., Beverly Hills, CA 90210. *Manager*—Envoy Entertainment, 1640 S. Sepulveda Blvd., Suite 530, Los Angeles, CA 90025. *Publicist*—PMK/HBH Public Relations, 700 San Vicente Blvd., Suite G910, West Hollywood, CA 90069. *Office*—c/o *One Tree Hill,* Warner Bros., 4000 Warner Blvd., Burbank, CA 91522.

Career: Actress. Appeared in television commercials for Swan's Crossing dolls, Dr. Pepper, and Eggo waffles.

Awards, Honors: *Soap Opera Digest* Award nomination (with Paul Anthony Stewart), favorite couple, 2000, for *The Guiding Light;* Teen Choice Award nominations, choice breakout TV star—female and choice TV sidekick, 2004, both for *One Tree Hill.*

CREDITS

Film Appearances:
(Uncredited) *I Love You, I Love You Not,* Avalanche Releasing, 1996.
Linda Halleck, *Thinner* (also known as *Stephen King's "Thinner"*), Paramount, 1996.
Marni Potts, *Bring It On Again,* Universal, 2004.

Television Appearances; Series:
Teenage Reva clone, *The Guiding Light* (also known as *Guiding Light*), 1998.
Michelle Bauer Santos Santos, *The Guiding Light* (also known as *Guiding Light*), 1998–2000.
(As Bethany Joy Lenz, then Bethany Galeotti) Haley James Scott, *One Tree Hill,* The WB, 2003—.

Film Work:
Sound, *Undercover Brother,* Universal, 2002.

Television Appearances; Movies:
Rose Cronin, *Mary and Rhoda*, 2000.

Television Appearances; Pilots:
1973, The WB, 1998.

Television Appearances; Specials:
Presenter, *The 26th Annual Daytime Emmy Awards*, CBS, 1999.

Television Appearances; Episodic:
Lady Julia, "A Knight to Remember," *Charmed*, The WB, 2001.
Gretchen, "Oops ... Noel Did It Again," *Felicity*, The WB, 2001.
Heather, *Off Centre*, The WB, 2001.
Salesgirl, "The Romeo & Juliet Episode," *Maybe It's Me*, The WB, 2002.
Claire Stasiak, "My Aim Is True," *The Guardian*, CBS, 2003.
Claire Stasiak, "What It Means to You," *The Guardian*, CBS, 2003.

Stage Appearances:
Appeared in *Annie; The Wizard of Oz; Gypsy; Cinderella; The Outsiders*.

RECORDINGS

Albums:
Preincarnate, 2002.

Released album on Epic Records, 2006.

Music Videos:
Appeared in 5ive's "When the Lights Go Out."

LEVINSON, Larry

PERSONAL

Addresses: *Office*—Larry Levinson Productions and Alpine Productions, 500 South Sepulveda Blvd., Suite 610, Los Angeles, CA 90049.

Career: Producer and executive. Larry Levinson Productions, Los Angeles, CA, president; Alpine Productions, producer.

Awards, Honors: Bronze Wrangler Award (with others), outstanding television feature film, Western Heritage awards, 1996, for *Streets of Laredo*; Camie Award (with others), Character and Morality in Entertainment awards, 2003, for *Love Comes Softly*; Camie Award (with others), 2005, for *Love's Enduring Promise*.

CREDITS

Television Executive Producer; Miniseries:
Gambler V: Playing for Keeps, CBS, 1994.
Streets of Laredo (also known as *Larry McMurtry's "Streets of Laredo"*), CBS, 1995.
Dead Man's Walk (also known as *Larry McMurtry's "Dead Man's Walk"*), ABC, 1996.
Rough Riders (also known as *Teddy Roosevelt & the Rough Riders*), TNT, 1997.
Johnson County War, The Hallmark Channel, 2002.
Roughing It (also known as *Mark Twain's "Roughing It"*), The Hallmark Channel, 2002.
Frankenstein, The Hallmark Channel, 2004.
King Solomon's Mines, The Hallmark Channel, 2004.
La Femme Musketeer, The Hallmark Channel, 2004.
Icon (also known as *Frederick Forsyth's "Icon"*), The Hallmark Channel, 2005.
Mysterious Island, The Hallmark Channel, 2005.
Supernova, The Hallmark Channel, 2005.
Blackbeard, The Hallmark Channel, 2006.
The Curse of King Tut's Tomb, The Hallmark Channel, 2006.

Television Executive Producer; Movies:
Rio Diablo, CBS, 1993.
Everything That Rises, TNT, 1998.
Hard Time, TNT, 1998.
Hard Time: Hostage Hotel (also known as *Hostage Hotel*), TNT, 1999.
Hard Time: The Premonition (also known as *The Premonition*), TNT, 1999.
Gentle Ben (also known as *Terror on the Mountain*), Animal Planet, 2002.
Night of the Wolf, Animal Planet, 2002.
Santa, Jr., The Hallmark Channel, 2002.
Audrey's Rain, The Hallmark Channel, 2003.
A Carol Christmas, The Hallmark Channel, 2003.
Gentle Ben 2: Danger on the Mountain (also known as *Black Gold*), Animal Planet, 2003.
Hard Ground, The Hallmark Channel, 2003.
The King and Queen of Moonlight Bay, The Hallmark Channel, 2003.
The Last Cowboy, The Hallmark Channel, 2003.
Love Comes Softly, The Hallmark Channel, 2003.
Monster Makers, The Hallmark Channel, 2003.
Mystery Woman, The Hallmark Channel, 2003.
Straight from the Heart, The Hallmark Channel, 2003.
A Time to Remember, The Hallmark Channel, 2003.
Angel in the Family, The Hallmark Channel, 2004.
A Boyfriend for Christmas, The Hallmark Channel, 2004.
Gone but Not Forgotten, 2004.

The Hollywood Mom's Mystery (also known as *The Dead Hollywood Moms Society*), The Hallmark Channel, 2004.

Just Desserts, The Hallmark Channel, 2004.

Life on Liberty Street, The Hallmark Channel, 2004.

The Long Shot: Believe in Courage, The Hallmark Channel, 2004.

Love, Clyde, The Hallmark Channel, 2004.

Love's Enduring Promise, The Hallmark Channel, 2004.

Murder without Conviction, The Hallmark Channel, 2004.

A Place Called Home, The Hallmark Channel, 2004.

Single Santa Seeks Mrs. Claus, The Hallmark Channel, 2004.

The Trail to Hope Rose, The Hallmark Channel, 2004.

Wedding Daze, The Hallmark Channel, 2004.

Annie's Point, The Hallmark Channel, 2005.

Back to You and Me, The Hallmark Channel, 2005.

Desolation Canyon, The Hallmark Channel, 2005.

Detective (also known as *Arthur Hailey's "Detective"*), 2005.

A Family of Strangers, The Hallmark Channel, 2005.

The Family Plan, The Hallmark Channel, 2005.

Fielder's Choice, The Hallmark Channel, 2005.

Jane Doe: Now You See It, Now You Don't, The Hallmark Channel, 2005.

Jane Doe: Til Death Do Us Part, The Hallmark Channel, 2005.

Jane Doe: Vanishing Act, The Hallmark Channel, 2005.

Jane Doe: The Wrong Face, The Hallmark Channel, 2005.

Love's Long Journey, The Hallmark Channel, 2005.

McBride: Anybody Here Murder Marty?, The Hallmark Channel, 2005.

McBride: The Chameleon Murder, The Hallmark Channel, 2005.

McBride: The Doctor Is Out ... Really Out, The Hallmark Channel, 2005.

McBride: Fallen Idol, The Hallmark Channel, 2005.

McBride: It's Murder, Madam, The Hallmark Channel, 2005.

McBride: Murder Past Midnight, The Hallmark Channel, 2005.

McBride: Tune In for Murder, The Hallmark Channel, 2005.

Meet the Santas, The Hallmark Channel, 2005.

Mystery Woman: At First Sight, The Hallmark Channel, 2005.

Mystery Woman: Game Time, The Hallmark Channel, 2005.

Mystery Woman: Mystery Weekend, The Hallmark Channel, 2005.

Mystery Woman: Redemption, The Hallmark Channel, 2005.

Mystery Women: Sing Me a Murder, The Hallmark Channel, 2005.

Mystery Woman: Snapshot, The Hallmark Channel, 2005.

Mystery Woman: Vision of a Murder, The Hallmark Channel, 2005.

Ordinary Miracles, The Hallmark Channel, 2005.

Out of the Woods, The Hallmark Channel, 2005.

The Poseidon Adventure, NBC, 2005.

Thicker Than Water, The Hallmark Channel, 2005.

Wild Hearts, The Hallmark Channel, 2005.

Falling in Love with the Girl Next Door, The Hallmark Channel, 2006.

Hidden Places, The Hallmark Channel, 2006.

Jane Doe: The Brigadoon Effect, The Hallmark Channel, 2006.

Jane Doe: The Harder They Fall, Hallmark Channel, 2006.

Jane Doe: Yes, I Remember It Well, The Hallmark Channel, 2006.

Murder 101, The Hallmark Channel, 2006.

Mystery Woman: Wild West Mystery, The Hallmark Channel, 2006.

Our House, The Hallmark Channel, 2006.

The Reading Room, The Hallmark Channel, 2006.

Television Supervising Producer; Movies:

MacShayne: Final Roll of the Dice, NBC, 1994.

MacShayne: Winner Take All, NBC, 1994.

Television Executive Producer; Pilots:

Executive producer, *Guys Like Us,* ABC, 1996.

Television Work; Other:

Some sources cite Levinson as the music producer for the animated program *Gnomes,* CBS, 1980.

Television Appearances; Miniseries:

First card player, *Gambler V: Playing for Keeps,* CBS, 1994.

Film Executive Producer:

Texas Rangers, Miramax/Dimension Films, 1999.

Dinotopia: Quest for the Ruby Sunstone (animated), Goodtimes Entertainment, 2005.

Porky's (also known as *Howard Stern Presents "Porky's"*), Gotham Entertainment Group, 2006.

Rock 'n' Roll High School (also known as *Howard Stern Presents "Rock 'n' Roll High School"*), 2006.

Film Character Creator:

Missing in Action, Cannon, 1984.

Braddock: Missing in Action III, Cannon, 1988.

WRITINGS

Screenplays:

Missing in Action 2: The Beginning, Cannon, 1985.

Teleplays:

Some sources cite Levinson as a writer for the series *Joanie Loves Chachi,* ABC, 1982–83.

LILLY, Evangeline 1979–

PERSONAL

Full name, Nicole Evangeline Lilly; born August 3, 1979, in Fort Saskatchewan, Alberta, Canada; raised in Abbotsford, British Columbia, Canada; father, a teacher and missionary (some sources cite a produce manager at a grocery store); mother, a teacher and missionary (some sources cite an operator of a day–care center or cosmetician). *Education:* University of British Columbia, degree in international relations. *Avocational Interests:* Running, swimming, surfing, ice skating, kayaking, canoeing, hiking, snowboarding, reading, writing, painting, music, nature, travel. Religion: Christian.

Addresses: *Agent*—Hylda Queally, Creative Artists Agency, 9830 Wilshire Blvd., Beverly Hills, CA 90212. *Publicist*—Alan Nierob, Rogers & Cowan Public Relations, 8687 Melrose Ave., Los Angeles, CA 90069.

Career: Actress. Worked as a film extra; Ford agency, worked as a model; appeared in commercials. Founder and operator of a humanitarian committee and worked as a missionary in the Philippines; worked as a flight attendant and a waitress and in automotive maintenance; volunteer with children's projects and affiliated with charities.

Awards, Honors: Named one of the breakout stars of 2004, *Entertainment Weekly,* 2004; named one of the hot 100 of 2005, *Maxim,* 2005; member of the cast of *Lost* that was named entertainer of the year, *Entertainment Weekly,* 2005; Golden Satellite Award nomination, best actress in a drama series, International Press Academy, 2005, Teen Choice Award nominations, choice television actress in a drama, choice female television breakout performance, and choice television chemistry (with Matthew Fox), all 2005, Saturn Award nominations, best actress on television, Academy of Science Fiction, Fantasy, and Horror Films, 2005 and 2006, Golden Globe Award, best television series—drama, and Screen Actors Guild Award, outstanding performance by an ensemble in a drama series, both with others, both 2006, all for *Lost.*

CREDITS

Television Appearances; Series:
J. D. girl, *Judgment Day,* G4techTV (also known as G4 Network), beginning 2002.
Benson's girlfriend, *Kingdom Hospital* (also known as *Stephen King's "Kingdom Hospital"*), ABC, 2004.

Katherine "Kate" Austen, *Lost,* ABC, 2004—.

Television Appearances; Movies:
Model in commercial, *Stealing Sinatra,* Showtime, 2003.

Television Appearances; Specials:
(In archive footage) Kate Austen, *Lost: The Journey,* ABC, 2005.
Presenter of the band the Tragically Hip, *Live 8 Canada,* multiple networks, 2005.

Television Appearances; Awards Presentations:
The 57th Annual Primetime Emmy Awards, CBS, 2005.
Presenter, *The 63rd Annual Golden Globe Awards,* NBC, 2006.
12th Annual Screen Actors Guild Awards (also known as *Screen Actors Guild 12th Annual Awards*), TNT and TBS, 2006.

Television Appearances; Episodic:
Wade's girlfriend, "Kinetic," *Smallville* (also known as *Smallville: Beginnings* and *Smallville: Superman the Early Years*), The WB, 2002.
(Uncredited) Party guest, "Morning After," *Tru Calling* (also known as *Heroine, Tru,* and *True Calling*), Fox, 2003.

Appeared as an extra in other programs, including *Dead Like Me* (also known as *Dead Girl*), Showtime; and *The L Word* (also known as *Earthlings*), Showtime.

Television Guest Appearances; Episodic:
Jimmy Kimmel Live, ABC, 2004.
The Late Show with David Letterman (also known as *The Late Show*), CBS, 2004.
Ellen: The Ellen DeGeneres Show (also known as *Ellen* and *The Ellen DeGeneres Show*), syndicated, 2005.
Entertainment Tonight (also known as *Entertainment This Week, ET, E.T., ET Weekend,* and *This Week in Entertainment*), syndicated, 2005.
Good Morning America (also known as *GMA*), ABC, 2005.
Late Night with Conan O'Brien, NBC, 2005.
T4, Channel 4 (England), 2005.
The Tonight Show with Jay Leno, NBC, 2005.
The View, ABC, 2005.
Live with Regis and Kelly, syndicated, 2005, 2006.

Television Appearances; Pilots:
Katherine "Kate" Austen, *Lost,* ABC, 2004.

Film Appearances:
Dead body, *The Long Weekend,* Gold Circle Films, 2005.

Appeared as an extra in other films, including *Freddy vs. Jason,* New Line Cinema, 2003; *The Chronicles of Riddick* (also known as *Pitch Black 2, Pitch Black 2: Chronicles of Riddick,* and *The Chronicles of Riddick: The Director's Cut*), Universal, 2004; and *White Chicks,* Columbia, 2004.

Stage Appearances:

Presenter of the band the Tragically Hip, *Live 8 Canada,* 2005.

OTHER SOURCES

Periodicals:

Hawaiian Style, August 29, 2005.
OK! Weekly, August 29, 2005; March 27, 2006, pp.48–51.
Parade, October 23, 2005, p. 15.
People Weekly, October 28, 2004; December 6, 2004, p. 184; September 5, 2005, p. 104.
Rolling Stone, October 6, 2005, pp. 50–52.
Self, April, 2005.
TV Guide, October 3, 2004, p. 33; December 19, 2004, p. 41.
USA Today, October 13, 2004, p. 3D.

LIMON, Iyari 1979–
(Iyana Perez Limon)

PERSONAL

Born July 8, 1979, in Guadalajara, Jalisco, Mexico; immigrated to the United States, c. 1980.

Addresses: *Agent*—Mitchell K. Stubbs and Associates, 8675 West Washington Blvd., Suite 203, Culver City, CA 90232.

Career: Actress. Radio Disney, host of U.S. tour, 2001; appeared in commercials in both English and Spanish. Appeared at conventions.

CREDITS

Television Appearances; Series:

Kennedy, *Buffy the Vampire Slayer* (also known as *BtVS, Buffy,* and *Buffy the Vampire Slayer: The Series*), UPN, 2002–2003.

Television Appearances; Movies:

(As Iyari Perez Limon) Esperanza Gomez, *On the Line,* ABC, 1998.
Zoe Gold, *Double Teamed,* The Disney Channel, 2002.

Television Appearances; Episodic:

Brenda, "Love among the Ruins," *ER* (also known as *Emergency Room*), NBC, 1995.
Lisa, "La logica de la sangre," *Reyes y Rey* (also known as *Reyes and Rey*), Telemundo, 1998.
Cindy, *Undressed* (also known as *MTV's "Undressed"*), MTV, 2000.
Iris, "Beauty Marks," *Cover Me: Based on the True Life of an FBI Family* (also known as *Cover Me*), USA Network, 2000.
Flaca, "Discharged," *Strong Medicine,* Lifetime, 2002.
Jennifer, "Don't Judge a Book by Its Cover," *The Brothers Garcia,* Nickelodeon, 2002.
Jennifer, "New Man on Campus," *The Brothers Garcia,* Nickelodeon, 2002.
Stephanie, "The Perfect Babysitter," *The Mind of the Married Man* (also known as *My Dirty Little Mind*), HBO, 2002.
Carmelita, "Girlfriend, Interrupted," *The Drew Carey Show,* ABC, 2004.
Louisa Cruz, "In the Dark," *Without a Trace* (also known as *Vanished*), CBS, 2004.
Wendy, "The Coconut Kapow," *Quintuplets,* Fox, 2005.
Shannon Grey, "Band of Gold," *Skater Boys,* Fox, 2006.

Also a guest in *Humphrey,* Telemundo; and *Solo en America,* Telemundo.

Television Appearances; Pilots:

Shannon Grey, "Sundown," *Skater Boys,* Fox, 2006.

Film Appearances:

Teen girl, *King Cobra* (also known as *Anaconda 2* and *Seth*), Trimark Pictures, 1999.
Jamie Vecino, *The Egg Plant Lady,* Family Theatre Productions, 2000.
Erica, *Death by Engagement,* Rounding 3rd Productions, 2005.

RECORDINGS

Music Videos:

Martina McBride, "Love's the Only House," 1999.

OTHER SOURCES

Periodicals:

Buffy the Vampire Slayer, December, 2003, pp. 40–44.

Electronic:

IyariLimon.com, http://www.iyarilimon.com, January 16, 2006.

LONDON, Jerri Lynn
See MANTHEY, Jerri

LOPEZ, Jennifer 1970(?)–
(J.Lo, J–Lo, Jennifer "J–Lo" Lopez)

PERSONAL

Full name, Jennifer Lynn Lopez; born July 24, 1970 (some sources cite 1969), in the Bronx, New York, NY; daughter of David (a computer specialist) and Guadalupe (a kindergarten teacher; maiden name, Rodriguez) Lopez; married Ojani Noa (an actor, model, and club manager), February 22, 1997 (divorced, 1998); married Cris Judd (a choreographer, dancer, and actor), September 29, 2001 (divorced, January 26, 2003); married Marc Anthony (a singer and actor), June 5, 2004; stepchildren: Arianna, Cristan, Ryan. *Education:* Studied dance; once enrolled at the Bernard M. Baruch College of the City University of New York. *Religion:* Roman Catholicism.

Addresses: *Office*—Nuyorican Productions, 1100 Glendon Ave., Suite 920, Westwood, CA 90024. *Agent*—International Creative Management, 8942 Wilshire Blvd., Beverly Hills, CA 90211. *Manager*—The Firm, 9465 Wilshire Blvd., Sixth Floor, Beverly Hills, CA 90212. *Publicist*—Baker/Winokur/Ryder, 9100 Wilshire Blvd., Sixth Floor West, Beverly Hills, CA 90212.

Career: Actress, singer, dancer, and producer. Nuyorican Productions, Westwood, CA, principal; worked as a model and appeared in commercials and print advertisements. Madre's (Cuban restaurant), Pasadena, CA, founder, 2002; creator of the perfumes Glow, 2002, Still, 2004, Miami Glow, 2005, and Live, 2005; creator of the fashion clothing line J–Lo by Jennifer Lopez, 2001, founder of the Sweetface Fashion Company, beginning 2001, and affiliated with JLO boutiques. Appeared in e–mail messages by Emazing. Honoree at the Noche de Ninos Gala, Children's Hospital Los Angeles, 2004. Worked at a law firm and a bank. Also known as J.Lo and J–Lo.

Awards, Honors: Independent Spirit Award nomination, best supporting female, Independent Features Project/West, 1995, for *My Family;* Bravo Award nomination, outstanding actress in a feature film, National Council of La Raza, 1996, for *Money Train* and *Jack;* Lone Star Film and Television Award, best actress, Lasting Image Award, Imagen Foundation, Golden Globe Award nomination, best performance by an actress in a motion picture—comedy or musical, and MTV Movie Award nomination, best breakthrough performance, all 1998, for *Selena;* ALMA Award, outstanding actress in a feature film, American Latin Media Arts awards, 1998, for *Selena* and *Anaconda;* Saturn Award nomination, best actress, Academy of Science Fiction, Fantasy, and Horror Films, and Blockbuster Entertainment Award nomination, favorite actress—action/adventure, both 1998, for *Anaconda;* ALMA Award, outstanding actress in a feature film in a crossover role, and MTV Movie Award nominations, best female performance and (with George Clooney) best kiss, all 1999, for *Out of Sight;* Hollywood Film Festival Award nomination, actress of the year, 1999; MTV Music Video Award, best dance video, 2000, for "Waiting for Tonight"; Bambi Award, Hubert Burdia Media, 2000; ALMA Special Achievement awards, female entertainer of the year, 2000 and 2001; Blockbuster Entertainment Award, favorite actress—science fiction, Saturn Award nomination, best actress, MTV Movie Award, best dressed category, and MTV Movie Award nomination, best female performance, all 2001, for *The Cell;* ALMA Award nomination (with others), outstanding host of a variety or awards special, 2001, for *The First Annual Latin Grammy Awards;* named one of the top twenty entertainers of 2001, E! Entertainment Television; Teen Choice Award nomination (with Matthew McConaughey), 2001, choice film chemistry, and Blimp Award, favorite female movie star, Kids' Choice awards, 2002, both for *The Wedding Planner;* ALMA Award nomination, outstanding actress in a motion picture, 2002, for *Angel Eyes;* Teen Choice Award nomination, choice actress in a drama or action adventure film, 2002, for *Enough;* ALMA Award nomination, outstanding performance in a music, variety, or comedy special, 2002, for *Jennifer Lopez in Concert;* ShoWest Award, female star of the year, National Association of Theatre Owners, 2002; named one of the most intriguing people of 2002, *People Weekly* magazine; named to the Power 100 list, *Premiere* magazine, 2002 and 2003; Image Award, outstanding actress in a motion picture, National Association for the Advancement for Colored People, Teen Choice Award nominations, choice actress in a comedy film, choice movie liar, and (with Ralph Fiennes) choice movie liplock, and Blimp Award nomination, favorite movie actress, all 2003, for *Maid in Manhattan;* American Music Award, best pop–rock female artist, 2003; Teen Choice Award nomination, choice crossover artist from music to acting, 2003; Teen Choice Award nomination (with Richard Gere), choice movie dance scene, 2005, for *Shall We Dance;* Teen Choice Award nominations, choice actress in a comedy film and (with Jane Fonda) choice movie chemistry, 2005, for *Monster–in–Law;* named one of the twenty–five most influential Hispanics in America, *Time* magazine, 2005; platinum record certification, Recording Industry Association of America, for the single "If You Had My Love."

CREDITS

Film Appearances:

Myra, *My Little Girl,* Hemdale, 1986.

Booker, *Lambada,* Warner Bros., 1990.

Grace Santiago, *Money Train,* Columbia, 1995.

The young Maria Sanchez, *My Family* (also known as *East L.A., My Family, Mi Familia,* and *Cafe con leche*), New Line Cinema, 1995.

Miss Marquez, *Jack,* Buena Vista, 1996.

Gabriela (Gabby), *Blood and Wine,* Twentieth Century–Fox, 1997.

Grace McKenna, *U Turn* (also known as *U Turn—Ici commence l'enfer*), Sony Pictures Entertainment, 1997.

Selena Quintanilla–Perez (title role), *Selena,* Warner Bros., 1997.

Terri Flores, *Anaconda,* Sony Pictures Entertainment, 1997.

Karen Sisco, *Out of Sight,* Universal, 1998.

Voice of Azteca, *Antz* (animated), DreamWorks, 1998.

Catherine Deane, *The Cell,* New Line Cinema, 2000.

Sharon Pogue, *Angel Eyes,* Warner Bros., 2000.

Mary Fiore, *The Wedding Planner* (also known as *Wedding Planner—verliebt, verlobt, verplant*), Columbia, 2001.

Marisa Ventura, *Maid in Manhattan* (also known as *Made in New York*), Columbia, 2002.

Slim Hiller, *Enough,* Columbia, 2002.

Ricki, *Gigli* (also known as *Tough Love*), Columbia/TriStar, 2003.

Gertrude Steiney, *Jersey Girl,* Miramax, 2004.

Paulina, *Shall We Dance,* Miramax, 2004.

Charlie, *Monster–in–Law,* New Line Cinema, 2005.

Jean Gilkyson, *An Unfinished Life,* Miramax, 2005.

Lauren, *Bordertown,* Capitol Films, 2006.

Puchi, *El cantante* (also known as *The Singer* and *Who Killed Hector Lavoe?*), Nuyorican Productions, 2006.

Bridge and Tunnel, New Line Cinema, 2006.

Some sources cite appearances in *America's Darlings,* New Regency Pictures/Storyline Entertainment, c. 2006; and as Sue Ellen Ewing, *Dallas,* Twentieth Century–Fox, 2007.

Film Producer:

Bordertown, Capitol Films, 2006.

El cantante (also known as *The Singer* and *Who Killed Hector Lavoe?*), Nuyorican Productions, 2006.

Reggaeton, 2007.

Film Work; Other:

Performer of songs that have appeared in films, television productions, and videos.

Television Appearances; Series:

Member of the Fly Girls dancers, *In Living Color,* Fox, beginning c. 1990.

Melinda Lopez, *Second Chances,* CBS, 1993–94.

Lucille, *South Central,* Fox, 1994.

Melinda Lopez, *Hotel Malibu,* CBS, 1994.

Television Appearances; Miniseries:

(In archive footage) Herself, *200 Greatest Pop Culture Icons,* VH1, 2003.

(In archive footage) Herself, *And You Don't Stop: 30 Years of Hip–Hop,* VH1, 2004.

Television Appearances; Movies:

Rosie Romero, *Nurses on the Line: The Crash of Flight 7* (also known as *Race against the Dark: The Crash of Flight 7*), CBS, 1993.

Television Appearances; Specials:

Host, *Coming Up Roses,* CBS, 1994.

Herself, *The Secret World of Antz,* 1998.

Herself, *Arista Records' 25th Anniversary Celebration,* 1999.

Herself, *The Latin Beat,* ABC, 1999.

Herself, *Mi gente! My People,* 1999.

Host, *100 Greatest Women of Rock & Roll,* VH1, 1999.

MTV Uncensored, MTV, 1999.

Herself, *Greatest Rock & Roll Moments,* VH1, 2000.

Herself, *TRL Uncensored,* MTV, 2000.

Host, *100 Greatest Pop Songs,* MTV, 2000.

Herself, *Jennifer Lopez in Concert,* NBC, 2001.

Herself, *MTV Icon: Janet Jackson,* MTV, 2001.

Herself, *MTV Snowed in 2001,* MTV, 2001.

Herself, *The Royal Variety Performance 2001,* Independent Television (England), 2001.

Herself, *Sean "Puffy" Combs,* Arts and Entertainment, 2001.

Herself, *Tito Puente: The King of Latin Music,* PBS, 2001.

Herself, *TRL Super Bowl,* CBS, 2001.

Puffy on Trial: Victory or No Way Out?, MTV, 2001.

Herself, *American Bandstand's 50th Anniversary Celebration,* ABC, 2002.

Herself, *Boogie: Jennifer Lopez* (also known as *Boogie Special: Jennifer Lopez*), 2002.

(Uncredited; in archive footage) Herself, *Hello, He Lied & Other Truths from the Hollywood Trenches,* American Movie Classics, 2002.

Herself, *Nobel Peace Prize Concert,* Arts and Entertainment, 2002.

Herself, *Primetime Special Edition: Jennifer Lopez,* ABC, 2002.

Herself, *USO Special for the Troops* (also known as *For the Troops: An MTV/USO Special*), MTV, 2002.

Herself, *Ben & Jen: A Dateline Special,* NBC, 2003.

Herself, *50 Sexiest Video Moments,* VH1, 2003.

Herself, *Fromage 2003,* MuchMusic, 2003.

Herself, *Jingle Ball* (also known as *Jingle Ball Rock*), Fox, 2003.

Herself, *The Stars' First Time ... on Entertainment Tonight with Mary Hart,* CBS, 2003.

Herself, *VH1 All Access: Behind the Red Carpet,* VH1, 2003.

Michael Jackson Number Ones, CBS, 2003.

(In archive footage) *Saturday Night Live: The Best of Chris Kattan,* NBC, 2003.

Herself, *En nochebuena con los Lunnis y sus amigos,* Television Espanola (Spain), 2004.

(In archive footage) Herself, *50 Most Awesomely Bad Songs ... Ever,* VH1, 2004.

(In archive footage) Herself, *Last Laugh '04,* Comedy Central, 2004.

Herself, *Maxim Hot 100,* VH1, 2004.

Herself, *Michael Jackson: The One,* CBS, 2004.

(In archive footage) Herself, *The N–Word,* Trio, 2004.

The Record of the Year 2004, Independent Television, 2004.

Herself, *Borrow My Crew,* MTV, 2005.

Herself, *Jennifer Lopez: Beyond the Runway,* MTV, 2005.

(In archive footage) Herself, *Showbiz Hissy Fits,* Channel 4 (England), 2005.

Herself, *Wendy Williams Is on Fire on the Red Carpet,* VH1, 2005.

MTV's Iced Out New Year's Eve 2005, MTV, 2005.

Red Carpet Confidential, CBS, 2005.

Television Appearances; Awards Presentations:
Host, *The 1995 NCLR Bravo Awards,* Fox, 1995.

Presenter, *The VIDA Awards,* NBC, 1995.

Presenter, *The 69th Annual Academy Awards,* ABC, 1997.

Presenter, *1998 MTV Movie Awards,* MTV, 1998.

Presenter, *The 1998 VH1 Fashion Awards,* VH1, 1998.

Presenter, *The 70th Annual Academy Awards,* ABC, 1998.

ALMA Awards, ABC, 1998.

1998 MTV Video Music Awards, MTV, 1998.

Host and presenter, *The 1999 ALMA Awards,* ABC, 1999.

Presenter, *The 41st Annual Grammy Awards,* CBS, 1999.

Presenter, *1999 MTV Video Music Awards,* MTV, 1999.

Presenter, *The 1999 Teen Choice Awards,* Fox, 1999.

Presenter, *The 71st Annual Academy Awards Presentation,* ABC, 1999.

The Fifth Annual Blockbuster Entertainment Awards, Fox, 1999.

The 1999 Billboard Music Awards, Fox, 1999.

The 1999 MTV Movie Awards, MTV, 1999.

VH1/Vogue Fashion Awards, VH1, 1999, 2000.

Host, *The First Annual Latin Grammy Awards,* CBS, 2000.

Presenter, *Fifth Annual ALMA Awards,* ABC, 2000.

Presenter, *The 42nd Annual Grammy Awards,* CBS, 2000.

Presenter, *MTV Video Music Awards 2000,* MTV, 2000.

Presenter, *My VH1 Music Awards,* VH1, 2000.

Presenter, *The 27th Annual American Music Awards,* ABC, 2000.

MTV Europe Music Awards 2000, MTV, 2000.

2000 Blockbuster Entertainment Awards, Fox, 2000.

Presenter, *The 58th Annual Golden Globe Awards,* NBC, 2001.

Presenter, *The 73rd Annual Academy Awards,* ABC, 2001.

48 degres edicion de los premios Ondas, 2001.

MTV Video Music Awards 2001, MTV, 2001.

Second Annual Latin Grammy Awards, 2001.

The Teen Choice Awards 2001, Fox, 2001.

The 28th Annual American Music Awards, ABC, 2001.

The 2001 Billboard Music Awards, Fox, 2001.

2001 Top of the Pops Awards, BBC, 2001.

Presenter, *The 74th Annual Academy Awards,* ABC, 2002.

MTV Europe Music Awards 2002 (also known as *MTV Europe Music Awards 2002 Barcelona*), MTV, 2002.

MTV Video Music Awards 2002 (also known as *VMAs 2002*), MTV, 2002.

Presenter, *17th Annual Soul Train Music Awards,* The WB, 2003.

Presenter, *The 75th Annual Academy Awards,* ABC, 2003.

(In archive footage) *MTV Europe Music Awards 2003,* MTV, 2003.

2003 Radio Music Awards, NBC, 2003.

Presenter, *MTV Video Music Awards 2004,* MTV, 2004.

Presenter, *The 61st Annual Golden Globe Awards,* NBC, 2004.

Nickelodeon Kids' Choice Awards '04 (also known as *Nickelodeon's 17th Annual Kids' Choice Awards*), Nickelodeon, 2004.

The 47th Annual Grammy Awards, CBS, 2005.

Presenter, *The 78th Annual Academy Awards,* ABC, 2006.

Television Guest Appearances; Episodic:
One of the Fly Girls, *Inside Edition,* syndicated, 1990.

The Rosie O'Donnell Show, syndicated, 1997, 1998, 1999, 2000.

"Jennifer Lopez: Waiting for Tonight," *Making the Video,* MTV, 1999.

TFI Friday (also known as *Thank Four It's Friday*), Channel 4 (England), 1999.

Guest host, *Rock across America,* VH1, 2000.

"Jennifer Lopez: Love Don't Cost a Thing," *Making the Video,* MTV, 2000.

Diary, MTV, 2000.

Saturday Night Live (also known as *NBC's "Saturday Night," Saturday Night Live '80, SNL,* and *SNL 25*), NBC, 2000, 2001.

"Show n degres 244," *Mundo VIP,* 2001.

Parkinson, BBC, 2001.

Rove Live, Ten Network (Australia), 2001.

Verstehen Sie Spass?, 2001.

The Tonight Show with Jay Leno, NBC, 2001, 2006.

"Cannes Festival 2002," *Leute heute,* 2002.

"Jennifer Lopez," *Rank,* E! Entertainment Television, 2002.

"Jennifer Lopez," *Revealed with Jules Asner,* E! Entertainment Television, 2002.

"The 25 Most Powerful People in Entertainment," *Rank,* E! Entertainment Television, 2002.

Intimate Portrait: Jennifer Lopez, Lifetime, 2002.

The Oprah Winfrey Show (also known as *Oprah*), syndicated, 2002, 2004.

Total Request Live (also known as *TRL* and *Total Request with Carson Daly*), MTV, 2002, 2005.

(In archive footage) "It's Good to be Ben Affleck," *It's Good to Be,* E! Entertainment Television, 2003.

"Suuri Hollywood–elokuvaspesiaali," *4Pop,* 2003.

"Wetten, dass ... ? aus Berlin," *Wetten, dass ... ?,* 2003.

Ant & Dec's Saturday Night Takeaway, Independent Television (England), 2003.

Ben Affleck & Matt Damon: The E! True Hollywood Story, E! Entertainment Television, 2003.

(In archive footage) *Celebrities Uncensored,* E! Entertainment Television, multiple episodes, beginning 2003.

Extra (also known as *Extra: The Entertainment Magazine*), syndicated, 2003.

(Uncredited) *Mad TV,* Fox, 2003.

(In archive footage) *101 Most Shocking Moments in Entertainment* (also known as *E's "101"*), E! Entertainment Television, 2003.

Project Greenlight 2, HBO, 2003.

Richard & Judy, Channel 4, 2003.

Tinseltown TV, International Channel, 2003.

"Jennifer Lopez," *Famous,* Arts and Entertainment, c. 2003.

(Archive footage) *Love Chain,* E! Entertainment Television, c. 2003.

Entertainment Tonight (also known as *Entertainment This Week, E.T., ET Weekend,* and *This Week in Entertainment*), syndicated, 2003, 2006.

(In archive footage) "Bodas recientes," *Que bodas!,* 2004.

"FYI: I Hurt, Too," *Will & Grace,* NBC, 2004.

"I Do," *Will & Grace,* NBC, 2004.

"Oh, No, You Di–in't," *Will & Grace,* NBC, 2004.

(In archive footage) *El show de Cristina,* multiple episodes in 2004.

Inside the Actors Studio, Bravo, 2004.

(In archive footage) *101 Biggest Celebrity Oops* (also known as *E's "101"*), E! Entertainment Television, 2004.

The Late Show with David Letterman (also known as *The Late Show* and *Late Show Backstage*), CBS, 2004, 2005.

Live with Regis and Kelly, syndicated, 2004, 2005.

Top of the Pops (also known as *All New Top of the Pops* and *TOTP*), BBC, 2004, 2005, 2006.

(In archive footage) "Lo latino," *La tierra de las 1000 musicas,* 2005.

"Monster–in–Law," *HBO First Look,* HBO, 2005.

"The Newest Designer for Tommy Hilfiger Is ... ," *The Cut,* CBS, 2005.

"Wetten, dass ... ? aus Erfurt," *Wetten, dass ... ?,* 2005.

(In archive footage) *CD:UK,* Independent Television, 2005.

(In archive footage) *Cinema mil,* TV3 (Television de Catalunya, Spain), 2005.

Corazon de ... , Television Espanola (Spain), 2005.

Ellen: The Ellen DeGeneres Show (also known as *Ellen* and *The Ellen DeGeneres Show*), syndicated, 2005.

Fashion Week Diaries, 2005.

(In archive footage) *Getaway* (also known as *United Travel Getaway*), Nine Network (Australia), 2005.

GMTV, Independent Television, 2005.

Magacine, 2005.

Matthew's Best Hit TV+, 2005.

(In archive footage) *Silenci?,* 2005.

Today (also known as *NBC News Today* and *The Today Show*), NBC, 2005.

The View, ABC, 2005.

(As Jennifer "J–Lo" Lopez) *The Film Programme* (also known as *Film 2006*), BBC, 2006.

Television Appearances; Pilots:

Melinda Lopez, *Second Chances,* CBS, 1993.

Lucille, *South Central,* Fox, 1994.

Melinda Lopez, "The Bed, the Bride, and the Body," *Hotel Malibu,* CBS, 1994.

Television Executive Producer; Series:

South Beach, UPN, 2006.

Television Executive Producer; Specials:

Jennifer Lopez in Concert, NBC, 2001.

Jennifer Lopez: Beyond the Runway, MTV, 2005.

Stage Appearances:

A Christmas Carol, McCarter Theatre, Princeton, NJ, between 1991 and 1993.

Major Tours:

Golden Musicals of Broadway (revue), c. 1988.

Synchronicity (musical), Japanese cities, c. 1988.

RECORDINGS

Videos:

Herself in music video "That's the Way Love Goes," *Janet Jackson: Design of a Decade 1986/1996,* A&M Video, 1996.

Herself, *Inside "Out of Sight,"* Universal Studios Home Video, 1998.

(And executive producer) Herself, *Jennifer Lopez: Feelin' So Good,* Sony Music Entertainment, 2000.

Herself, *Style as Substance: Reflections on Tarsem,* New Line Home Video, 2000.

Herself, *Jennifer Lopez: The Reel Me,* Sony Music Entertainment, 2003.

Herself, *More Than Enough,* Columbia/TriStar, 2003.

"Siempre hace frio," *Selena: Greatest Hits,* EMI Latin, 2003.

Herself in music video "That's the Way Love Goes," *From Janet, to Damita Jo: The Videos,* EMI Distribution/Ventura Distribution, 2004.

Albums:

On the 6, The Work Group/Sony, 1999, other versions also released.

Official Interview CD, Megaworld, 2000.

Star Profile, Master Tone Records, 2000.

J.Lo, Epic, 2001, other versions also released.

J to tha L–O! The Remixes, Epic, 2002, other versions also released.

This Is Me ... Then, Epic, 2002.

The Reel Me, Sony, 2003.

Rebirth, Sony, 2005.

Singles:

"Baila," 1998.

"Feelin' So Good," featuring Fat Joe and Big Pun, 1999.

"If You Had My Love," Sony Records, 1999.

"Waiting for Tonight," Work Group/ERG, 1999.

(With Marc Anthony) "No me ames," 1999.

"Let's Get Loud," 2000.

"Love Don't Cost a Thing," 2000.

(With Big Punisher) "It's So Hard," 2000.

"Ain't It Funny" (version one), 2001.

"Ain't It Funny" (version two remix), featuring Ja Rule, 2001.

"I'm Real" (version one), 2001.

"I'm Real" (version two remix), featuring Ja Rule, 2001.

"Play," 2001.

(With MTV Allstars/Artists against AIDS) "What's Going On?," c. 2001.

"Alive," 2002.

"It's Going to Be Alright," featuring Nas, 2002.

"Jenny from the Block," 2002.

"All I Have," featuring LL Cool J, 2003.

"Baby, I Love U," 2003.

"I'm Glad," 2003.

(With Ja Rule) "New York," c. 2004.

"Get Right" (version one), 2005.

"Get Right" (version two), featuring Fabolous, 2005.

"Hold You Down," featuring Fat Joe, 2005.

(With LL Cool J) "Control Myself," 2006.

Music Videos:

Janet Jackson, "That's the Way Love Goes," 1993.

Puff Daddy and the Family, "Been around the World," c. 1997.

"Baila," 1998.

"Feelin' So Good," featuring Fat Joe and Big Pun, 1999.

"If You Had My Love," 1999.

"Waiting for Tonight," 1999.

(With Marc Anthony) "No me ames," 1999.

"Let's Get Loud," 2000.

"Love Don't Cost a Thing," 2000.

(With Big Punisher) "It's So Hard," 2000.

Black Rob, "Dame espacio/Spanish Fly," 2000.

"Ain't It Funny" (version one), 2001.

"Ain't It Funny" (version two remix), featuring Ja Rule, 2001.

"I'm Real" (version one), 2001.

"I'm Real" (version two remix), featuring Ja Rule, 2001.

"Play," 2001.

(With MTV Allstars/Artists against AIDS) "What's Going On?" (version 2, concept video), c. 2001.

"Alive," 2002.

"It's Going to Be Alright," featuring Nas, 2002.

"Jenny from the Block," 2002.

"All I Have," featuring LL Cool J, 2003.

"Baby, I Love U," 2003.

"I'm Glad," 2003.

(With Ja Rule) "New York," c. 2004.

"Get Right" (version one), 2005.

"Get Right" (version two), featuring Fabolous, 2005.

"Hold You Down," featuring Fat Joe, 2005.

(With LL Cool J) "Control Myself," 2006.

WRITINGS

Albums:

On the 6, The Work Group/Sony, 1999, other versions also released.

J.Lo, Epic, 2001, other versions also released.

J to tha L–O! The Remixes, Epic, 2002, other versions also released.

This Is Me ... Then, Epic, 2002.

The Reel Me, Sony, 2003.

Rebirth, Sony, 2005.

Singles:

"Baila," 1998.

"Feelin' So Good," featuring Fat Joe and Big Pun, 1999.

"If You Had My Love," Sony Records, 1999.

"Waiting for Tonight," Work Group/ERG, 1999.

(With Marc Anthony) "No me ames," 1999.

"Let's Get Loud," 2000.

"Love Don't Cost a Thing," 2000.

(With Big Punisher) "It's So Hard," 2000.

"Ain't It Funny" (version one), 2001.

"Ain't It Funny" (version two remix), featuring Ja Rule, 2001.

"I'm Real" (version one), 2001.
"I'm Real" (version two remix), featuring Ja Rule, 2001.
"Play," 2001.
"Alive," 2002.
"It's Going to Be Alright," featuring Nas, 2002.
"Jenny from the Block," 2002.
"All I Have," featuring LL Cool J, 2003.
"Baby, I Love U," 2003.
"I'm Glad," 2003.
(With Ja Rule) "New York," c. 2004.
"Get Right" (version one), 2005.
"Get Right" (version two), featuring Fabolous, 2005.
"Hold You Down," featuring Fat Joe, 2005.
(With LL Cool J) "Control Myself," 2006.

Wrote songs that have appeared in films, television productions, and videos.

Video Music:

Jennifer Lopez: Feelin' So Good, Sony Music Entertainment, 2000.
Jennifer Lopez: The Reel Me, Sony Music Entertainment, 2003.

Nonfiction:

Appeared in other books.

OTHER SOURCES

Books:

Contemporary Hispanic Biography, Volume 1, Gale, 2002.
Contemporary Musicians, Volume 55, Thomson Gale, 2006.
Duncan, Patricia J., *Jennifer Lopez,* St. Martin's Press, 1999.
Furman, Leah, *Jennifer Lopez,* Chelsea House, 2001.
Johns, Michael Anne, *Jennifer Lopez,* Andrews & McMeel, 1999.
Tracy, Kathleen, *Jennifer Lopez,* ECW Books, 2000.

Periodicals:

Billboard, November 27, 1999, p. 93; December 4, 1999, p. 22.
Blender, April, 2005, pp. 74–84, 86.
Cosmopolitan, March, 1999, pp. 202–205; June, 2002, pp. 54–55, 57–58.
Entertainment Weekly, October 9, 1998, pp. 28–31; January 7, 2000, pp. 8–9.
Femme Fatales, September 1, 2000, pp. 8–11.
Glamour, September, 2002, pp. 263–64.
GQ, September, 1996.
Harper's Bazaar, December, 2002, pp. 190–99.
Hello!, August 20, 2002, pp. 38–42.
Hollywood Latino, December 12, 2003, p. 61.

IFQ: Independent Film Quarterly, May, 2003, pp. 22–25.
InStyle, June 1, 1999, p. 276; August 1, 2004.
Interview, April, 1997, p. 50.
Ladies' Home Journal, January, 2003.
Movieline, October, 1996; February, 1998; February, 1999, p. 59.
New York Post, June 1, 1999.
Parade, December 8, 2002, pp. 4–7.
People Weekly, May 10, 1999, p. 187; September 13, 1999, pp. 71–74; January 1, 2000, pp. 84–85; March 13, 2000, p. 146; May 14, 2001, p. 88; June 24, 2002, p. 136; December 30, 2002, p. 106; July 26, 2004, p. 58; August 9, 2004, p. 54; January 17, 2005, p. 70; March 7, 2005, p. 66; September 26, 2005, p. 68.
Premiere, August, 1998, pp. 72–75, 99; February, 1999; August, 2000.
Reader's Digest, August, 2003.
Redbook, January, 2002, pp. 58–62.
Rolling Stone, February 15, 2001, pp. 44–50, 86, 88.
Talk, March, 2000.
Teen People, May, 2000, pp. 68–92; summer, 2000, p. 42.
Time, August 22, 2005, p. 45.
TV Guide, December 21, 2002, p. 13; February 21, 2004, p. 33.
UMM, fall, 2002, pp. 56–62.
Us, April, 1997
US Weekly, October 15, 2001, pp. 40–41.
V, issue 38, 2005, p. 81.
Vanity Fair, June, 2001, p. 166.
Variety, August 2, 1999, p. 4.
W, October, 2001, pp. 238–40.

Electronic:

Jennifer Lopez, http://www.jenniferlopez.com, March 6, 2006.

LOPEZ, Priscilla 1948–

PERSONAL

Born February 26, 1948, in the Bronx, New York, NY; daughter of Francisco (a hotel banquet foreman) and Laura (maiden name, Candelaria) Lopez; married Vincent Fanuele (a trombonist and conductor), January 16, 1972 (some sources cite 1971); children: Alex, Gabriela. *Education:* Graduated from High School of the Performing Arts, New York City, 1965; studied theatre and dance.

Addresses: *Agent*—Jeff Berger, Writers and Artists Agency, 924 Westwood Blvd., Suite 900, Los Angeles, CA 90024.

Career: Actress, singer, dancer, and choreographer. Appeared in commercials.

Awards, Honors: Acting award in high school; Obie Award, *Village Voice,* 1975, Antoinette Perry Award nomination, best featured actress in a musical, 1976, and special *Theatre World* Award (with others), outstanding ensemble performance, 1976, all for *A Chorus Line;* Antoinette Perry Award, best featured actress in a musical, 1980, for *A Day in Hollywood/A Night in the Ukraine;* Rita Moreno HOLA Award for Excellence, 2001; acting award, Hispanic Organization of Latin Actors, 2002; Drama Desk Award nomination, outstanding solo performance, 2003, for *Class Mothers '68.*

CREDITS

Stage Appearances:
Dancer, *Breakfast at Tiffany's* (musical), Majestic Theatre, New York City, 1966.

Member of adult ensemble, *Henry, Sweet Henry* (musical), Palace Theatre, New York City, 1967.

Egyptian, *Her First Roman* (musical), Lunt–Fontanne Theatre, New York City, 1968.

Your Own Thing, 1969.

Understudy for Kathy, *Company* (musical), Alvin Theatre, New York City, 1970–72.

Myrrhine, *Lysistrata,* Brooks Atkinson Theatre, New York City, 1972.

Member of ensemble, *What's a Nice Country Like You Doing in a Place Like This* (revue), off–Broadway production, 1973.

Fastrada, *Pippin* (musical), Imperial Theatre, New York City, c. 1974–77.

Diana Morales, *A Chorus Line* (musical), New York Shakespeare Festival, Public Theatre, Estelle R. Newman Theatre, New York City, then Shubert Theatre, New York City, 1975, also produced in workshops.

Gino and member of ensemble (some sources cite role as Harpo Marx or Gino), *A Day in Hollywood/A Night in the Ukraine* (musical), John Golden Theatre, New York City, 1980, then Royale Theatre, New York City, 1981.

Lisa, *Key Exchange,* Orpheum Theatre, New York City, 1982.

Herself, *Night of 100 Stars* (also known as *Night of One Hundred Stars*), Radio City Music Hall, New York City, 1982.

Liliane La Fleur, *Nine* (musical; also known as *Nine the Musical*), 46th Street Theatre, New York City, c. 1982–84.

Joy/Shirley, *Buck,* American Place Theatre, New York City, 1983.

Norina, *Non–Pasquale,* New York Shakespeare Festival, Public Theatre, Delacorte Theatre, New York City, 1983.

Terry, *Extremities,* Westside Arts Center, Cheryl Crawford Theatre, New York City, 1983.

La Goulue and Paulette, *Times and Appetites of Toulouse–Lautrec,* American Place Theatre, New York City, 1985–86.

Elizabeth, *Be Happy for Me,* Douglas Fairbank Theatre, New York City, 1986.

"Series B," *Marathon '88,* Ensemble Studio Theatre, New York City, 1988.

Kate Sullivan, *Other People's Money,* Hartford Stage Company, Minetta Lane Theatre, New York City, 1989–91.

Song performer, *Night of One Hundred Stars III* (also known as *Night of One Hundred Stars*), Radio City Music Hall, 1990.

Antigone in New York, Vineyard Theatre, New York City, 1996.

Frida Kahlo, *Goodbye My Friduchita,* Coconut Grove Playhouse, Miami, FL, 1997–98, then retitled *The Passion of Frida Kahlo,* Directors Company, Arc-Light Theatre, New York City, 1999, later Gramercy Arts Theatre, New York City, 1999–2000.

Class Mothers '68 (solo show), A. E. Hotchner Studio Theatre, Washington University, St. Louis, MO, 1998, then Harold Clurman Theatre, New York City, 2002–2003.

Emma Blackstone, *Babes in Arms* (concert), City Center Theatre, New York City, 1999.

Herself, *A Tony Celebration* (cabaret act), Arci's Place, New York City, 2001.

Herself, *What I Did for Love* (cabaret act; also known as *Priscilla Lopez: What I Did for Love*), Arci's Place, 2001.

newyorkers, Manhattan Theatre Club Stage II, New York City, 2001.

Rosie, *Bye Bye Birdie* (musical), Cherry Country Playhouse, Muskegon, MI, 2002.

Ofelia, *Anna in the Tropics,* McCarter Theatre, Princeton, NJ, 2003, then Royale Theatre (now Bernard B. Jacobs Theatre), New York City, 2003–2004, also produced as a reading in the New Works Now! series.

Edna, *The Oldest Profession,* Signature Theatre Company, Peter Norton Space Theatre, New York City, 2004.

Panelist discussing *Anna in the Tropics, Broadway Talks* (interview show), 92nd Street Y, New York City, 2004.

Herself, *Seth's Broadway Chatterbox* (interview show), Don't Tell Mama, New York City, 2004.

Purgatorio, Reynolds Theatre, Duke University, Durham, NC, 2005.

Paquita, *Beauty of the Father,* Manhattan Theatre Club Stage II, beginning 2006.

Appeared in *The Boy Friend* and *The Sisters Rosenzweig,* Broadway productions; also participated in benefits and cabaret performances, including affiliation with the Friday Cabaret Series, Queens Theatre in the Park, 2000.

Stage Work:

Assistant, *Nine* (musical; also known as *Nine the Musical*), 46th Street Theatre, New York City, c. 1982–84.

Choreographer, *Times and Appetites of Toulouse–Lautrec*, American Place Theatre, New York City, 1985–86.

Film Appearances:

Theresa, *Cheaper to Keep Her,* American Cinema, 1980.

Aldonza, *Revenge of the Nerds II: Nerds in Paradise,* Twentieth Century–Fox, 1987.

Dr. Gail Gitterman, *Simple Justice,* Panorama Entertainment, 1989.

Loretta, *Chutney Popcorn,* 1999.

Victor's mother, *Just One Time,* 1999.

Jazz class teacher, *Center Stage* (also known as *Centre Stage, City Ballet,* and *The Dance Movie*), Columbia, 2000.

Veronica Ventura, *Maid in Manhattan* (also known as *Made in New York*), Columbia, 2002.

Mrs. Vitale, *Tony 'n' Tina's Wedding,* 2004.

Television Appearances; Series:

Rita, *Feelin' Good* (also known as *Feeling Good*), PBS, 1974.

Sister Agnes, *In the Beginning,* CBS, 1978.

Nurse Rosa Villanueva, *Kay O'Brien,* CBS, 1986.

Multiple roles, *Square One TV,* PBS, 1987–94.

Regina Corrado, a recurring role, *As the World Turns,* CBS, 2003.

Television Appearances; Movies:

Irene, *The Recovery Room,* 1985.

Nelly Gardato, *Doubletake,* 1985.

Wanda Orozco, *Intimate Strangers,* CBS, 1986.

Anita DeSimone, *Alone in the Neon Jungle* (also known as *Command in Hell*), CBS, 1988.

Martha, *Jesse,* CBS, 1988.

District attorney White, *Moment of Truth: Stalking Back* (also known as *Stalking Back: The Anello Family Story*), NBC, 1993.

Mary Ayala, *For the Love of My Child: The Anissa Ayala Story,* NBC, 1993.

Television Appearances; Specials:

Herself, *Night of 100 Stars* (also known as *Night of One Hundred Stars*), ABC, 1982.

Voice of Herself the elf, *The Special Magic of Herself the Elf* (animated), 1983.

Song performer, *Night of 100 Stars III* (also known as *Night of One Hundred Stars*), NBC, 1990.

Herself, "My Favorite Broadway: The Leading Ladies," *Great Performances,* PBS, 1999.

Television Appearances; Episodic:

Guest, *Dinah!* (also known as *Dinah! & Friends*), syndicated, 1976.

Debbie Ballantine, "Mike and Gloria Meet," *All in the Family* (also known as *Justice for All* and *Those Were the Days*), CBS, 1977.

Helen Klatle, "Eternally Yours," *Trapper John, M.D.,* CBS, 1984.

Sally Packard, "Kiss the Girls and Make Them Die," *Law & Order* (also known as *Law & Order Prime*), NBC, 1990.

Reasonable Doubts, NBC, c. 1992.

Judge Rona Shays, "Book of Renovation, Chapter 1," *L.A. Law,* NBC, 1993.

Judge Rona Shays, "How Much Is That Bentley in the Window," *L.A. Law,* NBC, 1993.

Judge Rona Shays, "Leap of Faith," *L.A. Law,* NBC, 1993.

Judge Rona Shays, "Rafael's Proposal," *L.A. Law,* NBC, 1993.

Carla, "Brazil," *Cosby,* CBS, 1998.

Television Appearances; Pilots:

Linda, "Hereafter," *A Year at the Top,* CBS, 1975.

Radio Appearances; Episodic:

Guest, *Radio Playbill,* Arts and Entertainment Channel, Sirius Satellite Radio, 2003.

WRITINGS

Stories for Stage Plays:

(With others) *A Chorus Line* (musical), New York Shakespeare Festival, Public Theatre, Estelle R. Newman Theatre, New York City, then Shubert Theatre, New York City, 1975, also produced in workshops.

(With others) *Class Mothers '68* (solo show), A. E. Hotchner Studio Theatre, Washington University, St. Louis, MO, 1998, then Harold Clurman Theatre, New York City, 2002–2003.

OTHER SOURCES

Books:

Notable Hispanic American Women, Book 1, Gale, 1993.

Periodicals:

New York Times, September 28, 1975.

Playbill, November 16, 1999; December 28, 2005.

LOWE, Chad 1968–

PERSONAL

Full name, Charles Lowe; born January 15, 1968, in Dayton, OH; son of Chuck and Barbara Lowe; brother of Rob Lowe (an actor); married Hilary Swank (an actress), September 28, 1997. *Education:* Attended high school in Santa Monica, CA; studied acting.

Addresses: *Office*—Accomplice Films, 1416 North La Brea Ave., Los Angeles, CA 90028. *Agent*—David Rose, Innovative Artists, 1505 10th St., Santa Monica, CA 90401.

Career: Actor. Accomplice Films, Los Angeles, partner. Appeared in public service announcements. Los Angeles Youth Network (homeless shelter), volunteer, beginning 1991.

Awards, Honors: Emmy Award, outstanding supporting actor in a drama series, and Q Award, best supporting actor in a quality drama series, Viewers for Quality Television, both 1993, for *Life Goes On.*

CREDITS

Television Appearances; Series:
Spencer Winger (title role), *Spencer* (also known as *Under One Roof*), NBC, 1984–85.
Jesse McKenna, *Life Goes On,* ABC, 1991–93.
Carter Gallavan, a recurring role, *Melrose Place,* Fox, 1996–97.
Host, *Celebrity Charades,* American Movie Classics, beginning 2005.

Television Appearances; Miniseries:
Kippie Petworth, *An Inconvenient Woman,* ABC, 1991.

Television Appearances; Movies:
Al Hamilton, *Flight 90: Disaster on the Potomac* (also known as *Flight No. 90* and *Florida Flight 90*), NBC, 1984.
Skip Lewis, *Silence of the Heart,* CBS, 1984.
Josh Sydney, *There Must Be a Pony,* ABC, 1986.
Billy Kincaid, *So Proudly We Hail* (also known as *Skinheads*), CBS, 1990.
Jeff Frost, *Captive* (also known as *Season of Fear*), ABC, 1991.
Jaan Toome, *Candles in the Dark,* The Family Channel, 1993.
Winton Powell, *Siringo,* 1994.

Eric, *Fighting for My Daughter* (also known as *Fighting for My Daughter: The Anne Dion Story*), ABC, 1995.
Stephen Wells, *Dare to Love* (also known as *I Dare to Die*), ABC, 1995.
Sergeant Lott, *In the Presence of Mine Enemies,* Showtime, 1997.
Commissioner Faulk, *Target Earth,* ABC, 1998.
Stan Warden, *The Apartment Complex,* Showtime, 1999.
John Denver, *Take Me Home: The John Denver Story,* CBS, 2000.
Edward Welles, *Acceptable Risk* (also known as *Robin Cook's "Acceptable Risk"*), TBS, 2001.
Phillip Fielder, *Fielder's Choice,* The Hallmark Channel, 2005.

Television Appearances; Specials:
Adam Cooper, "April Morning," *Hallmark Hall of Fame,* CBS, 1988.
Michael Wells, "No Means No," *CBS Schoolbreak Special,* CBS, 1988.
Night of 100 Stars III (also known as *Night of One Hundred Stars*), NBC, 1990.
Host, *Understanding HIV: Does Teen America Know the Facts?,* syndicated, 1992.
In a New Light, ABC, 1992.
In a New Light '93, ABC, 1993.
Rob Tarda, *The Show Formerly Known as The Martin Short Show,* NBC, 1995.
Roger, "Me and My Hormones," *ABC Afterschool Specials,* ABC, 1996.
Hollywood Hockey Cup, Comedy Central, 1996.

Television Appearances; Awards Presentations:
The 61st Annual Academy Awards Presentation, ABC, 1989.
The 72nd Annual Academy Awards, ABC, 2000.
The 2001 IFP/West Independent Spirit Awards, Independent Film Channel, 2001.
The 75th Annual Academy Awards, ABC, 2003.

Television Appearances; Episodic:
Sam Taylor, "Shoshoni Dreaming," *Snowy River: The McGregor Saga* (also known as *Banjo Patterson's "The Man from Snowy River"*), The Family Channel, 1995.
Sam Taylor, "The Trial of Hetti Lewis," *Snowy River: The McGregor Saga* (also known as *Banjo Patterson's "The Man from Snowy River"*), The Family Channel, 1995.
George Henry, "Do You See What I See?," *ER* (also known as *Emergency Room*), NBC, 1997.
George Henry, "Freak Show," *ER* (also known as *Emergency Room*), NBC, 1997.
George Henry, "Something New," *ER* (also known as *Emergency Room*), NBC, 1997.

Neville, "A Matter of Style," *The Hunger,* Showtime, 1997.

Arthur Bowers, "Miles to Go before I Sleep," *Touched by an Angel,* CBS, 1998.

Josh Miller, "The Covenant," *Poltergeist: The Legacy,* Showtime, Sci–Fi Channel, and syndicated, 1998.

Voices of Rokk Krinn and Cosmic Boy, "New Kids in Town," *Superman* (animated; also known as *The New Batman/Superman Adventures* and *Superman: The Animated Series*), The WB, 1998.

Craig Spence, "Boy Wonder," *Now and Again,* CBS, 1999.

Craig Spence, "Everybody Who's Anybody," *Now and Again,* CBS, 1999.

Craig Spence, "The Insurance Man Always Rings Twice," *Now and Again,* CBS, 1999.

Mr. Luke Grant, "Mo' Menace, Mo' Problems," *Popular,* The WB, 1999.

Mr. Luke Grant, "The Phantom Menace," *Popular,* The WB, 1999.

Mr. Luke Grant, "Truth or Consequences," *Popular,* The WB, 1999.

Mr. Luke Grant, "Under Siege," *Popular,* The WB, 1999.

Voice of first barking deer, "Born to Be Wild," *The Wild Thornberrys* (animated), Nickelodeon, 1999.

Guest, *The Martin Short Show,* syndicated, 1999.

Voice of Buck the Ibex, "Every Little Bit Alps," *The Wild Thornberrys* (animated), Nickelodeon, 2000.

Guest, *The Rosie O'Donnell Show,* syndicated, 2000.

Andy Harris, "Hate Puppet," *Night Visions,* Fox, 2001.

Jason Mayberry, "Pique," *Law & Order: Special Victims Unit* (also known as *Law & Order's Sex Crimes, Law & Order: SVU,* and *Special Victims Unit*), NBC, 2001.

Voice of Wade Pennington, "Crime Waves," *The Zeta Project* (animated), The WB, 2001.

Himself, *Intimate Portrait: Kellie Martin,* Lifetime, 2002.

Jimmy Scanlon, "Brothers in Arms," *Hack,* CBS, 2003.

Scott Mandeville, "Blood Brothers," *CSI: Miami,* CBS, 2003.

Lawrence Pierce, "Upstairs Downstairs," *Without a Trace* (also known as *Vanished*), CBS, 2004.

(In archive footage) Himself, *101 Biggest Celebrity Oops* (also known as *E's "101"*), E! Entertainment Television, 2004.

David Call, "Being Mrs. O'Leary's Cow," *Medium,* NBC, 2005.

Dr. George Henry, "The Providers," *ER* (also known as *Emergency Room*), NBC, 2005.

Guest, *The Big Idea with Donny Deutsch,* CNBC, 2005.

Guest, *The View,* ABC, 2005.

Appeared in episodes of *Instant Comedy with the Groundlings.*

Television Appearances; Pilots:

Craig Spence, "Origins," *Now and Again,* CBS, 1999.

Television Work; Series:

Creator and executive producer, *Celebrity Charades,* American Movie Classics, beginning 2005.

Television Director; Episodic:

"Dial 0 for Murder," *Hack,* CBS, 2003.

"Soulless," *Law & Order: Special Victims Unit* (also known as *Law & Order's Sex Crimes, Law & Order: SVU,* and *Special Victims Unit*), NBC, 2003.

"The Road Home," *Without a Trace* (also known as *Vanished*), CBS, 2006.

Film Appearances:

(Uncredited) Computer hacker, *Oxford Blues,* Metro–Goldwyn–Mayer/United Artists, 1984.

Billy Kelly, *Apprentice to Murder* (also known as *The Long Lost Friend* and *The Long Lost Friends*), New World, 1988.

Donny Trueblood, *True Blood,* Fries, 1989.

Stephen/Stephanie, *Nobody's Perfect,* Moviestore Entertainment, 1990.

Charlie Sykes, *Highway to Hell,* Hemdale Releasing, 1992.

LeGrand, *Driven,* Driven Productions, 1996.

Marty, *Do Me a Favor* (also known as *Trading Favors*), Quadra Entertainment, 1997.

Richard, *The Way We Are* (also known as *Quiet Days in Hollywood*), 1997.

VTV director, *The Others,* The Asylum/Cinequanon Pictures International, 1997.

J. J., *Suicide, the Comedy* (also known as *The Intervention*), Alibi Entertainment, 1998.

Doug, *Floating,* Phaedra Cinema, 1999.

The Audition (short film), 2000.

Parker Smith, *Your Guardian,* Junebug Films, 2001.

Bill Stone, *Unfaithful* (also known as *Infidele* and *Untreu*), Twentieth Century-Fox, 2002.

Orin Sanders, *Red Betsy,* Lang Features, 2003.

Film Director:

The Audition (short film), 2000.

The Space Between (short film), 2002.

(And producer) *Beautiful Ohio,* Accomplice Films/Boom Baby Productions, 2006.

Stage Appearances:

Coming of Age in Soho, New York Shakespeare Festival, Public Theatre, Martinson Hall, New York City, 1985.

Huckleberry Finn, *The Adventures of Huckleberry Finn* (also known as *Huckleberry Finn*), Williamstown Theatre Festival, Williamstown, MA, 1990.

John, *Grotesque Love Songs,* Workshop of the Players Art Theatre, New York City, 1990.

Night of 100 Stars III (also known as *Night of One Hundred Stars*), Radio City Music Hall, New York City, 1990.

Lieutenant Will Stephenson, *Burning Blue,* Samuel Beckett Theatre, New York City, 2002.

The Exonerated, Forty–Five Bleecker Street Theatre, New York City, between 2002 and 2004.

Appeared as Arthur Bartley in *Blue Denim,* Los Angeles.

RECORDINGS

Audiobooks:

Leif Enger, *Peace Like a River,* HarperAudio, 2001.

Joyce Carol Oates, *Big Mouth and Ugly Girl,* Harper, 2002.

WRITINGS

Screenplays:

The Space Between (short film), 2002.

OTHER SOURCES

Periodicals:

TV Guide, April 29, 2000, pp. 40–42.

LUDLOW, Ian
    See GOLDBERG, Lee

M

MacADAMS, Rachel
    See **McADAMS, Rachel**

MADIO, James 1975–

PERSONAL

Born November 22, 1975, in The Bronx, NY.

Addresses: *Agent*—Domain, 9229 Sunset Blvd., Suite 415, Los Angeles, CA 90069. *Manager*—Gekis Management, 4217 Verdugo View Dr., Los Angeles, CA 90065.

Career: Actor. Appeared in television commercials, including Nike, 1997, and Burger King, 1990.

Awards, Honors: Young Artist Award (with others), outstanding young ensemble cast in a motion picture, 1993, for *Hook*.

CREDITS

Film Appearances:
Don't Ask, Lost Boy, *Hook,* TriStar, 1991.
Billy Cardillo, *The Godson* (short film), AtomShock-Wave, 1992.
Young Mac, *Mac,* Samuel Goldwyn, 1992.
Joey Laplante, Bernie's son, *Hero* (also known as *Accidental Hero*), Columbia, 1992.
Every Good Boy (short film), 1994.
Pedro, *The Basketball Diaries,* New Line Cinema, 1995.
Eddie Fontaine, *The Gifted,* 1999.
If Tomorrow Comes, RGH/Lions Share Pictures, 2000.

Voices of second Great White and Hammerhead, *Shark Tale* (animated), DreamWorks, 2004.
Guest star, *Diva Dog: Pit Bull on Wheels* (documentary short film), 2005.
Young Mike, *Searching for Bobby D,* 2005.
Sam, *Single White Female 2: The Psycho,* Columbia TriStar, 2005.
Jimmy Boy, *West of Brooklyn,* 2006.
Lenny, *The Grasslands,* 2006.

Television Appearances; Series:
Bobby "Lazz" Lazzarini, *USA High,* syndicated, 1997–98.
Mike Powell, *Queens Supreme,* CBS, 2003.

Television Appearances; Miniseries:
Sergeant Frank Perconte, *Band of Brothers,* HBO, 2001.

Television Appearances; Specials:
(Uncredited) Himself, *The Making of "Band of Brothers"* (documentary), HBO, 2001.

Television Appearances; Episodic:
Jimmy Pellegrino, "It's a Wonderful Laugh," *Doogie Howser, M.D.,* ABC, 1991.
Silvio, "House Guests," *Blossom,* NBC, 1992.
Rip Russo, "Judgment Day," *The Commish,* ABC, 1992.
Anthony, "Blood Brothers: The Joey DePaolo Story," *Lifestories: Families in Crisis,* HBO, 1992.
Andy Costello, "Born Bad," *Law & Order,* NBC, 1993.
The Test, F/X, 2001.
Private Officer Jack Horton, "Capital Crime," *JAG,* CBS, 2002.
Max, "End Game," *Arli$$,* HBO, 2002.
Billy Sullivan, "London Calling," *Related,* The WB, 2006.

RECORDINGS

Video Games:
Voice of Private Smith, *Call of Duty 2: Big Red One,* Activision, 2005.

MAGUIRE, Tobey 1975–
    (Tobias Maguire)

PERSONAL

Full name, Tobias Vincent Maguire; born June 27, 1975, in Santa Monica, CA; son of Vincent (a cook) and Wendy (a secretary) Maguire. *Avocational Interests:* Yoga, cooking, poker, chess.

Addresses: *Office*—Maguire Entertainment, 9220 Sunset Blvd., Suite 300, Los Angeles, CA 90069. *Agent*—Richard Lovett, Creative Artists Agency, 9830 Wilshire Blvd., Beverly Hills, CA 90212. *Manager*—Eric Kranzler, Management 360, 9111 Wilshire Blvd., Beverly Hills, CA 90210. *Publicist*—I/D Public Relations, 8409 Santa Monica Blvd., West Hollywood, CA 90069.

Career: Actor. Maguire Entertainment, Los Angeles, principal. Appeared in commercials. Participant in poker tournaments. Some sources cite Maguire as an advisor for EdgeTV.

Awards, Honors: Young Artist Award nomination, best young actor in a new television series, Young Artist Foundation, 1993, for *Great Scott!;* Saturn Award nomination, best performance by a younger actor or actress, Academy of Science Fiction, Horror, and Fantasy Films, 1999, for *Pleasantville;* named to *Entertainment Weekly* magazine's It List, 1999 and 2001; Toronto Film Critics Association Award, best supporting actor, 2000, for *Wonder Boys;* Screen Actors Guild Award nomination (with others), outstanding performance by a cast in a theatrical motion picture, 2000, for *The Cider House Rules;* Teen Choice awards, choice actor in a drama or action adventure film and (with Kirsten Dunst) choice lip lock, and Teen Choice Award nomination (with Dunst), choice film chemistry, all 2002, MTV Movie Award (with Dunst), best kiss, Saturn Award nomination, best actor, MTV Movie Award nomination, best male performance, and Blimp Award nomination, favorite male butt kicker, Kids' Choice awards, all 2003, all for *Spider–Man;* named one of the most powerful people in Hollywood, *Entertainment Weekly* magazine, 2002 and 2003; Screen Actors Guild Award nomination (with others), outstanding performance by a cast in a motion picture, 2004, for *Seabis-*

cuit; Saturn Award and Empire Award nomination, both best actor, and Blimp Award nomination, favorite movie actor, all 2005, for *Spider–Man 2.*

CREDITS

Film Appearances:
(Uncredited) Lucas's goon, *The Wizard,* Universal, 1989.
Chuck Bolger, *This Boy's Life,* Warner Bros., 1993.
Al, *S.F.W.* (also known as *So Fucking What?*), Gramercy Pictures, 1994.
Drunken teenager, *Healer,* Healer Productions, 1994.
Jimmy Spencer, *The Adventures of the Red Baron* (also known as *Plane Fear* and *Revenge of the Red Baron*), New Horizons, 1994.
Rich Cooper, *The Duke of Groove* (short film), Chanticleer Films, 1995, also released in *4 Tales of 2 Cities* (four short films), 1995.
Harvey Stern, *Deconstructing Harry,* Fine Line Features, 1997.
J. T., *Joyride,* Live Film & Mediaworks/Showcase Entertainment/High Fliers Distribution, 1997.
Paul Hood, *The Ice Storm,* Fox Searchlight Pictures, 1997.
David/Bud Parker, *Pleasantville* (also known as *Color of Heart*), New Line Cinema, 1998.
Hitchhiker, *Fear and Loathing in Las Vegas,* Universal, 1998.
Homer Wells, *The Cider House Rules,* Miramax, 1998.
Ian, *Don's Plum* (also known as *Saturday Night Club*), 1998, Trust Films Sales, 2001.
Jake Roedel, *Ride with the Devil* (also known as *To Live On*), Universal, 1999.
James Leer, *Wonder Boys* (also known as *Die Wonder Boys* and *Wonderboys—Lauter Wunderknaben*), Paramount, 2000.
Lou, *Cats & Dogs,* Warner Bros., 2001.
Peter Parker/Spider–Man, *Spider–Man* (also known as *Spiderman* and *Spider–Man: The Motion Picture*), Columbia, 2002.
Red Pollard, *Seabiscuit,* Universal, 2003.
Peter Parker/Spider–Man, *Spider–Man 2,* Columbia, 2004, IMAX version released as *Spider–Man 2: The IMAX Experience.*
Billy Chaka, *Tokyo Suckerpunch* (short film), Sony Pictures Entertainment, 2006.
Tully, *The Good German,* Warner Bros., 2006.
Peter Parker/Spider–Man, *Spider–Man 3,* Sony Pictures Releasing, 2007.
Quiet Type, New Line Cinema, 2007.

Film Producer:
25th Hour (also known as *The 25th Hour*), Buena Vista, 2002.
Executive producer, *Seabiscuit,* Universal, 2003.
Whatever We Do (short film), 2003.

Tokyo Suckerpunch (short film), Sony Pictures Entertainment, 2006.
Quiet Type, New Line Cinema, 2007.

Television Appearances; Series:
Scott Melrod, *Great Scott!,* Fox, 1992.

Television Appearances; Miniseries:
Chuck Borchardt, *Seduced by Madness: The Diane Borchardt Story* (also known as *Murderous Passion: The Diane Borchardt Story* and *Seduced by Madness*), NBC, 1996.

Television Appearances; Movies:
Martin, *Spoils of War* (also known as *In Spite of Love*), ABC, 1994.
Peter Lively, *A Child's Cry for Help,* NBC, 1994.

Television Appearances; Specials:
(As Tobias Maguire) *Rodney Dangerfield: Opening Night at Rodney's Place,* 1989.
Ronald "Hot Rod" Brown, *Tales from the Whoop: Hot Rod Brown, Class Clown* (also known as *Hot Rod Brown, Class Clown*), Nickelodeon, 1990.
Older Danny, *Profiles,* ABC, 1994.
Canned Ham: Deconstructing Harry, Comedy Central, 1997.
Himself, *What Is a Producer?,* E! Entertainment Television, 2001.
(In archive footage) Peter Parker, *Jack Black: Spider–Man,* MTV, 2002.
Himself, *Behind the Scenes: Spider–Man the Movie* (also known as *Behind the Ultimate Spin*), 2002.
Himself, *Spider–Man: An MTV Movie Special,* MTV, 2002.
Himself, *Spidermania,* 2002.
Himself, *The Spider–Man Story,* Channel 5 (England), 2002.
Barbara Walters Presents: The 10 Most Fascinating People of 2002, ABC, 2002.
Before They Were Stars!, ABC, 2002.
Himself, *The True Story of Seabiscuit,* Arts and Entertainment, 2003.
Himself, *VH1 Goes Inside: Spider–Man,* VH1, 2004.
(In archive footage) *Saturday Night Life: The Best of Cheri Oteri,* NBC, 2004.

Television Appearances; Awards Presentations:
The 1999 MTV Movie Awards, MTV, 1999.
Presenter, *The 57th Annual Golden Globe Awards,* NBC, 2000.
Presenter, *The 72nd Annual Academy Awards,* ABC, 2000.
Presenter, *The 74th Annual Academy Awards,* ABC, 2002.
Presenter, *Nickelodeon Kids' Choice Awards '04,* Nickelodeon, 2004.
Presenter, *The 76th Annual Academy Awards,* ABC, 2004.
Presenter, *2004 MTV Movie Awards,* MTV, 2004.
Presenter, *The 63rd Annual Golden Globe Awards,* NBC, 2005.

Television Appearances; Episodic:
"The Missing Eye," *General Hospital,* ABC, 1979.
Parenthood, NBC, 1990.
Boy, "Sex, Lies and Teenagers," *Blossom,* NBC, 1991.
Jeff, "Valentine's Day," *Roseanne,* ABC, 1991.
Tripp O'Connell, "The Dead Letter," *Eerie Indiana,* NBC, 1991.
Jake and the Fatman, CBS, 1991.
Wild & Crazy Kids, Nickelodeon and syndicated, 1992.
Duane Parsons, "The Prodigal Son," *Walker, Texas Ranger,* CBS, 1994.
Sonny, "Family," *Tracey Takes On ... ,* HBO, 1996.
Host, *Saturday Night Live* (also known as *NBC's "Saturday Night," Saturday Night, Saturday Night Live '80, SNL,* and *SNL 25*), NBC, 2000.
Himself, "Cats & Dogs," *HBO First Look,* HBO, 2001.
Himself, "Spider–Man," *HBO First Look,* HBO, 2002.
Movie House (also known as *MTV's "Movie House"*), MTV, c. 2002.
Himself, "Seabiscuit," *HBO First Look,* HBO, 2003.
(In archive footage) Himself, *Celebrities Uncensored,* E! Entertainment Television, 2003.
Himself, "Spider–Man 2," *HBO First Look,* HBO, 2004.
(In archive footage) *Magazine,* [Spain], 2005.

Television Guest Appearances; Episodic:
The Rosie O'Donnell Show, syndicated, 2000.
Howard Stern, E! Entertainment Television, 2002.
Rove Live, Ten Network (Australia), 2002.
The Tonight Show with Jay Leno, NBC, 2002, 2003.
The Late Show with David Letterman (also known as *The Late Show* and *Late Show Backstage*), CBS, 2003.
The Oprah Winfrey Show (also known as *Oprah*), syndicated, 2003, 2004.
(In archive footage) *101 Biggest Celebrity Oops* (also known as *E's "101"*), E! Entertainment Television, 2004.
Eigo de shabera–night, 2004.
Extra (also known as *Extra: The Entertainment Magazine*), syndicated, 2004.
On–Air with Ryan Seacrest, syndicated, 2004.
Smap x Smap, Fuji Television, 2004.
This Morning (also known as *This Morning with Richard and Judy*), Independent Television (England), 2004.

Television Appearances; Pilots:
Scott Melrod, *Great Scott!,* Fox, 1992.

Television Work; Specials:
Executive producer, *Rock of Ages,* HBO, 2003.

Stage Appearances:
Thanksgiving Cries, 1991.

Radio Appearances:
The Howard Stern Radio Show, 2002.

RECORDINGS

Videos:
Himself, *The Cider House Rules: The Making of an American Classic,* Miramax, 1999.
Himself, *Wonder Boys: A Look between the Pages,* Paramount, 2000.
Himself, *The Making of "Seabiscuit"* (also known as *Bringing the Legend to Life: The Making of "Seabiscuit"*), Universal Studios Home Video, 2003.
Himself, *Seabiscuit: The Making of a Legend,* 2003.
Himself, *Seabiscuit: Racing through History,* Universal Studios Home Video, 2003.
Himself, *Hero in Crisis,* Columbia/TriStar Home Entertainment, 2004.
Himself, *Making the Amazing* (also known as *Making the Amazing: The Making of "Spider–Man 2"* and *Making the Amazing: "Spider–Man 2"*), Sony Pictures Home Entertainment, 2004.

Video Games:
Voice of Peter Parker/Spiderman, *Spider–Man,* 2002.
Voice of Peter Parker/Spiderman, *Spider–Man 2,* Activision, 2004.

OTHER SOURCES

Books:
Newsmakers, Issue 2, Gale, 2002.

Periodicals:
Cosmopolitan, May, 1999, p. 214.
Entertainment Weekly, March 3, 2000, pp. 39–40; December 20, 2002, pp. 18–19; July 25, 2003, pp. 24–30.
Interview, October, 1998, pp. 142–50.
Parade, July 20, 2003, pp. 6–8.
People Weekly, May 20, 2002, p. 67.
Playboy, August, 2003, pp. 55–59, 139–41.
Premiere, November, 1997, p. 48; May, 2002, pp. 50–56, 95.
Request, May, 2002, p. 10.
Time, May 20, 2002, p. 74; July 21, 2003, p. 56.
TV Guide, December 13, 2003, p. 14.
US, November, 1998, pp. 82–83.
USA Today, October 22, 1997, p. 60.
Variety, January 3, 2000, p. 57; April 7, 2003.
Vogue, September, 1999, pp. 430–32.
Women's Wear Daily, December 21, 1999, p. 4.

MANTHEY, Jerri 1970–
(Jerri Lynn London, Jerri Lyn)

PERSONAL

Born September 5, 1970, in Stuttgart, West Germany (now Germany); father, a career army officer; married Tony Krebill, 1989 (divorced). *Education:* Attended University of Maryland overseas branch in Munich, Germany; trained with Manu Tupou. *Avocational Interests:* Softball, wilderness camping, photography, reading, writing, painting, music.

Addresses: *Office*—Velocity Productions, Inc., P.O. Box 27785, Los Angeles, CA 90027–0785. *Contact*—c/o Andrew Briskin, Tango Blues Entertainment, 1051–A North Cole Ave., Hollywood, CA 90038.

Career: Actress. Velocity Productions, Inc., Los Angeles, founder; singer and musician with the band Deep Eddy; affiliated with the band Mutaytor; appeared in commercials, print advertisements, and photography shoots in periodicals. Worked as a personal chef, an employee of BoKoas restaurant, Los Angeles, and a model for Home Shopping Network; also affiliated with charities.

Member: Screen Actors Guild, American Federation of Television and Radio Artists, American Society of Composers, Authors and Publishers.

CREDITS

Television Appearances; Series:
Herself, *Survivor: The Australian Outback* (also known as *Survivor*), CBS, 2001.
Herself, *The Surreal Life,* The WB, 2002.
Herself, *Survivor: All–Stars* (also known as *Survivor*), CBS, 2004.
Sideline reporter, *Extreme Dodgeball,* Game Show Network, 2004.
Contestant, *Battle of the Network Reality Stars,* Bravo, 2005.

Television Appearances; Movies:
(As Jerri Lynn London) Claire, *That Championship Season,* Showtime, 1999.
Sandra Crescent, *Komodo vs. Cobra,* Sci–Fi Channel, 2005.

Television Appearances; Specials:
Herself, *Survivor: The Australian Outback—The Reunion* (also known as *Survivor: The Outback Reunion*), CBS, 2001.

Audience member, *Survivor: Africa—The Reunion* (also known as *Survivor 3: The Reunion*), CBS, 2002.
Cohost, *Seaside Survivor* (also known as *MTV's "Seaside Survivor"*), MTV, 2002.
Herself, *Survivor: Men vs. Women Rumble in the Jungle,* MTV, 2003.
Correspondent, *Red Carpet Emmy's Pre–Show,* E! Entertainment Television, 2004.
Herself, *Reality TV Secrets Revealed,* VH1, 2004.
Herself, *Survivor All–Stars America's Tribal Council,* CBS, 2004.
Herself, *QTN Holiday Reel,* Q Television, 2005.

Television Guest Appearances; Episodic:
"Stars of Reality TV Week," *Blind Date* (also known as *Cupid Confidential*), syndicated, 2001.
The Late Late Show with Craig Kilborn (also known as *The Late Late Show*), CBS, 2001.
The Rosie O'Donnell Show, syndicated, 2001.
The Test, FX Channel, 2001.
The Young and the Restless (also known as *Y & R*), CBS, 2001.
The Early Show, CBS, 2001, 2004.
Howard Stern, E! Entertainment Television, multiple episodes in 2001, 2004.
"Survivor," *VH1 Goes Inside* (also known as *VH1 Goes inside Survivor*), VH1, 2003.
The Joe Schmo Show, Spike TV, 2003.
The Other Half, syndicated, 2003.
Live with Regis and Kelly, syndicated, 2004.
Getaway (also known as *United Travel Getaway*), Nine Network (Australia), 2005.

Also a guest in *The Late Show with David Letterman* (also known as *The Late Show*), CBS; *Politically Incorrect with Bill Maher* (also known as *Politically Incorrect*), Comedy Central and ABC; and appeared in other programs, including *Talk Soup,* E! Entertainment Television.

Film Appearances:
Lana Lahera, *Mr. Lucke* (also known as *Mr. Lucky*), 1995.
(As Jerri Lynn) *Prey of the Jaguar,* Jfw Productions, 1996.
Evan, *The Limited* (short film), New Ground Productions, 2000.
Jen, *Destiny,* Destiny Productions, 2002.
Iron Janes, 2003.
Commitment Pledge (short film), 2004.
Henry Bump's Happy Toast (short film), c. 2004.
Judy, *Chloe's Prayer,* Merus Pictures, 2005.
Woman, *Widowmaker* (short film), Hollywood Ending Films, c. 2005.

Appeared in *Bargain Hunting,* Instant Films. Appeared in other films, including *Bonehead: Scotty, Jackers,* and *Mind of a Woman.* Some sources cite appearances in *The Sacred Hoop* and *The Shoot.*

Film Work:
Director and producer of *Mind of a Woman.*

Stage Appearances:
Dilly, *Lady Macbeth Gets a Divorce,* Beverly Hills Playhouse, Beverly Hills, CA, 2001.
Blow Girls, Sierra Stage, 2003.
Pieces (of Ass) (monologues), Dodger Stages, Stage 2, New York City, beginning c. 2004.
The Vagina Monologues (monologues), V–Day, Pacific Design Center, Silver Screen Theatre, Los Angeles, 2005.

Appeared in *Agnes of God, Plaza Suite,* and *Pygmalion,* all Huntsville Theatre, Huntsville, AL. Appeared in *I Love You, Mr. Klotz, The Lalapalooza Bird,* and *The Pajama Game* (musical), all New Ulm Theatre, New Ulm, West Germany (now Germany); also appeared in *You Can't Take It with You,* Munich Theatre, Munich, West Germany (now Germany).

Stage Work:
Codirector and coproducer of *Beautiful Chaos,* Hudson Theatre, Los Angeles.

Radio Appearances; Episodic:
The Howard Stern Radio Show, multiple episodes in 2001, 2004.

RECORDINGS

Videos:
Herself, *Survivor—Season Two: The Greatest and Most Outrageous Moments,* Castaway Television Productions, 2001.

Music Videos:
Faith Hill, "Piece of My Heart," 1994.
Def Leppard, "When Love and Hate Collide," 1995.
Jay Murphy Band, "Hit Bottom," 2004.

WRITINGS

Writings for the Stage:
With others, wrote *Beautiful Chaos,* Hudson Theatre, Los Angeles.

Nonfiction:
Author of "Jerri Manthey's Passion Plate," a weekly column for *CdKitchen.com,* 2005.

OTHER SOURCES

Periodicals:
People Weekly, August 23, 2004, p. 55.

Electronic:
Jerri Manthey, http://www.jerrimanthey.com, January 25, 2006.

MARIENTHAL, Eli 1986–

PERSONAL

Full name, Eli Kenneth Marienthal (some sources cite Eli David); born March 6, 1986, in Santa Monica, CA (some sources say Berkeley, CA); son of Joe and Lola Marienthal. *Education:* Attended Brown University; studied acting at American Conservatory Theatre's Young Conservatory. *Avocational Interests:* Snowboarding, rock climbing, ice hockey, and writing poetry.

Addresses: *Agent*—International Creative Management, 8942 Wilshire Blvd., Beverly Hills, CA 90211.

Career: Actor. Performed with Bay Area poetry group, Youth Speaks.

Awards, Honors: YoungStar Award nomination, best performance by a young actor in a comedy film, Fennecus Award nomination, vocal performance, 1999, for *Slums of Beverly Hills;* Annie Award, outstanding individual achievement for voice acting in an animated feature production, 1999, YoungStar Award, best young voice–over talent, Young Artist Award, best performance in a voice–over (TV or feature film)—young actor, 2000, all for *The Iron Giant;* Black Box Award, for *Cryptogram.*

CREDITS

Film Appearances:
(Film debut) Adrian, *First Love, Last Rites,* Strand Releasing, 1997.
Rickey Abromowitz, *Slums of Beverly Hills,* Fox Searchlight Pictures, 1998.
Spencer, *Jack Frost* (also known as *Frost*), Warner Bros., 1998.
Stifler's brother, *American Pie,* Universal, 1999.
Voice of Hogarth Hughes, *The Iron Giant* (animated), Warner Bros., 1999.
Stifler's brother, *American Pie 2,* Universal, 2001.
Dex Barrington, *The Country Bears,* Buena Vista, 2002.
Voice of Timothy "Tim" Drake/Robin, *Batman: Mystery of the Batwoman* (animated), Warner Bros., 2003.
Sam, *Confessions of a Teenage Drama Queen,* Buena Vista, 2004.

Television Appearances; Series:
Tucker Pierce (title role), *Tucker,* NBC, 2000.

Voice of Young Zee, *The Zeta Project* (animated), The WB, 2001.

Television Appearances; Movies:
Matthew Bartilson, *Unlikely Angel,* CBS, 1996.

Television Appearances; Specials:
Himself, *The Making of "The Iron Giant"* (documentary), The WB, 1999.

Television Appearances; Episodic:
John, "A House Divided," *Touched by an Angel,* CBS, 2000.
Voice of Dak, "Where's Terry?," *Batman Beyond* (animated; also known as *Batman of the Future*), The WB, 2000.
Voices of Derek Minna and computerized Stingray, "Two Wheels, Full Throttle, No Brakes," *Fillmore!* (animated; also known as *Disney's "Fillmore!"*), ABC, 2003.

Stage Appearances:
Appeared in *Missing Persons* and *The Life of Galileo,* both Berkeley Repertory Theater, Berkeley, CA; *Cryptogram,* Magic Theater, San Francisco, CA; *Hecuba, A Midsummer Night's Dream,* and *Every 17 Minutes the Crowd Goes Crazy,* all American Conservatory Theatre, San Francisco, CA.

OTHER SOURCES

Periodicals:
Boys' Life, August, 1999, p. 14.

MARTIN, Duane 1970–

PERSONAL

Born January 1, 1970, in Hollywood, CA (some sources cite Brooklyn, New York, NY); married Tisha Campbell (an actress), August 17, 1996; children: Xen (son). *Education:* Attended New York University.

Addresses: *Agent*—Pearl Wexler, The Kohner Agency, 9300 Wilshire Blvd., Suite 555, Beverly Hills, CA 90212. *Manager*—3 Arts Entertainment, 9460 Wilshire Blvd., Seventh Floor, Beverly Hills, CA 90212.

Career: Actor, producer, and writer. Played professional basketball for the New York Knicks.

Awards, Honors: BET Comedy Award nomination, outstanding supporting actor in a box office movie, Black Entertainment Television, 2004, for *Deliver Us from Eva;* BET Comedy Award nomination, outstanding lead actor in a comedy series, 2005, for *All of Us.*

CREDITS

Television Appearances; Series:
Vidal Thomas, *Out All Night,* NBC, 1992–93.
Milo Doucette, *Getting Personal* (also known as *Personal Days* and *The Way We Work*), Fox, 1998–99.
Sugar Hill, beginning 1999.
Robert James, Sr., *All of Us,* UPN, beginning 2003.

Television Appearances; Movies:
Jim, "Mr. Headmistress," *The Wonderful World of Disney,* ABC, 1998.
B. J. Teach, *Mutiny,* NBC, 1999.

Television Appearances; Specials:
Jordan, *Different Worlds: A Story of Interracial Love,* HBO, 1992.

Television Appearances; Awards Presentations:
Presenter, *Ninth Annual Soul Train Lady of Soul Awards,* The WB, 2003.
Third Annual BET Awards, Black Entertainment Television, 2003.
2003 Vibe Awards: Beats, Style, Flavor, UPN, 2003.
BET Comedy Awards, Black Entertainment Television, 2004.
The Second Annual Vibe Awards, UPN, 2004.
The 35th Annual NAACP Image Awards, Fox, 2004.
Presenter, *The 36th Annual NAACP Image Awards,* Fox, 2005.
BET Awards 2005, Black Entertainment Television, 2005.
The Second Annual BET Comedy Awards (also known as *2005 BET Comedy Awards*), Black Entertainment Television, 2005.

Television Appearances; Episodic:
Kenny, "All That Jazz," *Roc* (also known as *Roc Live*), Fox, 1992.
Duane, "It's Better to Have Loved and Lost It ... ," *Fresh Prince of Bel–Air,* NBC, 1993.
Guest host, *Later* (also known as *Later with Bob Costas, Later with Cynthia Garrett,* and *Later with Greg Kinnear*), NBC, 1994.
Dr. Duane, "I, Ooh, Baby, Baby," *Fresh Prince of Bel–Air,* NBC, 1995.
Mason, "The List," *Between Brothers,* Fox, 1997.
Ty Richardson, "Living Single Undercover," *Living Single* (also known as *My Girls*), Fox, 1997.
Preston Hall, "Fried Turkey," *Girlfriends,* UPN, 2000.

Elliott, "Phantom Menace," *One on One,* UPN, 2001.
Alan, "Greg's New Friend," *Yes, Dear,* CBS, 2002.
Himself, *Intimate Portrait: Tisha Campbell–Martin,* Lifetime, 2002.
Jake, "Abby Gets Her Groove Back," *Abby,* UPN, 2003.
Guest, *The Sharon Osbourne Show* (also known as *Sharon*), syndicated, 2004.
Guest, *The Wayne Brady Show,* syndicated, 2004.
Ashton Belluso, "The Vanishing," *The Ghost Whisperer,* CBS, 2006.

Appeared in an episode of *Against the Law,* Fox.

Television Appearances; Pilots:
Steve, *Moe's World,* ABC, 1992.
Vidal Thomas, *Out All Night,* NBC, 1992.
Maxwell Stewart, *A Guy Named Max,* ABC, 1996.
Newcomer, *Blind Men,* CBS, 2001.
Untitled John Ridley Project (also known as *Untitled John Ridley Drama Project*), ABC, c. 2002.
Robert James, Sr., *All of Us,* UPN, 2003.
I Got You, ABC, 2003.

Television Work; Series:
Producer, *Getting Personal* (also known as *Personal Days* and *The Way We Work*), Fox, 1998–99.

Film Appearances:
Willie Lewis, *White Men Can't Jump,* Twentieth Century–Fox, 1992.
Junior Phillips, *The Inkwell* (also known as *No Ordinary Summer*), Buena Vista, 1994.
Kyle–Lee Watson, *Above the Rim,* New Line Cinema, 1994.
Planesman first class Jefferson "R. J." Jackson, *Down Periscope,* Twentieth Century–Fox, 1996.
Brandon, *Fakin' da Funk,* Octillion Entertainment, 1997.
Joel Jones, *Scream 2* (also known as *Scream Again, Scream Louder,* and *Scream: The Sequel*), Dimension Films, 1997.
(Uncredited) First officer, *The Faculty* (also known as *Feelers*), Miramax, 1998.
Frankie, *Woo,* New Line Cinema, 1998.
Willie's agent, *Any Given Sunday* (also known as *Gridiron, The League, Monday Night, On Any Given Sunday,* and *Playing Hurt*), Warner Bros., 1999.
Phil, *The Groomsmen* (also known as *What Boys Like*), Visionbox Pictures, 2001.
Michael (Mike), *Deliver Us from Eva,* Focus Features, c. 2002.
Rad, *Ride or Die* (also known as *Hustle and Heat*), Destination Films, 2003.
Derrick, *The Seat Filler,* Momentum Experience, 2004.

Film Producer:
Ride or Die (also known as *Hustle and Heat*), Destination Films, 2003.

The Seat Filler, Momentum Experience, 2004.

RECORDINGS

Videos:
Himself, *Behind the Scenes of "Deliver Us from Eva,"* Universal Studios Home Video, 2003.

Music Videos:
Boyz II Men, "I'll Make Love to You," 1994.
K–Ci & JoJo, "This Very Moment," 2002.

WRITINGS

Screenplays:
Ride or Die (also known as *Hustle and Heat*), Destination Films, 2003.
The Seat Filler, Momentum Experience, 2004.

OTHER SOURCES

Books:
Who's Who among African Americans, 18th edition, Gale, 2005.

Periodicals:
Essence, November, 1994, p. 87.

McADAMS, Rachel 1976–
   (Rachel MacAdams)

PERSONAL

Some sources cite original name as Rachel MacAdams; born October 7, 1976, in London, Ontario, Canada; daughter of Lance (a truck driver) and Sandy (a nurse) MacAdams. *Education:* York University, B.F.A. (with honors); studied drama with David Rothenberg, at theatres, and at theatre camps. *Avocational Interests:* Travel, backpacking.

Addresses: *Agent*—Allison Band, United Talent Agency, 9560 Wilshire Blvd., Suite 500, Beverly Hills, CA 90212; (voice work) Special Artists Agency, 9465 Wilshire Blvd., Suite 890, Beverly Hills, CA 90212. *Manager*—Shelley Browning, Magnolia Entertainment, 1620 26th St., Suite 480, Santa Monica, CA 90404.

Career: Actress. Worked at a fast–food restaurant and at a golf course. Performed as a competitive figure skater as a child.

Awards, Honors: Drama award, c. 1995, for *I Live in a Little Town;* Genie Award nomination, best performance by an actress in a supporting role, Academy of Canadian Cinema and Television, 2002, for *Perfect Pie;* Gemini Award, best performance by an actress in a featured supporting role in a dramatic series, Academy of Canadian Cinema and Television, 2004, for *Slings and Arrows;* Teen Choice Award nomination, choice female breakout movie star, 2004, for *Mean Girls* and *The Notebook;* Teen Choice Award nominations, choice movie actress in a comedy, choice movie hissy fit, choice movie blush, and choice movie sleazebag, all 2004, MTV Movie awards, breakthrough female performance and best on–screen team (with others), and MTV Movie Award nomination, best villain, all 2005, all for *Mean Girls;* MTV Movie Award, best kiss (with Ryan Gosling) and MTV Movie Award nomination, best female performance, Teen Choice awards, choice movie actress in a drama, choice movie chemistry (with Gosling), choice movie love scene (with Gosling), and choice movie liplock (with Gosling), and Teen Choice Award nomination, choice movie dance scene (with Gosling), all 2005, for *The Notebook;* Golden Satellite Award nomination, outstanding actress in a supporting role in a comedy or musical, International Press Academy, 2005, for *The Family Stone;* ShoWest Award, supporting actress of the year, National Association of Theatre Owners, 2005; Hollywood Film Festival Award, breakthrough of the year, 2005; Saturn Award nomination, best actress, Academy of Science Fiction, Fantasy, and Horror Films, 2006, for *Red Eye;* Rising Star Award nomination, British Academy of Film and Television Arts, 2006.

CREDITS

Film Appearances:
Jessica, *The Hot Chick,* Buena Vista, 2002.
Patsy at the age of fifteen, *Perfect Pie* (also known as *La voie du destin*), Odeon Films, 2002.
Sally Garfield, *My Name Is Tanino,* Medusa Distribuzione, 2002.
Allie Hamilton, *The Notebook,* New Line Cinema, 2004.
Claire Cleary, *Wedding Crashers,* New Line Cinema, 2004.
Regina George, *Mean Girls* (also known as *Untitled "Queen Bees and Wannabees" Project*), Paramount, 2004.
Amy Stone, *The Family Stone,* Fox 2000 Pictures, 2005.
Lisa Reisert, *Red Eye,* DreamWorks, 2005.

Television Appearances; Series:
Kate McNab, *Slings and Arrows,* The Movie Network, beginning c. 2003.

Television Appearances; Movies:
Danielle, *Guilt by Association* (also known as *Coupable par amour*), Court TV, 2002.

Television Appearances; Specials:
Himself, *Reel Comedy: Wedding Crashers,* Comedy Central, 2005.

Television Appearances; Awards Presentations:
The 2005 MTV Movie Awards, MTV, 2005.
The 2005 Teen Choice Awards, Fox, 2005.

Television Appearances; Episodic:
Hannah Grant, "Food for Thought," *The Famous Jett Jackson,* The Disney Channel, 2001.
(As Rachel MacAdams) Christine Bickwell, "Atavus High," *Earth: Final Conflict* (also known as *EFC, Gene Roddenberry's "Battleground Earth," Gene Roddenberry's "Earth: Final Conflict," Invasion planete Terre,* and *Mission Erde: Sie sind unter uns*), syndicated, 2002.

Television Guest Appearances; Episodic:
Jimmy Kimmel Live, ABC, 2004.
"Wedding Crashers," *HBO First Look,* HBO, 2005.
Corazon de ... , Television Espanola (Spain), 2005.
Late Night with Conan O'Brien, NBC, 2005.
The Late Show with David Letterman (also known as *The Late Show*), NBC, 2005.
Live with Regis and Kelly, syndicated, 2005.
Total Request Live (also known as *TRL* and *Total Request with Carson Daly*), MTV, 2005.

Television Appearances; Pilots:
Appeared as Beth in *Shotgun Love Dolls,* MTV.

Stage Appearances:
I Live in a Little Town (one-act), Ontario Showcase of the Sears Drama Festival, Canada, c. 1995.
Child, *The Piper* (workshop), Necessary Angel Theatre Company, York University, Burton Auditorium, Toronto, Ontario, Canada, 2001.

Appeared in productions of the Original Kids Theatre, Canada.

RECORDINGS

Videos:
Herself, *"Mean Girls": Only the Strong Survive,* Paramount Home Video, 2004.

OTHER SOURCES

Periodicals:
Entertainment Weekly, June 18, 2004, pp. 52–53.
Interview, May, 2004, p. 66; July, 2005, pp. 54–59.
Maclean's, July 18, 2005, pp. 45–48.
Movieline's Hollywood Life, May, 2004, p. 20.
Newsweek, August 22, 2005, p. 77.
Parade, June 3, 2005, p. 18.
People Weekly, May 10, 2004, p. 31; July 12, 2004, p. 114; August 8, 2005, p. 112.

McAVOY, James 1979–

PERSONAL

Born 1979 (some sources cite January 1, 1979), in Scotstoun, Glasgow, Scotland; brother of Joy McAvoy (a singer). *Education:* Royal Scottish Academy of Music and Drama, graduated, 2000. *Avocational Interests:* Music and dance, boxing, fencing, rugby, other sports, The Lord of the Rings.

Addresses: *Agent*—Ruth Young, Peters Fraser & Dunlop, Drury House, 34–43 Russell St., London WC2B 5HA, England; Theresa Peters, William Morris Agency, One William Morris Place, Beverly Hills, CA 90212. *Manager*—Paul Coates, The Management Company, 2030 Pinehurst Rd., Los Angeles, CA 90068.

Career: Actor. Also a gymnast and acrobat. Worked as a baker.

Awards, Honors: British Comedy Award nomination, best television comedy newcomer, 2004, for *Shameless;* Audience Award, Edinburgh International Film Festival, 2004, for *Inside I'm Dancing;* Empire Award nomination, best newcomer, 2006, *The Chronicles of Narnia: The Lion, the Witch, and the Wardrobe;* Rising Star Award, British Academy of Film and Television Arts, 2006.

CREDITS

Film Appearances:
Kevin, *The Near Room,* Metrodome Distribution, 1995.
Local boy, *An Angel Passes by* (short film), c. 1996.
Anthony Balfour, *Regeneration* (also known as *Behind the Lines* and *Renaissance*), Alliance Communications, 1997.
Mike, *Swimming Pool—Der Tod feiert mit* (also known as *The Pool, The Swimming Pool,* and *Water Demon*), Senator Film, 2001, Artisan Entertainment, 2002.
Jay, *Bollywood Queen,* Redbus Film Distribution, 2002.
Carl Colt, *Wimbledon* (also known as *La plus belle victoire*), Universal, 2004.
Rory O'Shea, *Inside I'm Dancing* (also known as *Rory O'Shea Was Here*), Focus Features/Universal, 2004.

Simon Balcairn, *Bright Young Things,* ThinkFilm, 2004.

Hal in English version, *Strings,* Wellspring Media, 2005.

Mr. Tumnus, *The Chronicles of Narnia: The Lion, the Witch, and the Wardrobe,* Buena Vista, 2005.

Brian Jackson, *Starter for Ten,* Picturehouse, 2006.

Grey, *Significant Others* (also known as *My Mistress*), Wasted Talent, 2006.

Max, *Penelope,* Zephyr Films, 2006.

Nicholas Garrigan, *The Last King of Scotland,* Twentieth Century–Fox, 2006.

Tom Lefroy, *Becoming Jane,* Columbia/Miramax, 2006.

Josh Gilmore, *The Dead Wait,* Beyond Films/Rubicon Pictures, c. 2006.

Robert Ainsle, *Burns,* c. 2006.

Joe, *Twist of Fate,* 2007.

Television Appearances; Series:

Dan Foster, *State of Play,* BBC and BBC America, 2003.

Liam, *Early Doors,* BBC–2, 2003.

Steve, *Shameless,* Channel 4 (England), 2004–2005.

Television Appearances; Miniseries:

Sergeant Bloxham, *Lorna Doone,* BBC, 2000, Arts and Entertainment, 2001.

Private James Miller, *Band of Brothers,* HBO, 2001.

Josh Malfen, *White Teeth,* Channel 4 (England), 2002, broadcast on *Masterpiece Theatre* (also known as *ExxonMobil Masterpiece Theatre* and *Mobil Masterpiece Theatre*), PBS, 2003.

Leto Atreides II, *Children of Dune* (also known as *Frank Herbert's "Children of Dune," Dune—Bedrohung des Imperiums, Dune—Der Messias, Dune—Die Kinder des Wuestenplaneten,* and *Dune—Krieg um den Wuestenplaneten*), Sci–Fi Channel, 2003.

Television Appearances; Movies:

Joe Macbeth, *Macbeth,* BBC, 2005.

Television Appearances; Specials:

Steve, *Shameless Christmas Special,* Channel 4 (England), 2004.

Himself, *"T4" in Narnia,* Channel 4, 2005.

Television Appearances; Awards Presentations:

Himself, *The British Comedy Awards 2004,* Independent Television, 2004.

Himself, *Third Irish Film and Television Awards,* Radio Telefis Eireann (RTE, Ireland), 2005.

Television Appearances; Episodic:

Charlie, *Not Just Saturday,* Independent Television, 1996.

Martin Vosper, "Teacher," *Murder in Mind,* BBC, 2001.

Gowan Ross, "Payment in Blood," *The Inspector Lynley Mysteries* (also known as *The Inspector Lynley Mysteries: Payment in Blood* and *The Inspector Lynley Mysteries, Series 2*), BBC, 2002, broadcast on *Mystery!,* PBS, 2003.

Ray Pritchard, "The German Woman," *Foyle's War* (also known as *Foyle's War, Series I*), Independent Television, 2002, *Masterpiece Theatre* (also known as *ExxonMobil Masterpiece Theatre* and *Mobil Masterpiece Theatre*), PBS, 2003.

Guest, *Breakfast,* BBC, 2005.

Appeared as Gavin Donald in an episode of *The Bill.*

Stage Appearances:

Joe, *Lovers,* Royal Lyceum Theatre, Edinburgh, Scotland, 1999.

Gerald, *The Reel of the Hanged Man,* Traverse Theatre, Edinburgh, Scotland, 2000.

Mancunian Iggy, *Out in the Open,* Hampstead Theatre, London, 2001.

Private Steven Flowers, *Privates on Parade,* Donmar Warehouse Theatre, London, 2001–2002.

Ben, *Breathing Corpses,* Royal Court Theatre, Jerwood Theatre Upstairs, London, 2005.

Appeared as Romeo, *Romeo and Juliet,* and as Riff, *West Side Story* (musical), both Courtyard Theatre, Hereford, England. Appeared as Bobby Buckfast, *Beauty and the Beast,* Adam Smith Theatre, Kirkcaldy, Scotland; and as Ferdinand, *The Tempest,* Brunton Theatre Company.

OTHER SOURCES

Periodicals:

Big Issue, October 18, 2004, pp. 15–16.

Glasgow Herald, September 20, 2004.

Independent, January 28, 2004.

Irish Times, October 12, 2004.

Observer, December 5, 2004.

Radio Times, November 12, 2005, pp. 8–9.

Scotsman, September 18, 2004.

Sunday Herald, September 12, 2004.

McDERMOTT, Shiva Rose 1969(?)– (Shiva Rose McDerott, Shiva Rose)

PERSONAL

Original name, Shiva Gharibafshar; born c. 1969; daughter of Parviz Gharibafshar (a television host); married Dylan McDermott (an actor), November 19, 1995; children: Colette, Charlotte Rose. *Education:* University of California, Los Angeles, B.A., theatre and world arts;

attended California State University, Northridge. *Avocational Interests:* Charity work.

Addresses: *Manager*—Envoy Entertainment, 1640 S. Sepulveda Blvd., Suite 530, Los Angeles, CA 90025.

Career: Actress. Previously worked for Betsey Johnson (a clothing boutique), Los Angeles, CA. Resource (program that feeds the homeless), founding member, Los Angeles, CA; active in Amnesty International. Sometimes credited as Shiva Rose McDerott.

CREDITS

Film Appearances:
(As Shiva Rose) Sally Mae, *How to Get Laid at the End of the World,* 1999.
(As Shiva Rose) Gwen, *Black Days,* 2001.
(As Shiva Rose) Lola, *13 Moons,* Lot 47 Films, 2002.
(As Shiva Rose) Terri, *The First $20 Million Is Always the Hardest,* Twentieth Century–Fox, 2002.
Evie, *Red Roses and Petrol,* 2003.
Snow White, *DysEnchanted* (short film), 2004.
Toni, *Myron's Movie,* 2004.
Yvette, *Woman at the Beach* (short film), 2004.
(As Shiva Rose) Red, *Prospect,* 2004.
Layla, *David & Layla,* 2005.

Television Appearances; Movies:
(As Shiva Rose) Toot's girl, *61** (also known as *61*), HBO, 2001.

Television Appearances; Episodic:
(As Shiva Rose) Sally Bader, "The Battlefield," *The Practice,* ABC, 1998.
(As Shiva Rose) Reporter girlfriend, "The Race," *Gideon's Crossing,* ABC, 2000.
Irina Maldova, "Rush to Judgment," *The Division* (also known as *Heart of the City*), Lifetime, 2003.

Stage Appearances:
Hennie, *Awake and Sing,* Berkshire Theatre Festival, Stockbridge, MA, 2001.
Nurse, *The Talking Cure,* Mark Taper Forum, Los Angeles, 2004.

Also appeared as Alexandra, *The Swan,* Pacific Resident Theatre; Saida, *Necessary Targets,* Helen Hayes Theatre, New York City.

OTHER SOURCES

Periodicals:
Child, April, 2006.
InStyle, February, 2000.

McGAVIN, Darren 1922–2006

PERSONAL

Born May 7, 1922, in Spokane, WA; died February 25, 2006, in Los Angeles, CA. Actor, director, producer, and writer. McGavin appeared in a number of television series and plays, but he was best known for his role as Ralphie's father in *A Christmas Story,* the 1983 comedy that became a holiday favorite. McGavin worked as a painter of movie sets before pursuing acting. He made his stage debut in 1941 in *Lady Windermere's Fan* and continued to work regularly in theatre through the 1940s, 1950s, and 1960s. McGavin toured in *Death of a Salesman* in the late 1940s and in *The Music Man* in 1962, among others. Additionally, McGavin directed and produced plays. McGavin made his film debut in 1945 in *A Song to Remember* and appeared in dozens of films, including *Summertime,* the James Bond film *The Man with the Golden Arm,* and *Airport '77.* He also produced and directed *Happy Mother's Day—Love, George* and directed and wrote *American Reunion.* McGavin made his mark in television as well and starred in numerous series, performing the title role in the detective show *Mike Hammer* and the title role of Chicago reporter Carl Kolchak in *Kolchak: The Night Stalker.* Among McGavin's television movie appearances were *The Berlin Affair, Ike: The War Years,* and *The Return of Marcus Welby, M.D.* McGavin won an Emmy Award in 1990 for his portrayal of the title character's father in an episode of the series *Murphy Brown.*

PERIODICALS

Broadcasting & Cable, March 6, 2006.

McGUIRE, Mickey
See ROONEY, Mickey

MILLER, Sienna 1981(?)–
(Sienna Rose Miller, Sienna Rose)

PERSONAL

Full name, Sienna Rose Miller; born December 28, 1981 (some sources say 1982), in New York, NY; daughter of Ed (a banker) and Josephine (a drama school teacher and manager) Miller. *Education:* Studied acting at the Lee Strasberg Institute, 2000, and with Michael Margotta.

Addresses: *Agent*—Endeavor, 9601 Wilshire Blvd., 6th Floor, Beverly Hills, CA 90212; Peters Fraser & Dunlop, Drury House, 34–43 Russell St., London WC2B 5HA, England; Special Artists Agency, 9465 Wilshire Blvd., Suite 890, Beverly Hills, CA 90212.

Career: Actress. Previously worked as a model.

Awards, Honors: Teen Choice Award nomination, choice TV breakout star—female, 2003, for *Keen Eddie;* Empire Award nomination, best newcomer, 2005, for *Alfie* and *Layer Cake.*

CREDITS

Film Appearances:
(As Sienna Rose) Sharon, *South Kensington,* 2001.
Savannah, *High Speed,* 2002.
Sara, *The Ride* (also known as *Joy–Rider*), MediaTrade, 2002.
Tammy, *Layer Cake,* Sony Pictures Entertainment, 2004.
Nikki, *Alfie,* Paramount, 2004.
Francesca Bruni, *Casanova,* Buena Vista, 2005.
Edie Sedgwick, *Factory Girl,* Weinstein Company, 2006.
Camille Foster, *Camille,* 2006.

Television Appearances; Series:
Stacey, *Bedtime,* BBC1, 2002.
Fiona Bickerton, *Keen Eddie,* Fox, 2003.

Television Appearances; Episodic:
(As Sienna Rose Miller) Babe, "Long live the King," *The American Embassy,* Fox, 2002.
Herself, *Late Night with Conan O'Brien,* NBC, 2003.
Herself, *GMTV,* 2005.
Herself, *Corazon de ... ,* 2005.
Herself, *Live with Regis and Kelly,* syndicated, 2005.
Herself, *The Tonight Show with Jay Leno,* NBC, 2005.
Herself, *The Early Show* (also known as *The Saturday Early Show*), CBS, 2005.

Stage Appearances:
(West End debut) Celia, *As You Like It,* Wyndham Theatre, London, 2005.

Also appeared in *Cigarettes and Chocolate,* as Striker *The Striker,* and as Lady Sneerwell, *A School for Scandal,* all New York City; Sherry, *Independence,* Neighborhood Playhouse, New York City.

OTHER SOURCES

Periodicals:
People Weekly, January 24, 2005, p. 71; August 1, 2005, p. 58; August 8, 2005, p. 56.

MILLER, Troy
   (Troy T. Miller, Wilson Thomas)

PERSONAL

Addresses: *Office*—Dakota Films, 1040 North Las Palmas, Hollywood, CA 90038; Dakota North Entertainment, 4633 Lankershim Blvd., North Hollywood, CA 91602. *Agent*—Endeavor, 9601 Wilshire Blvd., Sixth Floor, Beverly Hills, CA 90212. *Manager*—Brillstein–Grey Entertainment, 9150 Wilshire Blvd., Suite 350, Beverly Hills, CA 90212.

Career: Producer, director, and writer. Dakota Films (also known as Dakota Pictures), Hollywood, CA, staff producer, writer, and director; Dakota North Entertainment, North Hollywood, CA, partner; also affiliated with the production company 18Husky.

Awards, Honors: Emmy Award nomination (with others), outstanding multicamera picture editing for a miniseries, movie, or special, 2004, for *The 76th Annual Academy Awards;* some sources also cite additional Emmy awards as well as several Annual CableACE Award nominations from the National Cable Television Association.

CREDITS

Television Work; Series:
Production assistant, *Fridays,* ABC, 1980–82.
First assistant director and location supervisor, *Not Necessarily the News,* HBO, c. 1983–90.
Executive in charge of production, *Pee–Wee's Playhouse,* CBS, 1986–91.
Executive in charge of production, *Top of the Pops,* CBS, 1987–88.
Associate producer, *Out of This World,* NBC and syndicated, 1987–90.
Director and producer, *Beach Boys: Endless Summer,* syndicated, beginning 1988.
Producer, *Hit Squad,* syndicated, beginning 1988.
Producer, *Comic Strip Live* (also known as *Comic Strip Prime Time*), Fox, c. 1989–91.
Producer, *The Super Mario Bros. Super Show!* (animated and live action; also known as *Club Mario*), syndicated, 1989–91.

Director and producer, *Unplugged* (also known as *MTV Unplugged*), MTV, beginning 1989.

Producer, *On the Television,* Nickelodeon, beginning 1990.

Director and producer, *The Sunday Comics,* Fox, 1991–92.

Producer and second unit director, *Arresting Behavior,* ABC, 1992.

Director and producer, *Mr. Show with Bob and David* (also known as *Mr. Show*), HBO, 1995–98.

Director and producer, *Saturday Night Special,* Fox, 1996.

Director and producer, *The Big Scary Movie Show,* Sci–Fi Channel, beginning 1996.

Director and producer, *The Bill Bellamy Show,* MTV, beginning 1996.

Director and producer, *HBO Comedy Half–Hour,* HBO, 1997–98.

Director of main title sequence, *Save Our Streets* (also known as *SOS in America*), NBC and syndicated, beginning 1997.

Executive producer and director, *The Best Commercials You've Never Seen* (series of specials; also known as *The Best Commercials You've Never Seen (and Some You Have)*), ABC, beginning 1998.

Executive producer, *Tenacious D,* HBO, 1999.

Creator and executive producer, *Viva la Bam,* MTV, beginning 2003.

Executive producer, *Reel Comedy* (series of specials), Comedy Central, beginning 2003.

Creative consultant, *The Showbiz Show with David Spade,* Comedy Central, 2005—.

Television Work; Movies:

Director, "Beverly Hills Family Robinson," *The Wonderful World of Disney,* ABC, 1998.

Executive producer and director, *Sorority,* MTV, 1999.

Producer, *Knee High P.I.,* Comedy Central, 2003.

Television Work; Specials:

Associate producer, *Harry Anderson's "Hello Sucker,"* Showtime, 1986.

Associate producer, *Robin Williams—An Evening at the Met,* HBO, 1986.

Associate producer, *Vanishing America* (also known as *Rich Hall's "Vanishing America"*), Showtime, 1986.

(As Troy T. Miller) Associate producer and line producer, *George Carlin: Playin' with Your Head,* 1986.

Director and line producer, *Don Rickles: Rickles on the Loose,* Showtime, 1986.

Line producer, *Young Comedians All–Star Reunion,* HBO, 1986.

Producer, *Mystery Magical Special* (also known as *Marc Summers' "Mystery Magical Special"*), Nickelodeon, 1986.

Executive in charge of production, *Pee–Wee's Playhouse Christmas Special,* CBS, 1988.

Executive in charge of production, *Madonna—Live! Blond Ambition World Tour* (also known as *Madonna: Blond Ambition World Tour Live*), HBO, 1990.

Producer, *World's Greatest Magicians ... at the Magic Castle* (also known as *Magic at the Magic Castle*), 1990.

Producer and first assistant director, *Tales from the Whoop: Hot Rod Brown Class Clown* (also known as *Hot Rod Brown, Class Clown*), Nickelodeon, 1990.

Supervising producer, *Life as We Know It!,* Comedy Central, 1991.

Supervising producer, *Public Enemy #2* (also known as *Public Enemy Number 2*), Showtime, 1991.

Director and producer, *Friends and Lovers,* NBC, 1994.

Director and producer, *Sports Illustrated Swimsuit '94: The 30th Anniversary Special,* ABC, 1994.

Director and producer, *Mr. Show with Bob and David: Fantastic Newness* (also known as *The Best of Mr. Show: Fantastic Newness* and *Fantastic Newness*), 1996.

Executive producer and director, *Mr. Show and the Incredible, Fantastical News Report* (also known as *The Best of Mr. Show: The Incredible, Fantastical News Report*), 1998.

Director and producer, *David Cross: The Pride Is Back,* HBO, 1999.

Executive producer, *Celebrity Weddings: InStyle,* Lifetime, 1999.

Executive producer, *The 21 Hottest Stars under 21,* ABC, 1999.

Executive producer and director, *The Television Show with John Henson,* ABC, 1999.

Executive producer and director, *Sleepover with Bob,* 1999.

Postproduction audio worker, *Tarzan in Concert with Phil Collins,* ABC, 1999.

Executive producer and director, *Super Nerds,* 2000.

Executive producer and director, *The 25 Hottest Stars under 25,* ABC, 2000.

Executive producer, *The 20 Teens Who Will Change the World,* The WB, 2001.

Director, *Reel Comedy: Stuck on You,* Comedy Central, 2002.

Executive producer and director, *David Blaine: Vertigo,* ABC, 2002.

Executive producer and director, *20: Entertainment Weekly's Best Holiday Movies,* 2004.

Executive producer and director, *20: Entertainment Weekly's Scariest Movies,* 2004.

Executive producer and director, *Celebrity Autobiography: In Their Own Words,* Bravo, 2005.

Executive producer and director, *EW's Guide: Guilty Pleasures,* 2005.

Television Work; Film Clips for Awards Presentations:

Director, *1993 MTV Movie Awards,* MTV, 1993.

Director, *1995 MTV Movie Awards,* MTV, 1995.

Director, *1996 MTV Movie Awards,* MTV, 1996.
Director of "The Designer" segment, *The VH1 Fashion Awards,* VH1, 1996.
Director, *1997 MTV Movie Awards,* MTV, 1997.
The 69th Annual Academy Awards, ABC, 1997.
Producer, *The 70th Annual Academy Awards,* ABC, 1998.
Director, *1999 MTV Movie Awards,* MTV, 1999.
"Creative Arts" montage, *The 49th Annual Primetime Emmy Awards,* CBS, 1999.
Director, *The 72nd Annual Academy Awards,* ABC, 2000.
Director, producer, and editor, *The 76th Annual Academy Awards,* ABC, 2004.

Television Director; Episodic:
"Greatest Song in the World," *Tenacious D,* HBO, 1999.
"The Road Gig," *Tenacious D,* HBO, 1999.

Director of episodes of *The Ben Stiller Show,* Fox; *Greg the Bunny,* Fox; *The Jenny McCarthy Show,* MTV; *The Real World* (also known as *MTV Real World...*), MTV; *Running the Halls,* NBC; and *Weird Science,* USA Network. Director of episodes of *Emerald Cove,* a series broadcast on *MMC* (also known as *The All New Mickey Mouse Club, Club MMC,* and *The Mickey Mouse Club*), The Disney Channel.

Television Work; Pilots:
Director and line producer (some sources cite associate producer), *The Noel Edmonds Show,* ABC, 1986.
Director and supervising producer, *SK8 TV* (also known as *Skate TV*), Nickelodeon, 1990.
Executive producer and director, *Deadline Now,* Fox, 1997.
Director, *American Adventure* (also known as *National Lampoon's "American Adventure"*), Fox, 2000.
Director and producer, *Battle of the Sitcoms,* Fox, 2000.
Executive producer, *The Near Future,* HBO, 2000.
Director, *Criminal Mastermind,* ABC, 2001.
Executive producer, *Contact: Talking to the Dead,* ABC, 2002.
Executive producer, *The Lemur,* Comedy Central, 2002.

Worked on other pilots.

Television Work; Other:
Producer, *Almost Vegas,* MTV, 1990.
Director, *Best Defense,* CBS, 1994.
Executive producer and director, *Big News,* 1995.
Producer, *The Big Day,* 1995.
Executive producer, *The Guys* (also known as *National Lampoon's "The Guys"*), 1996.

Film Director:
Break on through with JFK (short film), Dakota North Entertainment, 1998.
Jack Frost (also known as *Frost*), Warner Bros., 1998.

The Announcement, BBC Films, 2000.
Run Ronnie Run (also known as *Run Ronnie Run! The Ronnie Dobbs Story: A Mr. Show Movie*), New Line Cinema, 2002.
Dumb and Dumberer: When Harry Met Lloyd (also known as *Dumb & Dumberer, Dumb & Dumbest, Dumb & Dumber 2,* and *When Harry Met Lloyd: Dumb and Dumberer*), New Line Cinema, 2003.

Director of several short films.

Film Producer:
Break on through with JFK (short film), Dakota North Entertainment, 1998.
The Announcement, BBC Films, 2000.
Run Ronnie Run (also known as *Run Ronnie Run! The Ronnie Dobbs Story: A Mr. Show Movie*), New Line Cinema, 2002.
Dumb and Dumberer: When Harry Met Lloyd (also known as *Dumb & Dumberer, Dumb & Dumbest, Dumb & Dumber 2,* and *When Harry Met Lloyd: Dumb and Dumberer*), New Line Cinema, 2003.

Film Work; Other:
(As Wilson Thomas) Camera operator, *The Announcement,* BBC Films, 2000.

Some sources credit Miller as a technical advisor for the film *Modern Love,* Triumph Releasing, 1990.

RECORDINGS

Videos:
Director and producer, *Sports Illustrated 1994 Swimsuit Issue Video,* Dakota North Entertainment/WarnerVision Films, 1994.
Director, *Tenacious D: The Complete Masterworks,* Sony Music Entertainment, 2003.

Music Video Director:
Chris Rock, "Champagne," 1997.

WRITINGS

Teleplays; Series:
(Uncredited) *The Sunday Comics,* Fox, 1991–92.

Teleplays; Specials:
(As Wilson Thomas) *The Best Commercials You've Never Seen* (series of specials; also known as *The Best Commercials You've Never Seen (and Some You Have)*), ABC, 1998.

(Uncredited) *The Television Show with John Henson,* ABC, 1999.

(As Thomas) *The 21 Hottest Stars under 21,* ABC, 1999.

(As Thomas) *The 20 Teens Who Will Change the World,* The WB, 2001.

(Uncredited) *David Blaine: Vertigo,* ABC, 2002.

20: Entertainment Weekly's Best Holiday Movies, 2004.

20: Entertainment Weekly's Scariest Movies, 2004.

EW's Guide: Guilty Pleasures, 2005.

Teleplays; Pilots:

(As Wilson Thomas) *Contact: Talking to the Dead,* ABC, 2002.

Screenplays:

Dumb and Dumberer: When Harry Met Lloyd (also known as *Dumb & Dumberer, Dumb & Dumbest, Dumb & Dumber 2,* and *When Harry Met Lloyd: Dumb and Dumberer*), New Line Cinema, 2003.

Videos:

(Uncredited) *Sports Illustrated 1994 Swimsuit Issue Video,* Dakota North Entertainment/WarnerVision Films, 1994.

OTHER SOURCES

Electronic:

Dakota Films, http://dakotafilms.com, January 18, 2006.

MILLER, Wentworth 1972–

PERSONAL

Full name, Wentworth E. Miller III; born June 2, 1972, in Chipping Norton, Oxfordshire, England; son of Wentworth E. II (a lawyer and teacher) and Roxann (a special education teacher) Miller. *Education:* Princeton University, B.A., English, 1995.

Addresses: *Agent*—Endeavor, 9601 Wilshire Blvd., 6th Floor, Beverly Hills, CA 90212. *Manager*—Management 360, 9111 Wilshire Blvd., Beverly Hills, CA 90210. *Publicist*—PMK/HBH Public Relations, 700 San Vicente Blvd., Suite G910, West Hollywood, CA 90069.

Career: Actor. Toured with the Princeton Tigertones (an a capella group); previously worked as an office temp, a production associate, and a script reader.

Awards, Honors: Black Reel Award nominations, film: best actor and film: best breakthrough performance, 2004, both for *The Human Stain;* Golden Globe Award nomination, best performance by an actor in a television series—drama, Saturn Award nomination, best actor on television, Academy of Science Fiction, Fantasy & Horror Films, 2006, both for *Prison Break.*

CREDITS

Film Appearances:

Paris, *Romeo and Juliet,* 2000.

Young Coleman Silk, *The Human Stain* (also known as *Der Menschliche Makel* and *La couleur du mensonge*), Miramax, 2003.

Dr. Adam Lockwood, *Underworld,* Screen Gems, 2003.

Voice of EDI, *Stealth,* Columbia, 2005.

Television Appearances; Series:

Michael Scofield, *Prison Break,* Fox, 2005—.

Television Appearances; Miniseries:

David Scott, *Dinotopia,* NBC, 2002.

Television Appearances; Specials:

Server #1, *Room 302* (short film), Showtime, 2001.

David Scott, *Evolution: The Making of "Dinotopia,"* 2002.

David Scott, *Witness from Dinotopia,* 2002.

David Scott, *Discovering Dinotopia,* 2002.

Television Appearances; Pilots:

Paul Adams, *Ghost Whisperer,* CBS, 2005.

Michael Scofield, *Prison Break,* Fox, 2005.

Television Appearances; Episodic:

Gage Petronzi, "Go Fish," *Buffy, the Vampire Slayer* (also known as *BtVS, Buffy,* and *Buffy the Vampire Slayer: The Series*), The WB, 1998.

Nelson, "The Time the Truth Was Told," *Time of Your Life,* Fox, 1999.

Nelson, "The Time They Got E-Rotic," *Time of Your Life,* Fox, 2000.

Mike Palmieri, "Homecoming," *ER,* NBC, 2000.

Adam Rothchild Ryan, "All about Adam," *Popular,* The WB, 2000.

Adam Rothchild Ryan, "Ch–Ch–Changes," *Popular,* The WB, 2000.

Himself, *The Sharon Osbourne Show* (also known as *Sharon*), syndicated, 2003.

Himself, *The Tonight Show with Jay Leno,* NBC, 2005.

Ryan Hunter, "Common Thread," *Joan of Arcadia,* CBS, 2005.

Ryan Hunter, "Something Wicked This Way Comes," *Joan of Arcadia,* CBS, 2005.

RECORDINGS

Music Videos:

Appeared in Mariah Carey's "It's Like That" and "We Belong Together," both 2005.

OTHER SOURCES

Periodicals:
Hollywood Reporter, December 12, 2005.
Interview, February, 2005, p. 104.

MILOS, Sofia
  (Sophia Milos)

PERSONAL

Born September 27, in Zurich, Switzerland. *Education:* Attended the School of Business and Economics, Switzerland; studied acting at the Beverly Hills Playhouse. *Avocational Interests:* Painting, cooking, reading, and spiritual study.

Addresses: *Agent*—The Chasin Agency, 8899 Beverly Blvd., Suite 716, Los Angeles, CA 90048. *Manager*—Evolution Entertainment, 901 North Highland Ave., Los Angeles, CA 90038.

Career: Actress. Also worked as a model.

CREDITS

Film Appearances:
Kristin, *Out of Control* (also known as *Over the Line*), 1992.
Young Sophia, *Jane Austen's "Mafia!"* (also known as *Mafia!*), Buena Vista, 1998.
Woman in airport, *Svitati* (also known as *Screw Loose*), Columbia TriStar Home Video, 1999.
Sarah Putanesca, *Family Jewels* (also known as *Pride & Peril*), 2000.
Cheryl, *The Ladies Man* (also known as *The Ladies' Man*), Paramount, 2000.
(As Sophia Milos) Carmela Krailes, *Double Bang,* New City Releasing, 2001.
Lieutenant Dalia Barr, *The Order* (also known as *Jihad Warrior*), TriStar, 2001.
Celia Amonte, *Passionada,* Samuel Goldwyn Films, 2002.
Boss, *The Cross,* 2002.

Television Appearances; Series:
Fabiana Borelli, *Cafe Americain,* NBC, 1993–94.
Julia Karinsky, *Caroline in the City* (also known as *Caroline*), NBC, 1997–98.
Maria, *The Secret Lives of Men,* ABC, 1998.
Detective Yelena Salas, *CSI: Miami,* CBS, 2003–2005.

Television Appearances; Movies:
Barbara Steel, *Lo zio d'America,* 2002.
Part Time, 2004.

Television Appearances; Specials:
Matya, *Shadow–Ops,* UPN 1995.

Television Appearances; Pilots:
Paulie, *Thieves,* ABC, 2001.
Detective Yelena Salas, "MIA/NYC—NonStop," *CSI: NY,* CBS, 2004.

Television Appearances; Episodic:
Aurora, "The One with the Butt," *Friends,* NBC, 1994.
Stella, "Sweet Denial," *Platypus Man,* UPN, 1995.
Gale Heathe, "Lock and Load, Babe," *Vanishing Son,* syndicated, 1995.
Ali, "Earth Boys Are Easy," *Weird Science,* USA Network, 1995.
Jill, "The Box," *Strange Luck,* Fox, 1995.
Sarah, "The Award," *Mad about You,* NBC, 1996.
Julie, *Life with Roger,* The WB, 1996.
Dr. Angela Lopez, "The Doctor Is In," *Getting Personal,* Fox, 1998.
Marisol, "Dust, Lust, Destiny," *The Love Boat: The Next Wave,* UPN, 1998.
Annalisa Zucca, "Commendatori," *The Sopranos,* HBO, 2000.
Annalisa, "Funhouse," *The Sopranos,* HBO, 2000.
Sofia, "The Pants Tent," *Curb Your Enthusiasm,* HBO, 2000.
(As Sophia Milos) Richard's girlfriend, "Affirmative Action," *Curb Your Enthusiasm,* HBO, 2000.
Paulie, "The Long Con," *Thieves,* ABC, 2001.
Francesca, "Future Trade," *The Twilight Zone,* UPN, 2002.
Coco, "A Little Help from My Friends," *ER,* NBC, 2003.
Herself, *The Late Late Show with Craig Kilborn* (also known as *The Late Late Show*), CBS, 2003.
Herself, *Extra* (also known as *Extra: The Entertainment Magazine*), syndicated, 2003.
Herself, *The Sharon Osbourne Show* (also known as *Sharon*), syndicated, 2004.
Herself, "Fights of Fancy," *My Crazy Life,* E! Entertainment Television, 2005.
Richard's girlfriend, "The End," *Curb Your Enthusiasm,* HBO, 2005.

Also appeared in "Foreign Affair," *Too Something* (also known as *New York Daze*), Fox.

RECORDINGS

Video Games:
Voice of Miami Dade Police Department Homicide/Robbery Detective Yelena Salas, *CSI: Miami,* UBI Soft Entertainment, 2004.

MITCHELL, Daryl 1969–
(Chill, Daryl "Chill" Mitchell, Daryl M. Mitchell)

PERSONAL

Born July 16, 1969, in the Bronx, New York, NY; raised in Wyandanch, NY; father, a truck and bus driver; mother, a secretary; married Carol (a homemaker), 1998; children: Kamari, Desmin, Justin.

Addresses: *Agent*—William Morris Agency, One William Morris Place, Beverly Hills, CA 90212.

Career: Actor and musician. Performer with Groove B. Chill (hip–hop musical group), 1980s. All for Wheels (nonprofit organization), founder and public speaker; Daryl Mitchell Foundation (organization promoting awareness about spinal cord injuries), founder; Christopher Reeve Foundation, minority outreach spokesperson.

Awards, Honors: Image Award nomination, outstanding supporting actor in a comedy series, National Association for the Advancement of Colored People, 1996, for *The John Larroquette Show.*

CREDITS

Television Appearances; Series:
(As Daryl "Chill" Mitchell) T, *Here and Now,* NBC, 1992–93.
(As Daryl "Chill" Mitchell) Dexter Walker, *The John Larroquette Show* (also known as *Larroquette*), NBC, 1993–96.
Leo Michaels, *Veronica's Closet,* NBC, 1997–2000.
Eli Goggins, *Ed* (also known as *Stuckeyville*), 2002–2004.

Television Appearances; Miniseries:
(As Daryl "Chill" Mitchell) Older Abner, *Queen* (also known as *Alex Haley's "Queen"*), CBS, 1993.
Himself, *I Love the '80s: 3D,* VH1, 2005.

Television Appearances; Movies:
Dean "The Dream" Memminger, *Rebound: The Legend of Earl "The Goat" Manigault* (also known as *Rebound*), HBO, 1996.
Raul, "Toothless," *The Wonderful World of Disney,* ABC, 1997.
Voice of Moocher, "The Pooch and the Pauper," *The Wonderful World of Disney,* ABC, 2000.

Television Appearances; Specials:
"The First Commandment," *Cosmic Slop,* HBO, 1994.
(As Daryl "Chill" Mitchell) Himself, *Made You Look: Top 25 Moments of BET History,* Black Entertainment Television, 2005.

Television Appearances; Episodic:
Man in club, "Clair's Case," *The Cosby Show,* CBS, 1985.
(As Chill) Old Head, "Warning—A Double Lit Candle Can Cause a Meltdown," *The Cosby Show,* CBS, 1991.
Reginald Beggs, "The Fertile Fields," *Law & Order* (also known as *Law & Order Prime*), NBC, 1992.
(As Daryl "Chill" Mitchell) Chill, "The Philadelphia Story," *The Fresh Prince of Bel–Air,* NBC, 1994.
Macho militant man, "Home Again," *In the House,* NBC, 1996.
Mike, "Lucas Platonicus," *Cosby,* CBS, 1996.
Guest, *Politically Incorrect with Bill Maher* (also known as *Politically Incorrect*), ABC, 1998.
(As Daryl "Chill" Mitchell) "Comedians Number Three Special," *Weakest Link* (also known as *The Weakest Link USA*), NBC, 2001.
Player in wheelchair, "Mad Hops," *Law & Order: Criminal Intent* (also known as *Law & Order: CI*), NBC, 2004.
(As Daryl "Chill" Mitchell) Guest host, *The Late Late Show with Craig Kilborn* (also known as *The Late Late Show*), CBS, 2004.
The Wayne Brady Show, syndicated, 2004.
(As Daryl "Chill" Mitchell) Damien, "Wheeling and Dealing," *Eve* (also known as *Opposite Sex*), UPN, 2005.

Television Appearances; Pilots:
(As Daryl "Chill" Mitchell) T, *Here and Now,* NBC, 1992.
(As Daryl "Chill" Mitchell) Dexter Walker, *The John Larroquette Show* (also known as *Larroquette*), NBC, 1993.
Leo Michaels, *Veronica's Closet,* NBC, 1997.

Appeared as Leo Michaels in the unaired pilot of *Veronica's Closet.* Some sources cite an appearance in *Man in the Kitchen.*

Television Producer; Pilots:
Producer of pilots.

Film Appearances:
Chill, *House Party,* New Line Cinema, 1990.
(As Daryl M. Mitchell) *House Party 2,* New Line Cinema, 1991.
(As Daryl "Chill" Mitchell) Street photographer, *Boomerang,* Paramount, 1992.
Kayam, *Fly by Night,* Arrow Releasing, 1993.

Private first class Wally Holbrook, *Sgt. Bilko* (also known as *Sergeant Bilko*), Universal, 1996.

(As Daryl M. Mitchell) *A Thin Line between Love and Hate,* New Line Cinema, 1996.

White Lies, Buena Vista, 1996.

Angel, *The Way We Are* (also known as *Quiet Days in Hollywood*), Warner Bros., 1997.

(As Daryl "Chill" Mitchell) Roy, *Home Fries,* Warner Bros., 1998.

(As Daryl "Chill" Mitchell) Mr. Morgan, *10 Things I Hate about You,* Buena Vista, 1999.

Tommy Webber/Lieutenant Laredo, *Galaxy Quest,* DreamWorks, 1999.

Detective Chambers, *Lucky Numbers* (also known as *Numbers* and *Le bon numero*), Paramount, 2000.

Steve, *Black Knight,* Twentieth Century–Fox, 2001.

Lenny, *13 Moons,* Lot 47 Films, 2002.

(As Daryl "Chill" Mitchell) Officer Hamm, *The Country Bears,* Buena Vista, 2002.

Himself, *Nobody Wants Your Film* (documentary), 2005.

Mobile command officer Rourke, *Inside Man,* Universal, 2006.

Film Work:

Some sources cite work as a grip intern for *Kalifornia,* Gramercy Pictures, 1993.

Stage Appearances:

Alexander, *The Day the Bronx Died,* Long Wharf Theatre, New Haven, CT, 1991–92.

RECORDINGS

Albums; with Groove B. Chill:

Various artists, *Uptown Is Kickin' It,* Uptown/MCA, 1986.

Starting from Zero, A&M, 1990.

Various artists, *New Jack Swing Mastercuts Volume 2,* Mastercuts, 1992.

Prince Paul and various artists, *Hip Hop Gold Dust,* Antidote, 2005.

Singles; with Groove B. Chill:

"Why Me" (recording also includes "Bass Game" by Finesse & Synquis), MCA, 1986.

"Starting from Zero," 1990.

"Swingin' Single," A & M, 1990.

Music Videos:

(With Groove B. Chill) "Starting from Zero," 1990.

WRITINGS

Albums; with Groove B. Chill:

Starting from Zero, A&M, 1990.

Material with Groove B. Chill appeared in various recordings.

Singles; with Groove B. Chill:

"Why Me" (recording also includes "Bass Game" by Finesse & Synquis), MCA, 1986.

"Starting from Zero," 1990.

"Swingin' Single," A & M, 1990.

OTHER SOURCES

Books:

Who's Who among African Americans, 18th edition, Gale, 2005.

Periodicals:

Movieline, June, 1996, p. 81.

Parade, October 5, 2003, p. 26.

People Weekly, July 29, 2002, p. 89.

MOLLEN, Jenny 1979–

PERSONAL

Born May 30, 1979, in Phoenix, AZ.

Addresses: *Manager*—Leverage Management, 3030 Pennsylvania Ave., Santa Monica, CA 90404.

Career: Actress.

CREDITS

Film Appearances:

Ashley, *Billy Makes the Cut,* The Entourage, 2003.

Grace Robin, *Searching for Haizmann,* Centre Communications, 2003.

German D.E.B., *D.E.B.S.,* Samuel Goldwyn, 2004.

Lenna, *The Raven,* Lointerscope, 2004.

Jenny, *Return to the Living Dead 5: Rave to the Grave,* Denholm, 2005.

Marina Del, *Cattle Call* (also known as *National Lampoon's "Cattle Call"*), Showcase, 2005.

Wendy, *Fear Itself,* 2005.

Wendy, *Ring Around the Rosie* (video), Sony, 2006.

Television Appearances; Episodic:

18 Wheels of Justice, The Nashville Network, 2000.

Blonde, "Black 'n' Flu," *Strong Medicine,* 2001.

Nina Ash, "Unleashed," *Angel,* 2003.

Nina Ash, "Smile Time," *Angel,* 2004.
Nina Ash, "Power Play," *Angel,* 2004.
Lydia Kane, "Method to His Madness," *Medium,* 2005.

MOMOA, Jason 1979–

PERSONAL

Birth name Joseph Jason Namakaeha Momoa; born August 1, 1979, in Honolulu, HI; engaged to Simmone McKinnon, 2004.

Addresses: *Agent*—Agency for the Performing Arts, 9200 Sunset Blvd., Suite 900, Los Angeles, CA 90069.

Career: Actor.

CREDITS

Television Appearances; Series:
Jason Ioane, *Baywatch* (also known as *Baywatch Hawai'i* and *Baywatch Hawaii*), syndicated, 1999–2001.
Frankie Seau, *North Shore,* 2004.
Ronon Dex, *Stargate: Atlantis,* 2005—.

Television Appearances; Movies:
Jason Ioane, *Baywatch: Hawaiian Wedding,* 2003.
Kala, *Tempted* (also known as *Returning Lily* and *A Mother's Choice*), 2003.

Film Appearances:
Navarro, *Johnson Family Vacation,* Twentieth Century–Fox, 2004.

OTHER SOURCES

Periodicals:
TV Zone Special, July, 2005, pp. 70–72.

MOMSEN, Taylor 1993–

PERSONAL

Born July 26, 1993, in St. Louis, MO; daughter of Michael and Colette Momsen. *Avocational Interests:* Cinema, song and dance, soccer.

Addresses: *Agent*—Cunningham/Escott/Slevin & Doherty Talent Agency, 10635 Santa Monica Blvd., Suite 140, Los Angeles, CA 90025. *Manager*—The Collective, 9100 Wilshire Blvd., Suite 700 West, Beverly Hills, CA 90212.

Career: Actress. Helps the Humane Society and the Miracle Network Telethon benefitting children's hospitals.

Awards, Honors: Young Artist Award nomination, best performance in a feature film, Blockbuster Entertainment Award nomination, favorite female—newcomer, Saturn Award nomination, best performance by a younger actor, Academy of Science Fiction, Horror, and Fantasy Film, 2001, for *How the Grinch Stole Christmas.*

CREDITS

Film Appearances:
Honey bee swan, *The Prophet's Game,* Moonstone, 1999.
Cindy Lou, *How the Grinch Stole Christmas* (also known as *The Grinch, Dr. Seuss' "How the Grinch Stole Christmas"* and *Der Grinch*), United International, 2000.
Julie Moore, *We Were Soldiers* (also known as *Wir waren helden*), Paramount, 2002.
Alexandra, *Spy Kids 2: Island of Lost Dreams* (also known as *Spy Kids 2: The Island of Lost Dreams*), Miramax, 2002.
Gretel, *Hansel & Gretel,* Warner Bros., 2002.
Samantha Wallace, *Saving Shiloh,* Warner Bros., 2006.
Madison, *Doubting Thomas,* 2006.

Television Appearances; Series:
Hopper Watson, *Misconceptions,* The WB, 2006.

Television Appearances; Episodic:
Allie, *Early Edition,* CBS, 1997–98.
The Rosie O'Donnell Show, syndicated, 2000.

Television Appearances; Specials:
2000 Blockbuster Entertainment Awards, Fox, 2000.
Presenter, *The 2001 Genesis Awards,* Animal Planet, 2001.

RECORDINGS

Songs:
Recorded "Christmas, Why Can't I Find You," from *The Grinch Soundtrack;* "One Small Voice," and "Rudolph the Red–Nosed Reindeer," from *School's Out Christmas.*

MOON, Amy

PERSONAL

Career: Actress.

CREDITS

Film Appearances:
Ava, *Underworld*, Trimark, 1996.
Woman, *Woman's Solitude*, Laughing Fish, 1997.
Izzy, *Last Mistake*, 2000.
Photoshop staff member number two, *Welcome to Hollywood*, Phaedra, 2000.
Tina, *Rock Star 101*, Shadow Machine, 2001.
Bella, *Fueling the Fire*, 2002.
Jeseca, *Six: The Mark Unleashed*, Sunrise, 2004.

Television Appearances; Series:
Veruca, *Undressed* (also known as *MTV's Undressed*), 1999.

Television Appearances; Episodic:
Chloe Meisner, "Peak Experience," *Silk Stalkings*, USA Network, 1997.
Leeza, first witch, "Exit Strategy," *Charmed*, The WB, 2001.
Bernice Brown, *Spyder Games*, MTV, 2002.

MORAN, Michael

PERSONAL

Career: Producer.

CREDITS

Television Co–Executive Producer; Miniseries:
Frankenstein, The Hallmark Channel, 2004.
King Solomon's Mines, The Hallmark Channel, 2004.
La Femme Musketeer, The Hallmark Channel, 2004.
Icon (also known as *Frederick Forsythe's "Icon"*), The Hallmark Channel, 2005.
The Curse of King Tut's Tomb, The Hallmark Channel, 2006.

Television Work; Miniseries:
Producer, *Mysterious Island*, The Hallmark Channel, 2005.

Executive producer, *Blackbeard*, The Hallmark Channel, 2006.

Television Co–Executive Producer; Movies:
Santa, Jr., The Hallmark Channel, 2002.
Audrey's Rain, The Hallmark Channel, 2003.
A Carol Christmas, The Hallmark Channel, 2003.
Hard Ground, The Hallmark Channel, 2003.
The King and Queen of Moonlight Bay, The Hallmark Channel, 2003.
The Last Cowboy, The Hallmark Channel, 2003.
Love Comes Softly, The Hallmark Channel, 2003.
Monster Makers, The Hallmark Channel, 2003.
Mystery Woman, The Hallmark Channel, 2003.
Straight from the Heart, The Hallmark Channel, 2003.
A Time to Remember, The Hallmark Channel, 2003.
Angel in the Family, The Hallmark Channel, 2004.
A Boyfriend for Christmas, The Hallmark Channel, 2004.
Gone but Not Forgotten, 2004.
The Hollywood Mom's Mystery (also known as *The Dead Hollywood Moms Society*), The Hallmark Channel, 2004.
Just Desserts, The Hallmark Channel, 2004.
The Long Shot: Believe in Courage, The Hallmark Channel, 2004.
Love's Enduring Promise, The Hallmark Channel, 2004.
Murder without Conviction, The Hallmark Channel, 2004.
A Place Called Home, The Hallmark Channel, 2004.
Single Santa Seeks Mrs. Claus, The Hallmark Channel, 2004.
Annie's Point, The Hallmark Channel, 2005.
Detective (also known as *Arthur Hailey's "Detective"*), 2005.
Jane Doe: Now You See It, Now You Don't, The Hallmark Channel, 2005.
Jane Doe: Til Death Do Us Part, The Hallmark Channel, 2005.
Jane Doe: Vanishing Act, The Hallmark Channel, 2005.
Jane Doe: The Wrong Face, The Hallmark Channel, 2005.
Love's Long Journey, The Hallmark Channel, 2005.
McBride: Anybody Here Murder Marty?, The Hallmark Channel, 2005.
McBride: The Chameleon Murder, The Hallmark Channel, 2005.
McBride: The Doctor Is Out ... Really Out, The Hallmark Channel, 2005.
McBride: It's Murder, Madam, The Hallmark Channel, 2005.
McBride: Murder Past Midnight, The Hallmark Channel, 2005.
McBride: Tune In for Murder, The Hallmark Channel, 2005.
Meet the Santas, The Hallmark Channel, 2005.
Mystery Woman: At First Sight, The Hallmark Channel, 2005.

Mystery Woman: Game Time, The Hallmark Channel, 2005.

Mystery Woman: Mystery Weekend, The Hallmark Channel, 2005.

Mystery Woman: Redemption, The Hallmark Channel, 2005.

Mystery Women: Sing Me a Murder, The Hallmark Channel, 2005.

Mystery Woman: Snapshot, The Hallmark Channel, 2005.

Mystery Woman: Vision of a Murder, The Hallmark Channel, 2005.

Ordinary Miracles, The Hallmark Channel, 2005.

Out of the Woods, The Hallmark Channel, 2005.

Jane Doe: The Harder They Fall, The Hallmark Channel, 2006.

Murder 101, The Hallmark Channel, 2006.

Film Work:

Co–executive producer, *Dinotopia: Quest for the Ruby Sunstone* (animated), Goodtimes Entertainment, 2005.

MORTENSEN, Viggo 1958–

PERSONAL

Full name, Viggo Peter Mortensen, Jr.; born October 20, 1958, in New York, NY; son of Viggo Peter (a farm manager and in business) and Grace Mortensen; married Exene Cervenka (a singer, musician, composer, and actress), July 8, 1987 (divorced, March 13, 1998 [some sources cite 1997]); children: Henry Blake (an actor and musician). *Education:* St. Lawrence University, degree in government and Spanish literature, 1980; trained at Warren Robertson's Theatre Workshop, New York City. *Avocational Interests:* Horseback riding, ice hockey.

Addresses: *Agent*—Jenny Rawlings, Creative Artists Agency, 9830 Wilshire Blvd., Beverly Hills, CA 90212–1825.

Career: Actor. Perceval Press, cofounder, owner, and publisher, 2002—. Poet, musician, photographer, painter, and mural artist, with work exhibited at various venues, including the Robert Mann Gallery, New York City, 2000, the Richard F. Brush Art Gallery, Canton, NY, 2003, the Fototeca de Cuba, Havana, Cuba, 2003, at galleries in Florence, Italy, and Los Angeles, and in the film *A Perfect Murder;* performer at various venues and at poetry readings; photography appeared on album covers. Also a political activist. Worked as a flower seller, truck driver, and dock worker. Some

sources state that Mortensen worked as a translator for the Swedish Olympic hockey team at the 1980 Winter Olympics at Lake Placid, NY, 1980.

Member: Screen Actors Guild, Academy of Motion Pictures Arts and Sciences.

Awards, Honors: *DramaLogue* Award, c. 1987, for *Bent;* MTV Movie Award nomination (with Demi Moore), best fight, 1998, for *G.I. Jane;* Blockbuster Entertainment Award nomination, favorite supporting actor—suspense, 1999, for *A Perfect Murder;* named one of the top entertainers of 2001, *Entertainment Weekly;* Empire Award nomination, best actor, 2002, Phoenix Film Critics Society Award, best acting ensemble, and Screen Actors Guild Award nomination, outstanding performance by the cast of a theatrical motion picture, both with others, both 2002, for *The Lord of the Rings: The Fellowship of the Ring;* Saturn Award nomination, best actor, Academy of Science Fiction, Fantasy, and Horror Films, Golden Satellite Award nomination, best performance by an actor in a supporting role in a drama, International Press Academy, Empire Award nomination, best actor, and MTV Movie Award nomination, best actor, all 2003, Phoenix Film Critics Society Award, best acting ensemble, Online Film Critics Society Award, best ensemble, and Screen Actors Guild Award nomination, outstanding performance by the cast of a theatrical motion picture, all with others, all 2003, for *The Lord of the Rings: The Two Towers;* honored with a retrospective of his photography, Museum of Photographic Art, Denmark, 2003; National Board of Review Award (with others), best acting by an ensemble, 2003, Saturn Award nomination, best actor, and Empire award nomination, best actor, both 2004, Screen Actors Guild Award, outstanding performance by the cast of a theatrical motion picture, Broadcast Film Critics Association Award, best acting ensemble, and Phoenix Film Critics Society Award nomination, best ensemble acting, all with others, all 2004, all for *The Lord of the Rings: The Return of the King;* Golden Satellite Award nomination, outstanding actor in a motion picture drama, 2005, Saturn Award nomination and Empire Award nomination, both best actor, both 2006, all for *A History of Violence;* named one of the twenty–five most intriguing people, *Tropopkin* magazine.

CREDITS

Film Appearances:

(Scenes deleted) *Swing Shift,* Warner Bros., 1984.

Moses Hochleitner, *Witness,* Paramount, 1985.

(Scenes deleted) *The Purple Rose of Cairo,* Orion, 1985.

Jerome Stample, *Salvation! Have You Said Your Prayers Today?* (also known as *Salvation!*), Circle Releasing, 1987.

Connie Burke, *Prison,* Eden/Empire Pictures, 1988.

Green, *Fresh Horses,* Weintraub Entertainment Group, 1988.

Let's Get Lost (documentary), Zeitgeist Films, 1988.

Cameron Dove, *The Reflecting Skin* (also known as *L'enfant miroir*), Fugitive Features, 1990.

Hans, *Tripwire,* New Line Cinema, 1990.

John W. Poe, *Young Guns II* (also known as *Hell Bent for Leather* and *Young Guns II: Blaze of Glory*), Twentieth Century–Fox, 1990.

Tex, *Leatherface: The Texas Chainsaw Massacre III* (also known as *TCM 3* and *The Texas Chainsaw Massacre III*), New Line Cinema, 1990.

Frank Roberts, *The Indian Runner,* Metro–Goldwyn–Mayer/Pathe, 1991.

Carl Fraser, *The Young Americans,* PolyGram Filmed Entertainment, 1993.

John E. "Johnny" Faro, *Deception* (also known as *The Missing Link: Ruby Cairo* and *Ruby Cairo*), Majestic Pictures, 1993.

Lalin, *Carlito's Way,* Universal, 1993.

Ronnie, *Boiling Point* (also known as *L'extreme limite*), Warner Bros., 1993.

Wes, *Ewangelia wedlug Harry'ego* (also known as *Desert Lunch* and *The Gospel according to Harry*), Propaganda Films, 1993.

Homeless man, *Floundering,* A–pix Entertainment, 1994.

Phillip, *The Crew,* Cineville International/LIVE Entertainment, 1994.

Oh, What a Day! 1914 (short film), 1994.

Clay, *The Passion of Darkly Noon* (also known as *Darkly Noon* and *Die Passion des Darkly Noon*), Turner Home Entertainment, 1995.

Hombre, *Gimlet,* Buena Vista International, 1995.

Lucifer, *The Prophecy* (also known as *God's Army* and *God's Secret Army*), Dimension Films/Miramax, 1995.

Nick Davis/David Brandt, *American Yakuza,* First Look Pictures Releasing, 1995.

Weapons officer Lieutenant Peter "Weps" Ince, *Crimson Tide,* Buena Vista, 1995.

Worthless drug user, *Black Velvet Pantsuit,* Hodge Podge Productions, 1995.

Caspar Goodwood, *The Portrait of a Lady,* Gramercy Pictures, 1996.

Guy Foucard, *Albino Alligator,* Miramax, 1996.

Roy Nord, *Daylight,* Universal, 1996.

Juanito, *La pistola de mi hermano* (also known as *My Brother's Gun*), Intra Films, 1997.

Master chief John James "Jack" Urgayle, *G.I. Jane,* Buena Vista, 1997.

David Shaw, *A Perfect Murder* (also known as *Dial M for Murder*), Warner Bros., 1998.

Samuel "Sam" Loomis, *Psycho,* Universal, 1998.

Walker Jerome, *A Walk on the Moon* (also known as *Blouse Man, Kiss the Sky, Over the Moon,* and *La tentacion*), Miramax, 1999.

Eddie Boone, *28 Days,* Columbia, 2000.

Aragorn, *The Lord of the Rings: The Fellowship of the Ring* (also known as *The Fellowship of the Ring* and *The Lord of the Rings: The Fellowship of the Ring: The Motion Picture*), New Line Cinema, 2001.

Aragorn, *The Lord of the Rings: The Two Towers* (also known as *The Two Towers* and *Der Herr der Ringe: Die zwei Tuerme*), New Line Cinema, 2002.

Aragorn, *The Lord of the Rings: The Return of the King* (also known as *The Return of the King* and *Der Herr der Ringe: Die Rueckkehr des Koenigs*), New Line Cinema, 2003.

Frank T. Hopkins, *Hidalgo* (also known as *Dash*), Buena Vista, 2004.

(In archive footage) Himself, *Cheshmane John Malkovich 1: Viggo Mortensen,* P&P Productions, 2004.

Himself, *Ringens disipler* (short documentary), SF Norge, 2004.

Narrator, *Wild Horse Preservation* (short documentary), 2005.

Tom Stall, *A History of Violence,* New Line Cinema, 2005.

Himself, *As Smart as They Are: The Author Project* (documentary), pbnoj productions, 2005.

Himself, *Ringers: Lord of the Fans* (documentary), Sony Pictures Home Entertainment, 2005.

Capitan Diego Alatriste (title role), *Alatriste,* Estudios Piccaso/Origen Producciones Cinematograficas, 2006.

Television Appearances; Series:

Bragg, *Search for Tomorrow,* NBC, 1985.

Television Appearances; Miniseries:

Lieutenant at LeBoeuf, *George Washington,* CBS, 1984.

Television Appearances; Movies:

Delroy, *Once in a Blue Moon,* 1990.

James "Jimmy" Kowalski, *Vanishing Point,* Fox, 1997.

Television Appearances; Specials:

Tim, "High School Narc," *ABC Afterschool Specials,* ABC, 1985.

Himself, Aragon, and Strider, *Quest for the Ring,* Fox, 2001.

Himself, *A Passage to Middle–Earth: Making of "Lord of the Rings,"* Sci–Fi Channel, 2001.

(In archive footage) Aragorn, *Lord of the Piercing,* MTV, 2002.

Himself, *Making the Movie* (also known as *Making the Movie: "The Lord of the Rings"*), MTV, 2002.

The Lord of the Rings: The Two Towers, Return to Middle Earth, The WB, 2002.

Himself, *The Lord of the Rings: The Quest Fulfilled,* 2003.

(In archive footage) Himself and Aragorn, *DNZ: The Real Middle Earth,* TVN2 (New Zealand), 2004.

Himself, *America's First Horse: Hidalgo and the Spanish Mustang,* 2004.
Journey to Middle Earth: The Lord of the Rings, the Return of the King, Arts and Entertainment, 2004.

Television Appearances; Awards Presentations:
First Annual Spaceys, Space Channel, 2003.
2003 MTV Movie Awards, MTV, 2003.

Television Appearances; Episodic:
Eddie Trumbull, "Red Tape," *Miami Vice,* NBC, 1987.
El informal, 2001.
Charlie Rose (also known as *The Charlie Rose Show*), PBS, 2002, 2005.
Caiga quien caiga—CQC, 2003.
Frids film, TV3 (Denmark), 2003.
God kveld Norge, 2003.
Otro rollo con: Adal Ramones (also known as *Otro rollo*), 2003.
Tinseltown TV, International Channel, 2003.
Filmland, 2003, 2004.
4Pop, 2003, 2004.
Comme au cinema (also known as *Comme au cinema: le magazine* and *Comme au cinema: l'emission*), 2003, 2005.
Eigo de shabera-night, 2004.
Last Call with Carson Daly, NBC, 2004.
Lo + plus, 2004.
Richard & Judy, Channel 4 (England), 2004.
Sen kvaell med Luuk, 2004.
The Late Show with David Letterman (also known as *The Late Show* and *Late Show Backstage*), CBS, 2004, 2005.
"A History of Violence," *HBO First Look,* HBO, 2005.
Caiga quien caiga, 2005.
Corazon de ... , Television Espanola (Spain), 2005.
Dagens Danmark, 2005.
The Daily Show (also known as *The Daily Show with Jon Stewart* and *The Daily Show with Jon Stewart Global Edition*), Comedy Central, 2005.
Go' aften Denmark, 2005.
Go' morden Danmark, 2005.
Le grand journal de canal+, 2005.
Magacine, 2005.
(In archive footage) *Silenci?,* 2005.
Tout le monde en parle, 2005.

Stage Appearances:
Tybalt, *Romeo and Juliet,* Indiana Repertory Theatre, Indianapolis, IN, 1985–86.
Nazi captain, *Bent,* Coast Playhouse, West Hollywood, CA, c. 1987.
Live at Beyond Baroque, Beyond Baroque, Venice, CA, 1999.
Beyond Baroque Live 2, Beyond Baroque, 2004.

Radio Appearances; Episodic:
Man in the Moon, KCRW (Santa Monica, CA), 1993.

RECORDINGS

Videos:
Himself, *"Psycho" Path,* Universal Studios Home Video, 1999.
Himself and Aragorn, *The Making of "The Lord of the Rings,"* 2002.
(In archive footage) Himself, *The Saw Is Family: Making "Leatherface,"* Automat Pictures, 2003.
Himself, *Between Two Worlds: The Making of "Witness,"* Paramount Home Video, 2005.
Himself, *The Ring Comes Full Circle* (short), Sony Pictures Home Entertainment, 2005.

Video Games:
Voice of Aragorn, *The Lord of the Rings: The Two Towers,* Electronic Arts, 2002.
Voice of Aragorn, *The Lord of the Rings: The Return of the King,* EA Games, 2003.

Albums:
1991 (poetry), 1991.
Don't Tell Me What to Do (music and poetry), c. 1994.
(With others) *One Less Thing to Worry About* (music and poetry), TDRSmusic, 1997.
(With others) *Live at Beyond Baroque,* 1999.
One Man's Meat, TDRSmusic, 1999.
(With others; and producer) *The Other Parade* (music and poetry), 1999.
(With Buckethead) *Pandemoniumfromamerica,* Perceval Press, 2003.
(With others) *Beyond Baroque Live 2,* Perceval Press, 2004.
(With Buckethead) *Please Tomorrow,* Perceval Press, 2004.
(With Buckethead) *This That and the Other,* Perceval Press, 2004.
(With Buckethead) *Intelligence Failure,* Perceval Press, 2005.

Audiobooks:
Myth: Dreams of the World, 1996.
Various authors, *The New Yorker Out Loud,* Mouth Almighty/Mercury, 1998.
(Reader and author of introduction) Dave Eggers, editor, *The Best American Nonrequired Reading 2004,* Houghton Mifflin Audio, 2004.

WRITINGS

Poetry:
Ten Last Night, Illuminati, 1993.
(And illustrator) *Recent Forgeries* (with accompanying CD), Smart Art Press, 1998.
(And illustrator) *Coincidence of Memory,* Perceval Press, 2002.

Art Work:

Errant Vine, Robert Mann Gallery, 2000.

(And photographer) *SignLanguage,* Smart Art Press, 2002.

Un hueco en el sol, Fototeca de Cuba, Havana, Cuba, 2003.

Photography:

Hole in the Sun, Perceval Press, 2002.

45301, Perceval Press, 2003.

(With Mike Davis, James Mooney, and Sonny Richards) *Miyelo,* Perceval Press, 2004.

Mo Te Upoko–o–te–ika/For Wellington, Perceval Press, 2004.

Linger, Perceval Press, 2005.

Nonfiction:

(Author of introduction) Dave Eggers, editor, *The Best American Nonrequired Reading 2004,* Houghton Mifflin, 2004.

(And photographer) *The Horse Is Good,* Perceval Press, 2004.

(With others) *Twilight of Empire: Responses to Occupation,* Perceval Press, 2004.

(With others) *Strange Familiar: The Work of Georg Gudni,* Perceval Press, 2005.

Film Music:

"Aragorn's Coronation," *The Lord of the Rings: The Return of the King* (also known as *The Return of the King* and *Der Herr der Ringe: Die Rueckkehr des Koenigs*), New Line Cinema, 2003.

Albums:

1991 (poetry), 1991.

Don't Tell Me What to Do (music and poetry), c. 1994.

(With others) *One Less Thing to Worry About* (music and poetry), TDRSmusic, 1997.

(With others) *Live at Beyond Baroque,* 1999.

One Man's Meat, TDRSmusic, 1999.

(With others) *The Other Parade* (music and poetry), 1999.

(With Buckethead) *Pandemoniumfromamerica,* Perceval Press, 2003.

(With others) *Beyond Baroque Live 2,* Perceval Press, 2004.

(With Buckethead) *Please Tomorrow,* Perceval Press, 2004.

(With Buckethead) *This That and the Other,* Perceval Press, 2004.

(With Buckethead) *Intelligence Failure,* Perceval Press, 2005.

Music Contributor:

(Contributor to the accompanying audio CD) Georganne Deen, *Western Witch, Season of the* (also known as *Season of the Western Witch*), Perceval Press, 2003.

(And contributor to the accompanying audio CD) Mark Eleveld, editor, *Spoken Word Revolution: Slam, Hip Hop & the Poetry of a New Generation,* introduction by Billy Collins, Sourcebooks, c. 2003.

OTHER SOURCES

Books:

Newsmakers, Issue 3, Gale, 2003.

Periodicals:

Detour, September, 1997, pp. 66–70.

Entertainment Weekly, November 3, 1995, p. 79; June 19, 1998, p. 46; December 21, 2001, pp. 36–37; August 19, 2005, pp. 48–52.

GQ, April, 2004.

Interview, June, 1995, p. 70.

Los Angeles Magazine, December, 1998, p. 56.

Movieline, August, 1998, pp. 72–73.

Now, January 23, 2002, pp. 48–49.

Parade, February 29, 2004, pp. 4–5.

People Weekly, June 22, 1998, p. 31; November 28, 2005.

Premiere, February, 1997, pp. 68–69; January, 2003, pp. 48–54, 88; February, 2006, pp. 92–93.

Progressive, November, 2005, pp. 39–43.

Red, January, 2002.

Sun–Times (Chicago), May 31, 1998.

Time, September 1, 1997, p. 77.

Tropopkin, October, 1995.

TV Guide, February 28, 2004, p. 33.

USA Today, April 21, 1999.

Vanity Fair, January, 2004.

Variety, April 7, 2003, p. S48.

Washington Post, March 4, 2004, pp. C1, C8.

MUELLER–STAHL, Armin 1930–

PERSONAL

Born December 17, 1930, in Tilsit, East Prussia, Germany (now Sovetsk, Russia); immigrated to East Berlin; immigrated to West Germany (now Germany), 1980; son of Alfred (a bank teller) and Editta Mueller–Stahl; married Gabriele Scholz (a dermatologist), 1973; children: Christian (an actor). *Education:* Attended drama school, beginning in 1952; studied violin at the Berlin Conservatory. *Avocational Interests:* Painting.

Addresses: *Agent*—William Morris Agency, One William Morris Place, Beverly Hills, CA 90212.

Career: Actor and writer. Berliner Ensemble, Berlin, East Germany (now Germany), concert violinist, beginning in the early 1950s; songwriter, performing protest tunes in East Germany and elsewhere, including France, Africa, and South America. Performer at various venues and festivals. Worked as a music teacher and pianist. Exhibitions of his paintings include *Malerei und Zeichnung,* Buddenbrookhaus, Luebeck, Germany, 2001–02, and *Armin Mueller–Stahl: Paintings and Graphic Arts,* the Kunsthaus Luebeck and City of Los Angeles Cultural Affairs Department, 2005.

Member: Screen Actors Guild, Academy of Motion Picture Arts and Sciences.

Awards, Honors: State Prize, German Democratic Republic (East Germany [now Germany]), 1975; Film Award in Gold, outstanding individual achievement: actor (also known as Deutscher Filmpreis for Acting), German Film awards, 1982, for *Lola;* Chaplin Schuh prize, Association of German Film and Television Directors, 1982; Montreal World Film Festival Award, best actor, 1985, for *Bittere Ernte;* Silver Berlin Bear, best actor, Berlin International Film Festival, 1992, for *Utz;* San Diego Film Critics Society Award, best supporting actor, and Australian Film Institute Award, best actor in a supporting role, both 1996, Golden Satellite Award, best performance by an actor in a supporting role in a motion picture—drama, International Press Academy, Academy Award nomination, best actor in a supporting role, and Screen Actors Guild Award nomination (with others), outstanding performance by a cast, all 1997, all for *Shine;* Berlinale Camera, Berlin International Film Festival, 1997; Bavarian Television Award, 2002, Special Award, television event of the year, German Television awards, and Adolf Grimme Award in Gold, outstanding series or miniseries, both with others, both 2002, for *Die Manns—Ein Jahrhundertroman;* World Cinematography Award, Czech Critics awards, 2004.

CREDITS

Film Appearances:
Norbert, *Heimliche Ehe* (also known as *The Secret Marriage*), 1956.
Pierre, *Fuenf Patronenhuelsen* (also known as *Five Cartridges*), Deutsche Film–Aktiengesellschaft (DEFA), 1960.
Michael, *Koenigskinder* (also known as *And Your Love Too, Invincible Love,* and *Royal Children*), 1962.
Ulrich Settich, *... und Deine Liebe auch,* 1962.
Hoefel, *Nackt unter Woelfen* (also known as *Naked among Wolves* and *Naked among the Wolves*), DEFA, 1962, Lopert, 1967.
Christine, filmed in 1963, released by Verleih des Staatlichen Filmarchivs der DDR (East Germany [now Germany]), 1974.

Quintana, *Preludio 11* (also known as *Prelude Eleven*), 1964.
Sowjetischer Arzt, *Alaskafuechse,* 1964.
Dr. Achim Engelhardt, *Ein Lord am Alexander–Platz,* 1967.
Chris Howard, *Toedlicher Irrtum,* 1970.
The blind man, *Der Dritte* (also known as *The Blind Man* and *The Third*), DEFA, 1972.
Dr. Brock, *Januskopf,* 1972.
Dechant, *Die Hosen des Ritters von Bredow,* 1973.
Mr. Slavovitz, *Kit & Co.—Lockruf des Goldes* (also known as *Kit & Co.*), DEFA, 1974.
Roman Schtamm, *Jakob der Luegner* (also known as *Jacob the Liar, Jakub lhar,* and *Jakub luhar*), DEFA, 1975.
Wolfgang Schmidt, *Nelken in Aspik,* DEFA, 1976.
Dr. Volkmar Schmith, *Die Flucht* (also known as *The Flight*), DEFA, 1977.
Harald Liebe, *Der Westen leuchtet* (also known as *Lite Trap*), Cine–International, 1981.
Lawyer, *Un dimanche de flics* (also known as *A Cop's Sunday*), Societe Nouvelle Prodis, 1981.
Von Bohm, *Lola,* United Artists, 1981.
The father, *L'homme blesse* (also known as *The Wounded Man*), Gaumont, 1982.
Goedel, *Die Fluegel der Nacht* (also known as *Wings of Night*), 1982.
Max Rehbein, *Veronika Voss* (also known as *Die Sehnsucht der Veronika Voss*), United Artists, 1982.
Tetzlaff, *Viadukt* (also known as *Matushka* and *The Train Killer*), Matilm, 1982.
Sam, *Trauma,* Futura Filmproduktion, 1983.
SS Untersturmfuhrer Mayer, *Eine Liebe in Deutschland* (also known as *A Love in Germany* and *Un amour en Allemagne*), Triumph Films, 1983.
Arnold, *Tausend Augen* (also known as *Thousand Eyes*), Filmverlag der Autoren, 1984.
Kurz, *Die Mitlaeufer* (also known as *Following the Fuhrer*), Futura Filmproduktion, 1984.
Rita Ritter, 1984.
Gandhi, *An uns glaubt Gott nicht mehr* (also known as *God Does Not Believe in Us Any More* and *Wohin und zurueck—An uns glaubt Gott nicht mehr*), Roxie Releasing, 1985, originally a television movie, 1982.
Archduke Franz Ferdinand, *Oberst Redl* (also known as *Colonel Redl* and *Redl ezredes*), Orion Classics, 1985.
The blind director, *Der Angriff der Gegenwart auf die uebrige Zeit* (also known as *The Assault of the Present on the Rest of Time* and *The Blind Director*), Spectrafilm, 1985.
Count Pergen, *Vergesst Mozart* (also known as *Forget Mozart* and *Zabudnite na Mozarta*), Slovak, 1985.
Francois Korb and Andres Korb, *Glut* (also known as *Embers* and *Glut im Herzen*), 1985.
Leon Wolny, *Bittere Ernte* (also known as *Angry Harvest*), European Classics, 1985.
Chief of the gray men, *Momo,* Rialto Film, 1986.

Mr. Kehlmann, *Unser Mann im Dschungel* (also known as *The Jungle Mission* and *Amazonas Mission*), Cine–International, 1986, originally a television movie, 1985.

Axel Baumgartner, *Der Joker* (also known as *Lethal Obsession*), 1987.

Inspector Alex Glas, *Killing Blue* (also known as *Midnight Cop*), 1988.

Baron von Rastschuk, *Das Spinnennetz* (also known as *The Spider's Web*), Beta–Kirch, 1989.

Marno, *A Hecc* (also known as *Just for Kicks*), Hungarofilm, 1989.

Maxwell, *Schweinegeld* (also known as *C.A.S.H.: A Political Fairy Tale, Ein Marchen der Gebruder Nimm Schweinegeld,* and *Schweinegeld—Ein Maerchen der Gebrueder Nimm*), Filmverlag der Autoren, 1989.

Arno/Aaron Bronstein, *Bronsteins Kinder* (also known as *Bronstein's Children*), Tobis Filmkunst, 1990.

Michael Laszlo, *Music Box,* TriStar, 1990.

Sam Krichinsky, *Avalon,* TriStar, 1990.

Helmut Grokenberger, *Night on Earth* (also known as *LANewYorkParisRomeHelsinki* and *Une nuit sur terre*), Fine Line Features, 1991.

Inspector Grubach, *Kafka,* Miramax, 1991.

Doc, *The Power of One* (also known as *La puissance de l'ange*), Warner Bros., 1992.

Otto Linder, *Far from Berlin* (also known as *Loin de Berlin*), 1992.

Baron Kaspar Joachim von Utz (title role), *Utz,* First Run Features/Castle Rock Productions, 1993.

Title role, *Der Kinoerzaehler* (also known as *The Film Narrator* and *The Movie Teller*), Roxy Film, 1993.

Dimitri, *Red Hot,* SC Entertainment International, 1993.

Severo de Valle, *The House of the Spirits* (also known as *Aandernes hus, A casa dos espiritos,* and *Das Geisterhaus*), Miramax, 1993.

Joseph Kopple, *The Last Good Time,* Samuel Goldwyn, 1994.

Uncle Wilhelm, *Holy Matrimony,* Interscope Communications/PolyGram Filmed Entertainment, 1994.

Virgilus and Karol, *Taxandria,* Iblis Films, 1994.

Elizar Kane, *Theodore Rex* (also known as *T. Rex*), New Line Cinema, 1995.

Mr. Linzer, *A Pyromaniac's Love Story* (also known as *Burning Love*), Buena Vista, 1995.

Adolf Hitler/Andreas Kronsted, *Conversation with the Beast* (also known as *Gespraech mit dem Biest* and *Gespraech mit der Bestie*), 1996.

Count von Kaltenborn, *Der Unhold* (also known as *The Ogre* and *Le roi des aulnes*), Westdeutscher Rundfunk/Le Studio Canal/France 2 Cinema, 1996.

Elias Peter Helfgott, *Shine,* Buena Vista, 1996.

Anson Baer, *The Game,* PolyGram Filmed Entertainment, 1997.

Dimitri Vertikoff, *The Peacemaker,* DreamWorks, 1997.

Hanson, *Tanger—Legende einer Stadt* (documentary), Accolade Films/Paladin Films, 1997.

Morris Bober, *The Assistant,* Lions Gate Films, 1997.

Conrad Strughold, *The X–Files* (also known as *Blackwood, Fight the Future, X–Files: Blackwood, The X–Files: Fight the Future, X–Files: The Movie,* and *Aux frontieres du reel*), Twentieth Century–Fox, 1998.

Hannon Fuller and Grierson, *The Thirteenth Floor* (also known as *Abwaerts in die Zukunft*), Centropolis Entertainment, 1998.

Archbishop Werner, *The Third Miracle,* Sony Pictures Classics, 1999.

Dr. Kirschbaum, *Jakob the Liar* (also known as *Jakob le menteur*), TriStar, 1999.

(Uncredited) Ramier Beck, *Mission to Mars* (also known as *M2M*), Buena Vista, 2000.

Bertold "Barry" Bohmer, *The Long Run,* Universal, 2001.

(In archive footage) Himself, *Der Bayerische Rebell* (documentary), Neue Visionen Filmverleih, 2004.

Grandpa Randolph, *The Dust Factory,* Metro–Goldwyn–Mayer, 2004.

Otto, *The Story of An African Farm* (also known as *Bustin Bonaparte*), Freestyle Releasing, 2004.

Karl Winter, *Ich bin die Andere,* Concorde Filmverleih, 2006.

Nicoli Seroff, *Local Color,* Permut Presentations/Local Color Productions, 2006.

Von Leeb, *Leningrad,* c. 2006, also broadcast as a miniseries, Channel One Russia, 2006.

Sigmund Freud, *Sabina* (also known as *Where Love Reigns*), Becker Entertainment, c. 2007.

Film Work:

Director, *Conversation with the Beast* (also known as *Gespraech mit dem Biest* and *Gespraech mit der Bestie*), 1996.

Television Appearances; Series:

Juergen Lesstorff, *Wege uebers Land,* Deutscher Fernsehfunk (East Germany [now Germany]), 1968.

(Uncredited) Musikant, *Stuelpner–Legende,* [East Germany (now Germany)], 1973.

Bredebusch, *Das Unsichtbare Visier,* Deutscher Fernsehfunk, c. 1973–79.

Keibel, *Le gorille* (also known as *Codename: Gorilla, Il gorilla,* and *Le gorille se mange froid*), France 2, beginning 1990.

Host, *The Power of Knowledge,* Mitteldeutscher Rundfunk (Germany), 2005.

Television Appearances; Miniseries:

Hans Roeder (a legionnaire), *Flucht aus der Hoelle,* Deutscher Fernsehfunk (East Germany [now Germany]), 1960.

Wolfgang, *Wolf unter Woelfen,* [East Germany (now Germany)], 1964.

Kurt Lindow, *Die Verschworenen,* [East Germany (now Germany)], 1971.

Die sieben Affaeren der Dona Juanita, Deutscher Fernsehfunk, 1973.

Andreas Roth, *Collin,* 1981.

Himself, *Plaisir du theatre,* [France], 1983.

Wohin und zurueck, 1984.

General Petya Samanov, *Amerika* (also known as *Topeka, Kansas ... USSR*), ABC, 1987.

Karl Steputat, *Jokehnen oder Wie lange faehrt man von Ostpreussen nach Deutschland?,* [West Germany (now Germany)], 1987.

Joseph, *Jesus* (also known as *Die Bibel—Jesus* and *La bibbia: Jesus*), CBS, 2000.

Alessio, *Crociati* (also known as *Crusaders* and *Die Kreuzritter*), [Germany and Italy], 2001.

Thomas Mann, *Die Manns—Ein Jahrhundertroman,* [Germany, Austria, and Switzerland], 2001.

(In archive footage) *Unterwegs zue Familie Mann,* Bayerischer Rundfunk, Norddeutscher Rundfunk, and Westdeutscher Rundfunk, 2001.

Von Leeb, *Leningrad,* Channel One Russia, 2006, also released theatrically, c. 2006.

Television Appearances; Movies:

Die Letzte Chance (title means "The Last Chance"), 1962.

Reinhard Marschner, *Der Andere neben dir,* 1963.

Columbus 64, 1966.

Die Dame aus Genua, 1969.

Oberleutnant Heide, *Kein Mann fuer Camp Detrick,* 1970.

Father Klemm, *Die Eigene Haut,* 1974.

Robert, *Geschlossene Gesellschaft,* 1978.

Die Laengste Sekunde, 1980.

Gandhi, *Ferry oder Wie es war,* 1981.

Ja und Nein, 1981.

Ernest Kiel, *Die Gartenlaube* (also known as *Eugenie Marlitt und die Gartenlaube*), 1982.

Lyssek, *Flucht aus Pommern* (also known as *Flight from Pomerania*), 1982.

Ausgestossen, 1982.

Der Fall Sylvester Matuska, 1982.

Ich werde warten, 1982.

Gandhi, *An uns glaubt Gott nicht mehr* (also known as *God Does Not Believe in Us Any More* and *Wohin und zurueck—An uns glaubt Gott nicht mehr*), 1982, released as a theatrical film, Roxie Releasing, 1985.

Ruhe sanft, Bruno, 1983.

Dr. Konrad Ansbach, *Tatort—Freiwild,* 1984.

Dold, *Hautnah,* 1985.

Mr. Kehlmann, *Unser Mann im Dschungel* (also known as *The Jungle Mission* and *Amazonas Mission*), 1985, released as a theatrical film, Cine-International, 1986.

Dr. Leopold Jordan and Dr. Koerner, *Der Fall Franza* (also known as *Franza*), 1986.

Auf den Tag genau, 1986.

Gauner im Paradies, 1986.

Max Telligan, *Tagebuch fuer einen Moerder,* 1988.

Juror number four, *12 Angry Men,* Showtime, 1997.

Rabbi Adam Heller, *In the Presence of Mine Enemies,* Showtime, 1997.

Hans Koenig, *The Commissioner* (also known as *Der Commissioner—Im Zentrum der Macht*), The Movie Channel, 1998.

Mac, *Inferno* (also known as *Pilgrim*), UPN, 2000.

Television Appearances; Specials:

Himself, *Geiger, Gaukler, Gentleman,* [Germany], 2001.

(In archive footage) Himself, *Grosses Herz und grosse Klappe—Helga Feddersen,* Norddeutscher Rundfunk (Germany), 2001.

Television Appearances; Awards Presentations:

Himself, *The 69th Annual Academy Awards,* ABC, 1997.

Television Appearances; Episodic:

"Die Rache enes V–Mannes," *Sonderdezernat K1,* 1981.

"Morgengrauen" (parts two and three), *Ein Fall fuer zwei,* 1984.

"Stellen Sie sich vor, man hat Dr. Prestel erschossen," *Derrick,* 1984.

Emil, "Les volets verts," *L'heure Simenon,* 1988.

Guest, "Wetten, dass ... ? aus Duisburg," *Wetten, dass ... ?,* 1991.

Guest, "Wetten, dass ... ? aus Muenchen," *Wetten, dass ... ?,* 2002.

Guest, *Beckmann,* 2002.

Israeli prime minister Efraim "Eli" Zahavy, "The Birnam Woods," *The West Wing,* NBC, 2004.

Israeli prime minister Efraim "Eli" Zahavy, "N.S.F. Thurmont," *The West Wing,* NBC, 2004.

Israeli prime minister Efraim "Eli" Zahavy, "Third Day Story," *The West Wing,* NBC, 2004.

Israeli prime minister Efraim "Eli" Zahavy, "The Warfare of Genghis Khan," *The West Wing,* NBC, 2004.

Guest, *Die Johannes B. Kerner Show* (also known as *JBK*), 2004.

Stage Appearances:

Appeared at Theatre am Schiffbauerdamm, East Berlin, Germany, c. 1953; worked with Volksbuehne (a theatre company; name means "People's Stage"), East Berlin, 1954–c. 1979; appeared in East German productions as the Prince in *Emilia Galotti;* as Romeo in *Romeo and Juliet;* and as Andrei in *War and Peace.*

RECORDINGS

Audiobooks:

Hannah, 2004.

WRITINGS

Screenplays:
Conversation with the Beast (also known as *Gespraech mit dem Biest* and *Gespraech mit der Bestie*), 1996.

Novels:
Verordneter Sonntag, Severin & Siedler, 1981.
In Gedanken an Marie Louise: Eine Liebesgeschichte, 1998.
Hannah, 2004.

Nonfiction:
Verordneter Sonntag (memoir), 1979.
Drehtage: "Music Box" und "Avalon" (diaries), Luchterhand, 1991.
Unterwegs nach Hause: Erinnerungen (memoir), Marion von Schroeder, 1997.
Malerei und Zeichnung (exhibition catalogue), c. 2001.
Venice: Ein amerikanisches Tagebuch, 2005.

OTHER SOURCES

Books:
International Dictionary of Films and Filmmakers, Volume 3: *Actors and Actresses,* fourth edition, St. James Press, 2000.

Periodicals:
People Weekly, November 12, 1990, pp. 87–88, 90.
Playboy, March, 1991, pp. 36–42.

MYLES, Sophia 1980–

PERSONAL

Born March 18, 1980, in London, England. *Avocational Interests:* Horse riding, skiing, skating, swimming.

Addresses: *Agent*—Hamilton Hodell Ltd., 66–68 Margaret Street, 5th Floor, London, W1W 8SR, UK; International Creative Management, 8942 Wilshire Blvd., Beverly Hills, CA 90211; Special Artists Agency, 9465 Wilshire Blvd., Suite 890, Beverly Hills, CA 90212. *Manager*—Melanie Green Management and Productions, 425 N. Robertson Dr., Los Angeles, CA 90048.

Career: Actress.

CREDITS

Film Appearances:
Susan Price, *Mansfield Park,* Miramax, 1999.
Saucy wood nymph, *Guest House Paradiso,* Universal, 1999.
Victoria Abberline, *From Hell,* Twentieth Century–Fox, 2001.
Anne Kennedy, *The Abduction Club,* A–Film, 2002.
Erika, *Underworld,* Moonlight, 2003.
Louise Thompson, *Out of Bounds* (also known as *Dead in the Water* and *Out of Bounds*), Euro Video, 2004.
Lady Penelope, *Thunderbirds,* United International, 2004.
Erika, *Underworld: Evolution,* Pioneer, 2006.
Isolde, *Tristan + Isolde,* Twentieth Century–Fox, 2006.
Audrey, *Art School Confidential,* Miramax, 2006.

Television Appearances; Miniseries:
Lady Jane Grey, *The Prince and the Pauper,* BBC, 1996.
Saffron, *Big Women,* Channel 4, 1998.
Agnes Fleming, *Oliver Twist,* 1999.
Kate Nickleby, *Nicholas Nickelby,* Bravo and ITV, 2001.
Lizzie Carter, *Colditz,* ITV, 2005.
Dr. Sophie Amsden, *The Hades Factor,* CBS, 2006.

Television Appearances; Movies:
Gwenda Halliday, *Marple: Sleeping Murder,* 2005.

Television Appearances; Episodic:
Heather Conway, "No Hiding Place," *Heartbeat,* ITV, 2001.
Susan Gascoigne, "A Lesson in Murder," *Foyle's War,* ITV, 2002.
Madame Du Pompadour, "The Girl in the Fireplace," *Doctor Who,* BBC1, 2006.

N-O

NICHOLSEN, J. D.
(Jack Nichols, Jack Nicholsen)

PERSONAL

Married Cindy Matthews (a singer).

Addresses: *Contact*—c/o Cameron Family Singers, Cameron Public House, 408 Queen St. West, Toronto, Ontario M5V 2A7, Canada.

Career: Actor, musician, and sound designer. Leslie Spit Treeo, performer, beginning c. 1988; Cameron Family Singers, performer, 1997—.

Awards, Honors: Juno Award (with Leslie Spit Treeo), most promising group, Canadian Academy of Recording Arts and Sciences, 1991; Dora Mavor Moore Award nomination, sound design, Toronto Theatre Alliance, 2000, for *Book of Thoht*.

CREDITS

Film Appearances:
(With Leslie Spit Treeo) *Roadkill* (also known as *Roadkill: Move or Die*), Shadow Shows, 1989.
Old man Grossler, *Time of the Wolf* (also known as *L'enfant et le loup* and *L'heure du loup*), Animal Tales Productions/Apollo Media/Chesler–Perlmutter Productions, 2002.
Ted Andrews, *Blizzard,* Premiere Group, 2003.
Man in gray suit, *16 Blocks,* Warner Bros., 2006.

Film Appearances; as Jack Nicholsen:
Val, *The Last Supper,* Outsider Enterprises, 1994.

Jackson, *Soul Survivor* (also known as *Survivant dans l'ame*), Norstar Entertainment, 1995.
Luther Penrose, *Iron Eagle IV* (also known as *Aigle de fer IV*), Trimark Pictures, 1995.
Kehoe, *Sabotage,* Imperial Entertainment/New City Releasing, 1996.
Neil, *Big Deal, So What* (short film), 1996.
Ray, *Foxy Lady, Wild Cherry* (short film), Nightvision Films, 2000.
Sam, *Tribulation,* Artist View Entertainment/Cloud Ten Pictures/Riverside Distributors/Spring Arbor, 2000.

Film Appearances; as Jack Nichols:
Duane Bickle, *Perfectly Normal,* Four Seasons Entertainment, 1991.
Archer, *I Love a Man in Uniform* (also known as *A Man in Uniform*), IRS Media, 1994.

Television Appearances; Miniseries:
Firing range instructor, *Master Spy: The Robert Hanssen Story,* CBS, 2002.
Higbie, *Roughing It* (also known as *Mark Twain's "Roughing It"*), The Hallmark Channel, 2002.

Television Appearances; Movies:
G. E. Smith, *Gilda Radner: It's Always Something* (also known as *It's Always Something: The Gilda Radner Story*), ABC, 2002.
Mike Lout, *Jasper, Texas,* Showtime, 2003.

Television Appearances as Jack Nicholsen; Movies:
Zed, *No Contest,* HBO, 1994.
Holdup man, *First Degree,* HBO, 1996.
Photographer, *Naked City: A Killer Christmas,* Showtime, 1998.
Scuzzy, *Coming Unglued* (also known as *Let's Ruin Dad's Day*), Fox Family Channel, 1999.
Detective, *Zebra Lounge* (also known as *Rendez–vous au Zebra Lounge*), HBO, 2001.

Television Appearances; Episodic:

Buddy Beal, "Let's Do It Again," *Soul Food,* Showtime, 2002.

Paul, "Episode 2.16," *Queer as Folk* (also known as *Queer as Folk USA*), Showtime, 2002.

Rob, "The Producers," *Doc,* PAX TV, 2002.

Police officer, "Geoffrey Returns," *Slings and Arrows,* The Movie Network, 2003.

Beck, "A Whisper from Zoe's Sister," *Wild Card* (also known as *Zoe Busiek: Wild Card*), Lifetime, 2005.

Television Appearances; as Jack Nicholsen; Episodic:

Himself, "Gay Pioneers," *In the Life,* PBS, 1992.

Barney, "Last Rites: Part 1," *Street Legal,* CBC, 1994.

Junkie, "Killer Instinct," *Forever Knight,* syndicated, 1994.

Caulfield, "The Wild Bunch," *Due South* (also known as *Due South: The Series, Direction: Sud,* and *Un tandem de choc*), CTV and CBS, 1995.

Joey, "Odds," *Due South* (also known as *Due South: The Series, Direction: Sud,* and *Un tandem de choc*), CTV and CBS, 1998.

Deckard, "Virtual Justice," *Total Recall 2070* (also known as *Total Recall: The Series*), CTV and Showtime, 1999.

Freddy Forsythe, "Temple of Light," *Psi Factor: Chronicles of the Paranormal* (also known as *Psi Factor*), CanWest Global Television and syndicated, 1999.

Harrison Bridger, "Civil Disobedience," *Little Men,* PAX TV, 1999.

Harrison Bridger, "Stepping Out," *Little Men,* PAX TV, 1999.

Harrison Bridger, "The Weaker Sex," *Little Men,* PAX TV, 1999.

Karl Hansen, "Second Wave," *Earth: Final Conflict* (also known as *EFC, Gene Roddenberry's "Battleground Earth," Gene Roddenberry's "Earth: Final Conflict," Invasion planete Terre,* and *Mission Erde: Sie sind unter uns*), syndicated, 2000.

Television Appearances; as Jack Nicholsen; Pilots:

Airport hustler, *Due South,* CBS, 1994.

Anthony "Sandman" Gerson, *Dark Eyes,* ABC, 1995.

Stage Appearances:

Steel Kiss, Toronto, Ontario, Canada, 1987.

Civilization of a Shoeshine Boy, 1993.

Barndance Live, Blyth Festival Theatre, Blyth, Ontario, Canada, 1996.

The Convict Lover, 1997.

The Piano Man's Daughter, 1998.

Big Daddy, *Tequila Vampire Matinee* (musical), Regent Theatre, then Theatre Passe Muraille, Toronto, Ontario, Canada, both 2003.

Boyfriend, *Chronic,* Factory Theatre, Toronto, Ontario, Canada, 2003.

Oberon, *A Midsummer Night's Dream,* Festival of Classics, Coronation Park Theatre, Oakville, Ontario, Canada, 2005.

Othello, *Goodnight Desdemona (Good Morning Juliet),* Festival of Classics, Bronte Harbour Theatre, Oakville, Ontario, Canada, 2005.

The Foursome, Grand Theatre Mainstage, London, Ontario, Canada, 2005.

Also appeared in productions of the Crow's Theatre, Platform 9 Theatre, and Theatre Aquarius.

Stage Sound Designer:

Book of Thoht, Toronto, Ontario, Canada, c. 2000.

Small Returns, Theatre Passe Muraille, Toronto, Ontario, Canada, 2004.

RECORDINGS

Albums; with Leslie Spit Treeo:

Don't Cry Too Hard, EMI Music Canada/IRS Records/Capitol, 1990.

Book of Rejection, Capitol, 1992.

Albums; with Cameron Family Singers:

Saturday Matinee, CamFam Records, 2005.

Albums; with Others:

(As a member of Leslie Spit Treeo) "The Sound," *Roadkill* (soundtrack), c. 1989.

Singles; with Leslie Spit Treeo:

"Angel from Montgomery," Capitol, 1991.

"Heat," Capitol, 1991.

"UFO (Catch the Highway)," Capitol, 1991.

"In Your Eyes," EMI, 1992.

"Sometimes I Wish," EMI, 1992.

WRITINGS

Albums; with Leslie Spit Treeo:

Don't Cry Too Hard, EMI Music Canada/IRS Records/Capitol, 1990.

Book of Rejection, Capitol, 1992.

Albums; with Cameron Family Singers:

Saturday Matinee, CamFam Records, 2005.

Albums; with Others:

(As a member of Leslie Spit Treeo) "The Sound," *Roadkill* (soundtrack), c. 1989.

Singles; with Leslie Spit Treeo:
"Heat," Capitol, 1991.
"UFO (Catch the Highway)," Capitol, 1991.
"In Your Eyes," EMI, 1992.
"Sometimes I Wish," EMI, 1992.

O'DONNELL, Lawrence 1951(?)–
  (Lawrence O'Donnell, Jr.)

PERSONAL

Full name, Lawrence Francis O'Donnell, Jr.; born November 7, 1951 (some sources cite 1955), in Boston, MA; son of Lawrence Francis (an attorney) and Frances Marie (an office manager; maiden name, Buckley) O'Donnell; married Kathryn Hunter Harrold (an actress), 1994; children: Elizabeth Buckley Harrold. *Education:* Harvard University, B.A. (cum laude), 1976.

Addresses: *Agent*—Chris Silbermann, Broder/Webb/Chervin/Silbermann, 9242 Beverly Blvd., Suite 200, Beverly Hills, CA 90210.

Career: Producer and writer. Lawrence O'Donnell, Jr. Productions, producer. O'Donnell, O'Donnell & O'Donnell (law firm), Quincy, MA, paralegal assistant, 1976–78; Office of U.S. Senator Daniel Patrick Moynihan, director of communications, 1988, senior advisor, 1989–92; U.S. Senate, chief of staff of Committee on Environment and Public Works, 1992, Democratic chief of staff of Committee on Finance, 1993–95. Also a public speaker.

Member: Authors Guild, Writers Guild of America, Institute for Criminal Justice Ethics.

Awards, Honors: Humanitas Prize (with others), sixty-minute category, Human Family Educational and Cultural Institute, 2000, and Writers Guild of America Award nomination (with others), episodic drama category, 2001, both for "Take This Sabbath Day," *The West Wing;* Writers Guild of America Award nomination (with others), episodic drama category, 2001, for "Enemies," *The West Wing;* Emmy Award (with others), outstanding drama series, 2001, and Writers Guild of America Award nomination (with others), outstanding dramatic series, 2006, both for *The West Wing;* honorary D.H.L., Suffolk University, 2001.

CREDITS

Television Work; Series:
Technical consultant, *Feds,* CBS, 1997.

Coproducer, *The West Wing* (also known as *West Wing*), NBC, 2000.
Producer, *The West Wing* (also known as *West Wing*), NBC, 2000–2001.
Supervising producer, *First Monday,* CBS, 2002.
Creator and executive producer, *Mister Sterling,* NBC, 2003.
Executive producer, *The West Wing* (also known as *West Wing*), NBC, 2005–2006.

Executive story editor for the series *The West Wing* (also known as *West Wing*), NBC.

Television Work; Movies:
Associate producer, *A Case of Deadly Force,* CBS, 1986.

Television Appearances; Series:
Senior political analyst, *MSNBC Live* (also known as *MSNBC Dayside* and *MSNBC Right Now*), MSNBC, beginning c. 1996.

Television Appearances; Movies:
(As Lawrence O'Donnell, Jr.) Judge Leggett, *Mrs. Harris,* HBO, 2005.

Television Appearances; Specials:
(As Lawrence O'Donnell, Jr.) Himself, *Politics: A Pop Culture History,* VH1, 2004.

Television Appearances; Episodic:
Dr. Bartlet, "Two Cathedrals," *The West Wing* (also known as *West Wing*), NBC, 2001.
(As Lawrence O'Donnell, Jr.) Judge Franklin Brown, "Goodbye," *The Practice,* ABC, 2003.

While billed as Lawrence O'Donnell, Jr., appeared as Judge Calloway in "Privileged," an unaired episode of *The Lyon's Den,* NBC, 2003.

Television Guest Appearances; Episodic:
Scarborough Country, MSNBC, 2004.
Dennis Miller, CNBC, multiple appearances, 2004 and 2005.
The Al Franken Show, Sundance Channel, multiple appearances, 2005.
The Late Late Show with Craig Ferguson (also known as *The Late Late Show*), CBS, 2005.
Weekends at the DL, Comedy Central, 2005.

Appeared in *ABC News Nightline* (also known as *Nightline*), ABC; *The CBS Morning Show,* CBS; *Charlie Rose,* PBS; *Good Morning America* (also known as *GMA*), ABC; *The McLaughlin Group,* PBS; and *Today* (also known as *NBC News Today* and *The Today Show*), NBC. Appeared in episodes of other series, including programs hosted by Phil Donahue and Larry King.

Television Appearances; Pilots:
(As Lawrence O'Donnell, Jr.) Lee Hatcher, *Big Love*, HBO, 2006.

Radio Appearances; Episodic:
Himself, *The Al Franken Show*, Air America Radio, multiple episodes in 2005.

WRITINGS

Teleplays; with Others; Series:
The West Wing (also known as *West Wing*), NBC, 2000, 2004–2005.
Mister Sterling, NBC, 2003.

Teleplays; with Others; Episodic:
"Right to Die," *First Monday*, CBS, 2002.

Several episodes of the television series *The West Wing* (also known as *West Wing*), NBC were based on stories by O'Donnell.

Teleplays; with Others; Pilots:
Mister Sterling, NBC, 2003.

Screenplays:
(With Paul Redford) *The Crusaders* (based on a book by Jack Greenberg), New Line Cinema, 2007.

Nonfiction:
Deadly Force: The Wrongful Death of James Bouden, Jr.; A True Story of How a Badge Can Become a License to Kill, William Morrow and Company, 1983.

Contributor to periodicals, including *Boston, New York Times*, and *Vanity Fair*.

ADAPTATIONS

The television movie *A Case of Deadly Force* was based on O'Donnell's book *Deadly Force: The Wrongful Death of James Bouden, Jr.; A True Story of How a Badge Can Become a License to Kill*.

P

PALMER, Joel 1986–

PERSONAL

Born March 6, 1986, in Canada.

Addresses: *Agent*—Wendi Green, Abrams Artists Agency, 9200 Sunset Blvd., 11th Floor, Los Angeles, CA 90069.

Career: Actor. Appeared in commercials.

Awards, Honors: Young Artist Award nomination, best performance by an actor under ten in a feature film, Young Artist Foundation, 1996, for *Far from Home: The Adventures of Yellow Dog.*

CREDITS

Television Appearances; Miniseries:
Lonesome Dove, CBS, 1989.
Second boy, *Living with the Dead* (also known as *Talking to Heaven*), CBS, 2002.

Television Appearances; Movies:
Patrick Farrow, *Liar, Liar* (also known as *Liar, Liar: Between Father and Daughter*), CBS, 1992.
The Man Upstairs, 1992.
Adam, *Moment of Truth: A Child Too Many,* NBC, 1993.
Donald Wade, *Morning Glory,* 1993.
Tommy, *Final Appeal* (also known as *L'ultime proces*), NBC, 1993.
Jason Holc at the age of five, *Heart of a Child,* NBC, 1994.

Nelson, *Someone Else's Child* (also known as *Lost and Found*), Lifetime, 1994.
Chris Dion, *Falling from the Sky: Flight 174* (also known as *Freefall: Flight 174*), ABC, 1995.
David Jenks, *Seduction in a Small Town* (also known as *Harvest of Lies*), ABC, 1997.
Kevin Lane, *Loyal Opposition: Terror in the White House,* Fox Family Channel, 1998.
David, *Bang, Bang, You're Dead,* Showtime, 2002.

Television Appearances; Specials:
Cohost of the five–day special *Hopscotch.*

Television Appearances; Episodic:
Kevin Morris, "Conduit," *The X–Files,* Fox, 1993.
Corby, "True Colours," *Madison* (also known as *Working It Out at Madison*), CanWest Global Television, 1994.
Luke Wyatt, "Wild Horses," *Lonesome Dove: The Series,* CTV and syndicated, 1994.
Andrew Rosman, "Under the Bed," *The Outer Limits* (also known as *The New Outer Limits*), Showtime, Sci–Fi Channel, and syndicated, 1995.
Charlie/Michael Holvey, "The Calusari," *The X–Files,* Fox, 1995.
Kevin Colyer, "The Kid," *The Commish,* ABC, 1995.
David, "Sins of the Father," *Poltergeist: The Legacy,* Sci–Fi Channel, Showtime, and syndicated, 1996.
Jesse Venable, "Criminal Nature," *The Outer Limits* (also known as *The New Outer Limits*), Showtime, Sci–Fi Channel, and syndicated, 1998.
Jimmy, "Wages of Sin," *Dead Man's Gun,* Showtime, 1998.
Matt Thomas, "Still Waters," *Poltergeist: The Legacy,* Sci–Fi Channel, Showtime, and syndicated, 1999.
Phillip, "Small Friends," *The Outer Limits* (also known as *The New Outer Limits*), Showtime, Sci–Fi Channel, and syndicated, 1999.
Young Cade Foster, "Shadowland," *First Wave,* Sci–Fi Channel, 2000.

Appeared as Henry in *Beggars and Choosers,* Show-time; also appeared in episodes of *The Hat Squad,* CBS; *Sesame Street,* PBS; and *Street Justice,* syndicated.

Television Appearances; Pilots:
Mikey Crosetti, *Crow's Nest,* ABC, 1992.
Kevin Singer, *Final Run,* CBS, 1999.
Matthew Reynolds, *Family Law,* CBS, 1999.

Film Appearances:
Knight Moves (also known as *Face to Face* and *Knight Moves—Ein moerderisches Spiel*), Republic Pictures, 1992.
Silas McCormick, *Far from Home: The Adventures of Yellow Dog,* Twentieth Century–Fox, 1995.
Jeremy Melton, *Valentine* (also known as *Love Hurts* and *Valentine's Day*), Warner Bros., 2001.
Young Pete, *Dreamcatcher* (also known as *L'attrapeur de reves*), Warner Bros., 2003.

Appeared in the film *Swindled.*

Stage Appearances:
Lyle the shoeshine boy, *Hello, Dolly* (musical), c. 1989.

OTHER SOURCES

Periodicals:
Cult Times, June, 2001, p. 11.
Easy Living, March, 1997, pp. 5, 8, 9.
Fangoria, Volume 146, 1996, p. 49.
Maclean's, Volume 110, issue 2, 1997, p. 61.
Teen Beat, Volume 19, issue 10, 1997, p. 36; Volume 20, issue 1, 1997, p. 61.

PANABAKER, Kay 1990–

PERSONAL

Born May 2, 1990, in Orange, TX.

Addresses: *Agent*—Coast to Coast, Talent Group, 3350 Barham Blvd., Los Angeles, CA 90068.

Career: Actress.

Awards, Honors: Young Artist Award nomination, best performance in a television drama series, 2003, for *ER;* Young Artist Award nomination, best performance in a commercial, 2004; Young Artist Award nomination, best performance in a television series, 2005, for *Phil of the Future;* Young Artist Award, best performance in a television series, 2005, for *Summerland.*

CREDITS

Film Appearances:
Additional voices, *Monsters, Inc.,* Buena Vista, 2001.
Sam LaRoche, *Dead Heat* (also known as *Dead Heat—Todliches rennen*), Kinowelt, 2002.
George, *Nancy Drew: The Mystery in Hollywood Hills,* Warner Bros., 2007.

Television Appearances; Series:
Nikki Westerly, *Summerland,* The WB, 2004.

Television Appearances; Movies:
Emily Watson, *Life is Ruff,* 2005.
Jamie Bartlett, *How My Private, Personal Journal Became a Bestseller,* The Disney Channel, 2006.

Television Appearances; Pilots:
Nikki Westerly, *Summerland,* The WB, 2004.

Television Appearances; Episodic:
Melissa Rue, "The Letter," *ER,* NBC, 2002.
Kelly, "Child Island," *The Jamie Kennedy Experiment,* 2002.
Alice Brand, "Regarding Eric," *7th Heaven* (also known as *7th Heaven: Beginnings* and *Seventh Heaven*), The WB, 2002.
The girl, "Forgiving," *Angel,* The WB, 2002.
The girl, "Habeas Corpes," *Angel,* The WB, 2003.
Susie Jenkins, "Cold Comfort," *The Division* (also known as *Heart of the City*), Lifetime, 2003.
Carrie Bauer, "Moving Up," *The Brothers Garcia,* Nickelodeon, 2003.
Debbie Berwick, "You Say Toe–Mato," *Phil of the Future,* The Disney Channel, 2004.
Debbie Berwick, "Future Tutor," *Phil of the Future,* The Disney Channel, 2004.
Debbie Berwick, "Doggie Day–Care," *Phil of the Future,* The Disney Channel, 2004.
Debbie Berwick, "Neander–Phil," *Phil of the Future,* The Disney Channel, 2004.
Debbie Berwick, "Corner Pocket," *Phil of the Future,* The Disney Channel, 2005.
Elisha, "Penny for Your Thoughts," *Medium,* 2005.

PARAS, Lalaine
    See LALAINE

PECK, Austin 1971–

PERSONAL

Born April 9, 1971, in Honolulu, HI; married Tara Crespo, April 16, 2000; children: A. J., Roman.

Career: Actor.

Awards, Honors: Soap Opera Digest Award (with Christie Clark), hottest romance, 1997, for *Days of Our Lives.*

CREDITS

Television Appearances; Series:
Austin Reed, *Days of Our Lives* (also known as *Days* and *DOOL*), 1995–2002, 2005—.

Television Appearances; Episodic:
"Cancun," *Search Party,* E! Entertainment, 1999.
"Witch Way Out," *Sabrina, the Teenage Witch* (also known as *Sabrina* and *Sabrina Goes to College*), The WB, 2002.
Fantasy Dexter, *The District,* CBS, 2002–2003.
Ryder, "Sand Francisco Dreamin'," *Charmed,* 2003.
"Naughty vs. Nice," *Family Feud* (also known as *Family Fortunes*), syndicated, 2005.

Television Appearances; Movies:
Harmony, *Mystery Woman: Sing Me a Murder,* Hallmark Channel, 2005.

Television Appearances; Specials:
The 12th Annual Soap Opera Awards, NBC, 1996.
Host, *The 13th Annual Soap Opera Awards,* NBC, 1997.
Presenter, *The 14th Annual Soap Opera Awards,* NBC, 1998.
Presenter, *The 26th Annual Daytime Emmy Awards,* CBS, 1999.
Macy's Thanksgiving Day Parade, NBC, 1999.
The 31st Annual NAACP Image Awards, Fox, 2000.
Presenter, *The 27th Annual Daytime Emmy Awards,* ABC, 2000.

Film Appearances:
Patrick, *Are You a Serial Killer,* Durham, 2002.
Nick Jenkins, *Dating Games People Play,* Marc, 2004.
Dr. Scott, *Breaking Dawn,* Lions Gate, 2004.
Davis White, *Revenge,* Goblin Market, 2004.
Aidam McAllister, *Aimee Price,* White Swan, 2005.

PENN, Chris 1962–2006
(Christopher Penn)

PERSONAL

Full name, Christopher Shannon Penn; born June 10, 1962 (some sources cite October 10, 1965), in Los Angeles, CA; died January 24, 2006, in Santa Monica, CA; buried in Holy Cross Cemetery in Culver City, CA. Actor and producer. A member of a family of entertainers that included actor Sean, musician Michael, and director Leo, Penn appeared in dozens of films, beginning in 1979 in *Charlie and the Talking Buzzard.* More a character actor than a leading man, Penn was in a number of prominent films, including *Footlose, At Close Range,* which also starred his brother Sean and mother Eileen Ryan, the Quentin Tarantino film *Reservoir Dogs,* Jackie Chan's *Rush Hour,* and the comedy *Starsky & Hutch.* In 1999 he produced and acted in the film *The Florentine.* Penn worked primarily in films, but he also made noteworthy appearances in television. In addition to a recurring role in the series *The Brotherhood of Poland, New Hampshire* in 2003, Penn had roles in episodes of *Seinfeld, Will & Grace,* and *CSI: Miami. The Darwin Awards,* Penn's last film, premiered on the day of his death.

PERIODICALS

Entertainment Weekly, February 3, 2006.
People Weekly, February 6, 2006.

PETERSEN, William 1953–
(William L. Petersen)

PERSONAL

Full name, William Louis Peterson; born February 21, 1953, in Evanston, IL; parents in the furniture business; married Joanne Brady, 1974 (divorced, 1981); married Gina Cirone (a biology teacher), June 14, 2003; children: (first marriage) Maite (some sources spell name Mae–Tae). *Education:* Attended Idaho State University; trained with Steppenwolf Theatre Company, Chicago, IL; studied in Spain. *Avocational Interests:* Sports.

Addresses: *Office*—High Horse Films, 25135 Anza Dr., Santa Clarita, CA 91355. *Agent*—Tracey Jacobs, United Talent Agency, 9560 Wilshire Blvd., Suite 500, Beverly

Hills, CA 90212. *Publicist*—Jennifer Allen, PMK/HBH Public Relations, 700 San Vicente Blvd., Suite G910, West Hollywood, CA 90069 (some sources cite 8500 Wilshire Blvd., Suite 700, Beverly Hills, CA 90211).

Career: Actor and producer. Innisfree (theatre ensemble), cofounder; Remains Theatre Ensemble (formerly known as Ix), Chicago, IL, founding member of company (with others); High Horse Films, Santa Clarita, CA, founder and partner (with Cindy Chvatal). Song performer at Chicago Cubs games, Wrigley Field, Chicago, IL. Worked in forestry and at a newspaper. Testified in front of the United States Senate on behalf of funding for crime laboratories. Sometimes credited as William L. Petersen.

Member: Screen Actors Guild.

Awards, Honors: Jeff awards, outstanding ensemble performance, Joseph Jefferson awards Committee, c. 1982, for *Balm in Gilead,* and c. 1984, for *Moby Dick;* Jeff Award nomination, c. 1984, for *The Tooth of Crime;* Jeff Award, best actor 1985, for *The Belly of the Beast: Letters from Prison;* Jeff Award nomination, c. 1994, for *The Night of the Iguana;* Commitment to Chicago Award, 1995; Alan J. Pakula Award (with others), artistic excellence, Broadcast Film Critics Association, 2001, for *The Contender; TV Guide* Award nomination, actor of the year in a new series, 2001, Golden Satellite Award nomination, best performance by an actor in a drama series, International Press Academy, 2002, Emmy Award nomination (with others), outstanding drama series, 2002, 2003, and 2004, Screen Actors Guild Award nominations (with others), outstanding performance by an ensemble in a drama series, 2002, 2003, and 2004, Golden Laurel Award nominations (with others), television producer of the year award in episodic drama category, Producers Guild of America, 2003 and 2004, Golden Globe Award nomination, best performance by an actor in a television drama series, 2004, and Screen Actors Guild Award (with others), outstanding performance by an ensemble in a drama series, 2005, all for *CSI: Crime Scene Investigation.*

CREDITS

Television Appearances; Series:
Gil Grissom, *CSI: Crime Scene Investigation* (also known as *CSI, CSI: Las Vegas, CSI: Weekends,* and *Les experts*), CBS, 2000—.

Television Appearances; Miniseries:
Joseph P. Kennedy, Sr., *The Kennedys of Massachusetts,* ABC, 1990.
Gideon Walker, *Return to Lonesome Dove,* CBS, 1993.

Whip Dalton, *The Beast* (also known as *Peter Benchley's "The Beast"*), NBC, 1996.
Jackson Connolly, *Haven,* CBS, 2001.

Television Appearances; Movies:
Cecil "Stud" Cantrell, *Long Gone* (also known as *Stogies*), HBO, 1987.
Joe Starling, *Keep the Change,* TNT, 1992.
Stephen Guerin, *Curacao* (also known as *Deadly Currents*), Showtime, 1993.
Juror number twelve, *12 Angry Men,* Showtime, 1997.
Jake Bridges, *Gunshy,* Cinemax, 1998.
Joad, *The Staircase,* CBS, 1998.
John F. Kennedy, *The Rat Pack,* HBO, 1998.
Jeff, *Kiss the Sky,* The Movie Channel, 1999.

Television Appearances; Specials:
The Taming of the Shrew, 1987.
Jack Tremaine, *Present Tense, Past Perfect,* Showtime, 1996.
Himself, *CBS at 75,* CBS, 2003.
TV Guide's Greatest Moments 2004, ABC, 2004.

Television Appearances; Awards Presentations:
Presenter, *The 53rd Annual Primetime Emmy Awards,* CBS, 2001.
Presenter, *The 27th Annual People's Choice Awards,* CBS, 2001.
The 54th Annual Primetime Emmy Awards, NBC, 2002.
Presenter, *The 55th Annual Primetime Emmy Awards,* Fox, 2003.
The GQ Men of the Year Awards (also known as *Spike TV Presents GQ Men of the Year Awards 2003*), Spike TV, 2003.
Presenter, *The 57th Annual Primetime Emmy Awards,* CBS, 2005.
Presenter, *The 63rd Annual Golden Globe Awards,* NBC, 2005.

Some sources cite an appearance as a presenter at *The 56th Annual Primetime Emmy Awards,* ABC, 2004.

Television Appearances; Episodic:
Edward Sayers, "Need to Know," *The Twilight Zone,* CBS, 1986.
George, "Good Housekeeping," *Fallen Angels* (also known as *Perfect Crimes*), Showtime, 1995.
Guest, *The Rosie O'Donnell Show,* syndicated, 2000.
Guest, *Larry King Live,* Cable News Network, 2002.
Himself, *Charlie Rose* (also known as *The Charlie Rose Show*), PBS, 2003.
Himself, *On the Record with Bob Costas,* HBO, c. 2003.
Himself, *TV Land Moguls,* TV Land, 2004.

Appeared in "The Films of Michael Mann," *The Directors,* Encore.

Television Appearances; Pilots:

Gil Grissom, "Cross–Jurisdictions," *CSI: Miami,* CBS, 2002, originally broadcast as an episode of *CSI: Crime Scene Investigation* (also known as *CSI, CSI: Las Vegas, CSI: Weekends,* and *Les experts*), CBS, 2002.

Television Work; Series:

Producer, *CSI: Crime Scene Investigation* (also known as *CSI, CSI: Las Vegas, CSI: Weekends,* and *Les experts*), CBS, 2000–2002.

Supervising producer, *CSI: Crime Scene Investigation* (also known as *CSI, CSI: Las Vegas, CSI: Weekends,* and *Les experts*), CBS, 2001–2002.

Co–executive producer, *CSI: Crime Scene Investigation* (also known as *CSI, CSI: Las Vegas, CSI: Weekends,* and *Les experts*), CBS, 2003.

Executive producer, *CSI: Crime Scene Investigation* (also known as *CSI, CSI: Las Vegas, CSI: Weekends,* and *Les experts*), CBS, 2004–2005.

Television Work; Movies:

Producer, *Keep the Change,* TNT, 1992.

Film Appearances:

Katz & Jammer bartender, *Thief* (also known as *Violent Streets*), United Artists, 1981.

Richard Chance, *To Live and Die in L.A.,* Metro–Goldwyn–Mayer/United Artists, 1985.

FBI agent Will Graham, *Manhunter* (also known as *Red Dragon* and *Red Dragon: The Pursuit of Hannibal Lecter*), De Laurentiis Entertainment Group, 1986.

Russell, *Amazing Grace and Chuck* (also known as *Silent Voice*), TriStar, 1987.

Tom Hardy, *Cousins* (also known as *A Touch of Infidelity*), Paramount, 1989.

Sheriff Patrick Floyd "Pat" Garrett, *Young Guns II* (also known as *Hell Bent for Leather* and *Young Guns II: Blaze of Glory*), Twentieth Century–Fox, 1990.

Joey Coalter, *Hard Promises,* Columbia, 1991.

Frank Scanlan, *Passed Away,* Buena Vista, 1992.

Tony C., *In the Kingdom of the Blind, the Man with One Eye Is King* (also known as *In the Kingdom of the Blind*), Arrow Releasing, 1995.

(Uncredited) Jack, *Muholland Falls,* Metro–Goldwyn–Mayer, 1996.

Steve Walker, *Fear* (also known as *No Fear* and *Obsession mortelle*), Universal, 1996.

Governor Jack Hathaway, *The Contender,* Dream-Works, 2000.

Senator Ames Levritt, *The Skulls* (also known as *Le clan des skulls*), MCA/Universal, 2000.

Himself, *This Old Cub* (documentary), Emerging Pictures, 2004.

Film Producer:

Hard Promises, Columbia, 1991.

Stage Appearances:

Darkness at Noon, Chicago area production, c. 1976.

Dillinger, Victory Gardens Theater, Chicago, IL, 1978.

Heat, Victory Gardens Theater, 1978.

Towards the Morning, Victory Gardens Theater, 1978.

Indulgences in a Louisville Harem, Remains Theatre, Chicago, IL, 1980.

Stanley Kowalski, *A Streetcar Named Desire,* Stratford Festival of Canada, Stratford, Ontario, Canada, 1981.

Sixty–Six Scenes of Halloween, Remains Theatre, 1981.

Canticle of the Sun, Wisdom Bridge Theatre, Chicago, IL, c. 1981.

Joe Conroy, *Balm in Gilead,* Remains Theatre, Steppenwolf Theatre, Chicago, IL, c. 1981–82.

Gardenia, Goodman Theatre, Chicago, IL, 1982.

Jack Henry Abbott, *The Belly of the Beast: Letters from Prison,* Wisdom Bridge Theatre, 1983, Ivanhoe Theatre, Chicago, IL, 1985, John F. Kennedy Center for the Performing Arts, Washington, DC, 1985.

Captain Ahab, *Moby Dick,* Remains Theatre, 1984.

Eddie, *Fool for Love,* Steppenwolf Theatre, 1984.

James Lingk, *Glengarry Glen Ross,* Goodman Theatre, 1984.

Hoss, *The Tooth of Crime,* Remains Theatre, c. 1984.

Interrogator, *Days and Nights Within,* Organic Theatre, Chicago, IL, 1986.

Matti, *Puntila and His Hired Man,* Remains Theatre, Organic Theatre, 1986.

Paul, *Big Time,* Remains Theatre, 1987.

The Taming of the Shrew, 1987.

Bobby Gould, *Speed–the–Plow,* Remains Theatre, Wisdom Bridge Theatre, 1989.

Teach, *American Buffalo,* Remains Theatre, 1991.

Painter, *Once in Doubt,* Remains Theatre, 1992.

The Chicago Conspiracy Trial, Remains Theatre, 1992.

Reverend T. Lawrence Shannon, *The Night of the Iguana,* Goodman Theatre, c. 1994, Roundabout Theatre Company, Criterion Center Stage Right Theatre, New York City, 1996.

Ted, *Flyovers,* Victory Gardens Theatre, Chicago, IL, 1998.

Appeared in *As You Like It* and *Twelfth Night* (also known as *Twelfth Night, or What You Will*), both productions of the Illinois Shakespeare Festival; in *A Class C Trial in Yokohama,* Chicago Theatre Project and Remains Theatre; in *Waiting for Godot,* Remains Theatre; and as Joe in *The Time of Your Life.* Appeared in productions at Boise State University and Lewis and Clark College.

Major Tours:

Jack Henry Abbott, *The Belly of the Beast: Letters from Prison,* productions in Glasgow, Scotland, and London, including the American Festival, London, 1985.

Stage Director:
Farmyard, Remains Theatre, Chicago, IL, c. 1980.
Traps, Remains Theatre, 1983.

RECORDINGS

Videos:
Narrator, *Wrigley Field: Beyond the Ivy,* Midwest Artists Distribution, 2001.
Himself, *Inside "Manhunter,"* Anchor Bay Entertainment, 2001.
Himself, *Counterfeit World: Making "To Live and Die in L.A.,"* Metro–Goldwyn–Mayer Home Entertainment, 2003.
Narrator, *Blue Neon Night: Michael Connelly's Los Angeles* (also known as *Blue Neon Night*), Incline Entertainment, 2004.

Video Games:
(And co–executive producer) Voice of Gilbert "Gil" Grissom, *CSI: Crime Scene Investigation,* Ubi Soft Entertainment, 2003.
Voice of Gilbert "Gil" Grissom, *CSI: Crime Scene Investigation—Dark Motives,* 2004.

OTHER SOURCES

Periodicals:
American Film, August, 1990, pp. 48–49.
Good Housekeeping, June, 2003, p. 144.
Parade, March 31, 2002, p. 14.
People Weekly, March 11, 2002, p. 57.
Sports Illustrated, September 13, 2004, p. 23.
TV Guide, November 29, 2003, p. 8.
Velocity, July, 1998.

PIPER, Roddy 1954–
(Rowdy Roddy Piper)

PERSONAL

Original name, Roderick George Toombs; born April 17, 1954, in Saskatoon, Saskatchewan, Canada (not Glasgow, Scotland, as sometimes cited); father a police officer; married Kitty, 1979; children: six (some sources cite four). *Religion:* Christian. *Avocational Interests:* Playing the bagpipes.

Career: Actor. National Wrestling Alliance, professional wrestler, 1973–87; World Wrestling Federation (later known as World Wrestling Entertainment), began as professional wrestler, became color commentator, then interim president, c. 1995–96, and affiliated with the organization in later years; World Championship Wrestling, interim commissioner, 1997, storyline vice president, 1999; Extreme Wrestling Federation (also known as XWF; some sources spell name Xtreme Wrestling Federation), president, beginning c. 2000, and trainer of wrestlers; sometimes wrestled as the Masked Canadian early in his career. Appeared in commercials and appeared on various forms of merchandise. Mentor for other wrestlers. Also a boxer and installed billboards.

Awards, Honors: Named Americas wrestling champion, 1976–77, Americas tag champion, 1976–78, U.S. champion, 1978, Pacific Northwest tag champion, 1978–80, Pacific Northwest champion, 1979–80, Canadian tag champion, 1980, mid–Atlantic television champion, 1980, mid–Atlantic champion, 1981–82 and 1983, and U.S. mid–Atlantic champion, 1981 and 1983, all National Wrestling Alliance; named intercontinental champion, World Wrestling Federation, 1992, and U.S. Champion, World Championship Wrestling, 1999; inducted into the World Wrestling Entertainment Hall of Fame, 2005, and the SLAM! Wrestling Canadian Hall of Fame.

CREDITS

Television Appearances; Series:
(As Rowdy Roddy Piper) *World Wide Wrestling,* syndicated, 1980–84.
(As Rowdy Roddy Piper) Himself and host of "Piper's Pit" segments, *WWF Superstars of Wrestling,* TBS and syndicated, beginning 1984.
(As Rowdy Roddy Piper) Performer in live action segments, *Hulk Hogan's Rock 'n' Wrestling* (live action and animated; also known as *Rock 'n' Wrestling Saturday Spectacular*), CBS, c. 1985–87.
Cohost, *Saturday Night's Main Event* (also known as *Saturday Night Main Event*), NBC, c. 1990–92, Fox, c. 1992.
WWF Monday Night RAW, USA Network, 1994–96.
WCW Thunder, TBS, 1998–99.
WCW Monday Nitro (also known as *nWo Nitro, WCW Monday Nitro Live!,* and *World Championship Wrestling Monday Nitro*), TNT, 1998–2000.
Himself and host of "In the Pit with Piper" segments, *TNA Impact! Wrestling* (also known as *TNA Xplosion*), Spike TV, 2004–2005.
Celebrity Wrestling, Independent Television 2, beginning 2005.
WWE A.M. RAW, USA Network, beginning 2005.

Television Appearances; Movies:
Preacher, *The Highwayman* (also known as *Terror on the Blacktop*), NBC, 1987.
Maurice "The Brute" Steiger, *The Love Boat: A Valentine Voyage* (also known as *The Love Boat: A Summer Cruise*), CBS, 1990.

Ice, *No Contest,* HBO, 1994.
Randy, *Hard Time,* TNT, 1998.
Detective Deeks, *Jack of Hearts,* Aquarius (Greece), 2000.
Pastor Robert, *Three Wise Guys,* USA Network, 2005.

Television Appearances; Specials:
StarrCade, 1983.
(As Rowdy Roddy Piper) *WrestleMania* (also known as *WWF WrestleMania*), 1985.
(As Rowdy Roddy Piper) *WrestleMania 2,* pay–per–view, 1985.
WWF Wrestling Classic, pay–per–view, 1985.
WrestleMania III, pay–per–view, 1987.
(As Rowdy Roddy Piper) *Summerslam,* pay–per–view, 1988.
Survivor Series, pay–per–view, 1989.
WrestleMania V (also known as *WWF WrestleMania*), pay–per–view, 1989.
Royal Rumble, pay–per–view, 1990.
WrestleMania VI, pay–per–view, 1990.
Summerslam (also known as *Summerslam '91*), pay–per–view, 1991.
Survivor Series (also known as *WWF Survivor Series*), pay–per–view, 1991.
WrestleMania VII, pay–per–view, 1991.
(As Rowdy Roddy Piper) *Royal Rumble,* pay–per–view, 1992.
Summerslam, pay–per–view, 1992.
(As Rowdy Roddy Piper) *WrestleMania VIII,* pay–per–view, 1992.
(As Rowdy Roddy Piper) *King of the Ring* (also known as *WWF King of the Ring*), pay–per–view, 1994.
WrestleMania X (also known as *WWF WrestleMania X*), pay–per–view, 1994.
WrestleMania XI, pay–per–view, 1995.
Starrcade (also known as *WCW Starrcade*), pay–per–view, 1996.
WrestleMania XII (also known as *WWF WrestleMania XII*), pay–per–view, 1996.
Himself, *WCW Great American Bash,* pay–per–view, 1997.
Halloween Havoc, 1997.
(In archive footage) Himself, *Hitman Hart: Wrestling with Shadows,* Arts and Entertainment, 1998.
WCW Fall Brawl, pay–per–view, 1998.
(As Rowdy Roddy Piper) *WrestleMania XIX,* pay–per–view, 2003.
WWE Backlash, 2003.
WWE Judgment Day, pay–per–view, 2003.
TNA Wrestling: Victory Road, pay–per–view, 2004.
TNA Wrestling: Final Resolution, 2005.
(As Rowdy Roddy Piper) Himself, *WrestleMania 21,* pay–per–view, 2005.
(In archive footage) Himself, *WWE Unforgiven,* pay–per–view, 2005.

Television Appearances; Episodic:
(Uncredited) Himself, *Saturday Night Live* (also known as *NBC's "Saturday Night," Saturday Night,* and *SNL*), NBC, 1985.
Himself, *Saturday Night's Main Event* (also known as *Saturday Night Main Event*), NBC, multiple appearances, beginning 1985.
Himself, "Rowdy Roddy's Rotten Pipes," *The Super Mario Bros. Super Show!* (animated and live action), syndicated, 1989.
Bishop, "Broken Heart, Broken Mask," *Zorro* (also known as *The New Zorro* and *Les nouvelles aventures de Zorro*), The Family Channel, 1990.
Adrian Temple, "Metamorphosis," *Superboy* (also known as *The Adventures of Superboy*), syndicated, 1992.
Jimmy Snow, "Wild Card," *Silk Stalkings,* USA Network and CBS, 1992.
Anthony Gallen, "Epitaph for Tommy," *Highlander* (also known as *Highlander: The Series*), syndicated, 1993.
Commander Cash, "Robocop vs. Commander Cash," *Robocop* (also known as *RoboCop: The Series*), syndicated, 1994.
Cody "The Crusader" Conway, "Crusader," *Walker, Texas Ranger,* CBS, 1998.
(Uncredited) "Wrestling" (also known as "Professional Wrestling"), *Weird Weekends* (also known as *Louis Theroux's "Weird Weekends"*), BBC–2 and Independent Film Channel, c. 1998.
Marlon, "Small Friends," *The Outer Limits* (also known as *The New Outer Limits*), Showtime, Sci–Fi Channel, and syndicated, 1999.
Guest, *Mad TV,* Fox, 1999.
Daniel Boone, "The Rescue," *Mentors,* The Family Channel (Canada), 2000.
Coach Harold, "Grudge Match," *The Mullets,* UPN, 2003.
Himself, "The Man Show Boy Apologizes," *The Man Show,* Comedy Central, 2003.
WWE Velocity (also known as *Velocity*), Spike TV and Internet broadcast, 2003, 2005.
(As Rowdy Roddy Piper) *WWF Smackdown!* (also known as *Smackdown!, Smackdown! Xtreme, World Wrestling Federation Smackdown!,* and *WWE Smackdown!*), UPN, 2003, 2005, 2006.
Himself, "WrestleMania," *Hogan Knows Best,* VH1, 2005.
WWE Monday Night RAW, USA Network, multiple appearances in 2005.

Television Appearances; Pilots:
Rick McDonald, *Tag Team,* ABC, 1991.
Sergeant Lundy, *Daytona Beach,* ABC, 1996.

Film Appearances:
(Uncredited) Leatherneck Joe Brady, *The One and Only,* Paramount, 1978.
Quick Rick Roberts, *Body Slam,* De Laurentiis Entertainment Group/Worldvision Enterprises, 1987.
Sam Hell, *Hell Comes to Frogtown,* New World Pictures, 1987.

Nada (some sources cite Nana), *They Live* (also known as *John Carpenter's "They Live"* and *They Live!*), MCA/Universal, 1988.

Cowboy, *Buy & Cell,* Empire Pictures/New World Pictures, 1989.

Frank Rossi, *Back in Action,* Shapiro–Glickenhaus Home Video, 1994.

John Keller, *Immortal Combat* (also known as *Resort to Kill* and *Viaje para matar*), A–pix Entertainment, 1994.

Bartel, *Terminal Rush,* Triboro Entertainment Group, 1995.

Elmo Freech, *Tough and Deadly,* MCA–Universal, 1995.

Frank Gibson, *Marked Man,* LIVE Entertainment/ Starlight, 1995.

Lieutenant Jacob "Jake" Cornell, *Jungleground,* Norstar Releasing/Starlight, 1995.

Himself, *The Misery Brothers,* 1995.

Detective Cameron Grayson, *Sci–Fighters,* Triboro Entertainment Group, 1996.

First Encounter, Leo Home Video, 1997.

Mick Leddy, *Dead Tides,* LIVE Entertainment, 1997.

Dash Simms, *The Bad Pack,* Showcase Entertainment, 1998.

Nick Ford, *Last to Surrender,* New Films International, 1998.

Legless Larry, *Legless Larry & the Lipstick Lady,* 1999.

Miles, *Shepherd* (also known as *Cybercity*), Danforth Studios/VCL Communications, 1999.

L. T. Tyrell, *Honor,* Birch Tree Entertainment, 2005.

Yokum, *Shut Up and Shoot,* Birch Tree Entertainment, 2005.

Bronco Bill, *Domestic Import,* 2006.

Chief Fred Mears, *Blind Eye,* Skylight Films, 2006.

Jackson Smith, *Urban Legends: Goldfield Murders,* 18th Avenue Productions, 2006.

Trent Polly, *Sin–Jin Smyth,* Classic Pictures/Sunn Classic Pictures, 2006.

Some sources cite an appearance in *Dilemma,* c. 1999.

RECORDINGS

Videos:

Pro Wrestling Illustrated Presents Lords of the Ring: Superstars & Superbouts, Avid Video/Live Video, 1985.

Wrestling's Country Boys, Coliseum Video, 1985.

WWF Wrestling's Hottest Matches, Coliseum Video, 1992.

The Best There Is: Bret "Hitman" Hart 2, 1994.

WCW/nWo Superstar Series: Diamond Dallas Page— Feel the Bang!, Warner Bros., 1998.

(In archive footage) Nada in *They Live, Ultimate Fights from the Movies,* Flixmix, 2002.

(In archive footage) Himself, *The Ultimate Ric Flair Collection,* World Wrestling Entertainment, 2003.

Ultimate Pro Wrestling: Rage at the River (also known as *UPW: Rage at the River*), 2003.

(In archive footage) Himself, *The Monday Night War: WWE RAW vs. WCW Nitro* (also known as *The Monday Night War: WWE RAW Is WAR vs. WCW Monday Nitro*), World Wrestling Entertainment Home Video, 2004.

The Damn! Show (animated), Studio Works Entertainment, 2005.

Overload (also known as *UPW: Overload*), 2005.

WWE Hall of Fame, World Wrestling Entertainment Home Video, 2005.

WWE Legends: Greatest Wrestling Stars of the '80s, World Wrestling Entertainment Home Video, 2005.

Music Videos:

Cyndi Lauper, "The Goonies 'R' Good Enough," 1985.

Meat Loaf, Cyndi Lauper, and Rick Derringer, "Land of 1000 Dances," 1985.

Screamin' DeVilles, "Drive Drive 105," 2002.

WRITINGS

Nonfiction:

In the Pit with Piper: Roddy Gets Rowdy (autobiography), Berkley Publishing, 2002.

OTHER SOURCES

Books:

Lentz, Harris M., *Biographical Dictionary of Professional Wrestling,* McFarland & Company, 1997.

Morton, Gerald, and George M. O'Brien, *Wrestling to Rasslin': Ancient Sport to American Spectacle,* Bowling Green State University Press, 1985.

St. James Encyclopedia of Popular Culture, St. James Press, 2000.

Periodicals:

Entertainment Weekly, August 11, 1995, p. 61.

PITILLO, Maria 1965–

PERSONAL

Born January 8, 1965, in Elmira, NY; raised in Mahwah, NJ. *Education:* Studied acting with William Esper and Harold Guskin; studied voice with Robbie McCauley.

Addresses: *Agent*—William Morris Agency, One William Morris Place, Beverly Hills, CA 90212; Jonathan Howard, Innovative Artists, 1505 10th St., Santa Monica, CA 90401.

Career: Actress. Appeared in commercials and performed as a singer. Worked in the retail field.

CREDITS

Film Appearances:
Masseuse, *Wise Guys,* United Artists, 1986.
Angel, *Spike of Bensonhurst* (also known as *Throw Back!*), FilmDallas Pictures, 1988.
Ponytail girl, *Bright Lights, Big City,* Metro–Goldwyn–Mayer, 1988.
Olivia Honey, *She–Devil,* Orion, 1989.
Janey, *White Palace,* Universal, 1990.
Mary Pickford, *Chaplin* (also known as *Charlot*), TriStar, 1992.
Kandi, *True Romance* (also known as *Breakaway*), Warner Bros., 1993.
Deborah, *Natural Born Killers,* Warner Bros., 1994, director's cut of the film also released.
Flight attendant, *I'll Do Anything,* Columbia, 1994.
Kim, *Bye Bye, Love,* Twentieth Century–Fox, 1995.
Gloria McKinney, *Dear God,* Paramount, 1996.
Audrey Timmonds, *Godzilla,* TriStar, 1998.
Maggie, *Something to Believe In,* Warner Bros., 1998.
Betty, *Dirk and Betty,* AMCO Entertainment Group, 1999.
Vicki, *After Sex,* Cutting Edge Entertainment/Lantern Lane Entertainment/Splendid Pictures, 2000.

Television Appearances; Series:
Nancy Don Lewis, *Ryan's Hope,* ABC, 1987–89.
Robin, *Middle Ages,* CBS, 1992.
Gina Weston, *South of Sunset,* CBS, 1993.
Alicia Sundergard Star, *Partners,* Fox, 1995–96.
Casey Farrell, *House Rules,* NBC, 1998.
Tina Calcatera, *Providence,* NBC, 2001–2002.

Television Appearances; Movies:
Annie DeMarco, *The Lost Capone,* TNT, 1990.
Bridget, "Cooperstown," *TNT Screenworks,* TNT, 1993.
Maria Caprefoli, *Between Love & Honor,* CBS, 1995.
Teresa Walden Stamper, *Escape from Terror: The Teresa Stamper Story* (also known as *Crimes of Passion: Escape from Terror—The Teresa Stamper Story*), NBC, 1995.
Zee, *Frank & Jesse,* HBO, 1995.
Debbie McNeal, *The Christmas Secret* (also known as *Flight of the Reindeer*), CBS, 2000.

Television Appearances; Specials:
Vickie, "What If I'm Gay?," *CBS Schoolbreak Special,* CBS, 1987.

Television Appearances; Episodic:
Anna, "The Cell Within," *Miami Vice,* NBC, 1989.

Angel, "Aria," *Law & Order* (also known as *Law & Order Prime*), NBC, 1991.
Mimi, "The Man Who Said Hello," *Mad about You* (also known as *Loved by You*), NBC, 1993.
Guest, *Late Night with Conan O'Brien,* NBC, 1998.
Paula Hunt, "Civil War," *Ally McBeal,* Fox, 1999.
Rebecca Waters, "Weather Girl," *Early Edition,* CBS, 1999.
Paula, "Love Plus One," *Will & Grace,* NBC, 2000.
Laura, "The One with the Home Study," *Friends* (also known as *Across the Hall, Friends Like Us, Insomnia Cafe,* and *Six of One*), NBC, 2003.

Television Appearances; Pilots:
Chelsea, *Saturday's,* ABC, 1991.
Alicia Sundergard Star, *Partners,* Fox, 1995.
Casey Farrell, *House Rules,* NBC, 1998.
Meg, *In the Loop,* ABC, 1998.
Follow the Leeds (also known as *Suburban Sleuths*), Lifetime, 2003.
Allison, *The Angriest Man in Suburbia,* CBS, 2006.

Appeared as Maddy Chase in the pilot *It's about This Guy.*

Stage Appearances:
Appeared in regional theatre productions.

RECORDINGS

Videos:
Herself, *Godzilla: On Assignment with Charles Caiman,* Columbia/TriStar Home Video, 1998.

OTHER SOURCES

Periodicals:
Movieline, April, 1998, p. 12.
Total Film, August, 1998, pp. 26, 27.

POEHLER, Amy 1971–

PERSONAL

Born September 16, 1971, in Burlington, MA; daughter of Bill and Eileen Poehler; married Will Arnett, August 29, 2003. *Education:* Attended Boston College.

Addresses: *Agent*—United Talent Agency, 9560 Wilshire Blvd., Suite 500, Beverly Hills, CA 90212.

Manager—3 Arts Entertainment, 9460 Wilshire Blvd., 7th Floor, Beverly Hills, CA 90212.

Career: Actress.

Awards, Honors: Teen Choice Award nomination, choice comedian, 2005.

CREDITS

Television Appearances; Series:
Colby, *Upright Citizens Brigade,* Comedy Central, 1998.
Saturday Night Live (also known as *NBC's Saturday Night, SNL, SNL 25* and *Saturday Night Live '80*), NBC, 2001—.

Television Appearances; Episodic:
Susan, "Single White Male," *Spin City,* ABC, 1998.
Pink, *Zoe Loses It,* Cinemax, 2001.
"Upright Citizens Brigade," *Late Friday,* NBC, 2001.
Hillary, "So You Have a Boyfriend," *Undeclared,* Fox, 2002.
Hillary, "Hal and Hillary," *Undeclared,* Fox, 2002.
Celebrity Poker Showdown, Bravo, 2003–2004.
Wife of GOB, "Altar Egos," *Arrested Development,* Fox, 2004.
Wife of GOB, "Justice is Blind," *Arrested Development,* Fox, 2004.
Wife of GOB, "Best Man for the GOB," *Arrested Development,* Fox, 2004.
Wife of GOB, "Whistler's Mother," *Arrested Development,* Fox, 2004.
The Sharon Osbourne Show, syndicated, 2004.
60 Minutes (also known as *TV Land Legends: The 60 Minutes Interviews*), CBS, 2004.
The Tonight Show with Jay Leno, NBC, 2004.
Late Night with Conan O'Brien, NBC, 2004, 2005.
Ellen: The Ellen DeGeneres Show, syndicated, 2004, 2005.
Wife of GOB, "Motherboy XXX," *Arrested Development,* Fox, 2005.
Voice of Jenda, "Future–Drama," *The Simpsons* (animated), Fox, 2005.
Voice of grandma, "Where's Gary," *SpongeBob SquarePants* (animated; also known as *SpongeBob*), Nickelodeon, 2005.
Weekends at the DL, Comedy Central, 2005.
Jimmy Kimmel Live, ABC, 2005.

Television Appearances; Pilots:
Amy, *Apt. 2F,* 1997.
Sick in the Head, Trio, 2003.

Television Appearances; Specials:
Brilliant But Cancelled, Trio, 2002.

Saturday Night Live: The Best of Chris Kattan, NBC, 2003.
Mellinda, *Saturday Night Live: The Best of Christopher Walken,* NBC, 2004.
Cheryl Spander, *Saturday Night Live: Presidential Bash 2004,* NBC, 2004.
Saturday Night Live: The Best of Alec Baldwin, NBC, 2005.

Television Appearances; Miniseries:
Heroes of Comedy: Women on Top, Comedy Central, 2003.

Television Appearances; Movies:
Escape from It's a Wonderful Life (also known as *Escape from a Wonderful Life*), 1996.
A.S.S.S.S.C.A.T.: Improv, 2005.

Television Executive Producer; Movies:
A.S.S.S.S.C.A.T.: Improv, 2005.

Film Appearances:
Kirsten, *Saving Manhattan,* 1998.
Woman sprayed with hose, *Tomorrow Night,* Circus King, 1998.
Ruth, *Deuce Bigalow: Male Gigolo,* Buena Vista, 1999.
The Devil and Daniel Webster, Pyramid, 2001.
Susie, *Wet Hot American Summer,* Kinowelt, 2001.
Patty, *Martin & Orloff,* Harlem, 2002.
Mrs. George, *Mean Girls,* Paramount, 2004.
Natalie Vaderpark, *Envy,* Columbia, 2004.
Bank teller, *Wake Up, Ron Burgundy: The Lost Movie* (also known as *Anchorman: Wake–Up Ron Burgundy* and *Wake Up Ron Burgundy*), DreamWorks, 2004.
Doreen Moran, *Wild Girls Gone,* 2005.
Maggie Hoffman, *Mr. Woodcock,* New Line Cinema, 2006.
Southland Tales, United International, 2006.
Truck stop waitress, *Tenacious D in: The Pick of Destiny,* New Line Cinema, 2006.
Blades of Glory, DreamWorks, 2006.
The Heartbreak Kid, DreamWorks, 2006.

Film Producer:
Wild Girls Gone, 2005.

RECORDINGS

Videos:
"Mean Girls": Only the Strong Survive, Paramount Home Video, 2004.

Video Games:
Deer Avenger 2: Deer in the City, Simon & Schuster, 1999.

WRITINGS

Screenplays:
Wild Girls Gone, 2005.

Television Movies:
Escape from It's a Wonderful Life (also known as *Escape from a Wonderful Life*), 1996.
(And creator) *A.S.S.S.S.C.A.T.: Improv,* 2005.

Television Series:
(And creator) *Upright Citizens Brigade,* 1998.

POPE, Randy

PERSONAL

Addresses: *Office*—Sid & Marty Krofft Pictures, 4024 Radford Ave., Building 5, Suite 102, Studio City, CA 91604.

Career: Producer, assistant director, unit production manager, and special effects technician. Sid & Marty Krofft Pictures, Studio City, CA, senior vice president of production.

CREDITS

Television Work; Series:
Supervising producer, *Land of the Lost,* ABC, 1991–94.
Executive producer, *Family Affair,* The WB, 2002–2003.

Television Producer; Movies:
(And line producer) *California Casanova,* Cinemax, 1992.
A Carol Christmas, The Hallmark Channel, 2003.
Hard Ground, The Hallmark Channel, 2003.
The King and Queen of Moonlight Bay, The Hallmark Channel, 2003.
Mystery Woman, The Hallmark Channel, 2003.
(With others) *Recipe for Disaster,* PAX TV, 2003.
The Hollywood Mom's Mystery (also known as *The Dead Hollywood Moms Society*), The Hallmark Channel, 2004.
Just Desserts, The Hallmark Channel, 2004.
Life on Liberty Street, The Hallmark Channel, 2004.
Love's Enduring Promise, The Hallmark Channel, 2004.
Detective (also known as *Arthur Hailey's "Detective"*), 2005.
Mystery Woman: At First Sight, The Hallmark Channel, 2005.

Mystery Woman: Game Time, The Hallmark Channel, 2005.
Mystery Woman: Mystery Weekend, The Hallmark Channel, 2005.
Mystery Woman: Redemption, The Hallmark Channel, 2005.
Mystery Women: Sing Me a Murder, The Hallmark Channel, 2005.
Mystery Woman: Snapshot, The Hallmark Channel, 2005.
Mystery Woman: Vision of a Murder, The Hallmark Channel, 2005.
Out of the Woods, The Hallmark Channel, 2005.
The Poseidon Adventure, NBC, 2005.
Mystery Woman: Wild West Mystery, The Hallmark Channel, 2006.
Our House, The Hallmark Channel, 2006.

Television Unit Production Manager; Movies:
Hard Ground, The Hallmark Channel, 2003.
The King and Queen of Moonlight Bay, The Hallmark Channel, 2003.
Mystery Woman, The Hallmark Channel, 2003.
The Hollywood Mom's Mystery (also known as *The Dead Hollywood Moms Society*), The Hallmark Channel, 2004.
Just Desserts, The Hallmark Channel, 2004.
Life on Liberty Street, The Hallmark Channel, 2004.
Detective (also known as *Arthur Hailey's "Detective"*), 2005.
Mystery Woman: Snapshot, The Hallmark Channel, 2005.
Out of the Woods, The Hallmark Channel, 2005.

Television Location Manager; Movies:
Deceptions, Showtime, 1990.

Television Executive Producer; Pilots:
Electra Woman and Dyna Girl, The WB, 2001.

Film Coproducer:
Hangfire, Motion Picture Corporation of America, 1991.
Double Trouble, Motion Picture Corporation of America, 1992.
Just for Kicks, Metro–Goldwyn–Mayer, 2003.

Film Assistant Director:
Beach Balls, Concorde Pictures, 1988.
Deadly Dreams, Concorde Pictures, 1988.
Second assistant director, *The Drifter,* Concorde Pictures, 1988.
Catch Me If You Can, Management Company Entertainment Group, 1989.
Long xing tian xia (also known as *The Master* and *Wong fei hung*), Paragon Films, 1989.
Medium Rare, 1989.

First assistant director, *Ministry of Vengeance,* Concorde Productions, 1989.

First assistant director, *Hangfire,* Motion Picture Corporation of America, 1991.

First assistant director, *Double Trouble,* Motion Picture Corporation of America, 1992.

First assistant director, *Life on the Edge,* Festival Films, 1992.

Film Special Effects Work:

Special effects coordinator, *Passion in the Desert,* Fine Line Features, 1997.

Special effects technician, *Santa Fe,* Nu–Image Films, 1997.

Special effects technician, *Ghosts of Mars* (also known as *John Carpenter's "Ghosts of Mars"*), Screen Gems/Columbia/TriStar, 2001.

Film Work; Other:

Unit production manager, *Purple People Eater,* Concorde Pictures, 1988.

Location manager, *The Masque of the Red Death,* Concorde Productions, 1989.

RECORDINGS

Video Work:

Co–executive producer, *I Wish I Were a Football Player,* WarnerVision Entertainment/Kid Vision, 1995.

PROSKY, John

PERSONAL

Son of Robert (an actor) and Ida Prosky; brother of Andy Prosky (an actor).

Addresses: *Agent*—Michael Linden Greene, Michael Greene and Associates, 7080 Hollywood Blvd., Suite 1017, Hollywood, CA 90028.

Career: Actor.

CREDITS

Film Appearances:

Officer Tom Bostich, *Late for Dinner,* Columbia, 1991.

Collins, *Interceptor,* Trimark Pictures, 1992.

Captain Hulett, *Aurora: Operation Intercept,* Trimark Pictures, 1995.

Doctor, *The Nutty Professor,* Universal, 1996.

Police officer, *The Phantom,* Paramount, 1996.

First aide, *Fire down Below,* Warner Bros., 1997.

Forensic police officer, *Goodbye Lover,* Warner Bros., 1998.

Police officer, *Permanent Midnight,* Artisan Entertainment/Live Film & Mediaworks, 1998.

Larkin, *Brown's Requiem,* 1998, Avalanche Releasing, 2000.

MindHead executive, *Bowfinger* (also known as *Bowfinger's Big Thing*), MCA/Universal, 1999.

Gordon, *Grandfather's Birthday* (short film), 2000.

Orderly, *Lost Souls,* New Line Cinema, 2000.

Mr. Williamson, *Artificial Intelligence: AI* (also known as *A.I. Artificial Intelligence*), Warner Bros., 2001.

Sergeant, *Offside* (short film), EuropaCorp. Distribution, 2001.

Atheon technician, *Hulk,* Universal, 2003.

Brigadier general Lewis Armistead, *Gods and Generals,* Warner Bros., 2003.

Director, *The Battle of Shaker Heights,* Miramax, 2003.

Male commentator, *Bringing down the House* (also known as *In the Houze* and *JailBabes.com*), Buena Vista, 2003.

Old man, *Groom Lake* (also known as *The Visitor*), Shadow Entertainment, 2003.

Tom O'Malley, *Southside* (also known as *Cock & Bull Story*), Pantheon Entertainment, 2003.

Hotel manager, *The Last Shot,* Buena Vista, 2004.

Officer at horse corral, *Hidalgo* (also known as *Dash*), Buena Vista, 2004.

Brewer, *Heart of the Beholder,* Beholder Productions, 2005.

Some sources cite an appearance as a confessor in *The Flintstones in Viva Rock Vegas,* Universal, 2000; an appearance in the film *The Lords of Discipline,* Paramount, 1983; and an appearance in *Love Machine 4.0* (also known as *The Last Big Toe*), Existential Films, 2004.

Television Appearances; Movies:

Phil, *A Case of Deadly Force,* CBS, 1986.

Don, *In the Line of Duty: A Cop for the Killing* (also known as *A Cop for the Killing* and *In the Line of Duty: Blood Brothers*), NBC, 1990.

Controller, *Flight of Black Angel,* Showtime, 1991.

Sherman Bochs, *Sketch Artist II: Hands That See* (also known as *A Feel for Murder* and *Sketch Artist II*), Showtime, 1995.

Markham, *The Cold Equations,* Sci–Fi Channel, 1996.

Polygraph technician, *Forgotten Sins,* ABC, 1996.

Alpha the alien commander, *The Advanced Guard* (also known as *The Colony*), Sci–Fi Channel, 1998.

Harold Bly, *My Little Assassin,* Lifetime, 1999.

Tom Reynolds, *An American Daughter* (also known as *Trial by Media*), Lifetime, 2000.

Wayne Turner, *Gone but Not Forgotten,* 2004.

Charles Greene, *Jane Doe: Til Death Do Us Part,* The Hallmark Channel, 2005.

Television Appearances; Episodic:
Officer Randall Carlson, "Watts a Matter?," *L.A. Law,* NBC, 1990.

Mike Evans, "Sweet 16," *Life Goes On,* ABC, 1991.

Mr. Taylor, "Play Melville for Me," *Dream On,* HBO, 1991, also broadcast on Fox.

Fred Converse, "Up on the Roof," *NYPD Blue,* ABC, 1994.

Ted, "Resolutions," *My So–Called Life,* ABC, 1995.

Bart Simon, "V–Fibbing," *Chicago Hope,* CBS, 1996.

Brathaw, "For the Cause," *Star Trek: Deep Space Nine* (also known as *Deep Space Nine, DS9,* and *Star Trek: DS9*), syndicated, 1996.

Dr. Porter, "Dr. Feelgood," *High Tide,* syndicated, 1996.

Mark Smith, "Chapter Seventeen," *Murder One,* ABC, 1996.

Preston, "A Lilith Thanksgiving," *Frasier* (also known as *Dr. Frasier Crane*), NBC, 1996.

Bart Simon, "The Adventures of Baron Von Munchausen ... by Proxy," *Chicago Hope,* CBS, 1997.

Bart Simon, "Split Decisions," *Chicago Hope,* CBS, 1997.

Bart Simon, "Verdicts," *Chicago Hope,* CBS, 1997.

Dr. Vanderkelen, "On Wings of Angels," *The Burning Zone,* UPN, 1997.

Hale, "Well, Nothing to Fear but Death Itself," *Spy Game,* ABC, 1997.

Jon Barrow, "Above and Beyond," *JAG,* CBS, 1997.

Lottery official, "Mo' Money, Mo' Problems," *The Jamie Foxx Show,* The WB, 1997.

"Child's Play," *Silk Stalkings,* USA Network, 1997.

"Why Can't Even a Couple of Us Get Along?," *Brooklyn South,* CBS, 1997.

Duke Weatherill, "Illegal Tender," *Beverly Hills 90210,* Fox, 1998.

Duke Weatherill, "Ready or Not," *Beverly Hills 90210,* Fox, 1998.

Earl Potter, "Scribbles," *Beyond Belief: Fact or Fiction* (also known as *Beyond Belief* and *Strange Truth: Fact or Fiction*), Fox, 1998.

Jules Clegg, "Boom," *Pensacola: Wings of Gold,* syndicated, 1998.

Malloy, "My Best Friend's Funeral," *The Closer,* CBS, 1998.

Norman, "The Odd Couple: Part 1," *Just Shoot Me!,* NBC, 1999.

Professor Ward, "Just above My Head," *Moesha,* UPN, 1999.

Salinger, "All in the Family," *Profiler,* NBC, 1999.

Attorney Mitchell Kravits, "Germ Warfare," *The Practice,* ABC, 2000.

Attorney Mitchell Kravits, "Officers of the Court," *The Practice,* ABC, 2000.

Dr. Meighan, "Episode Eleven," *Titus,* Fox, 2000.

Fourth aide, "Shibboleth," *The West Wing,* NBC, 2000.

Rafe and Harve's doctor, "Barry's Big Surprise," *Strip Mall,* Comedy Central, 2000.

Rafe and Harve's doctor, "Tammy Babysits," *Strip Mall,* Comedy Central, 2000.

Stewart Grossman, "Overdue & Presumed Lost," *JAG,* CBS, 2000.

"Legacy: Part 2," *JAG,* CBS, 2000.

"Relic of Evil," *Good versus Evil* (also known as *GvsE* and *G vs. E*), Sci–Fi Channel, 2000.

Businessperson, "What If?," *Any Day Now,* Lifetime, 2001.

Congressperson, "Muse to My Ears," *Charmed,* The WB, 2001.

Gregory, "Famous Last Words," *Touched by an Angel,* CBS, 2001.

Malchus, "Red Sky," *Stargate SG–1,* Showtime and syndicated, 2001.

Mr. Guidry, "Hold on Tight," *Judging Amy,* CBS, 2001.

Otrin, "Friendship One," *Star Trek: Voyager* (also known as *Voyager*), UPN, 2001.

Robert Horowitz, "Two Clarks in a Bar," *NYPD Blue,* ABC, 2001.

Dr. George Ferragamo, "11:00 a.m.–12:00 p.m.," *24* (also known as *24 Hours*), Fox, 2002.

Dr. Stern, "Ben Don't Leave," *Felicity,* The WB, 2002.

Medical examiner, "Jump the Shark," *The X–Files,* Fox, 2002.

Mr. Connelly, "Blind Injustice," *Becker,* CBS, 2002.

Mr. Garth, "One Bracelet Don't Feed the Beast," *Lost at Home* (also known as *My Second Chance* and *Michael Jacobs' Untitled Project*), ABC, 2003.

Tipton, "The Perfect Crime," *Peacemakers,* USA Network, 2003.

"My Mother's Daughter," *For the People* (also known as *Para la gente*), Lifetime, 2003.

Dr. Bergin, "The Socratic Method," *House* (also known as *House, M.D.*), Fox, 2004.

Mr. Brooks, "Abby Normal," *ER* (also known as *Emergency Room*), NBC, 2004.

Mr. Brooks, "Drive," *ER* (also known as *Emergency Room*), NBC, 2004.

Mr. Brooks, "Just a Touch," *ER* (also known as *Emergency Room*), NBC, 2004.

Mr. Brooks, "One for the Road," *ER* (also known as *Emergency Room*), NBC, 2004.

Reverend John Haynes, "Fighting Words," *JAG,* CBS, 2004.

Wil Banner, "The People vs. Achmed Abbas," *The D.A.,* ABC, 2004.

"Soup to Nuts," *Oliver Beene,* Fox, 2004.

Banks, "Good Housekeeping," *The Closer,* TNT, 2005.

Glen Easley, "Frankenlaura," *Nip/Tuck,* FX Channel, 2005.

Mr. Guidry, "10,000 Steps," *Judging Amy,* CBS, 2005.

Mr. Seabrooks, "You're Fired!," *The Second Time Around,* UPN, 2005.

"The Commencement," *American Dreams* (also known as *Bandstand, Miss American Pie,* and *Our Generation*), NBC, 2005.

"For Richer, for Poorer," *American Dreams* (also known as *Bandstand, Miss American Pie,* and *Our Generation*), NBC, 2005.

"Starting Over," *American Dreams* (also known as *Bandstand, Miss American Pie,* and *Our Generation*), NBC, 2005.

Author, "Begin the Begin," *Grey's Anatomy* (also known as *Complications, Surgeons,* and *Under the Knife*), ABC, 2006.

Dr. Gorenberg, "Here's a Balloon for You," *Related,* The WB, 2006.

Dr. Gorenberg, "Not without My Daughter," *Related,* The WB, 2006.

Appeared as Waxman in "The Cure," an unaired episode of *Air America,* syndicated. Some sources cite appearances as Charles Davis, *Family Law,* CBS; as Carl Bellamy, *Michael Hayes,* CBS; as Norman Sayers, *Moloney,* CBS; and as a police officer, *Something Wilder,* NBC.

Television Appearances; Pilots:

"This Baby's Gonna Fly," *Presidio Med,* CBS, 2002.

Banks, *The Closer,* TNT, 2005.

Television Work; Series:

Additional voices, *Techi Muyo!* (anime; also known as *Techi Universe*), [Japan], beginning c. 1995, Cartoon Network, c. 2000–2005.

Stage Appearances:

Colonel Edmund Starling, *Camping with Henry and Tom,* Wind Dancer Theatre, Lucille Lortel Theatre, New York City, 1995.

Osip Mandelstam, *The Akhmatova Project,* Critical Mass Performance Group, Actors' Gang Theatre, Los Angeles, 2000.

Member of ensemble, *Pera Palas,* Theatre at Boston Court, Los Angeles, 2005.

Member of ensemble, *A Tale of Charles Dickens,* Antaeus Company, Los Angeles Theatre Works, 2005.

Appeared in *A Life in the Theatre,* Marilyn Monroe Theatre, Los Angeles.

Radio Appearances:

Member of ensemble for *A Tale of Charles Dickens,* Antaeus Company, Los Angeles Theatre Works.

R

REHERMAN, Lee 1966–

PERSONAL

Born July 4, 1966, in Louisville, KY.

Addresses: *Contact*—G4 Media c/o Arena, 11301 West Olympic Blvd., Suite 501, Los Angeles, CA 90064.

Career: Actor.

CREDITS

Film Appearances:
Krause, *Last Action Hero,* Columbia, 1993.
Hans Saxer, *Ski Hard* (also known as *Downhill Willie* and *Ski Nuts*), BMG Video, 1995.
Matt Rakowski, *Heaven & the Suicide King,* Third Millenium, 1998.
Steele Manheim, *Champions,* A–Pix, 1998.
Big Ed, *Crossfire,* Scorpio, 1998.

Television Appearances; Series:
Hawk, *American Gladiators* (also known as *Gladiators*), syndicated, 1993–97.
Host, *Rollerjam,* The Nashville Network, 1999.
Host, *X.F.L.* (also known as *Xtreme Football League*), NBC, 2001.
Host, *USA's Cannonball Run 2001* (also known as *USA's Cannonball Run 2001 Race Across America*), USA Network, 2001.
Host, *Arena,* G4, 2002.
Host, *That Yin Yang Thing,* 2005.

Television Appearances; Movies:
Motorcycle cop, *Hard Time,* 1998.

Deputy, *Detective* (also known as *Arthur Hailey's Detective*), 2005.

Television Appearances; Episodic:
Hawk, "Gladiators," *Ellen* (also known as *These Friends of Mine*), 1995.
Fist, *Mad TV,* Fox, 1995.
Sweeney brother number one, *Caroline in the City,* NBC, 1998–99.
John Storm, "Last Man Standing," *The Net,* USA Network, 1999.
Mark, "Welcome to Bent Copper," *Soldier of Fortune, Inc.* (also known as *S.O.F. Special Ops Force, S.O. F., Inc.* and *SOF, Inc.*), syndicated, 1999.
Yuri Volkoff, "Vienen," *The X Files* (also known as *The X–Files*), 2001.
Captain, "There's No Place Like Plrtz Glrb," *Angel* (also known as *Angel: The Series*), 2001.
Doorman, "Red Light on the Wedding Night," *Gilmore Girls* (also known as *Gilmore Girls: Beginnings*), 2001.
Ludwig Morgal, "Dead Soldiers," *The Shield,* FX Channel, 2003.
Carl, "Saturday Afternoon Fever," *That's So Raven* (also known as *Absolutely Psychic* and *That's So Raven!*), The Disney Channel, 2003.
Sergeant Tuers, "Hung Out to Dry," *Navy NCIS: Naval Criminal Investigative Service* (also known as *NCIS* and *NCIS: Naval Criminal Investigative Service*), 2003.
Turbo, *Eve,* UPN, 2003–2004.
Celebrity wrestler, "Maddie Checks In," *The Suite Life of Zack and Cody*), The Disney Channel, 2005.
Soldier, *Charmed,* The WB, 2005.

Also appeared in *Family Feud.*

Television Appearances; Specials:
Host of annual show, *American Veteran Awards,* History Channel, 2002.

RIEGERT, Peter 1947–

PERSONAL

Born April 11, 1947, in the Bronx, New York, NY; son of Milton (a food wholesaler) and Lucille (a piano teacher) Riegert. *Education:* University at Buffalo the State University of New York, B.A., 1966.

Addresses: *Agent*—John S. Kelly, Bresler, Kelly and Associates, 11500 West Olympic Blvd., Suite 352, Los Angeles, CA 90064; (voice work) Special Artists Agency, 9465 Wilshire Blvd., Suite 890, Beverly Hills, CA 90212.

Career: Actor. Performer with the improvisational comedy group War Babies. Worked as an English teacher, social worker, waiter, and a political aide.

Member: Screen Actors Guild, Actors' Equity Association.

Awards, Honors: Emmy Award nomination, outstanding supporting actor in a miniseries or special, 1993, for *Barbarians at the Gate;* Screen Actors Guild Award (with others), outstanding performance by the cast of a theatrical motion picture, 2001, for *Traffic;* Academy Award nomination (with Ericka Frederick), best short film, live action, 2001, for *By Courier;* Festival Award, best first feature, Marco Island Film Festival, 2004, for *King of the Corner;* Golden Eagle Award, Marco Island Film Festival, 2004.

CREDITS

Film Appearances:
Donald "Boon" Schoenstein, *Animal House* (also known as *National Lampoon's "Animal House"*), Universal, 1978.
Eric McMurkin, *Americathon,* United Artists, 1979.
Sam Maguire, *Chilly Scenes of Winter* (also known as *Head over Heels*), United Artists, 1979.
Jason Cooper, *National Lampoon Goes to the Movies* (also known as *National Lampoon's "Movie Madness"*), United Artists, 1981.
Mac MacIntyre, *Local Hero,* Warner Bros., 1983.
Walter Giammanca, *Le grand carnaval* (also known as *The Big Carnival*), Carthago Films, 1983.
Tim, *The City Girl,* Moon Pictures, 1984.
Dr. Harris Kite, *Cudzoziemka* (also known as *The Stranger* and *El extrano*), Columbia, 1987.
Michael Pozner, *Un homme amoureux* (also known as *A Man in Love* and *Un uomo innamorato*), Gaumont, 1987.

Sam Posner, *Crossing Delancey,* Warner Bros., 1988.
Baby Elroy as an adult, *That's Adequate,* Southgate Entertainment, 1989.
Eric, *Oltre l'oceano* (also known as *Beyond the Ocean*), Medusa Distribuzione, 1990.
Robert Benham, *A Shock to the System,* Corsair Pictures, 1990.
Aldo, *Oscar,* Buena Vista, 1991.
Larry, *The Object of Beauty,* Avenue Entertainment, 1991.
Captain Gregory Fanducci, *The Runestone,* Hyperion Pictures, 1992.
Peter Syracusa, *Passed Away,* Buena Vista, 1992.
Marius Fisher, *Utz,* First Run Features/Castle Rock Productions, 1993.
Doctor, *White Man's Burden* (also known as *Bleeding Hearts* and *Fatal Destiny*), Savoy Pictures, 1994.
Lieutenant Mitch Kellaway, *The Mask,* New Line Cinema, 1994.
Dad Dunlap, *Pie in the Sky,* Fine Line Features, 1995.
Steve, *Coldblooded* (also known as *The Reluctant Hitman*), IRS Releasing, 1995.
Mel Feynman, *Infinity,* First Look Pictures, 1996.
Minor, *Hi–Life,* Lions Gate Films, 1998.
Attorney Michael Adler, *Traffic* (also known as *Traffic—Die Macht des Kartells*), USA Films, 2000.
Barry, *In the Weeds,* Moonstone Entertainment, 2000.
Dr. Peters, *Passion of Mind,* Paramount Classics, 2000.
Larry, *How to Kill Your Neighbor's Dog,* Artistic License, 2000.
C–Scam, Landscape Films, 2000.
Leo Spivak, *King of the Corner* (also known as *The Pursuit of Happiness*), Pursuit Films, 2004.

Appeared in the short film *A Director Talks about His Film.*

Film Director and Producer:
By Courier (short film), Two Tequila Productions, 2000.
King of the Corner, Pursuit Films, 2004.

Television Appearances; Series:
Walter Cooper, *Middle Ages,* CBS, 1992.
Ted Fisher, *The Beast,* ABC, 2001.
State assemblyman Ronald Zellman, a recurring role, *The Sopranos,* HBO, 2001–2002.

Television Appearances; Miniseries:
Jacob Rubinstein/Jake Rubin, *Ellis Island,* CBS, 1984.

Television Appearances; Movies:
Eric Ross, *News at Eleven,* CBS, 1986.
Herbie, *Gypsy* (musical), CBS, 1993.
Peter Cohen, *Barbarians at the Gate,* HBO, 1993.
Rabbi Cooper, *The Infiltrator,* HBO, 1995.
Sidney Wiltz, *An Element of Truth,* CBS, 1995.
Porker, *North Shore Fish,* Showtime, 1996.

Lieutenant Coop Cooper, *Face Down,* Showtime, 1997.

Irving Mansfield, *Scandalous Me: The Jacqueline Susann Story* (also known as *Jacqueline Susann, la scandaleuse*), USA Network, 1998.

Richard Luckman, *The Baby Dance,* Showtime, 1998.

Stan, *Jerry and Tom* (also known as *Tom and Jerry*), Showtime, 1999.

Marty Forkins, *Bojangles,* Showtime, 2001.

Rabbi, *Club Land,* Showtime, 2001.

Decker, *Bleacher Bums* (also known as *The Cheap Seats*), Showtime, 2002.

Mel, *Surrender Dorothy,* CBS, 2006.

Television Appearances; Specials:

Table Settings, HBO, c. 1983.

Richard M. Nixon, "Concealed Enemies," *American Playhouse,* PBS, 1984.

W. Eugene Smith, "W. Eugene Smith: Photography Made Difficult," *American Masters* (also known as *American Masters: W. Eugene Smith: Photography Made Difficult*), PBS, 1989.

Himself, *Burt Lancaster: Daring to Reach,* Arts and Entertainment, 1996.

Himself, *Burt Lancaster,* American Movie Classics, 1997.

Himself, *Behind the Movies: Animal House,* NBC, 2001.

Himself, *Unseen Untold: National Lampoon's "Animal House,"* Spike TV, 2003.

Zeb, "Back When We Were Grownups," *Hallmark Hall of Fame,* CBS, 2004.

(In archive footage) *Mouthing Off: 51 Greatest Smartasses,* Comedy Central, 2004.

(In archive footage) *Live from New York: The First 5 Years of Saturday Night Live,* NBC, 2005.

Television Appearances; Awards Presentations:

Himself, *The 2001 IFP/West Independent Spirit Awards,* Independent Film Channel, 2001.

Television Appearances; Episodic:

Groucho Marx, *Feelin' Good,* PBS, 1974.

Igor, "Change Day," *M*A*S*H,* CBS, 1977.

Igor, "War of Nerves," *M*A*S*H,* CBS, 1977.

Gus Rosenthal as an adult, "One Life, Furnished in Early Poverty," *The Twilight Zone,* CBS, 1985.

Bill, "The Hit List," *Trying Times,* PBS, 1989.

Jerold Dixon, "Deceit," *Law & Order* (also known as *Law & Order Prime*), NBC, 1996.

Kimbrough, "The Finale: Part 1," *Seinfeld,* NBC, 1998.

Jay Rydell, "The Cut Man Cometh," *Sports Night,* ABC, 2000.

Defense attorney, "Shrunk," *Law & Order* (also known as *Law & Order Prime*), NBC, 2003.

Voice of Max Weinstein, "When You Wish upon a Weinstein," *Family Guy* (animated; also known as *Padre de familia* and *Padre del familia*), Fox, 2003.

Chauncey Zeirko, "Conscience," *Law & Order: Special Victims Unit* (also known as *Law & Order's Sex Crimes, Law & Order: SVU,* and *Special Victims Unit*), NBC, 2004.

Chauncey Zeirko, "Lowdown," *Law & Order: Special Victims Unit* (also known as *Law & Order's Sex Crimes, Law & Order: SVU,* and *Special Victims Unit*), NBC, 2004.

Chauncey Zeirko, "Sick," *Law & Order: Special Victims Unit* (also known as *Law & Order's Sex Crimes, Law & Order: SVU,* and *Special Victims Unit*), NBC, 2004.

Chauncey Zeirko, "Design," *Law & Order: Special Victims Unit* (also known as *Law & Order's Sex Crimes, Law & Order: SVU,* and *Special Victims Unit*), NBC, 2005.

Appeared as Marshall Rifkin in *LateLine,* NBC and Showtime.

Television Appearances; Pilots:

Alan Baker, *Mystery Dance,* ABC, 1995.

Stage Appearances:

Honey Boy, *Dance with Me* (musical), Mayfair Theatre, New York City, 1975–76.

Danny Shapiro, *Sexual Perversity in Chicago/The Duck Variations,* Cherry Lane Theatre, New York City, 1976–77.

S. Vogel, Sauvage Sagar, and Vincenzo Chiaruggi, *Censored Scenes from King Kong* (musical), Princess Theatre, New York City, 1980.

Sunday Runners in the Rain, New York Shakespeare Festival, Public Theatre, Anspacher Theatre, New York City, 1980.

Marty Sterling, *Isn't It Romantic!,* Marymount Manhattan Theatre, New York City, 1981.

Key Exchange, Westwood Playhouse (later known as the Geffen Playhouse), Los Angeles, 1982.

Table Settings, c. 1983.

Marty, *La Brea Tarpits,* Workshop of the Players Art Theatre, New York City, 1984.

Sandy, *A Hell of a Town,* Westside Arts Theatre Upstairs, New York City, 1984.

The Cherry Orchard, Goodman Theatre, Chicago, IL, 1985.

Festival of Original One–Act Comedies, Manhattan Punch Line Theatre, New York City, 1985.

The Spanish Prisoner, New Theatre Company, Goodman Theatre, 1985.

Barney Rosen, *A Rosen by Any Other Name,* American Jewish Theatre, New York City, 1986.

Goldberg, *The Birthday Party,* Classic Stage Company, Classic Stage Company Theatre, New York City, 1987.

Axel Hammond, *The Nerd,* Helen Hayes Theatre, New York City, 1987–88.

Goldberg, *The Birthday Party,* and prisoner, *Mountain Language* (double–bill), Classic Stage Company, Classic Stage Company Theatre, 1989.

Jerry, *Road to Nirvana,* Circle Repertory Theatre, New York City, 1991.

Walter Abrahmson, *An American Daughter,* Cort Theatre, New York City, 1997.

Bobby Gould, *The Old Neighborhood* (consists of *The Disappearance of the Jews, Jolly,* and *Deeny*), Booth Theatre, New York City, 1997–98.

Celebration [and] *The Room* (double–bill), American Conservatory Theater, Geary Theater, San Francisco, CA, 2001.

Appeared in *Call Me Charlie,* The Performing Garage, New York City; and as Chico Marx, *Minnie's Boys* (musical), Playhouse in the Park, Philadelphia, PA.

Stage Work:

Director, *Sexual Perversity in Chicago,* American Conservatory Theater, San Francisco, CA, 2006.

RECORDINGS

Videos:

Himself, *The Yearbook: An "Animal House" Reunion,* Universal Studios Home Video, 2000.

Donald "Boon" Schoenstein, *Where Are They Now? A Delta Alumni Update,* Universal, 2003.

Audiobooks:

Andrea Barrett, *The Voyage of the Narwhal,* Random House, 1999.

WRITINGS

Screenplays:

By Courier (short film), Two Tequila Productions, 2000.

OTHER SOURCES

Periodicals:

Playbill, November 19, 1997.

ROBINSON, Ann 1935–

PERSONAL

Born May 1, 1935, in Hollywood, CA; father, a bank employee; married Jaime Bravo (a matador), 1957 (divorced, 1967); married Joseph Valdez (a real estate broker), 1987; children: (first marriage) Jaime, Jr. (a sports director), Estefan A. (an actor).

Career: Actress. Worked as a stunt performer; appeared in commercials; frequent guest at conventions.

CREDITS

Film Appearances:

(Uncredited) Girl at pool in home movie, *The Damned Don't Cry,* Warner Bros., 1950.

(Uncredited) Salesclerk, *I Was a Shoplifter,* Universal International Pictures, 1950.

(Uncredited) *A Life of Her Own,* Metro–Goldwyn–Mayer, 1950.

(Uncredited) Clarisse Carter, *Goodbye, My Fancy,* Warner Bros., 1951.

(Uncredited) Gloria, *I Want You,* RKO Radio Pictures, 1951.

(Uncredited) Hat check girl at Mocambo's, *Callaway Went Thataway* (also known as *The Star Said No*), Metro–Goldwyn–Mayer, 1951.

(Uncredited) Girl at palace, *Son of Ali Baba,* Universal International Pictures, 1952.

(Uncredited) *The Cimarron Kid,* Universal International Pictures, 1952.

(Uncredited) Girl in bar, *City beneath the Sea,* Universal International Pictures, 1953.

Lucille Grellett, *Bad for Each Other,* Columbia, 1953.

Nancy, *The Glass Wall,* Columbia, 1953.

Sylvia Van Buren, *The War of the Worlds,* Paramount, 1953.

Officer Grace Downey, *Dragnet* (later known as *The Original Dragnet*), Warner Bros., 1954.

Rose Fargo, *Gun Brothers,* United Artists, 1956.

Valerie, *Julie,* Metro–Goldwyn–Mayer, 1956.

Judy, *Gun Duel in Durango* (also known as *Duel in Durango*), United Artists, 1957.

Cleo, *Damn Citizen,* Universal International Pictures, 1958.

Showgirl, *Imitation of Life,* Universal International Pictures, 1959.

Dr. Van Buren, *Midnight Movie Massacre* (also known as *Attack from Mars*), filmed c. 1984, released in 1988.

Herself, *The Fantasy Film Worlds of George Pal* (documentary), Arnold Leibovit Entertainment, 1985.

Dr. Sylvia Van Buren, *Attack of the B–Movie Monster,* 1985.

Party guest, *My Lovely Monster,* 1990.

Dr. Sylvia Van Buren, *The Naked Monster,* Heidelberg Films, 2005.

Grandmother, *War of the Worlds,* Paramount, 2005.

Some sources state that Robinson appeared in other films, including *Black Midnight,* Monogram Pictures, 1949; *The Story of Molly X,* Universal International Pictures, 1949; *Peggy,* Universal International Pictures, 1950; *An American in Paris* (musical), Metro–Goldwyn–Mayer, 1951; and *A Place in the Sun.*

Film Work:

Stunt rider for Shelley Winters, *Frenchie,* Universal International Pictures, 1950.

Stunt performer in other films. Some sources state that Robinson was a member of a dialogue loop group for various films, including *L'etrusco uccide ancora* (also known as *The Dead Are Alive, The Etruscan Kills Again, Overtime, Das Geheimnis des gelben Grabes,* and *Die Etrusker*), Inex Film/Mondial, dubbed version released by National General Pictures, 1972; *Supervivientes de los Andes* (also known as *Survive!*), Aviant Films/Paramount, c. 1976; *Volver a empezar* (also known as *Begin the Beguine, Starting Over, To Begin Again,* and *Volver a empezar (Begin the Beguine)*), Warner Bros., c. 1982, subtitled version released by Twentieth Century–Fox, 1983; and *Tough Guys.*

Television Appearances; Series:

Helen Watkins, *Fury* (also known as *Brave Stallion*), NBC, c. 1955–60.

Television Appearances; Specials:

Herself, *Hollywood Aliens & Monsters* (also known as *To the Galaxy and Beyond with Mark Hamill*), Arts and Entertainment, 1997.

(Uncredited; in archive footage) Sylvia Van Buren, *Watch the Skies! Science Fiction, the 1950s, and Us,* TCM, 2005.

Television Appearances; Episodic:

Queen Juliandra, "The Cold Sun," *Rocky Jones, Space Ranger* (also known as *Silver Needle in the Sky*), syndicated, 1954.

Queen Juliandra, "Inferno from Space," *Rocky Jones, Space Ranger* (also known as *Silver Needle in the Sky*), syndicated, 1954.

Queen Juliandra, "Out of the World," *Rocky Jones, Space Ranger* (also known as *Silver Needle in the Sky*), syndicated, 1954.

Joan Carter, "Mountain Fortress," *Cheyenne,* ABC, 1955.

Liz, "The Deceiving Eye," *Stage 7,* CBS, 1955.

Margaret Perry, "The Bitter Rival," *Studio 57* (also known as *Heinz Studio 57*), The DuMont Network, 1955.

Josie Howard, "The David Tremayne Story," *The Millionaire* (also known as *If You Had a Million*), CBS, 1956.

Queen Juliandra and Noviandra, "The Robot of Regalio," *Rocky Jones, Space Ranger* (also known as *Silver Needle in the Sky*), syndicated, 1956.

Paula, "Deadline," *Cheyenne,* ABC, 1957.

Anne Carter, "Borrowed Time," *The Texan,* CBS, 1960.

Julia Garcia, "Incident of the Challenge," *Rawhide,* CBS, 1960.

Miss Baxter, "The Deadly Key," *Shotgun Slade,* syndicated, 1960.

Sally Somers, "Rodeo," *The Man and the Challenge,* NBC, 1960.

Vivian Page, "The Case of the Slandered Submarine," *Perry Mason,* CBS, 1960.

Gloria Hale, "Double Image," *Surfside 6,* ABC, 1961.

Helen Cox, "Ambition," *Alfred Hitchcock Presents,* NBC, 1961.

Hetty Doane, "Billy Buckett, Incorporated," *The Life and Legend of Wyatt Earp* (also known as *Wyatt Earp*), ABC, 1961.

Joanna Cochrane, "Portrait in Leader," *Peter Gunn,* ABC, 1961.

Penelope Carmody, "A Slight Case of Chivalry," *Surfside 6,* ABC, 1961.

"Angel," *Sugarfoot* (also known as *Tenderfoot*), ABC, 1961.

"And If I Die," *Ben Casey,* ABC, 1962.

Manager, "Walk among Tigers," *77 Sunset Strip,* ABC, 1963.

Sylvia Van Buren, "Thy Kingdom Come," *War of the Worlds* (also known as *War of the Worlds: The Second Invasion*), syndicated, 1988.

Sylvia Van Buren, "To Heal the Leper," *War of the Worlds* (also known as *War of the Worlds: The Second Invasion*), syndicated, 1988.

Sylvia Van Buren, "The Meek Shall Inherit," *War of the Worlds* (also known as *War of the Worlds: The Second Invasion*), syndicated, 1989.

Some sources cite appearances in episodes of other series, including *Adam-12,* NBC; *Bachelor Father,* CBS, NBC, and ABC; *Biff Baker, U.S.A.,* CBS; *The Bob Cummings Show,* CBS; *The Burns and Allen Show,* CBS; *Days of Our Lives* (also known as *Cruise of Deception: Days of Our Lives, Days,* and *DOOL*), NBC; *Four Star Playhouse,* CBS; *General Hospital,* ABC; *Gilligan's Island,* CBS; *It's a Great Life,* NBC; *My Little Margie,* CBS and NBC; *Police Woman,* NBC; *Waterfront,* syndicated; and *The Web,* CBS and NBC.

Television Appearances; Pilots:

Night Stick, 1959.

RECORDINGS

Videos:

Herself, *The Sky Is Falling: The Making of "The War of the Worlds,"* Paramount Home Video, 2005.

Herself, *Steven Spielberg and the Original "War of the Worlds,"* DreamWorks Home Entertainment, 2005.

OTHER SOURCES

Periodicals:

Starlog, issue 195, 1993.

Electronic:
Ann Robinson's Home Page, http://annrobinson.com, January 18, 2006.

RODRIGUEZ, Michelle 1978–

PERSONAL

Full name, Michelle Marie Rodriguez; born July 12, 1978, in Bexar County, TX; raised in the Dominican Republic, Puerto Rico, and Jersey City, NJ; daughter of Rafael (in the military) and Carmen Rodriguez. *Education:* Studied business. *Avocational Interests:* Travel, in–line skating, dancing, painting, video games.

Addresses: *Agent*—International Creative Management, 8942 Wilshire Blvd., Beverly Hills, CA 90211. *Publicist*—True Public Relations, 6725 Sunset Blvd., Suite 570, Los Angeles, CA 90028.

Career: Actress and voice performer. Worked as a film extra and at a toy store.

Awards, Honors: National Board of Review Award, best breakthrough performance by an actress, 2000, Breakthrough Award, Gotham awards, Independent Features Project, 2000, Acting Prize, best female performance, Deauville Film Festival, 2000, Sierra Award, best female newcomer, and Sierra Award nomination, best actress, both Las Vegas Film Critics Society, 2000, Independent Spirit Award, best debut performance, Independent Features Project/West, 2001, Black Reel Award nomination, best actress in a theatrical film, Foundation for the Advancement of African Americans in Film, 2001, and Online Film Critics Society Award nomination, best cinematic debut or breakthrough performance, 2001, all for *Girlfight;* Chicago Film Critics Association Award nomination, most promising actress, 2001; Teen Choice Award nomination, film—choice breakout performance, 2001; ALMA Award nomination, outstanding actor or actress in a television movie or miniseries, American Latin Media Arts awards, 2002, for *3 A.M.;* MTV Movie Award nomination (with Kate Bosworth and Sanoe Lake), best onscreen team, 2003, for *Blue Crush;* Imagen Award, best supporting actress in a film, Imagen Foundation, 2004, for *S.W.A.T.;* member of the cast of *Lost* that was named entertainer of the year, *Entertainment Weekly,* 2005; Golden Globe Award, best television series—drama, and Screen Actors Guild Award, outstanding performance by an ensemble in a drama series, both with others, both 2006, for *Lost.*

CREDITS

Film Appearances:
Diana Guzman, *Girlfight,* Screen Gems, 2000.

Letty, *The Fast and the Furious* (also known as *Racer X, Reline,* and *Street Wars*), Universal, 2001.
Eden, *Blue Crush* (also known as *Surf Girls, Surf Girls of Maui,* and *Untitled Surf Project*), Universal, 2002.
Rain Ocampo, *Resident Evil* (also known as *Resident Evil: Ground Zero* and *Resident Evil the Movie*), Sony Pictures Entertainment, 2002.
Chris Sanchez, *S.W.A.T.,* Columbia, 2003.
Teresa, *Control,* Lions Gate Films, 2004.
Voice, *Sian Ka'an* (animated), Paramount, 2005.
Katarin, *BloodRayne,* Romar Entertainment, 2006.
Nicki, *The Breed,* First Look Media, 2006.
Mariah, *Grapefruit Moon,* Americana Productions/My Own Worst Enemy, 2007.

Some sources cite appearances in *Cradle Will Rock,* Buena Vista, 1999; *For Love of the Game,* MCA/Universal, 1999; and *Summer of Sam* (also known as *The Son of Sam*), Buena Vista, 1999.

Television Appearances; Series:
Voice of Liz Ricardo, *IGPX: Immortal Grand Prix* (anime; also known as *IGPX* and *Immortal Grand Prix*), Cartoon Network, beginning 2003.
Ana–Lucia Cortez, *Lost,* ABC, 2005—.

Television Appearances; Movies:
Salgado (cab driver), *3 A.M.,* Showtime, 2001.

Television Appearances; Specials:
Herself, *The Fast and the Furious Movie Special,* Black Entertainment Television, 2001.
Herself, *Sizzlin' Sixteen 2001,* E! Entertainment Television, 2001.
Herself, *Women of the Beach,* E! Entertainment Television, 2002.
Herself, *E! Entertainer of the Year 2003,* E! Entertainment Television, 2003.

Television Appearances; Awards Presentations:
The 10th Annual IFP Gotham Awards, Bravo, 2000.
The 2001 IFP/West Independent Spirit Awards, Independent Film Channel, 2001.
Presenter, *17th Annual IFP/West Independent Spirit Awards,* Independent Film Channel, 2002.
Presenter, *2002 ABC World Stunt Awards,* ABC, 2002.
Presenter, *Third Annual Taurus World Stunt Awards,* USA Network, 2003.
2004 MTV Movie Awards, MTV, 2004.
2004 Taurus World Stunt Awards, 2004.
Video Game Awards 2004, Spike TV, 2004.
The 57th Annual Primetime Emmy Awards, CBS, 2005.
12th Annual Screen Actors Guild Awards (also known as *Screen Actors Guild 12th Annual Awards*), TNT and TBS, 2006.

Television Guest Appearances; Episodic:

Herself, *The Tonight Show with Jay Leno*, NBC, 2001, 2002, 2006.

Herself, "S.W.A.T.," *HBO First Look*, HBO, 2003.

Herself, *Tinseltown TV*, International Channel, 2003.

(In archive footage) Herself, *Celebrities Uncensored*, E! Entertainment Television, 2004.

Punk'd, MTV, 2005.

RECORDINGS

Videos:

Herself, *Film–Fest DVD: Issue 5—Cannes 2000 & SXSW*, 2000.

Herself, *Playing Dead: "Resident Evil" from Game to Screen*, Columbia/TriStar Home Video, 2002.

Music Videos:

Ja Rule, "Always on Time," c. 2001.

Lenny Kravitz, "If I Could Fall in Love," 2002.

Video Games:

Voice of Rosie Velasco, *True Crime: Streets of LA*, Activision, 2003.

Voice of Calita, *Driv3r* (also known as *Driver 3*), Infogrames Entertainment, 2004.

Voice of marine, *Halo 2*, Microsoft, 2004.

OTHER SOURCES

Periodicals:

Cosmopolitan, October, 2000, pp. 218–20.

Femme Fatales, September, 2001, pp. 13–14.

Gallery, December, 2002, pp. 62–64.

Interview, September, 2000, p. 165; September, 2003, pp. 206–209.

Movieline, October, 2000, pp. 56–57.

Newsweek, October 2, 2000, p. 71.

People Weekly, November 6, 2000, p. 182; October 17, 2005, p. 143.

Talk, June/July, 2000.

Time, October 2, 2000, p. 88.

Time Out New York, 5, 2000.

TV Guide, November 28, 2005, pp. 14–18.

ROONEY, Mickey 1920–
   (Mickey McGuire, Joe, Jr. Yule, Mickey Yule)

PERSONAL

Original name, Joseph "Joe" Yule, Jr.; name legally changed, 1932; born September 23, 1920, in Brooklyn, New York, NY; son of Joe (a vaudeville performer) and Nell (a vaudeville performer; maiden name, Carter) Yule; married Ava Gardner (an actress), January 10, 1942 (some sources cite 1941; divorced May 21, 1943); married Betty Jane Rase, September 30, 1944 (divorced June 3, 1949); married Martha Vickers (an actress), June 3, 1949 (divorced September 25, 1951); married Elaine Mahnken (some sources cite Elaine Devry; an actress), 1952 (divorced May 18, 1958); married Barbara Ann Thomason (some sources spell surname Thompson), December 1, 1958 (died January 3, 1966); married Margie Lane, September 10, 1966 (divorced 1967); married Carolyn Hockett, 1969 (divorced 1974); married Janice Darlene "Jan" Chamberlain (a singer, songwriter, and actress), July 28, 1978; children: (second marriage) Mickey Rooney, Jr. (an actor and musician; also known as Joseph Yule III), Timothy "Tim" (an actor); (third marriage) Theodore "Teddy" (an actor); (fifth marriage) Kelly Ann, Kerry Yule, Michael Joseph Kyle, Kimmy Sue; (seventh marriage) Jimmy, Jonelle; stepchildren: (eighth marriage) Christopher Aber (an actor), Mark Aber (a musician). *Education:* Attended Mrs. Lawlor's School for Professional Children. *Avocational Interests:* Golf, horses and horse racing, animals and animal rights causes, painting.

Addresses: *Agent*—Robert Malcolm, The Artists Group, Ltd., 2049 Century Park East, Suite 4060, Los Angeles, CA 90067.

Career: Actor. Made his stage debut at the age of fifteen months. Appeared in commercials and print advertisements. Singer at various venues. Participant and speaker at various events, parades, and festivals, including the Judy Garland Festival, Grand Rapids, MN, 1999 and 2000. Mickey Rooney Tabas Hotel, Downingtown, PA, co-owner. Some sources state that Rooney was involved with a health food company, an advertising firm, and the World Poker Tour Invitational. *Military service:* U.S. Army, served during World War II.

Member: Screen Actors Guild, American Society of Composers, Authors and Publishers.

Awards, Honors: Juvenile Academy Award (with Deanna Durbin), 1938; Academy Award nomination, best actor in a leading role, 1939, for *Babes in Arms*; Academy Award nomination, best actor in a leading role, 1943, for *The Human Comedy*; Academy Award nomination, best actor in a supporting role, 1956, for *The Bold and the Brave*; Golden Laurel Award nomination, top male action star, Laurel awards, Producers Guild of America, 1958, for *Baby Face Nelson*; Emmy Award nomination, best single performance by a lead or supporting actor, 1958, for "The Comedian," *Playhouse 90*; Emmy Award nomination, best single performance by an actor, 1959, for "Eddie," *Alcoa Theatre*; Golden Laurel Award nomination, top male supporting performance, 1963, for *Requiem for a*

Heavyweight; Golden Globe Award, best male television star, 1964; Academy Award nomination, best actor in a supporting role, 1979, for *The Black Stallion;* Special *Theatre World* Award, Antoinette Perry Award nomination, and Drama Desk Award nomination, both best actor in a musical, all 1980, for *Sugar Babies;* Emmy Award, outstanding lead actor in a limited series or special, and Golden Globe Award, best performance by an actor in a miniseries or motion picture made for television, both 1982, for *Bill;* honorary Academy Award, 1982; Emmy Award nomination, outstanding lead actor in a limited series or special, 1984, for *Bill: On His Own;* Former Child Star Lifetime Achievement Award, Young Artist awards, Young Artist Foundation, 1991; Gemini Award nomination, best performance by an actor in a continuing leading dramatic role, Academy of Canadian Cinema and Television, 1992, for *The Black Stallion;* Francois Truffaut Award, Giffoni Film Festival, 1996; Hollywood Film Legend Award, Hollywood Christmas Parade, 2000; named mayor for life, Girls and Boys Town alumni, 2003; John Payne Lifetime Achievement Award, Blue Ridge Southwest Virginia Vision Film Festival, 2004; special award for service during World War II, National D–Day Memorial, 2004; received multiple on the Hollywood Walk of Fame; recipient of other awards and honors.

CREDITS

Film Appearances:
Midget, *Not to be Trusted,* 1926.

(Uncredited) *Orchids and Ermine,* 1927.

(As Mickey McGuire) Boy, *Sin's Pay Day,* Mayfair, 1932.

(As Mickey McGuire) Buddy Whipple, *High Speed,* Columbia, 1932.

King Charles V, *My Pal the King,* Universal, 1932.

(Uncredited) Mickey Fitzpatrick, *The Beast of the City,* Metro–Goldwyn–Mayer, 1932.

Midge, *Fast Companions* (also known as *Caliente* and *The Information Kid*), Universal, 1932.

Emma, Metro–Goldwyn–Mayer, 1932.

Arthur Wilson, *The Big Chance,* Arthur Greenblatt Distribution Service/States Rights Independent Exchanges, 1933.

(As Mickey McGuire) Buddy Malone, *Officer Thirteen,* 1933.

(Uncredited) Freckles, *The Life of Jimmy Dolan* (also known as *The Kid's Last Fight*), Warner Bros., 1933.

Jimmy O'Hara, *The Big Cage,* Universal, 1933.

Otto Peterson as a child, *The World Changes,* Warner Bros., 1933.

Willie, *The Chief* (also known as *My Old Man's a Fireman*), Metro–Goldwyn–Mayer, 1933.

Young Ted Hackett III, *Broadway to Hollywood* (also known as *March of Time, Ring up the Curtain,* and *Show World*), Metro–Goldwyn–Mayer, 1933.

The Bowery, United Artists, 1933.

Blackie at the age of twelve, *Manhattan Melodrama,* Metro–Goldwyn–Mayer, 1934.

(Uncredited) Boy swimmer, *Chained,* Metro–Goldwyn–Mayer, 1934.

(Uncredited) Boy with dog, *The Lost Jungle,* 1934.

Freddy, *Blind Date* (also known as *Her Sacrifice*), Columbia, 1934.

Gladwyn Tootle, *Love Birds,* Universal, 1934.

(Scenes deleted) Jerry, *Upperworld* (also known as *Upper World*), Warner Bros., 1934.

Messenger, *I Like It That Way,* Universal, 1934.

Mickey, *Death on the Diamond,* Metro–Goldwyn–Mayer, 1934.

Tommy, *Beloved,* Universal, 1934.

William "Willie" Miller, *Hide–Out,* Metro–Goldwyn–Mayer, 1934.

Willie, *Half a Sinner,* Universal, 1934.

(Uncredited) Country boy, *Rendezvous,* 1935.

Eddie, *Reckless,* Metro–Goldwyn–Mayer, 1935.

Freckles, *The County Chairman,* Twentieth Century–Fox, 1935.

Jimmy Thurger, *Riffraff,* Metro–Goldwyn–Mayer, 1935.

Jimmy, *The Healer* (also known as *Little Pal*), Monogram, 1935.

Himself, *Pirate Party on Catalina Island,* 1935.

Puck, *A Midsummer Night's Dream,* Warner Bros., 1935.

Tommy Miller, *Ah, Wilderness!,* Metro–Goldwyn–Mayer, 1935.

Dick Tipton, *Little Lord Fauntleroy,* United Artists, 1936.

Fred "Snappy" Sinclair, *Down the Stretch,* Warner Bros., 1936.

James "Gig" Stevens, *The Devil Is a Sissy* (also known as *The Devil Takes the Count*), Metro–Goldwyn–Mayer, 1936.

Dan Troop, *Captains Courageous,* Metro–Goldwyn–Mayer, 1937.

Jerry Crump, *Live, Love and Learn,* Metro–Goldwyn–Mayer, 1937.

Himself, *Cinema Circus,* Metro–Goldwyn–Mayer, 1937.

Shockey Carter, *Hoosier Schoolboy* (also known as *Forgotten Hero* and *Yesterday's Hero*), Monogram, 1937.

Swifty, *Slave Ship,* Twentieth Century–Fox, 1937.

Timmie "Tim" Donovan, *Thoroughbreds Don't Cry,* Metro–Goldwyn–Mayer, 1937.

Chick Evans, *Hold That Kiss,* Metro–Goldwyn–Mayer, 1938.

Himself, *Hollywood Handicap,* 1938.

Mickey, *Stablemates,* Metro–Goldwyn–Mayer, 1938.

Mike O'Toole, *Love Is a Headache,* Metro–Goldwyn–Mayer, 1938.

Terry O'Mulvaney, *Lord Jeff* (also known as *The Boy from Barnardo's*), Metro–Goldwyn–Mayer, 1938.

Whitey Marsh, *Boys Town,* Metro–Goldwyn–Mayer, 1938.

Huckelberry Finn, *The Adventures of Huckleberry Finn* (also known as *Huckleberry Finn*), Metro–Goldwyn–Mayer, 1939.

Mickey Moran, *Babes in Arms* (musical), Metro–Goldwyn–Mayer, 1939.

James "Jimmy" Connors, *Strike Up the Band* (musical), Metro–Goldwyn–Mayer, 1940.

Himself, *Rodeo Dough,* 1940.

Thomas Alva "Tom" Edison, *Young Tom Edison,* Metro–Goldwyn–Mayer, 1940.

(In archive footage) *Trifles of Importance,* 1940.

Tommy "Tom" Williams, *Babes on Broadway* (musical), Metro–Goldwyn–Mayer, 1941.

Whitey Marsh, *Men of Boys Town,* Metro–Goldwyn–Mayer, 1941.

Timothy Dennis, *A Yank at Eton,* Metro–Goldwyn–Mayer, 1942.

Danny Churchill, Jr., *Girl Crazy* (musical; also known as *When the Girls Meet the Boys*), Metro–Goldwyn–Mayer, 1943.

Homer Macauley, *The Human Comedy,* Metro–Goldwyn–Mayer, 1943.

Himself, *Show Business at War* (also known as *The March of Time Volume IX, Issue 10*), 1943.

Master of ceremonies at show, *Thousands Cheer* (musical), Metro–Goldwyn–Mayer, 1943.

Mike Taylor, *National Velvet,* Metro–Goldwyn–Mayer, 1944.

Mickey the Great (short film), 1946.

Himself, *Screen Snapshots Series 27, No. 3: Out of This World Series,* 1947.

Tommy McCoy, *Killer McCoy,* Metro–Goldwyn–Mayer, 1947.

Lorenz Hart, *Words and Music* (musical), Metro–Goldwyn–Mayer, 1948.

Richard Miller, *Summer Holiday* (musical), Metro–Goldwyn–Mayer, 1948.

Billy Coy, *The Big Wheel,* United Artists, 1949.

Daniel "Dan" Brady, *Quicksand,* United Artists, 1950.

Freddie Frisby, *He's a Cockeyed Wonder,* Columbia, 1950.

Johnny Casar, *The Fireball* (also known as *The Challenge*), Twentieth Century–Fox, 1950.

J. Dennis "Denny" O'Moore, *My Outlaw Brother* (also known as *My Brother, the Outlaw*), Eagle Lion Classics, 1951.

Stanley Maxton, *The Strip,* Metro–Goldwyn–Mayer, 1951.

Mike Donnelly, *Sound Off,* Columbia, 1952.

Augustus "Geechy" Cheevers, *A Slight Case of Larceny,* Metro–Goldwyn–Mayer, 1953.

Francis "Moby" Dickerson, *All Ashore,* Columbia, 1953.

Herbert Tuttle, *Off Limits* (also known as *Military Policeman*), Paramount, 1953.

Himself, *Screen Snapshots: Mickey Rooney—Then and Now* (also known as *Mickey Rooney, Then and Now*), 1953.

Himself, *Screen Snapshots: Spike Jones in Hollywood,* 1953.

Barnaby "Blix" Waterberry, *The Atomic Kid,* Republic Pictures, 1954.

Eddie Shannon, *Drive a Crooked Road,* Columbia, 1954.

Mike Forney, *The Bridges at Toko–Ri,* Paramount, 1954.

Reverend William Macklin II, *The Twinkle in God's Eye,* Republic Pictures, 1955.

David Prescott, *Francis in the Haunted House,* Universal, 1956.

Dooley, *The Bold and the Brave,* RKO Radio Pictures, 1956.

Frank Sommers, *Magnificent Roughnecks,* Allied Artists, 1956.

Himself, *Screen Snapshots: Playtime in Hollywood,* 1956.

Lester M. "Baby Face Nelson" Gillis (title role), *Baby Face Nelson,* United Artists, 1957.

Master sergeant Yancy Skibo, *Operation Mad Ball,* Columbia, 1957.

Gus Harris, *A Nice Little Bank That Should Be Robbed* (also known as *How to Rob a Bank*), Twentieth Century–Fox, 1958.

John "Killer" Mears, *The Last Mile,* United Artists, 1959.

"Little Joe" Braun, *The Big Operator* (also known as *Anatomy of the Syndicate*), Metro–Goldwyn–Mayer, 1959.

Nick Lewis (the Devil), *The Private Lives of Adam and Eve,* Universal, 1960.

Steven Conway, *Platinum High School* (also known as *Rich, Young and Deadly* and *Trouble at Sixteen*), Metro–Goldwyn–Mayer, 1960.

Beetle McKay, *Everything's Ducky,* Columbia, 1961.

Johnny Burke, *King of the Roaring '20s: The Story of Arnold Rothstein* (also known as *The Big Bankroll* and *King of the Roaring Twenties*), Allied Artists, 1961.

Mr. Yunioshi, *Breakfast at Tiffany's,* Paramount, 1961.

Army, *Requiem for a Heavyweight* (also known as *Blood Money*), Columbia, 1962.

Ding "Dingy" Bell, *It's a Mad Mad Mad Mad World* (also known as *It's a Mad, Mad, Mad, Mad World*), United Artists, 1963.

Terence Scanlon, *The Secret Invasion,* United Artists, 1964.

(In archive footage) Himself, *Hollywood: My Home Town,* 1965.

(In archive footage) Himself, *Inside Daisy Clover,* Warner Bros., 1965.

Norman Jones, *24 Hours to Kill* (also known as *Twenty–Four Hours to Kill*), Seven Arts, 1965.

Peachy Keane, *How to Stuff a Wild Bikini,* American International Pictures, 1965.

Gunnery sergeant Ernest Wartell, *Ambush Bay,* United Artists, 1966.

Adramalek, *L'arcidiavolo* (also known as *The Devil in Love* and *Il diavolo innamorato*), Warner Bros./Seven Arts, 1968.

"Blue Chips" Packard, *Skidoo,* Paramount, 1968.

W. W. J. Oglethorpe, *The Extraordinary Seaman,* Metro–Goldwyn–Mayer, 1968.

Vienna (short film), 1968.

Cockeye, *The Comic* (also known as *Billy Bright*), Columbia, 1969.

Wilfred Bashford, *80 Steps to Terror* (also known as *80 Steps to Jonah*), Warner Bros., 1969.

Indian Tom, *The Cockeyed Cowboys of Calico County* (also known as *A Woman for Charley*), Universal, 1970.

Himself, *Hollywood Blue,* 1970.

B. J. Lang, *The Manipulator* (also known as *B. J. Lang Presents* and *B. J. Presents*), Maron Films, 1971.

Himself, *Mooch Goes to Hollywood* (also known as *Mooch*), 1971.

Voice of Scarecrow, *Journey Back to Oz* (animated), Filmation, 1971.

Guardian angel, *Richard,* Aurora City, 1972.

Preston Gilbert, *Pulp,* United Artists, 1972.

Rocky Mastrasso, *The Godmothers,* 1972.

Cohost and narrator, *That's Entertainment!,* Metro–Goldwyn–Mayer, 1974.

Gas station attendant, *Thunder County* (also known as *Cell Block Girls, Convict Women, Swamp Fever,* and *Women's Prison Escape*), Prism Entertainment, 1974.

Laban, *Rachel's Man* (also known as *Ish Rachel*), 1974.

(Uncredited) Himself, *Just One More Time,* 1974.

Juego sucio en Panama (also known as *Ace of Hearts* and *As de corazon*), 1974.

Marty, *Bons baisers de Hong Kong* (also known as *From Hong Kong with Love*), 1975.

Himself, *Hooray for Hollywood* (also known as *Hollywood and the Stars* and *Hollywood on Parade*), Cinamo, Inc., 1975.

(In archive footage) Himself, *It's Showtime* (also known as *Crazy Animals, Jaws, Paws, Claws, Wonderful World of Those Cukoo Animals,* and *World of Those Cuckoo*), United Artists, 1976.

Himself, *That's Entertainment!, Part II,* Metro–Goldwyn–Mayer, 1976.

Trigger, *Find the Lady* (also known as *Call the Cops!* and *Kopek and Broom*), 1976.

Lampie, *Pete's Dragon* (live action and animated), Buena Vista, 1977.

Gus, *The Magic of Lassie,* International Picture Show Company, 1978.

Daad El Shur, *Arabian Adventure,* Associated Film Distributors, 1979.

Henry Dailey, *The Black Stallion,* United Artists, 1979.

Spiventa, *The Domino Principle* (also known as *The Domino Killings* and *El domino principe*), Avco–Embassy, 1979.

The railway engineer, *The Emperor of Peru* (also known as *Odyssey of the Pacific, Treasure Train, La traversee de la Pacific,* and *L'empereur de Perou*), Cine–Pacific, 1981.

Voice of Todd, *The Fox and the Hound* (animated), Buena Vista, 1981.

(In archive footage) *Hollywood Outtakes,* 1984.

Voice of Mr. Cherrywood, *The Care Bears Movie* (animated), Samuel Goldwyn, 1985.

(In archive footage) *That's Dancing!,* 1985.

Barney Ingram, *Lightning, the White Stallion* (also known as *The White Stallion*), Cannon, 1986.

Erik's grandfather, *Erik the Viking* (also known as *Erik viking*), Orion, 1989.

Elmer, *Home for Christmas,* New World Pictures, 1990.

Junior, *My Heroes Have Always Been Cowboys,* Samuel Goldwyn, 1991.

Barry Reilly, *The Milky Life* (also known as *La vida lactea*), 1992.

Chief of police, *Maximum Force,* PM Home Video, 1992.

Joe Petto, *Silent Night, Deadly Night 5: The Toy Maker,* Still Silent Films, 1992.

Narrator, *The Magic Voyage* (animated; also known as *Pico and Columbus* and *Die Abenteuer von Pico und Columbus*), Atlas Film, dubbed version released by Hemdale Film Corporation, 1992.

Pat Jensen, *The Legend of Wolf Mountain,* Hemdale Releasing, 1992.

Voice of Flip, *Little Nemo: Adventures in Slumberland* (animated), Hemdale Releasing, 1992.

Zeke, *Sweet Justice* (also known as *Killer Instincts*), Triboro Entertainment Group, 1992.

Gabriel, *Making Waves,* 1994.

Grandpa James Spencer, *Revenge of the Red Baron* (also known as *The Adventures of the Red Baron* and *Plane Fear*), New Horizons Home Video, 1994.

Host, *That's Entertainment III,* Metro–Goldwyn–Mayer, 1994.

Himself, *A Century of Cinema,* 1994.

Himself, *Radio Star—die AFN–Story,* 1994.

O. B. Taggart, *The Legend of O. B. Taggart* (also known as *The Outlaws: Legend of O. B. Taggart*), Northern Arts Entertainment, 1994.

Professor Mort Sang, *Killing Midnight,* 1997.

(Scenes deleted) *Kings of the Court,* Tennis Classics, 1997.

Derelict, *The Face on the Barroom Floor,* 1998.

Fugly Floom, *Babe 2: Pig in the City* (also known as *Babe in Metropolis* and *Babe 2*), Universal, 1998.

Griffith, *Michael Kael contre la World News Company* (also known as *Michael Kael in Katango* and *Michael Kael vs. the World News Company*), Bac Films, 1998.

Tollkeeper, *Animals and the Tollkeeper* (also known as *Animals*), Magnolia Mae, 1998.

Holy Hollywood, 1999.

Internet Love, 2000.

Voice of Sparky, *Lady and the Tramp II: Scamp's Adventure* (animated), Walt Disney Home Video/Buena Vista Home Video, 2001.

Prospector, *Topa Topa Bluffs,* 2002.

(Uncredited; in archive footage) Himself, *Hollywood's Magical Island: Catalina* (documentary), 2003.

Simon/Henry, Sr., *Paradise,* Sunset International, 2003.

Grandpa, *A Christmas Too Many,* Echelon Entertainment, 2005.

Himself, *Hedy Lamarr: Secrets of a Hollywood Star* (documentary; also known as *Hedy Lamarr: The Secret Communication*), Tre Valli Filmproduktion, 2005.

David McCord, *Strike the Tent,* Strongbow Pictures/
Solar Filmworks, 2006.

Max, *To Kill a Mockumentary,* Pizza Guy Films/Angry
Irish Productions/SoDak Productions, 2006.

Savy (some sources cite Senoi), *The Thirsting,* Cin-
emavault Releasing International, 2006.

Brooks, *Bamboo Shark,* Mental Ward Film Productions,
c. 2006.

Night at the Museum, Twentieth Century–Fox, c. 2006.

Some sources cite an appearance in a version of *Heidi.*

Film Appearances in Role of Andrew "Andy" Hardy:

A Family Affair (also known as *Skidding* and *Stand Ac-
cused*), Metro–Goldwyn–Mayer, 1937.

Andy Hardy's Dilemma (short film; also known as *Andy
Hardy's Dilemma: A Lesson in Mathematics ... and
Other Things*), Metro–Goldwyn–Mayer, 1938.

Judge Hardy's Children, Metro–Goldwyn–Mayer, 1938.

Love Finds Andy Hardy, Metro–Goldwyn–Mayer, 1938.

Out West with the Hardys, Metro–Goldwyn–Mayer,
1938.

You're Only Young Once, Metro–Goldwyn–Mayer,
1938.

Andy Hardy Gets Spring Fever, Metro–Goldwyn–Mayer,
1939.

The Hardys Ride High, Metro–Goldwyn–Mayer, 1939.

Judge Hardy and Son, Metro–Goldwyn–Mayer, 1939.

Andy Hardy Meets Debutante, Metro–Goldwyn–Mayer,
1940.

Andy Hardy's Private Secretary, Metro–Goldwyn–
Mayer, 1941.

Life Begins for Andy Hardy, Metro–Goldwyn–Mayer,
1941.

Andy Hardy's Double Life, Metro–Goldwyn–Mayer,
1942.

The Courtship of Andy Hardy, Metro–Goldwyn–Mayer,
1942.

(In archive footage of screen test) *Personalities,* 1942.

Andy Hardy's Blonde Trouble, Metro–Goldwyn–Mayer,
1944.

Love Laughs at Andy Hardy (also known as *Uncle Andy
Hardy*), Metro–Goldwyn–Mayer, 1946.

Andy Hardy Comes Home, Metro–Goldwyn–Mayer,
1958.

(In archive footage) *Alone. Life Wastes Andy Hardy*
(short film), Canyon Cinema, 1998.

**Film Appearances in Role of Mickey "Himself"
McGuire; Billed Variously as Mickey Yule, Mickey
McGuire, or Mickey Rooney:**

Mickey's Battle, 1927.

Mickey's Circus, 1927.

Mickey's Eleven, 1927.

Mickey's Minstrels, 1927.

Mickey's Pals, 1927.

Mickey in Love, 1928.

Mickey in School, 1928.

Mickey's Athletes, 1928.

Mickey's Babies, 1928.

Mickey's Big Game Hunt, 1928.

Mickey's Little Eva, 1928.

Mickey's Movies, 1928.

Mickey's Nine, 1928.

Mickey's Parade, 1928.

Mickey's Rivals, 1928.

Mickey's Triumph, 1928.

Mickey's Wild West, 1928.

Mickey the Detective, 1928.

Mickey's Big Moment, 1929.

Mickey's Brown Derby, 1929.

Mickey's Explorers, 1929.

Mickey's Great Idea, 1929.

Mickey's Initiation, 1929.

Mickey's Last Chance, 1929.

Mickey's Menagerie, 1929.

Mickey's Midnite Follies, 1929.

Mickey's Mix–Up, 1929.

Mickey's Northwest Mounted, 1929.

Mickey's Strategy, 1929.

Mickey's Surprise, 1929.

Mickey's Bargain, 1930.

Mickey's Champs, 1930.

Mickey's Luck, 1930.

Mickey's Master Mind, 1930.

Mickey's Merry Men, 1930.

Mickey's Musketeers, 1930.

Mickey's Warriors, 1930.

Mickey's Whirlwinds, 1930.

Mickey's Winners (also known as *Mickey Wins the
Day*), 1930.

Mickey the Romeo, 1930.

Mickey's Crusaders, 1931.

Mickey's Diplomacy, 1931.

Mickey's Helping Hand, 1931.

Mickey's Rebellion, 1931.

Mickey's Sideline, 1931.

Mickey's Stampede, 1931.

Mickey's Thrill Hunters, 1931.

Mickey's Wildcats, 1931.

Mickey's Big Business, 1932.

Mickey's Busy Day, 1932.

Mickey's Charity, 1932.

Mickey's Golden Rule, 1932.

Mickey's Holiday, 1932.

Mickey's Travels, 1932.

Mickey's Ape Man, 1933.

Mickey's Big Broadcast, 1933.

Mickey's Covered Wagon, 1933.

Mickey's Disguises, 1933.

Mickey's Race, 1933.

Mickey's Tent Show, 1933.

Mickey's Touchdown, 1933.

The Lost Jungle (serial), Mascot, 1934.

Mickey's Medicine Man, 1934.

Mickey's Rescue, 1934.

Mickey's Derby Day, 1936.

Film Director:
My True Story, Columbia, 1951.
(Uncredited) *The Bold and the Brave,* RKO Radio Pictures, 1956.
The Private Lives of Adam and Eve, Universal, 1960.

Film Producer:
The Atomic Kid, Republic Pictures, 1954.
The Twinkle in God's Eye, Republic Pictures, 1955.
Associate producer, *Jaguar,* Republic Pictures, 1956.

Film Work; Other:
Performer of songs that have appeared in films, television productions, and videos.

Television Appearances; Series:
Mickey Mulligan, *The Mickey Rooney Show* (also known as *Hey Mulligan*), NBC, 1954–55.
Mickey Grady, *Mickey,* ABC, 1964–65.
Host, *NBC Follies,* NBC, 1973.
Oliver Nugent, *One of the Boys,* NBC, 1982.
Henry Daley, *The Black Stallion* (also known as *The Adventures of the Black Stallion, The New Adventures of the Black Stallion,* and *L'etalon noir*), YTV (Canada) and The Family Channel, c. 1990–93.
Voice of Talbut, *Kleo the Misfit Unicorn* (animated), [Canada], c. 1997–98.

Television Appearances; Miniseries:
John Paul Jones, *Bluegrass,* CBS, 1988.
D. W. (the director), *Luck of the Draw: The Gambler Returns,* NBC, 1991.
Himself, *MGM: When the Lion Roars* (also known as *The MGM Story*), TNT, 1992.
(Uncredited; in archive sound footage) *Life with Judy Garland: Me and My Shadows* (also known as *Judy Garland: L'ombre d'une etoile*), ABC, 2001.
Himself, *The 100 Greatest Family Films,* Channel 4 (England), 2005.

Television Appearances; Movies:
Nelson Stool, *Evil Roy Slade,* NBC, 1971.
Old Bailey, "Donovan's Kid," *Disney's Wonderful World* (also known as *Disneyland, The Disney Sunday Movie, The Magical World of Disney, Walt Disney, Walt Disney Presents, Walt Disney's Wonderful World of Color,* and *The Wonderful World of Disney*), NBC, 1979.
The Maker, *My Kidnapper, My Love* (also known as *Dark Side of Love*), NBC, 1980.
Bill Sackter, *Bill,* CBS, 1981.
Guest, *Senior Trip,* CBS, 1981.
Jack Thum, *Leave 'em Laughing,* CBS, 1981.
Bill Sackter, *Bill: On His Own,* CBS, 1983.
Mike Halligan, *It Came upon the Midnight Clear,* syndicated, 1984.

Jack Bergan, *The Return of Mickey Spillane's "Mike Hammer,"* CBS, 1986.
James Turner (Jimmie the hermit), *Little Spies,* ABC, 1986.
Himself, *There Must Be a Pony,* ABC, 1986.
Father Flanagan, *Brothers' Destiny* (also known as *Long Road Home* and *The Road Home*), 1995.
Boss Ed, *The First of May,* Showtime, 1998.
Wellington, *Boys Will Be Boys,* c. 1998.
Sage, *Sinbad: The Battle of the Dark Knights,* syndicated, 1999.
Movie Mason, *Phantom of the Megaplex,* The Disney Channel, 2000.

Television Appearances; Specials:
George M. Cohan, *Mr. Broadway* (musical), NBC, 1957.
Title role, *Pinocchio* (musical), NBC, 1957, simulcast on radio.
Himself, *Glamorous Hollywood,* 1958.
Voice of Kris Kringle, *Santa Claus Is Comin' to Town* (animated), ABC, 1970.
(In archive footage) Himself, *Hollywood: The Dream Factory,* 1972.
Fol–de–Rol, ABC, 1972.
Voice of Santa Claus, *The Year without a Santa Claus* (animated), ABC, 1974.
Himself, *Backlot USA* (also known as *Dick Cavett's "Backlot"*), CBS, 1976.
Voice of Santa Claus, *Rudolph and Frosty's Christmas in July* (animated), 1979.
Himself, *From Raquel with Love,* ABC, 1980.
Himself, *Hollywood der Erinnerungen,* [West Germany (now Germany)], 1980.
Himself, *All–Star Comedy Birthday Party from West Point* (also known as *Bob Hope's All–Star Comedy Birthday Party from West Point*), NBC, 1981.
Himself, *Night of 100 Stars* (also known as *Night of One Hundred Stars*), ABC, 1982.
Ringmaster, *Circus of the Stars #7,* CBS, 1982.
Bob Hope Special: Bob Hope in "Who Makes the World Laugh?" Part II, NBC, 1984.
Himself, *The Spencer Tracy Legacy: A Tribute by Katharine Hepburn* (also known as *The Spencer Tracy Legacy*), PBS, 1986.
Himself, *Stand–Up Comics Take a Stand!,* The Family Channel, 1988.
Master of ceremonies, *Miss Hollywood Talent Search,* syndicated, 1989.
Himself, "The Disney–MGM Studios Theme Park Grand Opening," *The Magical World of Disney,* NBC, 1989.
When We Were Young ... Growing Up on the Silver Screen, PBS, 1989.
(In archive footage) Himself, *The Wonderful Wizard of Oz: 50 Years of Magic,* CBS, 1990.
The Family Channel's Fall Sneak Preview, The Family Channel, 1990.

Himself, *Benny Hill: The World's Favorite Clown,* BBC, 1991.

Himself, *A Closer Look: Elizabeth Taylor,* NBC, 1991.

Himself and Ding "Dingy" Bell, *Something a Little Less Serious: A Tribute to "It's a Mad Mad Mad Mad World,"* 1991.

Burt Reynolds' Conversations with ... , CBS, 1991.

(In archive footage) Himself, *The Carol Burnett Show: A Reunion,* CBS, 1993.

Host, *Remember When,* PBS, 1995.

Himself, *The First 100 Years: A Celebration of American Movies,* HBO, 1995.

Here Comes the Bride ... There Goes the Groom, CBS, 1995.

Himself, "Musicals Great Musicals: The Arthur Freed Unit at MGM," *Great Performances,* PBS, 1996.

The 1997 Hollywood Christmas Parade, syndicated, 1997.

67th Annual Hollywood Christmas Parade, UPN, 1998.

Himself, *AFI's 100 Years ... 100 Laughs: America's Funniest Movies,* CBS, 2000.

(In archive footage) *Elizabeth Taylor: England's Other Elizabeth,* PBS, 2000.

Himself, *The Hollywood Christmas Parade,* 2000.

Grand marshal, *The Hollywood Christmas Parade,* 2002.

(Uncredited; in archive footage) Himself, *Cleavage,* 2002.

Himself, *Gossip: Tabloid Tales,* Arts and Entertainment, 2002.

(Uncredited; in archive footage) Himself, *Joan Crawford: The Ultimate Movie Star,* TCM, 2002.

Himself, *Hollywood Legenden,* 2004.

Voice of Santa, *The Happy Elf* (animated), NBC, 2005.

Himself, *Silent Hollywood: Cult, Stars, Scandals,* Bayerischer Rundfunk (Germany), c. 2006.

Television Appearances; Awards Presentations:

Presenter, *The 29th Annual Academy Awards,* NBC, 1957.

Himself, *The Kennedy Center Honors: A Celebration of the Performing Arts,* CBS, 1979.

Presenter, *The 52nd Annual Academy Awards,* ABC, 1980.

The 34th Annual Tony Awards, CBS, 1980.

The 55th Annual Academy Awards, ABC, 1983.

America's All-Star Tribute to Elizabeth Taylor (also known as *America's Hope Award*), ABC, 1989.

Presenter, *The 48th Annual Golden Globe Awards,* PBS, 1991.

Presenter, *Family Film Awards,* CBS, 1996.

American Veteran Awards, History Channel, 2002.

The 75th Annual Academy Awards, ABC, 2003.

(Uncredited) *The 76th Annual Academy Awards,* ABC, 2004.

Television Appearances; Episodic:

"Saturday's Children," *Celanese Theatre,* ABC, 1952.

Himself, *The Milton Berle Show* (also known as *The Buick–Berle Show* and *Texaco Star Theatre*), NBC, 1956.

Title role, "Eddie," *Alcoa Theatre,* NBC, 1957.

Host, "The Miracle Worker," *Playhouse 90,* CBS, 1957.

Red McGivney, "The Lady Was a Flop," *Schlitz Playhouse of Stars* (also known as *Herald Playhouse, The Playhouse,* and *Schlitz Playhouse*), CBS, 1957.

Sammy Hogarth, "The Comedian," *Playhouse 90,* CBS, 1957.

Guest, *The Ed Sullivan Show* (also known as *Toast of the Town*), CBS, 1957, 1958, 1960, 1962, 1965.

Himself, *What's My Line?,* CBS, 1957, 1958, 1960, 1966.

Himself, "The Mickey Rooney Show," *December Bride,* CBS, 1958.

Himself, "The Dean Martin Variety Show I," *Startime* (also known as *Ford Startime* and *Lincoln–Mercury Startime*), NBC, 1959.

Samuel T. Evans, "The Greenhorn Story," *Wagon Train* (also known as *Major Adams, Trail Master*), ABC, 1959.

Al Roberts, "The Money Driver," *General Electric Theater* (also known as *G.E. Theater*), CBS, 1960.

Himself, "Billy Barty," *This Is Your Life,* NBC, 1960.

Samuel T. Evans, "Wagons Ho!," *Wagon Train* (also known as *Major Adams, Trail Master*), ABC, 1960.

Himself, *The Revlon Revue* (also known as *Revlon Presents* and *Revlon Spring Music Festival*), CBS, 1960.

Augie Miller, "Somebody's Waiting," *The Dick Powell Show* (also known as *The Dick Powell Theatre*), NBC, 1961.

George Bick, "Ooftus Goofus," *Naked City,* ABC, 1961.

Jack Daley, "I Thee Kill," *The Investigators,* CBS, 1961.

(In archive footage) Himself, "USO—Wherever They Go!," *The DuPont Show of the Week,* NBC, 1961.

Mike Zampini, "Who Killed Julie Greer?," *The Dick Powell Show* (also known as *The Dick Powell Theatre*), NBC, 1961.

Richard Winslow, "Shore Patrol Revisited," *Hennesey,* CBS, 1961.

Steve Margate, "The Paper Killer," *Checkmate,* CBS, 1961.

Guest, *The Jackie Gleason Show* (also known as *You're in the Picture*), CBS, 1961.

Arnold, "Calamity Circus," *Frontier Circus,* CBS, 1962.

Himself, "Modern Prison Sketch," *The Jack Benny Program* (also known as *The Jack Benny Show*), CBS, 1962.

Himself, "The Top Banana," *Pete and Gladys,* CBS, 1962.

Putt–Putt Higgins, "Special Assignment," *The Dick Powell Show* (also known as *The Dick Powell Theatre*), NBC, 1962.

Guest, *The Andy Williams Show,* NBC, 1962.

Babe Simms, "Five, Six, Pick up Sticks," *Alcoa Premiere,* ABC, 1963.

Grady, "The Last Night of Jockey," *The Twilight Zone,* CBS, 1963.

Sheriff Williams, "The Hunt," *Kraft Suspense Theatre,* NBC, 1963.

Sweeney Tomlin, "Everybody Loves Sweeney," *The Dick Powell Show* (also known as *The Dick Powell Theatre*), NBC, 1963.

Guest, *The Judy Garland Show,* CBS, 1963.

Panelist, *Laughs for Sale,* ABC, 1963.

Archie Lido, "Who Killed His Royal Highness?," *Burke's Law* (also known as *Amos Burke, Secret Agent*), ABC, 1964.

George M. Cohan, "The Seven Little Foys," *Bob Hope Presents the Chrysler Theater* (also known as *The Chrysler Theater* and *Universal Star Time*), NBC, 1964.

Harry White, "Silver Service," *Combat!,* ABC, 1964.

Hoagy Blair, "Funny Man with a Monkey," *Arrest and Trial,* ABC, 1964.

Pan Macropolus, "Incident at the Odyssey," *Rawhide,* CBS, 1964.

Guest, *The Jonathan Winters Show,* NBC, 1964.

Himself, *The Hollywood Palace,* ABC, 1964, 1965, 1966, multiple appearances in 1967.

Lefty Duncan, "Kicks," *Bob Hope Presents the Chrysler Theater* (also known as *The Chrysler Theater* and *Universal Star Time*), NBC, 1965.

Charlie Paris, "This'll Kill You," *The Fugitive,* ABC, 1966.

Himself, "Lucy Meets Mickey Rooney," *The Lucy Show* (also known as *The Lucille Ball Show*), CBS, 1966.

Eddie Julian, *The Jean Arthur Show,* CBS, 1966.

Shindig, ABC, 1966.

Guest, *The Carol Burnett Show* (also known as *Carol Burnett and Friends*), CBS, 1967, 1968.

Guest, *The Dean Martin Show* (also known as *The Dean Martin Comedy Hour*), NBC, 1968.

Guest, *The Jackie Gleason Show* (also known as *The Honeymooners*), CBS, 1969.

Les, "Cynthia Is Alive and Living in Avalon," *The Name of the Game,* NBC, 1970.

Himself, "Mickey Rooney Episode," *The Red Skelton Show* (also known as *The Red Skelton Hour*), CBS, 1970.

Guest, *The Mike Douglas Show,* syndicated, multiple episodes in 1970.

Guest, *Rowan & Martin's "Laugh–In"* (also known as *Laugh–In*), NBC, 1970.

Guest, *The Merv Griffin Show,* CBS, 1970, syndicated, 1971.

Guest, *The Tonight Show Starring Johnny Carson* (also known as *The Best of Carson*), NBC, multiple appearances beginning c. 1970.

"The Manufactured Man," *Dan August,* ABC, 1971.

August Kolodney, "Rare Objects," *Night Gallery* (also known as *Rod Serling's "Night Gallery"*), NBC, 1972.

Himself, "Judy Garland," *The Hollywood Greats* (also known as *Hollywood Greats*), BBC, 1978.

Santa Claus, "A Christmas Presence," *The Love Boat,* ABC, 1982.

Himself, "Mickey Rooney," *This Is Your Life,* syndicated, 1984.

True Confessions, syndicated, 1986.

Himself, "Mickey Rooney," *This Is Your Life,* Independent Television (England), 1988.

Rocco, "Larceny and Old Lace," *The Golden Girls,* NBC, 1988.

Guest, *Reflections on the Silver Screen with Professor Richard Brown,* American Movie Classics, 1990.

Hearts Are Wild, CBS, 1992.

Family Edition, The Family Channel, c. 1992.

Matt Cleveland, "Bloodlines," *Murder, She Wrote,* CBS, 1993.

Mr. Dreghorn, "Arrest Ye Merry Gentlemen," *Full House,* ABC, 1994.

Himself, *Gottschalk Late Night,* RTL (Germany), 1994.

Himself, "Mickey Rooney: Hollywood's Little Giant," *Biography* (also known as *A&E Biography: Mickey Rooney*), Arts and Entertainment, 1995.

Voice of himself, "Radioactive Man," *The Simpsons* (animated), Fox, 1995.

Gobe, "The Heart of the Elephant: Parts 1 & 2," *Conan* (also known as *Conan the Adventurer*), syndicated, 1996.

Harold Lang, "A Shaolin Treasure," *Kung Fu: The Legend Continues,* syndicated, 1996.

Himself, "Carmen Miranda: The South American Way," *Biography* (also known as *A&E Biography: Carmen Miranda*), Arts and Entertainment, 1996.

Himself, "Mickey Rooney," *Private Screenings,* TCM, 1997.

Voice of Ole Lukoje, "The Snow Queen," *Stories from My Childhood* (animated; also known as *Mikhail Baryshnikov's "Stories from My Childhood"*), PBS, 1997.

Dr. George Bikel, "Exodus," *ER* (also known as *Emergency Room*), NBC, 1998.

Lucius, "Lucky in Love," *Mike Hammer, Private Eye,* 1998.

Mr. Hardy, "The Follies of WENN," *Remember WENN,* American Movie Classics, 1998.

Himself, *Elizabeth Taylor: The E! True Hollywood Story,* E! Entertainment, 1998.

Himself, *Intimate Portrait: Donna Reed,* Lifetime, 1998.

Art Sumski, "Life Insurance," *Safe Harbor,* 1999.

Himself, "Judy Garland: Beyond the Rainbow," *Biography* (also known as *A&E Biography: Judy Garland*), Arts and Entertainment, 1999.

Old man, "Goodbye, My Friend," *Chicken Soup for the Soul,* PAX TV, 1999.

Himself, "Retribution," *Norm* (also known as *The Norm Show*), ABC, 2000.

Himself, *Intimate Portrait: Ava Gardner,* Lifetime, 2000.

Guest, *Larry King Live,* Cable News Network, 2001.

Himself, *Intimate Portrait: Judy Garland,* Lifetime, 2001.

Himself, *Last Days of Judy Garland: The E! True Hollywood Story,* E! Entertainment Television, 2001.

Guest, "Wetten, dass ... ? aus Leipzig," *Wetten, dass ... ?,* 2002.

Himself, *Liza Minnelli: The E! True Hollywood Story,* E! Entertainment Television, 2002.

(Uncredited) Himself, "The Hangman's Noose," *The Contender,* NBC, 2005.

Himself, "Hollywood Goes to War," *War Stories with Oliver North,* Fox News Channel, 2006.

Appeared as Harry Burton, *Jack's Place,* ABC; appeared as himself in "Mickey Rooney," an episode of *Celebrity Golf* (also known as *The Golf Channel Presents "Celebrity Golf with Sam Snead"*), NBC, later broadcast on The Golf Channel; appeared in other programs, including *Hollywood Squares* and various news telecasts.

Television Appearances; Pilots:
The Mickey Rooney Show, ABC, 1964.

Superhero, *Return of the Original Yellow Tornado,* 1967.

Ready and Willing, NBC, 1967, later broadcast on *Three in One,* CBS, 1973.

Uncle Mickey Durbin, "Hereafter," *A Year at the Top,* CBS, 1975.

Mike O'Malley (title role), *O'Malley,* NBC, 1983.

Television Director:
Directed episodes of the series *Happy,* NBC.

Stage Appearances:
The Tunnel of Love, 1963.

See How They Run, Alhambra Dinner Theatre, Jacksonville, FL, 1973, 1974.

Three Goats and a Blanket, Little Theatre on the Square, Sullivan, IL, 1976.

Mickey, *Sugar Babies* (musical revue), Mark Hellinger Theatre, New York City, 1979–82.

Himself, *Night of 100 Stars* (also known as *Night of One Hundred Stars*), Radio City Music Hall, New York City, 1982.

Clem Rogers, *The Will Rogers Follies* (musical), Palace Theatre, New York City, between 1991 and 1993.

Lend Me a Tenor (musical), Chicago area production, 1993.

Crazy for You (musical), Royal Alexandra Theatre, Toronto, Ontario, Canada, 1995.

Hollywood Goes Classical (concert), Los Angeles Music Center, Dorothy Chandler Pavilion, Los Angeles, 2000.

Singular Sensations, Village Theatre, New York City, 2003.

Also appeared in other productions, including *Gifts from the Attic* (musical), Minneapolis, MN; and in *W.C.*

Major Tours:
George M! (musical), U.S. cities, c. 1970.

Mickey, *Sugar Babies* (musical revue), U.S. cities, 1983–87.

Two for the Show, U.S. cities, 1989.

The Sunshine Boys, U.S. cities, 1990.

The Mind with the Naughty Man, Canadian cities, 1994.

The Wizard, Professor Marvel, and other roles, *The Wizard of Oz* (musical), U.S. and Canadian cities, 1997–99.

Let's Put On a Show! (musical revue; also known as *Mickey Rooney: Let's Put On a Show!;* some sources cite original title as *The One Man, One Wife Show*), various international cities, beginning c. 1998.

Toured in vaudeville as Joe Yule, Jr., and later as Mickey Rooney with his family; toured in vaudeville with Sid Gold, 1932.

Radio Appearances; Specials:
Title role, *Pinocchio* (musical), NBC, 1957, simulcast on television.

Radio Appearances; Episodic:
"Strike Up the Band" (musical), *Lux Radio Theatre,* 1940.

"Babes in Arms" (musical), *Lux Radio Theatre,* 1941.

"Babes in Arms" (musical), *Screen Guild Theatre,* 1941.

RECORDINGS

Videos:
Himself, *Hollywood's Children,* 1982.

(In archive footage) Himself, *1930s: Music, Memories & Milestones,* 1988.

(In archive footage) Himself, *Oscar's Greatest Moments,* 1992.

Himself, *That's Entertainment! III Behind the Screen,* Metro–Goldwyn–Mayer, 1994.

(In archive footage) *Judy Garland's Hollywood,* 1997.

(In archive footage) *Broadway's Lost Treasures,* Acorn Media, 2003.

(In archive footage) *Judy Duets,* Kultur Films, 2005.

Appeared in various recordings and collections of videos and DVDs.

Albums; with Others:
Girl Crazy (original soundtrack recording), Decca, 1944.

Sugar Babies: The Burlesque Musical (original cast recording), c. 1983.

(With Judy Garland) *Mickey and Judy,* c. 1991.

The Wizard of Oz (cast recording), TVT, 1998.

Appeared in other recordings, including *Pinocchio* (original television cast recording), Columbia.

Singles; with Judy Garland:
"Could You Use Me" (B side of "Embraceable You"), Decca, 1944.
"Treat Me Rough" (B side of "But Not for Me"), Decca, 1944.

Audiobooks:
Hanno Schilf, *Silent Night,* 1994.

WRITINGS

Screenplays:
The Godmothers, 1972.
The Legend of O. B. Taggart (also known as *The Outlaws: Legend of O. B. Taggart*), Northern Arts Entertainment, 1994.

Film Music:
Composer, *Sound Off,* Columbia, 1952.
Songs, *The Twinkle in God's Eye,* Republic Pictures, 1955.
Songs, *The Bold and the Brave,* RKO Radio Pictures, 1956.
Song "I'm So in Love with You," *Baby Face Nelson,* United Artists, 1957.
Songs "Lazy Summer Night," "The Octavians," "U Gotta Soda," and "Unkwinit," *Andy Hardy Comes Home,* Metro–Goldwyn–Mayer, 1958.

Television Music; Specials:
Song "Love Is Being Loved," *Kathie Lee Gifford's "Lullabies for Little Ones,"* PBS, 1996.

Writings for the Stage:
(With Donald O'Connor) *Two for the Show,* tour of U.S. cities, 1989.
(With Jan Chamberlain Rooney) *Let's Put On a Show!* (musical revue; also known as *Mickey Rooney: Let's Put On a Show!;* some sources cite original title as *The One Man, One Wife Show*), tour of various international cities, beginning c. 1998.

Songs:
Wrote songs, including "Oceans Apart," a song performed by Judy Garland.

Nonfiction; Autobiographies:
I.E.,: An Autography, Putnam, 1965.
Me and You, 1990.
Life Is Too Short, Villard Books, 1991.

Contributor to periodicals, including *Newsweek.*

Novels:
The Search for Sonny Skies, Carol Publishing, 1994.

OTHER SOURCES

Books:
International Dictionary of Films and Filmmakers, Volume 3: *Actors and Actresses,* fourth edition, St. James Press, 2000.
Marill, Alvin, *Mickey Rooney: His Films, Television Appearances, Radio Work, Stage Shows, and Recordings,* McFarland and Co., 2004.
Marx, Arthur, *The Nine Lives of Mickey Rooney,* Stein & Day, 1986.

Periodicals:
Interview, May, 1992.
New York Times, July 7, 1993.
People Weekly, July 26, 1993, p. 65.

Electronic:
Mickey Rooney, http://www.mickeyrooney.com, February 23, 2006.

ROSE, Shiva
      See MCDERMOTT, Shiva Rose

ROSE, Sienna
      See MILLER, Sienna

RYAN, Roz 1951–

PERSONAL

Original name, Rosalyn Bowen; born July 7, 1951, in Detroit, MI; daughter of Thomas and Gertrude Bowen (employees of the Board of Education); married and divorced twice; children: Dante Reid.

Addresses: *Agent*—Gerry Koch, The Gage Group, 14724 Ventura Blvd., Suite 505, Los Angeles, CA 91403; (commercials) Leanna Levy, Cassell–Levy, Inc., 843 North Sycamore Ave., Los Angeles, CA 90038.

Career: Actress and voice performer. Nightclub and cabaret performer, including performances of "All about the Music" and "A Personal Moment." Member of the musical group El Riot and singer at various venues; also a singer at benefit performances.

Awards, Honors: Carbonell Award, best supporting actress in a musical, 1986, for *Cole Porter Requests the Pleasure;* Carbonell Award, best actress in a musical, 1992, and ari–Zoni Award (some sources call award Zoni Award), both for *Blues in the Night;* Barrymore Award nomination, outstanding supporting actress in a play, Theatre Alliance of Greater Philadelphia, 1997, for *Seven Guitars.*

CREDITS

Stage Appearances:
Ain't Misbehavin' (musical), Plymouth Theatre, New York City, 1981, then Belasco Theatre, New York City, 1981–82.
Edna Burke and Effie Melody White in the musical *Dreamgirls* (musical), Imperial Theatre, New York City, 1984–85.
Party guest, *Cole Porter Requests the Pleasure* (musical), Coconut Grove Playhouse, Miami, FL, c. 1986.
Lady from the road, *Blues in the Night* (musical), Coconut Grove Playhouse, c. 1992.
Gospel singer, landlady and woman knitting, *Violet* (musical), Playwrights Horizons, Anne G. Wilder Theatre, New York City, 1997.
Louise, *Seven Guitars,* Philadelphia Theatre Company, Philadelphia, PA, 1997, also produced at the Coconut Grove Playhouse
Ghost of Christmas present, *A Christmas Carol* (musical; also known as *A Christmas Carol—The Musical*), Theatre at Madison Square Garden, New York City, 1998.
Quilly, *The Old Settler,* The Old Globe, San Diego, CA, 1998.
Bertha Williams, *One Mo' Time* (musical), Williamstown Theatre Festival, Williamstown, MA, 2001, then Longacre Theatre, New York City, 2002.
Matron Mama Morton, *Chicago: A Musical Vaudeville* (musical), Shubert Theatre, New York City, 2002–2003, then Ambassador Theatre, New York City, 2003, 2004.
Violet (concert), Playwrights Horizons, New York City, 2003.
The Barry Z Live Variety Show, Gramercy Theatre, New York City, 2004.
So in Love: A Night of Romance at the Rainbow Room (benefit), Rainbow Room, New York City, 2006.
Mabel, *The Pajama Game* (musical), Roundabout Theatre Company, American Airlines Theatre, New York City, 2006—.

Appeared as Miss Hannigan in the musical *Annie.* Affiliated with the Carolina Arts Festival.

Major Tours:
Matron Mama Morton, *Chicago* (musical), U.S. cities, beginning 2003, and in Portugal.

Toured as Miss Hannigan in the musical *Annie,* U.S. cities; appeared in *Ain't Misbehavin'* (musical), Israeli and European cities; as the lady from the road, *Blues in the Night* (musical), Japanese cities; as Effie and Nell, *Broadway Tonight,* South American and Dutch cities; and as Bloody Mary, *South Pacific* (musical), international cities.

Stage Work:
Worked with development workshops for musicals.

Television Appearances; Series:
Sister Amelia Herebrink, *Amen,* NBC, 1986–91.
Mrs. Dixon, *The Good News* (also known as *Good News*), UPN, 1997–98.
Voice of the president, a recurring role, *Buzz Lightyear of Star Command* (animated; also known as *Disney/Pixar's "Buzz Lightyear of Star Command"*), UPN and syndicated, 2000.
Chickie, *Danny* (also known as *American Wreck* and *Community Center*), CBS, 2001.
Flo Anderson, *All about the Andersons,* The WB, 2003–2004.
Narrator, *A2Z,* VH1, beginning c. 2004.

Television Appearances; Specials:
Judge, *The 1988 Miss Teen USA Pageant,* CBS, 1988.
1990 King Orange Jamboree Parade, NBC, 1990.
The Sixth Annual Sears Soul Train Christmas Special, UPN, 2003.

Television Appearances; Episodic:
Panelist, *The New Hollywood Squares,* syndicated, 1989.
Loretta Eakins, "Rehearsal of Fortune," *Sparks* (also known as *Sparks, Sparks, Sparks*), UPN, 1997.
Merle, "The Truth about Lies," *The Journey of Allen Strange,* Nickelodeon, 1998.
Voice of Thalia, "Hercules and the Muse of Dance," *Hercules* (animated; also known as *Disney's "Hercules"*), ABC and syndicated, 1998.
Voice of park ranger, "Monkey Fist Strikes," *Kim Possible* (animated; also known as *Disney's "Kim Possible"*), The Disney Channel, 2002.
Voice of Wade's mother, "Crush," *Kim Possible* (animated; also known as *Disney's "Kim Possible"*), The Disney Channel, 2002.
Josephine Baylor, "The Big Practice What You Preach Episode," *Half & Half,* UPN, 2004.
Voice of Wade's mother, "Mother's Day," *Kim Possible* (animated; also known as *Disney's "Kim Possible"*), The Disney Channel, 2004.
Loretta McKee, "Unknown Soldier," *JAG,* CBS, 2005.
Mae, "Debates and Dead People," *Barbershop,* Showtime, 2005.
Mae, "Family Bussiness," *Barbershop,* Showtime, 2005.
Mae, "Madonna Is a Ho," *Barbershop,* Showtime, 2005.

Herself, *Bid Whist Party Throwdown,* TV One, 2005.
Herself, "Sherman Hemsley," *Living in TV Land,* TV Land, 2006.

Appeared as a guest in *The Tonight Show,* NBC.

Television Appearances; Pilots:
Sister Amelia Herebrink, *Amen,* NBC, 1986.
Mrs. Dixon, *The Good News* (also known as *Good News*), UPN, 1997.
Chickie, *Danny* (also known as *American Wreck* and *Community Center*), CBS, 2001.
Flo Anderson, *All about the Andersons,* The WB, 2003.

Television Work; Series:
Song performer, including performer of title theme, *Hercules* (animated; also known as *Disney's "Hercules"*), ABC and syndicated, 1998–99.

Film Appearances:
Voice of Thalia, *Hercules* (animated), Buena Vista, 1997.
Nurse, *Went to Coney Island on a Mission from God ... Be Back by Five,* 1998, Phaedra Cinema, 2000.
Voice of Thalia, *Hercules: Zero to Hero* (animated), Walt Disney Pictures, 1999.
Nikita's Blues (short film), 1999.
Mildred Williams, *Nikita Blues,* York Entertainment, 2001.
Voice of Wade's mother, *Kim Possible: The Secret Files* (animated), Walt Disney Home Entertainment, 2003.

Some sources cite appearances in *The Cotton Club,* Orion, 1984; and *Dark Indigo.*

Film Work:
Coproducer, *Nikita Blues,* York Entertainment, 2001.

RECORDINGS

Albums; with Others:
(With the group El Riot) "Do It Right," *Searching for Soul,* Ubiquity Records, c. 2005.

Video Games:
Voice of Thalia, *Hercules,* 1997.

WRITINGS

Albums; with Others:
(With the group El Riot) "Do It Right," *Searching for Soul,* Ubiquity Records, c. 2005.

OTHER SOURCES

Electronic:
Black Pages Today, http://blackpagestoday.com, January 26, 2006.
BroadwayStars, http://www.broadwaystars.com, May 28, 2004.
RozRyan.com, http://www.rozryan.com, January 18, 2006.

S

SABELLA, Paul

PERSONAL

Career: Producer, animator, director, and actor. Hanna–Barbera, senior vice president in charge of animation projects; began working with Jonathan Dern at Metro–Goldwyn–Mayer, 1992; Metro–Goldwyn–Mayer Animation, cofounder and cohead (with Dern), 1993–c. 2000; SD Entertainment (an animation studio), partner and cofounder (with Dern), 2000.

CREDITS

Film Animator:
In a Nutshell (animated short; also known as *La noix de Bongolie*), 1971.
Tiki Tiki (animated), Faroun Films, 1971.
Man: The Polluter (animated), National Film Board of Canada, 1973.
A Room Full of Energy (animated short; also known as *De l'energie de ci, de la*), 1982.
International production executive, *Monster in My Pocket: The Big Scream* (animated short), Kidmark, 1992.

Film Producer:
An All Dogs Christmas Carol, Metro–Goldwyn–Mayer Family Entertainment, 1998.
Tom Sawyer, 2000.
Noddy Saves Christmas (animated short), Kidtoon Films, 2004.
Noddy and the Island Adventure (animated), 2005.

Film Director:
A Room Full of Energy (animated short; also known as *De l'energie de ci, de la*), 1982.
All Dogs Go to Heaven 2 (animated), 1996.

Babes in Toyland (animated), Metro–Goldwyn–Mayer, 1997.
An All Dogs Christmas Carol (animated), Metro–Goldwyn–Mayer Family Entertainment, 1998.
Tom Sawyer (animated), Metro–Goldwyn–Mayer, 2000.

Film Work; Other:
Key animator and sequence director, "Captain Sternn," *Heavy Metal* (animated), 1981.
Executive producer, *Candyland: Great Lollipop Adventure* (animated), Hasbro, 2005.
Executive producer, *Dinotopia: Quest for the Ruby Sunstone* (animated), Goodtimes Entertainment, 2005.

Film Appearances:
Himself, *Imagining "Heavy Metal"* (documentary short), 1999.

Television Executive Producer; Series:
A Pup Named Scooby Doo (animated), ABC, 1988.
"Monster Tails" and "Fender Bender 500," *Wake, Rattle & Roll* (animated), syndicated, 1990.
Timeless Tales from Hallmark, USA Network, 1990.
Tom and Jerry Kids Show (animated), Fox, 1990.
The Adventures of Don Coyote and Sancho Panda (animated), syndicated, 1990.
Bill & Ted's Excellent Adventure (animated), CBS, 1990.
Gravedale High (also known as *Rick Moranis in Gravedale High*), NBC, 1990.
The Pirates of Dark Water (animated), 1991.
Dark Water (animated), Fox, 1991.
The Addams Family (animated), ABC, 1992.
The Pink Panther (animated), syndicated, 1993.
All Dogs Go to Heaven: The Series (animated), syndicated, 1996.
The Lionhearts (animated), syndicated, 1998.
Robocop: Alpha Commando (animated), syndicated, 1998.
Action Man (animated), Fox, 2000.

Make Way for Noddy (animated), 2001.

Also produced *The Smurfs* and *Foofur.*

Television Co–Executive Producer; Series:
Yo Yogi (animated), NBC, 1991.
Fish Police (animated), CBS, 1992.

Television Producer; Series:
Make Way for Noddy (animated), 2001.
Say It With Noddy (animated), 2005.

Television Work; Series:
International production executive, *Tom and Jerry Kids Show* (animated), Fox, 1990.
Animation consultant, *Young Robin Hood* (animated), syndicated, 1991.
Creative supervisor, *The Lionhearts,* syndicated, 1998.
Creative producer, *Alien Racers* (animated), 2005.

Television Work; Movies:
International production executive, *Jonny's Golden Quest* (animated), USA Network, 1993.
International production executive and supervising animation director, *I Yabba–Dabba Doo!* (animated), ABC, 1993.
Producer and codirector, *Tom Sawyer* (animated), The Nashville Network, 2000.

Television Work; Specials:
Character lead, *The Selfish Giant* (animated), CBS, 1973.
Animator, *The Little Mermaid* (animated), CBS, 1974.

Television Appearances; Series:
Voice of Willie the Whale, *Mickey Mouse Works* (animated), ABC, 1999.
Voice of Willie the Whale, *House of Mouse* (animated), ABC, 2001.

SCHNEIDER, Rob 1963–

PERSONAL

Full name, Robert M. Schneider; born October 31, 1963, in San Francisco (some sources cite Pacifica), CA; son of Marvin (a real estate broker) and Pilar (a teacher) Schneider; married London King (a model and actress), 1988 (divorced 1990); married Helena, October, 2002; children: (first marriage) Chloe Autumn. *Education:* Attended community college. *Avocational Interests:* Collecting.

Addresses: *Agent*—Endeavor, 9601 Wilshire Blvd., Sixth Floor, Beverly Hills, CA 90212–2020.

Career: Actor, comedian, and writer. From Out of Nowhere, partner. As a stand–up comedian, performed in comedy clubs as an opening act for various performers, including Jay Leno, Jerry Seinfeld, and Dana Carvey, San Francisco, CA; appeared in television commercials. Co–owner of The DNA Lounge (dance club) and Eleven (restaurant), both San Francisco, CA. Worked as a shoe salesperson.

Awards, Honors: Emmy Award nominations (with others), outstanding writing in a variety or music program, 1990, 1991, and 1992, all for *Saturday Night Live;* Blockbuster Entertainment Award nomination, favorite actor—comedy, 2000, for *Deuce Bigalow: Male Gigolo.*

CREDITS

Film Appearances:
Voyeur Martian, *Martians Go Home,* Taurus Entertainment, 1990.
Chuck Neiderman, *Necessary Roughness,* Paramount, 1991.
Cedrick the bellman, *Home Alone 2: Lost in New York* (also known as *Home Alone II*), Twentieth Century–Fox, 1992.
(Uncredited) Erwin, *Demolition Man,* Warner Bros., 1993.
Iggy, *Surf Ninjas* (also known as *Surf Warriors*), New Line Cinema, 1993.
Woodrow Tyler, *The Beverly Hillbillies,* Twentieth Century–Fox, 1993.
Herman "Fergie" Ferguson, *Judge Dredd,* Buena Vista, 1995.
Executive officer Martin T. "Marty" Pascal, *Down Periscope,* Twentieth Century–Fox, 1996.
Volpe, *The Adventures of Pinocchio* (live action and animated; also known as *Carlo Collodi's "Pinocchio," Die Legende von Pinocchio,* and *Pinocchio*), Metropolitan Filmexport, 1996.
The agent, *Sammy the Screenplay,* 1997.
Tommy Hendricks, *Knock Off,* Sony Pictures Entertainment, 1998.
Townie, *The Waterboy,* Buena Vista, 1998.
Title role, *Deuce Bigalow: Male Gigolo,* Buena Vista, 1999.
Nazo, *Big Daddy* (also known as *Guy Gets Kid*), Columbia, 1999.
Television producer, *Muppets from Space,* Columbia, 1999.
Townie, *Little Nicky,* New Line Cinema, 2000.
Marvin, *The Animal,* Columbia, 2001.
Clive/Jessica, *The Hot Chick,* Buena Vista, 2002.
(Uncredited) Nazo, *Mr. Deeds* (also known as *Deeds* and *Mister Deeds*), Columbia, 2002.

Voices of Chinese waiter and narrator, *Eight Crazy Nights* (animated; also known as *Adam Sandler's "Eight Crazy Nights"*), Columbia, 2002.

San Francisco hobo, *Around the World in 80 Days,* Buena Vista, 2004.

Ula, *50 First Dates,* Columbia, 2004.

Bill, *American Crude,* Sheffer–Kramer Productions, 2005.

Title role, *Deuce Bigalow: European Gigolo,* Columbia, 2005.

Punky, *The Longest Yard,* Paramount, 2005.

(Uncredited; in archive footage) Himself, *The Aristocrats,* ThinkFilm, 2005.

Gus, *The Benchwarmers,* Sony Pictures Releasing, 2006.

Yuri, *Grandma's Boy,* Twentieth Century–Fox, 2006.

Rob Schneider's Hard R, 2006.

Title role, *Big Stan,* Crystal Sky Pictures/Silver Nitrate Pictures, 2007.

Some sources cite an appearance in the film *DysFunktional Family* (also known as *Eddie Griffin: Dys–Funktional Family*), Miramax, 2003.

Film Work:

Coproducer, *The Animal,* Columbia, 2001.

Executive producer, *Rob Schneider's Hard R,* 2006.

Director and producer, *Big Stan,* Crystal Sky Pictures/Silver Nitrate Pictures, 2007.

Television Appearances; Series:

Saturday Night Live (also known as *NBC's "Saturday Night," Saturday Night, Saturday Night Live '80, SNL,* and *SNL 25*), NBC, 1991–94.

Jamie Coleman, *Men Behaving Badly* (also known as *It's a Man's World*), NBC, 1996–97.

Voice, *Kid Notorious* (animated), Comedy Central, 2003.

Television Appearances; Movies:

Steve, *Susan's Plan* (also known as *Dying to Get Rich*), Cinemax, 1999.

Television Appearances; Specials:

The 13th Annual Young Comedians Show Hosted by Dennis Miller (also known as *The 13th Annual Young Comedians Show*), HBO, 1989.

Saturday Night Live: All the Best for Mother's Day, NBC, 1992.

The Second Annual Saturday Night Live Mother's Day Special, NBC, 1993.

Comedy Central Spotlight: Kelsey Grammar, Comedy Central, 1996.

Host, *Sports Illustrated Swimsuit '97,* TNT, 1997.

Host, *Canned Ham: The Waterboy,* Comedy Central, 1998.

Host, *Sports Illustrated Swimsuit '98,* NBC, 1998.

Saturday Night Live: Bad Boys (also known as *The Bad Boys of Saturday Night Live*), NBC, 1998.

(In archive footage) *Saturday Night Live: The Best of Chris Farley,* NBC, 1998.

(In archive footage) *Saturday Night Live: The Best of Phil Hartman,* NBC, 1998.

Canned Ham: Big Daddy, Comedy Central, 1999.

The Making of "Big Daddy" (also known as *HBO Look: The Making of "Big Daddy"*), HBO, 1999.

(In archive footage) *Saturday Night Live: The Best of Adam Sandler,* NBC, 1999.

(In archive footage) *Saturday Night Live: The Best of Dana Carvey,* NBC, 1999.

(In archive footage) Multiple characters, *Saturday Night Live: Game Show Parodies,* NBC, 1999.

Saturday Night Live: 25th Anniversary (also known as *Saturday Night Live: 25th Anniversary Primetime Special*), NBC, 1999.

Comedy Central Presents: The N.Y. Friars Club Roast of Hugh Hefner, Comedy Central, 2001.

Reel Comedy: The Animal, Comedy Central, 2001.

Tiny Elvis, *Elvis Lives,* NBC, 2002.

Voice of Rinky–Dink–Dink, *The Electric Piper* (animated musical), Nickelodeon, 2003.

(In archive footage) Bob from accounting, *Saturday Night Live: The Best of Christopher Walken,* NBC, 2004.

Ula, *Reel Comedy: 50 First Dates,* Comedy Central, 2004.

(In archive footage) *Saturday Night Live: The Best of Tom Hanks,* NBC, 2004.

Multiple characters, *Back to Norm,* Comedy Central, 2005.

Live from New York: The First 5 Years of Saturday Night Live, NBC, 2005.

MTV Movie Awards 2005 Pre–Show, MTV, 2005.

Reel Comedy: Deuce Bigalow European Gigolo, Comedy Central, 2005.

(In archive footage) *Saturday Night Live: The Best of Alex Baldwin,* NBC, 2005.

WrestleMania 21, pay–per–view, 2005.

Television Appearances; Awards Presentations:

The 43rd Annual Primetime Emmy Awards Presentation, Fox, 1991.

Presenter, *The Second Annual Blockbuster Entertainment Awards,* UPN, 1996.

The Fifth Annual Blockbuster Entertainment Awards, Fox, 1999.

Imhotep in *The Mummy* parody, *The 2001 MTV Movie Awards,* MTV, 2001.

Presenter, *Nickelodeon's 14th Annual Kids' Choice Awards,* Nickelodeon, 2001.

Host, *The Teen Choice Awards 2005,* Fox, 2005.

Presenter, *2005 MTV Movie Awards,* MTV, 2005.

Presenter, *Asian Excellence Awards,* AZN, 2006.

Television Appearances; Episodic:

Jeremy, "House Number," *227,* NBC, 1989.

Leonard Kraleman, "Professor Doolittle," *Coach,* ABC, 1990.

Leonard Kraleman, "Leonard Kraleman: All–American," *Coach,* ABC, 1991.

Bob, "The Friars Club," *Seinfeld,* NBC, 1996.

Contestant in celebrity tournament, *Jeopardy!,* syndicated, 1997.

Ross Fitzsimmons, "Happy Trails," *Ally McBeal,* Fox, 1998.

Host/Dick Thistle, *Later* (also known as *Later with Bob Costas, Later with Cynthia Garrett,* and *Later with Greg Kinnear*), NBC, 1998.

Sin City Spectacular (also known as *Penn & Teller's "Sin City Spectacular"*), ABC, 1998.

"Big Daddy," *HBO First Look,* HBO, 1999.

Himself, "Da Best of Ali G," *The 11 O'Clock Show* (also known as *Da Best of Ali G*), Channel 4 (England), 2000.

"Comedians Special," *Weakest Link* (also known as *The Weakest Link USA*), NBC, 2001.

Himself, *Intimate Portrait: Lela Rochon* (also known as *Intimate Portrait: Lela Rochon Fuqua*), Lifetime, 2001.

"50 First Dates," *HBO First Look,* HBO, 2004.

(In archive footage) *101 Most Unforgettable SNL Moments* (also known as *E's "101"*), E! Entertainment Television, 2004.

Himself, "Episode 1202: Rob Schneider, Tyrese Gibson, Jenners," *Cribs* (also known as *MTV Cribs*), MTV, 2005.

Damage Control, MTV, 2005.

Television Guest Appearances; Episodic:

Late Night with David Letterman, NBC, 1987.

The Rosie O'Donnell Show, syndicated, 1996.

The Tonight Show with Jay Leno, NBC, 1996, 2001, 2004, 2005, 2006.

Late Night with Conan O'Brien, NBC, 1998, 1999, 2002, 2005.

"Elvis Presley," *Dennis Miller Live,* HBO, 2000.

The Panel, 10 Network (Australia), 2001.

Rove Live, 10 Network, 2001.

The Daily Show (also known as *The Daily Show with Jon Stewart* and *The Daily Show with Jon Stewart Global Edition*), Comedy Central, 2002.

Saturday Night Live (also known as *NBC's "Saturday Night," Saturday Night Live '80, SNL,* and *SNL 25*), NBC, 2002.

Last Call with Carson Daly, NBC, 2002, 2004.

The Late Late Show with Craig Kilborn (also known as *The Late Late Show*), CBS, 2003.

Primetime Glick, Comedy Central, 2003.

RI:SE, Channel 4 (England), 2003.

"El sacrificio," *Big Brother VIP: Mexico* (also known as *BB Vip* and *BB Vip 2*), 2004.

Howard Stern, E! Entertainment Television, 2004.

The Late Show with David Letterman (also known as *The Late Show* and *Late Show Backstage*), CBS, 2004.

On–Air with Ryan Seacrest, syndicated, 2004.

Otro rollo con: Adal Ramones (also known as *Otro rollo*), 2004.

Real Time with Bill Maher, HBO, 2004.

The Sharon Osbourne Show (also known as *Sharon*), syndicated, 2004.

Tinseltown TV, International Channel, 2004.

The Andy Milonakis Show, MTV, 2005.

Cold Pizza, ESPN2, 2005.

Dancing with the Stars, ABC, 2005.

Live with Regis and Kelly, syndicated, 2005.

Monday Night Raw (also known as *Raw Is War, WWE Raw Is War, WWF Raw, WWF Raw Is War,* and *WWF Warzone*), Spike TV, 2005.

The Paul O'Grady Show, Independent Television (England), 2005.

Total Request Live (also known as *Total Request with Carson Daly* and *TRL*), MTV, 2005.

The View, ABC, 2005.

Late Night with Jimmy Kimmel, ABC, 2006.

Rome Is Burning (also known as *Jim Rome Is Burning*), ESPN, 2006.

Radio Appearances:

Presenter, *Bay Area Music Awards,* 1994.

The Howard Stern Radio Show (episodic), 2004.

RECORDINGS

Videos:

Ula, *The Dating Scene,* Columbia/TriStar Home Entertainment, 2004.

(Uncredited; in archive footage) Adolf Hitler, *Saturday Night Live: The Best of Mike Myers,* Europa Filmes 2005.

Music Videos:

Adam Sandler, "Steve Polychronopolous," 1996.

The Village People, "In the Navy," 1996.

Neal McCoy, "Billy's Got His Beer Goggles On," 2005.

Albums; with Others:

(Performer and coproducer) Adam Sandler, *They're All Gonna Laugh at You,* Warner Bros./Wea, 1993.

(Performer) Adam Sandler, *What the Hell Happened to Me!,* Warner Bros./Wea, 1996.

Singles; with Others:

Adam Sandler, "Steve Polychronopolous," 1996.

Video Games:

Voice, *A Fork in the Tale,* AnyRiver Entertainment, 1997.

WRITINGS

Screenplays:

Deuce Bigalow: Male Gigolo, Buena Vista, 1999.
The Animal, Columbia, 2001.
The Hot Chick, Buena Vista, 2002.
(And story) *Deuce Bigalow: European Gigolo,* Columbia, 2005.
Rob Schneider's Hard R, 2006.

Film Music:

Song "Ula's Luau Song," *50 First Dates,* Columbia, 2004.

Teleplays; Series:

(With others) *Saturday Night Live* (also known as *NBC's "Saturday Night," Saturday Night, Saturday Night Live '80, SNL,* and *SNL 25*), NBC, 1989–94.

Teleplays; Specials:

(With others) *Saturday Night Live: All the Best for Mother's Day,* NBC, 1992.
Sports Illustrated Swimsuit '97, TNT, 1997.
(With others) *Saturday Night Live Remembers Chris Farley,* NBC, 1998.

Albums; with Others:

Adam Sandler, *They're All Gonna Laugh at You,* Warner Bros./Wea, 1993.

OTHER SOURCES

Periodicals:

Computer Life, February, 1997.
Entertainment Weekly, March 21, 1997, p. 77.
People Weekly, April 15, 1991; March 18, 1996, p. 77; February 10, 1997, p. 37; February 24, 1997; April 21, 1997, p. 92.
Rolling Stone, November 28, 1996, p. 139.

SCHOOLEY, Robert
(Bob Schooley)

PERSONAL

Married; has children.

Addresses: *Agent*—Danny Greenberg, William Morris Agency, One William Morris Place, Beverly Hills, CA 90212. *Manager*—Ellen Goldsmith–Vein, Gotham Group, 9255 Sunset Blvd., Suite 515, Los Angeles, CA 90069.

Career: Writer and producer. Frequent partner of Mark McCorkle. Worked at Sesame Place (a theme park), Langhorne, PA.

Awards, Honors: Annie Award nomination (with Mark McCorkle), outstanding individual achievement for writing in an animated television production, International Animated Film Society, 1998, for "The Perfect Gift," *Great Minds Think for Themselves;* Video Premiere Award nomination (with others), best animated video premiere, DVD Exclusive awards, 2001, for the film *Buzz Lightyear of Star Command: The Adventure Begins;* Daytime Emmy Award nomination (with others), outstanding special class animated program, 2001, for the television series *Buzz Lightyear of Star Command;* Emmy Award nomination (with others), outstanding animated program for programming less than one hour, 2003, and Daytime Emmy Award nominations (both with others), outstanding special class animated program, 2003, and outstanding children's animated program, 2004 and 2005, all for *Kim Possible.*

CREDITS

Television Work with Mark McCorkle; Series:

Story editor, *Bonkers* (animated; also known as *Disney's "Bonkers"*), syndicated, beginning 1993.
Story editor, *Aladdin* (animated; also known as *Disney's "Aladdin"*), CBS and syndicated, 1994–95.
Story editor, *Great Minds Think for Themselves* (animated; also known as *Genie's Great Minds* and *Genie's Great Minds Think for Themselves*), ABC, beginning 1997.
Segment producer and story editor, "Find Out Why," *One Saturday Morning* (also known as *Disney's "One Saturday Morning"*), ABC, 1997–98.
Producer and executive story editor, *Hercules* (animated; also known as *Disney's "Hercules"*), ABC and syndicated, 1998–99.
(As Bob Schooley) Executive producer, *Buzz Lightyear of Star Command* (animated; also known as *Disney/Pixar's "Buzz Lightyear of Star Command"*), UPN and syndicated, 2000–2001, ABC, 2001.
(As Bob Schooley) Creator, executive producer, and story editor, *Kim Possible* (animated; also known as *Disney's "Kim Possible"*), The Disney Channel, between 2002 and 2004, also broadcast on *ABC Kids,* ABC.
Character creator, *Lilo & Stitch: The Series* (animated; also known as *The Adventures of Lilo & Stitch*), The Disney Channel, beginning c. 2003.

Television Sound Recording Assistant:

"The Halloween Door," *The Real Ghostbusters* (episode of an animated series; also known as *The Real*

Ghost Busters and *Slimer! And the Real Ghost-busters*), ABC, 1989.

Camp Candy (animated series), NBC, 1989–91, syndicated, 1992–93.

Television Work with Mark McCorkle; as Bob Schooley; Animated Movies:

Creator and executive producer, *Kim Possible: A Stitch in Time* (also known as *Disney's "Kim Possible: A Stitch in Time"*), The Disney Channel, 2003.

Creator, executive producer, and story editor, *Kim Possible: So The Drama* (also known as *Disney's "Kim Possible: So the Drama"*), The Disney Channel, 2005.

Film Producer:

(With Mark McCorkle; as Bob Schooley) *Buzz Lightyear of Star Command: The Adventure Begins* (animated), Buena Vista Home Entertainment, 2000.

RECORDINGS

Video Game Work:

Coproducer, *Buzz Lightyear of Star Command,* Activision, 2000.

WRITINGS

Teleplays; with Mark McCorkle; Series:

The Super Mario Bros. Super Show! (animated and live action; also known as *Club Mario*), syndicated, 1989–91.

(And with Mike Medlock) *Swamp Thing: The Animated Series* (animated; also known as *Swamp Thing*), Fox, 1991.

Great Minds Think for Themselves (animated; also known as *Genie's Great Minds* and *Genie's Great Minds Think for Themselves*), ABC, beginning 1997.

(And lyricist for the song "I Want It My Way"; as Bob Schooley) *Kim Possible* (animated; also known as *Disney's "Kim Possible"*), The Disney Channel, between 2002 and 2004, also broadcast on *ABC Kids*, ABC.

Teleplays; with Mark McCorkle; as Bob Schooley; Movies:

Kim Possible: So The Drama (animated; also known as *Disney's "Kim Possible: So the Drama"*), The Disney Channel, 2005.

Teleplays; with Mark McCorkle; Specials:

New Kids on the Block Christmas Special (animated), ABC, 1990.

Teleplays; with Mark McCorkle; Episodic:

"20,000 Leaks under the City," *Teenage Mutant Ninja Turtles* (animated; also known as *Teenage Mutant Hero Turtles* and *Teenage Mutant Ninja Turtles: The Series*), syndicated, 1989.

(As Bob Schooley) "Busters in Toyland," *The Real Ghostbusters* (animated; also known as *The Real Ghost Busters* and *Slimer! And the Real Ghostbusters*), ABC, c. 1990.

Also the uncredited coauthor of episodes of other series.

Teleplays; with Mark McCorkle; Pilots:

New Kids on the Block (animated), ABC, 1990.

Screenplays; with Mark McCorkle:

(Story) *The Return of Jafar* (animated; also known as *Aladdin 2*), Buena Vista Home Entertainment, 1994.

Aladdin and the King of Thieves (animated), Walt Disney Home Video/Buena Vista Home Video, 1996.

Additional material, *The Lion King II: Simba's Pride* (animated), Walt Disney Home Video/Buena Vista Home Video, 1998.

(And with others; as Bob Schooley) *Buzz Lightyear of Star Command: The Adventure Begins* (animated), Buena Vista Home Entertainment, 2000.

(As Bob Schooley) *Kim Possible: The Secret Files* (animated), Walt Disney Home Entertainment, 2003.

(And with others; as Bob Schooley) *Sky High,* Buena Vista, 2005.

Some sources state that Schooley worked on the screenplays for *Big Sir,* New Line Cinema; *Enchanted,* Buena Vista; and *Hip Hop Nanny,* Buena Vista.

Comic Books:

Kim Possible: Royal Pain & Twin Factor, Book 4, Tokyo-Pop, 2003.

(With Mark McCorkle) *Kim Possible Cine–Manga,* TokyoPop, Volumes 1–2, 2003, Volume 7, 2004.

Kim Possible Cine–Manga: Animal Attraction and All the News, TokyoPop, 2004.

Additional volumes of the "Kim Possible" book series were created by Schooley and Mark McCorkle and adapted for print by others.

OTHER SOURCES

Electronic:

ABC Media Net, http://www.abcmedianet.com, January 25, 2006.

SEYFRIED, Amanda 1985–

PERSONAL

Born December 8, 1985, in Allentown, PA.

Addresses: *Agent*—Innovative Artists, 1505 10th St., Santa Monica, CA 90401. *Manager*—GHJ Management, 405 E 54th St., Suite 3H, New York, NY 10022.

Career: Actress.

Awards, Honors: Bronze Leopard Award, best actress, Locarno International Film Festival, Best Ensemble Award nomination (with others), Gotham Awards, 2005, for *Nine Lives;* MTV Movie Award, best on–screen duo (with others), 2005, for *Mean Girls.*

CREDITS

Television Appearances; Series:
Lucinda Marie "Lucy" Montgomery, *As the World Turns,* 2000.
Joni Stafford, *All My Children* (also known as *All My Children: The Summer of Seduction*), ABC, 2002–2003.
Sarah Henrickson, *Big Love,* HBO, 2006.

Television Appearances; Episodic:
Joni Stafford, *Soap Center,* SoapNet, 2003.
Tandi McCain, "Outcry," *Law & Order: Special Victims Unit* (also known as *Law & Order: SVU* and *Special Victims Unit*), 2004.
Pam, "Detox," *House, M.D.* (also known as *House*), Fox, 2005.
Lilly Kane (recurring), *Veronica Mars,* 2005.
Rebecca, "A Good Convict Is Hard to Find," *Wildfire,* 2006.
Rebecca, "Dangerous Liaisons," *Wildfire,* 2006.

Television Appearances; Awards Presentations:
18th Annual Soap Opera Digest Awards, SoapNet, 2003.
The 30th Annual Daytime Emmy Awards, ABC, 2003.
2005 MTV Movie Awards, MTV, 2005.

Film Appearances:
Karen Smith, *Mean Girls,* United International, 2004.
Samantha, *Nine Lives,* Magnolia, 2005.
Mouse, *American Gun,* IFC, 2005.
Julie Beckley, *Alpha Dog,* New Line Cinema, 2006.
In Search of, Independent Dream, 2006.

RECORDINGS

Videos:
"Mean Girls": Only the Strong Survive, Paramount Home Video, 2004.

SIEMASZKO, Nina 1970–

PERSONAL

Full name, Antonina Jadwiga Siemaszko; born July 14, 1970, in Chicago, IL; sister of Casey Siemaszko (an actor); married. *Education:* Attended DePaul University. *Avocational Interests:* Marathon running, snowboarding, surfing.

Addresses: *Agent*—David Rose, Innovative Artists, 1505 10th St., Santa Monica, CA 90401.

Career: Actress.

CREDITS

Film Appearances:
Karen Lundahl, *One More Saturday Night,* Columbia, 1986.
Marilyn Lee Tucker, *Tucker: The Man and His Dream,* Paramount, 1988.
Natalie, *License to Drive,* Twentieth Century–Fox, 1988.
Merilee, *Lost Angels,* Orion, 1989.
Blue McDonald, *Wild Orchid II: Two Shades of Blue* (also known as *Wild Orchid 2: Blue Movie Blue*), Triumph Releasing, 1992.
Cassie, *Bed & Breakfast,* Hemdale Releasing, 1992.
Dolores, *Little Noises,* Monument Films, 1992.
(Scenes deleted) Undercover police officer, *Reservoir Dogs,* Miramax, 1992, scenes appear on the DVD *Reservoir Dogs Special Edition,* Artisan Entertainment, 2002.
Bank teller, *Twenty Bucks,* Triton Pictures, 1993.
Tamsen, *The Saints of Fort Washington,* Warner Bros., 1993.
Gal, *Floundering,* A–pix Entertainment/Strand Releasing, 1994.
Suzzi, *Airheads,* Twentieth Century–Fox, 1994.
Beth Wade, *The American President,* Columbia, 1995.
Maria, *Power of Attorney,* Prism Pictures, 1995.
Nina, *Love and Happiness,* Phaedra Cinema, 1995.
Shelly, *Kiss & Tell* (also known as *Lucid Days*), Phaedra Cinema, 1996.
Voice, *The Long Way Home* (documentary), Seventh Art Releasing, c. 1996.

Jennifer, *Suicide Kings* (also known as *Boys Night Out* and *Bred and Bored*), New Films International, 1997.

Tiffany, *Johns,* First Look Pictures Releasing, 1997.

Angela, *George B.,* 1997, York Entertainment, 2001.

Newscaster, *Goodbye Lover,* Warner Bros., 1998.

Paperlily, 1998.

Rosa Frankfurter, *Jakob the Liar* (also known as *Jakob le menteur*), Columbia/TriStar, 1999.

Betty Fuego, *The Big Tease* (also known as *J m'appelle Crawford*), Warner Bros., 2000.

Television Appearances; Series:

Eleanor "Ellie" Bartlet, *The West Wing* (also known as *West Wing*), NBC, between 2001 and 2005.

Television Appearances; Miniseries:

Janey, *Lonesome Dove,* CBS, 1989.

Mia Farrow, *Sinatra,* CBS, 1992.

Mona Ramsey, *More Tales of the City* (also known as *Armistead Maupin's "More Tales of the City"*), Showtime and Channel 4 (England), 1998.

Television Appearances; Movies:

Leeanne Dees, *Baby Brokers,* NBC, 1994.

Jenny Sloan, *Sawbones* (also known as *Prescription for Murder* and *Roger Corman Presents "Sawbones"*), Showtime, 1995.

Jenny Todd, *Runaway Car* (also known as *Out of Control*), Fox, 1997.

(Uncredited) Upset woman at convention, *Breast Men* (also known as *The Silicon Wars*), HBO, 1997.

Holly Proudfit, *Sleep Easy, Hutch Rimes,* Showtime, 2000.

Marla Obold, *The Darkling,* USA Network, 2000.

Roberta, *A Carol Christmas,* The Hallmark Channel, 2003.

Cassie Hillman, *Mystery Woman: Game Time,* The Hallmark Channel, 2005.

Cassie Hillman, *Mystery Woman: Mystery Weekend,* The Hallmark Channel, 2005.

Cassie Hillman, *Mystery Woman: Sing Me a Murder,* The Hallmark Channel, 2005.

Cassie Hillman, *Mystery Woman: Snapshot,* The Hallmark Channel, 2005.

Cassie Hillman, *Mystery Woman: Vision of a Murder,* The Hallmark Channel, 2005.

Cassie Hillman, *Mystery Woman: At First Sight,* The Hallmark Channel, 2006.

Cassie Hillman, *Mystery Woman: Redemption,* The Hallmark Channel, 2006.

Cassie Hillman, *Mystery Woman: Wild West Murder,* The Hallmark Channel, 2006.

Television Appearances; Specials:

Polly Stockman, "An Enemy of the People," *American Playhouse,* PBS, 1990.

Voice, "Children Remember the Holocaust" (also known as "Nothing but Sun"), *CBS Schoolbreak Special,* CBS, 1995.

Herself, *Happy Birthday Oscar Wilde,* BBC, 2004.

Television Appearances; Episodic:

Trudy, "Just Like That," *The Red Shoe Diaries* (also known as *Zalman King's "Red Shoe Diaries"*), Showtime, 1992.

Stella Bishop, "Creep Course," *Tales from the Crypt* (also known as *HBO's "Tales from the Crypt"*), HBO, 1993.

Gloria McKinnon, "You Gotta Have Heart," *Chicago Hope,* CBS, 1994.

Holly, "What Kind of Day Has It Been?," *Sports Night,* ABC, 1999.

New Age masseuse, "How Much Is That Sex Act in the Window," *Cold Feet,* NBC, 1999.

Dorinda Patterson, "Springing Tiny," *The Huntress,* USA Network, 2000.

Debra Johnson, "Family Ties," *NYPD Blue,* ABC, 2001.

Suzanna Clemons, "The Men from the Boys," *The Guardian,* CBS, 2001.

Teresa Wyatt, "Fork You Very Much," *Philly,* ABC, 2001.

Christy Wolinsky, "Baggage Claim," *Judging Amy,* CBS, 2004.

Linley Parker, "Bloodlines," *CSI: Crime Scene Investigation* (also known as *CSI, CSI: Las Vegas, CSI: Weekends,* and *Les experts*), CBS, 2004.

Julie Vera, "Superstar," *Cold Case,* CBS, 2006.

Television Appearances; Pilots:

Charlotte Kessler, *The Pastor's Wife,* Fox, 1995.

Stage Appearances:

The Sound of Music (musical), Chicago, IL, c. 1974.

Also appeared in *A Christmas Carol* and *A Cry of Players,* both Goodman Theatre, Chicago, IL. Performed at the Polish–language RefRen Theatre, Chicago, IL.

RECORDINGS

Video Games:

Voice of pedestrian, *Grand Theft Auto: San Andreas* (also known as *Grand Theft Auto V, GTA 4, GTA: San Andreas,* and *San Andreas*), Rockstar Games, 2004.

OTHER SOURCES

Periodicals:

Celebrity Sleuth, Volume 6, issue 7, 1993, pp. 78–79.

SIMMONS, Chelan 1982–
(Chelan Simmon)

PERSONAL

Born October 29, 1982, in Vancouver, British Columbia, Canada.

Career: Actress and model.

CREDITS

Television Appearances; Series:
Crystal, a recurring role, *Edgemont,* Fox Family Channel, 2001, CBC, 2001–2002.

Television Appearances; Miniseries:
Laurie Ann Winterbarger, *It* (also known as *Stephen King's "It"*), ABC, 1990.

Television Appearances; Movies:
Jennifer Martin, *Ratz,* Showtime, 2000.
Amber Henson, *Video Voyeur: The Susan Wilson Story,* Lifetime, 2002.
Helen Shyres, *Carrie,* NBC, 2002.
Amber, *Snakehead Terror,* Sci–Fi Channel, 2004.
Jen, *Monster Island,* MTV, 2004.
Emily Palmer, *Caved In,* Sci–Fi Channel, 2005.
Jenny, *Chupacabra: Dark Seas* (also known as *Chupacabra Terror*), Sci–Fi Channel, 2005.

Television Appearances; Specials:
Herself and Ashley, *Death's Design: Making "Final Destination 3,"* Cinemax, 2006.

Television Appearances; Episodic:
Attractive teenage girl, "Dead," *2gether: The Series* (also known as *2gether*), MTV, 2001.
(As Chelan Simmon) Cindy, "Dances with Squirrels," *The Sausage Factory* (also known as *MTV's "Now What,"* *Much Ado about Whatever,* and *Special Ed*), The Comedy Network (Canada) and MTV, 2001.
Second girl, "The Eve," *Special Unit 2* (also known as *SU2*), UPN, 2001.
Felice Chandler, "Drone," *Smallville* (also known as *Smallville: Beginnings* and *Smallville: Superman the Early Years*), The WB, 2002.
Gretchen Speck–Horowitz, "Pink Flamingos," *Wonderfalls* (also known as *Maid of the Mist* and *Touched by a Crazy Person*), Fox, 2004.
Gretchen Speck–Horowitz, "Wax Lion," *Wonderfalls* (also known as *Maid of the Mist* and *Touched by a Crazy Person*), Fox, 2004.

Rhonda, "Devoted," *Smallville* (also known as *Smallville: Beginnings* and *Smallville: Superman the Early Years*), The WB, 2004.
The devil and spokesmodel, "The UFOlogist," *The Collector,* CityTV and Space, 2005.
Jill, "Bloody Mary," *Supernatural,* The WB, 2005.
Voice, "Now You See Him, Now You Don't," *Zixx: Level Two* (animated; also known as *Zixx*), YTV (Canada), 2005.
Voice of babysitter, "Trust No One," *Zixx: Level Two* (animated; also known as *Zixx*), YTV, 2005.
Mara, "The Tower," *Stargate: Atlantis,* Sci–Fi Channel, The Movie Network (Canada), and Movie Central Network (Canada), 2006.

Television Appearances; Pilots:
Faith, *The Sports Page,* Showtime, 2001.
Hillary, *Kyle X/Y* (also known as *Kyle XY*), ABC Family Channel, 2006.

Film Appearances:
Cindy Thompson, *Bingo,* TriStar, 1991.
Girlfriend, *The Harp* (short film), JB Productions 2005.
Susie, *The Long Weekend,* Gold Circle Films, 2005.
Ashley, *Final Destination 3,* New Line Cinema, 2006.
Vivica, *Dr. Dolittle 3,* Twentieth Century–Fox Home Entertainment, 2006.
Waitress, *John Tucker Must Die,* Twentieth Century–Fox, 2006.
Blonde girl, *Wind Chill,* Revolution Studios, 2007.

Internet Appearances; Series:
Rhonda, *Smallville: Chloe Chronicles,* America Online, beginning 2003.

OTHER SOURCES

Electronic:
Chelan Simmons, http://www.chelansimmons.com, December 1, 2005.

SIMS, Molly 1973–

PERSONAL

Born May 25, 1973, in Murray, KY; daughter of Jim and Dottie Sims. *Education:* Attended Vanderbilt University.

Addresses: *Agent*—William Morris Agency, One William Morris Place, Beverly Hills, CA 90212. *Manager*—Untitled Entertainment, 331 N. Maple Dr., Third Floor, Beverly Hills, CA 90210.

Career: Actress. Appeared in many commercials for Old Navy and print ads for CoverGirl cosmetics.

CREDITS

Film Appearances:
Injured girl, *Frank McKlusky, C.I.* (video), Buena Vista, 2002.
Mrs. Feldman, *Starsky & Hutch,* Warner Bros., 2004.
Angie, *Venus & Vegas,* Luis Moro, 2005.
The Benchwarmers, Sony, 2006.
What Love Is, Big Sky, 2006.

Television Appearances; Series:
Host, *Mission: Makeover,* MTV, 1998.
Host, *House of Style,* MTV, 2000—.
Delinda Deline, *Las Vegas,* NBC, 2003.

Television Appearances; Episodic:
The Andy Dick Show, MTV, 2001.
The Late Late Show with Craig Kilborn, CBS, 2001, 2002.
Tracy, "Holy Sheep," *Andy Richter Controls the Universe,* Fox, 2002.
Janet, "Eye of the Beholder," *The Twilight Zone,* UPN, 2003.
The Tonight Show with Jay Leno, NBC, 2003.
Late Night with Conan O'Brien, NBC, 2003, 2005.
"Top 10 TV Cars," *TV Land's Top Ten,* TV Land, 2004.
Last Call with Carson Daly, NBC, 2005.
Live with Regis and Kelly, syndicated, 2005.
Jimmy Kimmel Live, ABC, 2004, 2005.

Television Appearances; Specials:
Presenter, *Sports Illustrated's Sportman of the Year,* CBS, 2000.
Host, *MTV Fashionably Loud: Spring Break, Cancun 2001,* ABC, 2001.
The Victoria's Secret Fashion Show, ABC, 2001.
MTV's New Year's Eve 2002, MTV, 2001.
Host, *MTV Fashionably Loud: Sports Illustrated Edition,* MTV, 2002.
Host, *World's Sexiest Athletes,* ESPN, 2002.
MTV's Mardi Gras, MTV, 2002.
Macy's 4th of July Spectacular, NBC, 2003.
Intimate Portrait: Vanessa Marcil (documentary), Lifetime, 2003.
Interviewee, *Sport's Illustrated Swimsuit 2003,* Spike, 2003.
Maxim Hot 100, NBC, 2003.
Sports Illustrated 40th Anniversary Swimsuit Special: American Beauty, Spike, 2004.
New Year's Eve with Carson Daly, NBC, 2004.
Host, *50 Hottest Vegas Moments,* E! Entertainment, 2005.
Celebrity judge, *Miss USA 2005,* NBC, 2005.

Television Appearances; Awards Presentations:
Host, *2003 Radio Music Awards,* NBC, 2003.
Host, *2004 Radio Music Awards,* NBC, 2004.
Presenter, *The 61st Annual Golden Globe Awards,* NBC, 2004.

RECORDINGS

Videos:
Herself/Mrs. Feldman, *Starsky & Hutch: A Last Look,* Warner Bros., 2004.

SQUILLANTE, Steven 1973–
 (Steve Squillante)

PERSONAL

Born June 14, 1973, in Bronxville, NY. *Education:* Attended Emerson College and Harvard University.

Career: Producer and executive. Dimension Films, worked as Los Angeles assistant, then as coordinator of development, manager of production and development, director of production and development, and executive in charge of production, until 2001; worked as senior vice president for production and development for Larry Levinson Productions and Alpine Media, beginning c. 2001; IDG Films, partner; worked as intern and creative assistant.

CREDITS

Television Co–Executive Producer; Miniseries:
Frankenstein, The Hallmark Channel, 2004.
La Femme Musketeer, The Hallmark Channel, 2004.
Supernova, The Hallmark Channel, 2005.

Television Co–Executive Producer; Movies:
Gentle Ben (also known as *Terror on the Mountain*), Animal Planet, 2002.
Night of the Wolf, Animal Planet, 2002.
Santa, Jr., The Hallmark Channel, 2002.
Audrey's Rain, The Hallmark Channel, 2003.
(As Steve Squillante) *A Carol Christmas,* The Hallmark Channel, 2003.
Gentle Ben 2: Danger on the Mountain (also known as *Black Gold*), Animal Planet, 2003.
Hard Ground, The Hallmark Channel, 2003.
The King and Queen of Moonlight Bay, The Hallmark Channel, 2003.
The Last Cowboy, The Hallmark Channel, 2003.
Love Comes Softly, The Hallmark Channel, 2003.

Monster Makers, The Hallmark Channel, 2003.
Mystery Woman, The Hallmark Channel, 2003.
Straight from the Heart, The Hallmark Channel, 2003.
A Time to Remember, The Hallmark Channel, 2003.
A Boyfriend for Christmas, The Hallmark Channel, 2004.
Gone but Not Forgotten, 2004.
(As Steve Squillante) *The Hollywood Mom's Mystery* (also known as *The Dead Hollywood Moms Society*), The Hallmark Channel, 2004.
Just Desserts, The Hallmark Channel, 2004.
(As Steve Squillante) *Life on Liberty Street,* The Hallmark Channel, 2004.
The Long Shot: Believe in Courage, The Hallmark Channel, 2004.
Love, Clyde, The Hallmark Channel, 2004.
A Place Called Home, The Hallmark Channel, 2004.
(As Steve Squillante) *The Trail to Hope Rose,* The Hallmark Channel, 2004.
Wedding Daze, The Hallmark Channel, 2004.
Back to You and Me, The Hallmark Channel, 2005.
Detective (also known as *Arthur Hailey's "Detective"*), 2005.
The Family Plan, The Hallmark Channel, 2005.
Out of the Woods, The Hallmark Channel, 2005.
The Poseidon Adventure, NBC, 2005.
Thicker Than Water, The Hallmark Channel, 2005.
Falling in Love with the Girl Next Door, The Hallmark Channel, 2006.
Hidden Places, The Hallmark Channel, 2006.

Television Production Executive; Movies:
(As Steve Squillante) *Gone but Not Forgotten,* 2004.

Film Producer:
Creative producer of "Cryptkeeper" sequences, *Ritual* (also known as *Tales from the Crypt Presents: Revelation* and *Tales from the Crypt Presents: Voodoo*), Miramax/Dimension Films, 2001.
(As Steve Squillante) Executive producer, *Children of the Corn: Revelation,* Dimension Films, 2001.
Dinotopia: Quest for the Ruby Sunstone (animated), Goodtimes Entertainment, 2005.
Porky's (also known as *Howard Stern Presents "Porky's"*), Gotham Entertainment Group, 2006.
Rock 'n' Roll High School (also known as *Howard Stern Presents "Rock 'n' Roll High School"*), 2006.
Witchblade, Platinum Studios/Relativity Media/Top Cow Entertainment, 2007.

Some sources cite Squillante as an executive producer of the film *Deader,* Dimension Films/Buena Vista Home Entertainment, c. 2005; and as a producer of the film *Witchblade 2,* Platinum Studios/IDG Films/Relativity Media/Top Cow Entertainment.

Film Executive in Charge of Production:
The Crow: Salvation (also known as *The Crow III—Toedliche Erloesung*), Dimension Films, 2000.

Equilibrium (also known as *Cubic*), Miramax/Dimension Films, 2002.

WRITINGS

Screenplays:
(With others) *Porky's* (also known as *Howard Stern Presents "Porky's"*; based on an earlier film), Gotham Entertainment Group, 2006.

Contributed material to films.

STAPLETON, Maureen 1925–2006

PERSONAL

Full name, Lois Maureen Stapleton; born June 21, 1925, in Troy, NY; died of Chronic pulmonary disease, March 13, 2006, in Lenox, MA. Actress. Award-winning, respected actress Stapleton began her long career on the stage, making her Broadway debut in 1946 in a production of *The Playboy of the Western World.* She won her first Antoinette Perry Award in 1951 for her portrayal of Serafina Delle Rose in Tennessee Williams' *The Rose Tattoo.* Stapleton made her film debut in the United Artists' film *Lonelyhearts* in 1959, and her performance gained her an Academy Award nomination for best supporting actress. She tirelessly worked in theatre and films as well as television throughout her long career. Among her best-known films are *Airport,* Woody Allen's *Interiors,* Warren Beatty's *Reds,* and *Cocoon.* She received Academy Award nominations for best supporting actress for her work in *Airport* and *Interiors* and finally won the award in 1982 with her performance in *Reds.* On stage Stapleton appeared in several other Tennessee Williams' plays, including *Twenty-Seven Wagons Full of Cotton* and *Orpheus Descending.* Over the years she also worked with Neil Simon, and she won an Antoinette Perry Award for *The Gingerbread Lady* in a role written for her. Stapleton's television appearances ranged from episodic guest roles to lead roles in movies, such as Beatrice Asher in *Queen of the Stardust Ballroom* and Kate Thornton in *The Gathering.*

PERIODICALS

Entertainment Weekly, March 24, 2006.
Time, March 27, 2006.
Variety, March 20, 2006.

STERLING, Maury

PERSONAL

Born in Mill Valley, CA.

Addresses: *Agent*—Innovative Artists, 1505 10th St., Santa Monica, CA 90401.

Career: Actor.

CREDITS

Film Appearances:
Sandman One, *Outbreak,* Warner Bros., 1995.
Van Jaspers, *Full Moon Rising,* Moondog, 1996.
Skinny guy, *Bulletproof,* United International, 1996.
Man in cell, *Somebody Is Waiting,* Redhead, 1996.
Donny, *Behind Enemy Lines,* Orion, 1998.
Communications tech, *Impostor,* Dimension, 2002.
Private First Class Dennis A. Gerber, *Hart's War,* Metro–Goldwyn–Mayer, 2002.
Maury, *March 1st* (short), 2002.
Roger, *Frankie and Johnny Are Married,* IFC, 2004.
Paul, *The Old Man and the Studio* (short), Diag, 2004.
Grant, *Illusion,* entitled entertainment, 2004.
Craig, *Come as You Are,* Eleventh Hour, 2005.
Hoss, *Dead Meat* (also known as *Andre the Butcher*), 2005.
Lester Tremor, *Smokin' Acres,* Universal, 2006.

Television Appearances; Series:
Vaughn Lerner, *Alright Already,* 1997.

Television Appearances; Episodic:
"This Little Piggy," *Picket Fences,* 1995.
David, *The Naked Truth,* 1995.
Eddie Hunter, "The Pink Flamingo Kid," *Boy Meets World,* 1996.
Morgan, "Relationship of Fools," *Boston Common,* 1996.
Mark Waring, "Inhuman Nature," *Dark Skies,* NBC, 1996.
Mordecai, "Davy Jones," *The Single Guy,* NBC, 1996.
Martin Donner Kingston, "Murder in the Air," *Diagnosis Murder,* 1997.
Donny Beaulieu, "Jarod's Honor," *The Pretender,* NBC, 1997.
Edward 'Eddie' Williams, "I Do," *Touched by an Angel,* 1998.
Policeman, *Two of a Kind,* ABC, 1998.
Airman Simpkins, "True Callings," *JAG,* CBS, 1999.
Harlowe, "Lady Evil," *G vs E* (also known as *Good vs Evil*), USA Network, 1999.
Barney, "Parting Gifts," *Angel* (also known as *Angel: The Series*), 1999.
"Run, Val, Run," *V.I.P.* (also known as *V.I.P.—Die Bodyguards*), syndicated, 2000.
Mr. Adams, "Star Search," *Do Over,* 2002.
Paul Zimberg, "Boys to Men," *Judging Amy,* CBS, 2002.
Mr. Molineaux, "Random Acts of Violence," *CSI: Crime Scene Investigation* (also known as *C.S.I.* and *CSI: Weekends*), CBS, 2003.

"Fire and Ice," *Crossing Jordan,* NBC, 2003.
Spencer Carls, "Motion Sickness," *Judging Amy,* CBS, 2003.
Tarquin, "Exile," *Enterprise* (also known as *Star Trek: Enterprise*), syndicated, 2003.
"Exposure," *Without a Trace,* 2004.
Dr. Nelson, "Just a Touch," *ER,* NBC, 2004.
Dr. Nelson, "Abby Normal," *ER,* NBC, 2004.
Pot dealer, "Grinding the Corn," *Six Feet Under,* HBO, 2004.
Blind man, "Natasha Charles," *Nip/Tuck,* FX Channel, 2004.
Lord Dyson, "The Bare Witch Project," *Charmed,* The WB, 2004.
Lewis, "Mr. Monk Goes to Vegas," *Monk,* USA Network, 2005.
"A Lie Agreed Upon: Part 2," *Deadwood,* 2005.

Also appeared as Doug, "The Six–Month Itch," *Townies,* ABC.

Television Appearances; Movies:
Store clerk, *Columbo: A Trace of Murder,* 1997.

Stage Appearances:
Incident at Vichy, The Complex, Theatre Row, Hollywood, CA, 1993.
Out at Sea, The Complex, Theatre Row, 1994.
Meat, The Powerhouse Theatre, Santa Monica, CA, 1996.
Modigliani, The Lost Studio, Los Angeles, 1996.
The Madman and the Nun, The Powerhouse Theatre, 1999.
Earl Rogers, *Crazy Drunk,* Inside the Ford, Los Angeles, 2002.

STERLING, Mindy 1953–
(Mindy Stirling)

PERSONAL

Full name, Mindy Lee Sterling; born July 11, 1953, in Paterson, NJ; raised in Miami, FL; daughter of Dick Sterling (a singer and stand–up comedian); mother, a dancer; married Brian L. Gadson; children: Max. *Education:* Studied acting.

Addresses: *Agent*—Mark Scroggs, David Shapira and Associates, 193 North Robertson Blvd., Beverly Hills, CA 90211.

Career: Actress and voice performer. The Groundlings (improvisational comedy group), member of company and teacher, beginning c. 1984. Appeared in community theatre productions in Miami, FL. Appeared in commercials.

Awards, Honors: Blockbuster Entertainment Award nomination, favorite supporting actress—comedy, 2000, for *Austin Powers: The Spy Who Shagged Me.*

CREDITS

Film Appearances:
First fan, *The Devil and Max Devlin,* Buena Vista, 1981.
Sister Oma and the Clarions, *UFOria,* Universal, c. 1985.
Woman in bookstore, *House* (also known as *House: Ding Dong, You're Dead*), New World Pictures, 1986.
Tentative woman, *Warlock,* Trimark Pictures, 1989.
Debbie Rollins, *The Favor* (also known as *The Favour* and *The Indecent Favour*), Orion, 1994.
Cindee, *Man of the Year,* Seventh Art Releasing, 1995.
Nanny with dog, *The Crazysitter* (also known as *Two Much Trouble*), 1995.
Frau Farbissina, *Austin Powers: International Man of Mystery* (also known as *Austin Powers—Das Schaerfste, was Ihre Majestaet zu bieten hat*), New Line Cinema, 1997.
Iris Clark, *Drop Dead Gorgeous* (also known as *Gnadenlos schoen*), New Line Cinema, 1998.
Frau Farbissina, *Austin Powers: The Spy Who Shagged Me* (also known as *Austin Powers 2: The Spy Who Shagged Me*), New Line Cinema, 1999.
Lady bowler, *Idle Hands,* Columbia, 1999.
Casting director, *The Audition* (short film), 2000.
Clamella, *How the Grinch Stole Christmas* (also known as *Dr. Seuss' "How the Grinch Stole Christmas,"* *The Grinch,* and *Der Grinch*), Universal, 2000.
Doris, *The Sky Is Falling,* Showcase Entertainment, 2000.
Mona Finch, *Barstow 2008,* Firebuilder Pictures/ Monkeyfactory, 2001.
Ramona, *Totally Blonde,* Panorama Entertainment/V Releasing, 2001.
Frau Farbissina, *Austin Powers in Goldmember* (also known as *Austin Powers: Goldmember*), New Line Cinema, 2002.
(Uncredited) Old woman in confessional, *EuroTrip* (also known as *The Ugly Americans,* *Untitled Berg, Schaffer, Mandel Project,* and *Untitled Montecito Project*), DreamWorks, 2004.
Lydia, *Getting Played,* New Line Home Video, 2005.
Mrs. Walsh, *The 12 Dogs of Christmas,* Screen Media Ventures, 2005.
Bernice Kimmelman, *Domestic Import,* 2006.
Mrs. Burris, *Cook–Off!,* 2006.
Patricia Riley, *The Enigma with a Stigma,* Digital Motion Picture Studio, 2006.

Voice of female ox, *Ice Age: The Meltdown* (animated), Twentieth Century–Fox, 2006.

Television Appearances; Series:
Dusty's Treehouse, syndicated, c. 1973.
Office manager, *Kristin,* NBC, 2001.
Fifi, *On the Spot,* The WB, 2003.
Voice of Aunt Mellie, *Higglytown Heroes* (animated), The Disney Channel, beginning 2004.

Some sources cite an appearance in the animated program *Red Hot Tomatoes.*

Television Appearances; Miniseries:
Herself, *I Love the '90s,* VH1, 2004.

Television Appearances; Movies:
Mary, *Working Tra$h,* Fox, 1990.
Fresno specialist, *Not Like Us,* 1995.
Lupe Horowitz, *30 Days until I'm Famous,* VH1, 2004.

Television Appearances; Specials:
Himself, *Canned Ham: The Spy Who Shagged Me* (also known as *Canned Ham Presents: Austin Powers— The Spy Who Shagged Me,* *Comedy Central's "Canned Ham": The Dr. Evil Story,* *The Dr. Evil Story,* and *Spyography: The Dr. Evil Story*), Comedy Central, 1999.
Herself, *Reel Comedy: Austin Powers in Goldmember,* Comedy Central, 2002.

Television Appearances; Awards Presentations:
Herself, *VH1 Big in '03,* VH1, 2003.
The 2004 Teen Choice Awards, Fox, 2004.

Television Appearances; Episodic:
"Wheels of Fortune," *B.J. and the Bear,* NBC, 1979.
Hostess, "First Date," *Perfect Strangers,* ABC, 1986.
LaWanda, *Evening Shade,* CBS, c. 1991.
Writer, "The Flirt Episode," *The Larry Sanders Show,* HBO, 1992.
Writer, "Hey Now," *The Larry Sanders Show,* HBO, 1992.
Clara Meade, "The Poker Game," *Saved by the Bell: The College Years,* NBC, 1993.
Clara Meade, "A Question of Ethics," *Saved by the Bell: The College Years,* NBC, 1993.
Woman, *The Second Half,* NBC, 1993.
Jill Peterman, *Good Advice,* CBS, 1994.
Coach, "Cheers Looking at You, Kid," *Family Matters,* ABC, 1995.
Denise's mom, "Single White Teenager," *Sister, Sister,* ABC, 1995.
Mrs. Fleckner, "Some Assembly Required," *Nick Freno: Licensed Teacher,* The WB, 1996.

Wedding planner, "The One with Barry and Mindy's Wedding," *Friends,* NBC, 1996.

June, "Makin' Whoopie," *Ellen* (also known as *These Friends of Mine*), ABC, 1997.

Maxine, "Again with the Black Box," *Alright Already,* The WB, 1997.

Mrs. Martin, *Hiller and Diller,* ABC, 1997.

Mrs. Walton, *Hiller and Diller,* ABC, 1997.

Instant Comedy with the Groundlings, FX Channel, 1998.

Guest, *The Martin Short Show,* syndicated, 1999.

(As Mindy Stirling) Voices of second lemur and newscaster, "Bogged Down," *The Wild Thornberrys* (animated), Nickelodeon, 2000.

Lona, *Manhattan, AZ,* USA Network, 2000.

Mrs. Lubitz, "The Gift Piggy," *Just Shoot Me!,* NBC, 2001.

Ms. Lynch, "Uncle Chuck," *Even Stevens,* The Disney Channel, 2001.

Guest, "Mike Myers," *Revealed with Jules Asner,* E! Entertainment Television, 2002.

Voice of Countess von Verminstrasser, "Lice," *Invader ZIM* (animated), Nickelodeon, 2002.

Ylva Gallo, "The Martini Shot," *She Spies* (also known as *B.A.I.T.*), NBC, 2002.

Guest, *Pyramid,* syndicated, multiple appearances, between 2002 and 2004.

Female house owner, "The Neighbors," *Hidden Hills,* NBC, 2003.

Casting director, "Joey and the Big Audition," *Joey,* NBC, 2004.

Mrs. Leonard, "Department Investigation: Part 2," *Reno 911!,* Comedy Central, 2004.

Mrs. Leonard, "President Bush's Motorcade," *Reno 911!,* Comedy Central, 2004.

Commentator, *101 Most Unforgettable SNL Moments* (also known as *E's "101"*), E! Entertainment Television, 2004.

Team player, *World Cup Comedy,* PAX TV, 2004, 2005.

Judge Foodie, "Food for Thought," *That's So Raven!* (also known as *Absolutely Psychic*), The Disney Channel, 2005.

Ms. Fennell, "Hair Tease," *Cuts,* UPN, 2005.

Voice of Enid Clinton, "The Once and Future Thing, Part 1: Weird Western Tales," *Justice League* (animated; also known as *JL, JLA, Justice League of America,* and *Justice League: Unlimited*), Cartoon Network, 2005.

Voice of Enid Clinton, "The Once and Future Thing, Part 2: Time, Warped," *Justice League* (animated; also known as *JL, JLA, Justice League of America,* and *Justice League: Unlimited*), Cartoon Network, 2005.

Sherry, "Gambling n' Diction," *The King of Queens,* CBS, 2006.

Appeared in episodes of other series; appeared as Nancy Haley in "The Feud," an unaired episode of *Hidden Hills,* NBC. Some sources cite an appearance as Superintendent Bell in *Unfabulous,* Nickelodeon; and appearances in *On the Television,* Nickelodeon, 1990; *The Downer Channel,* NBC, 2001; and *Cybill,* CBS.

Television Appearances; Pilots:
Office manager, *Kristin,* NBC, 2001.

Fifi, *On the Spot,* The WB, 2003.

Headmistress Moira Grodnickel, *Haversham Hall,* The Disney Channel, 2006.

Voices of Geraldine and Aggie, *Amazing Screw–On Head* (animated), Sci–Fi Channel, 2006.

Some sources cite an appearance in the animated pilot *Dog Town.*

Television Appearances; Other:
Mom Zumwalt, *Beyond Family,* Fox, 1995.

Stage Appearances:
Weena Savannah Shanker, *Beverly Winwood Presents the Actors Showcase,* Groundlings Theatre, Los Angeles, 2002.

RECORDINGS

Video Games:
Several voices, including those of Oracle Ulinara, Darmen Sproutmore, Merchant Novak, Kogna Bonesplit, and Oosa Gutwrench, *EverQuest II,* Sony Online Entertainment, 2004.

Voices of Aunt May and others, *Spider–Man 2,* Activision, 2004.

STEWART, Jon 1962–

PERSONAL

Original name, Jonathan Stewart Leibowitz; name legally changed; born November 28, 1962, in New York, NY; raised in Trenton (some sources cite Lawrenceville), NJ; son of Donald (a physicist) and Marion (a teacher and educational consultant) Leibowitz; married Tracey McShane (a veterinary technician), 2000; children: Nathan Thomas, Maggie Rose. *Education:* College of William and Mary, B.S., psychology. *Religion:* Judaism. *Avocational Interests:* Crossword puzzles.

Addresses: *Office*—Busboy Productions, 436 West 45th St., Third Floor, New York, NY 10036. *Agent*—Steve Levine, International Creative Management, 8942 Wilshire Blvd., Beverly Hills, CA 90211; (voice) Special

Artists Agency, 9465 Wilshire Blvd., Suite 890, Beverly Hills, CA 90212; (literary) Trident Media Group, 152 West 57th St., Carnegie Hall Tower, 16th Floor, New York, NY 10019. *Manager*—James Dixon, Dixon Talent, Inc., 436 West 45th St., Third Floor, New York, NY 10036. *Publicist*—Matthew Labov, Baker/Winokur/Ryder, 9100 Wilshire Blvd., Sixth Floor, West Tower, Beverly Hills, CA 90212.

Career: Actor, comedian, writer, and producer. Busboy Productions, New York City, principal; stand–up comedian at various venues; opening performer for various acts; provided voice–overs for commercials. Worked as the operator of a puppet show, bartender, bicycle repairperson, a van driver for a caterer, and in a laboratory.

Awards, Honors: George Foster Peabody Broadcasting awards (with others), Henry W. Grady School of Journalism and Mass Communications, University of Georgia, 2000 and 2005, Emmy Award nominations (with others), outstanding variety, music, or comedy program, 2001 and 2002, Emmy awards (with others), outstanding writing for a variety, music, or comedy program, 2001, 2003, 2004, and 2005, Emmy Award nomination (with others), outstanding writing for a variety, music, or comedy program, 2002, Emmy Award nominations, outstanding individual performance in a variety or music program, 2002, 2003, and 2005, Emmy awards (with others), outstanding variety, music, or comedy series, 2003, 2004, and 2005, Television Critics Association Award (with others), outstanding achievement in comedy, 2003, Television Critics Association awards, outstanding individual achievement in comedy, 2003 and 2005, Television Critics Association Award (with others), outstanding achievement in news and information, 2004, Television Critics Association Award nominations (with others), program of the year, 2003, 2004, and 2005, Television Critics Association Award nominations (with others), outstanding achievement in news and information, 2003 and 2005, Television Critics Association Award nomination, outstanding individual achievement in comedy, 2004, Television Critics Association Award nominations (with others), outstanding achievement in comedy, 2004 and 2005, and honor roll mention for campaign reporting, *Columbia Journalism Review*, 2004, all for *The Daily Show*; American Comedy Award nomination, funniest leading or supporting male performer in a television special, network, cable, or syndication, 2001, for *The Daily Show with Jon Stewart: Indecision 2000*; Teen Choice Award nomination, choice television personality, 2002; Commie Award, funniest person of the year, Comedy Central Network, 2003; named one of the entertainers of the year and the second funniest person in the United States, both *Entertainment Weekly*, 2004; named one of the 100 greatest stand–up comedians of all time, Comedy Central, 2004; honorary doctorate, College of William and Mary, 2004; Book of the Year

Award, *Publishers Weekly*, 2004, Thurber Prize for American Humor, 2005, and Quill Book awards, humor and audio categories, 2005, all with David Javerbaum, Ben Karlin, and others, all for *The Daily Show with Jon Stewart Presents America (the Book): A Citizen's Guide to Democracy Inaction*; Grammy Award (with others), best comedy album, National Academy of Recording Arts and Sciences, 2005, for *The Daily Show with Jon Stewart Presents ... America: A Citizen's Guide to Democracy Inaction*.

CREDITS

Television Appearances; Series:
Host, *Short Attention Span Theater*, Comedy Central, c. 1990–92.
Host, *You Wrote It, You Watch It*, MTV, beginning 1992.
Host, *The Jon Stewart Show*, MTV, beginning 1993.
Host, *The Jon Stewart Show*, syndicated, 1994–95.
Himself, *The Larry Sanders Show*, HBO, 1996–98.
Host, *The Daily Show* (also known as *The Daily Show with Jon Stewart* and *The Daily Show with Jon Stewart Global Edition*), Comedy Central, 1999—.

Television Appearances; Miniseries:
(In archive footage) *Heroes of Jewish Comedy*, Comedy Central, 2003.
(In archive footage) *Comedy Central Presents: 100 Greatest Stand–Ups of All Time*, Comedy Central, 2004.

Television Appearances; Movies:
Todd Zalinsky, *Since You've Been Gone*, ABC, 1998.
It's a Very Muppet Christmas Movie, NBC, 2002.

Television Appearances; Specials:
The 14th Annual Young Comedians Show, HBO, 1991.
Comedy Battle of the Sexes, Lifetime, 1992.
Announcer, *Third Annual Rock n' Jock B–Ball Jam* (also known as *MTV's "Third Annual Rock n' Jock B–Ball Jam"*), MTV, 1993.
Host, *Countdown to Comic Relief*, Comedy Central, 1995.
Interviewer, "Spring Break Rocks," *MTV's Spring Break '95*, MTV, 1995.
Comics Come Home, Comedy Central, 1995.
In a New Light: Sex Unplugged, ABC, 1995.
The State's 43rd Annual Halloween Special, CBS, 1995.
Jon Stewart: Unleavened, HBO, 1996.
Panelist, *What's Wrong with Sports in America?*, Comedy Central, 1997.
George Carlin: 40 Years of Comedy, HBO, 1997.
Host, *Elmopalooza*, ABC, 1998.
Comic Relief VIII, HBO, 1998.
Host, *The Daily Show with Jon Stewart Interview Special: Billy Crystal*, Comedy Central, 1999.

Host, *The Daily Show with Jon Stewart: The Greatest Millennium,* Comedy Central, 1999.

Himself, *Canned Ham: Big Daddy,* Comedy Central, 1999.

Frank DeCaro's "Out at the Movies" Fabulous Big "O" Buffet, Comedy Central, 1999.

MTV Uncensored, MTV, 1999.

Radio City Music Hall's Grand Re–Opening Gala, NBC, 1999.

25 Lame, MTV, 1999.

Host, *The Daily Show with Jon Stewart: Indecision 2000,* Comedy Central, 2000.

MTV20: Live and Almost Legal, MTV, 2001.

The Daily Show with Jon Stewart Presents Frank De-Caro: The Big O! True West Hollywood Story, Comedy Central, 2002.

Host, *Re–Decision 2003: The California Recall,* Comedy Central, 2003.

Comedy Central Roast of Denis Leary, Comedy Central, 2003.

MTV Bash: Carson Daly, MTV, 2003.

Night of Too Many Stars, NBC, 2003.

Richard Pryor: I Ain't Dead Yet, #%$#@!!* (also known as *Richard Pryor: I Ain't Dead Yet, #*%$#@!!—Uncensored*), Comedy Central, 2003.

Uncensored Comedy: That's Not Funny!, Trio, 2003.

Himself, *Feeding the Beast: The 24–Hour News Revolution,* Trio, 2004.

Host, *Election Night 2004: Prelude to a Recount,* Comedy Central, 2004.

Host, *Indecision 2004: Midway to the Election Spectacular,* Comedy Central, 2004.

Host, *Race from the White House 2004,* Comedy Central, 2004.

Choose or Lose Presents: The Best Place to Start, MTV, 2004.

(In archive footage) *Last Laugh '04,* Comedy Central, 2004.

(In archive footage) *Mouthing Off: 51 Greatest Smart-asses,* Comedy Central, 2004.

Last Laugh '05 (also known as *Comedy Central's "Last Laugh '05"*), Comedy Central, 2005.

ReAct Now: Music & Relief, MTV and VH1, 2005.

Television Appearances; Awards Presentations:

Presenter, *1994 MTV Music Video Awards,* MTV, 1994.

Host, *The 1995 Billboard Music Awards,* Fox, 1995.

Presenter, *The 16th Annual CableACE Awards,* TNT, 1995.

Presenter, *The 18th Annual CableACE Awards,* TNT, 1996.

Presenter, *12th Annual American Comedy Awards,* Fox, 1998.

Presenter, *The 51st Annual Primetime Emmy Awards,* Fox, 1999.

The 1999 MTV Movie Awards, MTV, 1999.

Host, *The 43rd Annual Grammy Awards* (also known as *2001 Grammy Awards*), CBS, 2001.

Host, *The 44th Annual Grammy Awards,* CBS, 2002.

The 54th Annual Primetime Emmy Awards, Fox, 2002.

Host, *The 55th Annual Primetime Emmy Awards,* Fox, 2003.

(In archive footage) *The Award Show Awards Show,* Trio, 2003.

Comedy Central Presents: The Commies (also known as *Comedy Central's "First Annual Commie Awards"* and *The Commies*), Comedy Central, 2003.

The GQ Men of the Year Awards (also known as *Spike TV Presents "The GQ Men of the Year Awards"*), Spike TV, 2003.

Presenter, *The 56th Annual Primetime Emmy Awards,* ABC, 2004.

Presenter, *The 2004 MTV Video Music Awards,* MTV, 2004.

Presenter, *The 57th Annual Primetime Emmy Awards,* CBS, 2005.

Host, *The 78th Annual Academy Awards,* ABC, 2006.

Television Appearances; Episodic:

Fan mail man, "Bologna Feet," *The State,* MTV, 1994.

Andrew, "Twins," *NewsRadio* (also known as *News Radio* and *The Station*), NBC, 1997.

Bobby, "Kissing Cousins," *The Nanny,* CBS, 1997.

Himself, "Mayonnaise," *Space Ghost Coast to Coast* (live action and animated; also known as *SGC2C*), Cartoon Network, 1997.

Himself, "A White Man Set Them Free," *Mr. Show* (also known as *Mr. Show with Bob and David*), HBO, 1997.

Voice, "Guess Who," *Dr. Katz: Professional Therapist* (animated), Comedy Central, 1997.

Pulp Comics: Dave Attell, Comedy Central, 1997.

Mitch Parker, "Wall Street," *Spin City* (also known as *Spin*), ABC, 1999.

Who Wants to Be a Millionaire, ABC, 2000.

Panelist, *Costas Now,* HBO, 2005.

Television Guest Appearances; Episodic:

The Late Show with David Letterman (also known as *The Late Show* and *Late Show Backstage*), CBS, 1994, 2005.

"The Dumbing of America," *Dennis Miller Live,* HBO, 1995.

Guest host, *The Late Late Show,* CBS, 1995.

Where's Elvis This Week?, BBC, 1996.

Howard Stern (also known as *The Howard Stern Radio Show*), E! Entertainment Television, 1996, 1998, 1999.

The Rosie O'Donnell Show, CBS, multiple appearances from 1996 through 2002.

"Bad Habits," *Dennis Miller Live,* HBO, 1997.

"Hypochondria," *Dennis Miller Live,* HBO, 1998.

Late Night with Conan O'Brien, NBC, multiple appearances from 1998 through 2000.

"The Making of 'Big Daddy,'" *HBO First Look,* HBO, 1999.

Charlie Rose (also known as *The Charlie Rose Show*), PBS, multiple appearances from 1999 through 2004.

"Hillary Clinton," *Dennis Miller Live,* HBO, 2000.

60 Minutes, CBS, 2001.

Larry King Live, Cable News Network, 2001, 2004, 2006.

"Religious Zealots," *Dennis Miller Live,* HBO, 2002.

Guest host, *Saturday Night Live* (also known as *NBC's "Saturday Night," Saturday Night, Saturday Night Live '80, SNL,* and *SNL 25*), NBC, 2002.

(Uncredited) *Contest Searchlight,* Comedy Central, 2002.

The Tonight Show with Jay Leno, NBC, 2002.

Now (also known as *Now with Bill Moyers*), PBS, 2003.

Primetime Glick, Comedy Central, 2003.

ABC News Nightline (also known as *Nightline*), ABC, 2004.

Crossfire, Cable News Network, 2004.

The O'Reilly Factor, Fox News Channel, 2004.

The Oprah Winfrey Show (also known as *Oprah*), syndicated, 2004, 2005.

The Colbert Report, Comedy Central, 2005.

This Week, BBC, 2005.

"Best of 02/20–02/24," *Howard Stern on Demand,* In Demand, 2006.

Corazon de ... , Television Espanola (Spain), 2006.

The Film Programme (also known as *Film 2006*), BBC, 2006.

Also appeared in episodes of *Comics Come Home,* Comedy Central; and *Full Mountie* (also known as *Jack Dee's "Full Mountie"*).

Television Executive Producer; Series:

The Jon Stewart Show, MTV, beginning 1993.

The Jon Stewart Show, syndicated, 1994–95.

(With others) *The Daily Show* (also known as *The Daily Show with Jon Stewart* and *The Daily Show with Jon Stewart Global Edition*), Comedy Central, 1999—.

The Colbert Report, Comedy Central, 2005—.

Television Executive Producer; Specials:

Jon Stewart: Unleavened, HBO, 1996.

(With others) *The Daily Show with Jon Stewart: The Greatest Millennium,* Comedy Central, 1999.

(With others) *Frank DeCaro's "Out at the Movies" Fabulous Big "O" Buffet,* Comedy Central, 1999.

(With others) *The Daily Show with Jon Stewart Presents Mo Rocca's Back to School Special,* Comedy Central, 2001.

(With others) *The Daily Show with Jon Stewart Presents Steve Carell Salutes Steve Carell,* Comedy Central, 2001.

(With others) *Out at the Movies Fabulous Big "O" Special: Miscast Away,* Comedy Central, 2001.

The Frank DeCaro Big "O" Special: A Fable, Comedy Central, 2003.

Election Night 2004: Prelude to a Recount, Comedy Central, 2004.

Indecision 2004: Midway to the Election Spectacular, Comedy Central, 2004.

Television Work; Awards Presentations:

Segment producer, *The 51st Annual Primetime Emmy Awards,* Fox, 1999.

Film Appearances:

Skater, *Mixed Nuts* (also known as *Lifesavers*), TriStar, 1994.

(Scenes deleted) *The First Wives Club,* Paramount, 1996.

Enhancement smoker, *Half Baked,* MCA/Universal, 1998.

Professor Edward Furlong, *The Faculty* (also known as *Feelers* and *Untitled Kevin Williamson/Robert Rodriguez Project*), Miramax/Dimension Films, 1998.

Trent, *Playing by Heart* (also known as *Dancing about Architecture* and *If They Only Knew*), Miramax, 1998.

Henry, *Wishful Thinking,* Miramax, 1999.

Himself, *Barenaked in America,* The Shooting Gallery, 1999.

Kevin Gerrity, *Big Daddy* (also known as *Guy Gets Kid*), Columbia, 1999.

(Uncredited) Dean, *Committed* (also known as *Non Stop Girl*), Miramax, 2000.

Pizza man, *The Office Party* (short film), 2000.

Voice of Godfrey, *The Adventures of Tom Thumb and Thumbelina* (animated), Miramax, 2000.

Reg Hartner, *Jay and Silent Bob Strike Back* (also known as *VA5* and *View Askew 5*), Miramax/Dimension Films, 2001.

Marion Frank Stokes, *Death to Smoochy* (also known as *Toetet Smoochy*), Warner Bros., 2002.

Himself, *Gigantic (A Tale of Two Johns)* (documentary), Cowboy Pictures/Plexifilm, 2003.

Himself, *Oh, What a Lovely Tea Party* (documentary), View Askew Productions, 2004.

(In archive footage) Himself, *Outfoxed: Rupert Murdoch's War on Journalism* (documentary), MoveOn.org, 2004.

Himself, *The Aristocrats,* ThinkFilm, 2005.

Voice of Zeebad for English version, *The Magic Roundabout* (animated; also known as *Sprung! The Magic Roundabout* and *Pollux—Le manege enchante*), 2005, The Weinstein Company, 2006.

Himself, *Wordplay* (documentary), IFC Films, 2006.

Voice of Zeebad, *Doogal* (animated), The Weinstein Company, 2006.

Radio Appearances:

Howard Stern (also known as *The Howard Stern Radio Show*), 1996, 1998, 1999, 2006.

RECORDINGS

Videos:

Wanda Sykes: Tongue Untied, 2003.

(Uncredited; In archive footage) *Saturday Night Live: The Best of Tracy Morgan,* Lions Gate Films Home Entertainment, 2004.

Indecision 2004, Comedy Central Home Entertainment/ Paramount Home Entertainment, 2005.

Audiobooks:

(With others) *The Daily Show with Jon Stewart Presents ... America: A Citizen's Guide to Democracy Inaction,* Warner Adult, 2004.

WRITINGS

Teleplays; with Others; Series:

The Sweet Life, HBO Comedy Channel, beginning 1989.

The Jon Stewart Show, MTV, beginning 1993.

The Jon Stewart Show, syndicated, 1994–95.

The Daily Show (also known as *The Daily Show with Jon Stewart* and *The Daily Show with Jon Stewart Global Edition*), Comedy Central, 1999—.

Teleplays; Specials:

Jon Stewart: Unleavened, HBO, 1996.

(With others) *Election Night 2004: Prelude to a Recount,* Comedy Central, 2004.

Teleplays; with Others; Awards Presentations:

The 43rd Annual Grammy Awards (also known as *2001 Grammy Awards*), CBS, 2001.

The 78th Annual Academy Awards, ABC, 2006.

Videos; with Others:

Indecision 2004, Comedy Central Home Entertainment/ Paramount Home Entertainment, 2005.

Audiobooks; with Others:

The Daily Show with Jon Stewart Presents ... America: A Citizen's Guide to Democracy Inaction, Warner Adult, 2004.

Humor:

Naked Pictures of Famous People (humorous essays), Rob Weisbach Books, 1998.

(With David Javerbaum, Ben Karlin, and the staff of *The Daily Show*) *The Daily Show with Jon Stewart Presents America (the Book): A Citizen's Guide to Democracy Inaction,* Warner Books, 2004.

OTHER SOURCES

Books:

Authors and Artists for Young Adults, Volume 57, Thomson Gale, 2004.

Newsmakers, Issue 2, Gale, 2001.

Periodicals:

Columbia Journalism Review, January/February, 2003, pp. 27–29.

Crain's New York Business, November 14, 2005, p. 1.

Entertainment Weekly, September 16, 1994, p. 49; November 11, 1994, pp. 36–39; August 21, 1998, p. 9; January 8, 1999, pp. 36–37; June 13, 2003, p. 82; October 31, 2003, pp. 30–35; December 31, 2004, p. 44; January 20, 2006, pp. 16–17.

Esquire, July, 2001, p. 62.

InStyle, February 1, 1999, p. 95.

Nation, May 5, 2003, p. 24.

New Statesman, October 10, 2005, pp. 42–43.

Newsweek, July 31, 2000, p. 60; December 29, 2003.

New York, January 10, 1994, p. 36; July 10, 1994, p. 17.

New Yorker, February 11, 2002, pp. 28–34.

People Weekly, April 4, 1994, pp. 99–100; October 31, 1994, p. 13; January 23, 1995, p. 90; November 23, 1998, p. 47; May 10, 1999, p. 160; January 10, 2006.

Playboy, March, 2000, p. 63.

Rolling Stone, January 26, 1995; October 28, 2004, pp. 58–64.

Time, January 18, 1999, p. 88; May 12, 2003, p. 87; September 27, 2004; April 18, 2005, p. 117.

Toronto Star, October 8, 2005, p. A22.

TV Guide, October 17, 2004, pp. 28–31, 32–35; January 16, 2006, pp. 74–78, 151–53.

USA Weekend, June 9, 2000, p. 8.

Variety, October 21, 2002, pp. A14–A15.

Village Voice, March 7, 1995.

Washington Post, May 2, 2002, pp. C1, C10.

STIRLING, Mindy
See STERLING, Mindy

STRONG, Tara 1973–
(Tara Charendoff, Tara Charendoff–Strong)

PERSONAL

Original name, Tara Lyn Charendoff; born February 12, 1973, in Toronto, Ontario, Canada; married Craig Strong (an actor and voice artist), May 14, 2000;

children: Sammy James, Aden Joshua. *Education:* Attended a school for the performing arts.

Addresses: *Agent*—International Creative Management, 8942 Beverly Blvd., Suite 155, Beverly Hills, CA 90211; VOX, Inc., 5670 Wilshire Blvd., Suite 820, Los Angeles, CA 90036.

Career: Actress, voice artist, and singer. Appeared in commercials. Appeared in the series of short comedy spots titled *Johnnie Talk,* Nickelodeon; provided the voice of Page for the segment "Page's Word of the Day" on *Playhouse Disney.* Provided voice characterizations for products, including the voice of Bubbles for Powerpuff Girls merchandise and the voice of Miranda for DivaStarz merchandise. Also known as Tara Charendoff–Strong.

Awards, Honors: Annie Award nomination, outstanding individual achievement for voice acting in an animated television production, International Animated Film Society, 1999, for *The Powerpuff Girls;* Annie Award nomination, outstanding individual achievement for voice acting by a female performer in an animated television production, 2001, for *The Fairly OddParents;* Annie Award nomination, outstanding individual achievement for voice acting by a female performer in an animated feature production, 2001, for *The Little Mermaid II: Return to the Sea;* Interactive Achievement Award, outstanding female achievement in character performance, Academy of Interactive Arts and Sciences, 2004, for *Final Fantasy X–2;* Annie Award nomination, outstanding voice acting in an animated television production, 2004, and Daytime Emmy Award nomination, outstanding performer in an animated program, 2006, both for *Jakers! The Adventures of Piggley Winks.*

CREDITS

Television Appearances; Animated Series:
Voice of Bubbles and cohost of live action segments, *Cartoon Cartoon Fridays* (also known as *CCF* and *Fridays*), Cartoon Network, beginning c. 1999.
Multiple voices, *Family Guy* (animated; also known as *Padre de familia* and *Padre del familia*), Fox, beginning 2000.
Voice of Tara Byron, *Da Mob,* Fox Family Channel, beginning 2001.
Voice of Timmy Turner, *The Fairly OddParents* (also known as *The Fairly GodParents, The Fairly Odd Parents,* and *Oh My! GodParents*), Nickelodeon, 2001—.
Voices of Bebe Proud, Cece Proud, Puff, and others, *The Proud Family,* The Disney Channel, beginning 2001.

Voice of Ingrid Third, *Fillmore!* (also known as *Disney's "Fillmore!"*), ABC, 2002–2004.
Voices of Tara and others, *Kim Possible* (also known as *Disney's "Kim Possible"*), The Disney Channel, between 2002 and 2005.
Voices of Dannan O'Mallard and Molly Winks, *Jakers! The Adventures of Piggley Winks,* PBS, beginning 2003.
Voices of Dylan Prescott "Dil" Pickles and others, *All Grown Up* (also known as *Rugrats All Grown Up*), Nickelodeon, beginning 2003.
Voices of Omi and others, *Xiaolin Showdown,* The WB, beginning 2003.
Multiple voices, *Codename: Kids Next Door,* Cartoon Network, between 2003 and 2004.
Voices of Raven and others, *Teen Titans,* Cartoon Network, 2003—.
Voice of Wendy, *The Infinite Darcy,* beginning 2004.
Voices of Ember McLean, Penelope Spectra, Star, and others, *Danny Phantom,* Nickelodeon, beginning 2004.
Voices of Terrence and others, *Foster's Home for Imaginary Friends,* Cartoon Network, 2004—.
Voices of Toot Braunstein and Princess Clara, *Drawn Together,* Comedy Central, 2004—.
Voice of Jake, *Angelica and Susie's Pre-School Daze* (also known as *Angelica and Susie's School Daze* and *Pre-School Daze*), beginning 2005.
Voice of Ben Tennyson (title role), *Ben 10,* Cartoon Network, 2005—.
Voices of Dawn Swatworthy and Maria, *The Buzz on Maggie,* The Disney Channel, 2005—.
Voices of Roger and others, *The Life and Times of Juniper Lee,* Cartoon Network, 2005—.
Multiple voices, *Camp Lazlo,* Cartoon Network, 2005—.

Television Appearances; Animated Series; as Tara Charendoff:
Voice of Sophia Tutu, *The Raccoons* (also known as *Les aventures de Raccoons*), CBC and The Disney Channel, 1985–90.
Voice of Frances, *Rupert the Bear,* beginning 1986.
Voices of Carol, Rebecca, Anna, and others, *The Care Bears Family* (also known as *The Care Bears*), ABC, 1986–88, syndicated, 1988–90.
Voice of Bridget, *Sylvanian Families,* syndicated, 1987.
Voice of Carly, *Maxie's World,* syndicated, beginning 1987.
Voice of Ame, *My Pet Monster* (also known as *P'tit monstre*), [Canada], also broadcast on ABC, 1987–88.
Voice of Hello Kitty, *Hello Kitty's Furry Tale Theater,* CBS, 1987–88.
Voice of young Celeste, *Babar,* CanWest Global Television, HBO, and France 3, beginning 1989.

Voices of Claire Brewster, Bertha, and Little Miss Warden, *Beetlejuice,* ABC, 1989–92.

Voice of Cloe, *Madeline,* Fox Family Channel, beginning c. 1990.

Voices of Dotty and Prissy, *Piggsburg Pigs!,* Fox, 1990–91.

Voices of Hip Koopa and Hop Koopa, *Captain N & the Adventures of Super Mario Bros. 3,* NBC, 1990–91.

Voice of Mary Jane, *Bill & Ted's Excellent Adventures,* CBS, 1990–91, Fox, 1991–92.

Host and voice of mouse, *Here's How!,* TVOntario and NBC, beginning 1991.

Voices of Hip Koopa and Hop Koopa, *Captain N and the New Super Mario World,* NBC, 1991–92.

Voice of Laura, *ProStars,* NBC, 1991–92.

Voice of Jenny Lawson, *Tales from the Cryptkeeper,* ABC, 1993–95, also broadcast in Canada.

Voice of Yumi Francois, *Tekkaman Blade 2* (anime), beginning c. 1994.

Voice of Agent Heather, *Gadget Boy and Heather* (also known as *Gadget Boy*), syndicated, beginning 1995.

Voice of Tutu, *Little Bear,* YTV (Canada) and Nickelodeon, beginning 1995.

Voice of Barbara Gordon/Batgirl, *Batman: Gotham Knights* (also known as *The New Adventures of Batman*), The WB, beginning 1997.

Voice of Barbara Gordon/Batgirl, *The New Batman Superman Adventures* (also known as *The New Batman/Superman Adventures*), The WB, beginning 1997.

Voice of Brenda, *Pepper Ann* (also known as *Disney's "Pepper Ann"*), ABC, beginning 1997.

Voice of Kylie Griffin, *Extreme Ghostbusters,* syndicated, beginning 1997.

Voice, *Channel Umptee–3,* The WB, beginning 1997.

Voices of Spot, Irma Chicken, Two Tone, and Vendela DeVil, *101 Dalmatians: The Series* (also known as *101 Dalmatians*), ABC, 1997, then syndicated, 1997–98.

Voice of Timmy McNulty, *Rugrats,* Nickelodeon, 1997–2001.

Voice of Agent Heather, *Gadget Boy's Adventures in History* (also known as *Gadget Boy*), History Channel, beginning 1998.

Voices of Mina and others, *Oh Yeah! Cartoons,* Nickelodeon, beginning 1998.

Voice of Dylan Prescott "Dil" Pickles, *Rugrats,* Nickelodeon, 1998–2004.

Voices of Bubbles and others, *The Powerpuff Girls* (also known as *PPG* and *Youlide–Chui nu*), Cartoon Network, 1998—.

Voice of Shareena Wickett, *Detention,* The WB, beginning 1999.

Voice of the title role, *Stevie Stardust,* [Germany], beginning 1999.

Voices of Sanjay and Penny, *The Kids from Room 402* (also known as *La classe en delire*), Fox Family Channel, c. 1999–2001.

Television Appearances; Live Action Series:

(As Tara Charendoff) Tara Harrison, *Mosquito Lake,* CBC, beginning 1989.

Television Appearances; Miniseries:

(As Tara Charendoff) Sarah, *Family Pictures,* ABC, 1993.

Television Appearances; Animated Movies:

(As Tara Charendoff) Voice of Lena, *Scooby–Doo on Zombie Island,* Cartoon Network, 1998.

Voices of Timmy Turner, first fairy, and kids, *Nickelodeon Presents the Fairly OddParents in: Abra Catastrophe!* (also known as *Abra–Catastrophe, The Fairly OddParents in Abra Catastrophe!,* and *The Fairly OddParents Movie*), Nickelodeon, 2003.

Voice of Timmy Turner, *The Jimmy Timmy Power Hour,* Nickelodeon, 2004.

Voices of young Timmy Turner, Paula Poundcake, Vicky and Tootie's mother, and others, *Nickelodeon Presents the Fairly OddParents in: Channel Chasers,* Nickelodeon, 2004.

Voices of Bebe Proud, Cece Proud, and Cashew, *The Proud Family Movie,* The Disney Channel, 2005.

Voice of Timmy Turner, *The Jimmy Timmy Power Hour 2: When Nerds Collide* (also known as *The Jimmy Timmy Power Hour 2*), Nickelodeon, 2006.

Voice of Timmy Turner, *The Jimmy Timmy Power Hour 3: The Jerkinators* (also known as *The Jimmy Timmy Power Hour 3*), Nickelodeon, 2006.

Television Appearances; Live Action Movies; as Tara Charendoff:

Vida Sparrows, *A Town Torn Apart* (also known as *Doc: The Dennis Litky Story*), NBC, 1992.

Lucille, *Reform School Girl,* Showtime, 1994.

Tina at the age of sixteen, *Thicker Than Blood: The Larry McLinden Story* (also known as *The Larry McLinden Story*), CBS, 1994.

Gwen, *Sabrina Goes to Rome,* ABC, 1998.

Gwen, *Sabrina Down Under,* ABC, 1999.

Lula, *Can of Worms,* The Disney Channel, 1999.

Television Appearances; Animated Specials:

Voice of Dylan Prescott "Dil" Pickles, *The Rugrats: All Growed Up,* Nickelodeon, 2001.

Voice of Dylan Prescott "Dil" Pickles, *Rugrats: Still Babies after All These Years,* Nickelodeon, 2001.

Voice of Sprout Speevak, *Crash Nebula,* Nickelodeon, 2004.

Voices of Timmy Turner and Baby Flappy Bob, *Nickelodeon Presents the Fairly OddParents in School's Out! The Musical* (musical), Nickelodeon, 2004.

Television Appearances; Live Action Specials:
(As Tara Charendoff) Host and announcer, *AidScare/ AidsCare,* CBC, c. 1994.

Television Appearances; Animated Episodes:
Voice of Cindy, *Lloyd in Space* (also known as *Disney's "Lloyd in Space"*), The Disney Channel, 2000.

Voice of little boy, "The Legend of Ha Long Bay," *The Wild Thornberrys* (animated; also known as *The Thornberrys*), Nickelodeon, 2000.

Voices of Candy and Christy, *The Weekenders,* The Disney Channel, 2000.

Voices of girls and lady, "Jack in Wonderland," *Samurai Jack,* Cartoon network, 2001.

Voice, "Tarzan and the Enemy Within," *The Legend of Tarzan* (also known as *Disney's "The Legend of Tarzan"*), UPN and syndicated, 2001.

Voice of Ariella Third, *Fillmore!* (also known as *Disney's "Fillmore!"*), ABC, 2002.

Voice of first Jane, "Fun with Jane and Jane," *King of the Hill,* Fox, 2002.

Voice of honey bee, "Black Widows," *Totally Spies!* (also known as *Totally Spies Undercover!*), ABC Family Channel, 2002.

Voices of Terry and Chris, "Roller Ghoster Ride," *What's New, Scooby–Doo?,* The WB, 2002.

Voice, *Ozzy & Drix,* The WB, 2002.

Voice of Alexandra Viggi, "Pompeii and Circumstance," *What's New, Scooby–Doo?,* The WB, 2003.

Voice of Christina, "Head over Heels," *Spider–Man* (also known as *Spider–Man: The New Animated Series*), MTV, 2003.

Voice of Christina, "Heroes and Villains," *Spider–Man* (also known as *Spider–Man: The New Animated Series*), MTV, 2003.

Voice of Katma–Tui, "The Green Loontern," *Duck Dodgers* (also known as *Duck Dodgers in the 24 1/2th Century*), Cartoon Network, 2003.

Voice of Ozmo, "Duck Codgers/Where's Baby Smartypants?," *Duck Dodgers* (also known as *Duck Dodgers in the 24 1/2th Century*), Cartoon Network, 2003.

Voice of queen, "Wild Cards: Part 1," *Justice League* (animated; also known as *JL, JLA,* and *Justice League of America*), Cartoon Network, 2003.

Voice of Sara, "Twilight: Part 2," *Justice League* (animated; also known as *JL, JLA,* and *Justice League of America*), Cartoon Network, 2003.

Voice of angel, "Angel: Experiment 624," *Lilo & Stitch: The Series* (animated; also known as *The Adventures of Lilo & Stitch*), The Disney Channel, 2004.

Voice of little girl, "Dis–Harmony/Collect All 5!," *Hi Hi Puffy AmiYumi,* Cartoon Network, 2004.

Voice of Tina Fey, "Iraqathon," *This Just In,* Spike TV, 2004.

Voice of Trudy Lowe, "Recipe for Disaster," *What's New, Scooby–Doo?,* The WB, 2004.

Voices of Comet and Pulsar, "Ultra Chicks," *Megas XLR* (also known as *LowBrow*), Cartoon Network, 2004.

Voices of Herieffenie and others, *Grim & Evil* (also known as *The Grim Adventures of Billy & Mandy*), Cartoon Network, c. 2004.

Voice of cheerleader, "The Kids Are All Wrong/Win, Lose, or Duck," *Duck Dodgers* (also known as *Duck Dodgers in the 24 1/2th Century*), Cartoon Network, 2005.

Voice of Counselor Dish, "Of Course You Know, This Means War and Peace: Parts 1 & 2," *Duck Dodgers* (also known as *Duck Dodgers in the 24 1/2th Century*), Cartoon Network, 2005.

Voice of Ellomold the Enchantress, "MMORPD/Old Mc-Dodgers," *Duck Dodgers* (also known as *Duck Dodgers in the 24 1/2th Century*), Cartoon Network, 2005.

Voice of Gabriella, "Pedigree, Schmedigree," *Brandy & Mr. Whiskers,* The Disney Channel, 2005.

Voice of Hermione, "One Crazy Summoner/Guess What's Coming to Dinner," *Grim & Evil* (also known as *The Grim Adventures of Billy & Mandy*), Cartoon Network, 2005.

Voice of Mom Howler, "The Howler Bunny," *Brandy & Mr. Whiskers,* The Disney Channel, 2005.

Voices of Bebe Proud, Cece Proud, and Puff, "Spats: Experiment #397," *Lilo & Stitch: The Series* (animated; also known as *The Adventures of Lilo & Stitch*), The Disney Channel, 2005.

Voices of intern, Dr. Paula Bowman, and housewife, "Quiller Instinct," *Stroker and Hoop,* Cartoon Network, 2005.

Voices of the oracle twins, "Body Guard Duty," *American Dragon: Jake Long* (also known as *ADJL, American Dragon, Disney's "American Dragon: Jake Long," Jake Long: American Dragon,* and *Last Dragon*), The Disney Channel, 2005.

Voices of Veronica and the oracle twins, "Dragon Breath," *American Dragon: Jake Long* (also known as *ADJL, American Dragon, Disney's "American Dragon: Jake Long," Jake Long: American Dragon,* and *Last Dragon*), The Disney Channel, 2005.

Voices of Veronica and the oracle twins, "Eye of the Beholder," *American Dragon: Jake Long* (also known as *ADJL, American Dragon, Disney's "American Dragon: Jake Long," Jake Long: American Dragon,* and *Last Dragon*), The Disney Channel, 2005.

Voices of Veronica and the oracle twins, "Hong Kong Knights," *American Dragon: Jake Long* (also known as *ADJL, American Dragon, Disney's "American Dragon: Jake Long," Jake Long: American Dragon,* and *Last Dragon*), The Disney Channel, 2005.

Voice of Johnny, "Patriot Act," *Justice League: Unlimited* (also known as *Justice League*), Cartoon Network, 2006.

Some sources state that Strong provided a voice for the animated program *Clifford the Big Red Dog* (also known as *Clifford*), PBS and BBC.

Television Appearances; Animated Episodes; as Tara Charendoff:

Voice of Illyana Rasputin, "Red Dawn," *X–Men,* Fox, 1993.

Voice, *The Busy World of Richard Scarry,* Canadian television and Showtime, c. 1993.

Voice of poodle, "Poodle Panic," *Shnookums and Meat Funny Cartoon Show,* syndicated, 1995.

Voice of little girl, "Compassion: Legend of the Dipper" (also known as "Compassion"), *Adventures from the Book of Virtues* (also known as *The Book of Virtues*), PBS, c. 1996.

Voice of Kazrina, "Ice Will Burn," *The Real Adventures of Jonny Quest* (also known as *Jonny Quest: The Real Adventures*), TBS, TNT, and Cartoon Network, 1996.

Voice of little girl, "Jubilee's Fairy Tale Theatre," *X–Men,* Fox, 1996.

Voices of Scarlet Witch and Wanda Maximoff, "Family Ties," *X–Men,* Fox, 1996.

Voices of Skids and Sally Blevins, "No Mutant Is an Island," *X–Men,* Fox, 1996.

Voice of Susie McIder, *Quack Pack* (also known as *Disney's "Quack Pack"*), The Disney Channel, 1996.

Voice of Paige Guthrie, "Hidden Agendas," *X–Men,* Fox, 1997.

Voices of Timmy McNulty and Teddy McNulty, "America's Wackiest Home Movies/The 'Lympics," *Rugrats,* Nickelodeon, 1997.

Voice of Billy, "Life in the Fast Lane," *King of the Hill,* Fox, 1998.

Voice of Irina Kafka, "The Haunted Sonata," *The Real Adventures of Jonny Quest* (also known as *Jonny Quest: The Real Adventures*), TBS, TNT, and Cartoon Network, 1998.

Voice of James, "Good Hill Hunting," *King of the Hill,* Fox, 1998.

Voice of Nurse Trudy, "Fakin' It," *The Angry Beavers,* Nickelodeon, 1998.

Voice of Kimmi, "Three Coaches and a Bobby," *King of the Hill,* Fox, 1999.

Voice of Martha, "Frankenfrog," *Oh Yeah! Cartoons,* Nickelodeon, 1999.

Voice of Mina, "Mina and the Count," *Oh Yeah! Cartoons,* Nickelodeon, 1999.

Voice, "Ask Edward," *Oh Yeah! Cartoons,* Nickelodeon, 1999.

Voice of little Becky Benson, *Recess* (also known as *Disney's "Recess" Created by Paul and Joe*), The Disney Channel, 1999.

Multiple voices, *Cow and Chicken,* Cartoon Network and TeleToon, 1999, 2000.

Voice of Bonnie Lepton, "Eye of the Tempest," *Buzz Lightyear of Star Command* (animated; also known as *Disney/Pixar's "Buzz Lightyear of Star Command"*), UPN and syndicated, 2000.

Voice of giggling girl, "Episode Two (a.k.a. The Clipshow wherein Dante and Randal Are Locked in the Freezer and Remember Some of the Great Moments in Their Lives" (also known as "The Clips Show"), *Clerks* (also known as *Clerks: The Cartoon* and *Clerks: Uncensored*), ABC, 2000.

Voice of giggling girl, "Episode Four (a.k.a. A Dissertation on the American Justice System by People Who Have Never Been inside a Courtroom, Let Alone Know Anything about the Law, but Have Seen Way Too Many Legal Thrillers)," *Clerks* (also known as *Clerks: The Cartoon* and *Clerks: Uncensored*), ABC, 2000.

Provided voice, *Alf Tales,* NBC; and voice, *Wish Kids,* USA Network. Provided the voice of giggling girl for "Episode Five (a.k.a. Dante and Randal and Jay and Silent Bob and a Bunch of New Characters and Lando Take Part in a Whole Bunch of Movie Parodies, including, but Not Exclusive to, *The Bad News Bears, The Last Starfighter, Indiana Jones and the Temple of Doom,* Plus a High School Reunion," and "The Last Episode Ever," both unaired episodes of *Clerks* (also known as *Clerks: The Cartoon* and *Clerks: Uncensored*), ABC.

Television Appearances; Live Action Episodes; as Tara Charendoff:

Angela, "Sing for Me, Olivia," *Street Legal,* CBC, 1986.

Sydney, "Junkyard Blues," *T and T,* syndicated and The Family Channel, c. 1988.

"Kids Just Want to Have Fun," *Katts and Dog* (also known as *Rin Tin Tin: K–9 Cop*), CTV and The Family Channel, 1988.

"Dying for Fame," *Forever Knight,* CBS, 1992.

Elizabeth, "Secret Place," *Kung Fu: The Legend Continues,* syndicated, 1993.

Nicole (some sources cite Jackie), "Black or White or Maybe Grey," *Ready or Not* (also known as *Les premieres fois*), CanWest Global Television and Showtime, c. 1993.

Lorna, "Homework," *Party of Five,* Fox, 1994.

Emily, "Out, Out, Damn Radio Spot!," *Maybe This Time,* ABC, 1995.

Voice of exercise lady, "My Mother the Alien," *3rd Rock from the Sun* (also known as *Life as We Know It* and *3rd Rock*), NBC, 1996.

Voice of Molly Dolly, "Good Will Haunting," *Sabrina, the Teenage Witch* (also known as *Sabrina* and *Sabrina Goes to College*), ABC, 1998.

Voice of puppy, *Puppies Present: Incredible Animal Tales,* 1998.

Voice of unborn baby, *Candid Camera,* CBS, c. 1998.

Girl with Ouija board, "The Occupant," *Touched by an Angel,* CBS, 1999.

Appeared as Millie Waters, "The Wild Thing," *The Judge;* as Donna Charter, *Heart of Courage* (also known as *Courage au coeur*), Discovery Channel Canada; as Shelly, *Missing Treasures;* and as Marla, *Top Cops,* CBS; also appeared in episodes of *Brainstorm,* TVOntario; *The Campbells,* syndicated; *Dog House,* YTV (Canada); and *E.N.G.,* CTV and Lifetime. Some sources cite an appearance in *Earth: Final Conflict* (also known as *EFC, Gene Roddenberry's "Battleground Earth," Gene Roddenberry's "Earth: Final Conflict," Invasion planete Terre,* and *Mission Erde: Sie sind unter uns*), syndicated.

Television Appearances; Pilots:

(As Tara Charendoff) Voice of giggling girl, *Clerks* (animated; also known as *Clerks: The Cartoon* and *Clerks: Uncensored*), Comedy Central, 2002.

Provided the voices of Cassidy and Cody for the animated pilot *Clayton,* UPN.

Television Additional Voices; Animated Series; as Tara Charendorff:

WishKid Starring Macaulay Culkin (also known as *Wish Kid*) NBC, 1991–92.
Ace Ventura: Pet Detective, CBS and Nickelodeon, beginning 1995.
Adventures from the Book of Virtues (also known as *The Book of Virtues*), PBS, beginning 1996.
The Real Adventures of Jonny Quest (also known as *Jonny Quest: The Real Adventures*), TBS, TNT, and Cartoon Network, c. 1996–99.
Healthspells, beginning c. 1997.
Sonic Underground, UPN, c. 1998–99.

Animated Film Appearances:

Voice of Barbara Gordon/Batgirl, *Batman Beyond: Return of the Joker* (also known as *Batman of the Future: Return of the Joker* and *Return of the Joker*), Warner Bros., 2000.
Voice of Bo the baby for English version, *Sen to Chiriho no kamikakushi* (also known as *Miyazaki's "Spirited Away," Sen, Sen and the Mysterious Disappearance of Chihiro, Spirited Away,* and *The Spiriting Away of Sen and Chihiro*), Toho Company/Buena Vista International, 2001.
Voice of Hazel, *Tarzan & Jane,* Buena Vista Home Video, 2002.
Voice of Nibbles, *Tom and Jerry: The Magic Ring,* Warner Home Video, 2002.
Voice of schoolgirl, *The Wild Thornberrys Movie,* Paramount, 2002.
Voices of baby Moeritherium, Roshan, and Start, *Ice Age,* Twentieth Century–Fox, 2002.
Voice of Bubbles, *The Powerpuff Girls* (also known as *The Powerpuff Girls Movie*), Warner Bros., 2002.
Voice, *The Hunchback of Notre Dame II,* Buena Vista Home Video/Walt Disney Home Video, 2002.

Voice of Barbara Gordon/Batgirl, *Batman: Mystery of the Batwoman,* Warner Bros., 2003.
Voice of Britina, *Kim Possible: The Secret Files,* Walt Disney Home Entertainment, 2003.
Voice of Bubbles, *Powerpuff Girls: Twas the Fight before Christmas,* Warner Home Video, 2003.
Voice of Dylan Prescott "Dil" Pickles, *Rugrats Go Wild!,* Paramount, 2003.
Voice of Lucas, *Creepy Freaks* (short film), Raichert Media, 2003.
Voices of Misha, "Beyond," a crew woman, "Final Flight of the Osiris," and a nurse, "World Record," *The Animatrix* (also known as *The Animatrix: Beyond, The Animatrix: Final Flight of the Osiris,* and *The Animatrix: World Record*), Warner Bros., 2003.
Voice of Essy, *Kaena: Le prophetie* (anime; also known as *Axis, Gaena, Gaiena,* and *Kaena: The Prophecy*), Bac Films, 2004, released in a special edition DVD by Studio Canal, 2004.
Voice of hotel maid, *Comic Book: The Movie,* Miramax Home Entertainment, 2004.
Voice of young Victoria, *Van Helsing: The London Assignment* (short film; also known as *Van Helsing Animated*), Universal Home Video, 2004.
Voice of Mara, *Dinotopia: Quest for the Ruby Sunstone,* Goodtimes Entertainment, 2005.
Voice of Vicky Vale, *The Batman vs. Dracula: The Animated Movie,* Warner Bros., 2005.
Voice of Zorra, *Hoodwinked* (also known as *Hoodwinked! The True Story of Red Riding Hood*), The Weinstein Company, 2005.
Voice, *The Joy Warrior,* JM Entertainment, 2005.
Pooh's Heffalump Movie (also known as *The Heffalump Movie*), Buena Vista, 2005.
Voice of Timmy Turner, *Untitled Fairly OddParents Project,* Paramount, c. 2007.

Animated Film Appearances; as Tara Charendoff:

Voice of Dylan Pickles, *The Rugrats Movie,* Paramount, 1998.
Voices of Kaya and factory girls, *Mononoke–hime* (anime; also known as *Princess Mononoke*), Miramax/Dimension Films, 1999, originally released in Japan by Toho Company, 1997.
Voice of Dylan Prescott "Dil" Pickles, *Rugrats in Paris: The Movie—Rugrats II* (also known as *Rugrats in Paris: The Movie* and *Rugrats in Paris—Der Film*), Paramount, 2000.
Voice of Melody, *The Little Mermaid II: Return to the Sea,* Buena Vista Home Video/Walt Disney Home Video, 2000.

Live Action Film Appearances; as Tara Charendoff:

Reena, *The Long Road Home* (also known as *Le retour de l'exil*), Oasis International, 1989.
Student in pageant, *Married to It,* Orion, 1993.

Tina, *Skin Deep,* Daruma Pictures, 1994.

Carla Morgan, *Senior Trip* (also known as *National Lampoon's "Senior Trip"* and *La folle excursion de National Lampoon*), New Line Cinema, 1995.

Some sources cite an appearance as a waitress in *Desiree's Wish;* and an appearance in *The Sadness of the Moon,* Daruma Pictures.

Film Additional Voices:

(As Tara Charendoff) *Black Mask,* English version, Odeon Films, 1999, originally released as *Hak hap,* 1996.

(As Tara Charendoff) *Mononoke–hime* (anime; also known as *Princess Mononoke*), Miramax/ Dimension Films, 1999, originally released in Japan by Toho Company, 1997.

101 Dalmatians II: Patch's London Adventure (animated; also known as *101 Dalmatians: The Animated Sequel*), Walt Disney Home Video, 2003.

Film Producer:

Some sources cite Strong as the producer of *Desiree's Wish.*

Stage Appearances:

Belinda, *A Christmas Carol* (musical), Young People's Theatre, Toronto, Ontario, Canada, c. 1990.

Appeared in *Abi Men Zeyt Zich* (also known as *Good to See You*), in *Hello Tel–Aviv,* and in *A Night of Stars,* all Toronto Jewish Theatre, Toronto, Ontario, Canada; and as Gracie, *The Music Man,* Limelight Dinner Theatre.

Internet Appearances; Series:

Voices of Barbara Gordon/Batgirl and Elizabeth Styles, *Gotham Girls,* Warner Bros. website, beginning 2002.

RECORDINGS

Video Games:

Voice of Mar, *Orphen: Scion of Sorcery,* Activision, 2000.

Voice of Melody, *Little Mermaid II,* THQ, Inc., 2000.

Voices of Yxunomei, Yxunomei as a child, and others, *Forgotten Realms: Icewind Dale,* 2000.

Voice, *Sacrifice,* Interplay Productions, 2000.

Voice of Barbara Gordon/Batgirl, *Batman: Vengeance,* 2001.

Voice of Bubbles, *The Powerpuff Girls: Chemical X–Traction,* BAM! Entertainment, 2001.

Voice of Bubbles, *Powerpuff Girls: Mojo's Pet Project,* BAM! Entertainment, 2001.

Voice of Rikku for English version, *Fainaru fantaji X* (also known as *FFX, Final Fantasy 10, Final Fantasy X,* and *Final Fantasy X International*), Square Enix, 2001.

Voice, *Pro Skater 3* (also known as *Tony Hawk's "Pro Skater 3"*), Activision, 2001.

Voice of Bowser Junior, *Super Mario Sunshine* (also known as *Mario Sunshine*), Nintendo, 2002.

Voices of Bubbles, a female child, and a female citizen, *The Powerpuff Girls: Relish Rampage,* BAM! Entertainment, 2002.

Voice of Mara, *Pirates: The Legend of Black Kat,* EA Games, 2002.

Voices of Chocolat and Goddess Poitreene for English version, *La pucelle* (also known as *La Pucelle: Tactics*), Mastiff, 2002.

Voice on tutorial, *Minority Report,* Activision, 2002.

Voice, *Pro Skater 4* (also known as *Tony Hawk's "Pro Skater 4"*), Activision, 2002.

Voice of Lucy, *Whacked,* c. 2002.

Voice of Barbara Gordon/Batgirl, *Batman: Rise of Sin Tzu,* Ubi Soft Entertainment, 2003.

Voice of Rikku for English version, *Final Fantasy X–2* (also known as *Fainaru fantajii X–2*), Square Enix, 2003.

Voices of Presea Combatir and Corrine for English version, *Tales of Symphonia,* Namco Hometek, 2003.

Voice, *Min'na no gorofu 4* (also known as *Hot Shots Golf Fore!* and *Minna Golf 4*), Sony Computer Entertainment America, 2003.

Voice of Rachel for English version, *Ninja gaiden,* Tecmo, 2004.

Voice of Timmy Turner, *The Fairly OddParents: Breakin da Rules,* THQ, Inc., 2004.

Voice of Timmy Turner, *The Fairly OddParents: Shadow Showdown,* THQ, Inc., 2004.

Voice of Timmy Turner, *Nicktoons Movin' Eye Toy,* THQ, Inc., 2004.

Voices of Keira and Seem, *Jak 3,* Sony Computer Entertainment America, 2004.

Voices of Lil' Red and fairy, *Shrek 2,* Activision, 2004.

Voice, *Champions of Norrath: Realms of EverQuest,* Sony Online Entertainment, 2004.

Voice, *Robotech: Invasion,* Vicious Cycle Software, 2004.

Voices, *Shark Tale,* 2004.

Voice of Blink, *X–Men Legends II: Rise of Apocalypse,* Activision, 2005.

Voice of KAEDE Smith for English version, *Killer7,* 2005.

Voice of Keira, *Jak X: Combat Racing,* Naughty Dog, 2005.

Voice of Rikku, *Kingdom Hearts II,* Square Enix, 2005.

Voice of Sakura Mizrahi, *Xenosaga Episode II: Jenseits von Gut und Boese,* Namco Hometek, 2005.

Voice of Sheegor, *Psychonauts,* Majesco Sales, 2005.

Voice of Timmy Turner, *Nicktoons United,* 2005.

Voice, *Chicken Little,* Buena Vista Games, 2005.

Voice, *Twisted Metal: Head–On,* Sony Computer Entertainment America, 2005.

Voices, *Champions: Return to Arms,* Snowblind Studios, 2005.

Video Games; as Tara Charendoff:
Voice of Daisy Mae, *Redneck Rampage Rides Again,* Interplay Productions, 1998.
Voice, *Vampire: The Masquerade—Redemption,* 2000.

Singles; with Others:
(With the Habonim Youth Choir) "Lo Yisa Goy (Lay Down Your Arms)," c. 2000.

OTHER SOURCES

Periodicals:
New York Times, August 15, 2004.
TV Guide, July 12, 2003, p. 6.
Working Mother, July/August, 2004, p. 15.

Electronic:
The Official Tara Strong, http://www.tarastrong.com, January 19, 2006.

T-V

TEJADA, Raquel
See WELCH, Raquel

THOMAS, J. Karen

PERSONAL

Education: Memphis State University, B.A.; trained at the Lee Strasberg Theatre Institute and the Broadway Dance Center.

Addresses: *Agent*—Boutique Talent, 10 Universal City Plaza, Suite 2000, Universal City, CA 91608; (commercial and voice work) Cunningham Escott Slevin Doherty, 10635 Santa Monica Blvd., Suites 130/135, Los Angeles, CA 90025; Michael Linden Greene, Michael Greene and Associates, 7080 Hollywood Blvd., Suite 1017, Hollywood, CA 90028.

Career: Actress and singer.

Member: Screen Actors Guild, American Federation of Television and Radio Artists, Actors' Equity Association.

Awards, Honors: Theatre Award (with others), outstanding ensemble, National Association for the Advancement of Colored People, 2002, for *Uncle Tom's Cabin; or, The Preservation of Favored Races in the Struggle for Life;* No Way Out Award nomination, best performance by a female actor, *"Adventures in Odyssey" HQ* and *The Soda Fountain* (Internet sites), c. 2004, for "Something's Got to Change," *Adventures in Odyssey.*

CREDITS

Television Appearances; Series:
(Uncredited) Jada, *Sunset Beach,* NBC, 1998, 1999.

Television Appearances; Movies:
Teacher, *Inferno,* UPN, 1998.
Corrine, *Mutiny,* NBC, 1999.
M. S. Washborough, *Gentle Ben* (also known as *Terror on the Mountain*), Animal Planet, 2002.
Ms. Washborough, *Gentle Ben 2: Danger on the Mountain* (also known as *Black Gold*), Animal Planet, 2003.
Winnie, *Life on Liberty Street,* The Hallmark Channel, 2004.
Ruby Bowe, *Detective* (also known as *Arthur Hailey's "Detective"*), 2005.
Professor Davis, *Sarang Song* (short), Showtime, 2006.

Television Appearances; Specials:
Lula Mae, *Black Filmmaker Showcase,* Showtime, 2004.
Announcer, *An Evening of Stars: Tribute to Stevie Wonder,* 2006.

Television Appearances; Episodic:
"G.I. Blues," *The Mississippi,* CBS, 1983.
Reporter, "Creep Throat," *Savannah,* The WB, 1996.
Reporter, "From Here to Paternity," *Savannah,* The WB, 1996.
Reporter, "Prince of Lies," *Savannah,* The WB, 1996.
Dogwoman, "The Adventures of Ratman and Gerbil or, Holy Homeboys in Outer Space," *Homeboys in Outer Space,* UPN, 1997.
Joan Farrell, "Citizen Canine," *Total Security,* ABC, 1997.
Lieutenant Teri Eastman, "The Exodus: Part 1," *Sliders,* Fox, 1997.
The operator, "Ellen's Deaf Comedy Jam," *Ellen* (also known as *These Friends of Mine*), ABC, 1997.
Karen Martin–Gray, "They Eat Horses, Don't They?," *Ally McBeal,* Fox, 1998.
Karen Shore, "Pops' Campaign," *The Wayans Bros.,* The WB, 1998.

Mrs. Keeling, "The One That Got Away," *NYPD Blue,* ABC, 1998.

Sheriff Dickson, "Buona Sera, Mr. Campbell: Part 2," *Melrose Place,* Fox, 1998.

"You Shoulda Seen My Daddy," *Any Day Now,* Lifetime, 1998.

Andrew's nurse, "Vigilance and Care," *Chicago Hope,* CBS, 1999.

Harriet Lane, "The Wendigo," *Charmed,* The WB, 1999.

Karen Martin–Gray, "Pyramids on the Nile," *Ally Mc-Beal,* Fox, 1999.

Cooing man, "Animal Planet: Part 2," *Jack & Jill,* The WB, 2000.

Dr. Cynthia Creighton, "To Halve or Halve Not," *City of Angels,* CBS, 2000.

Bartender, "The Invisible Man," *Providence,* NBC, 2001.

Dr. Janet Reuben, "Heart Problems," *That's Life,* CBS, 2001.

Hannah Parks, "Jeff," *Kate Brasher,* CBS, 2001.

Priscilla Carter, "Rage against the Machine," *The District,* CBS, 2001.

Prisoner transport officer, "April Showers," *ER* (also known as *Emergency Room*), NBC, 2001.

(As Karen Thomas) Dr. Blaine, "There's No Business Like No Business," *Philly,* ABC, 2002.

Airline representative, "The Friendly Skies," *Miracles* (also known as *The Calling*), ABC, 2003.

Prosecutor, "Sixteen Going on Seventeen," *Judging Amy,* CBS, 2003.

"Technical Corrections," *Mister Sterling,* NBC, 2003.

Ellen Turner, "Compulsion," *Criminal Minds,* CBS, 2005.

Mrs. Gurney, "Code of Ethics," *Crossing Jordan* (also known as *Untitled Tim Kring Project*), NBC, 2006.

Also appeared in *The Jamie Foxx Show,* The WB. Some sources cite an appearance as Donna Jean Polk in "A Final Arrangement," an episode of *In the Heat of the Night,* NBC, 1990 (while billed as Karen Thomas); some sources also cite an appearance as a SNCC woman in an episode of *I'll Fly Away,* NBC.

Television Appearances; Pilots:

Martha Simpson, *Nashville Beat,* The Nashville Network, 1990.

Film Appearances:

(Uncredited) Nurse, *Go,* Columbia/TriStar, 1999.

First class flight assistant, *The Shrink Is In,* New City Releasing, 2001.

The Tempest, Chaos Films, 2001.

Gottlieb, *Written in Blood,* Buena Vista Home Video, 2002.

Jamie's mom, *Leprechaun: Back 2 tha Hood* (also known as *Leprechaun: Back in da Hood* and *Leprechaun 6*), Lions Gate Films, 2003.

Sheila Stewart, *Woman Thou Art Loosed,* Magnolia Pictures, 2004.

Gift for the Living, 2005.

Promtoversy (short film), Power Up Films, 2005.

Herself, *Who Killed the Electric Car?* (documentary; also known as *EV Confidential*), Sony Pictures Classics, 2006.

Some sources cite appearances in other films, including *Blue Sky,* Orion, filmed in 1991, released in 1994; and *The Ways of Harmony.*

Stage Appearances:

Cassius, *Julius Caesar,* Jomandi Productions, Atlanta, GA, c. 1994.

Pinkie, *The Ties That Bind,* Alliance Theatre, Atlanta, GA, c. 1996.

The Tempest, Foliage Theatre Company, Los Angeles, 2001.

Nurse, *Romeo and Juliet,* Los Angeles Shakespeare Festival, Pershing Square, Los Angeles, 2002.

Topsy, *Uncle Tom's Cabin; or, The Preservation of Favored Races in the Struggle for Life* (also known as *Uncle Tom's Cabin*), Drama Department, Sacred Fools Theatre, Los Angeles, 2002.

Dreams & Visions (concert reading), Village Theatre, Lemerk Park, Los Angeles, 2002.

Beck, Occidental Studios Soundstage 4, Los Angeles, 2003.

Celebrity guest, *Power Up,* Beverly Hills Hotel Theatre, Beverly Hills, CA, 2005.

Yvette, *Mother Courage and Her Children,* Theatre at Boston Court, Pasadena, CA, 2005.

Appeared as Charlaine, *Ain't Misbehavin'* (musical), Charles Playhouse; as B. J., *Both Barrels: A Salvo of John Forster Songs* (also known as *Both Barrels*), Luna Park Theatre, West Hollywood, CA; as Velma Kelly, *Chicago* (musical), Chaffin's Barn Dinner Theatre, Nashville, TN; as Lorrell, *Dreamgirls* (musical), Jomandi Productions; as Miselaida, *Hair Pieces,* Hudson Theatre; in the title role, *Lysistrata,* Foliage Theatre Company, Los Angeles; as Puck, *A Midsummer Night's Dream,* Tennessee Repertory Company; and as the scarecrow, *The Wiz* (musical), Playhouse on the Square. Appeared as Josephine the singer extraordinaire (Josephine Baker) at the French Festival, Santa Barbara, CA, 2004 and 2005.

Radio Appearances; Episodic:

Elaine Washington, "The Mailman Cometh," *Adventures in Odyssey* (also known as *Odyssey USA*), multiple networks, 2003.

Elaine Washington, "The Mystery at Tin Flat," *Adventures in Odyssey* (also known as *Odyssey USA*), multiple networks, 2003.

Elaine Washington, "The Toy Man," *Adventures in Odyssey* (also known as *Odyssey USA*), multiple networks, 2003.

Elaine Washington, "No Way Out: Parts 1 & 2," *Adventures in Odyssey* (also known as *Odyssey USA*), multiple networks, 2004.

Elaine Washington, "Something's Got to Change," *Adventures in Odyssey* (also known as *Odyssey USA*), multiple networks, 2004.

RECORDINGS

Albums; with Others; Vocalist:

Nils, "Maybe There Are Reasons," *Blue Planet,* Ichiban Old Emd, 1998.

Wild Colonials, *Reel Life, Volume 1* (also known as *Reel Life, Volume 1—A Collection of Wild Colonials Film Music*), Chromatic Records, 2000.

Video Games:

Voice, *Extreme Skate Adventure* (also known as *Disney's "Extreme Skate Adventure"*), 2003.

Voices, *Star Wars: Knights of the Old Republic* (also known as *Star Wars: KOTOR*), LucasArts Entertainment, 2003.

OTHER SOURCES

Electronic:

J. Karen Thomas, http://www.jkarenthomas.com, January 26, 2006.

THOMAS, Wilson
See MILLER, Troy

THOMPSON, Reece 1988–
(Reese Thompson)

PERSONAL

Born November 22, 1988, in Canada.

Career: Actor and voice performer.

CREDITS

Film Appearances:

Voice of Hiroshi, *Junkers Come Here* (anime), Bandai/Madman Entertainment, c. 1994, released in the United States, c. 2003.

Young Beaver, *Dreamcatcher* (also known as *L'attrapeur de reves*), Warner Bros., 2003.

Child, *SuperBabies: Baby Geniuses 2* (also known as *Baby Geniuses* and *Baby Geniuses 2: Return of the Super Babies*), Triumph Films, 2004.

Singleton, *The Sandlot 2,* Twentieth Century–Fox, 2005.

Adolescent Carter, *In the Land of Women,* Warner Independent Pictures, 2006.

Hal Hefner, *Rocket Science,* Duly Noted/Rocket Science, 2006.

Some sources cite an appearance in *Undercover Brother,* Universal, 2002.

Television Appearances; Series:

Voice of young Connelly for English version, *Master Keaton* (anime), Nippon Television Network, 1998–99, broadcast in the United States beginning c. 2003.

Voice of Nicks Chaiplapat for English version, *Mugen no rivaiasu* (anime; also known as *Infinite Ryvius*), Bandai Channel and TV Tokyo, 1999–2000, also broadcast in English.

(As Reese Thompson) Voice of Taromaru for English version, *Inuyasha* (anime; also known as *Inu Yasha*), Nippon Television Network and Yomiuri TV, 2000–2004, Cartoon Network, beginning 2002, YTV (Canada), beginning 2003.

James, *I Love Mummy,* YTV, 2002–2003.

Voice of Tory Froid for English version, *Rockman.exe* (anime; also known as *MegaMan: NT Warrior, MegaMan: NT Warrior Axess, Rockman EXE,* and *Rockman.exe Axess*), TV Tokyo, c. 2002–2003, The WB, beginning c. 2003, also broadcast on TeleToon (Canada).

Voice of Vino Dupre for English version, *Mobile Suit Gundam Seed Destiny* (anime; also known as *Gundam Seed Destiny, Seed Destiny,* and *Kidou Senshi Gundam Seed Destiny*), Bandai, Mainichi Broadcasting, and TBS, 2004–2005.

Voice of Dwayne, *Zixx: Level Two* (animated; also known as *Zixx*), YTV, 2005.

Television Appearances; Miniseries:

Andy (abducted boy), *Living with the Dead* (also known as *Talking to Heaven*), CBS, 2002.

Television Appearances; Movies:

Harley Snider, *Thanksgiving Family Reunion* (also known as *Holiday Reunion, National Lampoon's*

"Holiday Reunion," National Lampoon's "Thanksgiving Family Reunion," and *National Lampoon's "Thanksgiving Reunion"*), TBS, 2003.

Television Appearances; Episodic:
Tommy, "Red Kiss," *Jeremiah,* Showtime, 2002.
Kevin, "Putting Out Fires," *Tru Calling* (also known as *Heroine, Tru,* and *True Calling*), Fox, 2003.
Jinto, "Hide and Seek," *Stargate: Atlantis,* Sci–Fi Channel, The Movie Network (Canada), and Movie Central Network (Canada), 2004.
Greg Venner, "Suffer the Children," *The 4400,* USA Network, 2005.

Television Appearances; Pilots:
Jinto, "Rising," *Stargate: Atlantis* (also known as *Stargate Atlantis: Rising*), Sci–Fi Channel, The Movie Network (Canada), and Movie Central Network (Canada), 2004.

OTHER SOURCES

Electronic:
The SciFi World, http://www.thescifiworld.net, November 15, 2005.

TOMAS, Jan
   See FORMAN, Milos

TOUSSAINT, Beth 1962–
   (Beth Toussaint Coleman)

PERSONAL

Born September 25, 1962; married Jack Coleman (an actor), June 21, 1996.

Addresses: *Agent*—Innovative Artists, 1505 10th Street, Santa Monica, CA 90401.

Career: Actress.

CREDITS

Film Appearances:
Shelly, *Berserker* (also known as *Berserker: The Nordic Curse*), Shapiro, 1987.
Lab technician, *Dead Heat,* Image, 1988.

Laurie Webber, *Project Shadowchaser II* (also known as *Armed and Deadly*), Nu–Image, 1995.
Karen Brennick, *Fortress 2* (also known as *Fortress 2: Re–Entry*), TriStar, 1999.
Valerie Miller, *Hijack* (also known as *The Last Siege*), Artisan, 1999.
Voice of female caller, *Scream 3,* Miramax, 2000.
(As Beth Toussaint Coleman) Mrs. Keefe, *Red Eye,* United International, 2005.

Television Appearances; Movies:
Charlene, *Blackmail,* 1991.
Karen, *Danger Island* (also known as *The Presence*), 1992.
Venus Maria, *Lady Boss* (also known as *Jackie Collins' "Lady Boss"*), 1992.
Nicole, *Green Dolphin Beat* (also known as *Green Dolphin Street*), 1994.
Paula Waite, *Breach of Conduct* (also known as *Tour of Duty*), 1994.
Vicki Morgan Sherry, *The Return of Hunter* (also known as *The Return of Hunter: Everyone Walks in L.A.*), 1995.

Television Appearances; Series:
Tracy Lawton, *Dallas,* CBS, 1988–89.
Veronica Koslowski, *Savannah,* The WB, 1996.

Television Appearances; Episodic:
"Sleeping Dragon," *Monsters,* syndicated, 1988.
Morgan Chase, "Coughing Boy," *Growing Pains,* ABC, 1989.
Jessica Barber, "Deals and Wheels: Part 1," *Booker* (also known as *Booker, P.I.*), Fox, 1989.
Ishara Yar, "Legacy," *Star Trek: The Next Generation* (also known as *Star Trek: TNG*), syndicated, 1990.
Dawn Rigel, "The Visitor," *MacGyver,* ABC, 1990.
Andrea Todd, "The Mother," *Matlock,* NBC, 1990.
"In the Name of Love," *21 Jump Street,* Fox, 1991.
Paula, "Rat Girl," *Cheers,* NBC, 1991.
Angela, "Dying Well Is the Best Revenge," *Nightmare Cafe,* NBC, 1992.
Anna Ruggiero, "Truth or Consequences," *Mann & Machine,* NBC, 1992.
Colleen Patterson, "Jake vs. Jake," *Melrose Place,* 1992.
The Round Table, NBC, 1992.
Karen Welsh, "The Heart Is a Lonely Sucker," *The Commish,* 1993.
Yolanda Bergstrom, "The Legacy," *Matlock,* ABC, 1993.
Nicole, "Triple Cross," *Fortune Hunter,* 1994.
Anna Sheridan, "Revelations," *Babylon 5,* syndicated, 1994.
Beth McMillan, "Bone of Contention," *Legend,* 1995.
Risa, *Marker,* UPN, 1995.
Gabriella Zane, "Dead Ringers," *Martial Law,* 1998.

Strip club's attorney, "I'm Not Emotional," *Any Day Now,* 1999.

VANN, Marc 1954–

PERSONAL

Born August 23, 1954, in Norfolk, VA; married Mary Easterling, 1985 (divorced, 1988).

Career: Actor.

CREDITS

Film Appearances:
Dutch's liquor henchman, *Hoodlum,* United Artists, 1997.
Deputy Jackson, *U.S. Marshals,* Warner Bros., 1998.
Gray, *Payback,* Paramount, 1999.
Decker, *The Forsaken* (also known as *The Forsaken: Desert Vampires*), Columbia TriStar, 2001.
Jerome, the angry guy, *Ghost World,* United Artists, 2001.
Roger, *Flying,* Bucktown, 2002.
Mr. One, *The Drop,* Arts and Letters, 2003.
Marc, *In Memory of My Father,* Interspot, 2005.
Kevin, *Art School Confidential,* Miramax, 2006.

Television Appearances; Episodic:
Phil Pritchard, "His Girl Thursday," *Early Edition,* CBS, 1996.
"First Loves," *Cupid,* ABC, 1998.
Sergeant David Korshak, "For the Children," *Seven Days* (also known as *Seven Days: The Series*), UPN, 1999.
Mr. Pinter, "Lois vs. Evil," *Malcolm in the Middle,* Fox, 2000.
Officer Wilbourne, "Blast from the Past," *Judging Amy,* CBS, 2000.
Harry Forsic, "Roll Out the Barrel," *NYPD Blue,* ABC, 2000.
Dan Vickers, "Kate," *Kate Brasher,* 2001.
Police detective, "*Hero Worship,*" JAG, CBS, 2002.
"The Chinese Wall," *The Guardian,* 2002.
Paul, "Proxy Prexy," *Frasier,* NBC, 2002.
Bob, "Partners," *The Shield,* FX Channel, 2003.
Hal Duncan, "Mr. Monk Goes to the Theater," *Monk,* USA Network, 2003.
Fergus Cook, "Slice of Life," *Dragnet* (also known as *L.A. Dragnet*), ABC, 2003.
Phillip Garnier, "Nobody's Perfect," *Karen Sisco,* ABC, 2003.

Doctor Sparrow, "Conviction," *Angel* (also known as *Angel: The Series*), The WB, 2003.
Doctor Sparrow, "Smile Time," *Angel* (also known as *Angel: The Series*), The WB, 2004.
Doctor Sparrow, "Shells," *Angel* (also known as *Angel: The Series*), The WB, 2004.
Terry Glazer, "Coming Home," *The Practice,* ABC, 2004.
Terry Glazer, "Pre–Trial Blues," *The Practice,* ABC, 2004.
Terry Glazer, "Mr. Shore Goes to Town," *The Practice,* ABC, 2004.
Paul Grady, "Old Yeller," *NYPD Blue,* ABC, 2004.
Michael Goddard, "Second Chances," *Crossing Jordan,* NBC, 2004.
Conrad Ecklie (recurring), *CSI: Crime Scene Investigation,* CBS, 2005.
District attorney Scott Berger, "Truly, Madly, Deeply," *Boston Legal,* ABC, 2005.

Television Appearances; Movies:
Robert Smith, *Since You've Been Gone,* 1998.
Nelson, *Stranger Inside,* HBO, 2001.
Young Buck, *When Billie Beat Bobby* (also known as *Billie Contre Bobby: La bataille des sexes*), ABC, 2001.
Detective Felton, *Just Ask My Children,* 2001.

Television Appearances; Pilots:
Phil Pritchard, *Early Edition,* CBS, 1996.

Stage Appearances:
As I Lay Dying, Steppenwolf Theatre Company, Mainstage Theatre, Chicago, 1995.
With and Without, Victory Gardens Theatre, Chicago, 1995.
The Cryptogram, Steppenwolf Theatre Company, Studio Theatre, Chicago, 1996.
The Libertine, Steppenwolf Theatre Company, Mainstage Theatre, 1996.

Appeared in *All The Rage, Light Up The Sky, The Notebooks of Leonardo DiVinci, All's Well That Ends Well, Three Sisters, Journey to the West,* and *Black Snow,* all Goodman Theatre, Chicago; *Night and Day, The Seagull,* and *Flyovers,* Victory Gardens Theatre, Chicago; and nearly 20 plays with the Center Theater Ensemble, Chicago.

VASSEY, Liz 1972–

PERSONAL

Born August 9, 1972, in Raleigh, NC; married David Emmerichs (a camera operator), May 2, 2004. *Education:* Attend the University of South Florida.

Addresses: *Agent*—Endeavor, 9601 Wilshire Blvd., 6th Floor, Beverly Hills, CA 90212. *Manager*—Kass & Stokes Management, 9229 Sunset Blvd., Suite 504, Los Angeles, CA 90069.

Career: Actress. Appeared in television commercials including, Tide, 1991, and a breakfast cereal, 1994; previously sang in piano bars in New York City. Neuroses to A T (a t–shirt company), co–owner (with Kristin Bauer, an actress).

Awards, Honors: Daytime Emmy Award nomination, outstanding juvenile female in a drama series, 1990, for *All My Children.*

CREDITS

Film Appearances:
Sylvia, *Calendar Girl,* 1993.
Julia, *9mm of Love* (short), 2000.
Renee O'Malley, *Pursuit of Happiness,* 2001.
Maggie Swanson, *Man of the House,* Columbia, 2005.

Television Appearances; Series:
Emily Ann Sago Martin, *All My Children,* ABC, 1988–91.
Lou Davis, *Brotherly Love,* 1995–96.
Tess Galaway, *Pig Sty,* 1995.
Kathy Baker, *Maximum Bob,* ABC, 1998.
Captain Liberty/Janet, *The Tick,* Fox, 2001.
Dawn Mitchell, *Push, Nevada,* ABC, 2002.
Dr. Carrie Allen, *Tru Calling,* Fox, 2005.
Wendy Simms, *CSI: Crime Scene Investigation,* CBS, 2005.

Television Appearances; Miniseries:
Suzy Atkins, *The Secrets of Lake Success,* 1993.

Television Appearances; Movies:
Chloe, *Love, Lies & Lullabies* (also known as *Sad Inheritance*), 1993.
Carla, *Saved by the Bell: Wedding in Las Vegas,* 1994.
Princess Tyra, *The Adventures of Captain Zoom in Outer Space,* 1995.

Television Appearances; Pilots:
Martin and Claudia, The WB, 1999.
Life with David J, CBS, 2001.
Rachael Dragan, *The Dragans of New York,* CBS, 2002.
Christine Ryder, *The Partners,* ABC, 2003.
Nikki Chambers, *Nikki & Nora,* UPN, 2004.
Marissa, *20 Things to Do Before You're 30,* UPN, 2005.
Dakota, *Cooked,* UPN, 2006.

Television Appearances; Episodic:
Cheers, 1982.
Candy, *Still the Beaver,* 1989.
Student, "Birdwoman of the Swamps," *Superboy,* 1989.
Dream On, HBO, 1990.
Paula Fletcher, "Raped—June 20, 1980," *Quantum Leap,* NBC, 1991.
Sis, *Walter & Emily,* 1992.
Kristin, "Conundrum," *Star Trek: The Next Generation,* 1992.
Marcie St. Claire, "The Pit and the Pendulum," *Beverly Hills, 90210,* Fox, 1992.
Rebecca Woods, "Sperm 'n' Herman," *Herman's Head,* Fox, 1992.
Mary, "Summer of '92," *Parker Lewis,* Fox, 1992.
Lorraine, "T–R–A Something, Something Spells Tramp," *Married ... with Children,* Fox, 1992.
Amy Madrid, "A Year to Remember," *Murphy Brown,* CBS, 1992.
Barbara Whitmore, "Goodbye Norma Jean—April 4, 1960," *Quantum Leap,* NBC, 1993.
Monica Evers, "Lone Witness," *Murder, She Wrote,* CBS, 1993.
Jane Rice, "Shadows," *Bodies of Evidence,* 1993.
Lexie, "Go Ahead, Fry Me," *Danger Theatre,* 1993.
Candace Bennett, "Love and Hate in Cabot Cove," *Murder, She Wrote,* CBS, 1993.
Stephanie Crosley, "I've Got a Crush on You," *Love & War,* 1994.
Courtney, "Hey, Nineteen," *Wings,* NBC, 1994.
Ilene Bennett, "Shaker," *Diagnosis Murder,* CBS, 1994.
Liz, "24 Hours," *ER,* NBC, 1994.
Liz, "Day One," *ER,* NBC, 1994.
Liz, "Going Home," *ER,* NBC, 1994.
Liz, "Into That Good Night," *ER,* NBC, 1994.
"Beam Me Up, Dr. Spock," *Dream On,* 1995.
Mona, the waitress, "Home," *Early Edition,* CBS, 1997.
Donna, "The Dating Game," *Home Improvement,* ABC, 1997.
Brenda, "Estrogen," *Fantasy Island,* ABC, 1998.
Kim, "Drop Dead Gorgeous," *Dharma & Greg,* ABC, 2000.
Wendy Dalrymple, "Escape from Witch Island," *Dawson's Creek,* The WB, 2000.
Bella Nicholson, "Skulls," *Veritas: The Quest,* ABC, 2003.
Kate, "The Last Thing You Want to Do Is Wind Up with a Hump," *Two and a Half Men,* CBS, 2003.

Stage Appearances:

Appeared in numerous regional productions, including *A Chorus Line; My Name Is Alice; Oklahoma; The Crucible; Two Gentlemen of Verona; Dames at Sea.*

VENITO, Larry

PERSONAL

Addresses: *Agent*—Chris Schmidt, Paradigm, 360 North Crescent Dr., North Building, Beverly Hills, CA 90210.

Career: Actor and voice performer. Appeared in commercials.

CREDITS

Film Appearances:
The Good Policeman, LK–TEL Video, 1991.
Hrbek, *Money for Nothing*, Buena Vista, 1993.
Vince, *Layin' Low*, Shooting Gallery, 1996.
Kos, *Above Freezing*, @radical.media/Cooler Pictures/ 3DD Entertainment, 1998.
Moogie, *Rounders*, Miramax, 1998.
Stanley, *Just the Ticket* (also known as *Gary & Linda*), United Artists, 1999.
New York man, *Men in Black II* (also known as *MIB 2* and *MIIB*), Columbia, 2002.
Louis, *Gigli* (also known as *Tough Love*), Columbia/ TriStar, 2003.
Voices of Giuseppe and first Great White, *Shark Tale* (animated; also known as *Sharkslayer*), Dream-Works, 2004.
Lenny, *The Honeymooners*, Paramount, 2005.
Manny the mechanic, *War of the Worlds*, Paramount, 2005.
Police officer, *Duane Hopwood*, IFC Films, 2005.

Some sources cite appearances in the films *Piece of Cake* and *Village Idiots*.

Television Appearances; Series:
Carmine Santucci, *Living in Captivity*, Fox, 1998.

Television Appearances; Miniseries:
Sal DiMaggio, *Witness to the Mob* (also known as *Der Pate von Manhattan*), NBC, 1998.

Television Appearances; Episodic:
"Baker's Dozen," *The Cosby Mysteries*, NBC, 1995.
Gabe, "Alice Doesn't Fit Here Anymore," *NYPD Blue*, ABC, 1997.
Jake Nathan, "One," *Law & Order: Criminal Intent* (also known as *Law & Order: CI*), NBC, 2001.
Julian Pisano, "Johnny Got His Gold," *NYPD Blue*, ABC, 2001.
Julian Pisano, "Lies Like a Rug," *NYPD Blue*, ABC, 2001.
Detective Wade, "Myth of Fingerprints," *Law & Order*, NBC, 2001.
Julian Pisano, "Jealous Hearts," *NYPD Blue*, ABC, 2002.
Julian Pisano, "Less Is Morte," *NYPD Blue*, ABC, 2002.
Ozzie, "Boss," *The Job*, ABC, 2002.
Alec Tyson, "Out of the Ashes," *Hack*, CBS, 2003.
Armored car guard, "Everybody Lies," *Third Watch*, NBC, 2003.
Detective Temson, "The Boxer," *The Jury*, Fox, 2004.
Detective Temson, "Three Boys and a Gun," *The Jury*, Fox, 2004.
Eddie, "Adjourned," *The Practice*, ABC, 2004.
Sonny King, "Everybody Loves Raimondo's," *Law & Order*, NBC, 2004.
Julian Pisano, "Rub a Tub Tub," *Blind Justice*, ABC, 2005.
Sonny Famigletti, "Doggone," *Blind Justice*, ABC, 2005.
Butter, "Mayham," *The Sopranos*, HBO, 2006.
James "Murmur" Zaccone, "Members Only," *The Sopranos*, HBO, 2006.

Appeared as Zanfagna in an episode of *New York Undercover* (also known as *Uptown Undercover*), Fox; also appeared in episodes of *All My Children*, ABC; *Another World*, NBC; *One Life to Live*, ABC; and *The Sweet Life*, HBO Comedy Channel. Appeared as Mr. Riordan in "Case by Case" and "Mad about You," both unaired episodes of *Queens Supreme*, CBS.

Television Appearances; Pilots:
Steve, *A Perfect Life*, UPN, 1995.
Carmine Santucci, *Living in Captivity*, Fox, 1998.
Mayor, *The Mayor of Oyster Bay*, ABC, 2002.
Benny Cool, *The Black Donnellys*, NBC, 2006.

Stage Appearances:
Member of Psychocompany, "Phantasies," *Young Playwrights Festival*, Playwrights Horizons Theatre, New York City 1990.
Vic and soda jerk, *Club Soda*, Workshop of the Players Art Theatre, New York City, 1991.
The Gravity of Means, Manhattan Class Company Theatre, New York City, 1996.
Michele, *Filumena* (also known as *Filumena: A Marriage Italian Style*), Blue Light Theatre Company, Williamstown Theatre Festival, Main Stage, Williamstown, MA, 1996, Theatre Four, New York City, 1997.

Also appeared in *Tales of the Lost Formicans*, River Arts Repertory Company.

RECORDINGS

Video Games:
Voice of third hoodlum, *Manhunt*, Rockstar Games, 2003.

VIBERT, Ronan

PERSONAL

Born in Cardiff, South Wales, UK; son of David (an artist) and Dilys (an artist; maiden name, Jackson) Vibert.

Addresses: *Manager*—Melanie Greene Management and Productions, 425 N. Robertson Dr., Los Angeles, CA 90048.

Career: Actor.

CREDITS

Film Appearances:
Party guest, *Sammy and Rosie Get Laid,* Cinecom, 1987.
Jim, *On the Black Hill,* Roxie Releasing, 1987.
Third businessman, *Empire State,* 1987.
Fletcher, *Remando al viento* (also known as *Rowing In the Wind* and *Rowing with the Wind*), Buena Vista Home Video, 1988.
Man in pig scene, *Queen of Hearts,* Cinecom, 1989.
Charles Fieldhouse, *The Grass Arena,* 1991.
Young, *Tale of the Mummy* (also known as *Talos the Mummy* and *Russell Mulcahy's "Tale of the Mummy"*), Dimension, 1998.
Wolfgang 'Wolf' Muller, *Shadow of the Vampire,* Lions Gate, 2000.
Joseph Willcombe, *The Cat's Meow,* Lions Gate, 2001.
Alice's boss, *Killing Me Softly,* Metro–Goldwyn–Mayer, 2002.
Stewart, *Shearing,* National Film and Television School, 2002.
Janina's husband, *The Pianist* (also known as *Der Pianist, Pinaista* and *Le Pianiste*), A–Film, 2002.
Voice of Laird, *Princess and the Pea,* KOAN, 2002.
MI6 Agent Calloway, *Lara Croft Tomb Raider: The Cradle of Life* (also known as *Lara Croft Tomb Raider: Die wige des lebens*), Paramount, 2003.
Caesar, *Gladiatress,* Europa, 2004.
Thorkel, *Beowulf & Grendel,* Grendel, 2005.
Bodkin, *Tristan + Isolde,* Gemini, 2006.

Television Appearances; Episodic:
Martin Lepweg, "Dangerous Games," *Van der Valk,* ITV, 1991.
Wilmot, "Safety in New York," *Jeeves and Wooster,* ITV, 1992.
Lindsey Parry–Davies, "Second Fiddle," *Lovejoy,* BBC, 1993.

Martin Williams, "Unknown Soldier," *Between the Lines* (also known as *Inside the Line*), BBC, 1994.
Martin, "The Chigwell Years," *Birds of a Feather,* BBC, 1994.
Le Gaucher, "The Virgine in the Ice," *Cadfael,* PBS/ITV, 1995.
"Horror in the Night," *Tales from the Crypt* (also known as *HBO's "Tales from the Crypt"*), HBO, 1996.
Vince, "I Do, I Do, I Do, I Do, I Do," *Gimme, Gimme, Gimme,* BBC, 1999.
Sir Trevor Benton, "The Frame," *Highlander: The Raven* (also known as *L' Immortelle*), syndicated, 1999.
Douglas Prideux, "Laurels Are Poison," *The Mrs. Bradley Mysteries,* 1999.
Robespierre, "A Good Name," *The Scarlet Pimpernel,* BBC, 2000.
"Cartier" Craig Booth, "The Amazing Larry Dunn," *Keen Eddie,* 2003.
Dr. Jonathan Lynch, "Subterraneans," *Waking the Dead,* 2005.
Mephistopheles (recurring), *Hex,* Sky, 2005.

Television Appearances; Miniseries:
Lee, *Traffik,* 1989.
Alan Stafford, *Resnick: Rough Treatment,* BBC, 1993.
Lord Richard, *The Buccaneers,* BBC and PBS, 1995.
Bull Meadows, *Big Women,* Channel 4, 1998.
The Squire, *The Canterbury Tales,* BBC, 1998.

Television Appearances; Movies:
Witchcraft, BBC, 1992.
Tom, *The Cloning of Joanna May,* 1992.
Robespierre (uncredited), *The Scarlet Pimpernel Meets Madame Guillotine,* 1999.
Robespierre (uncredited), *The Scarlet Pimpernel and the Kidnapped King,* 1999.
Trezzini, *Peter in Paradise,* 2003.
Joseph Conrad, *London,* 2004.

Television Appearances; Specials:
Victor Frankenstein, *Frankenstein: Birth of a Monster* (documentary), BBC, 2003.

VIGODA, Abe 1921–

PERSONAL

Born February 24, 1921, in New York, NY; son of Samuel (a tailor) and Lena (maiden name, Moses) Vigoda; married Beatrice Schy, February 25, 1968 (died 1992); children: Carol. *Education:* Studied acting at Theatre School of Dramatic Arts and American Theatre Wing.

Addresses: *Agent*—Fifi Oscard, Fifi Oscard Agency, 110 West 40th St., Suite 1601, New York, NY 10018; (voice) Cunningham/Escott/Slevin & Doherty Talent Agency, 10635 Santa Monica Blvd., Suite 140, Los Angeles, CA 90025.

Career: Actor. Appeared in commercials.

Member: American Federation of Television and Radio Artists, Screen Actors Guild, Actors' Equity Association, Friars Club.

Awards, Honors: Emmy Award nominations, outstanding continuing performance by a supporting actor in a comedy series, 1976 and 1977, both for *Barney Miller;* Emmy Award nomination, outstanding single performance by a supporting actor in a comedy or drama series, 1978, for "Goodbye, Mr. Fish: Part 2," an episode of *Barney Miller;* Israel Culture Award, 1979.

CREDITS

Film Appearances:
Waiter, *Trois chambres a Manhattan* (also known as *Three Rooms in Manhattan*), 1965.
Salvatore "Sal"/"Sally" Tessio, *The Godfather* (also known as *Mario Puzo's "The Godfather"*), Paramount, 1972.
Don Tolusso, *The Don Is Dead* (also known as *Beautiful but Deadly* and *The Deadly Kiss*), Universal, 1973.
John Dellanzia, *Newman's Law,* Universal, 1974.
Salvatore "Sal"/"Sally" Tessio, *The Godfather, Part II* (also known as *Mario Puzo's "The Godfather, Part II"*), Paramount, 1974.
Sergeant Rizzuto, *The Cheap Detective* (also known as *Neil Simon's "The Cheap Detective"*), Columbia, 1978.
Caesar, *Cannonball Run II,* Warner Bros., 1984.
Commercial spokesperson, *The Stuff,* New World, 1985.
Detective Edwards, *Vasectomy, a Delicate Matter* (also known as *Vasectomy*), Seymour Borde/Vandom International Pictures, 1986.
Mr. Wiseman, *Plain Clothes* (also known as *Glory Days*), Paramount, 1988.
Grandpa, *Look Who's Talking* (also known as *Daddy's Home*), TriStar, 1989.
Orel Benton, *Prancer,* Orion, 1989.
Louie Keaton, *Keaton's Cop,* Cannon Releasing, 1990.
Waponi chief, *Joe versus the Volcano* (also known as *Joe against the Volcano*), Warner Bros., 1990.
Grandpa Henry Bruggers, *Home of Angels,* Cloverlay Productions, 1993.
Pawnbroker, *Me and the Kid* (also known as *Taking Gary Feldman*), Orion, 1993.

Victor Malucci, *Fist of Honor,* PM Home Entertainment, 1993.
Voice of Salvatore "Sal the Wheezer" Valestra, *Batman: Mask of the Phantasm* (animated; also known as *Batman: The Animated Movie, Batman: The Animated Movie—Mask of the Phantasm, Batman: Mask of the Phantasm: The Animated Movie,* and *Mask of the Phantasm: Batman the Animated Movie*), Warner Bros., 1993.
Alaskan grandpa, *North,* Columbia, 1994.
Gus Molino, *Sugar Hill* (also known as *Harlem*), Twentieth Century–Fox, 1994.
Don Frito Layleone, *The Misery Brothers,* 1995.
Judge Powell, *Jury Duty,* Triumph Releasing, 1995.
Rudy, *Love Is All There Is,* Samuel Goldwyn, 1996.
Will Cassady, *Underworld,* Trimark Pictures, 1996.
Otis, *Good Burger,* Paramount, 1997.
Uncle Guy, *A Brooklyn State of Mind,* Miramax, 1997.
Zeus, *Me and the Gods* (also known as *Farticus*), Cinequanon Pictures, 1997.
Arty, *Just the Ticket* (also known as *Gary & Linda*), Metro–Goldwyn–Mayer, 1999.
The frog, *Chump Change,* Miramax, 2000.
Tea Cakes or Cannoli, Pellegrino Productions, 2000.
Angelo Giancarlo, *Crime Spree,* DEJ Productions/Viacom, 2003.

Some sources cite appearances in *Soho They Call It,* Mill at Bovina, c. 1998; and in *The End of the Bar* (also known as *Hung* and *My Angel Is a Centerfold*), Carbonated Films/Sub Q Films, 2002.

Television Appearances; Series:
Four Star Revue, NBC, c. 1950–51.
All–Star Revue, NBC, c. 1951–53.
Ezra Braithwaite/Otis Greene, *Dark Shadows,* ABC, 1969.
Detective Phil Fish, *Barney Miller* (also known as *The Life and Times of Captain Barney Miller*), ABC, 1975–77.
Phil Fish, *Fish,* ABC, 1977–78.
Joe Kravitz, *As the World Turns,* CBS, 1985.
Lyle DeFranco, *Santa Barbara,* NBC, 1989.
Judge Rinehart, *Lucky Luke,* [Italy], beginning c. 1993.

Television Appearances; Miniseries:
Paul Castellano, *Witness to the Mob* (also known as *Der Pate von Manhattan*), NBC, 1998.

Television Appearances; Movies:
Alikhine, *The Devil's Daughter,* ABC, 1973.
Dominic Morrell, *The Story of Pretty Boy Floyd* (also known as *Pretty Boy Floyd*), ABC, 1974.
Al Schneider, *Having Babies* (also known as *Giving Birth*), ABC, 1976.
Jake, *The Comedy Company,* CBS, 1978.
Nathan Perlmutter, *How to Pick Up Girls!,* ABC, 1978.

Mr. Frisch, *Death Car on the Freeway* (also known as *Wheels of Death*), CBS, 1979.

Herb, *Gridlock* (also known as *The Great American Traffic Jam*), NBC, 1980.

Television Appearances; Specials:

Detective Phil Fish, *Joys* (also known as *Bob Hope Special: Bob Hope in "Joys"*), NBC, 1976.

Dean Martin's Red Hot Scandals of 1928, NBC, 1976.

Guest, *Alan King's Final Warning*, ABC, 1977.

Circus of the Stars, CBS, 1977.

Circus of the Stars #2, CBS, 1977.

Dean Martin's Red Hot Scandals Part 2, NBC, 1977.

Carnival pitch man, *The Big Stuffed Dog*, NBC, 1980.

The Greatest Practical Jokes of All Time, NBC, 1990.

Night of 100 Stars III (also known as *Night of One Hundred Stars*), NBC, 1990.

Comedy Central Presents: The N.Y. Friars Club Roast of Rob Reiner, Comedy Central, 2000.

Comedy Central Presents the New York Friars Club Roast of Hugh M. Hefner, Comedy Central, 2001.

Late Night with Conan O'Brien: 10th Anniversary Special, NBC, 2003.

Television Appearances; Awards Presentations:

Mr. Big, *The Second Annual TV Land Awards: A Celebration of Classic TV* (also known as *The Second Annual TV Land Awards*), TV Land and Nickelodeon, 2004.

Mike Delfino, *The Third Annual TV Land Awards: A Celebration of Classic TV* (also known as *The Third Annual TV Land Awards*), TV Land, 2005.

Television Appearances; Episodic:

"Lunch Box," *Suspense*, CBS, 1949.

Mr. Samuelson, "Play It Again Samuelson," *The Sandy Duncan Show*, CBS, 1972.

Anton Valine, "A Matter of Principle," *Mannix*, CBS, 1973.

Abe Kemper, "The Two-Faced Corpse," *Hawaii Five-0* (also known as *McGarrett*), CBS, 1974.

Al Dancer, "The Kirkoff Case," *The Rockford Files* (also known as *Jim Rockford, Private Investigator*), NBC, 1974.

Michael Lance, "Something Less Than a Man," *The Rookies*, ABC, 1974.

Norman Kilty, "The Best Judge Money Can Buy," *Kojak*, CBS, 1974.

"The Street," *Toma*, ABC, 1974.

Mr. Couzellous, "Search and Destroy," *Cannon*, CBS, 1975.

Barlow, "Black Magic," *The Bionic Woman*, ABC, 1976.

Himself, *Break the Bank*, ABC, 1976.

Himself, *Dinah!* (also known as *Dinah! & Friends*), syndicated, 1976.

Himself, *Tattletales*, CBS, 1976.

Max, "Centerfold," *Vega$*, ABC, 1978.

Phil "the Dancer" Gabriel, "Rosendahl and Gilda Stern Are Dead," *The Rockford Files* (also known as *Jim Rockford, Private Investigator*), NBC, 1978.

Ben Ryan, "The Final Days," *Eight Is Enough*, ABC, 1979.

Charlie Fletcher, "The Gopher's Opportunity/Home Sweet Home/Switch," *The Love Boat*, ABC, 1979.

Grandpa Ben Rule, "Mary Ellen," *B. J. and the Bear*, NBC, 1979.

Joe Lange, "Goose for the Gander," *Fantasy Island*, ABC, 1979.

Phil Fish, "Burial," *Barney Miller* (also known as *The Life and Times of Captain Barney Miller*), ABC, 1979.

Ray Yellburton, "A Very Formal Heist," *Supertrain*, NBC, 1979.

Sid Gordon, "Pentagram/The Casting Director," *Fantasy Island*, ABC, 1979.

Howard Mattson, "The Million Dollar Fur Heist," *The Littlest Hobo*, syndicated, 1980.

Phil Fish, "Lady and the Bomb," *Barney Miller* (also known as *The Life and Times of Captain Barney Miller*), ABC, 1981.

Slick, "Stellascam," *Harper Valley P.T.A.* (also known as *Harper Valley*), NBC, 1981.

Mr. Corelli, "A Choice of Dreams," *Tales from the Darkside*, syndicated, 1986.

Mr. Wagner, "Back to Oblivion," *Superboy* (also known as *The Adventures of Superboy*), syndicated, 1988.

"The Dancer's Touch," *B. L. Stryker*, ABC, 1989.

Bill Cody, "Harry's Will," *MacGyver*, ABC, 1990.

George, "The Prodigal Father," *Murder, She Wrote*, CBS, 1990.

"The Gift," *Monsters*, syndicated, 1990.

"Last Race," *The Black Stallion* (also known as *The Adventures of the Black Stallion, The New Adventures of the Black Stallion*, and *L'etalon noir*), YTV (Canada) and The Family Channel, 1990.

Guest, *Late Night with Conan O'Brien*, NBC, multiple appearances beginning c. 1993.

Alfred Bartell, "You Can Call Me Johnson," *Diagnosis Murder*, CBS, 1994.

Detective Landis, "Remand," *Law & Order* (also known as *Law & Order Prime*), NBC, 1996.

Harry, "All about Christmas Eve," *Wings*, NBC, 1996.

Old man Lisa, "Grumpy Old Genie," *Weird Science*, USA Network, 1996.

(Uncredited) Himself, *Saturday Night Live* (also known as *NBC's "Saturday Night," Saturday Night, Saturday Night Live '80, SNL*, and *SNL 25*), NBC, 1996.

Charlie the Hat, "Long Live the King," *It's Good to Be King*, 1997.

Receptionist, "Clipped Wings," *Touched by and Angel*, CBS, 1997.

Albert Spokaine, "Jury Duty," *Promised Land* (also known as *Home of the Brave*), CBS, 1998.

Kalman Wertzel, "Farmer Buchman," *Mad about You* (also known as *Loved by You*), NBC, 1998.

The Reel to Reel Picture Show, PAX TV, 1998.

Viva Variety, Comedy Central, 1998.

Sal, "Norm, Crusading Social Worker," *The Norm Show* (also known as *Norm*), ABC, 1999.

Voice of himself, "The Kiss Seen around the World," *Family Guy* (animated; also known as *Padre de familia* and *Padre del familia*), Fox, 2001.

Guest, *Howard Stern* (also known as *The Howard Stern Radio Show*), E! Entertainment Television, 2005.

Television Appearances; Pilots:

Donzer, *Toma,* ABC, 1973.

Detective Phil Fish, *The Life and Times of Captain Barney Miller* (pilot for the series *Barney Miller*), broadcast on *Just for Laughs,* ABC, 1974.

Blind Uncle Morty, *Frankie the Squirrel* (short), c. 2005.

Stage Appearances:

Title role, *Richard III,* Public Theatre, Delacorte Theatre, New York City, c. 1960.

John of Gaunt, *Richard II,* Public Theatre, New York City, 1961.

Vagrant, *The Cherry Orchard,* Theatre Four, New York City, 1962–63.

Abbe Bossard and Francois, *A Darker Flower,* Pocket Theatre, New York City, 1963.

Hendricks, *The Cat and the Canary,* Stage 73, New York City, 1965.

Man animal, *The Persecution and Assassination of Jean–Paul Marat as Performed by the Inmates of the Asylum of Charentin under the Direction of the Marquis de Sade* (also known as *Marat–Sade*), Majestic Theatre, New York City, 1967.

Landau, *The Man in the Glass Booth,* Royale Theatre, New York City, 1968–69.

Inquest, Music Box Theatre, New York City, 1970.

Abraham Lincoln, *Tough to Get Help,* Royale Theatre, 1972.

Jonathan Brewster, *Arsenic and Old Lace,* Forty–Sixth Street Theatre, New York City, 1986–87.

Night of 100 Stars III (also known as *Night of One Hundred Stars*), Radio City Music Hall, New York City, 1990.

Poker player, *The Odd Couple* (benefit performance), National Actors Theatre, Belasco Theatre, New York City, 1991.

Radio Appearances; Episodic:

Guest, *Howard Stern* (also known as *The Howard Stern Radio Show*), 2005.

RECORDINGS

Videos:

Salvatore "Sal"/"Sally" Tessio, *The Godfather Trilogy: 1901–1980* (also known as *The Godfather Saga* and *The Godfather Trilogy;* consists of *The Godfather, The Godfather, Part II,* and *The Godfather: Part III*), 1992.

Video Games:

Salvatore "Sal"/"Sally" Tessio, *The Godfather: The Game,* Electronic Arts, 2006.

OTHER SOURCES

Periodicals:

People Weekly, March 24, 1997, p. 48.

W

WAINWRIGHT LOUDON III, 1946–
(Loudon Wainwright)

PERSONAL

Born September 5, 1946, in Chapel Hill, NC; son of Loudon S., Jr. (a magazine editor and columnist) and Martha T. (a yoga instructor) Wainwright; married Kate McGarrigle (a singer), 1973 (divorced 1977); married Suzzy Roche (a singer; divorced); children: (first marriage) Rufus (a singer, songwriter, and actor), Martha (a singer and songwriter); (second marriage) Lucy; (with Ritamarie Kelly) Alexandra. *Education:* Attended Carnegie–Mellon University, 1965–67.

Addresses: Agent—Dan Baron, Agency for the Performing Arts, 9200 Sunset Blvd., Suite 900, Los Angeles, CA 90069; (bookings) Rosebud Agency, P.O. Box 170429, San Francisco, CA 94117. *Manager*—Harriet Sternberg, Harriet Sternberg Management, 4530 Gloria Ave., Encino, CA 91436-2718.

Career: Singer, songwriter, guitarist, music producer, and actor. Began writing and performing music in Boston and New York City, 1968.

Awards, Honors: Grammy Award nomination, best contemporary folk recording, National Academy of Recording Arts and Sciences, 1986, for *I'm Alright;* Grammy Award nomination, best contemporary folk recording, 1987, for *More Love Songs.*

CREDITS

Film Appearances:
Gary, *The Slugger's Wife* (also known as *Neil Simon's "The Slugger's Wife"*), Sony Pictures Releasing, 1985.

Ferretti, *Jacknife,* Cineplex Odeon, 1989.
Guitar man, *28 Days,* Columbia, 2000.
(As Loudon Wainwright) Beamen, *Big Fish,* Columbia, 2003.
(As Loudon Wainwright) Second vocalist at Coconut Grove, *The Aviator,* Miramax, 2004.
(As Loudon Wainwright) Priest, *The 40 Year Old Virgin,* Universal, 2005.
(As Loudon Wainwright) Uncle Dale, *Elizabethtown,* Paramount, 2005.
Himself, *The Holy Modal Rounders: Bound to Lose,* 2006.

Film Song Performer:
Performer of songs that have appeared in films, television productions, radio productions, and videos.

Television Appearances; Series:
Resident singer, *Carrot Confidential,* BBC, beginning c. 1987.
(As Loudon Wainwright) Hal Karp, *Undeclared,* Fox, 2001–2002.

Television Appearances; Specials:
The Labor Day Show, PBS, 1991.
Broadway's Best, Bravo, 2002.
(Uncredited; in archive footage) Himself, *All I Want: A Portrait of Rufus Wainwright,* 2005.
(In archive footage) Himself, *Live from New York: The First 5 Years of Saturday Night Live,* NBC, 2005.

Television Appearances; Episodic:
Captain Calvin Spalding, "Rainbow Bridge," *M*A*S*H,* CBS, 1974.
Captain Calvin Spalding, "There Is Nothing Like a Nurse," *M*A*S*H,* CBS, 1974.
Captain Calvin Spalding, "Big Mac," *M*A*S*H,* CBS, 1975.
Musical guest, *Saturday Night Live* (also known as *NBC's "Saturday Night," Saturday Night, Saturday Night Live '80, SNL,* and *SNL 25*), NBC, 1975.

America 2Night, syndicated, 1978.

Guest, *The Tonight Show Starring Johnny Carson* (also known as *The Best of Carson*), NBC, 1984.

Norman, "Lifelines," *Soldier Soldier,* Independent Television (England), 1992.

Himself, *Austin City Limits,* PBS, 1999.

Jerome Trouper, "Love Is All Around: Parts 1 & 2," *Ally McBeal,* Fox, 2002.

Dr. Weidlinger, "Cuts Like a Knife," *Grounded for Life,* The WB, 2003.

Musical guest, *Late Night with Conan O'Brien,* NBC, 2005.

Celebrity Charades, American Movie Classics, 2005.

The Heaven and Earth Show, BBC, 2005.

Minister, "Renewing Vows," *According to Jim* (also known as *The Dad*), ABC, 2006.

Television Appearances; Pilots:

Dead man on telethon and Spinal Tap keyboard player, *The T.V. Show,* ABC, 1979.

(As Loudon Wainwright) Hal Karp, *Undeclared,* Fox, 2001.

Tom's father, *Other People's Business,* The WB, 2004.

Radio Appearances:

Appeared in radio productions, including appearances as a music commentator for National Public Radio.

Stage Appearances:

Jim, *Pump Boys and Dinettes* (musical), Princess Theatre, New York City, c. 1982–83.

Appeared in a production of *The Birthday Party.*

RECORDINGS

Albums:

Loudon Wainwright III (also known as *Album I*), Atlantic, 1970.

Album II, Atlantic, 1971.

Album III, Columbia/CBS, 1972.

Attempted Mustache, Columbia/CBS, 1974.

Unrequited, Columbia/CBS, 1975.

T Shirt, Arista, 1976.

Final Exam, Arista, 1978.

A Live One, Radar, 1979.

Fame and Wealth, Demon/Rounder, 1982.

I'm Alright, Demon/Rounder, 1985.

More Love Songs, Demon/Rounder, 1986.

Therapy, Silvertone/RCA, 1988.

History, Virgin, 1992.

Career Moves, Virgin, 1993.

Grown Man, Virgin, 1995.

One Man Guy: The Best of Loudon Wainwright III 1982–1986, MCI, 1995.

BBC Sessions, Fuel 2000, 1998.

Little Ship, Virgin, 1998.

Social Studies, Hannibal, 1999.

The Atlantic Recordings, Rhino Handmade, 2000.

Last Man on Earth, Red House, 2001.

So Damn Happy, Sanctuary, 2003.

Here Come the Choppers, Sovereign Artists, 2005.

Contributor to numerous compilation albums and recordings by other artists, including the Beat Farmers, Chris Harford, Willie Nile, and the Tony Trischka Band.

Singles:

"Dead Skunk," 1972.

"Y2K," c. 1999.

Other singles include "Jesse Don't Like It."

Album Producer; Albums by Loudon Wainwright III:

(With Milton Kramer) *Album II,* Atlantic, 1971.

Unrequited, Columbia/CBS, 1975.

T Shirt, Arista, 1976.

(With John Wood) *A Live One,* Radar, 1979.

Fame and Wealth, Demon/Rounder, 1982.

(With Richard Thompson) *I'm Alright,* Demon/Rounder, 1985.

(With Chaim Tannenbaum and Thompson) *More Love Songs,* Demon/Rounder, 1986.

(With Tannenbaum) *Therapy,* Silvertone/RCA, 1988.

(With Jeffrey Lesser) *History,* Virgin, 1992.

(With Lesser) *Career Moves,* Virgin, 1993.

(With Lesser) *Grown Man,* Virgin, 1995.

(With Stewart Lerman) *So Damn Happy,* Sanctuary, 2003.

WRITINGS

Film Music; Songs:

Dead Skunk (short animated film), 1973.

28 Days, Columbia, 2000.

Wrote songs that have appeared in films, television productions, radio productions, and videos.

Radio Music; Songs:

Composed songs for National Public Radio, beginning 1980s, and compiled on the album *Social Studies,* released by Hannibal, 1999.

Stage Music; Songs:

A Couple White Chicks Sitting around Talking, Astor Place Theatre, New York City, 1980–81.

Albums:

Loudon Wainwright III (also known as *Album I*), Atlantic, 1970.

Album II, Atlantic, 1971.

Album III, Columbia/CBS, 1972.

Attempted Mustache, Columbia/CBS, 1974.

Unrequited, Columbia/CBS, 1975.

T Shirt, Arista, 1976.

Final Exam, Arista, 1978.

A Live One, Radar, 1979.

Fame and Wealth, Demon/Rounder, 1982.

I'm Alright, Demon/Rounder, 1985.

More Love Songs, Demon/Rounder, 1986.

Therapy, Silvertone/RCA, 1988.

History, Virgin, 1992.

Career Moves, Virgin, 1993.

Grown Man, Virgin, 1995.

One Man Guy: The Best of Loudon Wainwright III 1982–1986, MCI, 1995.

BBC Sessions, Fuel 2000, 1998.

Little Ship, Virgin, 1998.

Social Studies, Hannibal, 1999.

The Atlantic Recordings, Rhino Handmade, 2000.

Last Man on Earth, Red House, 2001.

So Damn Happy, Sanctuary, 2003.

Here Come the Choppers, Sovereign Artists, 2005.

Contributor to numerous compilation albums and recordings by other artists, including the Beat Farmers, Chris Harford, Willie Nile, and the Tony Trischka Band.

Singles:

"Dead Skunk," 1972.

"Y2K," c. 1999.

Other singles include "Jesse Don't Like It."

OTHER SOURCES

Periodicals:

Entertainment Weekly, October 19, 2001, pp. 46–49.

Guardian (London), April 15, 2005.

Los Angeles Times, September 25, 2001.

People Weekly, March 2, 1998, p. 30.

Reader's Digest, October, 1988, p. 157.

Sunday Herald, June 20, 1999.

Uncut, May, 2005, p. 96.

Electronic:

Loudon Wainwright III, http://www.lwiii.com, February 26, 2006.

WALKEN, Christopher 1943–
(Chris Walken, Ronnie Walken, Christopher Wlaken)

PERSONAL

Original name, Ronald Walken; born March 31, 1943, in Astoria, Queens, New York, NY; son of Paul (a baker) and Rosalie (a baker) Walken; brother of Glenn Walken (an actor); married Georgianne Thon (a casting director, dancer, and production assistant), 1969. *Education:* Attended Hofstra University; trained at American National Theatre and Academy, at Actors Studio, New York City, and with Wynn Handman, New York City; studied dance. *Avocational Interests:* Cooking, painting, cats.

Addresses: *Agent*—International Creative Management, 8942 Wilshire Blvd., Beverly Hills, CA 90211. *Publicist*—I/D Public Relations, 8409 Santa Monica Blvd., West Hollywood, CA 90069.

Career: Actor and dancer. Worked as a child actor and catalogue model; as a teenager, worked as an assistant to a circus lion tamer. Held various jobs.

Member: Screen Actors Guild, Actors' Equity Association, American Federation of Television and Radio Artists.

Awards, Honors: Clarence Derwent Award, American Theatre Wing, 1966, for *The Lion in Winter; Theatre World* Award, most promising personality, 1967, for *The Rose Tattoo;* Drama Desk Award, outstanding performance, 1970, for *Lemon Sky;* Jeff Award, Joseph Jefferson awards, 1971, for *The Night Thoreau Spent in Jail;* Obie Award, best actor, *Village Voice,* 1975, for *Kid Champion;* New York Film Critics Award, best supporting actor, 1978, Academy Award, best actor in a supporting role, 1979, Golden Globe Award nomination, best motion picture actor in a supporting role, 1979, and Film Award nomination, best supporting actor, British Academy of Film and Television Arts, 1980, all for *The Deer Hunter;* Obie Award, best actor, 1981, for *The Seagull;* Saturn Award nomination, best actor, Academy of Science Fiction, Horror, and Fantasy Films, 1984, for *The Dead Zone;* Emmy Award nomination, outstanding lead actor in a miniseries or special, 1991, for "Sarah, Plain and Tall," *Hallmark Hall of Fame;* William Shakespeare Award for Classic Theatre, Shakespeare Theatre of Washington, DC, 1994; Actor Award, Gotham awards, Independent Features Project, 1995; Saturn Award nomination, best supporting actor, 1996, for *The Prophecy;* special mention, Malaga International Week of Fantastic Cinema, 1997, for *The Addiction;* Susan Stein Shiva Award, Public Theatre, New

York City, 1997; Master Screen Artist Tribute, USA Film Festival, 1998; Antoinette Perry Award nomination, best actor in a musical, 2000, for *James Joyce's "The Dead"*; Saturn Award nomination, best supporting actor, and MTV Movie Award nomination, best villain, both 2000, for *Sleepy Hollow*; American Comedy Award, funniest male guest appearance in a television series, 2001, for *Saturday Night Live*; MTV Video Music Award (with Michael Rooney and Spike Jonze), outstanding choreography, 2001, for "Weapon of Choice"; Screen Actors Guild Award, outstanding performance by a male actor in a supporting role, National Society of Film Critics Award, best supporting actor, Film Award, British Academy of Film and Television Arts, best performance by an actor in a supporting role, and Academy Award nomination, best actor in a supporting role, all 2003, for *Catch Me If You Can*; ShoWest Award, supporting actor of the year, National Association of Theatre Owners, 2003; named one of the 100 greatest movie stars, Channel 4 (England), 2003; received a star on the Hollywood Walk of Fame, 2004; Best Actor Award, Montreal World Film Festival, 2004, and Golden Satellite Award, best actor in a supporting role, drama, International Press Academy, 2005, both for *Around the Bend*; Marquee Award, CineVegas International Film Festival, 2005; named one of the twenty–five most intriguing people, *Tropopkin* magazine.

CREDITS

Film Appearances:

Me and My Brother, New Yorker, 1968.

The kid, *The Anderson Tapes*, Columbia, 1971.

Private James H. Reese, *The Happiness Cage* (also known as *The Demon within* and *The Mind Snatchers*), Cinerama, 1972.

(As Chris Walken) Robert, *Next Stop, Greenwich Village*, Twentieth Century–Fox, 1976.

Detective Rizzo, *The Sentinel*, Universal, 1977.

(As Christopher Wlaken) Duane Hall, *Annie Hall*, United Artists, 1977.

Russel (the Hustle), *Roseland*, Cinema Shares, 1977.

Nikanor "Nick" Chevotarevich, *The Deer Hunter*, Universal, 1978.

Eckart, *Last Embrace*, United Artists, 1979.

Nathan D. Champion, *Heaven's Gate* (also known as *Johnson County Wars*), United Artists, 1980.

Jamie Shannon, *The Dogs of War*, United Artists, 1981.

Mr. Rainbow, *Shoot the Sun Down*, 1981.

Tom, *Pennies from Heaven* (musical), United Artists, 1981.

Dr. Michael Anthony Brace, *Brainstorm*, Metro–Goldwyn–Mayer/United Artists, 1983.

Johnny Smith, *The Dead Zone*, Paramount, 1983.

(In archive footage) *Terror in the Aisles*, 1984.

Max Zorin, *A View to a Kill* (also known as *Ian Fleming's "A View to a Kill"*), Metro–Goldwyn–Mayer/United Artists, 1985.

Brad Whitewood, Sr., *At Close Range*, Orion, 1986.

Don Stevens, *Deadline* (also known as *Witness in the War Zone* and *War Zone—Todeszone*), Skouras Pictures, 1987.

Kyril Montana, *The Milagro Beanfield War*, Universal, 1988.

Sergeant Merwin J. Toomey, *Biloxi Blues* (also known as *Neil Simon's "Biloxi Blues"*), Universal, 1988.

Wesley Pendergrass, *Homeboy*, Twentieth Century–Fox, 1989.

Whitley Strieber, *Communion*, New Line Cinema, 1989.

Frank White, *King of New York*, New Line Cinema, 1990.

Title role, *McBain*, Glickenhaus Entertainment, 1991.

Robert, *The Comfort of Strangers* (also known as *Cortesie per gli ospiti*), Skouras Pictures, 1991.

Max Schreck, *Batman Returns*, Warner Bros., 1992.

Pasco Meisner, *Le grand pardon II* (also known as *Day of Atonement*), Vidmark Entertainment, 1992.

P. J. Decker, *All–American Murder*, Prism Entertainment, 1992.

Warren Zell, *Mistress* (also known as *Hollywood Mistress*), Tribeca Productions, 1992.

Bobby Cahn, *Wayne's World 2*, Paramount, 1993.

Don Vincenzo Coccotti, *True Romance* (also known as *Breakaway*), Warner Bros., 1993.

Captain Koons, *Pulp Fiction*, Miramax, 1994, alternate versions also released.

Vanni Corso, *A Business Affair* (also known as *Astucias de mujer*, *D'une femme a l'autre*, and *Liebe und Andere Geschaefte*), Castle Hill Productions, 1994.

Angel Gabriel, *The Prophecy* (also known as *God's Army* and *God's Secret Army*), Dimension Films, 1995.

Kim Ulander, *Search and Destroy* (also known as *The Four Rules*), October Films, 1995.

The man with the plan, *Things to Do in Denver When You're Dead*, Miramax, 1995.

Mr. Smith, *Nick of Time* (also known as *Counted Moments*), Paramount, 1995.

Peina, *The Addiction*, October Films, 1995.

Hickey, *Last Man Standing*, New Line Cinema, 1996.

The interviewer, *Basquiat* (also known as *Build a Fort, Set It on Fire*), Miramax, 1996.

Ray Tiempo, *The Funeral*, October Films, 1996.

United States officer, *Celluloide*, Civite, 1996.

Bill Hill, *Touch*, Metro–Goldwyn–Mayer/United Artists, 1997.

Caesar, *Mouse Hunt* (also known as *Mousechase*), DreamWorks, 1997.

Charles Barrett/Carlo Bartolucci, *Suicide Kings* (also known as *Boys Night Out* and *Bred and Bored*), New Films International, 1997.

Raymond "Ray" Perkins, *Excess Baggage*, Columbia, 1997.

Fox, *New Rose Hotel*, Avalanche Releasing, 1998.

Gabriel, *The Prophecy II* (also known as *God's Army II* and *Prophecy II: Ashtown*), Dimension Films, 1998.

Umberto Bevalaqua, *Illuminata,* Artisan Entertainment, 1998.

Uncle Bill Ferriter, *Trance* (also known as *The Eternal* and *The Eternal: Kiss of the Mummy*), Trimark Pictures, 1998.

Voice of Colonel Cutter, *Antz* (animated; also known as *Ants*), DreamWorks, 1998.

Calvin Webber, *Blast from the Past,* New Line Cinema, 1999.

Himself, *Cast and Crew* (short film), TVI's Productions, 1999.

Hessian horseman, *Sleepy Hollow,* Paramount, 1999.

Gabriel, *The Prophecy III: The Ascent* (also known as *God's Army III*), Dimension Films, 2000.

Victor "Vic" Kelly, *The Opportunists,* Fist Look Pictures Releasing, 2000.

Clem, *Joe Dirt* (also known as *The Adventures of Joe Dirt*), Columbia, 2001.

Count Cagliostro, *The Affair of the Necklace,* Warner Bros., 2001.

Hal Weidmann, *America's Sweethearts,* Columbia, 2001.

Lieutenant Ernie McDuff, *Scotland, Pa.,* Lot 47 Films, 2001.

Roy, *Jungle Juice,* Miracle Entertainment, 2001.

Frank Featherbed, *Plots with a View* (also known as *Plotz with a View, Undertaking Betty, Grabgefluester, Grabgefluester—Liebe kann Saerge,* and *Grabgefluester—Liebe versetzt Saerge*), Miramax, 2002.

Frank W. Abagnale, Sr., *Catch Me If You Can,* Dream-Works, 2002.

Reed Thimple, *The Country Bears,* Buena Vista, 2002.

Detective Stanley Jacobellis, *Gigli* (also known as *Tough Love*), Columbia/TriStar, 2003.

Hatcher, *The Rundown* (also known as *Welcome to the Jungle*), Universal, 2003.

Mike, *Poolhall Junkies,* Samuel Goldwyn, 2003.

Salvatore "Sal" Maggio, *Kangaroo Jack,* Warner Bros., 2003.

J-Man, *Envy,* DreamWorks, 2004.

Mike Wellington, *The Stepford Wives,* Paramount, 2004.

Rayburn, *Man on Fire,* Twentieth Century-Fox, 2004.

Secretary Cleary, *Wedding Crashers,* New Line Cinema, 2004.

Turner Lair, *Around the Bend,* Warner Bros., 2004.

Cousin Bo, *Romance and Cigarettes,* Metro-Goldwyn-Mayer, 2005.

Mark Heiss, *Domino,* New Line Cinema, 2005.

CIA agent, *Fade to Black,* Miramax, 2006.

Morty, *Click,* Sony Pictures Releasing, 2006.

Man of the Year, Universal, 2006.

Fang, *Balls of Fury,* c. 2007.

Film Work:

Coproducer, *New Rose Hotel,* Avalanche Releasing, 1998.

Stage Appearances:

(As Ronnie Walken) David, *J. B.,* American National Theatre and Academy Theatre, New York City, 1959.

(As Ronnie Walken) Clayton "Dutch" Miller, *Best Foot Forward* (musical), Stage 73, New York City, 1963.

(As Ronnie Walken) Chorus member, *High Spirits* (musical), Alvin Theatre, New York City, 1964–65.

Killer, *Baker Street* (musical), Broadway Theatre and Martin Beck Theatre, both New York City, 1965.

Claudio, *Measure for Measure,* New York Shakespeare Festival, Public Theatre, Delacorte Theatre, New York City, 1966.

Jack Hunter, *The Rose Tattoo,* New York City Center Drama Company, City Center Theatre, then Billy Rose Theatre, both New York City, 1966.

Philip (king of France), *The Lion in Winter,* Ambassador Theatre, New York City, 1966.

Unknown soldier, *The Unknown Soldier and His Wife,* Lincoln Center, Vivian Beaumont Theater, then George Abbott Theatre, both New York City, 1967.

Achilles, *Iphigenia in Aulis,* Circle in the Square Downtown, New York City, 1967–68.

Felton, *The Three Musketeers,* Stratford Festival of Canada, Stratford, Ontario, Canada, 1968.

Lysander, *A Midsummer Night's Dream,* Stratford Festival of Canada, 1968.

Romeo, *Romeo and Juliet,* Stratford Festival of Canada, 1968.

Priest, *The Chronicles of Hell,* APA Repertory Company, Ann Arbor, MI, 1969.

Rosencrantz, *Rosencrantz and Guildenstern Are Dead,* Parker Playhouse, Fort Lauderdale, FL, 1969.

The Comedy of Errors, San Diego Shakespeare Festival, San Diego, CA, 1969.

Julius Caesar, San Diego Shakespeare Festival, 1969.

Alan, *Lemon Sky,* Playhouse Theatre, New York City, 1970.

Posthumus Leonatus, *Cymbeline* (also known as *The Tale of Cymbeline*), New York Shakespeare Festival, Public Theatre, Delacorte Theatre, 1971.

Thoreau, *The Night Thoreau Spent in Jail,* Goodman Theatre, Chicago, IL, 1971.

Scenes from American Life, Forum Theatre, New York City, 1971.

Title role, *Caligula,* Yale Repertory Theatre, New Haven, CT, 1971–72.

George, *The Judgment,* American Place Theatre, New York City, 1972.

Oedipus, *The Palace at 4 a.m.,* John Drew Theatre, East Hampton, NY, 1972.

Sinstov, *Enemies,* Lincoln Center, Vivian Beaumont Theater, 1972.

Achilles, *Troilus and Cressida,* New York Shakespeare Festival, Mitzi E. Newhouse Theatre, New York City, 1973.

Bassanio, *The Merchant of Venice,* Lincoln Center, Vivian Beaumont Theater, 1973.

Title role, *Houdini,* Lenox Art Center, Lenox, MA, 1973.

Jack Clitheroe, *The Plough and the Stars,* Lincoln Center, Vivian Beaumont Theater, 1973.

Dance of Death, Long Wharf Theatre, New Haven, CT, 1973.

Miss Julie, Long Wharf Theatre, 1973.

Antonio, *The Tempest,* New York Shakespeare Festival, Mitzi E. Newhouse Theatre, 1974.

Title role, *Hamlet,* Seattle Repertory Theatre, Center Playhouse, Seattle, WA, 1974.

Title role, *Macbeth,* New York Shakespeare Festival, Mitzi E. Newhouse Theatre, 1974.

Title role, *Kid Champion,* New York Shakespeare Festival, Public Theatre, Anspacher Theatre, New York City, 1975.

Chance Wayne, *Sweet Bird of Youth,* Brooklyn Academy of Music, Brooklyn, New York City, then Rebehak Harkness Theatre, New York City, 1975, John F. Kennedy Center for the Performing Arts, Washington, DC, c. 1975, Academy Festival Theatre, Chicago, IL, 1976.

Gregers Werle, *The Wild Duck,* Yale Repertory Theatre, 1978.

Measure for Measure, Yale Repertory Theatre, 1979.

Trigorin, *The Seagull,* New York Shakespeare Festival, Public Theatre, Estelle R. Newman Theatre, New York City, 1980.

Title role, *Hamlet,* American Shakespeare Theatre, Stratford, CT, 1982.

Henry Percy (Hotspur), *Henry IV, Part I,* American Shakespeare Theatre, 1982.

Leonard Charteris, *The Philanderer,* Yale Repertory Theatre, 1982.

Title role, *Ivanov,* Williamstown Theatre Festival, Williamstown, MA, 1983.

The director, *Cinders,* New York Shakespeare Festival, Public Theatre, LuEsther Hall, New York City, 1984.

Mickey, *Hurlyburly,* Promenade Theatre, then Ethel Barrymore Theatre, both New York City, between 1984 and 1985.

A Bill of Divorcement, Westport Country Playhouse, Westport, CT, 1985.

Billy Einhorn, *The House of Blue Leaves,* Mitzi E. Newhouse Theatre, 1986.

Stanley Kowalski, *A Streetcar Named Desire,* Williamstown Theatre Festival, 1986.

Uncle Vanya, American Repertory Theatre, Cambridge, MA, 1988.

Caius Marcius Coriolanus (title role), *Coriolanus,* New York Shakespeare Festival, Public Theatre, Anspacher Theatre, New York City, 1988–89.

William Makepeace Ladd III, *Love Letters,* Promenade Theatre, 1989.

Night of 100 Stars III (also known as *Night of One Hundred Stars*), Radio City Music Hall, New York City, 1990.

Iago, *Othello,* New York Shakespeare Festival, Public Theatre, Delacorte Theatre, 1992.

Title role, *Him* (solo show), New York Shakespeare Festival, Public Theatre, LuEsther Hall, 1995.

Gabriel Conroy, *James Joyce's "The Dead"* (musical), Playwrights Horizons, Belasco Theatre, New York City, 1999–2000.

Piotr Nikolayevich Sorin, *The Seagull,* New York Shakespeare Festival, Public Theatre, Delacorte Theatre, 2001.

Major Tours:

Riff, *West Side Story* (musical), c. 1960.

Television Appearances; Series:

(As Ronnie Walken) Kevin Acton, *The Wonderful John Acton,* NBC, 1953.

(As Ronnie Walken) Michael "Mike" Bauer (shared role with brother Glenn Walken), *The Guiding Light* (also known as *Guiding Light*), CBS, 1954–56.

Voice of Dr. Mayhem, *Defenders of Dynatron City* (animated), Fox, beginning c. 1992.

Television Appearances; Miniseries:

Max Zorin, "I Love 1985," *I Love 1980s,* BBC–2, 2001.

Marcus Porcius Cato, *Julius Caesar* (also known as *Caesar* and *Guilio Cesare*), TNT, 2002.

Himself, *The 100 Greatest Movie Stars,* Channel 4 (England), 2003.

Himself, *The 100 Greatest War Films,* Channel 4, 2005.

Television Appearances; Movies:

Puss, *Cannon Movie Tales: Puss in Boots* (musical; also known as *Puss in Boots*), 1988.

Jack Shanks, *Scam,* Showtime, 1993.

Bruno Buckingham, *Wild Side,* HBO, 1996.

James Houston, *Vendetta,* HBO, 1999.

Max, *Kiss Toledo Goodbye,* Starz!, 1999.

Television Appearances; Specials:

Lamprocles, "Barefoot in Athens," *Hallmark Hall of Fame* (also known as *George Schaefer's "Showcase Theatre: Barefoot in Athens"*), NBC, 1966.

Felton, *The Three Musketeers,* [Canada], 1969.

The Hessian, "Valley Forge," *Hallmark Hall of Fame,* NBC, 1975.

Harry Nash, "Sense of Humor: Who Am I This Time?," *American Playhouse,* PBS, 1982.

"Celebrating Gershwin" (also known as "The Jazz Age" and "'S Wonderful"), *Great Performances,* PBS, 1987.

(In archive footage) *Happy Anniversary 007: 25 Years of James Bond,* ABC, 1987.

Night of 100 Stars III (also known as *Night of One Hundred Stars*), NBC, 1990.

Jacob Witting, "Sarah, Plain and Tall," *Hallmark Hall of Fame,* CBS, 1991.

Jacob Witting, "Skylark" (also known as "Sarah, Plain and Tall: Skylark"), *Hallmark Hall of Fame,* CBS, 1993.

The Second Annual Saturday Night Live Mother's Day Special, NBC, 1993.

Himself, *Anatomy of Horror,* UPN, 1995.

The Secret World of Antz, NBC, 1998.

Jacob Witting, "Sarah, Plain and Tall: Winter's End," *Hallmark Hall of Fame,* CBS, 1999.

Saturday Night Live: 25th Anniversary (also known as *Saturday Night Live: 25th Anniversary Primetime Special*), NBC, 1999.

Narrator, *David Blaine: Frozen in Time,* ABC, 2000.

Himself, "The Papp Project," *American Masters,* PBS, 2001.

Rusty, "Engine Trouble," *Reflections from Ground Zero,* Showtime, 2002.

(Uncredited; In archive footage) *Best Ever Bond,* Independent Television (England), 2002.

(In archive footage) *Saturday Night Live: The Best of Will Ferrell,* NBC, 2002.

Comedy Central Roast of Denis Leary, Comedy Central, 2003.

The Making of "Man on Fire," 2004.

(In archive footage) *Saturday Night Live: The Best of Cheri Oteri,* NBC, 2004.

(In archive footage) *Saturday Night Live: The Best of Christopher Walken,* NBC, 2004.

(In archive footage) *Saturday Night Live: The Best of Tom Hanks,* NBC, 2004.

Himself, *Reel Comedy: Wedding Crashers,* Comedy Central, 2005.

Television Appearances; Awards Presentations:

The 51st Annual Academy Awards, ABC, 1979.

Presenter, *The 43rd Annual Primetime Emmy Awards,* Fox, 1991.

Presenter, *50th Annual Golden Globe Awards,* TBS, 1993.

Presenter, *The 54th Annual Golden Globe Awards,* NBC, 1997.

The 54th Annual Tony Awards, CBS, 2000.

Presenter, *MTV Video Music Awards 2001,* MTV, 2001.

The 15th Annual American Comedy Awards, Comedy Central, 2001.

The 75th Annual Academy Awards, ABC, 2003.

Presenter, *On Stage at the Kennedy Center: The Mark Twain Prize Celebrating Lorne Michaels,* PBS, 2005.

Television Appearances; Episodic:

(As Ronnie Walken) "The Muldoon Matter," *The Motorola Television Hour* (also known as *The Motorola TV Hour* and *Motorola TV Theatre*), ABC, 1954.

(As Ronnie Walken) Chris, "Robin Hood and Clarence Darrow, They Went out with Bow and Arrow," *Naked City,* ABC, 1963.

Walt Kramer, "Run, Johnny, Run," *Hawaii Five-0* (also known as *McGarrett*), CBS, 1970.

Ben Wiley, "Kiss It All Goodbye," *Kojak,* CBS, 1977.

Himself, *Inside the Actors Studio,* Bravo, 1995.

Rotten TV, VH1, 2000.

"Man on Fire," *HBO First Look,* HBO, 2004.

(In archive footage) *101 Most Unforgettable SNL Moments* (also known as *E's "101"*), E! Entertainment Television, 2004.

Appeared in other programs, including episodes of *The Colgate Comedy Hour,* NBC; *Ernie Kovacs,* NBC and CBS; *Mama,* CBS; *Omnibus,* CBS, ABC, and NBC; and *Philco Television Playhouse,* NBC.

Television Guest Appearances; Episodic:

Guest host, *Saturday Night Live* (also known as *NBC's "Saturday Night," Saturday Night, Saturday Night Live '80, SNL,* and *SNL 25*), NBC, multiple appearances between 1990 and 2003.

Late Night with David Letterman, NBC, 1992.

The Rosie O'Donnell Show, syndicated, 1997.

Late Night with Conan O'Brien, NBC, 2000, 2003, 2004.

The Movie Chart Show, 2001.

Live with Regis and Kelly, syndicated, 2004.

The Late Show with David Letterman (also known as *The Late Show* and *Late Show Backstage*), CBS, 2005.

Today (also known as *NBC News Today* and *The Today Show*), NBC, 2005.

Television Director; Specials:

Popcorn Shrimp, Showtime, 2001.

RECORDINGS

Videos:

Guardian angel in "Bad Girl" music video, *Madonna: The Video Collection 93:99,* 1999.

Sleepy Hollow: Behind the Legend, Mandalay/Paramount, 2000.

Breaking the Silence: The Making of "Hannibal," Metro–Goldwyn–Mayer Home Entertainment, 2001.

Performer in "Weapon of Choice" music video, *The Work of Director Spike Jonze,* Palm Pictures, 2003.

A Perfect World: The Making of "The Stepford Wives," Paramount Home Video, 2004.

The Rundown: Rumble in the Jungle (short), Universal, 2004.

The Rundown: Running down the Town (short), Universal, 2004.

The Rundown: Walken's World (short), Universal, 2004.

Stepford: A Definition, Paramount Home Video, 2004.

The Stepford Husbands, Paramount Home Video, 2004.

It's a Good Day: The Making of "Around the Bend," Warner Home Video, 2005.

Vengeance Is Mine: Reinventing "Man on Fire," Twentieth Century–Fox Home Entertainment, 2005.

Music Videos:

Madonna, "Bad Girl," 1993.

Fatboy Slim, "Weapon of Choice," 2001.

Video Games:

Voice of David Hassan, *Privateer 2: The Darkening,* Electronic Arts, 1996.

Voice of Detective Vince Magnotta, *Ripper,* Take 2 Interactive, 1996.

Voice of George, *True Crime: Streets of LA,* Activision, 2003.

Voice of Gabriel Whitting, *True Crime: New York City,* Activision, 2005.

Audiobooks:

"The Raven," *Closed on Account of Rabies: Poems and Tales of Edgar Allan Poe,* Mercury/Universal, 1997.

WRITINGS

Screenplays:

The Prophecy (also known as *God's Army* and *God's Secret Army*), Dimension Films, 1995.

Author of other screenplays.

Writings for the Stage:

Him (solo show), New York Shakespeare Festival, Public Theatre, LuEsther Hall, New York City, 1995.

Teleplays; Specials:

Popcorn Shrimp, Showtime, 2001.

OTHER SOURCES

Books:

International Dictionary of Films and Filmmakers, Volume 3: *Actors and Actresses,* fourth edition, St. James Press, 2000.

Periodicals:

Details, December, 1993, pp. 145–47, 198–200.

Empire, issue 60, 1994, pp. 46–47; December, 1997, pp. 62–63.

Entertainment Weekly, March 17, 2000, pp. 30–35; October 22, 2004, p. 14.

Esquire, January, 1981.

Feature, April, 1979.

Film Comment, July/August, 1992.

Films Illustrated, March, 1979.

Interview, August, 1977; February, 1979; March, 1988, p. 76; July, 1993; June, 2004, pp. 68–73.

Mademoiselle, December, 1980.

Movieline, December, 1993; November, 1998, pp. 56–59, 82–83, 91.

Movieline's Hollywood Life, May, 2004, pp. 80–83.

New York, June 15, 1981.

New York Daily News, March 24, 1988, pp. 1, 62.

New Yorker, January 9, 1995.

New York Times, December 26, 1978; June 24, 1992.

People Weekly, May 26, 1986, pp. 59–62.

Photoplay, July, 1985.

Playboy, September, 1997, pp. 51–59.

Premiere, issue 237, 1996, p. 82; July, 2004, pp. 104–108, 128.

Rolling Stone, March 8, 1979.

Sight & Sound, January, 1997.

Starlog, October, 1992.

Tropopkin, October, 1995.

Village Voice, January 15, 1979.

Washington Post, July 24, 2005, pp. N1, N5.

WALTER, Lisa Ann 1963–

PERSONAL

Born August 3, 1963, in Silver Spring, MD (some sources cite the state of Pennsylvania); father a geophysicist; married Sam Baum (a producer and writer; divorced, 1999); children: (with Baum) Jordan, Delia; Simon, Spencer. *Education:* Catholic University of America, B.F.A. *Avocational Interests:* Dancing, music, reading, gourmet cooking.

Addresses: *Agent*—Ruthanne Secunda, United Talent Agency, 9560 Wilshire Blvd., Suite 500, Beverly Hills, CA 90212; (voice work) Special Artists Agency, 9465 Wilshire Blvd., Suite 890, Beverly Hills, CA 90212. *Manager*—McKeon–Valeo–Myones Management, 9150 Wilshire Blvd., Suite 102, Beverly Hills, CA 90212.

Career: Actress. Began stage career as a singer at the age of six. Stand–up comedienne in *Fabulous Women of Comedy,* Toyota Comedy Festival, Catch a Rising Star, New York City. Stand–up comedienne at other venues, including the Comic Strip, New York City, the Laugh Factory, Los Angeles, and Nick's Comedy Club, Boston, MA. Worked as a singing waitress in Washington, DC and in sales.

CREDITS

Film Appearances:

One Crazy Summer (also known as *Greetings from Nantucket*), Warner Bros., 1986.

Claudine, *Eddie,* Buena Vista, 1996.

Chessy, *The Parent Trap* (also known as *Disney's "The Parent Trap"*), Buena Vista, 1998.

Principal Perry, *Get Your Stuff,* Ariztical Entertainment, 2000.

Janet, *Early Bird Special,* Early Bird Special LLC, 2001.

Debbie, *Bruce Almighty,* Universal, 2003.

Sexy feminist executive, *Farm Sluts* (short film), Mad–Hoc Media, 2003.

Bobbie, *Shall We Dance,* Miramax, 2004.

Dee Dee Rutherford, *The Trouble with Dee Dee* (also known as *Dee Dee Rutherford*), Hunt and the Kill, 2005.

Sara, *Coffee Date,* Coffee Date Productions, 2005.

Sheryl, *War of the Worlds,* Paramount, 2005.

Carol, *Graduation,* Blueline Films, 2006.

Sergeant Burch, *Room 6,* CFQ Films/Haunted Hospital Productions/Mindfire Entertainment, 2006.

Television Appearances; Series:

Lisa McGinnis, *My Wildest Dreams* (also known as *Something's Gotta Give*), Fox, 1995.

Lisa Ann Hunter, *Life's Work,* ABC, 1996–97.

Rachel Glass, *Breaking News,* produced by TNT in 2000–2001 (but never aired), broadcast on Bravo, 2002.

Cassandra Gilman, *Emeril,* NBC, 2001.

Television Appearances; Specials:

The Walt Disney World Very Merry Christmas Parade, ABC, 1996.

Politically Incorrect with Bill Maher After Party, ABC, 2001.

Television Appearances; Episodic:

Guest, *The Rosie O'Donnell Show,* syndicated, 1996.

Audrey Cranston, "How Long Has This Been Going On?," *The Love Boat: The Next Wave,* UPN, 1998.

Herself, *Hollywood Squares* (also known as *H2* and *H2: Hollywood Squares*), syndicated, 1998.

Nurse, "Interior Decorator," *Curb Your Enthusiasm,* HBO, 2000.

Herself, "Comedians #2 Special," *Weakest Link* (also known as *The Weakest Link USA*), NBC, 2001.

Rita Harper, "Hot Flash," *Strong Medicine,* Lifetime, 2001.

Rose Gluck, "Sons and Lovers," *Las Vegas* (also known as *Casino Eye*), NBC, 2004.

As a comedienne, appeared in episodes of various series, including *Caroline's Comedy Hour,* Arts and Entertainment; *Comedy on the Road,* Arts and Entertainment; *Politically Incorrect with Bill Maher* (also known as *Politically Incorrect*), Comedy Central and ABC; and *USA Up All Night* (also known as *Up All Night*), USA Network. Also appeared in *Fox after Breakfast* (later known as *The Vicki Lawrence Show*), Fox; *Later* (also known as *Later with Bob Costas, Later with Cynthia Garrett,* and *Later with Greg Kinnear*), NBC; and *The Test,* FX Channel.

Television Appearances; Pilots:

Lisa Ann Hunter, *Life's Work,* ABC, 1996.

Cassie Baltic, *Late Bloomer,* 1997.

Wake Up!, CBS, 1998.

Rachel Glass, *Breaking News,* pilot produced by TNT in 2000 (but never aired), broadcast on Bravo, 2002.

Cassandra Gilman, *Emeril,* NBC, 2001.

Appeared in the pilot *Regular Joe.*

Television Work; Series:

Character creator, *My Wildest Dreams* (also known as *Something's Gotta Give*), Fox, 1995.

Creator and producer, *Life's Work,* ABC, 1996–97.

Television Work; Pilots:

Producer, *Wake Up!,* CBS, 1998.

Stage Appearances:

Appeared as Brandy in a production of *Battery,* off–Broadway; appeared in regional theatre and dinner theatre productions.

Radio Appearances; Episodic:

Appeared in radio programs, including *The Steve & Vikki Morning Show,* Star 94 FM (Atlanta, GA).

RECORDINGS

Videos:

Performer and producer, *The Naughty Show,* 2005.

WRITINGS

Teleplays:

(Story with Warren Bell) *Life's Work* (pilot), ABC, 1996.

As a comedienne, contributed material to episodes of various series, including *Caroline's Comedy Hour,* Arts and Entertainment; *Comedy on the Road,* Arts and Entertainment; and *USA Up All Night* (also known as *Up All Night*), USA Network.

Video Scripts; with Others:

The Naughty Show, 2005.

WALTERS, Jerrie
See WITHERS, Jane

WARBURTON, Patrick 1964–
(Patrick Wharburton)

PERSONAL

Born November 14, 1964, in Paterson, NJ; son of John Warburton (a doctor) and Barbara Lord (an actress); married Cathy (a homemaker), 1991; children: Talon Patrick, Alexandra Catherine, Shane, Gabriel. *Education:* Graduated from college. *Religion:* Roman Catholicism.

Addresses: *Agent*—Jim Hess, Paradigm, 360 North Crescent Dr., North Building, Beverly Hills, CA 90210; (voice work) Sutton, Barth & Vennari, 145 South Fairfax Ave., Suite 310, Los Angeles, CA 90036. *Manager*—Delores Robinson, Delores Robinson Entertainment, 9250 Wilshire Blvd., Suite 220, Beverly Hills, CA 90210. *Publicist*—Liza Anderson, Warren Cowan and Associates, 8899 Beverly Blvd., Suite 919, Los Angeles, CA 90048.

Career: Actor and voice performer. Performed in regional theatre productions. Worked as a model and appeared in advertisements and public service announcements. Voice for ride attractions at Walt Disney theme parks, including *Soarin' over California,* Disney's California Adventure, Anaheim, CA, and *Soarin',* EPCOT Center, Lake Buena Vista, FL.

Awards, Honors: Annie Award nomination, outstanding individual achievement for voice acting by a male performer in an animated feature production, International Animated Film Society, 2001, for *The Emperor's New Groove;* Outstanding Achievement Award, best actor, New York VisionFest, 2005, for *The Civilization of Maxwell Bright.*

CREDITS

Film Appearances:
Richard Abdee, *Dragonard,* 1987.
Richard Abdee, *Master of Dragonard Hill,* Cannon, 1989.
Balford, *Scorchers,* Goldcrest, 1991.
Charlie's brother, *Dickwad,* Taylor–Made Productions, 1994.
Rookie police officer, *American Strays,* A–pix Entertainment, 1996.

Horace Tutt, Jr., *Camouflage,* PM Entertainment Group, 1999.
Richard Hudson, *The Woman Chaser,* Inwood Films, 1999.
Al Burnett, *The Dish,* Warner Bros., 2000.
Steven Stone, *Scream 3* (also known as *Ghostface* and *Scream 3: Ghostface Killer*), Miramax/Dimension Films, 2000.
Voice of Kronk, *The Emperor's New Groove* (animated; also known as *Kingdom in the Sun* and *Kingdom of the Sun*), Buena Vista, 2000.
Voices of little green men, *Buzz Lightyear of Star Command: The Adventure Begins* (animated), Buena Vista Home Entertainment, 2000.
Mark McKinney, *Joe Somebody,* Twentieth Century–Fox, 2001.
Vincent, *Dirt* (also known as *Dumber Than Dirt*), 2001, New Light Entertainment, 2006.
Agent Tee, *Men in Black II* (also known as *MIB 2* and *MIIB*), Columbia/TriStar, 2002.
Head of gay conspiracy, *Run Ronnie Run* (also known as *Run Ronnie Run! The Ronnie Dobbs Story: A Mr. Show Movie*), New Line Cinema, 2002.
Officer Walker Kramitz, *Big Trouble,* Buena Vista, 2002.
Jack, *I'd Rather Be in Philadelphia,* Mozart Pictures, 2003.
Voice of Mr. Steve Barkin, *Kim Possible: The Secret Files* (animated), Walt Disney Home Entertainment, 2003.
(Scenes deleted) *A Mighty Wind* (also known as *Untitled Christopher Guest Project*), Warner Bros., 2003, scenes included on the DVD of the film.
(As Patrick Wharburton) Bubba, *The Ruining,* Troma Films, 2004.
Rudy Buckmaster, *Bob Steel,* 2004.
Voice of Patrick, *Home on the Range* (animated; also known as *Sweating Bullets*), Buena Vista, 2004.
Voice of Superman, *Hindsight Is 20/20...* (animated short film), 2004.
Voice of Superman, *A Uniform Used to Mean Something* (animated short film), 2004.
Larry Burgess, Sr., *Rebound,* Twentieth Century–Fox, 2005.
Maxwell Bright, *The Civilization of Maxwell Bright* (also known as *Sex & Violence*), Sneak Preview Entertainment, 2005.
Voice of alien police officer, *Chicken Little* (animated), Buena Vista, 2005.
Voice of Joe Swanson, *Family Guy Presents: Stewie Griffin—The Untold Story* (animated; also known as *Family Guy: The Movie*), Twentieth Century–Fox, 2005.
Voice of Kronk, *Kronk's New Groove* (animated), Buena Vista Home Video, 2005.
Voice of Royal Pain, *Sky High,* Buena Vista, 2005.
Voice of wolf, *Hoodwinked* (animated; also known as *Hoodwinked! The True Story of Red Riding Hood*), The Weinstein Company, 2005.

Dr. Seth Douglass, *First Time Caller,* 19th Hole Entertainment/Boy in the Drain Productions, 2006.

Voice of Blag, *The Wild* (animated), Buena Vista, 2006.

Voice of Ian, *Open Season* (animated), Sony Pictures Releasing, 2006.

Voice of prince, *Happily N'ever After* (animated), Vanguard Films Production, 2006.

Cad, *Underdog,* Walt Disney Pictures, 2007.

Voice, *Bee Movie* (animated), DreamWorks, 2007.

Film Work:

Production assistant, *Salsa,* Cannon, 1988.

Television Appearances; Series:

Eric, *Dave's World,* CBS, 1993–97.

David Puddy, *Seinfeld,* NBC, 1995–98.

Johnny Johnson, a recurring role, *NewsRadio* (also known as *News Radio* and *The Station*), NBC, 1998–99.

Sonny Mayfield, *Maggie Winters,* CBS, 1998–99.

Voice of Joe, *Family Guy* (animated; also known as *Padre de familia* and *Padre del familia*), Fox, 1999–2002, 2005—.

Voices of Buzz Lightyear and little green men, *Buzz Lightyear of Star Command* (animated; also known as *Disney/Pixar's "Buzz Lightyear of Star Command"*), UPN and syndicated, 2000–2001, ABC, 2001.

Title role, *The Tick,* Fox, 2001–2002.

Voice of Mr. Steve Barkin, *Kim Possible* (animated; also known as *Disney's "Kim Possible"*), The Disney Channel, 2002–2005.

Jeb Denton, *Less Than Perfect,* ABC, beginning 2003.

Voice of Brock Samson, *The Venture Bros.* (animated), Cartoon Network, 2004.

Voice of Ripley "Rip" Smashenburn, *Game Over* (animated; also known as *Meet the Breaknecks*), UPN, 2004.

Voice of Mr. X, *The X's* (animated), Nickelodeon, 2005—.

Voice of Kronk, *The Emperor's New School* (animated; also known as *The Emperor's New Skool*), The Disney Channel, 2006—.

Television Appearances; Movies:

Scott Mercereau, *Rise and Walk: The Dennis Byrd Story,* Fox, 1994.

Morgan, *The Apartment Complex,* Showtime, 1999.

Eddie "Steady" Everett, "Angels in the Infield," *The Wonderful World of Disney,* ABC, 2000.

Television Appearances; Specials:

Pool boy, *Battle in the Erogenous Zone,* Showtime, 1992.

Harry Anderson: The Tricks of His Trade, CBS, 1996.

E! Rock-n-Roll: Behind the Scenes, E! Entertainment Television, 1999.

Hollywood Unites: An E! News Special, E! Entertainment Television, 2001.

Reel Comedy: Big Trouble, Comedy Central, 2002.

A Merry Mickey Celebration, ABC, 2003.

Television Appearances; Episodic:

Blaster, "The Leap Home: Part 2 (Vietnam)—April 7, 1970," *Quantum Leap,* NBC, 1990.

"The Torrid Zone," *Anything but Love,* ABC, 1991.

Billy, "The Lisa and Billy Story," *Grapevine,* CBS, 1992.

Bo, "A Year to Remember," *Murphy Brown,* CBS, 1992.

Glenn, "Northwest Passages," *Northern Exposure,* CBS, 1992.

Chuck, "What Are Friends for?," *Nurses,* NBC, 1993.

Craig, "Gone with a Whim: Parts 1 & 2," *Designing Women,* CBS, 1993.

Craig, "Too Dumb to Date," *Designing Women,* CBS, 1993.

Sam, "Love among the Tiles," *Mad about You* (also known as *Loved by You*), NBC, 1993.

Duane, "It Don't Mean a Thing If It Ain't Got That Swing," *Love & War,* CBS, 1993.

Brent, "The Spa," *Ellen* (also known as *These Friends of Mine*), ABC, 1995.

Jack, "Thirty Kilo Man: Parts 1 & 2," *Ellen* (also known as *These Friends of Mine*), ABC, 1995.

Meter reader, "A Night at the Opera," *Grace under Fire* (also known as *Grace under Pressure*), ABC, 1995.

Kurt, *Hiller and Diller,* ABC, 1997.

Dan, "Sex and Violence," *House Rules,* NBC, 1998.

Voice of Lastrigon, "Hercules and the Prom," *Hercules* (also known as *Disney's "Hercules"*), syndicated, 1998.

Voice of security guard, "Escaping Dog Trick," *Teacher's Pet* (also known as *Disney's "Teacher's Pet"*), ABC, 2000.

Azoth the Avenger, "Azoth the Avenger Is a Friend of Mine," *The Twilight Zone,* UPN, 2002.

Burt Landon, "Company Picnic," *Malcolm in the Middle,* Fox, 2002.

Nick Sharpe, "Goodbye: Part 1," *8 Simple Rules ... for Dating My Teenage Daughter* (also known as *8 Simple Rules*), ABC, 2003.

Nick Sharpe, "Queen Bees and King Bees," *8 Simple Rules ... for Dating My Teenage Daughter* (also known as *8 Simple Rules*), ABC, 2003.

Bill Harris, "Bill's Back," *Happy Family,* NBC, 2003.

Guest, *The Wayne Brady Show,* syndicated, 2004.

Voice of Cash Tankinson, "JTV," *The Batman* (animated), The WB, 2005.

The Daily Buzz, syndicated, 2005.

Voice of Cash Tankinson, "Cash for Toys," *The Batman* (animated), The WB, 2006.

Appeared in episodes of other series, including *Late Night with Conan O'Brien,* NBC.

Television Appearances; Pilots:

Eric, *Dave's World,* CBS, 1993.

Sam, *Death & Taxes,* NBC, 1993.

J. P., *Stop and Go,* CBS, 1998.
Blind Men, NBC, 1998.
Jeff of the Universe, Fox, 1999.
Title role, *The Tick,* Fox, 2001.
Bud, *These Guys,* ABC, 2003.
Voice of Brock Samson, "The Terrible Secret of Turtle Bay," *The Venture Bros.* (animated), Cartoon Network, 2003.
Voice of Mr. X, "AAIIEE, Robot/Mission: Irresponsible," *The X's* (animated), Nickelodeon, 2005.

RECORDINGS

Videos:

Agent T, *Men in Black Training Video: Australia,* Columbia/TriStar Home Video, 2002.
Agent T, *Men in Black Training Video: Germany,* Columbia/TriStar Home Video, 2002.
Agent T, *Men in Black Training Video: Japan,* Columbia/TriStar Home Video, 2002.
Agent T, *Men in Black Training Video: UK,* Columbia/TriStar Home Video, 2002.
Himself, *The Bench: Life before "Seinfeld,"* Columbia/TriStar Home Video, 2004.
Himself, *World Domination: The "Family Guy" Phenomenon,* Twentieth Century–Fox Home Entertainment, 2005.

Video Games:

Voice of Buzz Lightyear, *Buzz Lightyear of Star Command,* Activision, 2000.
Voice of Kronk, *Emperor's New Groove,* Disney Interactive/PCB Productions, 2001.
Voice of Lok, *Tak and the Power of Juju,* Nickelodeon Productions, 2003.
Voice of Mozer, *Metal Arms: Glitch in the System,* Vivendi Universal Games, 2003.
Voice of Lok, *Tak 2: The Staff of Dreams,* THQ, Inc., 2004.
Game show host, *Who Rules? The Game,* The Cannery, 2005.
Voice of Lok, *Tak 3: The Great Juju Challenge,* THQ, Inc., 2005.

OTHER SOURCES

Periodicals:

Entertainment Weekly, February 13, 1998, p. 49.
People Weekly, February 23, 1998, p. 83.
Xpose, February, 2002.

WAYANS, Damien
(Damien Dante Wayans)

PERSONAL

Born in New York, NY; son of Nadia Wayans; nephew of Damon, Dwayne, Keenen Ivory, Kim, Marlon, and Shawn Wayans (all in the entertainment industry); cousin of Damon, Jr. and Michael Wayans (in the entertainment industry). *Education:* Attended St. Anthony's High School, Jersey City, NJ.

Addresses: *Agent*—Aaron Kaplan, William Morris Agency, One William Morris Place, Beverly Hills, CA 90212.

Career: Actor, director, and writer.

Awards, Honors: BET Comedy Award nominations, outstanding writing for a comedy series and outstanding directing for a comedy series, Black Entertainment Television Network, both with others, both 2004 and 2005, for *My Wife and Kids.*

CREDITS

Television Work; Series:
Executive story editor, *My Wife and Kids* (also known as *Wife and Kids*), ABC, 2003–2004.
Supervising producer, *My Wife and Kids* (also known as *Wife and Kids*), ABC, 2004–2005.

Television Work; Episodic:
Director, *My Wife and Kids* (also known as *Wife and Kids*), ABC, episodes between 2002 and 2005.

Television Appearances; Movies:
Snow Lurcher, *Passing Glory,* TNT, 1999.
Bo Drew, *Freedom Song,* TNT, 2000.

Television Appearances; Awards Presentations:
BET Comedy Awards, Black Entertainment Television, 2004.
The Second Annual BET Comedy Awards (also known as *BET Comedy Awards*), Black Entertainment Television, 2005.

Television Appearances; Episodic:
"Toy Soldiers," *New York Undercover* (also known as *Uptown Undercover*), Fox, 1996.
"Heartbeat," *413 Hope St.,* Fox, 1997.
Shaun, "Norm vs. the Boxer," *The Norm Show* (also known as *Norm*), ABC, 1999.
Trey Langdon, "Brothers under Arms," *NYPD Blue,* ABC, 2000.

Film Appearances:
Child running in the house, *Eddie Murphy Raw* (also known as *Raw*), Paramount, 1987.
Cadet Deak Williams, *Major Payne,* Universal, 1995.

Cousin with bag, *Don't Be a Menace to South Central While Drinking Your Juice in the Hood* (also known as *Don't Be a Menace*), Miramax, 1996.

(As Damien Dante Wayans) Tec, *Malibu's Most Wanted* (also known as *Suckaz*), Warner Bros., 2003.

The Last Meal (short film), c. 2004.

(As Damien Dante Wayans) Isiaha, *Edison,* Nu–Image Films/Redbus Film Distribution, 2005.

Man about Town, Media 8 Entertainment, c. 2006.

Film Work:

Director and producer, *The Last Meal* (short film), c. 2004.

WRITINGS

Teleplays; with Others; Series:

My Wife and Kids (also known as *Wife and Kids*), ABC, 2002–2004.

Screenplays:

The Last Meal (short film), c. 2004.

WAYANS, Kim 1961–

PERSONAL

Born October 8, 1961, in New York, NY; daughter of Howell and Elvira Wayans; sister of Damon, Dwayne, Keenen Ivory, Marlon, Nadia, and Shawn (all in the entertainment industry). *Education:* Wesleyan University, Middletown, CT, graduated (cum laude).

Addresses: *Agent* Karen Forman, Agency for the Performing Arts, 9200 Sunset Blvd., Suite 900, Los Angeles, CA 90069.

Career: Actress, singer, director, writer, and editor. Stand–up comedienne at comedy clubs, including the Improv.

Awards, Honors: BET Comedy Icon Award (with other members of the Wayans family), outstanding career body of work and overall contributions to the comedy genre, Black Entertainment Television Network, 2004; BET Comedy Award nominations, outstanding writing for a comedy series and outstanding directing for a comedy series, Black Entertainment Television Network, both with others, both 2004 and 2005, for *My Wife and Kids.*

CREDITS

Television Appearances; Series:

Allison, a recurring role, *A Different World,* NBC, 1987–88.

Multiple characters, *In Living Color,* Fox, 1990–93.

Tonia Harris, *In the House,* NBC, c. 1995–96, UPN, c. 1996–98.

Mom, *Waynehead* (animated), The WB, 1996–97.

Television Appearances; Specials:

Multiple characters, *The Best of Robert Townsend & His Partners in Crime,* HBO, 1991.

It's Hot in Here: UPN Fall Preview, UPN, 1996.

Voices of Jackie–in–the–Box and Lula, *The Steadfast Tin Soldier: An Animated Special from the "Happily Ever After: Fairy Tales for Every Child" Series* (animated), HBO, 2000.

Television Appearances; Awards Presentations:

Presenter, *Soul Train Comedy Awards,* 1993.

American Comedy Honors, Fox, 1997.

BET Comedy Awards, Black Entertainment Television, 2004.

The Second Annual BET Comedy Awards (also known as *BET Comedy Awards*), Black Entertainment Television, 2005.

Television Appearances; Episodic:

Cameo Candette, "Lost and Found: Parts 1 & 2," *China Beach,* ABC, 1988.

Nicki, "Over Your Dead Body," *Dream On,* HBO, 1990, also broadcast on Fox.

Host, *Soul Train,* syndicated, 1993.

Sheila, "Farmer's Daughter," *The Wayans Bros.,* The WB, 1995.

Cousin Sheila, "A Country Christmas," *The Wayans Bros.,* The WB, 1998.

Rhonda, "There's Something about Rhonda," *Getting Personal,* Fox, 1998.

Random Acts of Comedy, Fox Family Channel, 1999.

Mystic ruler, "New Kids on the Planet," *Cousin Skeeter,* Nickelodeon, 2000.

Guest, *The Oprah Winfrey Show* (also known as *Oprah*), syndicated, 2004.

Television Appearances; Pilots:

Multiple characters, *In Living Color,* Fox, 1990.

Not the Bradys, NBC, 2003.

Television Work; Series:

Story editor, *My Wife and Kids* (also known as *Wife and Kids*), ABC, 2001–2002.

Executive story editor, *My Wife and Kids* (also known as *Wife and Kids*), ABC, 2002–2003.

Supervising producer, *My Wife and Kids* (also known as *Wife and Kids*), ABC, 2003–2005.

Television Work; Episodic:

Director, *My Wife and Kids* (also known as *Wife and Kids*), ABC, episodes between 2004 and 2005.

Film Appearances:

Customer in chair, *Hollywood Shuffle* (also known as *Robert Townsend's "Hollywood Shuffle"*), Samuel Goldwyn, 1987.

(Uncredited) Interviewed fan, *Eddie Murphy Raw* (also known as *Raw*), Paramount, 1987.

Nightclub singer, *I'm Gonna Git You, Sucka,* Metro–Goldwyn–Mayer, 1988.

Herself, *Wisecracks* (documentary), Alliance International Pictures, 1992.

Andie Norman, *Talking about Sex,* 1994.

Diane, *A Low Down Dirty Shame* (also known as *Mister Cool*), Buena Vista, 1994.

"Unemployment," *Floundering,* A–pix Entertainment/Strand Releasing, 1994.

Mrs. Johnson, *Don't Be a Menace to South Central While Drinking Your Juice in the Hood* (also known as *Don't Be a Menace*), Miramax, 1996.

Bettina, *Critics and Other Freaks* (also known as *Critics Choice*), Niuwirth Pictures, 1997.

Latisha Jansen, *Juwanna Mann,* Warner Bros., 2002.

Film Work:

Production assistant, *I'm Gonna Git You, Sucka,* Metro–Goldwyn–Mayer, 1988.

WRITINGS

Teleplays; with Others; Series:

Special material, *In Living Color,* Fox, 1991–92.

My Wife and Kids (also known as *Wife and Kids*), ABC, 2002–2005.

Short Stories:

Author of short stories.

OTHER SOURCES

Electronic:

Black Film, http://blackfilm.com, June, 2002.

WEAVER, Blayne 1976–

PERSONAL

Born in 1976, in Bossier City, LA.

Addresses: *Agent*—Vox, Inc., 5670 Wilshire Blvd., Suite 820, Los Angeles, CA 90036; The Agency Group, 9348 Civic Center Dr., 2nd Floor, Beverly Hills, CA 90210.

Career: Actor, writer, director, executive producer. Co–owner of Secret Identity Productions.

CREDITS

Television Appearances; Series:

Voice of Peter Pan, *House of Mouse* (animated), ABC, 2001.

Television Appearances; Movies:

Jeff Bowman, *The Flood: Who Will Save Our Children?,* 1993.

Tommy Calloway, *The Good Old Boys,* 1995.

Caddy, *Winchell,* 1998.

Television Appearances; Episodic:

Private first class Douglas, "War Cries," *JAG,* NBC, 1995.

Jeffrey, "You Bet Your Life," *ER,* NBC, 1997.

Luke Serone, "Broken Hearts," *Chicago Hope,* CBS, 1998.

"The Chalkboard," *Beyond Belief: Fact or Fiction* (also known as *Beyond Belief*), Sci–Fi Channel, 1998.

Second year medical student, "Time of Death," *Mds,* 2002.

Voice of D. J. (uncredited), "Precedent Nixin," *The King of Queens,* CBS, 2004.

Probation officer Darrell Baum, "The Good Wives Club," *Navy NCIS: Naval Criminal Investigative Service* (also known as *NCIS* and *NCIS: Naval Criminal Investigative Service*), CBS, 2004.

Film Appearances:

Charlie, *Manic,* IFC, 2001.

Voice of Peter Pan, *Mickey's Magical Christmas: Snowed In at the House of Mouse* (animated), Buena Vista Home Video, 2001.

Voice of Peter Pan, *Return to Never Land* (animated), Buena Vista, 2002.

Voice of Peter Pan, *Mickey's PhilharMagic* (animated), Walt Disney, 2003.

Voice of Peter Pan, *The Lion King 1 ½* (video; also known as *Lion King 3: Hakuna Matata!*), Buena Vista Home Video, 2004.

Clark Kent/Superman, *Losing Lois Lane,* Secret Identity, 2004.

Kirk Hastings, *Outside Sales,* Secret Identity, 2005.

Film Director:

Losing Lois Lane, Secret Identity, 2004.

Outside Sales, Secret Identity, 2005.

Film Executive Producer:

Losing Lois Lane, Secret Identity, 2004.

Outside Sales, Secret Identity, 2005.

RECORDINGS

Video Games:
Peter Pan, *Kingdom Hearts II,* Square Electronic Arts, 2005.

WRITINGS

Screenplays:
Manic, 2001.
Losing Lois Lane, Secret Identity, 2004.
Outside Sales, Secret Identity, 2005.

WEAVER, Dennis 1924–2006

PERSONAL

Full name, Billy Dennis Weaver; born June 4, 1924, in Joplin, MO; died of prostate cancer, February 24, 2006, in Ridgway, CO. Actor, producer, and director. Weaver was best known for his roles as western lawmen: he appeared as Deputy Chester Goode in the television series *Gunsmoke* for nine seasons, from 1955 to 1964, and in the 1970s played the title role of Deputy Sam McCloud in the series *McCloud.* Weaver began his acting career on Broadway in 1950 but soon headed to Hollywood, where he starred in both films and television. Weaver made his mark in series television, including *Kentucky Jones, Gentle Ben, Emerald Point N.A.S.,* and *Buck James.* He appeared in numerous television movies, such as *Duel, Ishi: The Last of His Tribe,* and *The Return of Sam McCloud,* which he also co-executive produced. Weaver directed several episodes of *Gunsmoke.* Though Weaver was known primarily for his television work, he starred in dozens of feature films, including *The Bridges at Toko-Ri, Seven Angry Men, Touch of Evil,* and *Gentle Giant.* Weaver served as president of the Screen Actors Guild in the early 1970s and was founder and president of LIFE (Love Is Feeding Everyone), an anti-hunger organization. An avid environmentalist, Weaver built a solar-powered home in Colorado with recycled tires and cans.

PERIODICALS

Broadcasting & Cable, March 6, 2006.
People Weekly, March 13, 2006.
Variety, March 6, 2006.

WELCH, Raquel 1940–
(Raquel Tejada)

PERSONAL

Original name, Jo Raquel Tejada; born September 5, 1940, in Chicago, IL; daughter of Armand and Josepha (Hall) Tejada; married James Westley Welch, May 8, 1959 (divorced, 1964); married Patrick Curtis, February 14, 1967 (divorced, 1971); married Andre Weinfeld (a producer, cinematographer, and director), July 5, 1980 (divorced, September 1990); married Richard Palmer (a restaurateur), July 17, 1999 (separated, August, 2003); children: (first marriage) Damon, Tahnee (an actress); (second marriage) two. *Education:* Graduated La Jolla High School, La Jolla, CA, 1957; studied theater arts at San Diego State College; studied ballet with Irene Clark.

Addresses: *Agent*—Cunningham/Escott/Slevin & Doherty Talent Agency, 10635 Santa Monica Blvd., Suite 140, Los Angeles, CA 90025; Innovative Artists, 1505 10th St., Santa Monica, CA 90401. *Manager*—Media Four, 8840 Wilshire Blvd., 2nd Floor, Beverly Hills, CA 90211.

Career: Actress, singer, producer, and writer. Curtwel Productions, founder (with Patrick Curtis); Raquel Welch Productions, Inc. (also known as RWP, Inc.), founder and owner; served as television spokesperson for Equal Sweetener, 1994; appeared in print ads for Foster Grant sunglasses, 1968, and Raquel Welch Signature Collection Wigs & Extensions. Owns wig and beauty product lines; previously worked as a model at Neiman–Marcus in Dallas, TX, a weather reporter in San Diego, CA, and as a cocktail waitress.

Member: Actors' Equity Association, Screen Actors Guild.

Awards, Honors: Golden Laurel Award nominations, Producers Guild of America, female new face, 1967, female star, 1968; Golden Globe Award, best motion picture actress in a musical or comedy, 1975, for *The Three Musketeers;* Bronze Wrangler (with others), fictional television drama, Western Heritage Awards, 1983, for *The Legend of Walks Far Woman;* Golden Globe Award nomination, best performance by an actress in a miniseries or motion picture made for television, 1988, for *Right to Die;* Star on the Hollywood Walk of Fame, 1994; Lifetime Achievement Award, Imagen Foundation Awards, 2001; American Media Arts Award (ALMA) nomination (with Bobby Cannavale), outstanding host of a variety or awards special, National Council of LaRaza, 2001, for *The 2000 Hispanic Heritage Awards.*

CREDITS

Film Appearances:
Call girl, *A House Is Not a Home,* Embassy, 1964.
(Uncredited) College student, *Roustabout,* Paramount, 1964.

Do Not Disturb, Twentieth Century–Fox, 1965.

Jeri, *A Swingin' Summer,* United Screen Artists, 1965.

Cora Peterson, *Fantastic Voyage* (also known as *Microscopia* and *Strange Journey*), Twentieth Century–Fox, 1966.

Tania Mottini, *Shoot Loud, Louder ... I Don't Understand* (also known as *Spara Forte, Piu Forte ... Non Capisco*), Embassy, 1966.

Elena, "Queen Elena," *The Queens* (also known as *Sex Quartet, Le Fate,* and *Les ogresses*), Royal, 1966.

Lillian Lust, *Bedazzled,* Twentieth Century–Fox, 1967.

Fathom Harvill, *Fathom,* Twentieth Century–Fox, 1967.

Loana, *One Million Years B.C.,* Twentieth Century–Fox, 1967.

Herself, *Think Twentieth* (documentary short), Twentieth Century–Fox, 1967.

Nini, "La belle epoque" (also known as "The Gay Nineties"), *The Oldest Profession* (also known as *Love Through the Centuries, The Oldest Profession in the World, Das Alteste Gewerbe der Welt, L'amore attraverso i secoli, L'amour a travers les ages,* and *Le plus vieux metier du monde*), Goldstone/VIP, 1967.

Maria Stoner, *Bandolero!,* Twentieth Century–Fox, 1968.

Juliana, *The Biggest Bundle of Them All,* Metro–Goldwyn–Mayer, 1968.

Kit Forrest, *Lady in Cement,* Twentieth Century–Fox, 1968.

Michele, *Flare Up* (also known as *Flareup*), Metro–Goldwyn–Mayer, 1969.

Sarita, *100 Rifles,* Twentieth Century–Fox, 1969.

Slave driver/Priestess of the Whip, *The Magic Christian,* Commonwealth United, 1970.

Title role, *Myra Breckinridge* (also known as *Gore Vidal's "Myra Breckinridge"*), Twentieth Century–Fox, 1970.

Title role, *Hannie Caulder,* Paramount, 1971.

Magdelena, *Bluebeard* (also known as *Barbablu, Blaubart,* and *Barbe–bleue*) Vulcano, 1972.

Detective Eileen McHenry, *Fuzz,* United Artists, 1972.

Diane "K. C." Carr, *Kansas City Bomber,* Metro–Goldwyn–Mayer, 1972.

(Uncredited) Juliet, "I Who Have Nothing," *The Special London Bridge Special,* 1972.

Alice, *The Last of Sheila,* Warner Bros., 1973.

Constance, *The Three Musketeers* (also known as *The Queen's Diamonds, The Three Musketeers: The Queen's Diamonds,* and *Los tres mosqueteros*), Twentieth Century–Fox, 1974.

Constance, *The Four Musketeers* (also known as *The Revenge of Milady, The Four Musketeers: Milday's Revenge, The Return of the Three Musketeers,* and *Los cuatro mosqueteros*), Twentieth Century–Fox, 1975.

Queenie, *The Wild Party,* American International Pictures, 1975.

Jugs (Jennifer), *Mother, Jugs, and Speed,* Twentieth Century–Fox, 1976.

Jane Gardner, *L'animal* (also known as *The Animal* and *Stuntwoman*), Cerito Films/Les Films Christian Fechner, 1977.

Lady Edith, *Crossed Swords* (also known as *The Prince and the Pauper*), Warner Bros., 1978.

Elena, *Restless* (also known as *The Beloved* and *Sin*), 1978.

You and Me Together, 1979.

(Uncredited) Herself, *Fist of Fear, Touch of Death,* Aquarius Releasing, 1980.

Hero for Hire, 1990.

(Uncredited) Herself, *Naked Gun 33 1/3: The Final Insult,* Paramount, 1994.

100 Years of Horror: Giants and Dinosaurs (documentary), Passport Video, 1996.

Herself, *Flesh and Blood,* Anchor Bay Entertainment, 1997.

Ms. Grace Kosik, *Chairman of the Board,* Trimark Pictures, 1998.

Jacqueline, *What I Did for Love* (also known as *Folle d'elle*), UGC–Fox Distribution, 1998.

Herself, *Get Bruce!,* Miramax, 1999.

Host, *Hollywood at Your Feet: The Story of the Chinese Theatre Footprints* (documentary), Image Entertainment, 2000.

(Uncredited) Herself, *The Best of "So Graham Norton,"* 2000.

Hortensia, *Tortilla Soup,* Samuel Goldwyn, 2001.

Mrs. Windham Vandermark, *Legally Blonde,* Metro–Goldwyn–Mayer, 2001.

(Uncredited) Herself, *The Kid Stays in the Picture* (documentary), USA Films, 2002.

Raquel Welch in the Valley of the Dinosaurs (documentary short), Warner Bros., 2002.

Herself (actor), *Jim Brown All American* (documentary), HBO Sports, 2002.

Herself, *Sex at 24 Frames Per Second* (documentary; also known as *Playboy Presents Sex at 24 Frames Per Second: The Ultimate Journey Through Sex in Cinema*), Image Entertainment, 2003.

Christine DeLee, *Forget About It,* 2005.

Film Producer:
Hannie Caulder, Paramount, 1971.

Television Appearances; Series:
On Top All Over the World, 1984–85.

Dianna Brock, *CPW* (also known as *Central Park West*), CBS, 1996.

Host, *Sex and the Silver Screen,* Showtime, 1996–97.

Aunt Dora, *American Family* (also known as *American Family: Journey of Dreams*), PBS, 2002–2004.

Television Appearances; Miniseries:
Herself, *Retrosexual: The 80's,* VH1, 2004.

Herself, *Hollywood Women* (documentary), ITV, 1994.

Television Appearances; Movies:

Walks Far Woman, *The Legend of Walks Far Woman*, NBC, 1982.

Emily Bauer, *Right to Die*, NBC, 1987.

Leda Beth Vincent, *Scandal in a Small Town* (also known as *The Education of Leda Beth Vincent*), NBC, 1988.

Rachel Baxely, *Trouble in Paradise*, CBS, 1989.

(Uncredited) Voice of Shelly Milstone, *Hollyrock–a–Bye Baby* (animated), ABC, 1993.

Paula Eastman, *Judith Krantz's "Torch Song"* (also known as *Torch Song*), ABC, 1993.

Elizabeth Kane, *Tainted Blood*, USA Network, 1993.

Television Appearances; Specials:

Host, *Raquel!*, CBS, 1970.

The Bob Hope Show, NBC, 1970.

Little Orphan Annie, Brenda Starr, and Dragon Lady, *Funny Papers*, 1972.

Host, *Really Raquel*, CBS, 1974.

The McLean Stevenson Show, NBC, 1975.

Mac Davis Christmas Special ... When I Grow Up, NBC, 1976.

The Bob Hope Comedy Special, NBC, 1976.

Bob Hope Special: The Bob Hope Special from Palm Springs (also known as *Bob Hope Special* and *Bob Hope Special from Palm Springs*), NBC, 1978.

A Tribute to Neil Simon, HBO, 1978.

The Bob Hope Special, NBC, 1979.

The Muppets Go Hollywood, 1979.

Bob Hope's Overseas Christmas Tours: Around the World with the Troops—1941–1972, NBC, 1980.

Mac Davis 10th Anniversary Special: I Still Believe in Music, NBC, 1980.

From Raquel with Love (also known as *Raquel*), ABC, 1980.

Herself, *Margret Dunser, auf der Suche nach den Besonderen*, 1981.

Broadway Plays Washington!, PBS, 1982.

(Uncredited) Actress of *The Wild Party*, *The Wandering Company*, 1984.

The Barbara Walters Special, ABC, 1985.

The Bob Hope Christmas Special, NBC, 1985.

The Night of 100 Stars II (also known as *Night of One Hundred Stars*), ABC, 1985.

Interviewee, *Secrets Women Never Share*, NBC, 1987.

The Crystal Light National Aerobic Championships, syndicated, 1987.

Night of 100 Stars III (also known as *Night of One Hundred Stars*), NBC, 1990.

Bob Hope: The First Ninety Years (also known as *Bob Hope: The First 90 Years*), NBC, 1993.

"The World of Jim Henson" (documentary), *Great Performances*, PBS, 1994.

Flesh and Blood: The Hammer Heritage of Horror, 1994.

Legends in Light (documentary), TNT, 1995.

Oops! The World's Funniest Outtakes 4, Fox, 1996.

The Funniest of the World's Funniest Outtakes, Fox, 1997.

Hollywood Glamour Girls, E! Entertainment Television, 1998.

Dudley Moore: The E! True Hollywood Story, E! Entertainment Television, 1999.

Biography: Raquel Welch, Arts and Entertainment, 1999.

(Uncredited) Herself, *Hollywood Screen Tests: Take 1*, 1999.

FY2K: Graham Norton Live, Channel 4, 1999.

The Fourth Annual Celebrity Weddings: In Style, ABC, 2000.

(Uncredited) Herself, *The 72nd Annual Academy Awards Pre–Show*, ABC, 2000.

The Twentieth Century Fox: The Blockbuster Years, AMC, 2000.

Herself, *Intimate Portrait: Raquel Welch*, Lifetime, 2001.

(Uncredited) Herself, *Cleopatra: The Film That Changed Hollywood* (documentary), AMC, 2001.

(Uncredited) Herself, *Bob Hope at 100*, BBC, 2003.

100 Years of Hope and Humor, NBC, 2003.

Playboy's 50th Anniversary Celebration, Arts and Entertainment, 2003.

Television Appearances; Awards Presentations:

Presenter, *The 39th Annual Academy Awards*, ABC, 1967.

Presenter, *The 42nd Annual Academy Awards*, ABC, 1970.

Presenter, *The 44th Annual Academy Awards*, NBC, 1972.

Presenter, *The 45th Annual Academy Awards*, NBC, 1973.

Presenter, *The 46th Annual Academy Awards*, NBC, 1974.

Presenter, *The 47th Annual Academy Awards*, NBC, 1975.

Presenter, *The 50th Annual Academy Awards*, ABC, 1978.

Presenter, *The 55th Annual Academy Awards*, ABC, 1983.

The 38th Annual Tony Awards, CBS, 1984.

The 39th Annual Emmy Awards, 1987.

The 61st Annual Academy Awards Presentation, ABC, 1989.

The 16th Annual People's Choice Awards, CBS, 1990.

The 5th Annual American Comedy Awards, ABC, 1991.

The 49th Annual Golden Globe Awards, TBS, 1992.

Presenter, *The 14th Annual CableACE Awards*, Lifetime, 1993.

The 49th Annual Tony Awards, CBS, 1995.

Presenter, *The 51st Annual Tony Awards*, CBS, 1997.

Co–host, *The 2000 Hispanic Heritage Awards*, NBC, 2000.

Presenter, *The 2001 ALMA Awards*, ABC, 2001.

Television Appearances; Pilots:
Diana Brock, *Central Park West,* CBS, 1995.

Television Appearances; Episodic:
Billboard girl, *The Hollywood Palace,* ABC, 1964.
Saloon girl, "Ryker," *The Virginian* (also known as *The Men From Shiloh*), NBC, 1964.
Lieutenant Wilson, "McHale the Desk Commander," *McHale's Navy,* ABC, 1964.
Stewardess, "Witch or Wife?," *Bewitched,* ABC, 1964.
Miss France, "Hugger–Mugger, by the Sea," *The Rogues,* NBC, 1964.
"Wendy Sails in the Sunset," *Wendy and Me,* ABC, 1965.
"Sam's Nephew," *The Baileys of Balboa,* CBS, 1965.
Mystery guest, *What's My Line?,* CBS, 1967.
The Dean Martin Show (also known as *The Dean Martin Comedy Hour*), NBC, 1969.
Cameo, "Fade–In," *Bracken's World,* NBC, 1969.
Evening at Pops, PBS, 1970.
The Dick Cavett Show, ABC, 1970.
Guest performer, *Rowan & Martin's Laugh–In,* NBC, 1971.
Herself, *V.I.P.–Schaukel,* 1972.
Herself, *Parkinson,* BBC, 1972.
The Tonight Show Starring Johnny Carson (also known as *The Best of Carson*), NBC, 1974, 1976, 1979, 1980, 1984, 1988.
Cher, CBS, 1975.
Guest host, *Saturday Night Live* (also known as *SNL*), 1976.
The Muppet Show, syndication, 1978.
Captain Nirvana of the Necroton Black Army, "Mork vs. the Necrotons: Parts 1 & 2," *Mork and Mindy,* ABC, 1979.
On Top of the World, 1985.
Fame, Fortune & Romance, 1986.
Cynthia Gibson, *Evening Shade,* CBS, 1993.
Diana Stride, "Top Copy," *Lois and Clark: The New Adventures of Superman* (also known as *Lois and Clark* and *The New Adventures of Superman*), ABC, 1995.
Voice, "Cinderella," *Happily Ever After: Fairy Tales for Every Child,* HBO, 1995.
Vesta Spellman, "Third Aunt from the Sun," *Sabrina, the Teenage Witch* (also known as *Sabrina* and *Sabrina Goes to College*), ABC, 1996.
Herself, "The Summer of George," *Seinfeld,* NBC, 1997.
Abby Lassiter, "Porn in the U.S.A.," *Spin City,* ABC, 1997.
Abby Lassiter, "A River Runs through Me," *Spin City,* ABC, 1998.
Guest, *Politically Incorrect with Bill Maher,* ABC, 1998.
The Hollywood Fashion Machine, E! Entertainment Television, 1999.
Abby Lassiter, "Balloons Over Broadway," *Spin City,* ABC, 2000.
The O'Reilly Factor, Fox News, 2004.
Larry King Live, CNN, 2004.

Jackie, "Vanity Unfair," *8 Simple Rules ... for Dating My Teenage Daughter* (also known as *8 Simple Rules*), ABC, 2004.
Herself, *Your World w/Neil Cavuto,* Fox News, 2005.

Also appeared in *Hollywood Squares.*

Stage Appearances:
(As Raquel Tejada) Title role, *Ramona,* Hemet, CA, 1959.
Woman of the Year, Palace Theatre, New York City, 1981.
The Night of 100 Stars II (also known as *Night of One Hundred Stars*), Radio City Music Hall, New York City, 1985.
Night of 100 Stars III (also known as *Night of One Hundred Stars*), Radio City Music Hall, 1990.
Easter Bonnet Competition: A Salute to 100 Years of Broadway, Minskoff Theatre, New York City, 1994.
Title roles, *Victor/Victoria,* Marquis Theater, New York City, 1997.
Epifania, *The Millionairess,* Orpheum Theatre, Foxboro, MA, 1998.

Major Tours:
The Millionairess, U.K. cities, 1995.

Cabaret:
Raquel Welch: Live in Concert, Sands Hotel, Atlantic City, NJ, 1985.

Major Tours; Cabaret:
Raquel Welch: Live in Concert, U.S. and European cities, 1985–86.

RECORDINGS

Videos:
Herself, *Raquel: Total Beauty and Fitness,* HBO Home Video, 1984.
Herself, *Fozzie's Muppet Scrapbook,* 1984.
Herself, *Muppet Video: The Kermit and Piggy Story,* Playhouse Home Video, 1985.
Herself, *A Week with Raquel,* HBO Home Video, 1986.
Herself, *Lose 10 Lbs. in 3 Weeks,* HBO Home Video, 1988.
Herself, *Raquel: Body & Mind,* HBO Home Video, 1989.

WRITINGS

Television Specials:
From Raquel With Love (also known as *Raquel*), ABC, 1980.

Nonfiction:

Raquel: The Raquel Welch Total Beauty and Fitness Program, Holt, Rinehart and Winston (New York City), 1984.

(With Margaret Atwood and Graeme Gibson) Jill Bobrow, *St. Vincent and the Grenadines: Bequia, Mustique, Canouan, Mayreau, Tobago Cays, Palm, Union, PSV: A Plural Country,* photographs by Dana Jinkins, W. W. Norton (New York City), 1985.

OTHER SOURCES

Books:

Contemporary Hispanic Biography, Vol. 1, Gale Group, 2002.

International Directory of Films and Filmmakers, Volume 3: Actors and Actresses, 2nd ed., St. James Press (Detroit, MI), 1992.

Periodicals:

Parade Magazine, March 17, 2002, p. 22.

People Weekly, August 2, 1999, p. 110.

WHITE, Michole
(Michole Briana White, Michole Diana White)

PERSONAL

Born in Chicago, IL.

Career: Actress. Appeared in commercials.

Awards, Honors: Drama Desk Award and Obie Award, *Village Voice,* both outstanding ensemble performance, both with others, 2000, for *Jitney.*

CREDITS

Film Appearances:

(As Michole Briana White) Kathleen, *Encino Man* (also known as *California Man*), Buena Vista, 1992.

First young mother, *Everybody Can Float,* Buena Vista, 1995.

Maria, *Courage under Fire,* Twentieth Century–Fox, 1996.

(As Michole Briana White) First emergency room nurse, *Volcano,* United Artists, 1997.

Lark Medley, *Vacant Lot,* Urban Entertainment Group, 2000.

(As Michole Briana White) Coventry administrator, *25th Hour* (also known as *The 25th Hour*), Buena Vista, 2002.

(As Michole Briana White) Nadiyah, *She Hate Me,* Sony Pictures Classics, 2004.

Frankie, *The Breakup Artist,* 2004, Lantern Lane Entertainment, 2006.

Patty, *Into the Fire,* Slowhand Cinema Releasing, 2005.

Television Appearances; Series:

Angela, *Muscle,* The WB, 1995.

Fatima Kelly, *100 Centre Street* (also known as *101 Centre Street*), Arts and Entertainment, 2001–2002.

Television Appearances; Movies:

Schoolgirl, *Something to Live for: The Alison Gertz Story* (also known as *Fatal Love*), ABC, 1992.

(Uncredited) Taffy, *Final Shot: The Hank Gathers Story,* syndicated, 1992.

Lisa, *Out of Darkness,* ABC, 1994.

Austin, *Convict 762,* Sci–Fi Channel, 1997.

Television Appearances; Episodic:

(As Michole Briana White) Lisa, "Community Action," *The Fresh Prince of Bel–Air,* NBC, 1991.

(As Michole Briana White) Tasha Johnson, "Do the Spike Thing," *L.A. Law,* NBC, 1991.

Cynthia, "Scenes from a Wedding," *The Wonder Years,* ABC, 1992.

(As Michole Briana White) Lindsey, "P.S. I Love You," *The Fresh Prince of Bel–Air,* NBC, 1992.

(As Michole Briana White) Melissa, "Muskrat Love," *Family Matters,* ABC, 1993.

Olivia Imogene Jones, "Am I My Sister's Keeper?," *Living Single* (also known as *My Girls*), Fox, 1994.

Robin, "Blue Blossom," *Blossom,* NBC, 1994.

Thelma, "Uptown Fright Night," *Martin,* Fox, 1995.

Alyssa, "Two Mammograms and a Wedding," *Ellen* (also known as *These Friends of Mine*), ABC, 1996.

Karen, "Love, African–American Style," *The Parent 'Hood,* The WB, 1996.

Doris, "AKA Superman," *Lois & Clark: The New Adventures of Superman* (also known as *Lois & Clark* and *The New Adventures of Superman*), ABC, 1997.

Karen, "Home Loan," *The Parent 'Hood,* The WB, 1997.

Olivia, "A Family Affair," *Built to Last,* NBC, 1997.

Olivia Imogene Jones, "Never Can Say Goodbye," *Living Single* (also known as *My Girls*), Fox, 1997.

Alyson Griffin, "The Ties That Bind," *Chicago Hope,* CBS, 1998.

Janine, "Sam I Am," *Getting Personal* (also known as *Personal Days* and *The Way We Work*), Fox, 1998.

(As Michole Briana White) Mrs. Thomas, "To Protect ... ," *Third Watch,* NBC, 2002.

(As Michole Diana White) Tamara Semple, "Careless," *Law & Order: Special Victims Unit* (also known as *Law & Order's Sex Crimes, Law & Order: SVU,* and *Special Victims Unit*), NBC, 2004.

(As Michole Briana White) Agent Ramos, "The Counterfeit Reality," *Numb3rs* (also known as *Numbers*), CBS, 2005.

(As Michole Briana White) Cindy, "Progeny," *Threshold,* CBS, 2005.

Appeared as Brenda, *Simon,* The WB; and in episodes of other series, including *Sweet Justice,* NBC.

Television Appearances; Pilots:
Angela, *Muscle,* The WB, 1995.
Deborah Ganier, *Copshop,* PBS, 2004.

Stage Appearances:
(As Michole Briana White) Rena, *Jitney,* Mark Taper Forum, Los Angeles, 2000, Second Stage Theatre, Union Square Theatre, New York City, 2000–2001.

Appeared as Albertine, *Five Times;* in *Dearborn Heights,* Showtown Festival; *The Father,* Strindberg Festival; *For Colored Girls Who Have Considered Suicide When the Rainbow Is Enuf,* Coffeehouse Theatre; *The Trip,* Friends and Artists Festival, then the Complex; and in *Women behind Bars,* Los Angeles area production. Also appeared in *As You Like It, Blood Wedding, The Country Wife, The Lesson, A Midsummer Night's Dream, Scapino,* and *Shakespeare's Lovers.*

Major Tours:
Rena, *Jitney,* U.S. cities, 1999.

WILSON, Demond 1946–

PERSONAL

Full name, Grady Demond Wilson; born October 13, 1946, in Valdosta, GA; raised in Harlem, New York, NY; married Cicely Loise Johnston, 1973; children: six. *Education:* Attended a high school for the performing arts. *Religion:* Christian.

Career: Actor and writer. Appeared in commercials. Became a minister of religion, c. 1983; Restoration House of America (rehabilitation organization), founder, 1994. *Military service:* U.S. Army; served in Vietnam.

CREDITS

Television Appearances; Series:
Lamont Sanford, *Sanford and Son,* NBC, 1972–77.
Raymond "Ray" Ellis, *Baby, I'm Back!,* CBS, 1978.
Oscar Madison, *The New Odd Couple,* ABC, 1982–83.

Television Appearances; Specials:
NBC team member, *Battle of the Network Stars,* ABC, 1976.
ABC team member, *Battle of the Network Stars XIII,* ABC, 1982.
Himself, *American Soundtrack: Rhythm, Love and Soul,* 2003.

Television Appearances; Episodic:
Horace, "Edith Writes a Song," *All in the Family* (also known as *Justice for All* and *Those Were the Days*), CBS, 1971.
Simmons, "Underwater," *Mission: Impossible,* CBS, 1971.
Himself, *Rowan & Martin's "Laugh–In"* (also known as *Laugh–In*), NBC, 1972.
Guest, *The Tonight Show Starring Johnny Carson,* NBC, 1972, 1973.
Himself, "Celebrity Roast: Jack Benny," *The Dean Martin Show,* NBC, 1974.
Himself, "Celebrity Roast: Redd Foxx," *The Dean Martin Show,* NBC, 1974.
Himself, *All–Star Baffle* (also known as *Baffle*), NBC, 1974.
Bart, "The Brotherhood of the Sea/Letter to Babycakes/Daddy's Pride," *The Love Boat,* ABC, 1979.
Jesse, "Black Sheep/Hometown Doc/Clothes Make the Girl," *The Love Boat,* ABC, 1981.
Himself, *Redd Foxx: The E! True Hollywood Story,* E! Entertainment Television, 1999.
Himself, "Redd Foxx: Say It Like It Is," *Biography* (also known as *A & E Biography: Jim Carrey*), Arts and Entertainment, 2000.
Kenneth Miles, "L.A. Bound," *Girlfriends* (also known as *My Girls*), UPN, 2004.
Kenneth Miles, "New York Unbound," *Girlfriends* (also known as *My Girls*), UPN, 2004.
Kenneth Miles, "Who's Your Daddy?," *Girlfriends* (also known as *My Girls*), UPN, 2004.
Guest, *Praise the Lord* (also known as *TBN's "Praise the Lord"*), Trinity Broadcasting Network, 2004, 2005.

Some sources cite appearances in episodes of other series, including *The Hollywood Squares,* syndicated, between 1972 and 1978; *Sanford Arms,* NBC, 1977; *Grady,* NBC; *The Red Foxx Comedy Hour,* ABC; and *Sanford,* NBC.

Television Appearances; Pilots:
Raymond "Ray" Ellis, *Baby, I'm Back!,* CBS, 1978.

Some sources cite an appearance in *Mannix,* CBS, 1967.

Film Appearances:
Charlie Blossom, *The Organization,* Metro–Goldwyn–Mayer/United Artists, 1971.

Rupert, *Dealing: Or the Berkeley–to–Boston Forty–Brick Lost–Bag Blues,* Warner Bros., 1972.
Driver, *Full Moon High* (also known as *Moon High*), Filmways Pictures/Larco Productions, 1981.
Agent Schamper, *Me and the Kid,* Orion, 1993.
Prisoner, *Hammerlock,* Castle Hill Productions, 2000.

Stage Appearances:
The Green Pastures, Broadway Theatre, New York City, c. 1951.
Touchstone, *As You Like It,* c. 1960.
First drug user, *Five on the Black Hand Side,* American Place Theatre, St. Clement's Theatre, New York City, 1969–70.
Dudder, *Underground,* New York Shakespeare Festival, Public Theatre, New York City, 1971.

Major Tours:
Toured in *The Boys in the Band.*

WRITINGS

Juvenile Fiction:
John Neuman Smith, CAP Publishing and Literary Company, 1999.
Lil' Mowande, CAP Publishing and Literary Company, 1999.
Mr. Fish Takes a Wife, CAP Publishing and Literary Company, 1999.

Nonfiction:
New Age Millennium, CAP Publishing and Literary Company, 1998.

Screenplays:
Author of *The Legend of Ned Turner.*

OTHER SOURCES

Electronic:
CNN Entertainment/People Weekly, http://archives.cnn.com, October 15, 2002.

WITHERS, Jane 1926–
(Jerrie Walters)

PERSONAL

Born April 12, 1926, in Atlanta, GA; daughter of Lavinia Ruth Withers; married William P. Moss, Jr., September 20, 1947 (divorced, 1954); married Kenneth Errair, 1955 (died, 1968); children: (first marriage) 3, (second marriage) 2.

Career: Actress.

Awards, Honors: Star on the Walk of Fame; Former Child Star Lifetime Achievement Award, Young Artists Awards, 1980; DVD Premiere Award nomination (with others), best original song, 2003, for *The Hunchback of Notre Dame II.*

CREDITS

Film Appearances:
(Uncredited) *Handle with Care,* Fox, 1932.
(Uncredited) *Zoo in Budapest,* Fox, 1933.
Little girl at premiere (uncredited), *Tailspin Tommy,* Universal, 1934.
Little girl playing hopscotch (uncredited), *It's a Gift,* Paramount, 1934.
Peola's frontrow classmate (uncredited), *Imitation of Life,* Universal, 1934.
Joy Smythe, *Bright Eyes,* Fox, 1934.
Child, *The Good Fairy,* Universal, 1935.
Ginger, *Ginger,* Fox, 1935.
Della, *The Farmer Takes a Wife,* Fox, 1935.
Young girl (uncredited), *Redheads on Parade,* Fox, 1935.
Paddy O'Day, *Paddy O'Day,* Twentieth Century–Fox, 1935.
Peg Gurgle, *Can This Be Dixie?,* Twentieth Century–Fox, 1936.
Florence Atwater, *Gentle Julia,* Twentieth Century–Fox, 1936.
Judy Devlin, *Little Miss Nobody,* Twentieth Century–Fox, 1936.
Pepper Jolly, *Pepper* (also known as *Public Nuisance No. 1*), Twentieth Century–Fox, 1936.
Corky Wallace, *The Holy Terror,* Twentieth Century–Fox, 1937.
Angel, *Angel's Holiday,* Twentieth Century–Fox, 1937.
Arnette Flynn, *Wild and Wooly,* Twentieth Century–Fox, 1937.
Judith Frazier, *45 Fathers,* Twentieth Century–Fox, 1937.
Checkers, *Checkers,* Twentieth Century–Fox, 1937.
Gypsy, *Rascals,* Twentieth Century–Fox, 1938.
Jane Rand, *Keep Smiling,* Twentieth Century–Fox, 1938.
Jerry Darlington, *Always in Trouble,* Twentieth Century–Fox, 1938.
Mary Jane Patterson, *The Arizona Wildcat,* Twentieth Century–Fox, 1939.
Sally Murphy, *Boy Friend,* Twentieth Century–Fox, 1939.
Addie Fippany, *Chicken Wagon Family,* Twentieth Century–Fox, 1939.
Colette, *Pack Up Your Troubles* (also known as *We're in the Army Now*), Twentieth Century–Fox, 1939.
Hollywood Hobbies, Metro–Goldwyn–Mayer, 1939.
Jane Wallace, *High School,* Twentieth Century–Fox, 1940.

Jane Pritchard, *Shooting High,* Twentieth Century–Fox, 1940.

Jane, *Girl From Avenue A,* Twentieth Century–Fox, 1940.

Eadie–May, *Youth Will Be Served,* Twentieth Century–Fox, 1940.

Patricia Randall, *Small Town Deb,* Twentieth Century–Fox, 1941.

Jane Drake, *Golden Hoofs,* Twentieth Century–Fox, 1941.

Penny Wood, *Her First Beau,* Columbia, 1941.

Kitty Russell, *A Very Young Lady,* Twentieth Century–Fox, 1941.

Hedda Hopper's Hollywood No. 2, Paramount, 1941.

Hedda Hopper's Hollywood No. 4, Paramount, 1942.

Jane Campbell, *Young America,* Twentieth Century–Fox, 1942.

Kathy Martindale, *The Mad Martindales,* Twentieth Century–Fox, 1942.

Ann Winters/Penelope Ryan, *Johnny Doughboy,* Republic, 1942.

Clavdia Kurina, *The North Star* (also known as *Armored Attack*), RKO, 1943.

Kitty O'Hara, *My Best Gal,* 1944.

Mary Elliott, *Faces in the Fog,* Republic, 1944.

Screen Snapshots Series 25, No. 3: Fashions and Rodeo, Columbia, 1945.

Geraldine Cooper, *Affairs of Geraldine,* Teakwood, 1946.

Pat Marvin, *Danger Street,* Paramount, 1947.

Vashti Snythe, *Giant,* Warner Bros., 1956.

Screen Snapshots: Hollywood Small Fry, Columbia, 1956.

Liz, *The Right Approach,* Twentieth Century–Fox, 1961.

Lieutenant Grace Blodgett, *Captain Newman, M.D.,* Universal, 1963.

Voice of Laverne, *The Hunchback of Notre Dame* (animated), Buena Vista, 1996.

Voice of Laverne, *The Hunchback of Notre Dame II* (animated; video), Buena Vista Home Video, 2002.

Boxes, StarVehicle, 2005.

Television Appearances; Series:

Voice of Clarabelle Cow, *Mickey Mouse Works* (animated), ABC, 1999.

Voice of Clarabelle Cow, *House of Mouse* (animated), ABC, 2001.

Television Appearances; Episodic:

"Everybody Loves My Baby," *The Chevrolet Tele–Theatre* (also known as *Chevrolet Television Theatre, Chevrolet on Broadway* and *The Broadway Playhouse*), NBC, 1949.

Aunt Jan, "The Pink Burro," *The United States Steel Hour* (also known as *The U.S. Steel Hour*), CBS, 1959.

"The Frankie Adventure," *The Aquanauts* (also known as *Malibu Run*), CBS, 1961.

Sue Ann Baines, "A Possibility of Oil," *General Electric Theater* (also known as *G.E. Theatre*), CBS, 1961.

Betty Hamilton, "A Very Special Girl," *General Electric Theater* (also known as *G.E. Theatre*), CBS, 1962.

Edith Swinney, "How to Get Rid of Your Wife," *The Alfred Hitchcock Hour,* CBS, 1963.

Team captain, *The Match Game,* NBC, 1963.

Billie, "The Apartment House," *Summer Playhouse,* CBS, 1964.

Fanny Pike, "Pike's Pique," *The Munsters,* CBS, 1964.

Pamela Thornton, "Grandpa's Lost Wife," *The Munsters,* CBS, 1966.

"Celebrity Roast: Ralph Nader," *The Dean Martin Show* (also known as *The Dean Martin Comedy Hour*), NBC, 1974.

Gladys, "Invisible Maniac/September Song/Peekaboo," *The Love Boat,* ABC, 1980.

Roxy McGuane, "Murder in the Saddle," *Hart to Hart,* ABC, 1981.

Marge Allen, "Who Killed J. B. Fletcher?," *Murder, She Wrote,* CBS, 1991.

Alma Sobel, "Ship of Thieves?," *Murder, She Wrote,* CBS, 1993.

Esther Baker, *Amazing Grace,* NBC, 1995.

Television Appearances; Movies:

Helen Drummond, *All Together Now,* ABC, 1975.

Television Appearances; Specials:

Mitzi: A Tribute to the American Housewife, CBS, 1974.

Mrs. Minney, *The Winged Colt,* ABC, 1977.

Aunt Daisy, *Zack & the Magic Factory,* ABC, 1981.

When We Were Young ... Growing Up on the Silver Screen (documentary), PBS, 1989.

Shirley Temple: America's Little Darling (documentary), PBS, 1992.

Betty Grable: Behind the Pin–Up (documentary), Arts and Entertainment, 1995.

Interviewee, *Shirley Temple: The Biggest Little Star* (documentary), Arts and Entertainment, 1996.

Interviewee, *Alice Faye: The Star Next Door* (documentary), Arts and Entertainment, 1996.

20th Century–Fox: The First 50 Years (documentary), AMC, 1997.

Interviewee, *Hollywood at Your Feet: The Story of the Chinese Theatre Footprints,* AMC, 2000.

RECORDINGS

Videos:

Memories of 'Giant', Warner Home Video, 1998.

Return to 'Giant', Warner Home Video, 2003.

WRITINGS

Screenplays:

(As Jerrie Walters) *Small Town Deb,* 1941.

WRENN, James W.
(James Wrenn, Jim Wrenn)

PERSONAL

Addresses: *Contact*—5007 Junius St., Dallas, TX 75214.

Career: Cinematographer. Also worked as a second unit photographer.

Member: Texas Association of Film and Tape Professionals.

CREDITS

Television Cinematographer; Miniseries:
Cinematographer, *Oklahoma Passage,* OETA (PBS), 1989.

Television Second Unit Director of Photography; Miniseries:
Streets of Laredo (also known as *Larry McMurtry's "Streets of Laredo"*), CBS, 1995.
Helen of Troy, USA Network, 2003.

Television Cinematographer; Movies:
Across Five Aprils (also known as *Civil War Diary*), The Family Channel, 1990.
Gentle Ben (also known as *Terror on the Mountain*), Animal Planet, 2002.
Night of the Wolf, Animal Planet, 2002.
Audrey's Rain, The Hallmark Channel, 2003.
Gentle Ben 2: Danger on the Mountain (also known as *Black Gold*), Animal Planet, 2003.
(As Jim Wrenn) *Love Comes Softly,* The Hallmark Channel, 2003.
Monster Makers, The Hallmark Channel, 2003.
Straight from the Heart, The Hallmark Channel, 2003.
A Time to Remember (also known as *Turning Homeward*), The Hallmark Channel, 2003.
Angel in the Family, The Hallmark Channel, 2004.
(As James Wrenn) *Gone but Not Forgotten,* 2004.
A Place Called Home (also known as *'Til the River Runs Dry*), The Hallmark Channel, 2004.
Back to You and Me, The Hallmark Channel, 2005.
The Family Plan, The Hallmark Channel, 2005.
Fielder's Choice, The Hallmark Channel, 2005.
Meet the Santas, The Hallmark Channel, 2005.
Thicker Than Water, The Hallmark Channel, 2005.
Hidden Places, The Hallmark Channel, 2006.
The Reading Room, The Hallmark Channel, 2006.
Wild Hearts, The Hallmark Channel, 2006.

Television Cinematographer; Specials:
The Quest for Freedom (short), 1992.
Scrooge and Marley (musical), syndicated, 2001.

Film Cinematographer:
Dakota, Miramax, 1988.
Harley, Warner Bros., 1990.
Sioux City (also known as *Ultimate Revenge*), IRS Releasing, 1994.

Film Director of Photography:
Second unit director of photography, *Keys to Tulsa,* Gramercy Pictures, 1997.
Additional unit director of photography, *Texas Rangers,* Miramax/Dimension Films, 2001.

Y-Z

YOON–JIN, Kim
    See KIM, Yoon–jin

YULE, Joe, Jr.
    See ROONEY, Mickey

ZIEGLER, Karen
    See BLACK, Karen

Cumulative Index

To provide continuity with *Who's Who in the Theatre*, this index interfiles references to *Who's Who in the Theatre*, 1st–17th Editions, and *Who Was Who in the Theatre* (Gale, 1978) with references to *Contemporary Theatre, Film and Television*, Volumes 1–70.

References in the index are identified as follows:

CTFT and volume number—*Contemporary Theatre, Film and Television*, Volumes 1–70
WWT and edition number—*Who's Who in the Theatre*, 1st–17th Editions
WWasWT—*Who Was Who in the Theatre*

347

Cumulative Index

E

H

M

Cumulative Index

Cumulative Index

U

W

Cumulative Index